ISBN 978-1-332-21263-7
PIBN 10298989

WILLS, REGISTERS

AND

ONÜMENTAL INSCRIPTIONS

OF THE PARISH OF

BARWICK-IN-ELMET,

Co. YORK.

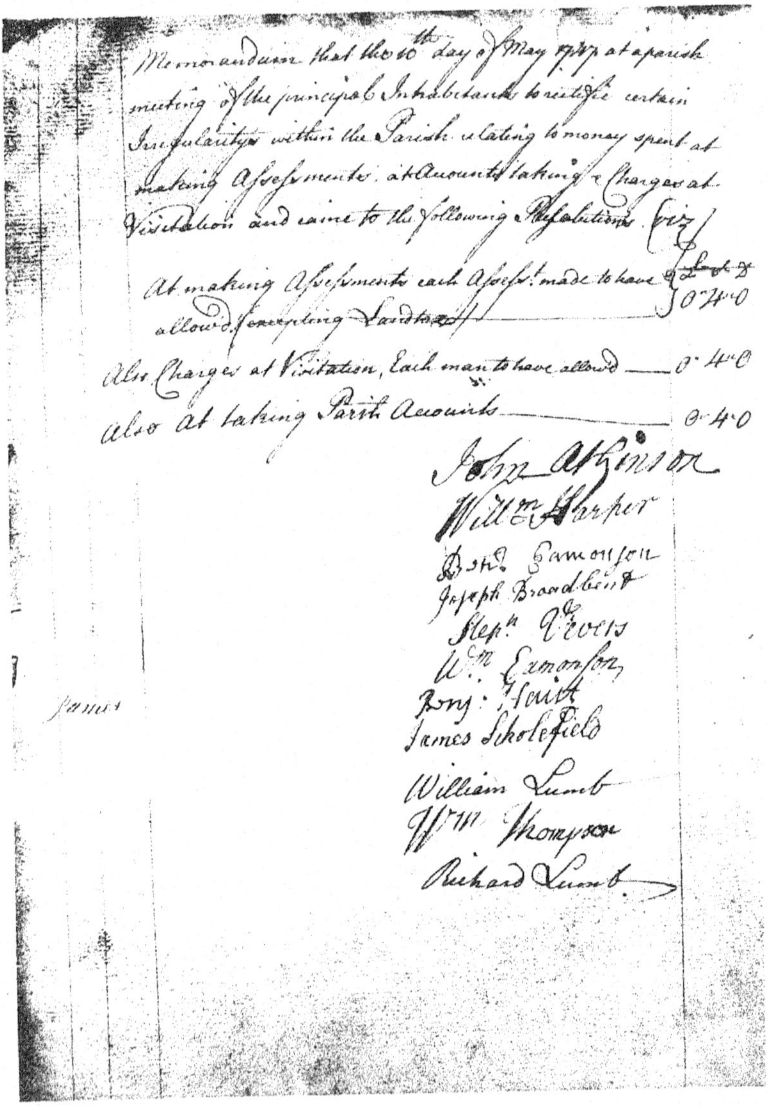

Memorandum that the 10th day of May 1757 at a parish meeting of the principal Inhabitants to rectifie certain Irregularitys within the Parish relating to money spent at making Assessments, at Accounts taking & Charges at Visitation and came to the following Resolutions (viz)

	£ s d
At making Assessments each Assesst. made to have allowed (excepting Landtax)	0 4 0
Also Charges at Visitation, Each man to have allowed	0 4 0
Also at taking Parish Accounts	0 4 0

John Atkinson
Willm Harper
Richd Gamonson
Joseph Broadbent
Stephn Devers
Wm Exmonson
Benj: Smith
James Scholefield
William Lumb
Wm Thompson
Richard Lumb

James

Resolutions passed at parish meetings at

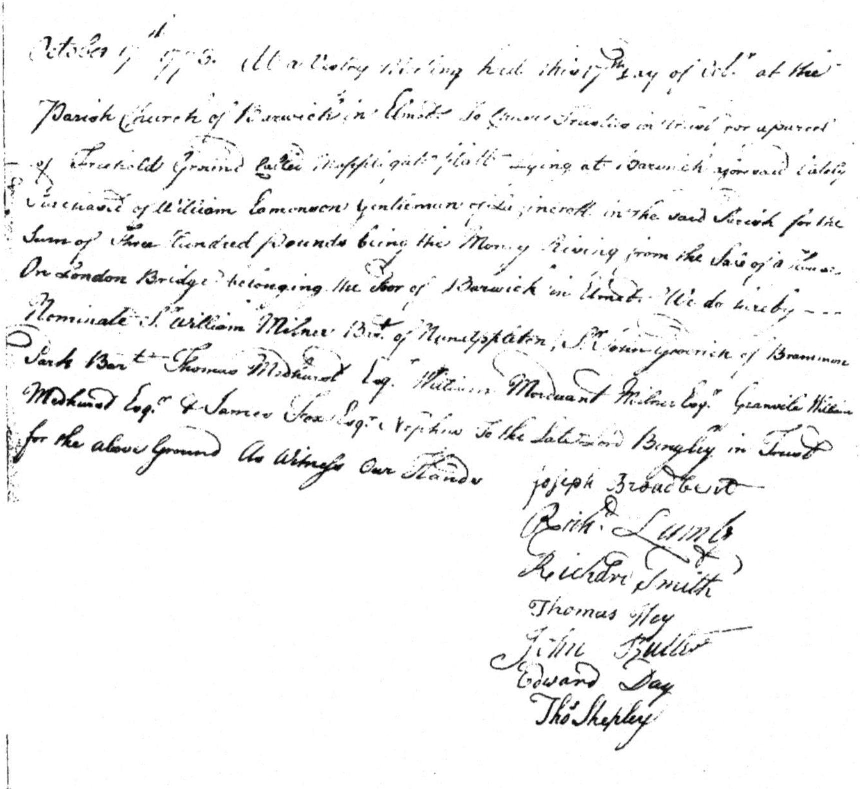

October 17th 1773. At a Vestry Meeting held this 17th day of Octr at the Parish Church of Barwick in Elmet to chuse Trustees in Trust for a parcel of Freehold Ground called [illegible] Hall lying at Barwick aforesaid lately purchased of William Edmonson Gentleman of Scarcroft in the said Parish for the Sum of Three Hundred Pounds being the Money Arising from the Sale of a House On London Bridge belonging the Poor of Barwick in Elmet. We do hereby Nominate Sr William Milner Bart of Nunappleton, Sr [illegible] of Bramham Park Bart Thomas Medhurst Esqr William Mordaunt Milner Esqr Granville Wheler Medhurst Esqr & James Fox Esqr Nephew to the Late Lord Bingley in Trust for the above Ground As Witness Our Hands

Joseph Broadbent
Richd Lumb
Richard Smith
Thomas Hey
John Fuller
Edward Day
Thos Shepley

-in-Elmet, 1747 and 1773, with signatures.

WILLS, REGISTERS

AND

MONUMENTAL INSCRIPTIONS

OF THE PARISH OF

BARWICK-IN-ELMET,

CO. YORK.

EDITED BY

GEORGE DENISON LUMB, F.S.A.

Hon Secretary of the Yorkshire Parish Register Society, Hon Treasurer of the Thoresby Society, Member of the Council of the Yorkshire Archæological Society, etc, Editor of the Leeds, Adel, Kippax, Methley and Rothwell Registers

PRIVATELY PRINTED FOR SUBSCRIBERS.

LEEDS, 1908.

KNIGHT AND FORSTER, PRINTERS, LEEDS.

PREFACE.

The present Volume contains extracts from Wills proved in the chequer and Prerogative Court of the Archbishop of York, to the year 1750, and from a few Wills proved in the Prerogative Court of Canterbury; also copies of the Parish Registers from 1653 to 1812, with the existing transcripts for earlier years, and the Monumental Inscriptions in the Church and Churchyard.

The Editor desires to thank Messrs. William Brown, F.S.A., and W. T. Lancaster, F.S.A., for assistance kindly rendered in respect of some of the earliest Wills, and also to thank the Rector, the Rev. F. S. Colman, M.A., for his kindness in allowing the Registers to be printed, and for the facilities he has most readily afforded for transcription and collation. Mr. Colman has written an excellent History of the Parish which is now being printed for the Thoresby Society.

G. D. L.

ERRATA.

P. 35, bottom line of footnote. For "20 June" *read* "31 July."

P. 101, footnote. The will of George Pearson is printed p. 49. It is not in the printed index of York Wills.

P. 111, bottom line of footnote. Insert "p. 646" after "Money," and delete "p. 646" after "Papers."

P. 122, line 7. For "Emett" *read* "Elmett"

P. 209, footnote, line 2. For "Richard" *read* "Robert."

P. 319, 4 lines from the bottom. Delete brackets.

P. 344, line 21. For "1778" *read* "1788."

P. 362, 11 lines from the bottom. Insert "1800" after "Nov. 2."

P. 392, line 21. For "Beann" *read* "Bean."

CONTENTS.

BARWICK-IN-ELMET.

WILLS.

WILLIAM CANON, Rector, 1404–1420.

Testamentum Willelmi Canon',* rectoris ecclesie parochialis de Berwyk in Elmett.

[Reg. Bowet, fo. 376*d.*]

In Dei nomine Amen. Sexto die mensis Novembris, anno Domini millesimo $cccc^{mo}$ xix, ego, Willelmus Canon', rector ecclesie parochialis de Berwyk in Elmett, Eboracensis diocesis, compos mentis et sane memorie, facio et ordino testamentum meum in hunc modum. In primis lego et commendo animam meam Deo omnipotenti et Beate Marie, matri ejus, ac omnibus suis Sanctis; corpusque meum sepeliendum in choro ecclesie predicte, ex parte australi summi altaris ejusdem chori. Item lego nomine mortuarii mei meliorem equum meum. Item lego pro expensis meis funeralibus quinque marcas monete Anglicane. Item lego summo altari ecclesie mee antedicte unum missale secundum usum ecclesie Eboracensis, ita quod executores mei non impediantur seu molestentur per aliquem in libera disposicione et execucione testamenti et bonorum meorum. Et si impediantur vel molestentur, volo tunc quod dicti executores mei hujusmodi missale vendant, et precium ejus in celebracionem divinorum pro anima mea convertatur. Item lego nove fabrice ecclesie cathedralis Eboracensis $xiij^s$ $iiij^d$. Item lego fabrice ecclesie mee antedicte $xiij^s$ $iiij^d$. Item lego fabrice ecclesie parochialis de Alne $xiij^s$ $iiij^d$. Item lego fabrice ecclesie parochialis de Elughton $xiij^s$ $iiij^d$. Item lego eidem ecclesie unum ordinale secundum usum ecclesie cathedralis Eboracensis. Item lego cuilibet ordini Fratrum Mendicancium civitatis Eboracensis vj^s $viij^d$. Item lego Fratribus Mendicantibus de Pontefracto vj^s $viij^d$. Item lego Custancie de Kereby, consanguinee mee, x^{li} argenti, vj coclearia argenti, ij meliores lectos, iiij lodices, iiij linthiamina, et ij *mattres*, j pelvim cum lavacro, j togam furratam cum capucio, quam elige e voluerit, ac medietatem vaso um omnium et utensiliorum coquine mee. Item lego Johanni Cras, clerico, j portiforium cum nota de usu ecclesie Eboracensis antedicte, ac quinque marcas monete. Item lego domino Roberto Otlay, rectori ecclesie Sancti

* The figure of William Canon was formerly in stained glass in the East window of Barwick Church.

Martini in Conyngstrete, civitatis Eboracensis meliorem ciphum meum murreum, argento ligatum et deauratum. Item lego Willelmo de Yolton, servienti meo, x marcas argenti et ij quarteria frumenti. Item lego domino Willelmo Milford, capellano, xx^{s}. Item lego Willelmo filio Willelmi Hesille de Eboraco ij^{s}. Item lego Willelmo filio Willelmi Yolton iij^{s} iiij^{d}. Item lego Johanni Cook juniori, servienti meo, x^{s} argenti et j quarterium frumenti. Item lego Philippo Webster, servienti meo, x^{s} argenti et j quarterium frumenti. Item lego clerico parochiali de Berwyk supradicta ij^{s} argenti. Item lego Willelmo Langtoo, servienti meo, vj^{s} viij^{d} et j quarterium frumenti. Item lego Elisote Webster, ad sustentacionem ejusdem, vj^{s} viij^{d}. Item lego cuilibet executorum meorum subscriptorum pro labore suo j marcam argenti. Residuum vero bonorum meorum superius non legatorum, debitis meis persolutis, do et lego in celebracione missarum et aliorum divinorum pro anima mea et animabus omnium benefactorum, et [ad] distribucionem pauperum in hiis parochiis quibus bona illa adquisivi, secundum discrecionem et disposicionem executorum meorum predictorum. Hujus autem testamenti mei perimplendi ordino, facio, et constituo discretum virum, magistrum Johannem de Thornton, vicarium Pontefracti, dominum Johannem Spanyelle, capellanum, et Edmundum Cook de Walton, meos executores. Hiis testibus, domino Willelmo Kymstan, capellano, Willelmo Beroby, notario publico, et Johanne Harpyn, Eboracensis diocesis. Datum sub sigillo meo apud Berwyk predictam die et anno Domini supradictis. *Probacio.* Probatum fuit presens testamentum apud Cawod, primo die mensis Junii, anno Domini M^{o}cccc^{mo}xx^{mo}, et commissa fuit administracio omnium bonorum ipsius defuncti tempore mortis sue executoribus in testamento nominatis, in forma constitucionis legati super hoc edite. Et facta fuit littera in forma debita, etc.

John Chapman.

Testamentum domini Johannis Chapman nuper de Thirsk, capellani defuncti. Dimiss' est nullo inventario exhibito.

[ii. 293b.] In Dei omine Amen. vij^{o} die mensis Januarij Anno Domini millesimo cccc^{mo} lij^{o} Ego Dominus Johannes Chapman compos mentis et sane memorie condo testamentum meum in hunc modum. In primis lego animam meam Deo Omnipotenti beate Marie et omnibus sanctis et corpus meum sepeliendum in cimiterio Omnium Sanctorum de Barwike et lego portatorium meum pro mortuario meo. Item lego quinque cereos quinque librarum cum iiij^{or} torchiis ad ignendum circa corpus meum et post mortem meam seruiendum sacramento. Item lego iiij^{or} presbiteros ad portandum me ad ecclesiam et quemlibet eorum habere ijs. Item lego xiiij presbiteros esse ad exequias meas et missam et quilibet eorum habere viij denarios. Item lego viij^{o} clericos parochiales esse ad exequias et missam meam, habere quilibet eorum iiij^{d}. Item lego illi presbitero qui celebrat missam et sepilit me vj^{s} viij^{d}. Item iij presbiteris ad celebrandum pro me xxj marcas. Item lego v marcas *to y^{e}*

stypyll' ecclesie de Barwike. Item lego pro fenestra factura in cancellario xl^s. Item lego ymagini beate Marie cum filio suo in manu sua dextera ante Altare ecclesie de Tadcast' iiij^{or} marcas. Item lego ecclesie de Adeill' vj^s viij^d. Item lego ecclesie de Tong' unum nobile. Item lego Elyott Harde quinque marcas. Item lego filie Thome Marshall' de Harwod xl^s. Item lego Willelmo coco Rectoris de Barwike x^s. Item lego iiij^{or} marcas ad distribuendum pauperibus pro anima mea. Item lego iiij^{or} marcas pro pane et cerevisia ad faciendum pro me. Item lego Willelmo Boswell xl^s. Item lego Willelmo Carter xl^s. Residuum vero omnium bonorum meorum non legatorum post mortem meam do et lego Willelmo Bosewell et Willelmo Carter ut ipsi ordinent et disponant prout salute anime mee quomodo salubrius & sanccius videatur ut a domino Deo omnipotenti [etc.] ad remissionem anime mee et omnium fidelium defunctorum. In cuius rei testimonium huic scripto sigillum meum presentibus apposui. Datum apud Berwik vij^o die Januarij Anno Domini millesimo cccc^{mo} lij^o. Probatum fuit presens testamentum penultimo die mensis Marcij Anno Domini &c. Liiij^o, et commissa administracio executoribus in eodem testamento nominatis juratis in forma juris.

RICHARD BURNHAM, Rector, 1432–1457.

[ii. 348a.] In Dei nomine Amen. Anno Domini millesimo cccclvij^{mo} Ego Ricardus Burnham Rector ecclesie parochialis de Barwike in Elmett compos mentis et sane memorie condo testamentum meum in hunc modum. In primis lego animam meam Deo omnipotenti, Et corpus meum ad sepeliendum in ecclesia parochiali ubi me obire contigerit. Item lego nomine mortuarij mei quod jus est et consuetudo patrie. Item lego fabrice ecclesie Cath. Ebor. vj^s viij^d. Item lego fabrice ecclesie Lincon' (*sic*) vj^s viij^d. Item fabrice ecclesie Sancti Wilfridi Ripon' iij^s iiij^d. Item lego fabrice ecclesie Sancti Johannis Beũ iij^s iiij^d. Item fabrice ecclesie Beate Marie de Suthwell' iij^s iiij^d. Item lego iiij^{or} ordinibus Fratrum Mendicancium Ebor. iiij^s. Item lego Fratribus de Pontefracto xij^d. Et volo quod expense mee funerales fiant secundum discrecionem executorum meorum. Huins autem testamenti mei executores meos facio & constituo Ric̃m Waterton armigerum de Coringham Magistrum Robertum Thornton, Aliciam Constable, sororem meam et Johannem Grenefeld seniorem armigerum. Item lego ecclesie de Barwike predicta nouum missale meum pro uno capellano ad celebrandum pro anima mea per unum annum. Item lego dessis chori edificand' xx^s. Item lego (*ad*) campanile edificandum xxs. Residuum omnium bonorum meorum non legatorum committo in manus executorum meorum prenominatorum. Hijs testibus, Johanne Dawson, Domino Johanne Saunder capellano parochiali de Barwike, et aliis. Dat. apud Barwike vicessimo die mensis Aprilis Anno Domini, etc., quinquagesimo septimo. Et commissa administracio Ricardo Waterton armigero executori in eodem testamento nominato jurato in forma juris Reseruata potestate consimilem administracionem committendi ceteris coexecutoribus in huiusmodi testamento nominatis cum venerint in forma juris accepturi.

Date of Probate not given.—Will before, of Wm. Spencer, proved May 25, 1457, and Will of Master John Barnyngham next after, proved May 28.

---

[1]John Grenefeld.

[iii. 301b.] In Dei nomine Amen. Anno Domini millesimo ccccmo sexagesimo quarto die xviijo mensis Octobris. Ego Johannes Grenefeld sane memorie et bone mentis condo testamentum meum in hunc modum. In primis do et lego animam meam Deo beate Marie et omnibus sanctis corpusque meum sepeliendum in choro ecclesie parochialis de Berwyk in Elmet. Item volo quod Margareta uxor mea habeat omnia terras et tenementa mea tam libera quam illa terras et tenementa secundum consuetudinem manerii necnon firmas et redditus ad terminum annorum durante vita dicte Margarete, salvo semper quod ipsa vel heredes mei solvat seu solvant Willelmo Grenefeld fratri meo annuatim durante vita sua vij marcas, prout plenius continetur in quadam carta per Johannem Grenefeld patrem nostrum sibi inde confecta. Item volo quod Johannes filius meus habeat post decessum Margerete uxoris mee omnia terras et tenementa mea in villa et campis de Altoftes sibi et heredibus de corpore suo legitime procreatis et si contingat predictum Johannem sine herede de corpore suo legitime procreato obire tunc volo quod omnia predicta terre et tenementa in villa et campis predictis remaneant rectis heredibus meis. Item do et lego residuum bonorum meorum Margarete uxori mee ut illa disponat prout sibi placuerit. Hiis testibus Willelmo Ryther generoso Willelmo Derley et aliis. [*Probate granted* 19 *March* 1464-5, *to Margaret, the widow.*]

Thomas Grene.

[iii. 518b.] In Dei nomine Amen. Sexto die Marcij Anno Domini Mocccc^{mo}xxxvijo. Ego Thomas Grene compos mentis mee condo ordino & facio testamentum meum in hunc modum. In primis lego et comendo animam meam Deo omnipotenti beatissimeque Virgini Marie & omnibus sanctis corpusque meum sepeliendum in ecclesia mea parochiali de Barwyk. Item lego iiij^{or} lb cere ad comburendum die cepulture mee. Item lego pro mortuario meo optimum meum animal. Item lego cappellano parochiali celebranti circa corpus meum die sepulture mee xij^{d}. Et clerico parochiali iiij^{d}. Item do et lego Roberto filio meo j togam de sangwyn pro corpore meo aptatam. Residuum vero omnium bonorum meorum superius non legatorum primitus debitis meis persolutis & expensis meis funera-

(1) The Greenfields were the owners of Barnbow prior to the Gascoignes, to whom they sold their estate The following inscriptions were, according to Dr Johnstone's MS., on tombstones in Barwick Church:—Orate pro animabus Joh. Grenefeld et Johanne uxoris sue que ob. in fest St. Sim. et Jud. 1442. Orate pro anima Joh Grenefeld, servientis ad legem qui ob. 23 Oct., 1464.
William Greenfield Archbishop of York (1304—1315), was of this family.

libus perimpletis do & lego executrici mee subscripte ad faciendum inde et disponendum pro salute anime mee prout coram summo iudice voluerint respondere. Huius autem testamenti mei executricem facio videlicet Johannam uxorem meam ad omnia premissa in forma predicta fideliter faciendum & perimplendum. In cuius rei testimonium sigillum meum apposui. Dat. die & anno supradictis. [*Proved* 4 *May*, 1438.]

HENRY ELLIS.[1]

[iv. 158b.] Item secundo die mensis Maij Anno Domini Millesimo cccc^{mo} septuagesimo primo comissa (*sic*) fuit ad^{o} omnium bonorum que fuerunt Henrici Elys nuper de Berwyk in Elmet ab intestato defuncti Agneti relicte et administratrici omnium bonorum dicti defuncti autoritate ordinaria deputata iurata (*sic*) in forma juris, &c.

WILLIAM HAWK, Rector, 1457-1472.

Testamentum magistri Willelmi Hawke sacre theologie professoris.

[iv. 171a]. In Dei nomine Amen. Decimo septimo die mensis Januarij Anno Domini millesimo cccc^{mo} septuagesimo primo Ego Magister Willelmus Hawk sacre Theologie professor ac Rector ecclesie parochialis de Berwyk in Elmet compos mentis et sane memorie ordino et facio testamentum meum in hunc modum. In primis, lego animam meam Deo omnipotenti beate Marie virgini et celestis curie omnibus sanctis corpusque meum sepeliendum in choro ecclesie predicte coram summo altari. Et lego sex libras in exequiis meis et messis pro anima mea celebrandis comburandas. Et lego nomine mortuarii venerabilissimo in Xpo patri et domino Domino nostro Eboracensi Archiepiscopo equum meum apud Medlay existentem vna cum sella freno occriis collobio et pug'. Item lego ad celebrandum pro anima in dicta ecclesia parochili vni presbitero idoneo per tempus trium annorum Dando eidem quolibet anno iiij^{li} xiij^{s} iiij^{d} si bona mea debitis et legatis meis persolutis ad hoc se extendant et sufficiant. Item lego Magistro Thome Sayls sacre Theologie professori monacho monasterii beate Marie Ebor. meum psalterium optimum manu mea conscriptum et glosatum per Hugonem de Vienna ad orandum pro anima mea. Item lego fabrice ecclesie de Berwyk xxiij^{s} iiij^{d} existentes in manibus yconomorum iam existencium dicte ecclesie. Item lego domui sive loco religioso sancti Andree Ebor. xiij^{s} iiij^{d}. Item lego loco religioso sancte Trinitatis Ebor. xiij^{s} iiij^{d}. Item lego cuilibet ordini sive domui Fratrum Mendicancium Trinitatis Ebor. iij^{s} iiij^{d}. Item lego gilde corporis Xpi iij^{s}. Item lego Roberti Fulliffh servienti meo unum domum sive mansum in villa de Berwyk una cum xij acris terre eidem pertinentibus. Item lego eidem Roberto unam equam albi coloris cum pulla eiusdem. Item lego uxori dicti Roberti unam

(1) His son, Thomas, added the bay window with the armorial glass, to Kiddal Hall, in 1501. For a pedigree of the Ellis family see the Genealogist, vol. xiv. p. 105.

vaccam. Item do et lego Elisabet Fullygh unam vaccam. Item do et lego Agneti Fullygh unam juvencam. Item do et lego Roberto Parker unam vaccam. Item lego Johanne Parker unam togarum mearum. Item do et lego Willelmo Fullygh pro servicio michi impenso unam vaccam tunicam et sibi togam competentem. Item do et lego Thome Pees tunicam caligas et camisiam. Item do et lego Magistro Willelmo Poteman officiali ij pawtener rynges dearg' et deaurat'. Item do et lego domino Johanni Broderton unam togam. Item do et lego Johanni Elys unam togam. Item do et lego domino Willelmo Steward unam togam. Residuum vero omnium bonorum meorum non legatorum do et lego executoribus meis quos ordino et facio magistrum Thomam Sayls sacre Theologie professorem et Robertum Fullygh servientem meum ut ipsi disponant omnia bona mea secundum discrecionem eorum ad utilitatem et salutem anime mee. Testibus Domino Willelmo Steward cappellano parochiali ibm. Willelmo Otlay clerico parochiali et aliis. Datum die et Anno Dni. supradictis. Probatum fuit presens testamentum xxij^{o} die mensis Januarij Anno Dñi. supradicto. Et commissa adm' Roberto Fullygh executori in eodem testamento nominato jurato in forma Juris &c. Magistro Thoma Sayls executore in dicto testamento nominato onus hujusmodi administracionis penitus recusante &c.

---

(1) RICHARD LASCY of Barwick, gentleman.

[v. 210.] Item vicesimo nono die mensis Januarij Anno Domini millesimo cccc^{mo}lxxxiij^{cio} supradicto commissa fuit administracio omnium bonorum que fuerunt Ricardi Lascy nuper de Berwyk in Elmett generosi ab intestato defuncti Agneti relicte et administratrici in bonis euisdem defuncti auctoritate ordinaria deputata in forma juris jurate.

---

(2) WILLIAM GASCOIGNE of Lasingcroft, Esq.

[v. 1a. Deed Poll. *Will illegible.*] 7 November, 1475. To all maner of men to whom this p'sent writing shall see here or com. Be it knawen that I, Wiłłm Gascoign of lasingcrofte, Esquire, make and ordance my will in the fourme that followes. That is to say. Where Sir Wiłłm Stapilton, Knyght, Wiłłm Skargill of ledes, John Vavaso^{r} of Newton, Esquiers, Nicholas More, gentilman, and Wiłłm Walwayn, chappelleyn, ar enfeffed by me the said Wiłłm Gascoign, Esquier, in the maner of lasingcrofte and in all the landę teñentę rentę s'uice w'in the said man' and also in all the landę teñentę rentę and s'uice in Abirford, P'lington, Kirkgarforth, West garthforth, Gartforth Morehouse, Mekelfeld and Milford which at any

(1) Glover in his *Visitation of* 1584, (p. 453, Foster's Edition) gives the inscription on Lacy's tombstone in Barwick Church, "Orate pro Ricardo Lacy, et Agnete et Elizabetha uxoribus suis" and also the Arms of Lacy impaling Sothill and Thwaites.

(2) For Pedigrees of the Gascoignes see Foster's *West Riding Pedigrees* and the various *Yorkshire Heralds* visitations. William Gascoigne was married, 4 Edward IV, to Joanetta, daughter of Sir William Beckwith of Clint, by Elizabeth, daughter of Sir William Plumpton of Plumpton. He was the son of John Gascoigne and Isabel, daughter and heiress of William Heton of Mirfield, who afterwards married Sir Ralph Greystock, Knight, Baron of Greystock. Administration to her effects was granted 3 August, 1473, to Sir Henry Vavasour, Thomas Thwaites, and William Scargill. See *Surtees Society*, Vol. 53, p. 20n.

tyme was myne the said Wiłłm Gascoign, Esquier And in all other maners, landꝭ, teñentes, rentes and s'uice which late wer Dame Isabell Graistok modur to me, the saide Wiłłm Gascoign, in the maners of Mirfeld, Westheton, Estheton and Ardislow, and in all lands, teñentꝭ in Polington to the entent and fulfill my last will shewed and declared to thame my foresaide feoffees by writinge under my seale. Be it knawen that Jenet, my wiff, haue a state of a rent charge of xiiijth markꝭ in the yere in name of hir thyrdꝭ at terme of hir lyve to be taken in the man' of Estheton and in all landes and teñentꝭ in the said man' of Estheton. And I will that Wiłłm, my son, haue a state of a rent charge of c^{s} in ye yere during his lyve to be taken in my chef place in P'lington, Milford, and in the teneñt in the holding of Richard Preston in Garthforth Morehouse, provided that the said Wiłłm shall take of the said sum of c^{s} but v mark during the tyme his susters be holpyn, also I will that Thoñs my son haue a state of a Rent charge of c^{s} in the yere during his lyve to be taken in the maner of Westheton, and in all the landes and teñentꝭ to the said Man' p'tenyng providing also that the said Thoñs shall take but yerely v mark to the said susters be holpyn. Also I will that all the p'fites and revenous of all the said maners, landis, rentꝭ and teñentꝭ except thes be fore except to be at disposicõn of my executores and my said feoffees to the entent to pay my dettꝭ. And for to pay and fulfill my legate in my testament comprissed and expressed. And ou' that of the surpleges of the said revenous for to be disposed to the helpinge and fortheringe of my said daughters. Also I will that my son and heire be rented and demened in his mariage and his demenyng aft' the discrecõns of my said feoffes and executors. And if he will not after thame be demened then I will my said feoffees take the p'fites of all the said mauers, landes, rentes, and teñents before rehersid to the valow of cc marke to enlarge the some of the mariage of my said daughters in my testament cõpressed. Also I will my said feoffees aft^{r} my legacꝭ in my testament expressed be fulfilled make astate unto my son and heire of the maner of Lasingcrofte with all other lands [&c.]. And also in all other landes [&c.] in Aberford, Perlington, Lutherton, Westgarthforth, Garthforth, Kirkgarthforth, Morehouse, Mekelfeld and Milford to hym and to the heires of his body lawfully begottyn. In default, "to next heires of my body lawfully begotyn." In default, "to the heires of John Gascoign my fader." In default, "to the right heires of Nicholas Gascoyn." [*Portion cut off*].

Direction to feoffees to make "a state to my son and heire" of the "maners of Mirfelde, Westheton, Estheton, and Ardislow, and of all other lands [&c.] in P'lington in Balne to hym & the heires of his body lawfully begotyn." In default, "to heires of my body lawfully begotyn." In default, "to heires of John Gascoign & Isabell his wife." In default, "to right heires of the said Isabell for evermore."

In witnesse wherof I the forsaid Wiłłm Gascoigne hath set to my seale gevyn the vij daye of Novembr, the yere of our lorde God M·cccclxxvth

[1] JOHN RILYE, Citizen and Haberdasher, of London.

[P.C.C. 31 Daughtry.] In the Name of God Amen. The Seauenteenth Daye of July, in the yeare of oure Lord God One Thowsande fiue hundred threscoare and seaventene, and in the nynetenth yeare of the reigne of our souereigne lady Elizabeth, by the grace of God, Quene of Englande, Fraunce and Irelande, defendor of the Faithe, etc. I, John Rylie, Citezin and haberdassher, of London, beinge sicke in bodie, but of good and perfecte remembraunce, laude and praise be giuen to Almightie God, do make and ordaine this my presente Testament conteyninge herein my last will in manner and forme followinge. That is to saye. First and principally I commend my Soule to Almightie God, my maker and Creator, and to his only Sonne Jesus Christ, my Sauiour and Redemer, in whome and by the mearitts of whose blessed death and passion I trust to be saued, And I will my bodie to be honestly brought to the place of my buriall wthin the parryshe Churche of St. Magnus the Marter, neare London Bridge, where I am a parrishioner, at the discreation of myne Executor hereunder named. Item I will there shalbe a Sermon made at my Buriall by some godly learned preacher, and I bequeath to him for his paines and labor Tenne shillinges. Item I giue and bequeath to thirtene poore men euerye of them a gowne, to be made of some good and stronge cloath, for theire most proffitt, and they to attend on my Bodie to the Earth. Item I give and bequeath to and amongst the poor prisoners in the fleet, where most need is, Fortye shillinges. Item I giue and bequeath to and amongst the poore people in Bedlam, Fortie shillinges. Item I giue and bequeath to my welbeloued frende John Challoner a blacke gowne. Item I giue and bequeath to Alice Mondaye, my late seruante, Tenne powndes. Item I give and bequeath to my Cosinn Wylton, Twentie poundes. Item I giue and bequeath to my welbeloued frende Mrs. Croscrowe, in Ireland, Twentye poundes. Item I give and bequeath to my frende Thomas Croscrowe Twentie poundes. Item I giue and bequeath to my seruaunte James Nott Tenne poundes. Item I giue and bequeath unto Johan Rylie ats Taylor, my kinswoman nowe in my house, Two hundred poundes of lawfull money of England, at one entire payment to be made unto her. Also I giue and bequeath to the same Johan all my household stuff, viz. Brasse, pewter, wollen and linnen, beddes, bedsteades and beddinge Excepte all myne Apparell. Also I giuc and bequeath to the same Johan Rylie ats Taylor, my lease, interest and tearme of my houses, landes and Tenements sett, lieing, and beinge in Longe Lane, in the parrishe of St George the Martir, in Sowthwerck, in the Countie of Surrye, wth all and singular their appurtenaunces: To haue and to houlde the same lease, houses, landes, and appurtenaunces to her and her Assignes. And the remainder of the

(1) The following Wills have been printed by the Thoresby Society—Elizabeth Nettleton, of Roundhay, 1517 (IX. 89). Robert Symkin, 1518 (IX. 90), and Rauff Aunger, of Barwick, 1529 (XI. 42). The Will of William Ellis, of Kiddall, 1535, has been printed by the Surtees Society (CVI. 48], and the Will of Timothy Bright, 1615, Rector of Barwick, by the Yorkshire Archæological Society (XVII. 52).

yeares to come after her death to John Taylor and Symon Taylor, her two sonnes, wth all the proffitts thereunto belonging duringe the continuaunce of the same lease. Item I gine and bequeath to my said Cosinn Johañ a salt of siluer guilte, one Tankerd of siluer guilte, one dozen of siluer spoones, parcell guilte. Item I giue and bequeath to Joħn Taylo[r] aforesaide my Cosinn, Fiftie poundes, and to thafforesaide Symoñ Taylor, my Cosinn, other Fiftie poundes, and to my Cosinne Margarett Taylor Fiftie poundes. Prouided alwayes and my will and mynd is Thatt all and euery the saide three seuerall Sommes of Fiftie poundes by me last bequeathed to my said Cosins Johñ Taylor, Symon Taylor and Margaret Taylor shalbe paide to the said Johañ Rylie aŧs Taylor, theire mother, forthw[th] to theire use. Item I giue and bequeath to the parson and Churchwardeins of the Towne of Barwicke in Elmett, in the Countie of Yorke, for the time being, and theire Successors, parsonns and Churchwardeins of the same parishe for euer, all that my nowe dwellinge house in London, commonly called by the Signe of the Cradle, sett and beinge in parishe of St. Magnus the Martir abouesaide, at the Northende of London Bridge, in the Bridge warde, To haue and to houlde the same house to the said parsonns and Churchwardeins, theire Successors and Assignes for euer, uppon this condicon: That the said parsonne and Churchwardeins, or one of them, theire Successors and Assignes, do in and uppon euery Sondaye for euer from and after thexpiracon of a lease by me made to William Owen of my said howse, gine and deliuer to Twelve poore parsons, parishioners of the saide Towne of Barwicke in Elmett, in the parryshe Churche, betwixt the redinge of the Epistle and gospell in the seruice time, one peny loafe of swete and wholsom̃e brede and one peny in money to euery one of them. And so from thenceforth to be giuen by the said parsoñ and Churchwardeins, theire Successors and Assignes for euermore, and not for any other intent or purpose. Item I will and my mynde and intent is, That the executor of this my testament shall, after thende of six monethes next after my decease, yearely euery yeare duringe the continuaunce of the lease of my said house, paye or cause to be paide to the said parsonne and Churchwardeins theire Successors or Assignes, Fiue poundes foure shillinges of lawfull money of England. And I will that they, the same parsonne and Churchwardeins, shall distribute the same on euery Sondaye to Twelue poor people, euerie one a penye, and a peanye lofe as aforesaide. And I will that the same my executor shall likewyse yearely duringe the continuaunce of the same lease, paye to the same Parsoñe and Churchewardeins and theire Successors, to make merry withall, amongst them, six shillinges. And my will and mynde is also that my saide kinswoman Johan Rylie aŧs Taylor and her Assignes shall haue thuse com̃oditie and occupieinge of the upper romes of my saide house duringe the saide lease of the same Willyam Owen, with free ingresse and egresse. Prouided alwaies and my wyll, mynde and intente is, That if the lawes of this Realme will not ne cannot permitt my bequest towchinge my said howse to the saide parsonne and Churchwardeins to be good and to stand in full effect to them. Then I giue and bequeath my saide house wth thappurtenaunces to my saide kynswoman Johan Taylor ats Rylie duringe her naturall life, and after her decease to Johñ and Symoñ, her Childreñ, and theire heires for euer. The Rest and Reasidue of all my goodes, Chattells and debtes, which I will shall remaine in my nowe dwellinge house in the Custodie of the said Johan and my ouerseers hereafter named, or twoo of them untill the saide Johañ my kinswoman be fullie satisfied and paide the legacies before by me willed unto her and her said Children (My Debtes paide, my other legacies herein performed, and my Funerall expences dischardged) I wholly giue and bequeath to my well beloued Cosinn, Henry Shawe of London, ymbroderer, whome of this my presente Testament and last will I make and ordaine my sole Executor. And for the better execucõn hereof I make and ordeine my trustie frendes Thomas Bagnall, Robert Stokes and Roberte Lydger, my Ouerseers, to see this my last will in all thinges performed as my trust is in them. And I giue and bequeath to euerye of my saide Ouerseers for theire paines therein to be taken Twentie poundes a pece of lawfull money of Englande, Also and finally I will and my mynde is, whatsoever is herein wrytten, interlined, augmented, of diminisshed by me or by the saide Thomas Bagnall by my appointement, That the same shalbe as parcell of this my last will and Testament, and shall stande in full force. In witnes whereof to this my presente Testament and last will, I, the saide John Rylie, haue sett my hande and seale. Yeouen the Day and yeare abouesaide, By me, John Rylie, By me, John Crimson, By me, Thomas Cooke, the Curate of St. Magnus, By me, Walter Wilcoks, By me, Willyam Owen. [*Proved 1 August, 1577, by John Jucent, notary public, procurator of Henry Shawe, the executor named.*]

HENRY TAYLYOR of Thorner, Clerk.

[xvij. 412a.] In the name of God Amen, the xiij day of January, in the yeare of or lord God, 1564. I, Henry Taylyor of Thorner, within the countie of Yorke, clarke, by the visitacon of Almyghtie God seike in bodie, of good and pfite rememberance do make this my last will and testament in maner and forme followinge. Fyrst I bequithe my soull to Almightie God and to all the celestiall company of heaven, and my bodie to be buried wthin the churche yeard of Barwicke in Elmet, nighe unto my ansesters. Also I gyve and bequithe unto Alice brahm̃, Eliž. Brahm̃ and Anne Mylner, all my goodę moveable and unmoveable, unbequest or gyven, I gyve them frelie to the said Alice, Eliž and Anne, whom I make my holle and full executrixes of this my last will and testament. Also my will is that all my goodę shalbe devided at the discrecon of the Right Worshipfull Sr Wittm Vavasor, Knight, whom I make supvisor of this my last will and testament, desyring hym of his worship to helpe thes poore children to ther Right, according to this my meanynge, and to have for his paynes one pece of gold. And further my will is, that Wittm Mylner shall have no occupacon nor dominion of any pte or pcell of my goodę, nor any other of his kyn. Witness[s] hereof Thomas Post, Francę Uttley, Oswald Holden, Wittm Bewerley, and others mo. [*Proved* 20 *March*, 1564-5.]

Thomas Gascoigne of Lasingcroft, Esq.[1]

[xvii. 536.] In the name of God Amen, the seavent day of Junij in the yeare of o[r] lord God 1565. I, Thomas Gascoigne of Lasingcroft in the countie of Yorke, esquier, holle of bodie and of good and pfite remẽberance do make this my last will and testament in maner and forme followinge. First I bequithe my soull to Allmyghtie God, my creator and redemer, and my bodie to be buried in the pishe church of Barwicke or elswhere yt shall please Almyghtie God. Item I bequithe to Eliz̃ my doughter, not begotten in matrimonye one hundreth markes of lawfull money of England, of the which said som̃e I will that xx[li] shalbe paid unto her at the day of hir mariage and other twentie poundę to be paid unto her twelve monethe after hir said mariage and the residew of the said som̃e of one hundreth markes to be paid accordinge to the promis and coueñat maid betwixt me, the said Thomas Gascoigne, and John Goodyere as by the said agrement yt dothe and may appeare. Item I gyve and bequithe to Margaret Hopton, my cosin, Sex poundę thirtene shillingę fourepence of lawfull Englishe money. Item I gyve and bequithe to hir sister, Dorithe Hopton, vj[li] xiij[s] iiij[d] of lawfull Englishe money. Item I gyve and bequithe to Isabell Womwell the yonger, Ten poundę of lawfull Englishe money. To eu[y] one of my household s'vutę, both man s'vnt, woman s'vnt and child, vj[s] viij[d] of lawfull Englishe money. To my brother Gascoigne, my gray ambling geldinge. To George Gascoigne, my blacke geldinge. To my brother John Gascoigne, one holle yeares rent of his ferme in P'lington, next & Im̃edyatlie after my deathe. Item I will and bequest Jane Gascoigne my wyf all maner and suche plaite as was hir fathers. To Xpofer Hopton, Thomas Doweman and Henrye Ellis, all my laudę, Tentę and hereditaments in Ardeslay, in the countie of Yorke, and all that my mano[r] of P'lington, with all my lands, teñtę and hereditamentę in P lingtou aforesaid, laite in the Tenure of Mathew Wentworthe and nowe in the Tenure and occupacon of John Gascoigne, and all that my messuage or teñ't, and all landes· tenements and hereditaments in P'lington aforesaid, now in the Tenure of Wittm Horberye, and all that my messuage, and all my laudę, Tenementę and hereditaments in P'lington aforesaid, now in the Tenure of Thomas Horberye, to have and to hold to them, there heires and assignes for and during the Terme of [*blank*] yeares, to thuse and intent that the said Xtofer Hopton,

---

(1) Thomas Gascoigne married Joan, daughter of William Ilson, of Gunby, and died circa 9 Sept, 1565. He was the son of John Gascoigne and Anne, daughter and co-heiress of John, third son of Sir Henry VaVasour of Haslewood. She was married secondly to Henry Ellis of Kiddall. His bequests to parsons and churchwardens, and the absence of religious bequests are some eVidence that he adhered to the National Church, and the family apparently remained in conformity until the time of Sir John Gascoigne, the first Baronet. The Micklefield or Sturton family were also adherents of the Church of England.

Thomas Doweman and Henrye Ellis, theire heires and assignes, shall yeyld and paye to the p'sonns hereafter naymed the sōmes of money to them gyven by this my last Will and Testament of the yssues, revenues and profitt*e* comyne and growynge of the said land*e*, Tent*e* and hereditament*e*. . . . . Item I gyve and bequithe to the poore and nedie people of Wytkirke p'ishe, xx^s^ yerlie, to be distributed and gyven to them during the terme of seaven yeares, so That the same sōme shalbe distributed by the p'son or curate therof, withe the churchwardens of the same. To the poore and nedie people of Barwicke, xx^s^ yerlie during seaven yeres, to be distributed and gyven by the curat and churchewardens of the same. To the poore and nedie people of Aberforth, xx^s^ yerlie to be distributed and gyven to them during the terme of seaven yeares as is aforesaid. To the poore & nedie people of Garforthe, xiij^s^ iiij^d^ yerlie, to be distributed and gyven to them duringe the terme of seven yeres as is aforesaid. To the reparacon & amendment of the highe waye aboute Lasyngcrofte, xx^s^ yearlie, to be gyven duringe the terme of twentie yeares next ensuing my deathe. To eu'y one of my brother John children xl^s^ of lawfull Englishe money. To euery one of my syster Awmbler children v^li^ xiij^s^ iiij^d^ of lawfull Englishe money. To Trowls Townesend seaven poundes of lawfull Englishe money, to be paid unto hym xx^s^ by yeare duringe seaven yeares. To Eliz. Doweman, my nece, xl^s^ of lawfull Englishe money. The Residue of my goodes unbequithed, my dettes and my legacis pformid and my funerall expenses deduct, I gyve to Wittm Gascoigne & Robt Barnebye, whom I make the sole executors of this my last will and Testament. Thes being witnesses. Thomas Dowman, George Leyton, John Craspe, Robt. Ball and others as Henrye Ellis, gent., and Wittm Robinson. [*Proved* 6 *May*, 1566.]

HENRY ELLIS, of Barwick, Gentleman.

[xvij. 818a.] In Dei noie, Amen, the Fyrste day of Junij, in the nynte yeare of the Reigne of o^r^ moste dread Sou'eigne ladie Eliz̃, queue of England, Fraunce and Ireland, Defender of the faithe, and supreme head of the churche of England. I, Henrye Ellis of Barwicke in Elmet, gent., constitutethe ordeynithe and makithe this my last will and Testament in maner and forme followinge, that is to saye. Fyrste I bequithe my soull to Almyghtie God my creator, to Jesū Christe my redemer, and to the hollie ghoste my comforter, and to all the hollie companye of heaven, also I bequithe my bodye to be buried within the Churche of Barwicke. Also I bequithe my good*e* to be devided in thre ptes, one pte to Agnes, my wyf, one to John Ellis my sonne, the thirde to declere my will vpō and to bringe me furth withall. Also I gyve to Franc*e* Mallet, my doughter in lawe, x^li^, to be taken of my pte Also I will that my brother, Richarde Gascon, have the custodye of my sonne, John Ellis pte, unto he be xxj yeares old or be marryed and keipe house, and his pte to be deliu'ed to hym, and yf it fortune John Ellis my sonne to dye before he keipe house or be maried and have no childe, Than I will that Francȩ Mallet, his sister, have his ꝑte. The Residew on my ꝑte unbequithed, my dettes and funeralls discharged, I gyve to Agnes, my wyf, and John, my sonne, whom I make my full executors of this my last will and testament. Witnesse herof I have wrytten this my last will and Testament and subscribed my nayme withe my owne hand, the yeare and day above wrytten. Rauf Aungell, Francis More, witness herof. [*Proved 22 June*, 1568.]

JOHN WILSON, of Roundhay, Husbandman.

[xxiii. 797.] In the name of God Amen, the nynetyne daye of Aprill, in the thirtie yere of the Reigne of o^r^ Sou'aigne ladie quene Elizabethe, by the grace of God of England, Frannce and Irelande, Defendres of the faithe, &c. Anno Dñi 1588. I, John Wilson of Roundhay, in the ꝑishe of Barwicke and Countie of Yorke, husbandman, being sicke of bodie but whole and ꝑfecte of myud, praysed be the lorde God, do ordeyne constitute and make this my last will and testament, in manner and forme followinge. First I geve and bequeath my soule to Almyghtie God, my maker and Redemer, and my bodie to be buried w^th^in my ꝑishe Churche yarde at Barwicke or els where it shall please my Executors. Also I will that my debtȩ be paide out of my whole goodes, then I will that my goodes be equallie devided into three ꝑtȩ, whereof I will that one ꝑte shalbe towardes the bringinge of me forthe and discharging of my funerall expencȩ. Also I will that Isabell, my wife, shall have one other ꝑte. And then I will that the thirde and last ꝑte of my goodes shalbe equallie devided amongest my children, that is to say Willm Wilson, Radulfe Wilson, Rychard Wilson, Mychaell Wilson, and Robt Wilsone, my sonnes, and Isabell Brame, my doughter, so that everyeone of these my foresaid children shall have to that portion of goodes w^c^he they haue had of me, there father, heretofore, the hole some of fortie poundes. That is to saye, to Willm Wilsone, my sonne, twentie poundes, for he haithe Received of me heretofore other xx^li^. Also I geve to Radulfe Wilson, my sonne, ten poundes, for he hathe Receaved heretofore xxx^ti^ poundes. Also I geue to Rycharde Wilson, my sonne, xxxj^tie^ poundȩ, for he hathe Receaved of me heretofore ix^li^. Also I gene to Mychall Wilson, my sonne, fortye poundȩ. Also I geue to Robt Wilson, my sonne, twentie poundes, for he haithe Received of me heretofore xx^li^. Also I geue to Peter Brame, my sonne-in-lawe, in the Right of Isabell, his wife, twentye poundes, for he hathe Received of me heretofore xx^li^. [Provision that in case the aforesaid third part shall be insufficient to pay each child £40, then the remainder of his owne and first part shall remain towards the payment thereof, and the remainder thereof shall be equally divided amongst his wife and children, William, Rycharde, Rauf, Mychaell and Robert, his sons, and Isabell Brame and Elizabeth Tottie, his daughters.] Also I geve and bequeath to Isabell, my wife, all my Leases duringe her life naturall, and after her decease to Mychaell Wilson, my sonne. And if it please God my said sonne Mychaell to dye wthout issue of his bodie lawfully begotten, Then I will that the Reu'sion of my said leases shall Remayne and come unto Isabell Brame my doughter and to her assigns. Also I geve and bequeathe to Elizabeth Wilson, my sister, one ewe and one lambe. Also I geue and bequeathe to eu'ye one of my Childers Children nowe lyvinge one ewe and one lambe. To Willm Glovers thre children thre gimber lambes. To Clemet Wilson thre children thre gymber lambes. To Nycholas Whalay, one gymber lambe. To Elizabethe Mathewe, one ewe and one lambe. To Roger Beu'ley, my man, one gymber lambe. To Sessellye Wilson, one gimber lambe. The Residue of my goodę, my dettę beinge paide, my funerall expenses discharged, I will shalbe equallie devided amonge my wife and forsaid children, whome I make executors of this my last will. And I hartelie Request Nycholas Beu'ley, John Tomlinson, Lawrence Askwth, and John Kyllingbeck to be the supvisors of this my last will, and that my foresaid wife and children shall in all causes and contrau'ses if any happen to arise hereafter refar themselfes holye to thes my forsaid supvisors. Thes beinge witnesses Nycholes Beu'ley, John Tomlinson, Lawrence Askwthe, John Kyllingbecke and Clemet Wilson. [*Proved* 19 *June*, 1588.]

ROBERT SETLE of Potterton, husbandman.

[xxiii. 145.] In the name of God Amen, Anno Dni. 1585. I, Robert Setle of Potterton, in the pishe of Barwicke in Elmett, within the dioces of Yorke, husbandman . . . . My body to be buryed wthin the Church yard of Barwicke aforesayd. Item I geve and bequethe unto Henry Setle, my sonne, xls. I geve to Elizabethe, my doughter, xls. To M'garet, my doughter, xls. To Anne Potter, one ewe hogge. To Barbary Potter, one Ewe hogge. To Mary Potter, one ewe hogg, and to Janet Potter, one ewe hogg, and the same to be delyuered ymediately after my decease, to be kepte together joyntely to the use of the sayd Anne, Barbary, Mary, and Janet, till any one of them be of Lawfull yeres. To Mary Setle, doughter of Richard Setle, one Ewe hogge. To Robert Setle, my brother sonne, my weddinge Jackett and one pair of hose. To my brother, Willm Settle, one Read Quy, in consideracon of one wedder and one ox wch I had of hym. I geve unto John Setle, sonne of Henry Setle, one Ewe. I geve unto Willm Setle, sonne of Lawrence Settle, one Ewe. Unto Michael Potter, one dublett. Unto Henry Setle, my sonne, one fether bedd. The Residew of all my goodes . . . . to Isabel, my wife, Henry, my sonne, Elizabeth and M'garet, my doughters, whom I make my full joynte executors. Also I will that my wife shall have the government and kepinge of all my sayd children during widowhead, and after she be married I will that my brother, Henry Setle, shall haue the kepinge and tuicon of them and their porcions, and also I will that Isabell, my wyfe, shall not Lett or sett over any pte or pcell of my Tenemente or other growndes and Tackę now in Lease but onely unto Henry, my

Brother. And further I will and requyre my sayd brother, Henry Setle, John Talyer, Witłm Hardcastell, and Richard Potter to be supervisors, and I will that everyone of them shall have for their paynes, xijd. Thes beynge Witnesses, Thomas Taite, Witłm Hayton and Leonard Briggę, with others. [*Proved* 5 *Feb.*, 1585-6.]

Richard Shanne of Potterton.

[xxiij. 405.] In Dei Nõie Amen. I, Richard Shanne of Potterton w^th^in the p'ishe of Barwicke in Elmet, in the countie of Yorke, sicke in bodie and of whole myud and p'fect memorie this instante last day of May, a thousand fyve hundrethe eyghtie sexe. . . my body to be buried in the mydle Alley in the churche of Barwicke aforesaid. Item that yf my syster Dorothie Johnson shall happen to be weddowe Then I do give unto her one cottaige house in Potterton layne with th'appurtenances nowe in the tenor of George Stilmã, and one acre and a halfe of lande to be laid unto yt, she to enioye the same duringe her widdowhead, and to paye twelve pence Rent yearlie. Itm I give and bequeathe my farmehold in Potterton togeither with my lease thereof . . . unto my brother Henrie Shann, excepte before bequiethed to my syster Dorothie, In consideration whereof the said Henrie shall contente and paye unto myne executoures or admi'stratoures the sōme of thirtie pounds . . . And also in consideration therof my mother Elizabeth Shanne, widdowe, shall by her seu'all acquittance release absolutlie to myne executors all debtę . . . I do owe unto her, And also in consideration thereof my said mother and brother Henrie shall provide and alowe unto my said wyfe and my two children sufficient meate and drink, And also the use of the chamber wherein I nowe do lye from my decease untill Martyne mas, wch shalbe in the yeare of our lord God one thousand fyve hundrethe foure score and seaven w^th^out paying any thinge for the same And I devise my demaine lands in Scoles together with my Lease thereof . . . to Frances Shanne and Katherine Shanne, my doughters. [Proviso that Elizabeth, his wife, should have the said demaine lands for 8 years, to enter so soon as Richard Slaters lease shalbe expired, and if she married again within the s^d^ term of 8 years she to pay the sum of 20s. by yeare to his said children. Neyther his said wyfe nor her assignes shall plowe and Ryve out the soile or grounde of the said demaine landes duringe the said terme of eyghte yeares. If children died under 21 without issue his said lands to go to his nephew, Roberte Shanne, he paying to everie one of Testators nephews fortie shillings]; And whereas one Land p'cell of the said demaine Landes nowe in the tenur of Witłm Evers shalbe to be entered unto at thannũcacõn of our Ladie next after the date hearof beinge a yeare soner then the Residue of the said p'misses should enter, the cōmoditie and occupacon of that same yeare in the said Land, I give and bequethe unto Elizabethe my said wyfe, she payinge the Quenes Rent yearlie for all the said demaine Landes duringe the said eyghte yeares. The custodie of the said demaine Lease I bequithe to my said brother Henrie Shanne to thuse of my said wyfe and children And a copie therof to the custodie of Wiłłm Vevers Itm I give to Elizabeth Shanne and Agnes Shanne, my neces, to eyther of them fyve shillings; To the said Frances and Katherine, my doughters, to eyther of them, fortie shillings; To everie one of my god children sexe pence; To my said brother Henrie Shanne, my Clooke and a paire of bootes. To the poure of the pishe of Barwicke sexe shillings eyghte pence. Itm I give the Residue of all my goodes and cattales . . unto Elizabeth my wife, Frances and Katherine my doughters, whome I make my full executoures. And I do make my said brother Henrie S. and Wiłłm Vevers to be supervisoures of the same Will and governores of my said children during their infances. Item I give to Elizabethe, my said wife, all such Rentes as Richard Slater oughte to paye duringe his terme of yeares yet unspente. Witnesses of this my Will, Richard Shanne, Thomas Tate, Leonard Brigges, John Hayton, Wiłłm Danyell, Richard Potter, Wiłłm Vevers and Henrie Shanne. [*Proved* 4 *April,* 1584.]

HENRY SETLE of Potterton, husbandman.

[xxiii. 561b.] In the name of God, Amen. The seaventh day of November, a thousand fyve hundreth eyghtie sexe, I, Henrie Setle of Potterton wthin the pishe of Barwicke in Elmet, in the Countie of Yorke, husbandman, beinge by the visitacon of God, sicke in bodie, but throughe his grace of good and pfect memorie, thanks be to God, do ordeyne and make this my last will and testament in maner and forme followinge, First, I bequieth my soule to the almyghtie Lord, trustinge throughe the merittę of his passion to be one of those that shalbe saved in the Latter day. And my bodie to be buried wthin the Churchyeard of Barwicke aforesaid. Item I give and bequieth to John, my sone, twentie shillinges. To Francis Settle, my sonne, twentie shillinges, and to Ric. Settle, one other of my sonnes, twentie shillinges, and to Marie, my doughter, twentie shillinges. Item I give to my nephew, Wiłłm Steele, the sonne of Lawrence Settle, tenne shillinges. Unto my brother Wiłłm, thre shillinges fourepence. Also I will that my said brother Wiłłm shall have Chamber Rowme for his Loudginge wher he nowe lyethe duringe the terme of my lease. Unto Helline, my wyfe, the lease of my farmehold for the better bringinge up of my younge children, she paying furthe of the same to euerie one of my foresaid Children tenne shillinges. The Residue of all goodes and cattalles . . . . I give and bequieth unto Elling, my wyfe, John, my sonne, Frances and Richard, my sonnes, and Marie, my doughter, whome I do ordeyne . . . . the full and joynt executoures of this my last will, and further, I will and requier John Talior, John Taliour, Richard Potter and Leonard Bridges to be supervisoures of this my last will. Item I will that everie one of them shall have for their paynes twelvepence. Provided alwayes and further my will is that my said wyfe and Isabell, my syster, shall endeavour themselves to take and renewe the Lease of the farme to the use of John Settle, my sonne, and Henrie Settle, the sonne of Robte, my brother. Thes beinge Witnesses, John Taite, John Talior, Leonard Briges, and Willm Dickson, and Richard Potter. [*Proved* 21 *Oct.*, 1587.]

JOHN BRAMHAM of Barnbow.

[xix. 467.] In Dei nõie Amen, scd. die Decembris Anno Dni Mcccclxxj. I, John Bramham of Barmebowe, crasyd in bodye, but thankꝭ be to God of hole mynd and good memorye, ordaince and mayks this my p'sent testament and last will in manner and forme following: fyrst I gyve and bequythe my sowlle to Allmyghtie God and to all the celestiall Companye of heaven and my bodye to be buried in the Churche yeard of all Sanctꝭ in Barwicke. Item I gyve to Thomas Broughe xxs. and all my working geare save one axe and one hatchett. Item I gyve to George Broughe xxs. and a gymber lambe. It' I gyve to Margrett Broughe xxs. and a gymber lambe. Item I gyve to John Bramhm̃, my son, one chiste. To Thomas Bramhm̃, my son, an other chiste. To John Daniell, my godson, xijd. To Isabell Harryson, my doughter, xijd. To Robt Bramh^9m, my brother, one browne jackett and a paire of showes. To Agnes, my wyfe, all the Corne in the barne to her own use, and the Resydew of all my goodꝭ herebefore not geven nor bequythed I gyve and Bequithe to Agnes, my wyfe, John Bramhm̃ and Thomas Bramhm̃, my souns, whom I ordane and mayke my hole executors of this my last will and testament. It' I make sup'visor of this my last will Willm Vevers. Thes being wytnes Willm Vevers, Robt Briggꝭ, Rychard Jeffrason, James Danyll, Steven Brame, Edward Sayver and John Cawdray. [*Proved* 14 *April*, 1572.]

WILLIAM SHANNE of Potterton, yeoman.

[xix. 500b.] In the name of God, Amen, the xvj^th day of Marche in the year of our lorde God a thowsande fyve hundrethe threscore and thirtene, I, Willm Shanne of Potterton, in the pishe of Barwicke in Elmett and countie of Yorke, yoman, of good and quyte mynde and also in helthe of bodie, laudes begyven to Allmyghtie God for the same, do ordene, constitute and mayke this my presente testamente and laste will, as well concerninge the order and disposic̃on of all that my farmeholde or tenement in Potterton aforesaid, and now in the occupac̃on of me, the said Willm Shanne, or of my assignes. And also of the tackꝭ, leases, and terme of years yet to come of and in the same. As also of all my other goodes, corne, cattels, rightes, credites, debtꝭ and moveables whatsoever, they be in manner and forme hearafter followinge. That ys to say. Firste I bequythe and moste hartelie com̃ende my soule unto Allmightie God the father that maid [me] and all the worlde. And to my saviour Jesus Christe, both God and man, that ordened me and all the worlde wth the price and effluction of his bloode. And to the holie ghoste the comforter of the meeke in all tribulacons. And my bodie to be buried in the pishe church yearde of Barwike in Ellmet aforesaid or els wheer yt shall please God according to my degree at the discrecion of my executrix and supvisoure. . .. I mayke and orden Elizabeth, nowe my wyfe, my executrix And I ordene and especiallie desier Mr Willm Ellis of Kiddall, the yonger, in the said countie, gentleman, and also my brother, Richarde Shanne, to be my supvisors of this my laste will and testamente to call upon my executrixe for the trewe pformance and execution of the same, and to order and helpe her in all suche thinges as shalbe requesite and necessarie aboute the same. And I bequythe, will, and gyve unto my said supervisors for ther paynes and frendeshipp herein fyve shillinges over and besides ther reasenable coste and charges by them at any tyme hearafter bestowed and maide aboute the execucon of this my present testamente. . . I bequythe unto my sone, Henry Shanne, all that cottaige or tenement wth thappurtenance nowe in the tenure of Robte Talior, sex acres of arrable lande lying and beynge in the feildes of Potterton aforesaid. That is to say, in everie feilde two acres late in the tenure of my sone, Richard Shanne, halfe an acre of medowe be yt more or lesse lyeinge in the ynge called Barwicke ynge. The sowthe ende of one oxe-house and also one pcell of grownde lyeinge befor the same to be used for a dongesteade. And also all that cottaige or tenemente and all the grounde thereunto belonginge wth thappurtenance in Potterton aforesaid nowe in the occupacon of Thomas Londe or of his assignes. And also one chamber nexte adjoyninge unto my garden and nowe in the occupacon of me the said Willm Shanne, all wch said cottages, &c., ar pcell of that my messuage, tenemente, or farmeholde in Potterton aforsaid, nowe in the occupacon of me the said testator. Also I will that my said sone, Henry Shanne, shall have two mares and two foles well kepte bothe winter and somer of in and uppon all that pte of my said farmeholde now in the occupacon of me the said testator. To have and to hold the said cottages, &c., unto my said sone, Henry Shanne, his executors, &c., ymmediatelie from and after the day of the decesse of me the said Willm Shann and the said Elizabeth, my wyfe, and the longer lyver of us unto the full ende and terme of all my years wch shalbe then to come and unexpired of and in the premisses by force and vertew of one Indenture of lease to me the said testator laytelie maide of all and singular the premisses by Edwarde Dacre of Croglie in the countie of Cūberlande, Esquier, as by the same Indenture of lease bearinge date the twentie day of Julye in the tente yeare of the reigne of oure said soveraigne ladie the queenes majestie that nowe is, more at large yt dothe and may appeare. The said Henry Shanne yeld-inge and payinge unto the occupiers or farmers of the caputall messuage of my said farmeolde the soīe of xijd of laufull mony of Englande at termes usuall. I bequythe unto my sone, Willm Shanne, and his assignes, all thos my two severall closes with th'appurtenance in Potterton aforsaid, the one called the quarrell close, the other the yuge close, and pcell of my said farmeolde ymmediatlie frome after the day of the decesse of me the said Willm Shanne, and of my said wyfe and the longer lyver of us as ys aforesaid, duringe all my years than to come of and in the same in manner and forme as my said sone Henry Shanne dothe occupie the cottages and others the premisses by this my presente testamente and laste will to him gyven as is aforsaid, yeldinge and payinge yearlie therfore unto the occupiers and farmers of my said caputall messuage of my said farmeolde the sum of vjd. at termes usuall. Itm I will gyve and assigne unto my doughter, Dorothie Shanne, her executors and assignes, all that cottaige or tenemente wth all the grounde and appurtenancę thervnto belonginge in Potterton aforsaid, nowe in the occupacon of John Dawson or of his assignes, ymmediatelie from and after the day of the decesse of me the said testator and my said wyfe, and the longer lyver of us, duringe all my yeares than to come of and in the same in manner and forme as my said sonnes, Henrye and Willm Shanne, dothe occupie the cottages, landes, tenementę and closes to them . . gyven and bequythed as is aforesaid, paynge therefore yearlie unto the occupiers and farmers of my said caputall messuaige of my said farmeholde the some of vjd. at termes usuall. Itm I bequyth, gyve and assigne unto the said Elizabethe, my wyfe, all the reste and Residewe of the said caputall messuaige of my said farmeholde in Potterton aforsaid duringe her naturall lyffe wth the remainder therof after her decesse unto my sonne, Richarde Shanne, his executors and assignes, together wth all my hole righte tytle and interest wch shalbe than to come of and in the same by force and vertue of the said Indenture of lease or otherwyse by any other meane, right or tytle. The said Elizabeth Shanne, my wyfe, and Richarde Shanne, ther executors and assignes, yeldinge and payinge yearlie therfore all and everie such rentes and other thinges as I the said testator aughte to do by colore of the said Indentur of lease or otherwise. And yf yt happen any of my said thre sones and doughter before named to decesse before they be married or wthoute issue of his hir or ther bodies laufullie begotten, than I will that the pte and porcon of my said farmeholde of him hir or them so decessinge shall remane to the nexte of my said sones by lyneall byrthe than lyvinge as folowethe, that ys to saye, Henrye to succede Richarde, Willm to succede Henry, and Richard to succede Willm . . . [other provisions respecting children and their wives]. Itm I bequith and gyve to my sone in lawe, Thomas Mindewell, one cowe, and to my grandechilde, Dorothie Mindewell, one Ewe and a lame. To my said sone, Henry Shanne, xls. in monye, one pare of stande bedstockę wth all the furniture to the bedd, and also one table wth two drawers thereunto belonginge. Item unto my said sone, Richarde Shanne, one pare of stande bedstockę. Unto my said doughter, Dorothie Shanne, xls. Unto my doughter, Anne Shanne, xls. All the reste and residewe of all and singuler my goodes. corne, cattelles, rightes, creditę, debtę and moveables whatsoever they be and not by this my presente testamente and laste will otherwyse gyven or devysed, shalbe equallie devided in thre ptes wherof I will one pte shalbe unto the said Elizabeth, my wyfe, and one other pte to all my said fyve children, viz., Richard, Henry, Willm, Dorothie, and Anne Shanne, equallie to be devided amonge them. And the third pte shalbe for the pformacon of this my presente testamente. The reste and residew therof my debtes, legacies, and fun'all expence paid, And this my laste will fulfilled, I gyve unto the said Elizabeth, my wyfe, neverthelesse I will that all my draughte of oxen, my yren Rawnge, one paire of cobirens, one pare of brigges, one table, one newe Iren bounde wane, one cupborde, one counter, and two paire of standinge bedstocke shall continue and be lefte at my said caputall messuaige or farmeholde to the use of my said executrix and her successor of and the same appointed by this my present testament. . . . . . . Thes beynge witnesses, Richard Danyell, Thomas Potter and Thomas Taytt, wth others, viz., John Tayte, Henry Kytchyn. Md that these bequeste hearafter named wear gyven after the maykinge up of this presente will. Imprimis I gyve and bequythe to my sonne, Willm Shanne, one paire of hose and one cote. Itm to my sone, Richarde Shanne, my Cloke. Itm to my sone, Henry Shanne, my purse and my key. Itm to my said sone Willm, his thre doughters, that is to say, Marie, Agnes and Elizabeth, and to every of them one ewe and one lame. Itm to Dorothie Mindevell one sheepe hogge. Itm to John Webster, my s'vante, one ewe and one lambe. Itm to my doughter, Dorothie Shanne, one bushell of wheate These beynge witnesses, viz., Thomas Potter and John Tayte. [*Proved* 28 *April*, 1574.]

JOHN SETLE of Potterton, husbandman.

[xix. 511a.] In the name of God, Amen the fourthe day of Januarie Anno Dñi 1572, and in the xiiij[th] year of queue Elizabethe, I, John Setle of Potterton, in the countie of Yorke, husbandman, unconstraned but of myne owne will do make this my laste will and testamente in maner and forme folowynge. Fyrste I bequythe my soule unto allmyghtie God and my bodie to be buried w[th]in the churche yearde of Barwicke in Elmet. Also I gyve to Elizabeth, my wyfe, my farmeholde duringe her lyfe naturall and after hir decesse to Robt, my sone. Also I gyve to Henry Setle, my sone, the other halfe of my farmeholde. Itm I gyve to Willm, my sone, iij[li] vj[s] viij[d] by legacy. Also I gyve to Janet, my doughter, by legacie, iij[li] vj[s] viij[d]. Also I gyve to Laurence Setle, my sone, x[s] that Thomas Hardecastle dothe owe. Also I will that my children shall peasablie take away all ther goode yt they have gotten besyde me. Also I will that the reste of my goode unbequythed be equallie devided emongste my children se my fun'all expence be discharged. Also I make Elizabethe, my wyfe, and Henry Setle, my sone, the full executors of this my laste will and testamente. Itm I gyve to the poore of Berwicke pishinge vjs. viijd. Also S[r] Xpofer Danbie dothe ow me xlviij[s] w[ch] shalbe devided emongste all my children, and to pve this will to be a true will I haue setto my marke wth my owne hande. Thes beinge witnesses, Sr Robte Hayton, clarke, Richard Danyell, Thomas Londe and Thomas Dyneley, wth others. [*Proved* 17 *June*, 1572.]

WILLIAM ELLIS of Kiddall, esq. (1)

[xix. 601a.] In the name of God Amen, the xijth yeare of Elizabethe by the grace of God quene of Englande, Anno Dñi a thowsande five hundrithe thre score and thirtene, I Willm Ellis of Kiddall, in the countie of Yorke, Esquier, sicke of bodie but whole of mynde and of sound and pfect memorie, do ordene and make this my laste will and testamente in mann9 and forme followinge. First I bequithe my sowle to Almightie God my lorde and maker, and to his sone my redemer and savioure by the merittę of whose passion my truste is to be saved and my bodie to be buried in the pishe churche of Barwicke in Elmett in the queare sometime caulled the Chantrie queare of the sowthe side of the saide churche. Itm I will that my bodie be broughte furthe in good and decent mann9 withoute any pompe and sumptiouse fun'all, and to the poore people of the said pishe in moste nede and penurie I do give and bequithe xxs the same to be destributed at the sighte and discretion of my executorę. Allso I will give and bequithe in consideraĉon of my tithes and other thinges forgotten to the churche iijs iiijd. Also I do give and bequithe by this my laste Will and testament to Willm Ellis, the soñe of Roger Ellis, and Mathewe More all and singuler those my landes and teñtę in Pomfrett of the cleare yearlie valewe of xxli, and by one Indenture maide betwene me the said Willm Ellis and Willm Ellis afforesaide the yonger and Martyne Anne of Frikley, in the said Countie of Yorke, esquier, bearinge date the xviijth day of Aprill in the xjth yeare of the reigne of oure sou9aigne ladie Elizabethe, by the grace of God quene of Englande, France, and Ireland, Defender of the fathe, &c., and speciallie res'ved by the said Indenture for me the saide Willm Ellis the elder to give, dispose and bequithe by my laste will and testamente or otherwisse at my will and pleasure. I do thearfore nowe wille and speciallie lymitt and appointe by this my saide laste wille and testamente that the said landes and tentę in Pomfrett afforesaide withe the rentes and pfittę shalbe frome the day of my deathe untill the full tearme of xxjtie yeares to such pson or psons as in this my saide will and testamente is sett furthe and declared, that is to say, to Willm Savell the soñe of xli to be paide to hime at the aige of xxtie yeares, that is to witt, xxxiijs iiijd for vj years to come. Itm to Marie Savell, sister of the saide Willm Savell, the some of xlli, that is to say, iiijli yearlie for x yeares, and untill the soñe of xlli be fullie satisfied and paide. Itm to Francę Ellis xlli, to be paide by iiijli yearlie and in tenne yeares for and untill the saide some of xlli be fullie satisfied and paide. Itm to Bridgett Savell vjli xiijs iiijd yearlie to be paide xxxiijs iiijd for iiijor yeares and untill the saide

(1) He married Margaret, daughter of [? John] Vavasour of the Wold; her will is the next one printed He died 15 Oct., 1573, without issue.

some be fullie satisfied and paide. Itm to Witłm Copley, Averay Copley, John Copley, Witłm Copley and Thoms Copley xx^li, that is to say, to eu'y of theme iiij^li, to be paide in five yeares, as it will rise subsequent eu'y paymente. Itm to Henrie Hodgson and his sone iij^li vj^s viij^d. Itm to Thoms Ellis, John Ellis, and Witłm Ellis, xx^li, that is to say, to eu'y of theme vj^li xiij^s iiij^d. Itm to Witłm Harte and John Harte xx^li, that is to say, to either of them x^li for and in consideracon of theire childes porcon whiche I will shalbe paide presentlie of my goodę and not of nor owte of the fore-saide landes. The Residewe of all my goodę and landes in and by this my laste will and testamente not bequithed my debtę and legacies paide and fun'allę made I do give to M'garett Ellis, my wiffe, and Witłm Ellis, soñe of Roger Ellis, whome I make my full executorę of this my laste will and testamente. Itm I will that Francę More have v^li to be reserved of the isshewes and pfittę of the afforesaide landes in Pomfrete, and of the firste money that shall ryse of the said landes after my deathe. Itm to the iiij^or children of Richard Bushe, that is to say, John, Anne, Susan, and Francę, iiij^li, that is to say, to eu'y of theme xx^s, to be taken of the landes afforesaide. Itm I give to Elizabethe Godyeare one of my best kyne or xl^s in money. Itm I do for the better sewertie and suer paymente of the legacies and bequestes before given furthe of my said Landes and tentę in Pomfrete by this my laste will and testamente, Lymitt assigne and appointe the afforesaide Witłm Ellis my executor, and Mathewe More my resaverę of all the rentę, issues and pfittę rysinge and groweinge of the said landes and tentę in Pomfrette. And I will that the saide Witłm and Mathewe shall yearlye accompte for the said rentę issues and profittę to and before the ordinarie and after the said accompte hadd and mayde pay and diseise the said money so by theme Resaved and accompted for accordinge to the purporte, tener, effect and trewe meanynge of this my laste will and testamente, and accordinge to the truste in theme put and reposed by me the testator. Itm I give to Witłm Bucktrote xx^s to be taken of my goodę. And I do make supvisoures of this my laste will and testamente Xpofer Vavasor, Henrie Copley, gentlemen, whome I do chardge soo farr furthe as I may to see my will pved and pformed, and as I speciallie truste theme and as they will dischardge the truste by me in theme reposed, and for theire paines hearin by theme to be taken I will they shall have theire costes borne of my goodę and allowed to theme by my executorę. And for theire paines I do give to either of theme one angell. Itm I will that James Harte shall have xl^s. I will and bequithe to Nicholas More one coulte fole of coller Iron gray. Itm I give and bequithe to John Bell, xl^s. Itm to Thoms Awklande xx^s. Itm to John Gilson, xx^s. Itm I give and bequithe to eu'y of the madens in my house vj^s viij^d. Itm I do give to Robert Hardcastle xl^s. Itm I give and bequithe to Edmonde Gibson xl^s. Itm to George Beckwithe I give xx^s. Itm I give to Witłm Londe x^s. Itm I give and bequithe to Thoms Favell vj^s viij^d. Itm I give and bequithe to John Goodyeare, the sone of John Goodyeare, xl^s. Theis being wytness, Wittm Power, Xpofer Vavasor, Mathewe More, and Henrie Copley. [*Proved* 3 *Nov.*, 1573.]

MARGARET ELLIS of Barwick,

[xix. 649a.] In the name of God Amen, the eighte daye of June in the yeare of oure Lorde God a thowsande five hundrithe threscore and fowertene, I, M'garett Ellis of Barwicke in Elmett in the dioces of Yorke, beinge of whole mynde and of good and pfecte memorie, p'sed be God, make my laste will and testamente in mann^r and forme followeinge. Firste I bequithe yelde upp and commende my sowle to thãndes of oure moste m'cifull and to his sone Jesus Christe the Redemer of Mankinde. And my bodie to be buried, &c. Itm I bequithe to Wittm Copley iij^li vj^s viij^d. To Marie Savell iij^li vj^s viij^d. To John Harte iij^li vj^s viij^d. To Averay Gascoigne iij^li vj^s viij^d. To Francę Ellis, doughter of Wittm Ellis, iij^d vj^s viij^d. To Elizabethe Goodyeare, wiffe to John Goodyeare, iij^li vj^s viij^d. To the poore folke of Barwicke in Elmett iij^s iiij^d. And the reste of all my goodę my husbande debtę and myne paide, my fun'all exspences dischardged, I give to John Gascoigne and Henrie Copley, gentlemã, whome I make my true and fathefull executorę off this my laste will and testamente. Theis beinge witness^s, Mathewe Norton, Henrie Wilson, James Harte and Thomas Dyneley, withe otherę. [*Proved* 1 *Oct.* 1574.]

RICHARD DANYELL of Potterton, husbandman.

[xix. 722a.] In the name of God Amen. The xiiij day of Aprill in the xvj yeare of the reigne of o^r Sou'eigne lady Eliz̃, by the grace of God, of Englande, Fraunce and Ireland, quene, Defender of the faithe, &c. And in the yeare of o^r lord God 1574. I, Richarde Danyell of Potterton, in the countye of Yorke, husbandman, seike in bodye but of good and pfyte memorye, thankę be to God, doythe ordayne, make and constitute this my last will and Testament in maner and forme followinge. The fyrst I comẽnde my soull to Almyghtie God my maker and to Jesũ Christ my redemer, and my bodye to be buried within the pishe churche yeard of Barwicke. Itm I gyve and bequithe to Isabell Bolton, laite wyf of Myles Bolton, one browne whye with calf. To Jane Danyell, my doughter, xl^s of lawfull moneye, also to Jennett Tottye, my goddoughter, a stryke of wheate and a bushell of malte. To Thomas Danyell, my godsonne, xij^d. Also to Wittm Taite, Richard Hemsworth and Richard Potter, and to eu'y of them iiij^d. To Thomas Danyell, my s'unt, one yowe and a lambe. To Robt Byckerdike, his children whiche he nowe haithe withe his wyf, my doughter, xl^s amongest them. Itm I gyve and bequithe to Wittm Danyell, my sonne, my messuage or Tenement whiche I nowe dwell in and also laithe bought of Robt Killingbecke. To have and to hold to hym̃ and to theires of his bodye lawfullie begotten, and for defaulte of suche yssue then to remayne to Jane Danyell, my said doughter, and to theires of her bodye lawfullie begotten, and for defaulte of such yssue then to remayne to the right heires of me the said Richard Danyell for euᵖ. To Witℓm Danyell, my said sonne, all my intrest and terme of yeares whiche I have yett to come in my leasse of Maynehouse garthe, whiche I did Taike of Mʳ Henrye Copley. To my said sone Witℓm all my intrest and terme of yeares yett to come in my leasse which I did Taike of Certayne arrable laudℓ, closses, and all other there appʳtenncℓ being the quenes Maᵗⁱᵉˢ landℓ lyinge and beinge in the lordshipp of Barwicke in the said countie of Yorke called the Demaynes. To my said doughter Jane xxˢ more in money. To Isabell Bickerdike, my doughter, wyf of Robt Bickerdike, xxˢ. Itm all the Residew of my goodℓ, my debtℓ paid and funeralls discharged, I gyve and bequithe to my said children Witℓm Danyell and Jane Danyell, whom I make, ordayne and constitute my executors of this my last will and Testament. Itm I gyve and will that my said executors do gyve to the poore mens boxe of Berwicke aforesaid iijˢ iiijᵈ. Also I will and desyre my frendℓ Robt Danyell and John Burneley to be supvisors of this my p'nte will. Itm I will that my said executors do gyve to the Poore of Barwicke and Potterton half a quarter of corne at the daye of my deathe. In witnes whereof I have putto my hand the daye and yeare abovesaid. Thes beinge witnessˢ, Thomas Dynelay, John Burnelay, Robarte Danyell, Witℓm Hodgeson, Thomas Potter and Thomas Barnebye. [*Proved* 9 *May*, 1574.]

ELIZABETH SETTLE of Potterton, widow.

[xxj. 347a.] In the name of God Amen. The xxijᵗʰ daye of January Anno Dni, 1578. I, Eliz̃ Settle of Potterton in the countye of Yorke, widowe, do ordayne and maike this my last will and Testament in maner and forme followinge. Fyrst I bequith my soulle to Almyghtie God and my bodye to be buryed in the churche yeard of Barwicke in Elmet. Also I gyve and bequithe to Witℓm Settle, my sonne, three poundℓ sex shillingℓ eighte pence and one acre of wheate and half an acre of waier corne. Also I gyve and bequithe to Lawrance Settle, my sonne, three poundℓ sex shillingℓ eight pence and one acre of wheate and half an acre of waier corne and one blanket and one sheitte. Also I will that Thomas Potter wyf shall have my bedd whiche I lye upon the daye and makinge hereof and three poundℓ sex shillingℓ eight pence. Also I gyve to Thomas Potter wyf and my sonne Henrye wyf all my harden yere and sameron to devide yt equallie emonge them. Also I gyve to Margaret Potter all my Rayment and one chiste. Also I will that Thomas Potter eldest doughter have one petticoate and Marye Lupton one petticoate, whiche shalbe maid upon my nowne wolle. Also I gyve to eu'y poore house in Potterton one pecke of corne. Also I gyve to Robt Settle, my sonne, one brasse potte and one fether bedde. Also I will that Marye Lupton shall have ijˢ viijᵈ. Also to Sʳ Robt Hayton viijᵈ, and to Thomas Dyneley viijᵈ. Also

I gyve more to Willm Settle, my sonne, one almerye. The Rest of all my goodę not bequest I gyve to Henrye Settle and Robt Settle, my sonnes, whom I maike my sole and onelye Executors of This my last will and Testament. Thes beinge witnesses, Sir Robarte Hayton, curate, Willm Daniell, John Tayte, John Hemysworthe, Robarte Ottes and Thomas Dyneley. [*Proved* 7 *May*, 1579.]

THOMAS POTTER of Potterton, husbandman.

[xxij. 602.] In Dei noie, Amen. The fyftenth daye of Auguste in the yeare of our lord God a thousand fyve hundrethe eyghtie foure. I, Thomas Potter of Potterton, in the Dioces of Yorke, husbandman, beinge by the visitacon of God sicke in bodie, but by his grace of good and perfect memorie, thankes be geven to God, do ordeyne, make and constitute this my last will and testament in maner and forme followinge. First I do bequiethe my soule to the Almightie Lord, trustinge that throughe the merrittę of his blessed passion to be one of those who shalbe saved. Itm I do also give and bequiethe my bodie to be buried w^th^in the churche yeard of Barwicke in Elmyt. Itm I do bequiethe my whole farmeholde to M'garet, my wyfe, Imediatlie frome and after the daye of my deathe for and duringe the tyme and terme of sexe yeares then nexte following fullie to be complett, determined and ended for the further mayntenance and better bringinge upe of my children, after wch tyme and terme of sexe yeares I will that my sonne Richard Porter and M'garet Porter, my said wyfe, shall occupie my aforesaid farmehold and Land joyntlie together for and duringe the terme of twentie yeares yf my wyfe kepe her selfe so longe widdowe. They or eyther of them yeldinge and payinge unto John Porter, my sonne, fortie shillinges at the feaste of St. Martyne the bushoppe nexte ensewinge after my decease. And to the rest of my children viz., Mychaell Potter, Andrewe Potter, Roberte Potter, Willm Potter, Elizabeth Potter, Agnes Potter, Marie Potter, Barbarey Potter and Janet Potter. And to everie one of them fortie shillinges so sone as they or everie one of them shall accomplishe the aige of twentie one yeares. Itm I will that my whole farmehold and Land, after the determinacon and end of the aforesaid [term] of twentie yeares before menconed, remaine unto my sonne Richard Potter fore ever. Itm I give unto Willm Settell, my wyffe brother, thre shillinges foure pence. The Residue of all my goodes and cattalles, moveable and unmoveable, my dettę and legacies paid and my fun'all expenses discharged, I frelie give and bequiethe unto M'garet, my wiffe, and Richard, my sone, whome I do ordeyn, constitute and make executoures of this my last will and testament. Itm I will and requier John Talior and Henrie Settle to be supvisoures of this my said will to see the same pformed. Thes beinge witnesses, Willm Danyell, John Taite, Willm Mawsone and Roberte Settell. [*Proved* 14 *Nov.*, 1584.]

WILLIAM SETTHELL, of Barwick.

[xxiij. 895.] In Dei Noie Amen. The — daye of Aprill, 1588, in Anno xxx° Elizabethe Regine, etc. I, William Setthell of Barwicke in Elmytt in the Countie of Yorke, beinge subiect to many deceases and infirmities in my bodie, and yet, praysed be God, of whole myud and p'fect memorye, do ordeyne and make this my last will and testament in maner and forme followinge. First I bequiethe my soule to Almightie God, trustinge that his great mercye and not the regore of his Justice for my synnes shalbe extended towards me, that by the merrittes of his most bitter passion and blond sheddinge I shalbe one of them that shalbe saved at the dreedfull day of Judgment. Itm I give and bequiethe unto Martyne Setthell, my sonne, one longe table with the frame and frames thereunto belonging, one corselett with the furnitur and one pyke, one Iron Range with all the pendles and peces of Iron therunto belonging. To the said Martyn my sonne, all and everye my demaine leases of Barwicke, and Scoles, viz., of litle Speightlies, highe Roodes, Jenkin flattes, Okenhead, wth all the arrable demaine land lyinge upon Basslingflatt, and also one lease of two beast gates in Barwyke Oxclosse. [Proviso that Rosamonde, his wife, should have them for her life, she paying the Queen's rents, also paying unto Helline Setthell, his mother, yearly, the sum of fyve pounds, and when the payment thereof shall end to pay unto his son, Martyne five marks during her said occupation. Proviso for renewal of lease and for entry in case of nonpayment of annuities.] I will that my lease of all the great Cloose of Speightlies and the lease of Manston becks shall be prysed as chattales. And my wyfe to have a third pte of the comoditie of bothe the same. Itm I give unto my mother the bed wherin she lyethe, sufficientlye furnished, one great presser, and the use of one waynscott chist duringe her lyfe. Itm I give unto the poore of Barwicke pish twentie shillinges. Itm I give to Maude Hayton fyve shillings. To Frances Setthell, my nece, one Quy or twenty sixe shillinges eighte pence. To Edward Browne my Russett Clooke and my graye hoose and two shillinges. The Residue of all my goodes and cattalls . . . I do give and bequiethe to Prudence Setthell and Robert Setthell, my children. And I ordeyne and make Thomas Setthell and Matthew Setthell, my bretheren, my executors, and I give unto eyther of them twentie shillinges and their charges. And I make John Grene, gentleman, and John Talor, my bretheren in lawe, supvisours of this my said will. And I give to my said brother Grene my sword and my dagger. And to my brother Taylor, one dagge[r] remayninge wth my said brother Grene and my Scotche sword. And lastlye I give to my sonne Martyne all my bookes. Testes, George Lewes, clarke, George Stylman, John Grene, Robert Jeffrasone, Wiłłm Poore, clarke. [*Proved* 17 *Oct*., 1588.]

WILLIAM MAWSON, of Potterton.

[xxiii. 907.] In the name of God Amen. 1587, The Secounde day of December. Wiłłm Mawson of Potterton w[th]in the pishe of

Barwicke in Ellmytt, beinge by the visitacon of God sicke in bodie but of good and p'fect memorie . . . And my bodie to be buried in the Church yeard of Barwike aforesaid. Itm I give and bequiethe unto John Mawson, my sonne, fortie shillinges; unto Elline, my wife, the benyfytt and use of my farme durynge my lease for the tuic̃on and better bringing upe of my said sonne. And further my will is that my said sonne John shall have my intrest for the renewinge of my foresaid leasse. Itm I will that my brother Christofer Mawson shall haue my Blewcot. The Residue of my goods and cattalls . . . I give and bequiethe unto Elline, my wyfe, and John, my sonne, whome I do ordeyne, make and constitute the full and joint executors of this my last will and Testament. Thes beinge witnesses, Henrye Shanne, John Caite and Wyllm Danyell. [*Proved* 2 *Nov.*, 1588.]

STEPHEN BRAME of Barnbow.

[xxiv. 743b.] In the name of God Amen, the first day of August in the yeare of our lord God and Savour Christ, 1590. I, Stephen Brame of Barmebowe w^th^in the county of Yorke, sicke in bodye but of good and pfect memorye, the lord be thanked, doe make and ordeyne this my last will and Testament in maner and forme as followethe. First I cõmitt my soule into the handes of Almightye God my Creator and redemer, and my bodye to be buryed in the Churche or Churche yeard of Barwicke in Elmet. Item I give and bequiethe to Thomas Broughe my sonne in lawe one Brounlye cowe called Blackwald in stead of one quy promyssed. Item I give to the said Thomas Broughe one Swarme of Bees. To Thomas Broughe thre children to everye child, two shillinges. I remytt Marye Broughe my doughter the geast of one cowe for wch she standes indetted unto me. To my sonne Henrye sixe poundes thirtene shillinges four pence in consideracon that the said Henrye shall instructe and teache my sonne Richarie ["suche Richard" in registered copy] the craft and occupacon he now usethe. To my youngest sonne Richard Tenne poundes. I give two yeares in my farmeholde unexpired after the decease of Gilian my wyfe, to my sonne Henrye. And yf he dye, the yeares then unexpired in my said farmehold I give to my secound sonne Richarie, and so consequently for want of Richarie to my youngest sonne Richard. And the residue of my goodes, my dettes, legacies and fun'all expenses discharged I give to my wyfe Juliane, my sonnes Henrye, Richarie and Richard, whome I make my full and whole executors. Fynallie I make, constitute and ordeyne Wittm Vevers and Robert Jeffrayson supervisours of this my last Will and Testament, and I give to eyther of them sixepence. Witnesses, Wittm Vevers, Robert Jeffraysone, Wittm Walker. [*Proved* 23 *Nov.*, 1591.]

RICHARD GASCOIGNE of Barnbow, esq.[1]

[xxv. 1245a.] In the name of God. In dei noie, Amen, the firste

(1) Richard Gascoigne married first Elizabeth, widow of Sir Henry Savile of Thornhill, and daughter and co-heiress of Thomas Sothill of Sothill. He married 2ndly Elizabeth, daughter and heiress of Robert West of Millington, and died without issue. He was the second son of John Gascoigne and Ann, daughter of Sir Henry Vavasour.

day, of Auguste in the yeare of our lord God one thousand fiue hundreth nintye, I, Richard Gascoigne of Barnebowe in the dioces and Countye of Yorke, Esquire, being at this p'sente sound and whole in bodye and of good and p'fecte myud and memorye, thankę be giuen to Allmightye God, callinge to my remembrance the uncertainetye and instabilitye of this world and knowinge that it is a thinge certaine that man shall dye and chainge this lyfe, but the tyme uncertaine when wee shall be called out of this miserable world, and desireinge to sett and ordaine some good staye and order as well concerneinge the order and disposic̃on of some pte of my messuages, landę, tenementę and hereditamtę wth their appurtn̄n̄cę in the Countye of Yorke, as also of all my goodę, cattellę and debtę, doe ordaine, constitute and make this my p'sente laste will and testament in manner and forme followinge. Firste and principally I committ my sinfull soule unto the greate mercye of Allmightye God and his onely begotten sonne our saiuor and redemer Jesus Christe, by whose death and moste paynfull bitter passion and sheddinge of his moste p'cious blood upon the Crosse for me and all mankynd, I hope to be saued and to be one of the inheritors of his moste glorious Kingdome amongste the moste blessed saintę in heauen. Et reposita est hec firma spes mea in sinu meo. My body to the earth from whence it came, to be buried wheresoever it shall please God to take me out of this transiterie lyfe. And whereas I haue by my Deede indented tripartite bearinge date the xxth day of Februarye in the fowretenth yeare of the raigne of our soueraigne Lady Queene Elizabeth, enfeoffed given and graunted unto Francis Gascoigne of Micklefield Esquire, Henrie Grice of Wakfeild, Wiłłm Beaumonte and John Barneby, gentlemen, and to there heires for ever, all that my capitall messuage comonlye called and knowne by the name of Barnebowe hall, wth all the members and appurtn̄n̄ces, and all other my laudę, tenemts and hereditantę, wth all their rightę and appurtenncę in Barwicke in Elmet, Scooles, Barnebowe, Potterton, Garforth and Ardesley wthin the said Countye of Yorke, wch lands in Potterton I lately purchased of one Edmund Brooke, and the landę in Ardesley wch I lately purchased of one Gilberte Tayler, and my landę in Garforth, lately purchased of one John Clerkeson, late Fairefax laudę, as by the said Deed indented Triptite it doth and may appeare to the use of me the said Richard Gascoigne and my assigns for tearme of my lyfe without impeachment of waste. And after my decease the said feoffees to be seazed to the uses of my will and of my coppiehould laudę in Barwicke, Scooles and Barnebowe surrendered to use of my will in trust to the use of James Birkeby, citizen and Alderman of the Cittye of Yorke and Elizabeth his wife, my neece, for tearme of her life, and after her decease to the use of Nicholas Gascoigne, eldest sonne of my brother George Gascoigne, for tearme of his life. And after his death to the use of John Gascoigne, eldest sonne to my brother John Gascoigne of Parlington, and to the heires males of his body lawfully begotten. Remainder to the use of Thomas Gascoigne, second son of my brother John Gascoigne, and of the heires males of the said Thomas. Remainder to the use of Leonard Gascoigne, one other of the sonnes of my said brother John Gascoigne, and of the heires males of the body of the said Leonard. Remainder to the heires males of the body of the said Nicholas Gascoigne. Remainder to the heires males of my said Brother George successively. . . . . With ultimate remainder To the use and behoofe of the right heires of me the said Richard Gascoigne for ever. And my will is that Christofer Coxson, my seruant, shall have one annuitye or yearely rente of xxs. goeinge out of my landę at Barwicke, accordinge to a surrender thereof by me made. Item I will giue and bequeath all my coppiehould landę wthin the lordshippes of Barwicke and Scooles and wthin the pishe of Barwicke wch I bought of John Newcomen th'elder, John Cawdrye, Henrie Harryson, Willm Viuers and Willm Ellis, or of all or any of them, to the said Nicholas Gascoigne for tearme of his lyfe. [Remainder to John Gascoigne the younger for tearme of his lyfe, *with other life estates and with similar remainders as previously mentioned.*] Trustees to stand and be seized of the said messuages, lands, &c., in Potterton, Garforth and Ardesley, which I purchased as aforesaid. To the use and behoofe of my said nephewe, Nicholas Gascoigne, for tearme of his lyfe, and after his decease To the use of the said John Gascoigne of Parlington, my brother, for tearme of his lyfe. [Remainder to John Gascoigne the younger, his son, and to the heirs male of his body, *with other remainders as before.*] I give and bequeath fortye shillingę p'cell of the yearely rent of foure poundę that is issueing and goeinge forth of one tenement or farmehould lyinge in Potterton, late in the tenure of John Settle, unto Thomas Rawson for tearme of his lyfe in consideracon of his seruice done to me and hereafter to be done to my heires if they will accepte of the same. Item I giue and bequeath the other fortye shillingę . . . unto Willm Liceter for tearme of his lyfe in consideracon of his seruice done to me . . . To Willm Rodehouse my seruant one annuitye or yearely rente of fortye shillingę duringe his lyfe issueinge and goeinge forth out of those landę at Garforth wch I bought of John Clarkeson, and of those laudę at Ardesley wch I bought of Gilbarte Tayler, in consideracon of his seruice done to me . . . [Power of entry and distress.] Itm I will that all my deade goods, vizt.—implements of husbandrye or househould stuffe at Barnebowe or Lasingcroft to the use of the said James Birkeby and Elizabeth his wife dureinge the life of the said Elizabeth, and after her decease to remaine to the said Nicholas Gascoigne for tearme of his estate in the said capitall messuage and premisses and then to follow the frehould as heirelomes to the said house of Barnebowe. And whereas I, the said Richard Gascoigne, have by my deede indented dated the twentye fourth day of Februarye in the one and twentye yeare of the raigne of our soueraigne Lady Elizabeth, the Quenes majestye that now is, giuen and graunted unto Richard Thompson, esq., and Thomas Hawkines, gent., one yearely rent charge of xxl issueinge out of my landę . . . in Barnebowe to the use of myself for tearme of my lyfe, And after my decease To the use and behoofe of John Newcomen, sonne of my sister Alice Newcomen, his heires and assignes for ever . . . Now my will is that my said cozen John Newcomen, his heires and assignes for ever, shall have . . . the said yearely rent of xx^{ty} pounds out of my said laudꝭ and tenm^{ts} in Barnbowe according to the purporte, true meaneinge and effecte of the said deed. [Provision to secure payment. Confirmation of Lease of cottage, tenmnt, or farme and certaine lands in Barnebowe to William Rodehouse for the tearme of xxj yeares to begin immediately after my decease, and of one other Lease to Stephen Brame of the tenement or farm with the laudꝭ thereto belonginge wherein he now inhabeteth for the tearme of xxj^{ty} yeares.] And for the true ꝑformance of this my laste will and testament I doe ordaine, constitute and make George Layton of Barroby, and Thomas Hawkins of Whixley, gentlemen, my whole and full executors . . . And for there paynes taken therein I giue to ether of them the some of six poundꝭ thirtene shillingꝭ and foure pence, provided they shall not take any of my goods to their own use and p'fitte. . . . But after my will p'formed I giue and bequeath to euery poore and needye house keeper in Barwicke ꝑishe, both man and woman, xijd., and to euery poore child they haue wch be not meete for seruice nor in seruice, iiijd. Itm I giue and bequeath to the poore of Aberforth and Garforth ꝑishes the lyke legacie and bequeste to euerye of them. To euery seruant in the house, both man and woman, over and besides there wages, xx^{s} if they have served me six yeares. If under six yeares then to euerye of them iij^{s} iiij^{d} for euery yeare soe served under six if they doe there seruice honestly and orderly untill Martinmass after my death. [Executors to make juste and due accompte yearely and from tyme to tyme to Richard Tompson late of Eshoulde, esq.] I will and bequeath to the said Richard Tompson for his paynes taken herein the some of vj^{l} xiij^{s} iiij^{d}. Itm I will that my Executors shall well and truely contente, satisfie and pay unto the daughters of my sisters Elizabeth Thompsonne and Grace Trowghton, to everye of them such some and somes of money as shall appeare by severall Bills of debt obligatorye written, signed and sealed wth my owne hand and seale, to be due and by me owing unto them. . . I will that all my debtꝭ beinge paid and legacies p'formed, and my funerall expenses beinge discharged, the surplusage of all my goodes . . (my household stuffe shall remaine as heire lombes to my house at Barnbowe onely excepted) shall be by my Executors bestowed upon Richard Gascoigne, one of my brothers, George Gascoigne, his younger sonnes, and upon my nephew, John Newcomen, in consideracõn of his charges to be bestowed upon my neece, his sister, Mary Newcomen, to be equally divided betwixt them at the discrecõn of my suꝑvisour, and moreouer my will is that Whereas my brother Robert Gascoigne doth owe unto me the iuste some of fortye poundꝭ sixtene shillingꝭ eight pence as may and doth appeare by a bill of debt. . that my executors shall pay wth that some to euery of my sisters Trowghtons thre daught^{rs} the sum of xiij^{l} vj^{s} viij^{d} apiece. And the rest of that debt I will shall remain to my said Brother himself as of my free gift. Itm I gine and bequeath to Willm Sampson of Parlington vj[l] xiij[s] iiij[d]. To Robt Howdell of Parlington fortye shillingę. To John Howdell of Parlington and his mother fortye shillingę. To Charles Norton of Parlington x[li]. To Isabell Walker my servant, accordinge to my promisse, if she doe her seruice accordingly, twentye poundę. To Stephen Brayme vj[li] xiij[s] iiij[d]. To George Cloughe and Alice, his wife, my neece, eight of my best oxen, six of my best kye, and one hundrethe sheepe. Unto Isabell Moore, my servant, vj[li] xiij[s] iiij[d]. To Elizabeth Goodyere, my servant, iiij[li] vj[s] viij[d]. Witnesses hereof Willm Power, Richard Darley, Richard Harwood, Richard Darley, yonger, Henry Grice, yonger.

Memorandum [Reciting the said will and the deed and surrender therein referred to] that on the second day of October, 1592, and in the xxxiiij[th] yeare of her Maiestyes Raigne, The said Richard Gascoigne did huius testandi expressly declare that his full myud and intente then was that the said James Birkeby and Elizabeth, his wife, should have his said copiehould landę, &c., w[th]in the lordshipp of Barwicke and Scoles, and w[th]in the pishe of Barwicke, and all his freehold laudę there duringe the lyfe of the said Elizabeth before the said Nicholas Gascoigne (the said former Clouse notw[th]-standinge), w[ch] said declaration and intente the said Richard Gascoigne did make and declare in the p'sence of us whose names are hereunder written, the said second day of October, 1592, the said Richard Gascoigne beinge then liueinge and of p'fecte memorye. In witnes whereof . . Richard Darley, Richard Harwood, clarke, Richard Darley, younger, Henry Gryce, younger, and George Clough. Alsoe the said Richard Gascoigne, the said second day of October . . . in the p'sence of the said witnesses did giue and bequeath to Lionell Carter xx[s] yearely duringe his lyfe, to be payd yearely unto the said Lionell forth of his, the said Richard Gascoigne, laudę. [*Proved* 28 *April*, 1593, by George Layton and Thomas Hawkins the executors.]

Richard Wilson of Potterton, yeoman.

[xxvi. 237a.] In the name of God Amen, I, Richard Wilson of Potterton, in the countye of Yorke, Yeoman, the fourteenth day of October in the yeare of our lord and saviour Christ one thowsand five hundreth ninety and five, being sicke in body but of good and pfect memory, God be thanked, therfore do ordaine and make this my last will and testament in manner and forme followinge. First I com̃itt my soule into the hands of Allmighty God my creator and redeemer. And my body to be buried in the Church or church yeard of Barwick in Elmet. Item I give and bequeath unto Jenet, my wyfe, one Cow called Marygould, one great pann and one cubbord, w[ch] cubbord my will and myud is shee shall haue dureinge her lyfe, And after the same to remaine to my daughter Agnes, now wyfe of Lyonell Dives, dureinge her lyfe, and after her decease unto Helen, daughter of the said Lyonell. Item I giue and bequeath unto my said wyfe Jenet one table and iij formes dureinge her lyfe, and after her decease unto Agnes, wyfe of the said Lyonell Divs, And after the decease of the said Agnes the same to remaine unto John, sonn of the said Lionell. Item I give unto my said wyfe one stand bed dureinge her lyfe, and after her decease the same to remane unto the said Agnes, wyfe of the said Lyonell Divs. Finally the residew of all my goods and chattells, my debtę, legacies, and fun'all expences discharged, I give and bequeath unto Agnes, wyfe of the said Lyonell Dyvs, my daughter, whome I make my full and whole executor by this my last will and testament. These beinge witnesses, Willm Daniell, George Stileman. [*Proved* 6 *March*, 1594-5.]

JOHN MITCHELL of Barwick, yeoman.

[xxvij. 574a.] In the name of God Amen, the vijth day of May in the yeare of or lord God 1598. I, John Mitchell of Barwicke in Elmett, in the Countie of Yorke, Yeoman, sicke in body but of good and pfect memorie, God be thanked, therefore do ordeyne and make this my last will and testament in manner and forme following. First I comitt my soule into the handę of Almightie God my Creator and redeemer, and my bodie to be buryed in the church or church-yard of Barwicke in Elmett. Itm I giue and bequeath unto my wife Katherin my lease of the milnes for and during the tearme of ten yeares next ensewing the dayt hereof towardę the bringing up and mayntenance of my children. And the residue of the tearme of yeares conteyned in the said Lease wth reu'con I give and bequeath unto my sonne Willm. And the residue of all my goodę and chattels, my debtę, legacies and funerall expences fullie discharged, I giue and bequeath unto my said wife Katherin, my children Anne, Elizabeth and Willm, whome I make my full and whole executors of this my last will and testament. And I noiate and appointe Robt Elred and Mathewe Cowp supvisors of this my last will and testament. Thes being witnesses, Robt Elred, Mathewe Cowp, Willm Walker. [*Proved* 20 *April*, 1599.]

JOHN THOMLINGSON of Roundhay, yeoman.

[xxvij. 587a.] In Dei nomine Amen, the xxth day of May, Anno Dni 1598. . . . . I, John Thomlingson of the Rounday, in the pish of Barwick in Elmett, wthin the countie of Yorke, yeoman, being of whole mynde and in good and pfect remembrance, laud and praise be given to Almightie God for the same. And calling to myud the uncertaintie of man's life and the vayne vanitie of this transitorie world howe shortlie we are cutt of and taken away from the same, I hane thought good to ordeyne and make this my psent testamt conteyning therein my last will in manner and forme followinge. First I giue and comend my soule to Almightie God my creator, and to or saviour Jesus Christ my redeemer, and to the holie ghoste, the comforter of the weake in all tribulacons, wch is to say three psons in trinitie and one in unitie. And I gine and bequeath my bodie to the earth from whence it came, and to be buried wthin the pish church of Barwicke aforesaid, in such convenient place as shalbe thought meet and convenient at the discretion of them whome I shall put in trust, which shalbe my wife, and of those wch shalbe the supvisorꝭ of this my last will. And I revoke and call backe again all former wills. . . . Item I bequeath unto M'grett, nowe my wife, and to her assignes, all that my teñte or farmehold wth th'appurtennñces in the Roundaye aforesaid that is in my occupacõn wch I take and have of Mr Xpofer Blithman, gentleman. And further I give unto my said wife all other my leases and tackꝭ which I have to come and expend of in and to all other laudꝭ, closes, meadowes and pastures wth there appurtenncꝭ wthin the aforesaid Countie of Yorke. [Residue to be divided into two parts, one for performance of will, and "I be well and honestlie brought furthe according to my degree at the day of my buriall," and the other unto Margaret, his wife.] Itm I gine and bequeath to my sister Jenett, her daughter three children, Charles Spenser, Marie Spencer and [*blank*] Spencer, to eu'ye one of them three poundꝭ a peice. Unto James Crosley of Otley, xxs. Unto Willm Thomlingson, son of Adam Thomlingson of Burley in Warkedale, xxs. Unto Henrie Thomlingson the younger of Ardington to two of his younger children to either of them one ewe sheepe, and to his sonne John, my godsonne, one ewe and a lambe. To Robt Holme my best coate. To Anne Holme, his daughter, three poundꝭ. Itm I giue all the rest of my appell to the poore wch standes most need to be bestowed upon them at the discretion of my wife, wth such other giftꝭ as I shall nõiate and appointe my wife to giue unto the said poore at such tyme when it shall please God to call me at my depting. All the rest and residue of the aforesaid p't before appointed for the pformance of this my p'sent testament and last will, my legacies and funerall expences being honestlie discharged and this my last will fulfilled. I will shall remaine wholie to the pp use and behoofe of M'grett, my wife, and her assignes. . . . I do ordeyne and make Margrett, my wife, my full and sole executrix. And I hartelie desire John Smithson of Burdett head, yeoman, and Adam Baynes of Knowstroppe to be supvisors of this my last will, to see the same executed and to call upon my wife to fulfill the same, and to help her wth there counsell and advise in all thingꝭ needfull and requisite about the same. And I further will that at any tyme whensoeu' my supvisorꝭ shalbe requested by my wife to travell or come to her to any place about the accomplishmt of this my last will that they shall haue there charges borne. And I giue unto the said John Smithson and Adam Baynes for there paines taking therein to either of them vjs viijd. In witness . . . Sealed and deliu'ed in the p'sence of John Smithson, Lawrence Middleton, Adam Baynes. [*Proved* 16 *May*, 1599.]

JOHN BURNELEY of Barwick.

[xxviij. 22b.] In the name of God Amen, the xxvijth day of November in the yeare of our lord and saviour Christ one Thowsand five hundreth fower score and six, I, John Burneley of Barwik in Ellmitt, w^th^in the countie of Yorke, sicke in bodie but of good and pfect remembraunce, God be thanked. . . . And my bodie to be buried where it shall please God. I give to my two sonnes, John and Robert, either of them xx^s^. To my wief Margerye one copper panne. To my seruant Andrew Brenton vj^s^ viij^d^, one paire of hose made and cloth to be annother payre, a tying coate of calf skynes and a Jerken. To my elder daughter Rosamond xl^s^ to be paid out of my laudę att Thorner in tenn yeares now next following, that is to say, eu^9^ie yeare iiij^s^. To my younger daughter Kathrine xl^s^, to be paid out of the Rentę of my land at Thorner, when as she is come to the age of xxj yeares or eles marrie, by the handę of whome soever shall inherrit my land. To my sonnes, John and Robert, and my two doughteres, Rosamond and Cathrine, xl^s^ equally to be devided amongst them, to be paid out of my aforesaid land at Thorner at the end and terme of a lease now devysed by whom soeu^9^ shall enjoy the same land. Item my said landę at Thorner I giue to my sonne Wiłłm and his heires, and for wante of issue to my second sonne John and to his heires, and for wante of issue I set them to my younger son Robert, and for defālt of thes my thre sonnes to myne eldest doughter Rosamond and her doughter, and for defalt of issue to my younger doughter Kathrine. And I will my wief Margaret receive the rentę of my laudę till my eldest sonne be at lawfull age, paying yearly fowre shillingę out of the same to the use of my eldest doughter Rosamond the space of tenne yeares now next following as aforesaid. Item I giue and bequeath my said wief to her use towardę the bringing upp of my children two acres of land lying in Parlynton felldę, demysed by John Tute for the terme of twentie yeares paying therefore yearly one pennye. And the Rest of my temperall goodę, my legacies and debtę and funerall expencies discharged, I gine to my wief Margaret and my two sonnes, John and Robert, and to my two doughters, Rosamond and Kathrine. I make and ordeyne my said wief Margaret and my two sonnes, John and Robert, my two doughters, Rosamond and Kathrine, my executores. Eynally I make and ordeyne Wiłłm Hart and Ralpe Dayniell overseers of this my will, And I gine to either of them xij^d^. Witnesses Mathew Belbrod and Wiłłm Walker. [*Proved* 20 *Dec.*, 1599.]

WILLIAM HUBYE of Roundhay, linen webster.

[xxviij. 141.] In Dei noie Amen. The fourth daie of Januarie in the yeare of o^r^ Lord God one Thousand fyue hundreth nyntie nyne. I, Wiłłm Hubye of the Roundhaie, in the countie of Yorke, Lynnen Webster, beinge sicke of body but of good and pfect remembrance, laude and praise be unto Almightie God, doe constitute, ordaine, and make this my present testam^t^ contayning therein my last will in mann^r^ and forme followings. Firste and principallie I doe giue and bequeath my soule into the hands of Almightie God my maker, Creator and redemer, and my bodie to be buried in the parish

Churchyeard of Barwicke in Elmett. Itm I bequeath to Marie, my wief, two kyne to her and to three of my youngest children, that is to saie, to Mathewe, Jane, and Elizabeth Huby, to be imploide to the educac̄on and bringinge up of the said children. And if my wife doe fortune to marie Then I will that my said wife shall paie to the said forenamed children to euerie one of them a pece thirtene shillingꝭ fower pence. And I further give to my eldest daughter Jane one greate panne. To my two eldest sonnes, John Hubye and James Hubye, to either of them a loombe wth all the geares to the same loomes belonging, to be equallie divided betwixt them. The rest of my goodꝭ not bequeathed, my debts beinge paid And my funerall expences discharged, I giue unto Marie, now my wiffe, And to John, my sonne, whome I make full executors of this my last will, and I hartelie desire Mr John Folkingame esqe, my good Mr, and his bedfellowe to be good to my wife and to my children, as my trust is in them. These beinge witnesses, Michaell Willson, James Barmbie and Laurence Mydleton, wth others. [*Proved 17 June*, 1600.]

JOHN PERKINSON of Shippen, yeoman.

[xxviij. 815a.] In the name of God Amen, the xxviijth daie of October in the yeare of our lord God 1602, I, John Perkinson of Shippen, yeom̄, sicke in bodye . . . my bodye to be buried in the churche yeard of Barwicke in Elmett when it shall please God to call me. Item I giue and bequeath unto Alice, my wief, xvjo ewe sheepe. The reste of all my goodꝭ moueable and unmoueable unbequested, my debtꝭ and legacꝭ, the coste of my buriall and all funerall expencꝭ discharged, I giue and bequeath unto Richard, my sonne, Alice and Elizabeth, my daughters, equallie amongst them. I make Alice, my wief, and Richard, my sonne, the executors of this my laste will. These being witnesses, George Layton, Christo[p]her Cockson, Willm Laycester and Willm Roodhouse. [*Proved 7 Dec.*, 1602.]

JOHN GASCOIGNE of Parlington esquire.[1]

[xxviij. 864a.] In the name of God, Amen. The thirde daie of Maie in the yeare of our lord God 1602. I, John Gascoigne of Parlington, wthin the dioces and Countie of Yorke, Esq., beinge at this presente of perfecte mynd and good remembrance (thankes be giuen to God therefore) callinge to mynde the great vanitie of this wretched worlde and instaabilitie thereof, but espetiallie my owne sundrie infirmities and presente weaknes, wch greatelie moue me to thinke that my tyme in this wretched worlde cannot continewe

(1) John Gascoigne married Maud, daughter of William Arthington, of Castley, and was the father of:—Sir John Gascoigne, the first Baronet; Thomas Gascoigne, who married Alice, daughter of Sir William Gascoigne, of Gawthorpe, and widow of Edmond Hazlewood, of Maydeswell; Alveray Gascoigne, of Garforth, married Awdrey, daughter of William Wittell, of Croydon; Leonard Gascoigne, baptised at Aberford Church 6 January, 1563–4, died unmarried 1 June, 1609, buried in St. Bride's Church, London; Lucy Gascoigne, baptised 1564, and buried 1565 at Aberford Church; Richard Gascoigne, baptised and buried at Aberford Church, 1566, and Mary, married to William Crofts, of Cloughton. He was buried at Barwick, 30 June, 1602.

longe, as allso desirous to sett some staye for disposinge of my worldlie goodꝭ, doe constitute, ordaine and make this my presente laste will and testam̃ in manner and forme followinge. Firste therefore I com̃end my soule unto the greate mercye of Allmightye God and his onelie begotten sonne our redemer and sauiour Jesus Christe by whose onelie most painefull passion and bitter death I hope to be saued and to be one of the Inheritors of his moste glorious Kingdome amongest the blessed Sainctꝭ in heaven. And this full hope and trust is setled in my harte, my bodye, to the earthe from whence it came, to be interred wthin the Churcheyeard at Barwicke. Itm I doe gine and bequeath unto Mawde, my faithfull and lovinge wief, my beste bedd wth all suche beddinge and furniture as belongeth to the same, and all suche furniture as is in this ꝑlor wherein I doe now lie. Itm I doe giue and bequeath unto her duringe her naturall lief all the laudꝭ wch I purchased latelye wthin Garford wth the whole ꝑfittꝭ of my Colemyne there. Itm I give and bequeath unto Thomas Gascoigne, my sonne, and to my doughter, his wief, either of them a golde Ringe of xx^{s} a peece. Itm I gine and bequeath unto Leonard Gascoigne, my youngest sonne, the some of xl^{li}. Itm I giue and bequeath unto Marie Crofte, my daughter, tenne poundꝭ. Itm I giue to Anne and Awdrye, my daughters in Lawe, eache of them a whye. Itm I giue and bequeath unto euerie one of my sonne John his children the some of vj^{li} xiij^{s} iiij^{d}. Unto the seauen children of my sonne Aluerey euerie one of them xx^{li}. Unto Robart Gascoigne, my brother, one golde Ringe. Unto my brother George Gascoigne, one golde Ringe. To my sister Tompson, one golde ringe. Unto Elizabeth Wentworthe, my neece, xl^{s}. Unto Marie Heselgreaue and to Mary Hoyle eyther of them one wyndle of breake corne. Unto Robart Coxon, my servant, iij^{li} xvj^{s} viij^{d}. Unto Elizabeth Goodyeare thelder and to Elizabeth Goodyeare, her daughter, to eyther of them xiij^{s} iiij^{d} a peece. To Margarett, my servante, xx^{s}. To Robert Sawer, my servante, xiij^{s} iiij^{d}. To Thomas Bywater, my servante, xiij^{s} iiij^{d}. Unto Michaell Hodgeson, my servante, xiij^{s} iiij^{d}. To Thomas Jackson xxvj^{s} viij^{d}. To the Vicar of Aberforthe xiij^{s} iiij^{d}. To the poore of the ꝑishe of Abberforthe and wthin Lotherington wch are my owne tenantꝭ, xx^{s}. To the poore of the ꝑishe of Barwicke xx^{s}. To the poore of the ꝑishe of Garforde xx^{s}. Unto the poore prisoners wthin the Castle and Kidcote at Yorke iij^{li} vj^{s} viij^{d}, to be distributed at the discretion of my welbeloved Cosen, Wiłłm Vavasour, esq^{e}, whome I doe intreate to be the suꝑviso^{r} of this my said Laste Will and testam̃. And for his paines therein soe to be taken I doe bequeath unto him one brasse of Angells. The reste of all my goodꝭ (my funerall expencꝭ defraied and my debtꝭ and legacꝭ discharged) I doe giue unto Maude, my welbeloued wief, and to Leonard Gascoigne, my youngest sonne, whome I doe constitute and make my executors of this my said laste will and testam^{t}. In witnesse whereof I haue hereunto putt my hande and seale in the p'sence of these whose [names] are hereunder written, Robart Gascoigne, John Gascoigne, Thomas Gascoigne, Aluerie Gascoigne. [*Proved* 3 *Feb.*, 1602-3.]

LEONARD SETHLE of Potterton, husbandman.

[xxx. 148b.] In the name of God Amen. The thirde daie of June in the yeares of the Raigne of our most dread Soueraigne Lord Kinge James . . . in the yeare of our lord God 1606. I, Leonard Sethle of Potterton, wthin the county of Yorke, husbandman, sicke in bodye but of good and pfecte remembrance praised be God . . . and my body to be buried in the Churcheyeard of Barwicke in Elmett at the discretion of my executr. Itm I giue and bequeath unto Richard Sethe, sonne of John Sethle, and Jenett Tayte, daughtr of Wiltm Tayte, one blacke Cowe. Unto John Sethle, my sonne, in full satisfaction of his filliall childę parte and porc̃on of my goodę, twoe quarters of Barley, twoe loades of wheate and twoe loades of Beanes of Leedę measure, and now growinge in and upon my farme in Potterton aforesaid. Unto my said sonne John one feather bedd whereon I now lye, twoe Couerlettę, twoe Coddę, twoe blancketę and a paire of sheetę. Itm I giue and bequeath unto Mary Sethle, daughter to my said sone, one gymer lambe or iijs iiijd to buye one wthall. And I nõiat and appointe Wiltm Sethle, my sonne, executor of this my laste will and testamt giuinge unto him the reste of my goodę, my debtę, legacę and Funerall expencę beinge firste discharged of the whole, and hopeinge that he will se the same pformed as my truste is in him. Witnesses, Richard Potter, Wiltm Shanne, John Smythe. Law: Daniell, Samuell Walbancke. [*Proved* 2 *Oct.*, 1606.]

LAURENCE ASKWITH of Roundhay, yeoman.

[xxx. 768b.] In the name of God Amen, the third day of October in the yere of or Lord one thousand sixe hundrethe and seaven, and in the fifte yere of the Reigne of or Sou'aigne Lord Kinge James. I, Laurence Askwith of Rooundhey, in the countie of Yorke, yeomã, beinge sicke and crased in bodie, yet whole and pfect in mynde, thankes be unto God, doe make this my last will and testament in mann9 and forme followinge. First I doe yeeld and bequeath my soule unto Allmightie God and to his sonne Jesus Christe my onelie sauiour and Redeem9, faythfully trustinge through the merritę of his bitter passion to be ptaker of the eu'lastinge blisse of heaven. And my bodie to be buried where yt shall please my exequutors. And as touchinge the order and disposic̃on of my goodes and chattels my full mynde and will is that aswell the som̃e of sixe and twenty poundes wch I doe owe unto John Corbridge and Elizabeth Corbridge, my wife's Children, shalbe paid unto theim in mann9 and forme followinge, that is to saye, to the said John xiijli when he shall come to the age of one and twentie yeres, and to the said Elizabeth other thirteene poundes when she shall accomplishe the age of one and twentie yeres or fortune to be married, as also the rest of my other debtes to be paide wth as convenient speede as may be, and these debtes being discharged my mynde and will is that the Residue of my goodes shalbe devided equallie into three ptes, whereof the one pte I doe giue and bequeath unto my Children, and another pte unto Elizabeth, my said wife, and the thirde pte unto myselfe for the discharge of my legacies and fun'all expenses, out of my owne part last menconed I doe give unto my sonne Nicholas one blacke Coulte, and unto my sonne Robte twentie shillings. And also I give unto Lawrence, Sara, Suzan and the said Robte, my fower youngest children, eighteene ewes and other sheepe which Thomas Brooke hath to halfe pte. And to Lawrence Whawley ten shillings. And to Izabell Askw^th ten shillings. The residue of my said parte, my legacies and fun'all expenses discharged, I give and bequeath to my said wife and to my said fower youngest children equallie to be devided amongest them. And whereas I and my said sonne Nicholas are ioyntlie possessed of the farme wheron I nowe dwell for divers yeares yet to come and unexpired of the demise and grante of the Right Honorable the Lord Darcy, my mynde and will is with the consent and likeinge of my said sonne Nicholas that Elizabeth my wife shall have the occupacon of the said farme duringe her widoweheade towardes the mayntenance and bringing up of her younge children. And yf yt shall happen my said wife to marrie or dye that then the interest or terme of yeares shall returne unto my said sonne Nicholas. And further I doe ordeyne and make Elizabeth my said wife and my sonne Nicholas my full and lawfull Exequutors of this my last will and testament. These beinge witnesses, William Oglethorpe, Christopher Mather, Michaell Wilson, Lawrence West and Robert Sympson. [*Proved* 13 *Dec.*, 1608, *by Elizabeth Askwith the widow, power reserved to Nicholas Askwith.*]

HENRY WALKER of Kidhall Moorhouses, Wheelwright.

[xxxj. 676a.] In Dei nõine Amen, the xij^th day of February in the eight yeare of the Reigne of our Sou^eigne Lord James, &c. I, Henrie Walker of Kidhall Moorhouses, in the county of Yorke, wheelewright, sick in body but of good and pfect remembrance, thancke be geven to Almightie God, doe ordeyne and make this my last will and testament in manner and forme followeinge. First and principally I give and bequeath my sinfull soule into the handes of Almightie God my maker and redeemer, whoe hathe redemed mee and all mankynde, trusting after this liefe to be saved by the meritte of Christe passion, and my body to be buryed wth in the pishe Churchyeard att Barwicke in Elmett. Secondly I give and bequeath all my goodes, moveable and unmoveable whatsoeu^, unto Margarett, my wiefe. Itm I give unto Cuthbert, my sonne, all my apparell, all my workeinge towles and xx^s in money wth in one halfe yeare to be paid him after my death by my wiefe. The rest of all my goodes not bequeathed, my debte beinge paid and legacies and funerall expenses discharged, I give unto Margarett my wiefe, whom I doe make full and sole executrix of this my last will and testam^t. And I give unto Anthonie Styam a great mell and certeine rules wch I have. In witnes thereof I have hereuntto sett my hand the day and yeare abouesaid. Itm I give unto eu'ie one of Cuthbert Witham children xij[d] a peece. Witnesses hereof Anthony Styam, Thomas Rawson. [*Proved* 3 *Oct.*, 1611.]

RICHARD VEVERS of Potterton, tanner. (1)

[xxxj. 716b.] In the name of God Amen, the first day of March in the yeare of or Lord God eu'lastinge 1610. I, Richard Vevers of Potterton in the County of York, Tanner, sick in body but of good and pfect remembrance praised be God, knoweing that their is nothinge more Certeine then death nor nothinge more uncerteine then the houre of death, doeth therefore ordeyne, constitute and make this my last will and testament in mann' and forme followeing. First I commend my soule into the handes of Almightie God, trusting by the meritt*e* of his sonne Christ Jesus to be one of his faithfull and Elect servant*e*, and my body to be buryed in the Church or Churchyeard of Barwick in Elmett att the discretionne of my Executors. Itm I give and bequeath unto my twoe sonns Thomas Vevers and James Vevers to either of them Forty poundes to be paid forthe of my goodes and landes in full satisfaction of all their filiall childes ptes and porcons of my goodes. Unto Ellen, my wiefe, the third pte of all my laud*e* and goodes, my debt*e* first paid upon the whole. The rest of all my goodes I give and bequeath unto Ellen, my wiefe, Thomas Vevers and James Vevers, my souns, and I constitute and make Ellen, my wiefe, Thomas and James, my sonns, Executors of this my last will and testament. And I nomynate and appointe Richard Vevers of Scholes, my nephue, and Thomas Taite, my brother in lawe, supvisors of this my last will and testament, hopeing that they will see the same pformed as my trust is in them. And I give to either of them for their paynes twoe shillinges. In witness . . . Witnesses Richard Vevers, Franc*e* Setle, Samuell Walbanck, with others. [*Proved* 4 *Oct.*, 1611.]

JOHN HAIRE of Potterton, wheelwright.

[xxxij. 371b.] In the name of God Amen, the xj[th] daie of Nouember one thousand six hundreth and six. I, John Haire of Potterton w[th]in the Countie of Yorke, wheelewright, sicke of bodie but of whole and sound, of perfect minde and remembrance (thanckes be giuen to God), doe make my last will and testament in manner and forme followinge, that is to saie. First and principally I giue my soule into the handes of Allmightie God my maker, wth full hope of remission of all my sinnes by the death and passion of my onely lord and sauiour Jesus Christ my Redeemer. And my bodie to be buried in the parish Churchyeard of Barwicke in Elmett. And as touchinge the disposicon of my farme and good*e* my will and minde is that it shalbe in manner and forme followinge distributed, that is to saie, I giue and bequeath unto Margarett, my wiffe, my full right title and interest of my farme wherein I now dwell duringe her liffe naturall, and after her decease to Raiph, my sonne, his executors and

(1) A pedigree of the Vevers family is given in Platt and Morkill's Whitkirk, p 96.

assignes. Item I gine unto George, my sonne, xls. And to John and Arthure either of them xls, soe that they take the same in full satisfaccon of theire childes porcons, and upon the payment of the same doe seale and deliuer unto mine Executors a generall Acquittance for the same. Item I giue unto Xpofer, my sonne, and Thomasine, my daughter, to either of them xls if they be liueinge and doe call for the same, soe that they be content to accepte of it and take it as theire childes porcons. Item I gine unto Marie and Anne, my two daughters, by legacie to either of them xijd. Item I giue unto my sonne George his foure children to eurie of them iijs iiijd. Item I gine unto my sonne John his foure children to euerie of them iijs iiijd. Item I giue unto Agnes, the daughter of my sonne Arthure, one Ewe and a lambe, and to John, his sonne, a lambe. Item I giue unto my sonne Raiph all the workeinge tooles. The rest of my goodꝭ unbequeathed, my debtꝭ and legacies paid, I give Joyntlie unto Margarett, my wiffe, and Raiph, my sonne, and to the longer liner of them. And I doe make my said wiffe and Raiph, my sonne, ioyntly Executors of this my last will and testament, requestinge Mr John Ellis of Kiddall, Esq., and James Chambers, Vicar of Thorner, to be supuisors and ouerseers of this my last will and testament 1606. Witnesses James Chambers, Vicar of Thorner, Richard Veners, William Shanne, John Settle and William Hopwood. [*Proved 22 April*, 1613.]

MARGARET POTTER of Potterton, widow.

[xxxiii. 19a.] In the name of God Amen, the six and twentieth day of March in the yeare of our Lord God euꝰlasting 1614. I, Margarett Potter of Potterton, wthin the County of York, widowe, sick in bodie but of good and pꝰfect memory, praised be God, doe ordeyne and make this my last will and testamt in mannꝰ and forme tolloweing. First I comend my soule into the handꝭ of Almightie God, trusting by the merittꝭ of his sonne Christ Jesus to be one of his elect and chosen servantꝭ. And my body to be buryed in the Church or Churchyard of Barwick att the discretion of my Executors. Item I give and bequeth unto Jennett Potter, my doughter, all my household stuffe as Lynnen and Wollen, brasse and pewther, wooden stuffe and all other thingꝭ within the house except one litle brasse pott wch I give to my doughter Anne, the wiefe of Wiłłm Settle, and one other litle pott wch I give unto Robert Potter, my sonne. Item I give and bequeath unto Andrew Potter, another of my sonns, one branded stottꝭ. Item I give unto Barbary Potter, nowe the wiefe of Christofer Waterworth, vjs viijd. Item I give unto Richard, John, Robert, Anne, Barbarey and Jennett Potter, my sonnes and doughters, euꝰy of them a siluꝰ spoone. Item I give to Andrew and Wiłłm Potter, twoe other of my sonns, to either of them iijs iiijd. Item I give to eu'y childe that I am grandmother unto, a lambe or for want of a lambe a younge sheep. Item I give to Ellen, doughter of Richard Potter, a gymꝰ sheep. Item I give to Richard Potter whom I am grandmother unto, one greate troughe in the chamber, and one Arke in the laith. Item I give and bequeath unto my said doughter Jennett, one red cowe called Cherrie. The rest of all my goodes as well moveable as unmoveable, corne and cattell, I give and bequeath to be equallye devyded amongst all my children, my debts and fun'all expencę first discharged. And I constitute and make Richard and Wittm Potter, my sonnes, and Jennett Potter, my doughter, Executors of this my last will, hopeing they will see the same pformed as my trust is in them. Witnesses hereof Wittm Daniell, Richard Potter, and Samuell Walbanck. [*Proved* 9 *April*, 1614.]

RICHARD SETTLE of Potterton, husbandman.

[xxxv. 497.] In the name of God Amen. The Seaven and Twentye day of August in the yeare of our Lord God eu'lasting 1617. I, Richard Settle of Potterton, wthin the Countie of Yorke, husbandman, sick of body but of good and pfect memorie praised be God, knowing that there is nothing more certaine then death, and nothing more uncertaine then the houre of death, doe therefore ordeine, constitute and make this my last will and testamt in mann9 and forme following. First I com̃end my soule into the hand of Allmightie God, Trusting by the merittę of his sone Christ Jesus to be one of his elect and faithfull s'uantę, and my body to be buryed in the Church or Churchyeard of Barwick in Elmet at the discrec̃on of my Executors. Itm I giue and bequeath unto John Settle, my sonne, all my land and my two stottę and an Ironbunn weane. Unto Anne Settle, my daughter, foure poundę. Unto Willia' Tate, my wife sonne, two yeues and two gimer Lambes. Itm I gine unto Mychaell Hopwood xijd, to William Settle xijd, to Thomas Potter xijd. Itm I gine to John Settle, my sonne, my younger mare, and doe make Bridget, my wife, full Executrix of this my will and Testamt. Itm my will and myud is, that Bridgett, my wife, shall be tutrix to John Settle, my sonne, dureing her widdowhoode, and ii shee marye then my will and mynd is that John Settle, my Brother, shall bee tutor and gardian unto my said sonne John, and shall from thenceforth haue and receaue the p'fittę of all my landę to thuse of my said sonne John, togeather wth his porc̃on dureing the noneage and minoritie of my said sonne. Witnesses Williã Vevers, Richard Potter and Peeter Cookson. [*Proved* 6 *Nov.*, 1619.]

RICHARD INGLE of Stocking.

[xxxvi. 399.] In the name of God, Amen, the second day of June in the seaventeenth yeare of the Reigne of or Sou'aigne Lord James by the grace of God, Kinge of England, France and Ireland, defendor of the faith, &c., and of Scotland the lijdo 1619. I, Richard Ingle of Stocking, within the pish of Barwicke and County of Yorke being sicke and deceased in body but of p'fect memory, Gods holy name be praised therefore, doe make this my last will and Testamt in manner and forme followeinge, vizt, first I give and commend my soule into the hands of Almighty God, trustinge faithfully thorow the meritt℮ and passion of his onely sonne and o^r^ onely savio^r^ Christ Jesus to be one of his elect servant℮. Itm my will and mind is that all my debts be paid out of my whole good℮ wch debt℮ are these followeinge. First to Mrs Anne Ellis xx^li^. Itm to Lawrence Glover of Rowndhey xj^li^ due at St Peter's day next. Itm to John Ingle, my sonne, vij^li^. Itm to Elizabeth Ingle, my daughter, v^li^. Itm to Jenett Ingle, my daughter, vj^li^. Itm to Anne Ingle, another of my daughters, v^li^. Itm to Euphame Browne, my sister in law, iij^li^. All the rest of my good℮, moveable and unmoveable, my debt℮, legacies and fun'all expences paid and discharged, I doe give and bequeath unto Jennett Ingle, my wiffe, and my said fower children, that is to say, the one halfe thereof to my said wiffe and thother halfe to my said fower children to be equally devided amongst them. And I make and ordeine the said Jennett, my wiffe, sole executrix of this my last will, revokeing all former wills. In witness . . . Witnesses Richard Taylo^r^, Richard Ingle, Junio^9^, Richard Muncie and Wm. Watterworth. [*Proved* 19 *April* 1621.]

JOHN SETLE of Potterton, yeoman.

[xxxvii. 450] In the name of God Amen, Augustij 25to 1622°. I, John Setle of Potterton, in the county of Yorke, yeoman, sicke in body but of good and p'fect memory, praised be God, do constitute, ordaine and make this my last will and testament in manner and forme following. First I comend my soule into the hands of Christ Jesus my Saviour, trusting by his meritt℮ to be one of his elect and choosenn servant℮, and my body to be buried in the Church or Church yeard of Barwicke at the discretion of my freinds. Item I give and bequeath unto Agnes, my daughter, and to such sonne or daughter as my wife Margery is now conceiued w^th^all, to either of them tenn pounds, to be paid by Robert Setle, my sonne and heire, out of my lands and tenement℮ in Potterton at such tyme as either of my said childrenn shall accomplish the age of one and twentie yeares or be married, and if either of them shall dye before the same come to be dew the whole some of twenty pounds to remaine to the then Survivor. Item for all my goods and chattells my will and minde is that they should be equallie devided amongst Margery, my wife, Agnes, my daughter, and my sonne or daughter not as yet borne, whom I make whole and sole executors. . . . In witnes . . . . Witnesses Willm Ball, Francis Setle, Richard Setle, Samuell Wallbanke. [*Proved* 8 *November*, 1623.]

HENRY TAILOR of Barwick.

[xxxix. 368b.] In the name of God Amen. The first of Januarie, 1623. I, Henrie Tailor of Barwicke, doe ordaine and make this my last will and testament in manner and forme followeing. In primis I giue to Margarett Tailor my best Cloake. Item I gine unto

Henrie Tailor my worst cloake wth my worst Jerkin and breeches. I gine more unto Margarett Tailor a little Chist. Itm I giue to Elizabeth Holine a pewter dubbler. Itm I giue to Thomas Holme my best doublett wth my one paire of Beddstockes in the nether Parlor. Itm I giue unto Willm Boulton iijs iiijd. Item I doe make my two sonnes William Tailor and Frauncis my whole and sole executors . . and unto them I gine all the remainder of my goodẹ, bills and bonde wth the debtes therein unto my two sonnes Willm and Frauncis, to thend that they bring my corpes honestlie forth and discharged my funerall expences. And alsoe that they giue unto my brother, Christopher Tailor, five shillinges out of the debtes wch I haue giuen them. Witnesses bee theis, Robte Lister, George Musgraue and Ingram Winterburne. [*Proved* 24 *March*, 1625-6.]

THOMAS HEMSWORTH of Potterton.

[xl. 69b.] In the name of God Amen, the eighteenth day of December in the yeare of our lord God one thowsand six hundred twentie and six. I, Thomas Hemsworth of Potterton, in the countie of Yorke, beinge sicke in bodie but whole of myud, laud and praise be given to Allmightie God, doe make this my p'sent Testamt concerneinge herein my last will in mannor and forme followinge, that is to say, first, I comend and comitt my soule into the handes of Allmightie God my maker and redeem̃, and my bodie to be buried in the church or churchyeard of Barwicke in Elmett in the same countie att the discretion of my executor hereafter named, in full confidence att the last day and generall resurecton of all flesh to have both bodie and soule revnited and maide to participate those ioyes which are prepaired for the elect. Next of my ꝑsonall estate I dispose on as followeth. First I give and bequeath unto John Kirkbie all that seaven poundes which he oweth me to the intent and purpose he enter sufficient securitie to myne executors hereafter named that once within a yeare after my departuer out of this naturall life he will buy a Cowe of three poundes price and put the same forward to be imployed for the best benifitt of Anne, now his daughter, or elles put out three poundes within the same tyme to her said profitt and pay whether soever of the same he shall put forward with the benifitt and pay thereof made when she shall accomplishe her Lawfull age of one and Twentie yeares or elles be married. Item I give and bequeath unto the said Anne, the daughter of the said John Kirkbie, five poundes which is in the hands of Richard Shanne, to be put forward once within a yeare after my decease by my executor hereafter named for the benefitt of her the said Anne, and paied to her withall the profitt thereof arriseinge when she shall accomplishe her lawfull age of one and Twentie yeares, or elles be married, and if she chaunce hereafter to depte this naturall life before eyther of the same happen then my myud and will is that Mary, now my neece, the wife of the said John Kirkbie, and the rest of her children shall have the one halfe thereof with all the profitt thereof arrisinge equally devided amongst them, and Mary, now the wife of my nephew John Hemsworth, and her children shall have the other halfe thereof with the bennefitt thereof arrisinge equally chaired [sic] and amongst them to be paid unto each of them att such tyme as they shall successively be capable to give a lawfull discharge for the same. Item to Anne Goodaile, my neece, Twentie shillinges out of that thirtie shillinges which I form'ly lent her husband. Item I give and bequeath unto Elizabeth Hemsworth, my neece, Twentie shillinges. Item I give and bequeath unto Mary and John Hemsworth, children of my nephew John Hemsworth, to eyther of them Twentie shillinges, and to John and Alice Kirkbie, the children of the said John Kirkbie, to eyther of them Twentie shillinges to be paid into the handes of the said John Kirkbie, theire father, once w^bin a yeare after my decease by myne executors hereafter named to be put forward by him for the best bennefitt of his said children, and to be paid unto them as they shall successively be inabled in the eie of the Lawe to make a sufficient discharge. Item my will and mynd is that if the three sonnes of my sister Issabell Dobson shall come to my buriall and helpe to carry my corpes to the Church, that soe many of them as shall come shall have xij^d for their paynes, otherwaies if they come not nothinge at all. Item I give and bequeath unto the said Elizabeth Dobson, my said sister, theire mother, if she be alive, twentie shillinges, if deed then I give and bequeath the same unto Jane, her daughter, to be put and paid once within a yeare after my decease into the hands of her brother Thomas to be desposed on by him for her best bennefitt and profitt. Item I give and bequeath unto Jane, John, Robert and Elizabeth, now the children of Charitie Wilson, to eu'y of them tenn shillinges, to be put forward once within a yeare after my deathe to their use. . . . And for the rest of my goodę, chattels, credittę and debtes not yett disposed on after my debtes paid, fun'alles defrayed and theise my legacies aforenamed trewly discharged accordinge to the purport an effect hereof, I give and absolutely bequeath all and singuller the same unto John Hemsworth, my nephew, whome of this my p'sent last will and testam^t I make the sole executor. . . . . Theise beinge witnesses, Richard Turner, Wiłłm Taite and Shanne [sic]. [*Proved* 18 *Oct.*, 1627.]

BREWEN BRIGGS of Roundhay, yeoman.

[xl. 198a.] In the name of God Amen, the three and twentieth day of May Anno Dni 1626. I, Brewen Briggę of Rowndhey, in the county of Yorke, yeom̃, being in p̧fect remembrance, thankes be given to God for the same, and callinge to mind the incertainty of this life doe ordayne and make this my testament and last will in manner and forme followeinge, that is to say. First I give and bequeath my soule to Allmighty God, and my body to be buried in the p̧ish Churchyeard of Barwicke in Elmett. Itm I give and bequeath to Mary Briggę, my eldest daughter, one cupboord standinge in Randall Briggs howse, tenn dublers, three candlesticks two saltę and one great brasse pott. Itm I give and bequeath unto Mary Briggs, wife of Lawrence Briggę, Robert Briggs, Jaine Briggs, Bridgett Briggs, Agnes Briggę and Thomas Briggę, children of the said Lawrence Briggs and Mary his wife, two parts of my farme wch I hold of the right honorable the lord Darcy, payinge the yearly rent of forty two shillings and one penny in the yeare. Itm I give to my sonne Beniamin Brigs nineteene shillings and fower pence, to be paid out of the third parte of my lease wch I hold of the lord Darcy, wch lease is in Rowndhey before recited, wch money shall be paid to him for helpinge to relieve his wife and the bringeinge up of his children for all the yeares which shalbe unexpired att the day of my death. And out of the third parte of my farme wch my sonne William Briggs nowe hath of me, and the said money soe bequeathed shalbe paid at the feastę of Thannuntiation and St Michaell the Arch: Angell, by equall porcons, that is to say, nine shillings eight pence att either feast day. Itm I give and bequeath unto my eldest daughter, Mary Briggs, ten shillings yearly, to be paid out of the third parte of my lease before recited in the occupacon of my sonne William Briggs, and to be paid att the daie before mencoñed (that is to say) five shillingę att either feast day. Itm I give and bequeath to my son John Briggę fower shillingę six pence in full satisfaccon of his childes porcon. Item I give and bequeath unto my sonne in lawe, Martin Morris, fower shillingę six pence in full satisfaccon of all that I will bestowe of him. Itm as for the rest of my goodę wch I have lefte undisposed of I give to William Briggs, my sonne, whom I make sole executor. . . . . Witnesses hereof, James Clough, Martin Clough. [*Proved* 1 *May*, 1628.]

LAWRENCE GLOVER of Roundhay, yeoman.

[xli. 265.] In the name of God Amen, the Tenth day of May . . . 1628. I, Lawrence Glover of roundhey, in the prish of Barwicke in Elmett and in the county of York, yeomã . . . . And I will that my bodye be buried in the prish church yeard of Barwicke aforesaid . . I give and bequeath to Willm Glover, my sonne, the lease of my farme with all other the rest of my goodę and chattalls . . . . And I doe make him my full and sole executor. Witnesses hereof Willm Briggę and Tristram Ascoughe. [*Proved* 7 *Jan*., 1630-1.]

MARY ELLIS of Barwick, gentlewoman.(1)

[xli. 282.] In the name of God Amen, the eightenth day of February in the yeare of our Lord God one thousand sex hundreth twenty nyne. I, Marie Ellis of Barwicke in Elmett, in the county of Yorke, gentlewoman, being growne now in yeares and by reason of old age, infirmities, sombhinge of body, but whole and sound of mynd and memorie, thankę and prayse be geven to God for the

(1) Mary Ellis was the widow of John Ellis, of Kiddal, and daughter of Martin Anne, of Frickley.

same, knowinge that I ame but a stranger here upon earth and must leave this world I knowe not when, and being desyrous to sett my house in order ere I die, and to dispose of that lyttle p̄sonall estate wc̄h it hath pleassed God to lend me in this lyffe, that after my death it may be distributed in peace according to my mynd, and to take alwaye all just causes of future differrencę that perhaps might els hereafter aryse amonge my children about the same if it weare lefte undisposed on, doe hereby make this my last will and testament in mann' and forme followinge, that is to saye, First and principally I com̄end my soule into the handę of Almighty God from whome I had it, assuredly trustinge through the merrittę of Christ Jesus my saviour and redemer to receyve free pardon of all my synnes, and after my decease to be admitted into the blest societie of his sayntę and electe s'vantę. And my body I com̄ytt to the earth from whence it came, and to be buried in the p̄rish Church of Barwicke in Elmett aforesaid, as neare unto my late husband as conveniently may be, then of my p̄sonall estate I dispose on as followeth. First I give and bequeath unto my sonnes Marttyn, Henry, Robert, Frauncis, Richard and Thomas Ellis, to every one of them twenty shillingę apiece, and to my daughter Marie, the wyfe of Thomas Cowp̄, twenty shillingę in full satisfaccon of all such filliall and childs porc̄ons as they or any of them myght lawfully challenge and of right ought to have out of my p̄sonall estate, and to be payd to every of them by my executor hereafter named. Item I give and bequeath to my sonne John Ellis his wyfe Twenty shillingę. To my daughter Laskewe, my daughter Burneley, and to my grand daughter Marie Ellis, daughter to my said son John Ellis, all myne apparrell and clothinge to be distrybuted amonge them at the discretion of my syster Holmes in such sorte as I have formerly geven directions to her for the distrybutinge of the same, save onlye my myud and will is that such thereof as she shall deeme unfytt for them be bestowed by her on Margarett, now my servant, unto which Margarett besydes I give and bequeath Twenty shillingę. Item I give and bequeath to my said syster Holmes my gould ringe to weare the same for a remembrance of my love after my death. The resydue of my said p̄sonall estate not yett disposed on after my debtę and these legacies discharged I freely give and wholly bequeath unto Samuell Ellis, my youngest sonne, out of the naturall affection I beare him and confident trust I repose in him, that after my death he will see me honestly brought forth and distrybute to the poor. And the said Samuell Ellis of this my present Testament I make and ordayne the whole executor, and this my said will and Testament may be more surely p̄formed according to my mynde I desyre my nephew Frauncis Tindall to be supervisor . . And I give and bequeath him for his paynes to be taken herein halffe a peece . . These beinge witnesses. Richard Turner, John Hardcastle and M'garett Robinson. [*Proved 7 Feb.*, 1630-1.]

RICHARD SETTLE of Potterton, tanner.

[xli. 327b.] In the name of God Amen, the thirtenth day of Septembr in the year of our lord God 1629. I, Richard Settle of Potterton, in the county of Yorke, Tanner, being sycke in body but whole in mynd, laude and prayse be geven to Almighty God therfore, doe make this my present Testament . . . First I comend my soule into the handę of Almighty God my maker and redemer, fully consyderinge not for any meritts of my owne but for his own merrytt sake manifested in the merittę of his sonne Christ Jesus, that he will receyve it into his tuiticon when it shall leave the pryson of my bodie. And I comytt my body to the earth from whence it came, And to be buried in the church or churchyarde of Barwicke in Elmett at the discrettion of my frendę in full confydence and assured hope at the generall resureccon of all flesh to have both body and soule Revnited and be maid to pticipate of those ioyes wch are prepared for the electe in the Kingdome of heaven. Next of my landę I dispose as followeth. First I devyse all and singular the same as well the singuler those lands wch I haue boughte as those wch I had in pte of my wyves portion unto Isabell, my wyfe, duringe her naturall lyfe unless that she marrie, and then I devyse all and singuler the same or so much thereof as the lawes of this lande will pmitt unto my eldest sonne and his heires for ever, to enter unto the same or so much therof as the lawes will permytt imediatly after the marriage. Item my will and myud is that the lease of the becke close beinge demeasne lands shalbe taken and renewed out of my psonall estaite in the name of Isabell, my said wyfe, and of the said Willm, my sonne, to haue and to hould unto the said Isabell, my wyfe, duringe her widdowhood, and after that she shall be maried or dye, whethersoever of the twaine shall sooner happen, to haue and to hold the said demeasne landę to the said Willm, my sonne, his executors and assignes for all and soe many of the yeares it shall be taken and renewed for as shalbe at eyther of the same then to expyre. Item my will and mynde is that after the demeasne lease be taken and renewed as aforesaid is declarede, that then the resydew and remainder of my said psonall estaite left behynde shall be devided into three equal partę, one pte whereof I give and frely bequeath unto the said Izabell, my said wyffe, in lieu of her third wch by the lawe she may challenge by reason of her marriage with me. the second third pte I give and bequeath unto Willm, John, Thomas, Samuell and Marie, my children, to be equally devided amongst them for their filliall or childę portions of my said psonall estaite, and out of the other third pte remayninge I give and bequeath unto the said Isabell, my wyffe, the sume of five poundę for a legacy, and unto the said Thomas, Samuell and Marie unto every one of them the sume of forty shillingę a peece for a legacie, and all the Resydue and remainder thereof not yett disposed on I give and absolutely bequeath unto the said Willm, John, Thomas, Samuell and Marie, to be equally pted amongst them for the augmentation and bettering of their portions. [Other provisions respecting his children's shares.] Isabell, my said wyfe

I ordayne and make the sole executrix, and unto whom I comytt the tuition and education of all my said children duringe ther minorities. . . . These beinge witnesses. Thomas Veuers, Thomas Taite, Richard Potter thelder, John Danyell and Richard Turner. [*Proved* 26 *February*, 1630-1.]

THOMAS TIRRINGTON of Shippen, labourer.

[xli. 436a.] In the name of God Amen, the last day of March in the yeare of our lord God 1631. I, Thomas Tirrington of Shippen, in the county of Yorke, laborer, beeinge sycke in body but whole in mynde . . . . and I comytt my body to the earth from whence it came, and to be buried in the Church or Churchyarde of Barwicke in Elmett in the said county of Yorke, at the discretion of my frendę. Next I give and bequeath unto Robert Sawer, one of my sonnes in lawe, and unto Jane, his wyffe, forty shillingę and whatsoever reckninge is due to me besydes I freely forgive them the same and absolutely give the same unto them in full satisfaccõn of all such parte as they or eyther of them might Lawfully challenge out of my ꝑsonall estaite. Item I give and bequeath unto Wiłłm Cawood, another of my sonnes in lawe, and Anne his wyfe, other forty shillingę in full satisfaccon . . . Item I give and bequeath unto Wiłłm Hargrave, another of my sonnes in lawe, and Marye, his wyffe, twenty shillingę in full satisfaccõn . . . Item I give and bequeath unto Anne, one of the daughters of the said Wiłłm Cawoode, my best hatt. Unto Henry, Wiłłm, Isabell, Elizabeth and Jane, the children of the said Robert Sawer, my said sonne in lawe, to every one of them Twoo shillingę. Unto Marie, Thomas, Anne, Dorathie, Fraunċis, M^{r}garett, Wiłłm, Alice and Isabell, the children of the said Wiłłm Cawood, my said sonne in lawe, to every one of them ij^{s}. Unto John, Thomas, Wiłłm, Robert, Marie, Jane and Elizabeth, the children of the said Wiłłm Hargrave, my said sonne in lawe, to every one of them ij^{s}. Unto Fraunces, Anne, Margarett and Thomas, the children of Thomas Tirrington, my naturall sonne, to every one of them ij^{s}. And to the childe now in the wombe of Margarett, his wife, if it shall lyve, twoo shillingę. Also and all and every of the said legacies to be payd to everie such of them once within a yeare after my decease by myne executor hereafter named as are of lawfull yeares of age to make my said executor lawfull discharges for the same. [Provision for legacies of minors to be paid to their fathers who should seal acquittances and enter into bonds for the due payment of the legacies, and that thereupon the executor should not be further liable.] The rest of my said ꝑsonal estate . . . . I freely give and absolutely bequeath unto the said Thomas Tirrington, my said naturall sonne, whome . . I make and ordayne the sole executor. . . . These witnesses R. Turner, Robt Johnson and Nycholas Shippen. [*Proved* 19 *May*, 1631.]

GEORGE PEARSON of Barwick, yeoman.

[Original.] Anno Domi 1633, February the 4th. In the name of God Amen. I, George Pearson in [of *erased*] Barwicke in Elmett, in the county of Yorke, yeoman, sicke in body and perfect in remembrance God be praised, do make this my last will and testament. Inprimis I bequeath my body to be Interred in the Church or Churchyard of Caluerley, and my soule I bequeath into the hands of my God and my Redeemer, to whose mercy my departinge soule will be taken. Itm those worldly goods with which God hath endowed me I bequeath them as followinge. In primis I giue unto Peter Wheelous tenne pounds. Item I giue to Jane Wheelous five pounds. Item I giue unto Willia Cowpland to the use of his children tenne pounds. Item I giue to Henry Croft tenne pounds. Item I giue to Henry Jefferson tenne pounds. Item I gine to Henry Waynman tenne pounds. Item I giue to John Croft tenne shillings. Item I giue to Robert Wilson of Mardon five pounds. Item I giue to the eldest brother of Henry Waynman and unto his yongest brother equally betwixt them both 5l. Item I gine unto the two children of Henry Wheelous tenne pounds to be equally distributed betwixt them. Item I gine to Thomas Knightson during his life the som of fiue pounds and after his decease he shall pay or his executors shall cause to be paid the some of fifty shillings equally to be distributed amonge the children of his wife now beinge. Item I giue unto Richard Veuers and Willia Veuers his sonne the some of twenty shillings equally betwixt them. Item I giue unto Richard Turner, parish clarke of Barwicke in Elmett, the some of twenty shillings. I give unto the children of Anne Knightson tenne pounds to be distributed equally amongst them. Item I bequeath and giue unto Richard Settle, the sonne of Anne Knightson, the some of fifty shillings. Item I giue unto Mr Grant of Calverley 5l. Item I gine unto Robert Harper three pounds sixe shillings and eight pence, being the Clearke of the said parish. Item I do constitute and ordaine Willia Bourman of Sturton and William Veuers of Potterton suprevisors of this my last will and testament, and I giue either of them the some of three pounds sixe shillings and eight pence for the seing of this my will discharged. Item I giuc unto James Forster, now the Curate of Barwicke in Elmett, the some of forty shillings. Ite I do chardge and wish my executors to bestowe tenne pounds of my buriall and funerall. Item I do constitute and ordaine Thomas Croft of Bradford and Henry Croft of Beeston [John Scott of Barwick my *erased*] full executors of this my last will and testament. In witnes whereof in the hearing of these witnesses I have sette my hand the day and yeare before mentioned. Item I give unto Mr Rawson and Mistris Rawson 2s. George Pearson, his marke. These witnesses, James Forster, John Scott, Willm Veners, Willm Veuers, Junr. [*Proved* 6 *Feb.*, 1635-6.]

RICHARD DIGHTON of Barwick, yeoman.

[Original.] In the name of God Amen, the fifth daye of Februarie Anno Dni 1644. I, Richard Dighton of Barwick in Elmett, in the countie of Yorke, yeoman, being diseased and infirme in bodie but whole and sounde in minde and of good and perfect remembrance, thankes and praise bee given to Almightie God therefore, and beeing desireous to sett my howse in order and settle the temporall estaite wherewith it hath pleased God to blesse mee in my life time, that all iust occasions of future differences that might arise about the same after my death if it weere left undisposed on, might bee alltogether prevented and avoided and utterly taken away, and to the intent and purpose that after my death it may bee disposed according to my minde doe hereby make and ordaine this my present last will and testament in manner and forme followeing, that is to saye, first I commend my soule into the handes of Almightie God my maker and redeemer, and I committ my bodie to the Earth from whence it came and to bee buried in the church or church yarde of whatsoeuer parish I shall happen to bee in when I shall die, at the discretion of my freindes and Executrix herein hereafter named. Then next of my temporall estate I dispose on as followeth, that is to say. First I give and bequeath unto Robert Dighton, my sonne, thirtie poundes in money in full satisfaction of his filiall or childes part or portion that of right hee may anyewaye challenge or claime out of my saide temporall estaite. And the residue and remainder thereof after my debts payed (if any bee) this my filiall or childes part or portion discharged and funeralls defrayed I hereby wholie give and absolutelie bequeath unto Margarett, now my wife. And thereupon I hereby declare and expresse that it is my minde and will that the securitie which shall hereafter bee yeilded by myne Uncle Palmes for the fiftie powndes which he oweth unto mee shalbee taken and made in the name of the saide Margarett, my wife, and to her use, to the intent and purpose that after my death in theise miserable and distracted times shee may bee thereby the better enabled, with out too much preiudice and damage to her owne estaite, to educate my saide sonne in good literature, and when in breeding in letters as well as yeares, hee shall be apt and meete to bee put apprentice to some fitting trade, that she may putt him apprentice at her owne cost and charges. And in case shee shall incline or dispose herself after my death to a second marriage with any other man, lest shee shoulde chance to match herself either with one surcharged with debts or of a waistfull disposition by means whereof my saide sonne may bee likelie or in danger to bee shortened, if not misse of some part of his said education in good letters or to have his said portion hereby bequeathed him in part abridged if not utterlie waisted by means thereof, then it is hereby declared and expressed to be my minde and will that my said wife shall bee cautelous and carefull (as my trust is in her) that before her second marriage she either yeilde herself or procure to bee yeilded good and sufficient Bonde or securitie to bee entered and delivered to my brother in lawe Richard Turner, or in his absence or neglect to my brother in lawe Willm Hardistie, to my said sonnes use for performance of his saide education and cost of his festing apprentice (as before is expressed) and for payement of the said thirtie poundes to helpe him to sett up his trade withall after hee shalbee soe putt apprentice. And in consideration of the especiall trust and great confidence which I repose in the said Margarett, now my wife, in regard of the tender love and care which I conceive shee beareth towards my saide sonne as well as my self, I hereby commit the tuition and education of my said sonne unto her the saide Margarett, now my wife, during his minoritie. And of this my p'sent last Will and Testament I hereby nominate, appoint, make and ordaine her the saide Margarett, now my wife, the sole executrix. Attested and confirmed hereby the day and yeare first aboue written under the hand of me, Richard Dighton. Theise witnesses R. Turner, Jo[n] Hardistye. [*Proved* 23 *Oct.*, 1645.]

SIR JOHN GASCOIGNE of Parlington, Baronet.[(1)]

[Attested Copy.] In Dei Nomine Amen. The Nyne and Twentieth day of August in the yeare of o[r] lorde God one thousand sixe hundred thirtie and five and in the Eleauenth yeare of the raigne of o[r] Soueraigne lord King Charles ouer England, &c. I, S[r] John Gascoigne of Parlington, w[th]in the dyocesse and county of Yorke, Barronett, being at this p̃nte in p̄fect health of body and mynde, thankes be to God therefore, and haning often tymes in my remembrance the Instabylity of this world, and greate uncertaynty of mans lyfe; But specially in this 79 yeare of my age, being laytely by God's goodnes well recouered of a sicknes verie dangerous to my age, and thereby feeling a declynacon in my body from all vayne hope of long tyme to live, and conceiuing the same to be unto me a mercifull admonicõn from Almyghty God that the dissolucon of my earthly bodie and chainge into another world cannot be long deferred, doe therefore desire soe to despose of my worldly estate, That my debts may be first discharged, And myselfe, after more carefully remembred by my children and poore freuds, Humbly therefore doe first commend my soule into the hands and mercie of Almighty God and his only sonne our redeemer and Sauior Jesus Christ, by whose bitter passion and painfull death I veryly hope to be saned and made an Inheritor of his blessed Kingdome in heauen, my body to be buried neare to my Father and mother in my Clossett w[th]in Barwicke Church, or where myne Exec[rs] and my eldest sonne, Thomas Gascoigne, shall thinke convenient to despose of the same. Item I doe giue and bequeath to Dame Anne, my louing and faythfull wyfe, all suche Jewells and ornam[ts] as herselfe hath euer used, and now hath of what kinde or

(1) Sir John Gascoigne of Lasingcroft, Parlington and Barnbow was advanced to the dignity of a baronet by King Charles I in 1635, died 3 May, 1637, and was buried at Barwick His funeral Certificate appears in the Yorks. Archælogical Journal, xiv 246. He married Anne, daughter of John Ingleby of Rudby, by his second wife Anne, daughter of William Clapham of Beamsley. They had issue (1) Sir Thomas Gascoigne, second Bart, of Barnbow, who was tried for high treason on a false accusation of a servant named Bolron, and was acquitted. An account of his trial is given in the York Depositions published by the Surtees Society, vol. xl. (2) John Gascoigne, Abbot of Lamspring; (3) Michael Gascoigne, a monk; (4) Francis Gascoigne, a secular priest; (5) Helen, wife of Gilbert Stapleton of Carleton; (6) Mary, wife of William Hauton; (7) Catherine, Abbess of Cambray; (8) Anne, wife of George Thwenge, (9) Margaret, died unmarried; (10) Christine Gascoigne.

fashion soeuer they be. Item I doe alsoe giue and bequeath unto my said wyfe twoe paire of Bedstocks and one Trundle Bed wthall bedding and furniture to them belonging, one low chaire wth lockers, one Table, one Cubberd, Sixe ioyned Stooles of Wallnuttree, one Cypresse Chyst, and two low coucred stooles for her owne chamber, at her owne choice. Item I doe also giue unto my said wyfe for her lyfe the use of one guilded syluer dishe, and after her decease I doe gine the use thereof to my sayd sonne Thomas Gascoigne during his lyfe, And after his decease to remayne an ayrelome to the heires of my house successiuely one after another. Item I doe giue and bequeath to my sayd sonne, Thomas Gascoigne, one gold ringe, and one greate siluer seale of Armes, of both wch is engrauen the Lucyes head. Item I doe alsoe giue to my sayd sonne all my Armors and furnitures for warres, of what sort or kinde soeuer. And whereas I haue by my late deede Indented bearing date the twentieth day of Marche in the Sixte yeare of his said Maties raigne ouer England, &c., made a lease to my late worthy and much honored good frends Sr Thomas Vauasour of Haslewood, Baronett, and Sr William Hungate of Saxton, Knight, now both deceased, of my demesne lands, Colepitts and Colemynes wthin Parlington, and of lands in Hillom, Beckhay, Lotherton and Abberford, and of my Mills in Abberford for the terme of one and twenty yeares for speedier payment of my debtes, and of suche legacies as I then Intended by my last will and testament to gine and bequeath. Now therefore I doe (accordingly) hereby declare gine and bequeath to John Gascoigne, my second sonne, twenty pounds, to Michaell Gascoigne, my third sonne, twenty poundes, and to Francis Gascoigne, my yongest sonne, twenty poundes. Item I doe gine and bequeath to Catherine Gascoigne, my daughter, fiftie poundes, and to Margarett Gascoigne, my yongest daughter, fiftie poundes. And whereas I haue heretofore by one other deede bearinge date the two and twentieth day of October in the Eighteenth yeare of the raigne of our late Soueraigne Lord King James ouer England, &c., giuen and granted to Thomas Meynell of North Kiluington, in the County of Yorke, Esquier, and to James Wright then of Barmebowe, in the said county, gent., theire heires and assignes, and to the heires and assignes of the suruiuior of them for euer, Those my two water Corne Mills, called Hillom Mills wth their appurts, And all those my fowerscore acres (more or less) of Chantry land, arable, meadowe, and pasture in Abberford butting and boundering upon the Ruyns of one decayed douecoote ioyned to the Parsonage Fould in Abberford, To the onely use of myselfe, and of my assignes for tearme of my lyfe wthoute impeachment of wast, And after my decease to suche other uses intentes and lymitacons as shouldbe by me in my last will, or by any other lawfull act in wryting in my lyfe tyme expressed lymytted or declared, as by the said Indenture more at large it doth and may appeare. Now therefore my intent and meaning is, and by this my last will I doe declare expresse and appoint, That if my sayd debts and legacies to my said children as aforesaid shall not be paid (as I veriely hope they will, out of my said goods, nor out of my said lease made of my sayd demesne lande and Coolemynes w^th^in Parlington as aforesaid (as undoubtedly I know they maie be) accordinge to my meaning therein expressed, That then (and no otherwise) the sayd Thomas Meynell and James Wright or myne exec[rs] shall sell the said Hillom Mills for making upp the whole soñe for the full payment of my said debts and legacies as aforesaid, and after all my debts and suche legacies as aforesaid truly payd and the sayd Mills not sould, Then that the whole benifitt and ꝑfitt of the said Mills shalbe equally deuided for the mayntaynance of George and John Gascoigne, two of the yonger sonnes of my said sonne Thomas Gascoigne, and to the longer liver of them, yf Thomas Gascoigne, my said sonne, shall yearely and euerie yeare from and ymmediately after my decease well and truly pay unto the said Francis Gascoigne, my yongest sonne, thyrty poundes ꝑ annũ during the terme of his naturall lyfe, but if default of payment be made of his yearely rente of thirtie poundes contrary to my true intent and meaning, Then and in such case my will and meaning is that my said sonne Francis Gascoigne shall haue the said Mills, and the whole benifitt and ꝑfitt thereof, according to an estate thereof formerly by me expressed and lymited to him, And from and after the decease of my said sonne Francis, and the decease of them the said George and John Gascoigne, two of the yongest sonnes of my said sonne Thomas Gascoigne, my will and meaning is, And I doe hereby expresse lymitt and declare that the said Mills wth thappurts shalbe and remayne to the use and behoofe of my right heires for euer. And as for and concerning my s[d] Chantry lands in Abberford w[ch] I haue lately leased by Indenture bearing date the first day of March in y[e] nynth yeare of y[e] raigne of o[r] Soueraigne lord King Charles ouer England, &c., unto my trusty and welbeloued seruant [1]Edmond Hickorngill and his ass[s] for y[e] terme of y[e] naturall liues of Richard, Edmond and Mathew Hickorngill, sons of y[e] s'd Edmond Hickorngill, and the longest liner of them, And yf the s'd Richard, Edmond and Mathew, sons of y[e] s'd Edmond, should dye w[th]in the terme of thirtie yeares then for and during soe manie yeares of y[e] number of thirty yeares as shouldbe then unexpyred to be accompted from y[t] date of y[e] s'd Indenture under y[e] rente of fowere pounds to be yearely payd unto the Kings Ma[tie] y[t] now is his heires and successors upon y[e] feast dayes of y[e] Annunciacon of o[r] blessed lady S[t] Mary the virgine and S[t] Michaell tharchayngell by equall porcons, and alsoe under y[e] rente of twenty markes to be yearely payd unto me my heires and asss upon y[e] said feast dayes by equall porcons as by y[e] said Indenture appeareth. [Confirmation of the said Indenture of Lease]. Neuertheles my intent and meaning is and I doe hereby lymytt and appoint that tenne poundes of all the said thirteene pounds six shillings and eight pence chantry rente shalbe yearly paid during the terme of one and twenty yeares next after

[1] He was father of the Rev. Edmond Hickorngill (1631—1708), junior fellow of Caius College, divine and pamphleteer, Chaplain to Lilburn's Regiment, 1653, successively baptist, quaker and deist, afterwards a soldier in Scotland and in Swedish service, ordained by Bishop Robert Sanderson 1661, and excluded 1685–8 —[Dictionary of National Biography.] For Hickeringill's account of himself see Thoresby's Correspondence ed. Hunter, II. p. 8.

my decease to my worthy and louing cosen Stephen Tempest of Rowndhay, Esquier, in accomplishm[t] of an agreem[t] betweene him and me made for the paym[t] thereof. And I doe hereby further hereby lymitt and appoint that the som̃e of three poundes sixe shillings and eight pence, being the remainder of the said thirteene poundes six shilling and eight pence rente, shalbe likewise yearely paid unto the poore people of the p̄ishe of Abberford during alsoe the terme of one and twenty yeares likewise next ensuing my decease. And from and immediately after the expyracon and determinacon of the estate of my said seruant Edmond Hickorngill of in and to the said chantry lands wth appurts, Then my will and meaning is And I doe hereby expresse lymitt and declare That they the said Thomas Meynell and James Wright and theire heires and the suruiuor of them and his heires shall stand and be seised of and in the said chantry lands w[th] thappurts, To the use and behoofe of my right heires for euer, And whereas upon my greate charges I haue renewed some leases and redeemed other leases and alsoe bought out some rente charges graunted out of my lands wherein for p[r]uenting of dangers and for better securing y[e] same I did some tymes use the name of John Gascoigne, my father, sometymes of some of my yonger children, and sometymes of some other frends, w[th] intencon in tymes conuenient to despose otherwise and to setle euery thing as occasions and just motiues might induce me to doe, since w[ch] tymes being enforced not only to needfull repaires of my seuerall houses, outhouses and Mills, all left unto me ruynous and in greate decay, but alsoe being necessarily drawne into noe lesse charges by marrying of my children, besides sundrie suits and troubles w[ch] haue falne heauily upon me, whereby I am now constrayned to alter my firste desynes in such manner as may best accord w[th] my p[r]sente estate, and indifferency amongst my children, Therefore p[r]suming of the vertuous disposition of my wyfe, and of them all to concurre w[th] me in a free and louing consent for the speedier paym[t] of my debts, and my more comfortable dep̄ture from them. I giue and bequeath to my exec[rs] Seauen yeares rents of one Annuity or rente charge of twentie poundes p̄ annũ in fee simple giuen away by Richard Gascoigne, my uncle, out of my lands in Barmebowe unto John Newcomen, late of Slatflatby in the county of Lyncolne, my cosen, deceased, from whome I redeemed the same in the name of John Gascoigne, my father, whoe by myne appointm[t] did assigne ouer the same to John Gascoigne, my second sonne, unto whome I did then intend the same noe longer, then untill I could better p'uide for him, as already long since I haue done. And after y[e] expyracon of seauen yeares or sooner if my debts and legacies shalbe payd, Then my will is and I doe hereby lymitt that Anne Gascoigne, my said wyfe (if she shall chance to liue at Barmbowe duringe her tyme here) shall haue and receiue the said yearely rente or Annuity of twenty poundes p̄ Annũ soe before by me redeemed, And after her decease I doe giue and bequeath the same to John Gascoigne, my second sonne, according to the deede thereof to him made by John Gascoigne, my father, if hee shalbe any wayes molested or interrupted, and shall not peaceably and quietly haue hold receiue and enioy one Annuity of thirtie pounds ꝑ Annũ by me already setled to and for his use during his lyfe, But if hee shall peaceably and quietly haue hold and enioy the said Annuity of thirty pounds ꝑ Annũ during his life, according to my meaning, Then my intent is And I doe hereby lymytt that John Gascoigne, my grandchild, eldest sonne to my sayd sonne Thomas Gascoigne, shall haue and receiue the sayd twenty pounds yearely rente out of Barmebowe ymmediately after the decease of my sayd wyfe, for and during his naturall lyfe, And after his decease then to remayne to the right heires of my selfe for euer. And for more speedy paymᵗ of all my said debts and legacies and noe longer I doe likewise giue and bequeath to my executors the rents and ꝓfitts of my demesne lands wᵗʰin the mannor of Scooles for seauen yeares alsoe next after my decease for fuller paymᵗ of my debts, After wᶜʰ payd I will that the said demesne lands and the rents and ꝓfitts of them shalbe conuerted and remane To the use and behoofe of the s'd dame Anne, my wyfe, during her tyme and tytle to the house and lands in Barmbowe, And after the determinacõn of her tyme, Then to remayne to Michaell Gascoigne, my third sonne, according to the lease of them by me taken in his name, if hee shall not peaceably and quietly haue hold receiue and enioy one Annuity of thirty poundes ꝑ Annũ by me already settled to and for his use during his life, But if hee shalbe noe wayes hindred of the said Annuity during his life according to my true meaning, Then my will is and I doe hereby lymitt that after the decease of my said wyfe and my debts and legacies payd the said demesne lands of Scooles shall ymmediately remayne and come (as my ꝑꝑ guift) unto the said Thomas Gascoigne, my sonne, and to none els. And whereas for that consideracons before expressed I did likewise in the names of Christine Gascoigne and Margarett Gascoigne, my two yongest daughters, and for the amendment of theire porcõns att that tyme redeeme from Audrey Gascoigne, late wyfe to Alueray Gascoigne my brother, deceased, and executrix of his last will and testament, a terme of twenty yeares to begyn after the expyracõn of one lease then in esse made before by my said brother Alueray to one Thomas Hemsworth, deceased, of one Farme or tenement in West Garford, the tytle and right whereunto is now in myselfe, althoughe hytherto I have and yet doe ꝑmitt and suffer Thomas Gascoigne, my sayd sonne, to receiue for my vse the rents thereof and to accompt unto me therefore, my full will and meaning therefore now is and I doe hereby declare That my said Execʳˢ shall haue and enioy all the said terme and remainder of yeares wᶜʰ after my death shalbe then to come and unexpyred to the only end intent and purpose to conuerte the rente and ꝓfitts thereof for payment of my debts and legacies and ꝑformance of this my last will and testament. Prouided alwayes that as soone as all my sayd debts and legacies shalbe truly and faythfully payd and discharged. Then my will is that Thomas Gascoigne, my said sonne, shall whollv haue and enioy the same. Item I giue and bequeath to Mary Layborne, my neece, one twoe and twenty shillings peece, and to her husband and her, either of them one gold ringe tor theire remembrance of me. Item I doe gine to the poore people of Abberford forty shillings. To the poore people of Wynmoore twenty shillings, to the poore people of Barwicke pishe twenty shillings, and to the poore people of Garford pishe and Cattell Moore twenty shillings to be destributed according to the descretion of dame Anne Gascoigne, my said wyfe, and Thomas Gascoigne, my said sonne. Item I doe giue and bequeath to Richard Clearkeson, Peter Slater, John Clearkeson, Richard Hickorngill, Richard Shakleton, Edward Barker, my seruants, euery one of them forty shillings a peece. Item I doe alsoe giue and bequeath to the Lady Barmby, M[rs] Ardington, Mary Thwaits, and Barbara Wharton euery one of them twenty shillings a peece. And I doe hereby constitute ordeyne and appoint that my said sonne Thomas Gascoigne, my welbeloued cosen Stephen Tempest, and the said Edmond Hickorngill, my seruant (who best understandeth my estate) be Executo[rs] of this my said will. And I doe hereby gine unto my said louing cosen Stephen Tempest for his loue and care to se my will pformed twenty loods of Cooles, and the said Edmond Hickorngill tenne poundes as aforesd for his fayethfull seruic thereby unto me to be done. And my further intent and meaning is, and I doe hereby expresse and declare, That if my s'd sonne Thomas Gascoigne shall louingly and faythfully pay yearely to John, Michaell and Francis Gascoigne, his yonger brethren, theire seuerall and respective Annuityes of xxx[li] a peece according to my declaracon and meaning in this my will, that then the estate and my lymytacons of them in Hillom Mills and in all my Chantry lands shall remayne and rest setled as is before expressed, or els if John, Michaell and Francis Gascoigne, my yonger sonnes, or any of them shalbe troubled or molested in theire quiett enioying of theire said seuerall annuityes of xxx[li] a peece by my said sonne Thomas, his occasion or meanes, then my meaning and intent is And I doe hereby declare lymitt and appoint That the said Thomas Meynell and James Wright and their heires shall stand and be seised of the said Hillom Mills and Chantry lands (after my debts and legacies payd) to the only use and behoofe of the said John, Michaell and Francis Gascoigne, my said yonger sonnes, for and during their seuerall naturall lifes and to the use of the suruiuor of them. And I doe desire my said louing cosen Stephen Tempest (according to my confidence reposed in him) that hee wilbe pleased to call myne executo[rs] to an accompt, and to Suruey theire doeings for hastning the speedie pformance of this my last will, unto whome (in hope of his loue and care soe to doe) I doe giue and bequeath twenty wayu loades of Cooles for his chamber fyre. And I doe acknowledge and declare this to be my last will and testament, recalling and reuooking all others as Scrowes and unpfecte papers. In witnes whereof to euery sheete to this my last will and testament being in number Seauen, I have subscribed my name and to the Labell (w[ch] fastneth it on the topp) haue sett my seale the day and yeare first aboue written. John Gascoigne. Signed sealed published and declared to be my last will in the presence of Wiłłm Smeaton, Edm. Hickorngill. [*Proved* 10 *Sept.*, 1637.]

RICHARD POTTER of Potterton, yeoman.

[Original.] In the name of God Amen, the seauententh daye of Octob[r] in the yeare of our Lord God 1638. I, Richard Potter of Potterton, in the countie of Yorke, Yeoman, being aged and something crazie in bodie, but whole and sownd in minde and of good and perfect remembrance, thankes and praise be giuen to Allmightie God therefor. Knoweing death to bee certaine and the howre of death uncertaine, and beeing desirous to sett myne howse in order before I dye that all inst occasions of future sewtes and differences might be taken awaye, and that my personall estaite which I shall leave behinde me may bee disposed after my death according to my mynde, doe hereby make and ordaine this my last will and testament in manner and forme followeing, that is to say. First I commende my soule into the hands of Allmightie God my maker and redeemer from whome I had it, and I committe my bodie to the Earth from whence it came, and to be buried in the Church or Church yarde of the parishe Church of Barwicke in Elmett in the Countie of Yorke, at the discretion of my freinds after my death. Next of my personall estaite I dispose on as followeth. First my will and minde is that all my said whole personall estaite shalbe equally divided in three equall parts, whereof I gine and bequeath one third part unto Gennett, now my wife, in lewe and consideration of her thirds out of the same which shee may challenge by the laws of this realme by reason of her marriage with mee. Item my will and mind is that the seconde thirde parte of my said personall estaite shall be equally divided among all my children that bee now liveing. Except that whereas Elizabeth, one of my daughters, or her husband Michaell Tod haue had on mee to the value of twentie six powns thirteene shillings fowre pence in money and pennieworthes one way and other and in keepeing Anne Tod theire daughter with meate drinke and apparell for 12 yeares at the least. My will and myud is That the said summe shalbee part and rated in the said Elizabeths share of the said second third part of my said personall estait, and that John Potter, Thomas Potter and Hellen Potter, beeing all the rest of my children that bee living, shall haue euerie one of them as much to themselues out of the said seconde thirde part to make theire shares equall with the said share of the said Elizabeth aforenamed. And after the same donne The residue and remaynder of the said second thirde part of my said personall estaite to bee equallie divided amonge all my said children afore recited. First I giue and bequeath unto Hellen, the daughter of Wiłłm Potter laite of Leeds, my sonne deceased, the sum̃e of twentie shillings to be putt forward for her by myne Executour hereafter named to the intent and purpose that the yearlie consideration thereof ariseing according to the limitation of the Statute shalbee yearly payed to or bestowed on her for and towards part of her maintenance in such sort as my said executoure shall se or deeme the same to bee best for her, And that the principall shalbee payed in to her when and assoone as shee shall hereafter accomplish her lawfull age of one and twentie yeares or within sixe monethes after that shee shalbee marryed whither soeuer of the same shall sooner happen. Item I giue and bequeath to the said Hellen Potter one of myne owne daughters one why stirke at her owne choyse to bee elected out of all the three why stirks which I haue. Item I glue unto Richard Potter, Alice and Genett Potter, the three childrenne of the said Jo. Potter, my sonne, unto Francis Potter, my grandchild whom I keepe, and to the said Anne Tod to euery one of them a gimmer hog. The rest of my goodes and chattells not yet disposed on after my debtes payed, theise my legacies discharged and funerall expenses defrayed, I wholie giue and bequeath to the said Jennett, now my wife, whome of this my present last will and testament I make and ordaine the sole executrixe. And in testimonie of the truith I haue hereunto putte myne hande the daye and yeare first above written. Richard Potter. Theise witnesses, P. Turner, Richard Shan. [*Proved May*, 1639.]

MICHAEL WILSON of Roundhay, yeoman.

[Original.] In the name of God Amen. I, Mighill Wilson of Rowndhay in the Cowntie of Yeorke, Yeoman, doe make this my last will and Testiment in manner and forme followinge. Inprimis I giue and bequeath my sowle unto Almighty god my maker, trustinge through the most bitter deth and passion of his sonn to be made ptaker of his euierlastinge Kingdom, Amen. And as towchinge the ordering and disposinge of that temporall estat which god hath lent me is as followeth. I doe giue and bequeath unto and amongest the Children of Thomas Howley of Woodkirke the sume of ten powndꝭ to be diuided amongest them share and share like all but the eldest which is to haue noe pt of it. Item I giue and bequeath unto George and Stephan Netherwod of Leedꝭ, Cloatherꝭ, the sume of fiue poundꝭ apece. Item I giue and bequeath to Urselley Tomeson and Ann the dawghterꝭ of William Killingbeck of Gleadow the sume of ten powndꝭ to be deuided eaqually amongest them, share and share like. I gine and bequeath all my right title and intrest of and in my Ferme which now I liue upon untto John Wilson my kinsman with all the corne theare upon growinge wth all my quick goodꝭ and cattel which I haue on it as also all my other moueableꝭ whatsoeuer within or about my house. Item I giue and bequeath unto Elizabeth Wilson, Margret and Ann, William and Isabell Wilson, all children unto William Wilson deceased, to euery one of them twentie shillingꝭ apece. Item I gine and bequeath unto Jennet Croft, the wife of James Croft, fiftie shillingꝭ to buy hir a dosson with. Also I gine unto Jane Niccolson twentie shillingꝭ. And I doe make John Wilson my sole executor and leaue him to pay all my debtꝭ and to discharge my funerall expenses with all the Legacies which I haue given. And I doe giue unto

John Wilson that fowre score poundℯ which James Netherwood and Nicholas Netherwood are to pay at my decease, w[th] all my go[o]dℯ and chattles bilℯ bondℯ and all other debtℯ whatsoever. And I haue to this my last will and Testement set my hand and seale the fiue and twentieth day of Febre: An. Do. 1639. Mighill Wilson. Sealed and deliuered in the p[r]sence of Henry Holmes, John Burnhill, Jennet Croft, Robert Askwith. [*Proved April* 1640.]

JOHN BALL of Potterton, blacksmith.

[Original.] In the name of God Amen, on or about the 23[th] daye of June Anno Domini 1644. John Ball of Potterton in the countie of York, blacksmith, beeing sicke in bodie but whole in minde and of good and perfect remembrance, being then desireous to settle his estaite in his life time that after his death it might bee ordered and disposed according to his minde and for preventing all causes and coloure of future differences and sewts at lawe that otherwise might arise between his then wife and others his freindes about the same if hee has left the same unordered or undisposed on in his life time, made his last will and testament noncupative in wordes in manner and forme followeing, that is to say[e], first after that hee has commended his soule into the hands of Almightie God his maker and redeemer, and was willing to leave and committ his bodie to the Earth and to bee buried in the parish church or Church yarde of Barwick in Elmett in the saide countie at the discretion of his executrix which hee afterwardes named and others his freindes. First hee gave and bequeathed all his weareing apparrell to his father and father's children, beeing his bretheren, to bee divided amongst them in such manner and sort as hee had or should in his life time give directions unto Elizabeth then his wife to dispose the same amongst them. Item he wholie gave and absolutelie bequeathed the residue of his whole estaite remaineing besides unto the saide Elizabeth then his wife, and to the childe in her wombe if shee then or afterwardes chanced to be conceived with childe by him and shoulde bringe forth a childe that lived, to bee equallie divided betweene them, that is to saye, the one half thereof to his then saide wife and the other half thereof to the saide childe in case his then said wife proved afterwardes to bee with childe by him and that the saide childe shoulde live, otherwise if shee did not prove to bee with childe by him or in case shee did and the saide childe lived not then hee wholie gave and absolutelie bequeathed all the residue of his whole estaite to his then saide wife for and in respect of the tender love and affection which hee bare unto her Except onely five shillinges out of the same which hee bequeathes for a legacie unto the childe of Richard Daniell of Potterton aforesaid which hee had then liveing by Francis, his wife, one of the Testatours sisters. And the saide John Ball made and ordained the saide Elizabeth then his saide wife of his saide last will and testament noncupative. the sole executrix. Attested by theise presents putt as shortly after the daye and yeare first aboue written into writeing as time and occasion woulde permitt under the handes of us witnesses whose names bee here unto subscribed. Willm Settle, Thomas Potter, Richard Daniell, his marke. [*Proved Feb.,* 1644-5.]

RICHARD SHAN of Potterton, yeoman.

[Original.] In Dei nomine Amen. I, Richard Shanne of Potterton in the countie of Yorke, yeoman, beeing sicke in bodie but whole and sownde in minde and of good and perfect remembrance, praise and thankes bee given to Allmightie God therefore, doe hereby make and ordaine this my last will and testament in manner and forme following, that is to saye, first I commende my soule into the handes of Allmightie God my maker and Redeemer in full confidence of eternall life by the onelie merits and passion of my blessed Saviour Christ Jesus, and I committ my bodie to the Earth and to bee buried in the parish-churche or Church yarde of Barwick in Elmett at the discretion of my freindes and Executours herein hereafter named. Item of the temporall estaite wherewith it hath pleased Allmightie God of his gratious goodness to endowe mee withall I dispose on as followeth, First I give and bequeath unto Francis, now my wife, the whole farme with the appurtenaunces which I now houlde by Lease graunted unto me by Sr John Ramsden Knight, my Landlorde, untill Richard, now my sonne, shall fullie accomplish and attaine unto his lawfull age of one and twentie yeares or els bee married, onelie upon the Condition that shee keepe her self my wife and bee unmarried to anie other man untill my said sonne shall come to his saide lawfull age or bee married. And in case my saide wife shall in the interim or at any time afterwardes after my death bee married to another man Then I hereby freelie give and absolutelie bequeath after any such her saide marriage the saide whole farme with the appurtenaunces unto him the saide Richard my sonne, Except onelie one thirde part thereof which shee the said Francis, my saide wife, may lawfullie challenge and have out of the same dureing her life by the standeing lawes of this Realme in leiwe of her thirds or third part thereof by reason of her marriage with me. And if in case my saide sonne shall depart this naturall life in his minoritie or before hee shalbe married without issue of his bodie lawfullie to bee begotten hereafter liveing after his death, Then I hereby freelie give and absolutelie bequeath in thiese cases twoe parts of my saide farme with the appurtenaunces into three to bee equallie divided and the other thirde part after my saide wifes death, unto Anne and Elizabeth, twoe of my daughters, to bee equallie divided betweene them, To the intent and purpose that they twaine and theire assignees shall equallie pay betweene them the summe of fourtie shillings apeece unto everie one of myne other daughters to witt to Marie, Martha, Francis and Margarett Shanne, fourtie shillings apeece for their better livelihood and preferments hereafter. And in case that they the said Anne and Elizabeth or either of them shall chance to decease in their or either on theire minorities or before they or either of them bee married without issue on their severall bodies hereafter lawfullie to bee begotten liveing after them or either of them, Then I hereby give and bequeath the purpartie or part in the saide farme with the appurtenaunces of both or either such of them that shall soe decease unto such of myne other daughters as in senioritie of yeares shalbee next unto them that shall soe dye. To the intent and purpose that such of them as hereby ought to enioy the purpartie or part of either of theire saide sisters that shall hereafter soe decease as aforesaid shall pay out of the same to the rest of my daughters before named in like sort and manner as such of them that shall soe decease hereby should have donne if they had lived or theire lawfull issue. And soe consequently to bee short my will and minde hereby further is declared and expressed to be that the purpartie or part in the saide farme with the appurtenaunces of everie such of my saide daughters as shall soe decease as aforesaid upon the same tearmes in like sort shall bee devolved and still discende from one of them to another according to theire senioritie in yeares. Item I give unto everie one of my saide sixe daughters to witte Anne, Mary, Elizabeth, Martha, Francis and Margarett fourtie powndes a peice out of my money in the howse and myne other goodes and chattells in full satisfaction of their severall filiall childes parts or portions out of the same, And the same to bee payed unto everie one of them when and as soone as each of them shall fullie accomplish theire severall lawfull ages of one and twentie yeares or els bee married. Item I give and bequeath unto the saide Richard, my sonne, out of my saide moneys in the howse and other goodes and chattels the summe of twentie powndes, And the same to bee payed unto him when and assoone as hee shall accomplish his lawfull age of one and twentie years. Provided allwayes neverthelesse that if anie one of my saide sixe daughters or my saide sonne shall chance to depart this naturall life in theire minorities or before they shall bee married, Then my will and minde hereby is that the purpartie or part of each one of them hereby given as shall soe depart this naturall life shalbee equallie divided amongst such of them all of my forenamed children as shall survive to the times before mentioned. Item I hereby give and bequeath unto Henrie Shanne, my Brother, one quarter of Mault, one paire of Bootes, my best Hatt and best sewte. And I hereby give unto Mary Knapton, my sister, twoe shillings, and to everie one of her children now liveing twelue pence a peece and to be payed within a yeare after my death into the handes of theire father or mother then liveing for theire childrens use upon either of theire Acquittances for the discharge thereof. And to Elizabeth, Edward and the rest of my sister Daniells children that shallbee alive after my death twelue pence a peece. And the same likewise to bee payed within a yeare after my death into the handes of theire father or mother if then liveing for their use upon either of their acquittances for the discharge thereof. And to the two children of Alice my sister deceased, to either of them xij^{d} a peice. And to Richard Knapton, my brother in lawe, one paire of Bootes. And to Richard Settle, my father in lawe, two shillinges, And to his sonne Robert Settle, my brother in lawe, other two shillinges. And the residue and remainder of my saide temporall estaite after my debts payed theise my saide childrens portions and legacies discharged and funerall expenses defrayed, I hereby give and absolutelie bequeath unto them the said Francis, now my saide wife, and Mary, my saide daughter. Except that she the said Francis, now my said wife, shall hereafter marry againe after my death, Then my will and minde hereby is that she the saide Francis shall have nothing out of the same, but the said Mary, my daughter, the whole residue and remainder thereof, And she the said Francis, now my saide wife, shall rest content onelie with her iust and full thirdes or thirde part of all and singular other my said goodes chattells and debts beeing as much by reason of her marriage with me as she can challenge or have of right by the standeing lawes of this Realme [in] case she shall bee married againe after my death. And of this my last will and testament I make and ordaine them the said Francis, now my wife, and Mary, my saide daughter, ioynt Executours. And I hereby committ the Tuition of all my saide Children and of theire portions and legacies unto her the saide Francis, nowe my wife, dureing all theire severall minorities onelie soe longe as she the saide Francis, now my saide wife, shall keepe her self my wife and bee unmarried to another. But my will and minde hereby further is if in case she the saide Francis, now my saide wife, shall after my death bee married againe to any other man whereby in liklihood shee may preiudice or become disabled by her saide marriage to doe all my said children right and pay what is due by this my last will and testament to all or any of them, Then I hereby committ the tuition of all my saide children theire portions and legacies after such her saide marriage unto my neare kinsemen John Twisleton of Micklefield, Willm Vevers of Scoles, and Ralph Collett of Barwick in Elmet aforesaid, unles she the said Francis now my said wife shall make seale and deliver unto them the said John Twisleton, Willm Vevers and Ralph Collett good reasonable lawfull and sufficient Bond or other securitie with able sureties before her said marriage, to and for the use and behoofe of all my saide children for the due performance of all theire Educations and payment of theire full portions and legacies unto everie one of my saide children according to the tenour and true intent and meaneing of this my p'sent Last will and Testament in all pointes. And to the ende and purpose that this my last will and testament shall and may the better bee executed and performed according to my minde, I doe hereby make and ordaine them the saide John Twisleton, Willm Vevers and Ralph Collett supervisours of this my last will and testament to see the same effectuallie performed according to my minde and according to the true intent and meaneing of this my last will and testament. In witness whereof I have hereunto sett myne hande and seale, Dated the Ninthe day of Aprill In the yeare of our Lord 1646. Richard Shan. Theise witnesses Robt Settle, Isacke Wood, Wm. Vevers, Ralphe Collett. [*Proved Nov.*, 1646.]

THOMAS WRIGHT of Winmoor.

[Original.] In the name of God Amen. I, Thomas Wright of Wynmore, in the pish of Barwicke, being sick of body but of pfeckt Rememberanc, thankes be to God, do ordaine and make this my last will and testament in maner and forme following. First I bequeath my soule to Allmightie God my maker and Redemer, hoping through his death and passion to obtain saluation, and for my bodie to be buried in the pish church yeard of Barwicke, and for my worldly goodes I bequeath and despose of in maner and forme following. First I gine unto my daughter Ester Wright all my dwelling houses with the barnes, stables, Cowhouses and outhouse, Croft and yeardes and all the appurteance belonging thereto, and likewise I gine and bequeath to my said daughter Ester Wright all the reve^{r}cions and remainder of one lease past to me by Michell Norton and Richard Norton with all my goods and chattils moueable and unmoueable, and I make my said daughter Ester Wright my whole and sole executrickes of this my last will and testament, whome I bequeath to my wife to haue the tuiss of my said daughter untill she shall accomplish full yeares of age, and when my debtes and funeall expences being payed out of the said goods and houseing then what doth remaine to my said child that my wife shall giue bonnd to pay itt when she shall accomplish full age. In witnes hereof I haue setto my hand and seale the xixth of February, 1648. Thomas Wright. Sealed and delv^{d} in p^{r}sence of William Clough, Christopher Grene, Willm Wright, Stephen Clough. [*Proved about July* 1649.]

THOMAS HOLMES of Roundhay, husbandman.

[Original.] In the Name of God Amen, the Fifth Day of September in the yeare of our Lord god accordinge to the course and compatacon of the church of England 1650. Seeinge that noethinge is more certeyne Then Death and noethinge more uncerteyne then the Houre and Tyme thereof, I therefore, Thomas Holmes of Rowndhey, within the Dioces of Yorke, Husbandman, beinge Sicke in bodye but of good and Perfect Remembrance, Laud and prayse be therefore giuen to Allmightie god doe ordeigne and make this my last will and Testament in manner and forme followinge. First and princepally I giue and comend my Soule into the hands of Allmighty God my Creator and maker assuredly Trustinge and faithfully beleuinge to Have full and free remission and forgiueness of all my Sinnes by the precious Death and bloodsheadinge of my alone Sauiour and Redemer Jesus Christ, the second pson in Trenitie, and by him alone and through his Merrites and passion to haue euerlastinge life amongest the blessed Scants and Childeren of God in the Kingdome of Heauen, And I comend my body to the Earth where of itt was made, hopeinge that the same shall haue Joyfull Resureccon att the last Day and the same to be Buried in Xpian Buriall. Now Touchinge the Desposicon of my worldly goods. First my will and minde is that all my Debts and funrall expences shall be paid and Discharged forth of my wholle goods and Chattels. Ittem my will and minde is That Mary, my wife, shall haue all the Dispossinge and good will of my farme Duringe her life after my Decease with The appʳtnncę in Rowndhey aforesaid now in the Tenure or occupacon of me the said Testator, Prouided allwayes and upon condicon and my will and minde is That John Holmes, my soñe, and his heirs lawfully begotten upon his body shall haue halfe of the farme with his mother after one whole yeare be past after my Decease, the said John payinge and Discharginge the halfe of All the rents Layes and assessmᵗˢ and all othere Duties beloiñge to the same, and for Defalt of such Issue for want of heirs my will and minde is that Wiłłm Holmes, my sonne, shall haue the goodwill of my farme after the Disease of my wife and my soñe John and his heirs lawfully begotten, and after the Desease of Mary, my wife, my will and minde is John, my sonne, shall haue all the goodwill of my farme and hes heirs duringe their Life. And I giue and bequeath unto Thomas, Wiłłm and Martin and Richard Holmes, my sonnes, euery one of them Twentie shillings a peece, and to my sonne Roberte 2ˢ 6ᵈ, and to my sonne Thomas Todd other Twentie shillings. Ittm I giue and bequeath unto Thomas Todd Children Ittm to Thomas, my Godsonne, 2ˢ 6ᵈ, and to the rest euᵉie one of them Twelpence a peece. Ittm I gine and bequeath to my sonne Thomas Hollmes children euᵉie one of them 1ˢ a peece, and to my sonne Richard Holmes chilldren euᵉie one of them 1ˢ a peece. Itm I giue and bequeath unto Martine Holmes, my sonne, 4ˡⁱ to be paid in four seuᵉall years after my Decease, that is to say, 1ˡ euᵉie yeare dureinge the said 4 yeares. Itm I giue and Bequeath unto Dorothy Burnhill, my god daughter, 1ˢ, and as for the Legicies which I haue giuen to eurie one of my chilldren aboue expressed my will and minde is that such Legicies as I haue giuen them shall be in full satisfacōn of euᵉie one of their fielliall pte or childs porcōn, and the sáme to be paid wᵗʰin one whole yeare after my Desease. Itm my will and minde is and I doe giue devise and bequeath unto John Holmes, my sonne, Halfe of all my Draught which I plew wᵗʰall with halfe of all the furniture thereunto belonging wᵗʰin one whole yeare after my discease, and I doe make and ordeyne the said Mary, my wife, sole executoʳ of this my last will and testament. And I doe hereby appoynte Lawrence Weste, Randall Briges and Wiłłm Burnhill and my son Wiłłm Holmes to be surpuisors of this my last will and Testament, desiringe them to doe their best Endeuors to haue this my last will and Testamt duely executed as they haue promised me and euen as I Trust them. Prouided Lastly and my will and minde is that if any of my said seuᵉall chilldren shall be discontented with this my last will and Testamᵗ and wᵗʰ the gifts bequests and legacies therein to them seuᵉally giuen and bequeathed or if they or any of them shall sue or cumber my Executor herein-before named for or about any other or greater pte or porcyn then I haue giuen them then my will and minde is that the Legicie gifte and bequest herein menconed of him or her that shall soe sue or be Discontented shall cease and be utterly voide, and then I giue and bequeath unto him or shee which shall soe sue or be discontented the sum̃e of Twelue pence onely in sattisfac̃on of hes or hir childes po^{r}con, and I doe giue and bequeath unto my Two seruants ather of them 1^{s} 6^{d} apeece. Ittm concerninge the Debts which I owe—Imp^{9}mes to Alura Howden 3^{li}. Ittm to Thomas Hardwicke 4^{s} 6^{d}. Ittm concerninge the Debts I haue oweinge, Inp^{9}rmies, Thomas Todd, my sonne in Lawe, oweth unto me 3^{li} 6^{s} 8^{d}. Ittm Thomas Holmes, my eldest sonne, is oweing unto me the sume of 2^{li} 10^{s} for a younge cowe. Ittm James Varley of Mickelewicke is owinge unto me ix^{s}. Ittm Richard Carner of Gleadstone is owinge unto me 7^{s}. Ittm Thomas Leyesseter of Mickelefield is owinge me 6^{s} for a wiñle of oates. Itm Addam Greenewood of Mickelfield is owing me 6^{s} for a winle of oates. Ittm John Ellies of S^{tnt} Ellin well att Mickellfield is owinge me 5^{s}. Ittm Mr Rawson of Mickelfield is owinge me 15^{s} for a sacke of Oates. Ittm Wiłłm March of Mickelefield is owinge me 2^{s} 6^{d} for a strocke of oates. Ittm Wiłłm Ellies of Mickelefield is owinge me 3^{s} 4^{d} for a Bushell of Oates. Ittm Thomas Funtanes of Mickelefield is owinge me 3^{s} 3^{d} for oates. Ittm Thomas Paniell of Mickelefield is owinge me 2^{s} 3^{d}. And this I doe declare to be my will in Regard I haue giuen eu^{9}ie one of my children a reasonable and equall ꝑte of my estate wth as much Indefferencie as I could Deuise. In Testimonye whereof I the said Testator haue hereunto sett my hand and seale the day and yeare aboue exp^{r}ssed. Thomas Holmes x. Witnesses hereof Lawrence Weste, Randall Briggs x, William Burnhill, Wiłłm Holmes, Jeremie Butler. [*Proved June,* 1651.]

WILLIAM ROYDHOUSE of Shippen.

[P.C.C. Wootton 193.] In the Name of God Amen. I, William Roydhouse of Shippon, in the parish of Barwicke in Elmett and Countie of Yorke, crazie in bodie but of perfect mind and memorie (Praised be God), doe ordaine and make this my last will and testament in manner and forme following. First I bequeath my soule into the hands of God my Creator and Jesus Christ my Redeemer, expecting salvac̃on only through his death and passion. And my bodie to be buried in the Church or Churchyarde of Barwicke in Elmett. For that temporall estate wherewith God hath of his goodnes blessed me I dispose of the same in manner following. For my freehold land at Kippax, being one cottage and garth with the appurtenances thereto belonging, purchased by me of Anne Taylour, and likewise three pasture gates purchased of Richard Barker with the appurtenances, being now in the tenure and occupac̃on of William Roydhouse, I give and bequeath after my decease to Matthew Crost, sonne of Bernard Crost, and his beires for ever, Provided that he pay yearly unto Elizabeth Rantree of Leeds the summe of fortie shillings during her naturall life at Martinmas and Whitsontide, twentie shillings at each time. And in case the said summe of fortie shillings per annum be not duely paid as intended It shalbe lawfull for the said Elizabeth Rantree to enter into the said house and lands and enioye the same during her naturall life. Item I give unto Richard Taylour, my nephew, one shilling for full satisfaction of all demands out of my estate. Item I give to Dorothie Brabenour, my niece, Maud Smith and Jennot Crost, my niece, twelve pence a piece in satisfaction of all demaunds out of my estate. Item I give and bequeath unto Michaell Smith and Christopher Smith, sonnes to my niece Maud Smith, to each of them the summe of twentie shillings a yeare during their naturall lives, to be paid at Martinmas and Whitsontide by my executor hereafter named. Item I give to John Smith, sonne of my said Niece Maud Smith, the summe of tenne pounds To be paid within one halfe yeare after my decease. Item I give and bequeath to Anne Croft, Mary Crost and Margaret Crost, daughters of Jennet Crost, my Niece, to each of them the sum̃e of Tenne pounds when they shall accomplish the age of twentie yeares if they be then alive. Item I give unto Gilbert Nunne of Methley, my Cosin, the summe of Twentie shillings. Item I give to William Nunne, my Cosin and Godsonne, the summe of twentie shillings. Item I give to Thomas Sharpe of Methley, my kinsman, the summe of twentie shillings. Item to Richard Hutchinson of Methley, my godsonne, the summe of five shillings. Item I give to Joseph Turner of Barwicke in Elmet, my godsonne, the summe of fortie shillings. Item I give and bequeath unto William Bridges of Saxton, clerke, the summe of twentie shillings. Item I give unto Mr. Edward Hickernegill of Abberford one standbed in which I lye, featherbed and all things belonginge to it, my owne chest, and one gray pacing fillie. Item for all my wood growing upon my copiehold land at Methley lately purchased from Sir Henry Savile, I give and bequeath unto Isabell Reame and her heires forever. Also I hereby further give and bequeath to the poore of the parish of Barwicke in Elmett at my funerall twentie shillings. Also I further hereby give and bequeath towards the mending of the highways betwixt my house and Laysingcroft fortie shillings, to be paid in Two yeares next after my death, to witt, twentie shillings in the yeare. And I also give and bequeath unto Maud Smithsonne of Leeds, my niece, Twentie shillings in the yeare during her naturall life to be paid by mine executrix hereafter named. For all the rest of my estate as bills, bonds, goods moveable and unmoveable and Chattels whatsoever (my funeralls defrayed and debts and legacies paid) I give and bequeath unto Isabell Keame, my Niece, whome I make sole executrix of this my last will and testament. In witnesse whereof I have sette this my hand and seale this twelfth day of Aprill, one thousande sixe hundred fiftie seaven. William Roydhouse. Witnesse hereof W. Bridges, Gabriell Layton, Seth Lofthouse, John Ewington, J. Turner. [*Proved* 4 *March*, 1657 (*English style*), *by Isabell Ream̃e, sole executrix named.*]

CHRISTOPHER SHORE of Barnbow, yeoman.

[P.C.C. Pell 283.] In the Name of God Amen, the sixteenth of Februarie in the yere of our Lord One Thousand six Hundred Fiftie and Seaven. Praise be given to Almightie God, I, Christopher Shore of Barmbowe, in the parish of Barwicke in Elmett in the Countie of York, Yeoman, sicke and Crasie in bodie, but of sound and perfect memorie and understanding, Glorie be given to God Almightie, Doe make and ordaine this my last will and testament in manner and forme followinge. First and especially I comend my sinfull Soule into the mercifull hands of Almightie God my creator and maker and of his sonne Jesus Christ my onely Saviour and Redeemer, through the onely merritts of whose bitter death and passion I verilie beleeve and hope to bee saved, and to bee made one of his electe in his blessed and heavenly kingdome, and my bodie to bee buried in the Church or Churchyard of Barwicke in Elmett aforesaid. Item as touching my poore worldly estate wherewith it hath pleased God to blesse mee, havinge bin a most unprofitable husband thereof hitherto and havinge and being like to leave behind mee a poor wife and a greate Charge of Children. Item I give will and bequeath unto Christopher Shore and Margarett Shore, my younger sonne and daughter, the Reversion and inheritance of two closes called the Moore close and of halfe a close called Beamonds close with all their appurtennces lyeing and being in Hutton Pannell in the said Countie of Yorke after the death and decease of Margarett Shore, widdowe, my Mother, and to their heyres and Assignes forever, to bee equallie devided betwixt them, which said Closes and premises with all their appurtenances I have by my deede bearinge date the second daye of Februarie in the yere of our Lord one thousand six Hundred Fiftie and Six settled conveyed and assured to their uses as aforesaid. Item whereas there remayneth deposited in the hands of Thomas Ramsden of Hemswath, in the said Countie, yeoman, the whole Summe of One Hundred poundes of current money in trust for the use benefitt and behoofe of Francis Shore, my Eldest Sonne, and to bee ymployed for the use of the said Francis Shore by vertue of certaine Articles of Agreement betwixt mee the said Christopher Shore And the said Thomas Ramsden bearing date the Eight and Twentieth daye of Maye in the yere of our Lord one Thousand six Hundred Fortie and Seaven. Now my will minde and desire is, And I doe give and bequeath Threescore pounds thereof to my said sonne Francis, and twentie pounds apeece thereof to Thomas Shore, my youngest sonne, And to Margaret Shore, my youngest daughter to be equallie devided betwixt them two for their filiall portions, And the consideracon of the said one Hundred poundes I give unto Alice, my wife, during the noneage and minoritie of my said Sonne Francis Shore. Item whereas I am possessed in the right of my wife Alice and of her children by her former Husband, Henry Shippen, of certaine goods and household stuffe (the proppertie whereof is not nor hath not by mee or her bin changed since the Coverture betwixt us) I leave give and bequeath wholly and all my Right therein to Alice, my lovinge Wife, to whome I giue all the Rest of my goods Chattells and debts, my debts by mee oweing and my funerall Expences first payed and discharged, And doe hereby ordaine and make her my sole

Executrix of this my last will and Testament, And doe Revoke and declare to be voyd all former wills by me made. In witnes whereof I haue hereunto putt my hand and Seale The daye and yere first aboue written. Christopher Shore. Sealed Signed and published to bee my last will and testament in the presence of us James Wrighte, John Errington, William Briame. [*Proved* 31 *May*, 1659, *by Alice Shore, the Relict and Executrix named.*]

JOHN SETTLE of Potterton, yeoman.

[l. 233.] Septemb[r] the 17th, 1668. In the name of God Amen. I, John Settle of Potterton, in the county of Yorke, yeoman, being sicke in body butt of good and perfect minde and memory, God be praised, doe make this my last will and Testament in manner and forme followinge. First and principally I committ my soule to God and my body to the ground, hopeing of a joyfull Resurrection in and through Christ my Lord. And as touchinge my worldly Estate whereof itt hath pleased God to bestowe upon mee, I give deuise and bequeath as followeth. Inprimis I give Elizabeth, my wife, all the houses barnes and Stables with the Garthes and Intacks dureing the tyme that she is my widow and unmarryed. And if she dye or marry Then my sonne, Richard Settle, to enter into the said p'misses for ever. Item I give my sonne Richard the Lowe beane Close adjoyneing to a close called the Spenfeild, belonginge to M[r] Ellis, withall my arrable Lands belonginge to the house wherein I now live in the three feilds belonginge to Potterton, with the Tann yarde and Fatts to him and his heires for ever. Item I give my sonne Joseph one house and backside in the Tenure and occupacon of James Wood, one Close called little Feild Close, with the meadow in the Ings, butt he not to enter till hee accomplish the Age of Twenty one yeares, and if he dye before the said age or without issue, then to retourne to my sonne Richard and his heires for ever. Item I give my daughter Sarah one close abuttinge on a Close called beane close in the Tenure and occupac̃on of Richard Daniell of Potterton aforesaid, withall the appurtenances thereunto belonginge, She not to enter until she accomplish the age of one and Twenty yeares, and if she dye before the said age or without issue Then to retourne to my sonne Richard and his heires for ever. Item I give my daughter Susann two closes, one called crosse close another called Wheate close, lyeing on the South of M[r] Ellis grounds, She not to enter till she accomplish the age of One and twenty yeares, and if she dye before the said age or without issue Then to retourne to my sonne Richard and his heires for ever. Item I constitute and ordaine my wife and sonne Richard joynt executors of this my last will and Testament, and they equally to enioy the said Lands dureing the tyme of my children's minority for and towards the payment of my debts. Witnesse Richard Vevers. [*Proved* 30 *July*, 1669.]

ROBERT SETTLE of Potterton, chandler.

[l. 275b.] In the name of God Amen, the Twentieth day of May One thousand six hundred sixty nyne. I, Robert Settle of Potterton, in the county of Yorke, Chandler, being crasie of body but whole in minde and of good and p'fect memory, praised be God, doe make and ordaine this my last will and Testament in manner and forme followinge. First I committ my soule to Allmighty God And my body to the Earth, and to be buryed in the Church or Church yarde of Barwicke after my death, att the discretion of my friends. Item I give and bequeath to my daughter, Mary Settle, Seaventy pounds to be paid out of my personall estate when she shall accomplish the Age of One and twenty yeares by my executors hereafter named, and to haue meate, drinke, and app'll as shall be necessary. Item I give and bequeath as a Legacie to my sonne, John Settle (Provided that my wife marry againe), Fourscore pounds to be paid out of my p'sonall estate. Item I give as a Legacie to Roger Carbutt Fourty shillings, to be paid to him the said Ro: Carbutt three mouthes after my decease. Item I giue to Hellen Carbutt tenn shillings att the same tyme. Item I giue to John Carter one shillinge and the silver buttons on the Buckskinne dublitt when he shall come to the age of one and twenty yeares. Item I give to Thomas Carter one shillinge when he shall come to the aforesaid age. Item I give to William Carter one shillinge to be paid as aforesaid. Item I give to Thomas Catterton one shillinge, to be paid in like mann[r]. Item I give to Thomas Taite my brother in Law, Five shillings to be paid three mouthes after my decease. Item I give to my cozen, John Taylor, Five shillings, to be paid as aforesaid. After the said portion paid and the said Legacies and my Funeralls discharged, I make Jane, my wife, and John Settle, my sonne, joynt executors of this my last will and testament. And I constitute and appoint my two wellbeloued Friends, Thomas Taite of Barwicke in Elmett, and John Taylor, younger, of the same, Feoffees in trust to see that my will and minde shall be done as in this my last will contained. In witnesse whereof I have sett my hand and seale y[e] day and yeare within written. Robert Settle. Witnesses William Settle, his marke, Hellen Bateson, her marke. [*Proved 21 Jan.*, 1669-70.]

ANNE POSTGATE of Roundhay, widow.

[lv. 203b.] In the name of God Amen. I, Anne Postgate of Roundhay, in the parish of Barwick in Elmet, widdow, being of good and perfect memorie, praised be God, doe make and declare this my last will and Testament in manner and forme following, revoaking thereby all other former wills and Testaments whatsoever. First I comend my soule into the hands of my Savio[r] Jesus Christ, and my bodie to be buried neare unto that of my dear Husbands, William Postgate, in the Church of Barwicke aforesaid, and as concerninge my Temporall estate First I giue and bequeath to my dear mother, Jane Wilson, widdow, Twentie pounds. Item I giue and bequeath to my sister, Mary Wilson, my Cabbinet and all my wearing clothes. Item I giue and bequeath to my Brother, William Wilson, five shillings. Item I giue and bequeath to my servant, Thomas Prince, the best Horse or Cow which I now haue or am possessour off. I giue and bequeath to my maide servant, Margrett Dearloue, Twentie shillings. Item I giue and bequeath to William Whelas Two shillings six pence. Item I giue and bequeath to John Maulume Two shillings six pence. And all the rest of my estate both reale and personall I entyerly giue and bequeath, my funerall expences being first deducted, to my sonne, John Postgate, whome by this my last will and Testament I solely leave to the Guardianshipp of S[r] John Savile of Copley, Bar[tt], whome by these and hereby I doe constitute and ordaine the sole executor of this my last will and Testament and Guirdian of my childe, John Postgate, excluding hereby all other person or persons whatsoever reposeing in him my Trust and confidence that hee will faithfully performe the same for my childs good, and according to my Will and True intencon. In witnesse whereof I haue hereunto set my hand and seale the first day of June, Anno Dom. one Thousand six hundred seaventie foure. Anne Postgate. Sealed Signed and delivered in the presence of us, Charles Killingbeck, William Hall, Mary Aspinwall, her marke, Thomas Gibson. [*Proved* 6 *July*, 1674.]

JOHN BURLAND of Barwick.

[lix. 304b.] In the name of God Amen, the Eighteenth day of March, in the yeare of our Lord God one thousand six hundred eighty and one, I, John Burland the elder of Barwick in Elmet, in the county of Yorke, being sicke and weake of body but of perfect minde and memory, thancks be given unto God therefore, doe make and ordaine this to be my last will and testament in manner and form followeing, that is to say. First and principally I give my soule into the handes of Almighty God whoe gave it me. And for my body I commend to the earth to be buried in Christian and decent manner in the Church yeard of Barwicke aforesaid, nothing doubting but at the generall resurrection I shall receive the same againe by the mighty power of God, and as touching such worldly estate wherewith it hath pleased God to bless me in this life, I give, devise, bequeath and dispose the same in manner and forme followeing. First I will that my funerall charges be paide and discharged. Item I give unto my sonne, William Burland, the sum̃e of tenn shillings. Item I give unto my sonne, Richard Burland, the sum̃e of tenn shillings. Item I give unto my sonne, John Burland, the sume of three poundes and two Maires which he hath in his owne possession, withall things which is belonging to husbandry and tooles and wood within the Shop, and one acree of hard corne lying and being in Potterton feild, and one rainge being in the said house of the aforesaid John Burland the elder, all those I give unto the afore John, my sonñe. Item I give unto my sonne, Thomas Burland, the sum̃e o f tenn shillings. And of this my last will I make and ordaine Mary, my daughter, my full and whole executrix. And I doe hereby vtterly disallow revoake and annull all and every other former testaments, wills, legacies, bequests and executors and executrixes by me in any wise before this time named willed and bequeathed, ratifying and confirmeing this and none other to be my last will and testament. In witness whereof I have hereunto set my hand and seale the day and yeare above written. Signed sealed published p'nounced and declared by the said John Burland the elder as his last will and testament in the presence of John Burland, his marke and seale, Jo: Tayler, P. Daniell, Thomas Knapton. [*Proved* 4 *June*, 1682.]

ELIZABETH THOMPSON of Barwick, widow.

[lxi. 67.] In the name of God Amen, I, Elizabeth Thompson of Barwick in Elmet, in the county of Yorke, widdow, being of perfect minde and memory, praised be God for the same, but calling to minde mine owne greate age and the uncertainty of this p'sent life doe make constitute ordaine and declare this my last will and testament in manner and forme following. First I give and bequeath my soule into the hands of Almighty God my maker, stedfastly hoping to enjoy everlasting life by the death and passion of Jesus Christ his onely sonn my alone Saviour. Secondly I comend my body to the earth whereof it was made to be decently buried in or very neare the grave of my second husband, John Timme, within the Church of Barwick aforesaid at the discretion of my executors hereafter named. Thirdly as for that worldly estate wherewith God hath blessed me, I dispose thereof in manner and forme following. First my will and minde is and I hereby give and bequeath unto my nephew, John Browne, sonn of Lidia Browne of St Maries parrish in Colchester, in the county of Essex, the sume of twenty pounds, or in case at his death before mine then to his daughter Elizabeth, and in case they both be dead before me then the said sum̃e of twenty pounds shall be paid to the youngest children of William Bridges, clerke, hereafter named, to be equally devided amongst them. I give unto the children of John Timme of Rotheram, Glover, late dec̃ed, the sum̃e of tenn pounds to be equally devided amongst them. And to each of the said John Timms sisters (to witt) Ellen, Dorothy, Alice, and Elizabeth, the sum̃e of twenty shillings a peece. Item I give to my neece, Rachel Garforth, tenn shillings, And to her sonn and daughter the sume of ten shillings a peece. Item I give to John Thompson of Water Popleton tenn shillings. To his sister Prince and daughter Elizabeth tenn shillings a peece. Item I give to Elizabeth, the wife of Richard Lovel, the sũme of five pounds. Item I give to Sarah Dineley, widdow, the sume of Eight pounds. Item I give five pounds a peece to the foure eldest children of William Briggs, clerke, hereafter named. Item I give forty shillings to be equally devided amongst the children of Susannah, the wife of Thomas Dunnington. Item I give one silver spoone markt J: T: to John, sonn of John Tate. Item I give the sume of halfe a crowne a peece to every Godchild of mine. Item I give to Joseph Fountaines of Leeds twenty shillings. To his sister, Mary Toppin, tenn shillings. To Thomas Horbury and Isabell, his wife, twenty shillings a peece. To James Orton, tenn shillings. To John Dineley tenn shillings. To Frances Varley tenn shillings. To Richard Bingy tenn shillings. To Margaret Dineley twenty shillings. To Thomas Watersons wife tenn shillings. To the two daughters of Thomas Prince of Haughton five shillings a peece. Item I give my wedding ring to Sarah, the wife of William Bridges, clerke. Item I give my bed and the furniture of it with the rest of my unpromised household goods to Sarah Dineley, widdow. Item I give to Robert Ball tenn shillings; All these legacies I doe order to be paid at the years end after my decease to such onely of the legacys as shall be then alive. And for the due performance thereof I doe charge my whole estate both reall and personall whatsoever, which being done and my funeral expences (which I order to be decent and suiteable to my quality) satisfied, I doe hereby give bequeath, devise and demise to my welbeloved freind William Bridges abovesaid, Clerk and Rector of Castleford, in the county of Yorke, and to his heires and assignes for ever, all that my halfe Messuage or Tenement with three cottages thereto belonging, and all the edifices, barnes, folds whatsoever thereto belonging, withall the other arrable Lands, Closes, pastures, gates, doles and parcels whatsoever, containeing by estimation aboute forty six acres, be they more or less, withall their appurtenances whatsoever thereto belonging, scituate lying and being in Potterton and Barwick or their feilds and territories, all which I lately purchased from William Hodgson, gent. Provided that the said William Bridges, his heires or assignes, yearely for ever forth of the said estate pay the sume of twenty shillings, twelve shillings whereof shall be yearly for the poorest sort, especially widdows, within the Towne of Barwick, to be distributed by twelve pence a peece, and the other eight shillings to be alike yearly distributed to the like poore within the Towne of Potterton; And I doe request the Minister and Churchwardens of Barwick to assist my heires or assignes in the faithfull distribution of the same, the first payment to beginn the first rent day after my decease; And soe tenn shillings to be paid as above every halfe yeare for ever after; And for the residue of my estate whatsoever I doe hereby give, bequeath and devise it unto the abovesaid William Bridges, his executors administrators or assignes, whome I doe hereby make constitute and ordaine sole executor of this my last will and testament. And I doe hereby revoke all my former wills and testaments whatsoever. In witness whereof I have declared and published this to be my last will and Testament, and have thereto set my hand and seale the twenty third day of July in the second yeare of the Raigne of our Soveraigne Lord James the Second by the Grace of God of England, Scotland, France and Ireland King, Defender of the Faith, Annoq. Dni 1686. Elizabeth Thompson, her marke. Sealed signed and published to be the last will and testament of the abovesaid Elizabeth Thompson in the presence of us, John Tayler, Matthew Isott, William Strickland, John Smith, jun., his marke. [*Proved* 8 *Apl.*, 1689.]

HENRY WRIGHT of Winmoorside, yeoman.

[lxi. 157b.] In the name of God Amen. I, Henry Wright of Winmooreside, in the parish of Barwick in Elmet, in the county of York, Yeoman, being sicke in body but of good and perfect memory, praised be given to Almighty God, doe make . . . First I will that my dear and loveing wife shall have the use of one third part in three parts to be devided of all my personall estate dureing the terme of her naturall life. Unto my son Henry Wright, 5s. Unto my son William Wright, tenn pounds. Unto my daughter Sarah Wright, twenty pounds. Unto my son in lawe Thomas Smith, five pounds. Residue unto my son Nathan Wright. He sole exõr. Dated 5 September, 1689. Witnesses George Wright, Samuell West, William Dixon. [*Proved* 11 *Oct.*, 1689.]

JOHN TAYLOR of Barwick, husbandman.

[lxi. 201b.] In the name of God Amen. I, John Taylor, juñ., of Barwick in Elmet, in the county of York, Husbandman, being very sick and weake of body but of good and perfect memory, praised be Almighty God, doe make and ordaine my last will and testament in manner and forme following (that is to say). First I give and bequeath my soule into the hand of Almighty God my Maker, hopeing by the merrits of his son Jesus Christ my Redeemer to participate those Joyes which are prepared for the elect. And my body to be buried in the Church or Churchyard of Barwick in Elmett, at the discretion of my freinds and Relations. And for my worldly estate wherewithall it hath pleased God to endow me, I give bequeath and dispose of as followeth, that is to say. First I give and bequeath unto Mary, my welbeloved wife, all my personall estate. Alsoe my will and minde is that my son John shall pay unto my daughter Ann fifty pounds out of the Lands which will descend upon him hereditorily. And doe make my said daughter Ann sole executrix of this my last will and Testament. In witness whereof I have hereto set my hand and seale the second day of January in the year of our Lord God 1689. Jo: Tayler. Sealed signed and declared in the p'sence of us, Will: Tayler, William Tayler, Jo: Tayler. [*Proved* 31 *Jan.*, 1689-90.]

ELIZABETH MASSIE of Barwick, spinster.

[lxi. 262b.] In the name of God Amen. I, Elizabeth Massie of Barwicke, in the county of Yorke, spinster, being sick and weake of body but of perfect minde and memory (praised be Almighty God for the same) doe make and ordaine this my last will and testament in manner and forme following. First and principally I commit my soul into the hands of Almighty God my maker, hopeing through the merits of my Saviour Jesus Christ to inherrit life everlasting, and my body I commit to the earth to be decently buried at the discretion of my executrix hereafter named. And as touching that temporall estate which it hath pleased God to bless me withall, I doe give and dispose thereof as followeth. First my will and minde is that my funerall expenses and reall debts shall be discharged and paid. Item I doe give and bequeath unto Margaret Dineley, my Aunt, five pounds as a legacy to be paid to her out of my personall estate within one year after my decease by my executrix hereafter named; Item I doe give and bequeath unto Jeremy Ball and Robert Ball, my two cousins, fifty shillings a peece, to be paid unto them out of my personall estate within one year after my decease by my executrix hereafter named. Item I doe give and bequeath unto Joseph Issott, my godson, twenty shillings to be paid unto him out of my psonall estate within one year after my decease by my executrix hereafter named. Item I doe give and bequeath unto Sarah Hodgson, my freind, three pounds to be paid unto her . . . Item I doe give and bequeath unto Mary Vagy, my servant, ten shillings to be paid her within one yeare. . . Item I doe give devise and bequeath all those my two messuages tenements or dwellinghouse scituate and being in Leeds in a Street there called Briggate, with their and either of their appurts, unto my dear and loveing mother, Mrs Sarah Wood, for and dureing her naturall life, And imeditely from and after her decease then to Alice Atkinson, the wife of Mr. Thomas Atkinson of Pontefract, if then living, And after her decease then to all children begotten or to be begotten of the said Mr Thomas Atkinson by Alice, his now wife, to be equally devided amongst them, and to their heirs for ever, paying out of the same one hundred pounds within one year after they shall enter to the above devised premisses unto such person or persons as shall be named in the last will and testament of my dear mother, Mrs Sarah Wood, to have the same. Item I doe give devise and bequeath unto my said dear and loveing mother, Mrs Sarah Wood, All that my Close of medow arrable or pasture lying and being at Beeston, in the said county of York, called or known by the name of the Hilly Close, with appurtenances, for and dureing her naturall life, and imediately from and after her decease then to Charles Hall, son of Mr Charles Hall, minister of Hucknall in the county of Derby, and to his heirs for ever. Item I doe give devise and bequeath unto my said dear and loveing mother, Mrs Sarah Wood, all those my five acres and a halfe of arrable pasture ground, be the same more or less, lying and being in the severall feilds of Shereburne in the said county of Yorke, and to her heirs for ever. All the rest of my temporall estate not already disposed of I doe hereby give devise and bequeath unto my dear and loveing mother, Mrs Sarah Wood, whome I doe make sole executrix of this my last will and Testament, revokeing all other former wills by me heretofore made. In wittness whereof I, the said Elizabeth Massie, have hereunto set my hand and seal this second day of September in the First year of the Raigne of our Soveraigne Lord and Lady King William and

Queen Mary, Annoq' Dni. 1689. Eliz: Massie. Sealed signd. published and declared in the p'sence of Willm Knapton, Jo: Tayler, Arth: Gargrave. [*Proved* 13 *May*, 1690.]

ROBERT LEIGH of Roundhay.

[lxiii. 426a.] In the name of God Amen. I, Robert Leigh of Roundhay, in the parish of Barwicke, in the County of Yorke, being of perfect mind and memory, praised be God, Do make this my last will and Testament in manner and forme following. First I comend my soule into the hands of Almighty God, hoping for salvacon through the meritts of my dear Saviour Jesus Christ, as for my worldly estate I give and bequeath in manner and Forme following. Impris I give and bequeath unto my brother, Thomas Leigh of Audwork in the parish of Anne, the sume of one shilling. Unto my sister, Mary Parker of Plumton, in the parish of Spofforth, the sume of Five shillings. Unto Robert Leigh, in the parish of Spofforth, son to my brother, John Leigh, lately deced, the sume of tenn shilling. Residue unto Ellener Barrow and Godfrey Stonehouse whome I make my sole executor . . Dated 29 March, 1705. Robert Leigh, his mke. Witness William Eamonson, Thomas Brame. Tho: Aspiwall. [*Proved* 26 *Feb*., 1706-7.]

ANDREW SLATER.

[lxiv. 188b.] In the name of God Amen, the Twelfth day of August, 1707. I, Andrew Slater, being sick in body but of perfect memory, praised be Almighty God . . I give unto Robert Slater, my eldest son, the sume of 12d., and Ann and Eliner, my two daughters, each of them 12d., to be paid within 12 months after my decease, my debts paid and funerall expences discharged. I doe appoint Peter, my son, Izabell, my daughter, sole exectors . . Andrue Slaiter, his mark. Test. Willm Vevers, Henry Bedall, his marke, Aquilla Blackburn, his m'k. [*Proved* 1 *Nov*., 1707.]

JAMES WINTER of Barwick, Chirurgeon.

[lxiv. 413.] In the name of God Amen, the 30th day of June, 1708. I, James Winter of Barwick in Elmitt, in the county of Yorke, Chirurgeon, being sicke of body but of perfect memory, Praised be God, doe make and ordaine this my last will and Testament in manner and form following. First I Bequeath my Soul into the hands of Almighty God my maker, hopeing that through the meritorious death and passion of Jesus Christ my onely Saviour and Redeemer, to receive free pardon and forgiveness of all my sins, and as for my Body, to be buried In Christian Buriall [at] the discretion of my Executors hereafter named. Item I give unto Samll King of Barwick in Elmett, my Great Bible. Item I give unto Pheby Hardcastle my silver spoon. Item I give to her doughter, Sarah Hardcastle, my Dimothy Down Bedd. All the Rest of my Goods,

Bills, Book Debts, and Estate whatsoever I die possessed on I give to my executors, Jn° Pitts of London, Cordwinder, and Mary Pitts, his sister, they paying my debts and funerall charges. In witness whereof I have hereunto sett my hand and seale the day and year above written. I also request Sam[ll] King to be superv[r] of this my last Will. James Winter. Witness, Elizabeth Balle, the marke of Martha Burrell. [*Proved* 10 *Aug.*, 1708.]

GEORGE HAIST of Barwick, Butcher.

[lxvi. 214b.] In the name of God Amen. I, George Haist of Barwick in Elmett, in the county of Yorke, Butcher, being in reasonable good health of body . . . . Item I give and bequeath unto my dear and Loveing wife, Mary Haist, and her assignes during the Terme of her naturall Life, All that my messuage dwellinghouse or tenement scituate and being in Barwick in Elmitt aforesaid, and all and singular the barnes, &c., which sometimes heretofore I bought of Robert Haigue of Barwick in Elmitt aforesaid, deceased, and alsoe all that my other messuage, &c., in Barwick in Elmett aforesaid, and all the buildings with the orchard and garth to the same belonging, which said orchard and garth lie between the lands of William Ellis, Esq., on both sides, together wth the little cottage scituate in the s[d] garth, which s[d] last menconed messuage, &c., I purchased of William Taite of Weatherby, in the said county of Yorke, Butcher, with all ways, &c., and from and after the decease of Mary, my said wife, I doe give and bequeath all and singular the said messuages, &c., unto my son, Richard Haist, his heires and assignes for ever. Item I give and bequeath unto him Twenty pounds. Unto my sone William Haist Twenty pounds. Unto my son George Haist Twenty pounds. To my daughter Elizabeth Ingam, wife of Peter Ingam, Twenty pounds. Unto my son John Haist Thirty pounds. Unto my son Phillip the like sum̃e of Thirty Pounds. Unto my son Joseph Haist the some of Twenty pounds. To my son Bengemen Haist Fifty pounds. Unto all my grandchildren five shillings a peice which shall be found alive at my decease. Residue of parsonall estate unto Mary, my said wife, and my said two sonns, Richard and Benjamin, equally. They to be joint executors. In witness, &c., the second day of Aprill, 1709. George Haiste, his marke and seale. Witnesses, William Hague, Jeremiah Ball, his marke, Thomas Knapton. [*Proved* 30 *March*, 1710.]

EDWARD HUNT of Lasingcroft, yeoman.

[Original.] In the name of God Amen, the 16th day of Nouember, 1693, according to the Computation of The Church of England. I, Edward Huntt of Lasingcroft, in the parich of Barwick in The Elmett and in the county of Yorke, Yomond, Being of perfect memory and Remembrance, praisid be God, Do make and ordaine this my Last will and Testament in maner and forme following, viz.

First I Bequeath my soule into the hands of Allmighty God my maker, hoping that Through the meritorious death and passion of Jesus Christ my sauiour and Redeemer to Receiue free pardon and foregiueness of all my sins, and as for my Body to be Buried in Christian Buriall att the Disicetion of my executors here after nominated. Item I giue to Anne Bentlife, wife to Matthew Bentlife, the sume of fiue shillings. I giue to Matthew Bentlife one shilling. I giue to three daughters of Matthew Bentlifes and Annes Bentlifes, his wife, the sume of three shillings. I giue to my sister, Mary Huntt, the sume of ten pounds. I giue to Margrey Huntt, wedow, one shilling. I giue to Thomas Huntt, eldest son to Margrey Huntt, the sume of one shilling. I gine to Petter Huntt one shilling. I gine to Anthony Huntt the sume of one shilling. I giue to Henry Huntt one shilling. I gine to Francas Huntt the sume of fiue shillings. I gine to Vollantine Shepin the sume of one shilling. I make Mary, my wife, sole executtor of this my Last will and Testament. In witness whereof I haue here unto sett my hand and seall the day and year aboue written, Revoking all other wills and Testaments. Edward Huntt, his mark. Witnessed by us William Gillson, John Gillson, Robert Gillson, his marke. [*Proved* 4 *Nov.*, 1694.]

October 15th, 1694.

A true Inventory of the goods cattels and chattels, moveable and unmoveable, of Edward Hunt, late deceased, of Lasingcroft, by Wiħ Morrett, Robt. Dawson, William Dawson, John Gillson.

	l.	s.	d.
Imp'mis his purse and Apparell	05	00	00
In the hall house one Table 6 Chaires one forme one Rainge	05	00	06
In the Kitchin one Rainge one paire of Racks 2 Spitts 3 brasspotts 3 brass panns wth all other huslements	05	00	00
In the Brew house one mast fatt one guilefatt, one pan with all other huslements	00	10	00
In the Milke house 10 Bowles one Churne 3 Barrills one ee e-press wth all other huslements ..	00	10	00
In the plohr one stand bedd feather bedd one pe of Sheets one paire of Blanketts one Coverlett	01	00	00
In one Butterie 2 Tearses 6 pewther dishes 2 flagons 2 tankerds 2 Candlesticks	00	15	00
In one chambr over the Kitchen one bed stead one feather bedd one boulster 2 pillowes one paire of blankets one Rugg 6 Chaires one presser 2 tables one Chest	02	00	00
In one chamber over the hall one halfe headed bedd one feather bedd one paire of blankettẹ one coverlett with other huslements ..	01	00	00
All the Corne in the Barne	30	00	00
All the hay in the Barne	05	00	00

	l.	s.	d.
4 Cowes 4-2 yeare old 4 Calves	12	00	00
3 Geldings 2 Maires..	10	00	00
One Waine 2 Cartes one plough wth all the Waine Geere and Plow Geere..	05	00	00
Malt in the Kilne	06	00	00
In the fould one sow six holdings..	01	10	00
the sume is—	82	05	06

Proved by Mary Hunt, Lasingcroft, wid., William Gilson of Poole, yeoman, et John Gilson of Lasingcroft, farmer, 5 Nov., 1694.

JOSEPH DIXON of Barwick, Schoolmaster.

[lxxvii. 61a.] In the name of God Amen. I, Joseph Dixon of Barwick in Elmet, in the county of York, Schoolmaster, being weak in body but of perfect mind and remembrance, praised be God, do make and ordaine this my last will and Testament in manner and form following. First my will and mind is that all my just and lawfull debts and funerall expences be lawfully discharged. Now as touching such worldly goods as it hath pleased Almighty God to bless me withall, I give and dispose of in manner following. First I give and bequeath unto my brother, Benjamin Dixon, the sume of Twelve pence. Item I give and bequeath unto Mary Newby of Barwick the sume of twelve pence. Item I give and bequeath unto my son John, and my daughter Elizabeth, the sume of Ten pounds to be equally divided betwixt them and paid them when they come at the age of Twenty one years, but if either of them happen to dye before they come at lawfull years of age, then my will and mind is that the survivor of them have the s^d^ Ten pounds as a Legacy. Item I give and bequeath unto my loveing wife, Anne, all my right and title that I have unto that messuage or Tenement otherwise called a halfe Burgess with all the appurtences wherein John Hunter dwells in the Market place in Leeds, in the County of York. Also all the right and Title that I have to a pew in the New Church in Leeds. Lastly I give and bequeath unto my loveing wife, Anne, all my personall Estate of Goods and Chattels, and I doe make her sole extrix . . . As likewise I leave my two and well beloved friends, Richard Hutchinson and Jonathan Wetherid, Trustees, to see that all things be carefully managed, and I do hereby revoke and adnull all other wills gifts and bequests by me made heretofore. As witness my hand and seal this Twenty sixth day of Aprill, in the year of our Lord one Thousand seven hundred and Twenty one. Joseph Dixon. Testes. Edward Shackleton, Matthew Hutchinson, William Ledger. [*Proved* 17 *May*, 1723.]

THOMAS BRAME of Roundhay, husbandman.

[lxxviii. 6.] In the name of God Amen. I, Thomas Brame of Roundhay, in the parish of Barwick in Elmett and dioces of York,

Husbandman, being visited with sickness but of sound memory, and having a mind to settle that estate God hath bestowed upon me, so that there may be no strife nor controversy among my relations for or about the same after my decease, have thought good to constitute and ordain this my last will and Testament in manner and form following, this twelfth day of June in the year of our Lord One Thousand Seven Hundred and Twenty four. Imp[rs] I committ my soul into the Hands of Almighty God, Creator and Governour of all things, and to Jesus Christ my only Saviour through the merits of whose most precious Blood I hope for the pardon of all my sins, and to the holy Ghost the Blessed Trinity, hoping for the Blessed resurrection promised at the Last Day, and my Body to the Christian Burial at the Discretion of my Executor whom I shall hereafter nominate and appoint. Itm I Give and Bequeath unto my daughter Anne the summ of Twenty pounds to be paid when she shall arrive at the age of Thirty years. Itm I give and bequeath unto my son Thomas the summ of Ten pound to be paid when he shall attain the age of Twenty seven years, Unto my son William the summ of Twenty pound to be paid when he shall arrive at the age of Twenty five years. Unto my son Henry the summ of Ten pounds in case he go on to serve his apprenticeship, to be paid him when he shall arrive at the age of Twenty three years, or if he go not on with his Trade or some other which may be supposed to be the like Expence, then my will is he shall be paid ten pound more when he shall attain the age of Twenty five years. Unto my son John the summ of Ten pound to be paid him when he shall arrive at the age of twenty three years, and if he chuse to have a Trade my will is he should have ten pound to put him apprentice, and if he do not chuse to have a Trade then to have ten pound more paid at the date of the above mentioned ten pound. And my will is that if any of my children should dye before the respective times of payment that then their portions so dying shall be equally divided amongst my surviving children. Itm my will is that all my just debts and funeral expences be paid. Itm my will is that Sarah, my dear wife, have three pounds a year, paid Quarterly by equal portions by my son Joseph, who I appoint sole executor of this my last will and Testament. Thomas Braime. Witnesses—John Kitchingman, Tho: Aspinall, Sam. Dodgson. [*Proved* 19 *December*, 1724.]

William Ellis of Kiddall, Esq.

[lxxix. 346.] In the name of God Amen. I, W[m] Ellis of Kiddall, in the West Rideing of the countie of York, Esq[r], being in perfect memory (blessed be God), doe make this my last will and testament in manner and form following (that is to say), first I bequeath my Spirit to the hands of Almighty God and my body to be Buryed in

---

(1) William Ellis of Kiddal married Mary, daughter of Sir William Lowther of Swillington. Their son, William Ellis, was High Sheriff of Yorkshire 1709, married Mary, daughter of Dutton Seaman, and was father of Captain Charles Ellis, Captain William Ellis, R.N., Henry Ellis, and six daughters.

my Chancell in the parish Church of Barwick, and Touching the distribution of my worldly goods I dispose of the same as followeth. First I will and desire that all my just debts and Funerall expences shall be truly paid. Itm I will give to my daughter, Mary Ellis, wife of my son, Wm Ellis of Rowall, Esqr, Twenty pounds to buy her mourning and other necessaries. Itm I give unto my Grandaughter, Elizabeth Ellis, who is now with me, One Hundred and sixty pounds, to be paid out of two bonds, one exicuted by Mr Danglas, the other by Mr Dauglas and Mr Joseph Scolfield, to dispose of as she thinks convenient towards discharging of her father's debts. Itm I give to my grandson, Captain Charles Ellis, my Bed and Bedding in the Chamber wherein I lie, and half a douzen Chairs and two Scrivtores in the same room, with the bed and bedding in my manservts room. Itm I give unto my grandaughter, Catherine Ellis, four Silver spoons, my silver cup with the cover to it, and a silver Tum'ler and a pair of Chest of Drawers which stand next the screwtore in my Lodging room. Itm I give to my grandaughter, Mary Smith, Twenty pounds of good and lawfull money of Great Brittain, to be paid her at the end of six months after my decease. Itm I give unto my grandson, Wm Ellis the seaman, my watch and my silver cup with my armes engraven on it, and also five pounds to buy him mourning, also I give him that Indenture he gave me made the Twentyethe day of February in the Eight year of the Reign of our Sovereign Lord George by the grace of God of great Britain, France and Ireland King, Defender of the Faith, Annoq' Dom: 1721, between Wm Ellis of Rowall, in the county of York, Esqr, Charles Ellis, Gent., eldest son and Heir apparent of the one part, and Willm Ellis, Gent., the younger, and Willm Ellis of Kiddall, in the said county, Esqre, of the other part, I doe hereby give all that one hundred pounds due to me by virtue of that Indenture to my said grandson, Willm Ellis the seaman, back again if he be alive at the time of my death, but in case he be dead then I give the said Indenture with the one hundred pounds due upon it to my four grandchildren, Henry, Willm, Francis and John Ellis, sons of my youngest son, Henry Ellis of London, Linnen draper. Also I give to my grandson, Henry Ellis of London, my little silver Tankard, also I give him five pounds to buy him mourning. Itm I give unto Mary, the daughter of Willm Dawson, one silver spoon. Itm I give unto Timothy Smith of Barwick, Jur, my black suit of apparll(to witt) one coat, two waiscoats, one pair of Brieches and also my best coat and Brieches. Itm I give unto my man Tho: my coat, waiscoat and Brieches which I constantly wear, and also one old gray coat. All the residue and remainder of what kind soever I give to my executor, and lastly I make and ordain my grandaughter, Elizabeth Ellis, who is now with me, my whole and sole executrix . . In witness whereof I have hereunto set my hand and seall this Twelvt day of February In the year of our Lord God seventeen Hundred and Twenty five. Wm Ellis. Witnesses Jno Daniel, Will: Appleyard, Tho: Appleyard. [*Proved* 25 *March*, 1726.]

JOHN PEARSON, Kiddal lane end, yeoman.

[lxxix. 154.] In the name of God, Amen. I, John Pearson of Kidhall lain end, in ye parish of Barwick in Elmit, in the county of York, Yeoman, tho' weak and infirm of Body yet of sound mind and perfect memory, praise be therefore given to Almighty God, do make and ordain this my p^r sent last will and Testam^t in mañer and form following. First and principally I comend my soul into the hands of Almighty God, hoping through the meritts, Death and passion of my savo^r Jesus Christ to have full and free pardon and forgiveness of all my sins, and to inherit everlasting life, and my body I comitt to the Earth to be decently Buried at the Discretion of my Exec^rs hereafter named, and as touching the Dissolution of all such temporall Estates as it hath pleased Almighty God to bestow upon me I give and dispose thereof as follows. First I will that my funeral charges shall be paid and discharged out of the same, as also all my lawfull debts. Item I give to my eldest son, Thomas, the sum of ten pounds to be paid to him by my exec^rs hereafter to be named at the end of twelve months after my death. I give in like mañer to my son John the like sum of ten pounds. Item I give unto my son John Easby of Righton one shilling, and to his three children now living to each of them five shillings to be paid in mañer as afores^d. and my will is that if either of my afores^d sons, Thomas or John Pearson, shall happen to dye before the expiration of the said year that his Legacie shall goe and be P^d to the survivor. All the rest and residue of my psonal estate goods and chattels w^t soever I do give and bequeath to my loving wife Mary, and to my son Robert, and I do hereby nominate and apoint them to be full and sole exec^rs . . I desire my Body may be buried in the parish church yard of Barwick afores^d. In witness . . . Eleventh day of June, 1726. John Preston [sic] mark. Sealed signed and published in ye presence of us, John Burland, Robert Knapton, Francis Holmes, Timo. Jackson, clerk. [*Proved* 27 *Augt.*, 1726.]

MARY HAGUE, widow.

[lxxix. 650b.] In the nam[e] of God Amen. I, Mary Hague, widow, relict of William Hague late of Barwick in Elmit . . First my will is that out of such personall estate my just debts and funerall charges shall first be paid and discharged, and dispose of the remainder as follows. First my best chist I give unto my son William, and all the remainder of my psonall Estate I give unto my daughter Mary, and do nominate and desire Abraham Marshall and Francis Holmes Trustees for my son and daughter and exec^rs, and I desire them to accept the charge and Trouble of such Tuterage, believing they will faithfully discharge their trust . . . [Dated] 21 day of Jan^y, 1727. [Witnesses] Timothy Jackson, Robert Knapton, Matt^w Watson. [*Proved* 15 *Mar.*, 1727-8.]

JOHN MAUDE of Penwell, husbandman.

[lxxx. 53a.] Dated 16 Sept., 1727. In the name of God Amen. I, John Maude of Penwell, in the parish of Barwick in Elmett, in the county of York, Husbandman . . Imp[rs] I give unto Anne Robson, my neice, the summ of Five pounds to be paid on her weding day whensoever it shall happen, And other five pounds to be paid at me and my wife Dorothy decease. Item I give to Mary Maude, my neice, the summe of Eight pound after me and my wife Dorothy decease. Itm I give unto Ruth Maude the summ [of] forty shillings to be paid at me and my wife Dorothy decease. Item I give unto Anne Maude, my neice, the summ of forty shillings to be paid at me and my wife Dorothy decease. Itm I give unto Thomas Maude, my halfe Brother, one freehold house and housing in Scarcroft after me and my wife Dorothy decease, and if the said Thomas Maude dye without Heirs then the said House and Housing to be equally divided amongst the Three sisters. Itm I give unto Charles Hopkinson of Bramham, my nephew, the summ of Twenty shillings to be paid at me and my wife Dorothy decease. Itm I give unto Anne Hopkinson the sum of twenty shillings to be paid at me and my wife Dorothy decease. Item Ralph Hopkinson the summ of Twenty shillings to be paid at me and my wife Dorothy decease. Item I give unto Joseph Maude, my own Brother, the summ of five shillings to be paid at me and my wife Dorothy decease. Item I give unto Dorothy Maude, my wife, one House at Stanks which hath three Dwellings in with a Barne and an Orchard and all belonging to the said House. Itm I leave unto Dorothy, my said wife, all goods and chattels whatsoever, and to be full executrix of this my last will and Testament. . . The mark of John Maude. [Witnesses] Sam: Eamanson, the mark of John Massye, Richard Robinson. [*Proved* 24 *June*, 1728.]

JOHN TAILFORTH of Barwick.

[lxxxi. 696b.] In the name of God Amen. The first day of October in the year of our Lord one thousand seven hundred and thirty, I, John Tailforth of Baricke in Elmet, in the County of York, being something weak in Body but of perfect mind and memory, thanks be given unto God therefore, do make and ordain this to be my last will and Testament in manner and form as following, that is to say, First and principally I give my Soul into the hands of Almighty God who gave it to me, and for my Body I commend it to the Earth to be buried in a Christian manner, nothing doubting but at the generall Resurrection I shall receive the same again by the mighty power of God, and as touching such worldly Estate wherewith it hath pleased Almighty God to bless me with in this life I give and bequeath and dispose the same in manner and form following. First I will that my funeral charges be paid and discharged. Item I ordain George Haist, senior, and William Tailforth to be my Executors, paying such Legacyes as shall be hereafter mentioned. Item I give unto Henry Tailforth twenty pound to be paid twelve months after my decease. Item I give unto Elizabeth Tailforth, the daughter of Henry Tailforth of [? Barroby], five pound to be paid in like manner. Item I give unto Ann Tailforth, the sume of five pound to be paid in like manner. Item I give unto William Tailforth the sum of five pound to be paid in like manner. Item I give unto George Haist, senior, the sum of five pound to be paid in like manner. Item I give unto Elizabeth Horsley the sum of five pound to be paid in like manner. Item I give unto William Asquith the sum of fifteen pound to be paid in like manner. Item I give unto Elisabeth Asquith the sum of five pound to be paid in like manner. Item I give unto Mary Asquith the sum of five pound to be paid in like manner. Item I give unto Ann Asquith the sum of five pound to be paid in like manner. Item I give unto Joseph Tailforth the sum of five pound to be paid in like manner. Item [I] give unto Elizabeth Batley the sum of five pounds to be paid in like manner. Item I give unto Mary, the daughter of James Tailforth, the sume of five pound to be paid in like manner. Item I give unto Benjamin Haist the sum of five pound to be paid in like manner. Item I give unto Elizabeth Ingam the sum of five pound to be paid in like manner. Item I give unto Daniel Tailforth the sum of five pound to be paid in like manner. Item I give unto Elizabeth, the daughter of Daniel Tailforth, the sum of five pound to be paid in like manner. Item I give unto William Pickerd the sum of two pound two shillings to be paid in like manner. Item I give unto Martha, the daughter of Thomas Tailforth, the sum of five pound to be paid in like manner. And if it so happen that any of them dye before the money be paid to go amongst the other sisters, and I do hereby this uterly revoke and disalow all and every other my last Wills and former Testaments, Legacies and bequeaths or excutors in any wise before this time mentioned willed and bequeathed, ratifying and confirming this and none other to be my last Will and Testament. Witness whereof I have hereunto set my hand and seal the day and year abovementioned writen. John Tailforth. Signed sealed and published and pronounced and declared by the said John Tailforth as his last will and Testament in the presence of us, George Watson, James Popleton, John Wood. [*Proved* 8 *February*, 1730-1]

JOHN MOUNSEY of Winmoorhead, joiner.

[lxxxii. 139b.] In the name of God Amen. I, John Mounsey of Winmorehead, in the parish of Barwick in Elmit and county of York, Joyner . . . . Itm I give to my wife, Mary Mounsey, the sume of twelve pounds upon condition that she deliver up all my p'sonall estate assetts and credits to my said Trustee to be in trust for my childe (except all my weareing apparell which I give to her my said wife besides the Twelve pounds afores^{d} to be paid to her in three months after my decease or sooner if money can be raised out of my personall Estate). Item I do appoint my daughter, Martha Mounsey, sole exect^{x} of this my will, and it is also my will and I do appoint my brother in law, Thomas Kilby of Bardsey, Trustee for my s^{d} childe, and it is also my desire that my daughter should be brought up with Sarah Scott of Barwick so long as she is free to take care of her, and Provided my s^{d} daughter shall happen to die before she be at adge or in the minority, then after the truste[e] be paid what shall be due to him I give the fourth part of what is then remaining to my Broth^{r}, Wm Mounsey, and his heirs, I also give other two of the s^{d} four parts if it happen as afores^{d} to my broth^{r}, Thomas Kilby, and the other fourth part I give to Sarah Scott of Barwicke for her care of my childe . . . , [Dated] Twenty second day of July, Anno Domi, 1730. And I do appoint Joseph Brame, Sam^{ll} Dodgson, and the s^{d} Thos Kilbie apprisers of my goods. John Mounsey. [Witnesses] Joseph Brame, Math^{w} Clarkson. [*Proved*, 16 *August*, 1731.]

WILLIAM DAWSON of Kiddal, gentleman.

[lxxxii. 198a.] In the name of God Amen, the nineteenth day of June in the year of our Lord one Thousand seven Hundred and Thirty one, I, Willm Dawson of Kidall, in the county of York, Gent., being something weak of Body but of p'fect mind and memory, thanks be given unto God therefore, do make and ordain this to be my Last will and Testam^{t} in mann^{r} and form following, that is to say, first and principally I give my soul into the hands of Almighty God who gave it to me, and for my Body I com̃end it to the Earth to be buried in a Christian manner, nothing doubting but at the Gen^{r}al Resurec̃con I shall receive the same again by the Mighty power of God, and as touching such worldly Estate wherewith it hath pleased God to bless me in this Life, I give bequeath and dispose the same in mann^{r} and form following. First I will that my fun^{r}al charges be paid and discharged. Item I ordain Elizabeth, my wife, exec^{r}, puting my Brother, David Dawson, in Trustee to Look after the children to see that such Legacys be paid as shall be hereafter menc̃ond. First I give to my wife, Elizabeth, that Land at Lotherton which my brother Thomas farms of me dureing her life, and afterwards to my son William. But in case he happen to dye before he come at age to be equally divided betwixt my two daught^{rs}. Item I give to my son Willm that Land which I have at Fenton and one hundred pounds, the yearly Rent of which is towards Bringing him up. Item I give to my daughter Mary the sum of One Hundred and Fifty pounds. Item I give to my daught^{r} Elizabeth the sum̃ of One Hundred and Fifty pounds, both which sum̃s are to be paid if in case the p'sonal estate will answer. And as for the wood which is upon the land at Lotherton it is my will that the wood should not be felled untill my son come at age, and then to dispose of it as he pleases, and if in case that any of my children hapen to dye before they come at age then to be equally devided amongst the rest, and if they all happen to dye before they come at age to go amongst my Broth^{rs} and sist^{rs} that are then Living. . . . Wm Dawson. [Witnesses]

John Wood, Robert Pearson, David Hutchinson. [*Proved* 14 *Oct.*, 1731.]

WILLIAM SIMPSON of Roundhay, husbandman.

[lxxxii. 220a.] In the name of God, Amen. I, William Simpson of Roundhey, in the county of York, Husbandman, being out of Health but of perfect understanding, do make this my last will and Testam^t^ (of what it hath pleased Almighty God to bestow on me) in manner and form following vizt. I give unto my dear and Loving wife Mary, the tenant right of my farm where I now dwell and all the Goods and Stock thereon, who I make Executrix of this my last will and Testam^t^. Excepting out of the Stock and Goods one silver Tumbler markt S.S., which I give and devise unto Sarah Blackburn, my daughter, and unto her and my son James Simpson I give all my money lent out in whose hands or on what security soever the same is, equally to be divided between them my sd son and daughter. To my son I likewise give the Sheep let out to John Appleyard. In case my sd Executrix name should be made use of to recover any of the said money lent out she shall be saved from any charge. In witness whereof I have hereunto set my hand and Seal this Sixth day of September in the fifth year of th' Reign of our Sovereign Lord King George the second over Great Britain, &c., Annoq' Dom. 1731, the s^d^ James and Sarah to bear half of the funeral charges. William Simpson. [Witnesses] Lancelot Judson, Mary Clarkson, Wm Smeaton.[*Proved* 18 *Jan.*, 1731–2.]

WILLIAM HARGRAVE of Roundhay, yeoman.

[lxxxiv. 378a.] In the name of God, Amen. I, William Hargraves of Roundhay, in the county of York, Yeoman, being of sound and perfect mind and memory, praised be God for the same, do make and ordain this my last Will and Testament in manner and form following, and also I cōmend my soul into the hands of Almighty God and maker, and for my Estate whit [sic] God of his Great goodness hath lent me, my will and mind is that the same be disposed of as follows. Item I give unto my son Christopher five shillings to be paid to him by my executrix hereafter named. It' I give unto my son William five shillings to be paid by my Executrix. It' I give unto my son Thomas Ten shillings to be paid by my Executrix. It' I give and bequeath unto my dear wife all the rest and residue of my Estate of what kind or nature soever. And I do make my dear wife whole and sole executrix . . . Dated 21 February, 1730. William Hargrave. Witnesses Hannah Hargrave, Samuel Renton, his mark, Isabella Wait. [*Passed Seal* 1 *November*, 1736.]

JOHN ELSTON ALIAS PHILLIPS of Roundhay.

[lxxxv. 343a.] In the name of God, Amen. I, John Elston als Phillips of Roundhay, in the parish of Berwick in Elmet and county of York, being in perfect memory and a tollerable state of Health, thanks be to God, least when I come to dye I shall not have due time to make a will, do constitute ordain and declare this my last will and Testament revoking hereby all former Wills and Testaments by me heretofore made in manner following. First and principally I recomend my soul to God and my Body to the Earth to be privatly buried, and as to my Temporal Estate and effects, my funeral expences and all my just and lawfull debts being duly and truly paid, I order and dispose of them in manner and form following. Imp^rs I give unto my nephew Henry Newsham five pounds. To my nephew John Newsham five pounds. To my nephew Thomas Newsham five pounds. To my nephew James Newsham five pounds. To my neece Eliz. Newsham five pounds, the like sum of five pounds I give unto my niece Ann Poslewate. It' I give unto Mrs Eliz. Aspinall Two pounds. It' I leave to Mr Tho: Aspinall three pounds and my old watch. It' I give amongst the servants of the said Mr Tho: Aspinall in case I dye in his house or board with him at the time of my death, and not otherwise, the sum of Twenty shillings to be disposed off as he deems proper amongst them. And lastly as to all other effects undisposed of and which I shall not otherwise dispose of I leave and bequeath them all unto my worthy good friend Cuthbert Constable of Burton Constable, in the county of York, Esqr, whom I appoint sole executor. . . . [Dated 15 January, 1737/8.] John Elston alias Phillips. [Witnesses] Thomas Steel. Mathew Norton. [*Proved* 4 *Sept.*, 1738.]

MICHAEL GRAVELEY of Barwick, yeoman.

[lxxxv. 494.] In the name of God. Amen. I, Michael Graverly of Barwick in Elmet, in ye county of York, Yeoman, being weak and Infirm in body but of sound and perfect mind and memory (praised be God), do make and ordain this my last will and Testament in manner following. Whereas I am seized in fee of and in certain copyhold messuages, lands, Tenements and hereditaments which are parcel and held of ye mannor of Temple Newsam in ye said county of York, And whereas I have surrendered into ye hands of ye Lord of ye same mannor by the hands of Lancelot Hudson one customary Tenant of ye same mannor by surrender bearing equal date herewith, All those my said messuages lands . . . To the use of my last will and Testament. Now therefore my will and meaning is And I do hereby give and devise All those my said messuages lands . . unto my son Michael Graveley, his heirs and assigns for ever. Subject nevertheless to I do hereby expresly charge ye same copyhold tenements and premises with ye payment of ye sum of Twenty pounds of lawful British money unto each and every of my said three daughters, Sarah Gravely, Elizabeth Gravely, and Margaret Gravely, when they shall respectively attain ye age of Twenty one years. [Proviso for survivorship and power of

---

Michael Graveley was buried 28 July, 1739. Apparently his widow married Richard Varley, of Barwick, farmer, 7 Oct., 1740. For Pedigree, see Thoresby Society's vol. 2, p. 54.

entry.] And all my personall estate . . I do truly give and bequeath unto my dear and loving wife, Ann Gravely, and unto my son, Michael Gravely, whom I do hereby make and appoint joint executors. . . . [Dated 25 July, 1739.] Michael Gravely. [Witnesses] Thos Bolland, Chris: Gravely, Wm Fleming. [*Proved* 23 *August*, 1739.]

SARAH SHARP of Barnbow Carrhead, widow.

[lxxxvii. 12.] In the name of God, Amen, the 25th day of December, 1739. I, Sarah Sharp of Barmbow Carrhead, in the parish of Barwick in Elmit, in the county of York, Widow, being very sick and weak in Body, but of perfect mind and memory, thanks be given unto God therefore, calling into mind the mortality of my body and knowing that it is appointed for all men once to dye, do make this my last will and Testament, that is to say, principally and first of all I give and recommend my soul into the hands of God Almighty that gave it, and my Body I recom̃end to the earth to be buryed in decent Christian Burial at the discretion of my Ex$\bar{e}^{rs}$, nothing doubting but at the Judgment I shall receive the same again by the mighty power of God, and as touching such worldly estate wherewith it hath pleased God to bless me in this Life, I give demise and dispose of the same in the following manner and form. Imprimis I give and bequeath unto Sarah Cloudsley (now being Town prentice) a pot and a pan, three pewther doublers, the Great chest, a little Box, a Bed and Beding now being in the parlour, and four pounds in money, to be livered to her and paid her when she approacheth twenty one years of age by my executor hereafter named, and I intrust Thomas Braim of Carrhead, and Samuel Braim, his son, to take care that my will be truly executed. Item I likewise constitute make and ordain Ellmor Balmer my sole executrix of this my last will and testament, all and singular my goods and chattels, utensills and debts by her freely to be possessed and enjoyed. . . . Sarah Sharp, her mark. [Witnesses] Tho: Braim, Hannah Braim, her mark. [*Proved* 1 *March*, 1739.]

ROBERT KNAPTON..

[lxxxvii. 681a.] December ye 9th, 1740. Mem^{r}andum. I, Robt Knapton, being in perfect memory though weak in body, have thought good to make this my last will . .. I give and bequeath to Robt, my second son, the sum of ten pounds to be paid him when he is at the age of twenty one years, also to John, my third son, the sum of Ten pounds when he is of the age of twenty one years. Also to Sarah, my daughter, the sum of fifteen pounds when she is at the age of twenty one years, and if any of them dye before they come to age that their portion shall fall in equall shares among the rest. As for Sarah, my beloved wife, so long as she thinks fit to stay with my executors, to have sufficient maintenance or other wayes to alow her thirty shillings a year dureing her life, and a fether bed and beding and a chest of drawers in the best parlor with some other necessary household goods, which said goods at her discease shall fall to Sarah, my daughter, and all the Rest of my goods, chatle, money, and personal estate whatsoever I give to Willm, my eldest son, and Thomas, my youngest son, as whole and sole executors of this my last will and testament, as witness my hand. Robert Knapton. [Witnesses] Will. Lum, his mark, Matw Watson. [*Proved* 11 *Aug.*, 1742.]

SAMUEL HAIST of Barwick, yeoman.

[lxxxviii. 192.] In the name of God, Amen. I, Samuel Haist of Barwick, in the county of York, Yeoman, being weak and infirm in Body . . . I give and devise all the messuages lands . . . being in Chapel Town otherwise called Chapel Allerton, in the parish of Leeds. I ordaine that child my wife Rebeccay is with to be aire off it . . . if a daughter co-heir, but if it prove a son my will is that my daughter Margrit shall have one hundred pounds out of the personal estate. . . . I order my wife Rebecca and the child that is not born executors if it be a son, if it be a daughter they shall be Joyn'd executors altogether. If it should chance they do both dye without aires then the land to go to my brother Richard Haist and his heirs, and my will is that if both the children dye then I give to my brother in law William Scoles children, Mary, Margrit, William, Samuel, Elizabeth, each of them Ten pounds, and to Henry Samson's children, Margaret, Mary, Catherine and Jane, the sum of fifteen pounds to be equally divided amongst them. . . . I make constitute my good friends Henry Samson, John Gelder, to be my executors in trust for my said children, and as a token of my love to them and for their kindness in accepting this trust I give to each of them one shilling. [Dated 28 March, 1743.] Samuel Haist. [Witnesses] Robt Cawood, John Wad. [*Proved* 7 *June*, 1743.]

WILLIAM BURTON of Barwick, husbandman.

[lxxxviii. 193a.] In the name of God, Amen, the Twenty day of February in the year of our lord 1742. I, William Burton of Berwick, husbandman . . . I order Alice, my wife, whole and sole executor, pay such legacyes [as] shall be hereafter mentioned, my will is that my sister, Sarah Burton, shall have Ten pounds paid Twelve months after my decease. I give unto Jane Walker, my sister, Ten pounds to be paid Twelve months after my decease. I give to Eliz. Knapton, the daughter of Thomas Knapton, Eigh[t] pounds to be paid Twelve months after my decease. I give to my nephew, Thomas Knapton, the son of Thomas Knapton, 2 pounds to be paid Twelve months after my decease. . . . . William Burton, his mark. [Witnesses] John Wood, Richard Varley, William Knapto[n]. [*Proved* 17 *June*, 1743.]

JOHN SMEATON of Barwick, yeoman.

[lxxxviii. 236b.] In the name of God, Amen. I, John Smeaton of the parish of Barrick in Elmit and countrey of York, Yeman, being in helth but callin to mind the unsartenty of this Life, do make this my last will and testiment in manor and form follring, forst I ordor that my dets and funerall expences be forst paide. I leave my estaite real and personall to my childor as the Coman Law directs, for want of such Issue I leave all my Estaite at Swillinton and latel Porston to Elinor Smeaton, my wife, for her liafe, and after my wife decease I leave and give to my nephew, John Smeaton, my estate at Swillinton, Litile Preston, and houses and lande at Leeds. I give and bequeath to my sister Gorge childor one hundred pounds a peese. All my goods in the House called House fornitor I give to my wife, E: Smeaton [also] a hors and a cow as she may chuse out of my stock. I give and bequeath to Joseph Broardbent, my Tenant right in my farm and all my stock in the farm, maner and other tillige, ded goods, quick goods which is not otherwarse dispose of in this will. Whereas I had Twentey pounds of Sara Willson, and Ten shillings intrest I received for it, I order my Executor to pay it when they com at aige, John Willson, Hannah Willson, chilldor of the said Sara Willson. Samuel Broardbent, John Broardbent, Hannah and Anne, sisters to Samuell Broadbent, Ten Guineys a peese. Will Walker I give to him Ten pounds if he sarve his prentiship out to my neuey Joseph Broadbent, according to his indentors, to home I assine him. I Leave pore five pounds to be paid by my Executor to paid at Witkirk the day of my funeral. I leave to my two cozens Two pounds Ten shillings a peese, Mary Holmes, Faith Plats. Nephew John Smeaton I make my executor, and if he dye afore he be Twenty yeare ould I order my bro. Smeaton, Franses Gorge, said Josep Broardbent executors in trust of my real and personal estaite to the use of my sistors chillder and said brother Smeaton childer by sale or otherwise. Forty pounds my wife hath now, twentey of which is now out in John Daniell hands in my name, I leave it to my owne wife, and if the three said executors come to have a Title I do order them or aney of them to pay my wife a hondred pound more then a Bond given her, and I revok all former wills by me maid. In witness whereof I hereunto put my hand and seale this Twenty sixt day of March, 1740. John Smeaton. [Witnesses] Joseph Story, Ann Story, Wm Tolson. [*Proved* 12 *Oct.*, 1743.]

Reg^d^ at Wakefield Deeds Reg^y^ 14 Sept., 1743, in Book 22, page 650, No. 850.

WILLIAM VEVERS of Scholes, gentleman.

[lxxxix. 279a.] I, William Vevers of Scoles, in the parish of Berwick in the county of York, Gentleman, do make and ordain

John Smeaton married Eleanor, daughter of Robert Nalson, of Methley, and died at Swillington. John Smeaton, his nephew and executor, was the celebrated engineer. See Thoresby Society, vol. ii., p. 53, and vol. xii., p. 186.

this my last Will and Testament. . . . I give and devise unto Richard Vevers, my son, and to the Heirs of his Body, All my freehold and copyhold estates whatsoever, scituate, lying, and being in the county of York, the county of the city of York, and in the county of Derby or elsewhere. . . Subject nevertheless unto the payment of Sixty pounds a year unto my loving wife Priscilla, during her natural life to be paid to her at two usual Feasts or days in the year, that is to say, at Whitsontide and Martinmas, by even and equal portions. . . . And in case my said son Richard Vevers happen to die without leaving issue of his Body, Then I give and devise all my said freehold and copyhold estates and every part thereof unto James Brook of Killingbeck, in the said county of York, Gentleman, and to his heirs and assigns for ever, Subject nevertheless to the payment of the said Sixty pounds a year as aforesaid. I also give unto my said loving wife Priscilla the sum of One Hundred pounds, and do hereby make my said wife Priscilla sole executrix. . . . [Dated 31 Jan^{y}, 1744–5.] William Vevers, his mark. [Witnesses] Mary Ward, Ann Dobson, Hen: Whittaker. [*Proved* 22 *March*, 1744–5.]

THOMAS JACKSON of Barwick.

[lcii. 31b.] In the name of God, Amen. I, Thomas Jackson of Barwicke, being weake in body but of sound mind and memory, thanks be to God for the same, do make this my last will and testament in manner and form following. First I recomend my soul to Almighty God and my Body to be buried in a decent manner, in firm hopes of a Resurrection to Eternal Life thro' Jesus Christ our Lord. Next I bequeath my personal estate to my beloved wife for her use while she continue my widow. If she marry again I leave my estate for the use of my children to the Trustees following, vizt, Wm Harper, Rect^{r} of Barwick, Thomas Mallison, my father Willm Jackson, desiring they would secure my estate for the sole use of my children, to be equally divided betwixt them when they shall arrive at the age of one and twenty years. If either of my children dye before they come to age, then the other shall have the whole. If they both dye before they come to age then the Estate shall be divided betwixt my Brother and sister. I leave my wife sole exec^{rx} of this my last Will. Before the Sealing of this will, from the power I have to leave her out of the surrender of the Estate, I desire to leave my daughter Mary Forty pounds, to be paid her as soon as her mother dies, or as soon as she comes to the age of one and Twenty years. Given under my hand and seal this 6th day of June, 1748. Thos Jackson. Signed Sealed and delivered in the presence of Ja^{s} Scholefield, Willm Knapton, Richd Lumb. Past the Seal 19th Sept^{r}, 1748.

GRANTS OF ADMINISTRATION, &c.

1509–10. Thomas Gascayng de Lasyngcroft parochie de Barwik, nuper decessit et nominavit Margaretam uxorem suam executricem, et xij° die mensis Januarii emanauit commissio decano ad probandum dictum testamentum, set non potuit pro matriculacione, et habet festum presens Beate Marie Virginis ad exhibendum inventarium. Non soluit pro approbacione nec commissionis. *In margin* Nota.

[? 1515.] William Taylor de Scolasse nuper decessit.

[? 1515.] John Taylor de Scolasse parochie de Barwyk nuper decessit.

12 Feb., 1563–4. Agnes Danyell, Barmbowe, widow; to James [Jacobus], her son.

28 Jan., 1567–8. Henry Andrewe, Barweke in Elmet; to Mathew Andrewe and Alice Newsome, brother and sister of deceased.

6 Oct., 1575. William Shan, Potterton; to Isabel Shan, his widow.

15 Jan., 1578–9. Thomas Talier, Potterton.

7 May, 1579. Richard Settell; to Katherine Settell, his widow.

21 July, 1581. Frances Powre, Barwicke in Elmet; to William Powre, clerk, her husband.

17 April, 1583. Agnes Scott, Potterton; to Peter Scott.

28 May, 1591. Thomas Raven, Barwick in Elmet; to Robert and John Raven, his brothers.

4 April, 1595. Henry Shan, Potterton; to Alice Shan, his widow.

29 Nov., 1595. Thomas Tate, Potterton; to Elizabeth Tate, his widow.

4 April, 1598. William Ingle, Morwick, parish Barwick in Elmett. Caveat.

3 November, 1600. John Mawson, Potterton; to John Tate, of Barwick in Helmet, to the use of Janet, Robert and Katherine Harrison, children of Thomas Harrison, late of Tadcaster.

11 March, 1605–6. Simon Wairde, Barwick in Elmit; to Peter Wairde.

2 May, 1606. Christopher Brighton, Barret in Elnit; to Janet Brighton, his widow.

8 May, 1606. Christopher Wade, parish Barwick in Elmet; to George Wade.

3 September, 1608. John Craven, Barwicke in Elmet; to Elizabeth Craven, his widow.

4 October, 1610. Christopher Hoowme, Roundhaigh, parish Barwick in Elmet; to Thomas Hoowme.

23 April, 1611. Thomas Tate, Potterton, Barwick in Elmet; to Brigit Tate, his widow.

3 October, 1611. Laurence Harrison, Lasincrofte, par. Barwick; to Isabella Harrison, his widow.

22 December, 1612. Clement Wilson, Roondhey; to Elizabeth Wilson and William Wilson.

8 July, 1614. William Shanne, Potterton; to Frances Shanne, his widow, for her own use and for Richard Shanne, William, Alvered, Henry, Mary, Margaret, and Alice Shanne, his children.

18 April, 1616. Elizabeth Askewithe, Rowndhey; to Elizabeth Askewithe, widow, her mother.

15 December, 1617. Henry Proctor, Barwicke in Elmitt; to Alice Proctor, his widow, for her own use and for George, Henry, and Francis Proctor, his children.

24 Nov., 1620. Robert Jefferson, Barwicke in Elmet; to Peter Bramhall and Ann, his wife, daughter of deceased.

31 Jan., 1620–1. William Norton, Stanckes; to Susan Norton, his widow.

21 May, 1623. Janet Ingle, of Stockinge, par. Barwick in Elmet; to John Ingle of the same place for his own use and for the use of Elizabeth, Ann, and Janet Ingle, daughters of deceased.

9 Dec^r, 1625. Matthew West, of Rowndhay; to Margaret West, his widow.

20 August, 1633. William Duffin, of Roundhey; to Alice Metcalfe, spinster.

20 August, 1633. William Briggs, of Roundhey; to Katherine, wife of Randall Briggs.

20 August, 1633. Thomas Dodgson, of Roundhey; to Jennet Dodgson, his widow.

8 November, 1633. George Procter, clerk, of Barwicke in Elmett; to Robert Procter, of Newton Morker.

24 July, 1634. Mary Briggs, of Roundhey; to Randolph Briggs, of Roundhey.

6 April, 1635. John Hague, of Barwicke; to Mary Hague, his widow.

4 August, 1635. Richard Kirke, of Barwick in Elmet; to Grace Kirke, his widow.

14 October, 1635. James Clough, of Roundhey; to Isabel Clough, his widow.

11 March, 1635–6. Curation of Mary Kirke, daughter of Richard Kirke, of Barwick; to William Brough, of Barwick.

6 May, 1636. Henry Brayme, of Barnebowe Carre; to William Brayme, of the same.

11 July, 1638. John Haige, of Barwick in Elmet; to Mary Haige, his widow, and for use of Mathew Haige, his son.

18 July, 1638. Richard and —— Settle, children of Francis Settle, of Barwick in Elmet; to Thomas Knight, of Barwick, for his own use and for Mary Settle and Katherine Settle, als. Stowe, wife of Samuel Stowe, sisters of deceased.

1638. Oct. 3. Francis Gowthwaite, of Parlington Hollings; to Anne Gowthwaite, for William Gowthwaite, of Parlington.

1638. Oct. 27. Ann Gowthwaite, of Lazincrofte, parish Barwick in Elmet; to William Gouthwaite, of Parlington.

1638. Dec. 6. John Wright, of Barwick in Elmet; to Elizabeth Wright, his widow.

1638–9. March 14. Martin Clough, of Winmoorhead, parish Barwick in Elmet, with tuition of Jane, Isabel, Robert, Elizabeth, Martin, Katherine, and James Clough, his children; to Elizabeth Clough, his widow.

1639. Oct. 4. Walter Leper, of Barnebow Carr; to Ann Leper, his widow.
1669. June 20. Lawrence Hill, of Stanks, Barwick in Elmet; to Helen Hill, widow, for her use and for John and Ann, his children.
1671. April 24. George Gascoine, of Shippen; to Sir Thomas Gascoine, Knight, during minority of Thomas and John Gascoine, children of deceased.
1673. June 2. Robert Haigh, of Barwick in Elmet; to Elizabeth Haigh, his widow.
1676-7. Jan. 12. Richard Vevers, of Potterton; to William Vevers, his son.
1683. June 14. James Prince, of Barwick in Elmet; to Alice Prince, his widow.
1685-6. Jan. 22. William Taylor, of Barwick in Elmet; to Robert Riddell.
1689. Aug. 22. Thomas Tate, of Barwick in Elmet; to Thomas Tate, his son.
1691. Aug. 10. Christopher Hill, of Barwick; to Margaret Hill, his widow.
1694. Dec. 22. Matthew Holmes, of Barwick in Elmet; to Mary Holmes, his widow.
1698. Oct. 6. Alice Banks, of Roundhay, Barwick in Elmet; to Peter Banks, her husband.
1699-1700. Feb. 3. Sara Dyneley, of Barwick in Elmet; to Phineas Lee, her sister's son.
1703. July 6. Robert Shore, of Barwick; to Arthur Shore.
1703. Dec. 1. Eliza Birkhead, of Barwick in Elmet; to John Birkhead.
1706-7. Mar. 12. George Spink, of Scholes, parish of Barwick; to Jeremiah and William, his sons.
1718. July 10. Michael Eastburne, of Winmoorside, parish Barwick in Elmet; to Dorothy, his widow.
1718. Aug. 9. Richard Tarbottom, of Barwick in Elmet; to Alice, his widow.
1720. Dec. 20. Mark Dennison, of Potterton; to Elizabeth, wife of Thomas Smith, his daughter. (Eliz. Dennison, his widow, renounced.)
1724. April 24. Richard Robinson, of Barwick in Elmet; to Rosamond, his widow.
1727-8. Jan. 26. Matthew Robinson, of Garforth side, par. Barwick; to Thomas Robinson, creditor.
1729. May 18. John Shippin, of Whinmoor, Barwick in Elmet; to Ann, his widow.
1731. Aug. 16. Tuition of the person and portion of Martha Mounsey, infant daughter of John Mounsey, of Barwick in Elmet; to Thomas Killey, her uncle.
1731. Oct. 14. Tuition of Mary, Elizabeth and William Dawson, children of William Dawson, late of Kidall, Barwick in Elmet; to Elizabeth Dawson, their mother.

1732. July 20. John Baynes, of Lazincroft, Barwick in Elmet; to William Fleming, principal creditor.

1732–3. March 1. Robert Scope, of Kiddall Lane end, Barwick in Elmet; to John Shutt, nephew.

1734. Oct. 9. Richard Vevers, of Potterton, Barwick in Elmet; to James Oates, principal creditor.

1735. June 28. John Burlend, of Potterton; to Elizabeth, his widow.

1739. Feb. 7. William Holmes, of Roundhay; to Martha, his widow.

1739. Aug. 23. Curation of person and portion of Michael Graveley, aged 15 years, son of Michael Graveley, of Barwick in Elmet; to Ann Graveley, widow, his mother.

1740. July 2. William Prince, of Roundhay, parish of Thorner; to Thomas Prince, his only brother.

1740–1. Feb. 27. William Johnson, of Scholes; to Mary, his widow.

1741–2. March 4. John Upton, of Morwick; to Matthew Upton, his son and principal creditor.

1742–3. Jan. 19. John Abbot, of Barwick in Elmet; to Mary, his widow.

1743. May 2. Robert Dodgson, of Barwick in Elmet; to Ann, his widow.

1743. June 11. Ann Dodgson, of Barwick in Elmet, widow; to Wm Walton and Ann, the wife of James Priestman, her son and daughter.

1743. June 15. Robert Dodgson, of Barwick in Elmet; to Ann Hudson, widow, his sister.

1744–5. Jan. 22. Joseph Lamb, of Barwick in Elmet; to Sarah, his widow.

1745. May 6. John Wood, of Winmoor, Barwick in Elmet; to William Watson in right of Mary, his wife, relict of deceased.

1745. Dec. 28. Robert Doughty, of Barwick in Elmet; to Jonas Doughty and Henry Doughty, his brothers.

BARWICK-IN-ELMET REGISTER.

TRANSCRIPTS AT YORK.

BAPTIZATI 1600

Marcij	Elizabeth Brayme fili Richi. Brayme bapti. 25
Aprilis	Thomas filius thome Tayte de Potter. bapti. 3°
	Thomas filius Johanni Ellis Armigr bapti. 6°
	Clara ffenton filia Abraha. bapti. 2°
	Richardus filius Cuthbt Massie bapti. 26
	Willimus Merley filius Christopheri bapti. 14°.
Maij	Elizabeth Couper filia Mathej bapti. 9°
	Samuelis Richmund fili Georgij bapti. 12°
	Sicely filia Alexandr Hutchinson bapti. 25°
Juiij	Martinus Wade de Barwicke bapti. 1°
	Johannes Potter fili Richi. bapti. 22°
Augustij	Robertus filius Johanni Ingle de Scholes bapti. 26°
	Maria filia Wittmi Shan de Potter. bapti. 27°
Septembris	Willmi. fili Willmi. Leadbeater bapti. 19°
Octobris	Richardus Houdill fill Mathei bapti. 15°
	Alicea fili Wittia Sawer bapti. 24°
	Alicea fitti Robti. Tayte bapti. 26°
	Gulielmus fili Richi Veners de Scholes bapti. 26°
	Samuelis filius Robti. Heage 29°
	Johannes filius Wittm ffeather 23°
Decembris	Michaelis filius Petri Hill 14°
	Georgius filius Anthony Styane et Elena Wilkinson Illegit. bapti. 24
	Jana West filia Mathei West 30°
Februarij	Willmi. fili Robti. ffeilde de Brownemore 22°
	Johannes fili Joh. Horsley 22°
Marcij	Isabell filia Robti. Sayner de scholes 25°

MARITI.

Octobris	ffranciscus Richardson et Alicia Shippen nupti fuerunt 14°
Nouembris	Gulielmus Hopwoode et Elizabetham Daye nupti fuerunt 23°
Januarij	Randulphus Winterburne et Elena Beuerley nupti fuerunt 2°

SEPULTI.

Maij	Rosamunda filia Richardi Kirke sepulta 6°
	Samuelis filius Georgij Richmund sepultus 23°
	Matheus Cauderowe de Schooles sep. 24°
Augustij	Editha Ingle uxor Johan de Schooles sepult. 27°
	ffrancisca filia Johanni Crauen 27°
	Robt filius Johis Ingle Infans sept. 29°
Septembris	Maria uxor Wittmi ffarburne 9°
	Wittm ffarburne de Barwicke sep. 11°

Octobris Maria filia volentyne Toppliffe 3°
Johannes infans Robt. Turner 18°
Jonie Infans Thome Rawson sept. 19°
ffeb. ffranciscus Kaye de Scholes sepult. 23°
Isabella Sayner de Scholes sept. 24
Francescus Kaye de Scho. sept. 23
Marcij Margeria Brigge uxor Leonardi sept. 7°

Barwicke in Elmet. A copie of the Register this p'sent yeare 1601 by os Robert Hayton, Curate

Willm. Daniel
Willm. Tayte
Law. West
Willm. Hopwood
Churchwardens

BAPTIZATI

Marcij Elizabeth filli Witt Rawson bapta. 29°
Aprilis Richardus Taylio' filius Thome de Barwicke 5to
Maij Tho: filius Joh. Robinsonne 12°
Junij Alicea filia Jo: Ellis de Kiddall Ar. 3°
Septembris Samuelis filius Henrici Brayme 13°
Michaelis filius Wittm Hopwode 29
Octobris Jana filia Wittm Grenewod de Scholes 16°
Suzanna Askwith filia Lawrencij de Roundhaye 22°
Wittm filius Willmi. Jeffraysõ de barwicke bapti. 28°
Nouember Wittm filius Wittm Leaceter 28
Januarij Isabella filia Roberti Crosse de Stancke 6°
Jeneta filia Christopheri Cockson 24
ffebruaij Jana filia Christopheri Merley 13°
Richardus filius Robti. White de Barwicke 14°
Jana filia Tho. Saunderson de Barwicke 14°
Wittmi filius Willm. Tayte de Scholes 17°
Ricardus filius Willmi. Broadley de Barwicke 21°
Vera Coopia Concordan' cũ originali Robt Haytõ, Curate

MARITI

Aprilis Samuellis Wallbancke et Katherina Mitchell 2°
Augustij Johannes Lawe et Elizabetha Elismought 23°
Septembris Wittm Daniell et Isabella Roydhouse 1°
Nouembris Lawrentius Glouer et Jana Chadwicke 17°
Decembris Johannes Dawson et Agneta Douglas 21°
Januarij Georgius Baynes et Elizabetha Hemsworth 19°

SEPULTI.

Aprilis Samuelis Heage filius Roberti de Barwicke 1°
Wittm Sawer de Barwicke 14°
Maij Jenet Mitton vidua de Barwicke 4°
Rauphe Worthington de Barwicke 15°
Junij Alicea filia Johanni Ellis de Kiddall 6°
Julij Elizabetha filia Mathei Couper de Barwicke 1°
Augustij Johannes Bedford de Roundhay 11°
Septembris Jana Mitton de Bãrk 6°
October Johannes filius Roberti Turner de Stancke 14

Nouembris Johannes filius Tho. Terrington 27°
ffebruarij Jana Bradbery 6°
Elena Hardcastell vidua de Barw. 14°
Elizabetha Hart 16
Johan filia Henrici Trott 24
Marcij Johannes filius Tho. Tompson 3°
Johànnes filius Johanni Horsley 19°

An extract out of the Register booke of all the christnings, marriages, and burialls in the parish of Barwicke in Elmett since the 25th daye of March, Anno Dñi 1631 to the 25th daie of March last past, 1632.

CHRISTENINGS Anno Domini 1631.

Anne, the daughter of John Scotte of Barwicke in Elmett, June 5th
Thomas, the sonne of Richard Potter of the same, June 12th
Marie, the daughter of Richard Shan of Potterton, June 13th
Thomas, the sonne of Wiłłm Taite of the same, June 17th
Anne, the daughter of Wiłłm Haige of Barwicke, June 19th
Alice, the daughter of Xpofer Ibbison of Potterton, eiusd' 26th
Wiłłm, the sonne of Tho. Tirrington of Shippen, July 24th
Richard, the sonne of Fran. Turner of Stankes, eod. die eiusd'
Grace, the daughter of Jo. Hemsworth of Potterton, August 21th
Anne, the daughter of Jo. Daniell of the same, August 28th
Henrie, the sonne of Henrie Shuttleworth of Scoles, September 22th
Matthew, the sonne of Gualter Leper of Barmebow, September 25th
Matthew, the sonne of Randall Constable of Grimsedike, October 2d
Richard, the sonne of Wm. Wilcocke of Garforth More, October 9th
Richard, the sonne of Richard Jackeson of Scoles, Nouember 27th
Jeremie, the sonne of Wiłłm Strickland of Scoles, December 1st
Elizabeth, the daughter of Jo. Daniell of Rhowndhey, eiusd' 4th
Elizabeth, the daughter of Rich. Taite of Potterton Moreside, Jan. 22
Anne, the daughter of Raiphe Dawson of Scoles, Februarie 5th
Margaret, the daughter of Peter Hill of Stanckes, eiusd' 12th
Hellen, the daughter of Jo. Feather of Scoles, eiusd' 22th

MARRIAGES Anno Domini 1631

Edward Eddeant and Margaret Auesonne, Maye 30th
Willm. Brigs of Barwick and Elizabeth Caluerley, June 29th
Thomas Redman and Sara Howdell of Shippen, August 1st
Jo. Smith and Jane Pearesonne of Barwick, October 2d
Peter Hill and Alice Hardcastle of Stankes, November 16th
Martine West and Grace Wilsonne of Rhowndhey, Januarie 26th
Henrie Wraye and Marie Dodshon of the same, eiusd' 27th
Willm. Prince and Anne Harrison of Barwick, eiusd' 29th
Raiph Collet and Anne Veuers, married with a license from the Court, February 13th

BURIALLS, Anno Domini 1631.

Thomas Tirrington of Shippen, Aprill 13th
Rich. Nutter of Barwick in Elmet, eiusd' 30th
Elizabeth, the wife of Cuth. Haige of Barwick, May 4th
Richard, the sonne of Wiłłm Brigs of Rhowndey, eiusd' 7th

Katherine Johnsonne of Scoles, June 3d
Elizabeth Bywater of the same, eiusd' 6th
Alice Crofte of Barwick in Elmett, June 9th
Richard Hurst of the same, eiusdem 14th
Elizabeth, the daughter of Anne Cooke, eiusd' 19th
Willm Haitonne of Wynnemore-side, July 10th
Rosamond, the daughter of Randall Brigs, eiusd' 17th
Martine, the sonne of Martine Clough, August 6th
Willm, the sonne of Rich. Taite of Scoles, eiusd' 12th
Susan Nortonne, widdowe, of Scoles aforesaid, September 6th
Francis, the daughter of Jo. More, eiusd' 20th
Anne, the wife of Willm Settle of Potterton, eiusd' 28th
Brian Isotteson of Barwicke in Elmett, October 26th
Elizabeth Grafton of Barwick aforesaid, Nouember 22th
Elizabeth, the daughter of Martine Cloughe, December 27th
Jo. Hardcastle of Barwicke in Elmett, Januarie 7th
Thomas, the sonne of Peter Hillam of Scoles, eiusd' 29th
Thomas, the sonne of Rich. Potter of Barwick, February 6th
Martine, the sonne of Rich. Slaiter of Stankes, eiusd' 12th
Marie, the wife of Willm Feather of Scoles, eiusd' 20th
Willm Duffeild of Rhowndheye, eiusdem 28th
Concordat cum originali. Datum apud Baruicum, 27° die mensis Septembris, examinat'qe per Jacobum Forster, clerum curat' ibidem et Henrici Roote, H. R. signũ, Richard Shan, Thomas Terringtoon, Willm Brigs, Gardianos veteres, Anno Domini 1631

A true copie or extract taken out of the register booke of all the christenings, marriages, and burialls within the parish of Barwicke in Elmet, within the countie of Yorke, from the fiue and twentieth daye of March, Anno Domini 1632, to the fiue and twentieth daie of March last past, Anno Domini Dei 1633.

CHRISTENINGES, 1632.

Martine, the sonne of James Atkinson of Pottertonne, Aprill 3d
Anne, the daughter of Willm Veuers of Scoles, eiusd' 8th
Elizabeth, the daughter of Richard Knapton of Barwicke, eiusd' 15th
Isabell, Marie and Katherine, daughters of Willm Brigs, eiusd' May 2d
Willm, the sonne of Robert Veners of Scoles, eiusd' 10th
Alice, the daughter of Francis Ellis, gent., of Kidhall, eiusd' 13th
Anne, the daughter of Tho. Robinson of Garforth more, eiusd' cod'
John, the sonne of John Smith of Barwicke in Elmett, June 10th
John, the sonne of Jo. Burnell of Rhowndhey, July 1st
Brian, the sonne of Jo. Mitchell of the same, eiusd' 8th
John, the sonne of Willm Slaiter of Barwicke in Elmett, eiusd' 25th
*John, the sonne of Thomas Shippen of Barmebowe, August 5th
Lawrence, the sonne of Christofer Lumme of Grimesdike, eiusd' 12th
Thomas, the sonne of Willm Prince of Barwicke, eiusd' 26th
Katherine, the daughter of Jo. More of the same, eiusd' eod'
Math. and Robt., the sonnes of Martine West of Rhowndhey, Sep. 1st
Willm, the sonne of Willm Brame of Barmebowe, eiusd' 2d

*William Schepyn was taxed 4d. at Barwick in the Poll Tax of 1379.

Marie, the daughter of Willm Burnell of Rhowndhey, eiusd' 23th
Elizabeth, the daughter of Michaell Hill of Stankes, eiusd' 30th
Rosamond, the daughter of Geo. Lister of Rhowndhey, eiusd' eod'
Willm, the sonne of Raiphe Collett of Barwicke, Nouember 11th
Elizabeth, the daughter of Martine Clough of Rhowndhey, eiusd' 25th
John, the sonne of Jo. Thompsonne of Garforth More, eiusd' eod'
Agnes, the daughter of Jo. Mawe of the same, December 23th
Aluerid, the sonne of Richard Veuers of Scoles, January 9th
Thomas, the sonne of Cuth. Brigs of Barwicke, eiusd' 13th
John, the sonne of Jo. Taylor of Morwicke, eiusd' 22th
John, the sonne of Aquila Ferrar of Scoles, eiusd' 27th
Geo., the sonne of Jo. Wright of Barwicke, eiusd' eod'
Rich., the sonne of Willm Brigs of Rhowndhey, February 11th
Rich., the sonne of Rich. Taite of Scoles, eiusd' 17th
Alice, the daughter of Walter Leeper of Barmebow, eiusd' eod'
Jo., the sonne of Jo. Ingle of Grimsedike, March 12th
Tho., the sonne of Thomas Jordaine of Scoles, eiusd' 13th

MARRIAGES.

Thomas Jordaine and Jaine Howdell of Scoles, May 27th
Geo. Handley and Hellen Veners of the same, eiusd' 28th
Leonard Pickering and Elizabeth Daniell of Barmebow, July 1st
Robert Bellabie and Elizabeth Smith of Wynmore, September 2d
Cuthbert Haige and Anne Wiley of Barwicke, November 30th
Jo. Potter and Mawde Whincop of Potterton, February 12th

BURIALLS.

Elizabeth, the wife of Willm Prince of Barwicke in Elmett, Aprill 3d
A child still borne, the issue of Leo. Thompsonne of Rhowd., eiusd' 18th
Isabell, the daughter of Willm Brigs of Barwicke, May 4th
Marie, another of the daughters of the said Willm, eiusd' 7th
Katherine, another of the daughters of the same, eiusd' 14th
Alice, the daughter of Francis Ellis of Kidhall, gent', eiusd' eod'
Thomas Dodgshonne of Rhowndehey, July 7th
Thomas Saundersonne of Barwicke in Elmett, August 1st
Anne, the wife of Richard Kirke of the same, eiusd' 8th
Jo. Haige of the towne of Barwicke in Elmett, September 7th
Richard Potter of the same towne was in like manner buried eiusd' 11
Edith, wife of the said Richard Potter, October 6th
Anne, the daughter of Rich. Potter of Potterton, eiusd' eod'
Joseph, the sonne of Willm Howdell of Scoles, eiusd' 7th
Anne, the daughter of Jo. Abdie of Barwicke, November 10th
Rich., the sonne of Willm Wilcocke of Garforth more, eiusd' 14th
Christofer Haige of the towne of Barwicke in Elmett, December 2d
Jane, the mother of Richard Cooke of Scoles, eiusd' 9th
Katherine Sainer, widdowe, of the same Towne, eiusd' 13th
Anne, the daughter of Thomas Robinson of Garforth, eiusd' 23th
Anne, the wife of Cuthbert Haige of Barwicke, January 9th
Thomas, the sonne of Alexander Robinson of Scoles, eiusd' 26th
Jo., the sonne of Jo. Norton of Barwicke in Elmett, February 25th
Alice Cowper, widdowe, of the same Towne, March 6th

Concordat cum originali exam[t] 22th Aprilis, Anno Domini 1633. per Jacobum Forster, clerum vicarium ibidem. Henric's Ellys, William Brame, William Glover, John Daniell, Gardianos, Anno Dni. 1632.

An Extract or true copie of all the christninges, marriages, and burialls within the parish of Barwicke in Elmett, the whole yeare last past, taken out of the Regester Booke of the said parishe, the 25th daie of March, Anno Domini 1634, from 25th March, 1633 to the 25th March, 1634.

CHRISTNINGS.

Richard, the sonne of Richard Hill of Stanks, 31 March
Marie, the daughter of Thomas Robinson of Scoles, eod' die
John, the sonne of George Haundeleye of Morwicke, 7 Aprilis
Margaret, the daughter of Richard Ingle of Scoles, eod. die
Katherine, the daughter of Randall Brigs of Rowndhey, 13 eiusd'
Hester, the daughter of Andrew Ellis of Barwicke, 23° eiusd'
Marie, the daughter of Richard Shippen of Barmebow, eod. die
Elizabeth, the daughter of Willm Massie of Stockeing, 25° eiusd'
John, the sonne of Richard Tailor of Barwicke, 16° May
John, the sonne of John Taite of Scoles, 30 eiusd'
Robert, the sonne of John Daniell of Potterton, 3° July
Laurence, the sonne of Leonard Pickering of Barmbow, 11° Augusti
Robert, the sonne of Willm Brigs of Barwicke, 18 eiusd'
Mathew, the sonne of John Bailie of Rhowndhey, eod' die
Joseph, the sonne of Willm Stricklande of Scoles, 25° eiusd'
Dorathie, the daughter of Francis Heardson of Barwicke, eod' die
Robert, the sonne of Henrie Shuttleworth of Scoles, eod' die
Elizabeth, the daughter of Alexander Robinson of Scoles, 8° Septem.
Marie, the daughter of John Kirkebie of Potterton, 15° eiusd'
Martine, the sonne of Willm Taite of Potterton, 23° Octobris
Thomas, the sonne of Tho. Robinson of Garforth moreside, 24° Nouembris
Thomas, the sonne of Henrie Haworth, eiusd' loci, eod' die
Thomas, the sonne of Richard Hargraue of Rowndhey, eod' die
Martine, the sonne of Edward Metcalfe of Rhowndhey, 15° Decembris
George, the sonne of Francis Ellis of Kidhall, gent., 23° January
Alice, the daughter of John Potter of Potterton, 2° Februarii
Anne, the daughter of Richard Willsonne of Scoles, 9° eiusd'
Elizabeth, the daughter of Rich. Shan of Potterton, 12° Martij
Elizabeth, the daughter of Tho. Bellas of Barwicke, eod. die
Elizabeth, the daughter of John Prince of Barwicke, 16° eiusd.
John, the sonne of Willm Gillsonne of Scoles, 23 eiusd'

MARRIAGES.

Richard Willsonne and Hellen Simpson of Scoles, 29° Junij
Richard Stead and Marie Tailor of Morwicke, 21° Augustij
Richard Turner and Mercie Addie of Barwicke, 22° eiusd'
Robert Richmond and Katherine Usher of Barwicke, 26° eiusd'
Willm Feather and Hellen Topcliffe of Scoles, 19° Septembris
Rich. Winders and Elizabeth Howdell of Potterton, 24° Nouembris

Brian Bullocke and Jane Gibson of Barwicke, 28° eiusd'
John Beedhill and Anne Hardcastle of Scoles, 27° January

BURIALLS.

Willm, the sonne of Mage Pollard of Abberforth, 19° May
John Stowe of Barwicke in Elmett, 24° eiusd'
Thomas, the sonne of Cuthbert Brigs of Barwicke, 25° eiusd'
Willm Brigs the elder of Rhowndhey, 29° eiusd'
James, the sonne of Willm Slaiter of Barwicke, 8° Julij
Margarett, the daughter of John Haige of Barwicke, 11° eiusd'
Margarett, the daughter of Tho. Bellas of Barwicke, 15° eiusd'
George, the sonne of John Wright of Barwicke, 17° eiusd'
Willm, the sonne of Ralph Collett of Barwicke, 23° eiusd'
Anne, the daughter of John Mawe of Garforth moreside, 2° Augusti
Marie, the daughter of Henrie Nicholson of Barwicke, 13° eiusd'
An infant, unbaptized, of Jo. Hemsworths of Potterton, 5° Octobris
John Holmes, a child brought up at Morwicke, 23° eiusd'
An Infant, unbaptized, of Ralph Haires of Potterton, 5° Nouembris
Elizabeth, the daughter of Alexander Robinson of Scoles, 28° eiusd'
Marie Brigs, single woman, at Rhowndheye, 29° eiusd'
*Elizabeth Askewicke, widdowe, of Rhowndhey, 23° Decembris
Elizabeth, the wife of Cuthbert Brigs of Barwicke, 25° eiusd'
Ignoramus Clapeham, gentleman, of Barmebow, 6° Januarij
Elizabeth, the daughter of Tho. Gascoigne, Esquier, 4 Februarij
John Mitton of Barwicke in Elmett, 2° Martij
Examinat' et concordat cum originali his testibus quorum noia et cognoiã subscribuntur. Ja. Forster, cler., ibid. Willm Veuers, Richard Massie M his marke, Lawrence West, Willm Daniell W his marke, Churchwardens.

An extract or true Copie taken out of the Register booke of the parishe of Barwicke in Elmett of all the Christenings, Marriages, and burialls within the said Mannor the yeare Anno Domini 1634.

CHRISTENINGS.

Isabell, the daughter of Richard Knapton of Barwicke in Elmett, 31th March
Rosamond, the daughter of Willm Braime of Barmeboughe, 3° Aprill
Marie, the daughter of Brian Bullocke of Barwicke in Elmett, 8° eiusd'
Anne, the daughter of Richard Taite of Potterton Moreside, 20 eiusd'
Stephen, the sonne of John Shoesmith of Stockeinge, 25 May
Richard, the sonne of Willm Veners of Scoles, 8 June
Peter, the sonne of Peter Hill of the Stankes, 22 eiusd'
Christofer, the sonne of Michaell Hill of the Stankes, 2 Julie
Josuah, the sonne of Richard Turner of Barwicke in Elmett, 6 eiusd'
Anne, the daughter of Samuell Braime of Barmeboughe, die eodem
Marie, the daughter of John Mawe of Garforth Moreside, 27 eiusd'
Marie, the daughter of Richarde Tailor of Barwick in Elmett, 4 August
Matthewe, the sonne of John Mitchell of Rhowndhey parke, 21 September

*Probate of her Will was granted at York 24 July, 1634, to Robert Askewith, her son, one of the executors On the 1 Sept, 1634, Probate of the Will of George Pearson, of Barwick in Elmet, was granted at York to Thomas Crofte and Henry Crofte, co-executors. In neither case is the Will on record.

Francis, the daughter of Leonard Thompsonne of Rhowndhey, 28 eiusd'
John, the sonne of Richard Jackeson of Barwicke in Elmett, 19 October
Margarett, the daughter of John Gowthwaite of Scoles, 2 Nouember
Wiłłm, the sonne of George Lister of Rhowndhey parke, 17 eiusd'
Martine, the sonne of Martine Cloughe of Rhowndhey, 19 eiusd'
Leonard, the sonne of Leonard Pickering of Barmebough, 7 December
Thomasine, the daughter of John Feather of Scoles, 14 eiusd'
Thomas, the sonne of John Taite of Scoles, 21 Januarie
John, the sonne of Wiłłm Glouer of Rhowndhey, 26 eiusd'
Martia, the daughter of John Smith of Barwicke in Elmett, 1 Februarie
Marke, the sonne of Wiłłm Brearecliffe of Barwicke in Elmett, 5 eiusd'
Katherine, the daughter of Alexander Robinsonne of Roall, eodem die
Peter, the sonne of John Beckett of Grimesdike, 16 eiusd'
Michaell, the sonne of John Bailie of Rhowndhey parke, eodem die
Richard, the sonne of George Handley of Morwicke, 22 eiusd'
Wiłłm, the sonne of John Rodes of Wynnemore, 1 March
Margarett, the daughter of Ralphe Haire of Potterton Moreside, 15 eiusd'
Margaret, the daughter of Alexander Robinsonne of Scoles, eodem die
Elizabeth, the daughter of Thomas Robinson of Garforth Moreside, eodem die

MARRIAGES.

James Dearedon of Stankes and Elizabeth Hardwicke, 29 September
John Simpsonne and Elizabeth Thompsonne of Garforth Moreside, 2 Nouember
Arthur Burtonne of Potterton and Anne Haire of Kidhall, 12 eiusd'
Alexander Robinsonne of Roall and Anne Nutter of Potterton, 21 Januarie

BURIALLS.

Elizabeth, the wife of John Thompsonne of Potterton, 27 Aprill
Magdalen Holidaye, widdowe, of Potterton, eodem die
Stephen, the sonne of John Shoesmith of Stockeinge, 28 Maye
Grace, the daughter of John Beedehill of Scoles, 5 June
Margarett, the wife of Michaell Willsonne of Rhowndhey, 6 eiusd'
Francis, the daughter of Lawrence Jenkinson of Barwick, 15 Julie
Susanna, the daughter of John Kirkeby of Pottertonne, 1 August
Richard, the sonne of Tho. Wood of Barwicke in Elmett, 4° eiusd'
Hellen, the daughter of Wiłłm Ball of Pottertonne, 7 September
Cuthbert Brigs of Barwick in Elmett, 2 Nouember
John, the sonne of Richard Jackesonne of Barwick in Elmet, 17 eiusd'
Alice, the wife of George Lister of Rhowndhey parke 25 eiusd'
Elizabeth Hewbie, widdowe, of Rhowndhey parke, 29 eiusd'
Jacobus Cloughe of Rhowndhey parke, 4 Januarie
The widow of Wothersomme, whose name is unknowne, 2 Februarie
Elizabeth Dollie of Barmeboughe, 5 eiusd'
Katherine, the daughter of Alexander Robinson of Roall, 7 eiusd'
Jaine Gaiforth, a poore apprentice, of Garforth Moreside, 27 eiusd'

Richard Kirke of Barwicke in Elmett, 1 March
Examinatur concordare cum originali. Per Willm Bridges, cler. ibid. Willm Daniell, William Veuers, Richard Massie, Laurence West, Gardianos.

BARWICKE IN ELMETT.

An Extract or true copie taken out of the Register Booke of the parish Church of Barwicke in Elmett in the Countie of Yorke of all the Christenings, Marriages, and Burialls which haue beene in the said parish the yeare last past, to wit, from the 25th daye of March, Anno Domini 1635, till the 25th daie of March, Anno Domini 1636.

CHRISTENINGES.

Edward, the sonne of John Haighe of Barwicke, Aprill 12
Robert, the sonne of Willm Prince of Barwick, Aprill 26
Alice, the daughter of Willm. Massie of Stocking, Aprill 28
Ralph, the sonne of Ralph Collett of Barwick, May 7
Willm., the sonne of Tho. Harrison of Barmbowe, May 17
Robert, the sonne of Mr. Shereburne of Braiton, May 27
Brigit, the daughter of Mart. West of Rowndhey, June 6
Thomas, the sonne of Willm. Brigs of Rhowndhey, June 21
John, the sonne of Tho. Terrington of Shippen, June 24
Willm, the sonne of Rich. Veuers of Winmoore, Julie 5
Margaret, the daughter of John Beedhill of Scoles, Julie 8
Elizabeth, the daughter of Henrie Roote of Barwick, Julie 19
Robert, the sonne of Willm Haighe of Barwicke, August 2
Richard, the sonne of John Potter of Pottertonne, August 23
Peter, the sonne of Willm. Strickland of Scoles, August 30
Catherine, the daughter of Jo. Jackson of Rowndhey, September 17
Johanna, the daughter of Rich. Shippen of Barmbow, September 25
Henrie, the sonne of Jo. Simpson of Garforth more, October 4
Francis, the daughter of Jo. Daniell of Potterton, October 4
Isabell, the daughter of Tho. Jordaine of Scoles, October 4
Marie, the daughter of Christofer Ibbison of Potterton, October 4
Marie, the daughter of Jo. Shoesmith of Stocking, Nouember 15
Jeffery, the sonne of Rich. Jackson of Barwicke, December 13
Lawrence, the sonne of Mich. Hill of Stanks, December 16
Marie, the daughter of Jo. Tailor of Morwicke, December 16
Eliz. and Jere, daughters of Willm. Taite of Potterton, Januarie 6
Hellen, the daughter of George Hillton of Morwick, Januarie 17
Jane, the daughter of Thomas Sainer of Scoles, Februarie 3
Thomas, the sonne of Jo. Corden of Barwick, Februarie 5
Willm., the sonne of Hen. Haworth of Garforth More, Februarie 7
Grace, the daughter of Robt. Bellabie of Winne-more, Februarie 14
Samuell, the sonne of John Wright of Barwicke, March 20

MARRIAGES.

James Forster, clerke, and Marie Rawson of Barwick, October 1
Willm Hurst and Anne Broadley of Barwick, Nouember 8
Thomas Veuers and Eliz. Rawsonne of Barwick, Januarie 13
Stephen Shippen and Isab. Mounsey of Morwick, Februarie 8

BURIALLS.

Walter Caluerleye of Barwicke in Elmett, April 11
Robert Settle of Pottertonne, Aprill 16
Thomas, the sonne of John Taite of Scoles, Aprill 18
Robert, the sonne of Cuthbert Haighe of Barwick, Maye 23
Robert, the sonne of Willm Prince of Barwick, June 5
Thomas Rawsonne of Barwick in Elmett, June 9
Margaret, the daughter of Jo. Beedhill of Scoles, Julie 11
Marie, the wife of Willm Ball of Potterton, August 8
Elizabeth Greenewood, widdow, of Scoles, August 10
Thomas Tailor of Barwick in Elmett, October 1
A childe, unbaptized, the sonne of Jo. Prince, October 17
Alexander, the sonne of Robert Lee of Leedes, October 18
Marie, the daughter of Jo. Kirkebie of Potterton, October 19
Robert Butler of Barwick in Elmett, December 8
Robert Eldred of Barwicke in Elmett, December 12
Hellen, the daughter of Jo. Feather of Scoles, January 11
Ralph Mawe of Garforth-more, Januarie 17
Marie, the daughter of Jo. Mawe of Garforth-more, January 20
Willm Broadley of Barwicke in Elmett, Januarie 22
Elizabeth Crauen, widdowe, of Barwicke, Februarie 18
Examinatur concordare cum Registro 25° die Martij, 1636. Testibus his subscriptis, Willm Bridges, Cler., Robert Askwith, Willm Veuers, Richard Cookesonne, Willm Haighe, Gardianos.

An Extract or true Copie taken out of the Register Booke of the parish Church of Barwick in Elmett in the Countie of Yorke of all the Christenings, Marriages, and Burialls which have beene the yeare last past from the 25th day of March, Anno Domini 1636, till the 25th daie of March, Anno Domini 1637, as followeth :

CHRISTENINGS.

Elizabeth, the daughter of Aquila Ferrar of Scoles, 3d Aprill
Margaret, the daughter of Willm Veuers of Scoles, 15th Maye
John, the sonne of Stephen Shippen of Morwick, 12th June
John, the sonne of Francis Simpsonne of Barwick, 19th eiusdem
Willm, the sonne of Richard Shanne of Potterton, 3d Julie
Robert, the sonne of Robert Veuers of Scoles, 14th eiusdem
Richard, the sonne of Willm Brearecliff of Barwick, 20th eiusdem
Marie, the daughter of John Kirkbie of Potterton, die eodem
Thomas, the sonne of Thomas Woode of Barwicke, 6th August
Alice, the daughter of Peter Calbecke of Potterton, 7th eiusdem
Anne, the daughter of Rich. Slaiter of Winmore, 14th eiusdem
Willm, the sonne of Thomas Shore of Grimesdike, 28d eiusdem
Marie, the daughter of Rich. Turner of Barwicke, 31th eiusdem
Elizabeth, the daughter of Willm Prince of Barwicke, 11th September
Dorothee, the daughter of John Stowen of Barwicke, die eodem
Randall, the sonne of Randall Brigs of Rhowndhey, 2th October
Marie, the daughter of Jo. Ingle of Grimesdike, die eodem
Janett, the daughter of Rich. Tailor of Barwicke, die eodem
Rich., the sonne of Samuell Taite of Potterton, 16th eiusdem

Anne, the daughter of Willm Burnell of Rhowndhey, 23th eiusdem
Hellen, the daughter of Geo. Handley of Morwicke, 5th Nouember
Alice, the daughter of James Spinke of Scoles, 12th eiusdem
Willm, the sonne of Rich. Knaptonne of Barwick, 14th eiusdem
John, the sonne of Brian Bullocke of Barwick, 18th eiusdem
Willm., the sonne of John Prince of Barwick, 4th December
Christian, the daughter of Leon. Pickring of Barmbow, 3d Januarie
Anne, the daughter of Randall Constable of Winmore, die eodem
Willm, the sonne of Alexander Robinson of Scoles, 13th eiusdem
Tho., the sonne of Tho. Fletcher of Garforth-moreside, 5th February
Richard, the sonne of John Gowthwaite of Scoles, 22th eiusdem
Thomas, the sonne of John Hardcastle of Barwick, 24th eiusdem
Dorothee, the daughter of Christ. Kelshay of Rhowndey, 9th March
Martine, the sonne of Martine West, of Rhowndey, 19th eiusdem
Francis, the sonne of Sam. Crabtree of Barmebowe, die eodem

MARRIAGES.

Samuell Crabtree and Marie Daniell of Barmebowe, 15th Maye
Seth Lofthouse and Francis Veners of Scoles, 27th June
Willm Taite and Elizabeth Daniell of Barwick, 24th Julie
Robert Sainer and Marie Walshe of Stankes, die eodem
Tho. Fletcher and Dorothee Machill of Garforth side, die eodem
James Dickensonne and Jane Tailor of Barwicke, 25th eiusdem
Henrie Archibalde and Anne Barker of Barwick, 10th August
Willm Brooke and Elizabeth Burton of Barwick, 24th eiusdem
Leonard Wynne and Elizabeth Thompsonne of Grimesdike, 29th September
Jame Prince of Barwick and Anne Taite of Scoles, 25th Nouember
John Tailor and Francis Feather of Barwicke, 11th February

BURIALLS.

Alice, the daughter of Richard Swaile of Potterton, 3d Aprill
Katherine, the daughter of Jo. Jacksonne of Rhowndhey, 27th eiusdem
Christofer Sainer of Scoles, 5th May
Anne Coll of Kidhall, 7th eiusdem
Dorothee, the wife of Richard Hill of Stanks, 27th eiusdem
Robert, the sonne of Willm Pearson of Osmondthick, 5th Julie
Mathew Simpsonne of Leeds, a stranger, 11th eiusdem
Johanna, the daughter of Richard Shippen of Barmbowe, 24th eiusdem
Willm, the sonne of Richard Shanne of Potterton, 26th eiusdem
Alexander Robinsonne of Scoles, 2d August
Elizabeth, the daughter of Willm Taite of Potterton, 11th eiusdem
Jane, the daughter of Rich. Wilsonne of Rhowndeye, 24th eiusdem
John Johnsonne of Stankes, 6th September
Richard, the sonne of Rich. Slaiter of Winmore, 16th eiusdem
Robert, the sonne of Robert Bellabie of Winmore, 30th eiusdem
Willm, the sonne of Willm Peirsonne of Osmondthick, 3d October
Jane, the wife of Richard Taite of Scoles, 15th eiusdem
John, the sonne of Stephen Shippen of Barwicke, die eodem
The childe of Arthur Burtõñe of Barwick, 12th Nouember

Margaret, the daughter of Kath. Sainer of Scoles, 12th December
Marie, the wife of Thomas Woode of Barwicke, 11th February
Margaret, the daughter of Fr. Robinsonne of Scoles, 7th March
Examinatur cum Registro vicesimo quinto die Martij, Anno Domini 1637, et concord' cum Originali sicut attestantur Williã Bridges, Minist. ibid, Martine Hardcastle, Martine Clough, William Veners, Willia. Taite, Churche Wardens.

BARWICK IN ELMETT.

An Excerpt or true copie out of the Register Booke of the parish Church of Barwicke in Elmet of all the Christenings, Marriages and Burialls that haue beene in the whole yeare last past within the saide parish from the 25th day of Marche, Anno Domini 1637, unto the 25th daye of March last past, Anno Domini 1638, as followeth :—

CHRISTENINGES.

*John, the sonne of John Bathurst of Barwick, gentleman, March 31th
Willm, the sonne of Thomas Shore of Grimesdike, Aprill 9th
John, the sonne of John Haighe of Barwicke, eiusd' 30th
Martia, the daughter of Willm Taite of Potterton, eiusd' eodem
Martha, the daughter of Richard Shan of Potterton, Maye 21th
Isabell, the daughter of John Simpsonne of Garforth more, June 25th
Agnes, the daughter of Robert Bellabie of Winne-more, August 6th
John, the sonne of Richard Shippen of Barmebowe, eiusd' 27th
George, the sonne of Thomas Bellasse of Barwicke, September 10th
Alice, the daughter of James Prince of Scoles, eiusd' 27th
John, the sonne of John Mawe of Garforth more, October 28th
Edith, the daughter of Ralph Collet of Barwicke, Nouember 5th
Cuthbert, the sonne of Willm Brearecliffe of Barwick, eiusd' 8th
Richard, the sonne of John Smith of Barwicke, eiusd' 19th
Robert, the bastard sonne of Robert Nowell of Barwick, eiusd' eodem
Hellen, the daughter of Thomas Collins of Wothersome, eiusd' 26th
Hellen, the daughter of John Rodes of Wynnemore, December 3d
Thomas, the sonne of Willm Braime of Barmebowe, eiusd' 17th
Jane, the daughter of Michaell Hill of Stankes, Januarie 1st
Jane, the daughter of Willm Bridges, clerke of Barwick, eiusd' 22th
Janett, the daughter of John Potter of Pottertonne, February 24th
Thomas, the sonne of John Stowen of Barwicke, eiusd' 25

MARRIAGES.

Thomas Tailor and Elizabeth Feather of Barwicke, May 11th
John Drurie and Isabell Stringer of Barwicke, Nouember 19th
Samuell Stowen and Katherine Settle of Barwicke, eiusd' 26th
Thomas Abbey and Margaret Hawell of Barwicke, Januarie 15th

BURIALLS.

Henrie Haworth of Garforth Moreside, Aprill 17th
John, the sonne of Jo. Bathurst of Barwicke, gentleman, eiusd' 18th
Sir John Gascoigne of Parlingtonne, Baronett, Maye 4th
Jane, the daughter of Willm Taite of Pottertonne, eiusd' 11th
Dorothee, the daughter of Jo. Stowen of Barwicke, eiusd' 25th

*See Pedigree, Thoresby's Ducatus, 2nd Ed., p. 16, and Yorks. Archaeological Journal, vi. p. 267.

Dame Anne Gascoigne, widdow, of Parlingtonne, June 3rd
Cicilie Waterworth of Morewicke, widdow, Julie 10th
Alice, the daughter of Cuthbert Brigs of Barwick, eiusd' 11th
Marie, the daughter of Willm Ball of Pottertonne, eiusd' 17th
Marie, the Relict of John Haighe of Barwicke, August 12th
Robert Elwoode of Rhowndeheye Parke, eiusd' 26th
Anne, the wife of Leonarde Thompsonne of Rhowndehey, September 13th
Lawrence Brigges of Rhowndehey Parke, October 13th
Anthonie Witham of Pottertonne Moreside, eiusd' 17th
Thomas Shore of Winne More side, Nouember 15th
Dorothee Todde of Winne more side, Widdowe, eiusd' 24th
A Male Childe of Willm Massie of Stockeinge, Februarie 6th
Robert Dineleye of Barwicke in Elmett, eiusd' 25th
A Male, unchristened, of Arthur Barton's of Barwick, March 3d
Jane, the wife of Robert Akid of Barwicke, eiusd' 13th
Examinatur concordare cum Registro ecclesie parochialis de Barwick in Elmett, decimo sexto die mensis Aprilis, Anno a Saluatoris nostri Jesu Christi incarnatione, 1638. Per Willm
Bridges, minist. Ibid, et Willm Veners, Martin Cloughe, Willm Taite, et Martin Hardcastle, Gardianos Ecclesie parochialis de Barwicke in Elmett.

BARWICK IN ELMETT, 1638.

A true and perfect Abstract or copie taken out of the Register Booke of the parish Church of Barwick in Elmett, in the countie of Yorke, of all the Christenings, Marriages, and Burialls that haue beene in the saied parish, the yeare last past, that is to saye, from the 25th daye of March in Anno Domini 1638, until the 25th daye of March in Anno Domini 1639, as followeth :—

CHRISTENINGES.

Jaine, the daughter of William Glouer of Rhowndheye, 19th Aprill
John, the sonne of Thomas Abbeye of Kidhall, 3d Maye
William, the sonne of Richard Jackesonne of Barwick in Elmett, 27th eiusdem
John, the sonne of John Bailye of Rhowndheye, 24th June
Johanna, the daughter of Samuell Stowen of Barwick in Elmett, 4th Julie
James, the sonne of Martine Cloughe of Rhowndheye, the 9th eiusdem
Richard, the sonne of Richard Andrewes of Garforth Moreside, 22th eiusdem
Hellen, the daughter of Thomas Robinsonne of Garforth Moreside, 23th eiusdem
Randall, the sonne of Randall Brigs of Rhowndheye, 2d September
John, the sonne of John Hardcastle of Barwicke in Elmett, 8th eiusdem
Edwarde, the sonne of John Shoesmythe of Stockeinge, 9th eiusdem
Maitia, the daughter of Robert Richmonde of Barwicke in Elmett, 16th eiusdem

Anne, the daughter of Christofer Kelsheye of Rhowndheye, 23th eiusdem
Johanna, the daughter of John Daniell of Pottertonne, 26th eiusdem
William, the sonne of Gualter Leaper of Barmebowe Carre, 29th eiusdem
Cuthbert, the sonne of Richard Mounsea of Wynne More, 30th eiusdem
Marie, the daughter of John Tailor of Morwicke, 14th October
Hellen, the daughter of Robert Chambers of Grimesdike, eodem die
Francis, the daughter of John Tailor of Barwicke in Elmett, 21th eiusdem
Martine, the sonne of John Drurie of Barwick in Elmett, 5th Nouember
John, the sonne of John Wrighte of Barwicke in Elmett, 11th December
Robert, the sonne of John Corden of Barwicke in Elmett, 21th eiusdem
Marie, the daughter of Martine Weste of Rhowndheye, 23th eiusdem
Marie and Margarett, the daughters of Elias Robert of Shippen, 7th Januarie
Anne, the daughter of John More of Barwicke in Elmett, 9th eiusdem
Vrsula, the daughter of Samuell Crabtree of Barmebowe Carre, 14th eiusdem
John, the sonne of John Feather of Scoles, 24th eiusdem
Ralphe, the sonne of William Veuers of Scoles, the 17th Februarie
Anne, the daughter of Brian Bullocke of Barwick in Elmett, 3d March
Edith, the daughter of Robert Lacock of Browne More, 17th eiusdem
Marie, the daughter of John Haighe of Barwick in Elmett, 25th eiusdem

MARRIAGES.

Thomas Woode and Margarett Watsonne of Barwicke in Elmett, 4th Aprill
Richard Mounesea and Susanna Waterworthe of Morwicke, 27th June
William Mounesea and Anne Franckeland of Morwicke, 30th Julie
Robert Sayner of Barmebowe and Isabell Sayner of Scoles, 11th September
Thomas Wansley and Anne Saundersonne of Barwicke in Elmett, 23th eiusdem
Thomas Akid and Marie Settle of Barwicke in Elmett, 28th eiusdem
Thomas Chapman and Jane Sparke of Leedes were married with a facultie, 14th Nouember
John Nortonne and Dorothie Barker of Barwicke in Elmett, 28th eiusdem
*Christofer Tempest, gent., and Alice Rawsonne of Barwick in Elmett 29th eiusdem
Jeremie Waterhouse and Anne Tailor of Morwicke, 30th eiusdem

BURIALLS.

John Prince of the towne of Barwicke in Elmett, 25th March

*See Pedigree of Tempest of Tong, in the Genealogist, vol. x., p. 52.

Robert Sayner of the towne of Pottertonne, 10th Aprill
Jane Mittonne, widdowe, of the towne of Barwicke in Elmett, 23th eiusdem
Thomas, the sonne of William Settle of Skiptonne in Crauen, a strainger, 6th Maye
A male childe, unchristened, the sonne of Henrie Croft of Barwick in Elmett, 10th eiusdem
Marie Hardcastle, the daughter of John Hardcastle of Barwicke in Elmett, 16th eiusdem
William Sayner of the towne of Scoles, 29th eiusdem
Elizabeth, the wife of William Brigs of Barwicke in Elmett, 5th June
Edith, the wife of Richard Hill of Speighleyes, 27th eiusdem
A male childe, unchristened, the sonne of John Midgleye of Wynmore 29th eiusdem
Johanna, the daughter of Samuell Stowen of Barwicke in Elmett, 5th Julie
Richard, the sonne of William Brearecliffe of Barwicke in Elmet, 9th eiusdem
Richard, the sonne of Francis Settle of Barwicke in Elmett, 11th eiusdem
Elizabeth Hardcastle, widdowe, of Barwicke in Elmett, 17th eiusdem
Anne Settle, the daughter of Francis Settle of Barwicke in Elmett, eodem die
Jane, the daughter of William Glouer of Rhowndeheye, 26th eiusdem
Marie, the daughter of Nicholas Shippen of Barmebowe, 12th August
Elizabeth, the wife of John Veuers of Barwicke in Elmett, 24th eiusdem
Elizabeth, the daughter of Robert Scowthrop of Scoles, 1st September
Anne, the daughter of Nicholas Shippen of Barmebowe, 5th eiusdem
A woman, being a strainger, whose name is unknowne, who died at Scoles, buried the 9th eiusdem
Margerie, the wife of Willm Taite of the towne of Potterton, 24th eiusdem
Johanna, the daughter of John Daniell of Pottertonne, 28th eiusdem
Mundaye Fidlinge, a strainger, who died at Rhowndhey, 30th eiusdem
Margaret, the wife of John Tailor of Morwicke, 18th October
Richard Potter of the towne of Pottertonne, 21th eiusdem
Franncis, the wife of John Tailor of Barwick in Elmett, 22th eiusdem
John Wright of the towne of Barwicke in Elmett, 30th eiusdem
William Hopwoode of Pottertonne Moreside, 16th December
Marie, ye wife of Elias Robert of Shippen, 9th December
John, the sonne of John Wright of Barwick in Elmett, 11th eiusdem
Anne, the daughter of John Taite of the towne of Scoles, 17th eiusdem
Anne Hodgshonne of Browne More, a widdowe, 11th Januarie
Willm Burland of the towne of Barwicke, 16th eiusdem
William Brearecliffe of Barwick in Elmett aforesaide, 17th eiusdem
A male childe, unbaptized, the sonne of Henrie Stephenson of Barmbowe, 1st Februarie
Jane Sainer, widdowe, of the towne of Rhowndheye, 6th eiusdem

Martine Wynders of Pottertonne, 16th eiusdem
Henrie Stephensonne of the towne of Barmebowe, 14th eiusdem
Dorothee, the daughter of John Watman, a stranger, 24th eiusdem
Martine Cloughe of the towne of Rhowndheye, 27th eiusdem
Elizabeth Hardcastle, widdowe, of Barwicke in Elmett, 17th March
Examinatur concordare cum Registro Ecclie parochialis de Barwicke in Elmett, vicesimo quinto die mensis Martij, Anno Dni. 1639. Per William Bridges, minist. ibid, John Tailor, Thomas Veuers, Richard Shan, John Hubye, Church-wardens.

An Extract taken out of the Register Booke of the parish church of Barwicke in Elmett, in the countie of Yorke, of all the christenings, marriages, and burialls that haue beene in the said parish the whole yeare, from the 25th daye of March, Anno Domini 1639 last past, till the 25th daye of March in Anno Domini 1640 instant as hereafter followeth :—

CHRISTENINGS.

Marie, the daughter of John Haighe of Barwicke in Elmet, 25th March
Thomas, the sonne of Richard Vevers of Scoles, 7th Aprill
Katherine, the daughter of Willm Haighe of Barwicke in Elmet, 13th eiusdem
Hester, the bastard daughter of Jane Norton of the same, 15th eiusdem
Marie, the daughter of Willm Mounesea of Morwicke, 21th eiusdem
Hellen, the daughter of George Handleye of Scoles, eodem die
Willm, the sonne of Thomas Akid of the same, 28th eiusdem
Peter, the sonne of Richard Willsonne of Rhowndheye, eodem die
Willm, the sonne of Willm Burnell of the same, 5th Maye
Francis, the sonne of Thomas Fletcher of Garforth More, eodem die
Thomas, the sonne of Samuell Taite of Pottertonne, 26th eiusdem
Richard, the sonne of Samuell Stowen of Barwick in Elmet, 16th June
Hellen, the daughter of Richard Knapton of the same, 24th eiusdem
Sara, the daughter of Willm Massie of Stockeinge, 21th Julye
Isabell, the daughter of Robert Sayner of Scoles, eodem die
Sara, the daughter of Richard Turner of Barwick in Elmet, 25th eiusdem
Marie, the daughter of Thomas Jordaine of Scoles, 4th August
Willm, the sonne of Willm Bridges, clerke, of Barwick in Elmet, 8th eiusdem
Elizabeth, the daughter of Thomas Sayner of Scoles, 27th eiusdem
Richard, the sonne of John Cullingworth of Rhowndhey, eodem die
John, the sonne of Willm Rowstonne of Grimesdike, eodem die
Dorothie, the daughter of John Norton of Barwick in Elmet, 1st September
Anne, the daughter of Roger Judsonne of Rhowndehey, 21th eiusdem
Willm, the sonne of John Ingle of Grimesdike, 13th October
Richard, the sonne of Richard Tailor of Barwicke in Elmet, 10th Nouember
Elizabeth, the daughter of Thomas Woode of the same, 27th eiusdem
Martine, the sonne of William Glover of Rhowndeheye, 3d December

Alice, the daughter of John Stowen of Barwick in Elmet, 31th eiusdem
John, the sonne of John Hall, a strainger, at Stankes, 5th Januarie
Wiłłm, the sonne of Francis Ellis, gent., of Kidhall, 19th eiusdem
Marie, the daughter of Francis Prince of Rhowndhey, 2d Februarie
John, the sonne of John Smith of Barwicke in Elmett, 16th eiusdem
Wiłłm, the sonne of Samuell Waterworth of Wyn-more, 23th eiusdem
Anne, the daughter of John Hardcastle of Barwick in Elmet, 26th eiusdem

MARRIAGES.

John Smith and Elizabeth Dineley of Barwicke in Elmett, 1st Maye
John Denysonne and Alice Wright of the same, 24th June
Thomas Tod of Leathley and Isabell Holmes of Rhowndhey, 10th Julie
Francis Prince and Francis Chambers of the same, 14th eiusdem
Richard Chapman and Isabell Bell of Barwick in Elmet, 22th eiusdem
Samuel Shenton and Elizabeth Wright of the same, 6th Octõber
Ch[r]istofer Lee of Holbecke and Margaret Smith of Rowndhey, 21th eiusdem
Robert Fletcher and Margaret Chambers of Wynmore, 31th eiusdem
Nicholas Browne and Johanna Crosland of Barwick in Elmet, 11th Nouember
Robert Greene and Alice Prince of the same, 30th eiusdem
Robert Barker and Margaret Dineley of the same, 1st Februarie

BURIALLS.

Hellen, the wife of Edward Knapton of Barwick in Elmet, 28th March
Henrie, the sonne of Richard Topcliffe of Scoles, 11th Aprill
John Pickarde of Barwicke in Elmett, 15th eiusdem
*Ralph Cooke the Elder, gentleman, of the same, 24th eiusdem
John, the sonne of John Hardecastle of the same, 1st Maye
Marie, the daughter of Wiłłm Mounsea of Morwicke, 8th eiusdem
Margarett, the wife of William Gillsonne of Scoles, 1st June
Walter Leaper of Barmebowe Carre, 6th eiusdem
Wiłłm, the sonne of Wiłłm Burnell of Rhowndeheye, 9th eiusdem
Francis Hodgesonne, a woeman servante of Barmebow, 18th eiusdem
Richard Shippen of Barmebowe aforesaide, 1st Julie
Marie, the daughter of Francis Simpsonne, lait of Barwick, 9th eiusdem
Thomas, the sonne of Thomas Fletcher of Garforth More, 14th eiusdem
Isabell, the wife of Robert Sayner of Scoles, 10th Auguste
Wiłłm, the sonne of Walter Leaper of Barmebowe Carre, 14th September
Anne, the wife of John Deardonne of Browne-More, 17th October
Wiłłm Hodgeshonne, a poore collyer of Barmebowe, 24th eiusdem
Martine, the sonne of Martine West of Rhowndeheye, 9th Nouember
A foemale, unchristened, the childe of Henrie Croft of Barwick, 10th eiusdem
Henrie Grave of Barwicke in Elmett aforesaide, eodem die

*Ralph Cooke was possessed of lands in Leeds, purchased from Thomas Wood of Beeston, subject to a mortgage for £700, which descended on his death to his brother William (? John). *Calendar of Committee for Advance of Money, Royalist Composition Papers*, p. 646. (*Yorks. Record Series*, XV. 16)

Martine, the sonne of Willm Glover of Rhowndeheye, 17th December
Marie, the daughter of Randall Brigs of the same, 31th eiusdem
Willm Slaiter of Barwicke in Elmett, 9th Januarie
John Geater, a strainger of Staunkes, 16th eiusdem
Katherine, the wife of Robert Richmonde of Barwicke, 17th eiusdem
Richard Hill of Speighleyes on Wynne More, 29th eiusdem
Christian, the daughter of Leonarde Pickeringe of Barmbow, eodem die
John, the sonne of John Jackesonne of Rhowndeheye, 8th Februarie
Frauncis, the wife of Henrie Hollmes of the same, 11th eiusdem
Elizabeth, the daughter of John Lumleye, a strainger, 15th eiusdem
William, the sonne of John Simpsonne, a strainger, 17th eiusdem
Robert Johnsonne of Stankes, haueing a facultie granted, eodem die
Willm, the sonne of Samuell Waterworth of Win-more, 20th eiusdem
Richard, the sonne of Randall Constable of the same, 26th eiusdem
Michaell Willsonne of Rhowndehey-Parke, 28th eiusdem
Margerie Blackburne, widdowe, of the same, 4th March
Examinatur concordare cum originali Registro, 25° die Martij, Anno Domini 1640, attestat' sub manũm subscriptione. W. Bridges, minist. Ibid, John Tailor, Thomas Veuers, Richard Shan, Jo. Hubye, Church Wardens.

An extract or true copie taken out of the Register Booke of the parish of Barwick in Elmett, of all such Christenings, Marriages, and Burialls as haue beene within the saide parish from the fiue and twentieth daye of March which was in Anno Domini 1640, unto the fiue and twentieth daie of March last past in Anno Domini 1641, as followeth :—

CHRISTENINGES.

Willm, the sonne of Aquila Ferrar of Scoles, 25th March
John, the sonne of James Atkinsonne of Potterton, 26th eiusdem
John, the sonne of John Smith of Barwick in Elmett, 30th eiusdem
Robert, the sonne of Ralph Collett of Barwick in Ellmet, 2d Aprill
James and Isabell, the children of James Spinke of Scoles, 12th eiusdem
Anne, the daughter of Christopher Kelshey of Rhowndhey, eodem die
Thomas, the sonne of Willm Butler of Rhowndehey, eodem die
Richard and Edward, the sonnes of Sam. Knapton of Barwick, 20th eiusdem
Elizabeth, the daughter of George Hiltonne of Morwick, 3d Maye
Anne, the daughter of James Prince of Scoles, eodem die
Anne, the daughter of Thomas Akid of Barwicke, 20th eiusdem
Grace, the daughter of Arthur Burton of Barwicke, 27th eiusdem
Cicilie, the daughter of Robert Bellabie of Wynmore, 7th June
Sara, the daughter of John Hardcastle of Barwicke, 28th eiusdem
Janett, the daughter of Thomas Fletcher of Garforth More, eod. die
Willm, the sonne of John Simpsonne of Garforth More, 19th Julie
James, the sonne of John Jacksonne of Rhowndeheye, 26th eiusdem
Robert, the sonne of Willm Stricklande of Scoles, 2d August
Marie, the daughter of Willm Taite of Pottertonne, 9th eiusdem

Joseph, the sonne of Robert Skeltonne of Grimesdike, 23th eiusdem
Margarett, the daughter of Thomas Shippen of Barmebowe, 9th September
Christofer, the sonne of Christofer Haxbie of Scoles, 12th eiusdem
Marie, the daughter of Thomas Collins of Wothersome side, 24th eiusdem
Willm, the sonne of John Dennisonne of Barwicke, 27th eiusdem
John, the sonne of Thomas Tailor of Barwicke, 1st October
Richard, the sonne of Robert Greene of Barwicke, eodem die
Tobias, the sonne of John Fentiman of Barwicke, 11th eiusdem
Robert, the sonne of Richard Taite of Scoles, 28th eiusdem
George, the sonne of Samuell Wood of Grimesdike, 1st Nouember
Henrie, the sonne of Robert Johnsonne of Scoles, 8th eiusdem
Anne and Susan, the daughters of Thomas Prince of Scoles, 16th eiusdem
John, the sonne of John Beedehall of Scoles, 22th eiusdem
John, the sonne of Samuell Stowen of Barwicke in Elmett, 1st December
Margarett, the daughter of Richard Shan of Potterton, 2d eiusdem
Willm, the sonne of John Smith of Barwick in Elmett, 6th eiusdem
Willm, the sonne of Samuell Shenton of Barwick in Elmett, 6th Januarie
Susanna, the daughter of Mr. Willm Bridges of Barwicke, 13th eiusdem
George, the sonne of Richard Haiste of Barwicke, 24th eiusdem
Richard, the sonne of Willm Ingle of Scoles, 2d Februarie
John, the sonne of Martine West of Rhowndehey, 7th eiusdem
Willm, the sonne of Richard Andrew of Garforth More, eodem die
Matthias, the sonne of Willm. Glouer of Rhowndehey, 28th eiusdem
Willm, the sonne of Thomas Lacock of Garforth more, eodem die

MARRIAGES.

Richard Settle the younger of Potterton and Anne Roote of Barwick, 9th June
Thomas Tailor of Morwick and Susanna Kirke of Addle, 23th Nouember
John Settle the younger and Marie Settle of Potterton, 16th December
Lawrence Turner and Jane Elwoode of Rhowndheye, 22th Januarie

BURIALLS.

Francis, the wife of Richard Settle the Elder of Potterton, 28th March
Alice, the wife of Edwarde Metcalfe of Rhowndeheye, 7th Aprill
Thomas Hodgesonne, a colyer, of Browne More, 14th eiusdem
Margaret, the daughter of Willm Willsonne of Rhowndehey, 15th eiusdem
James, the sonne of James Spinke of Scoles, 16th eiusdem
Isabell, the daughter [of] the said James Spinke of Scoles, 17th eiusdem
John, the sonne of John Kirkebie of Pottertonne, 19th eiusdem
Willm Brigs of Rhowndehey, 26th eiusdem
Richard, the sonne of Samuell Knapton of Barwick in Elmett, eodem die

Edward, the sonne of the saide Samuell Knapton, 3d Maye
Marie, the wife of Francis Turner of the Stankes, 28th June
Isabell, the wife of John Veuers of Scoles, 29th August
John Potter of the towne of Pottertonne, 14th September
Richard, the sonne of Richard Veuers, the younger, of Scoles, 15th eiusdem
Elizabeth, the wife of Thomas Collins of Wothersome parke side, 15th October
Robert, the sonne of Richard Taite of Scoles, 31th eiusdem
Barbara, the daughter of Isabell Howdell of Scoles, 17th Nouember
Susanna, the younger daughter of Thomas Prince of Scoles, 19th eiusdem
Anne, the elder daughter of the saide Thomas Prince, 6th December
Henrie, the sonne of Robert Johnsonne of Scoles, 13th eiusdem
John, the sonne of John Graye, a traveller in the countrie, 16th eiusdem
John Gawthrop, seruant to Willm Emmersonne of Scarcrofte, 31th eiusdem
Richard Ingle of Scoles, 3d Januarie
Francis, the wife of John Corden of Barwicke in Elmett, 11th eiusdem
Richard, the sonne of Richard Compton of Barmebowe, 6th Februarie
Elizabeth Eldred, widdowe, of Barwicke in Elmett, 27th eiusdem
Marie, the wife of Robert Bravener of Pottertonne, 7th March
Examinatur et Attestat' concordare cum originali Registro Ecclie parochialis Baruicensis, undecimo die Aprilis, Anno Domini millesimo sexcentesimo quadragesimo primo. Per W. Bridges, minist. Ibid, John Hardcastle, Willm. Taite, Willm Massye, Thomas Holmes, Gardianos ibidem.

A true and perfect Extract or copie to bee exhibited into the Exchequer of the Lord Archbishop of Yorke, his Grace, taken out of the Register Booke of the parish Church of Barwick in Elmett, in the countie of Yorke, of all the christenings, marriages, and burialls whiche have beene in the said parish from the 25th day of March wch was in Anno Domini 1641, unto the 25th day of March last past in Anno Domini 1642, as followeth :—

CHRISTENINGES.

John, the sonne of Richard Settle of Barwicke in Elmett, 31st March
Dorothee, the daughter of Willm Burnell of Rhowndehey, 4th Aprill
Thomas, the sonne of Thomas Wansley of Barwicke in Elmett, eodem die
Leonarde, the sonne of Leonarde Pickeringe of Barmebowe, 11th eiusdem
Hester, the daughter of Stephen Shippen of Barwicke in Elmett, 2nd Maye
Obediah, the sonne of Francis Oddie of Scoles, 9th eiusd'
John, the sonne of Samuell Knapton of Barwicke in Elmett, eodem die
Samuell, the sonne of Thomas Robinsonne of Garforth More, eodem die
Francis, the sonne of John Thompsonne of the same, 6th June

Margaret, the daughter of Robert Veuers of Scoles, 9th eiusd'
Elizabeth, the daughter of Samuell Waterworth of Wynmore, 17th eiusd'
Willm., the sonne of Samuell Crabtree of Barmebow Carre, 4th Julie
John, the sonne of John Drurie of Barwicke in Elmett, 18th eiusd'
Samuell, the sonne of Samuell Taite of Potterton, 25th eiusd'
Susanna, the daughter of Robert Chambers of Grimesdike, 1st August
Anne, the daughter of Peter Hill of the Stankes, 12th September
Elizabeth, the daughter of Mathew Haighe of Barwicke in Elmett, 16th eiusd'
Alice, the daughter of Thomas Shippen the younger of Barmebowe, 23th eiusd'
Willm, the sonne of Brian Bullock of Barwick in Elmett, 3d October
Alice, the daughter of John Haighe of the same, 7th Nouember
Beatrix, the daughter of John Stowen of the same, 12th December
Elizabeth, the daughter of John Gibsonne of the same, 26th eiusdem
Willm, the sonne of John Burlande of the same, 5th Januarie
Elias, the sonne of Elias Roberts of Shippen, 9th eiusdem
Joseph, the sonne of Richard Turner of Barwick in Elmett, 13th Februarie
Anne, the daughter of George Handeley of Scoles, 1st March
Robert, the sonne of John Feather of the same, 3d eiusdem
Margarett, the bastarde daughter of Marie Ellis of Barwicke in Elmett, 12th eiusdem
Thomas, the sonne of Thomas Horberrie of Rhowndehey, 22th eiusdem
Marie, the daughter of Thomas Akid of Barwicke in Elmett, 24th eiusdem

MARIAGES.

*Robert Bravener of Potterton and Dorothee Tailor of Stanks, 3d Maye
Mr. Richard Thomas and Mris Cooke of Barwicke in Elmett, 22th eiusdem
Mr. Samuell Jackesonne and Mris Edith Standeaven, 27th eiusdem
Thomas Shippen of Barmebowe and Marie Daniell of Barwick in Elmett, 28th eiusdem
John Burneley and Anne Mounsea of Barwick in Elmett aforesaide, 18th August
Thomas Nelsonne of Pontefract and Margaret Mallom of Barwick in Elmett aforesaide, 13th October
John Layefield of Potterton and Margaret Carother of Barmebow Carre, 18th eiusdem
John Gibsonne and Elizabeth Fletcher of Barwick in Elmett aforesaide, 19th eiusdem
John Prince of Barwick in Elmett and Marie Jennisonne of Garfourth 20th eiusdem
Willm Dickesonne and Elizabeth Garnett of Browne Moreclose, 31th eiusdem

* Walter Brabaner was taxed 4d. at Barwick in the Poll Tax of 1379.

Martine Prince and Jane Addisonne of Barwicke in Elmett, 17th Nouember
Francis Ingle of the parish of Leedes and Elizabeth Brigs of Rhowndhey, 18th eiusdem
Thomas Horberrie and Dorothee Smyth of Rhowndehey aforesaide, 24th eiusdem
Leonarde Cooke of Leedes and Marie Thwaites, 7th Februarie

Burialls.

Richard Tailor, the souldier, of Barwicke in Elmett, 27th March
Clarie Taite, widdowe, of Scoles, 6th Aprill
Alice, the wife of John Settle of Pottertonne, 25th eiusdem
Elizabeth, the daughter of Thomas Robinsonne of Garfourth More, 9th Maye
Richard Tate of Potterton More side 24th Maye
Francis, the sonne of John Thompsonne of Garfourth More side, 24th Julie
Alice Hardcastle, widdowe, of Barwicke in Elmett, 28th eiusdem
John, the sonne of Willm Hurst of Garfourth More side, 4th August
Henrie and Anne Bullock, the children of Brian Bullocke of Barwick in Elmett, 5th eiusdem
John, the sonne of James Atkinsonne of Pottertonne, 6th eiusdem
Grace, the wife of Martine West of Rhowndeheye, 11th eiusdem
Margarett West, widdowe, of Rhowndheye aforesaid, 21th eiusdem
Dorothee, the wife of George Browne of Rhowndhey aforesaide, 29th eiusdem
Rosamonde, the wife of Lawrence West of Rhowndhey aforesaide, 30th eiusdem
Richard Ingle the younger of Scoles, 1st September
Willm, the sonne of John Prince of Barwick in Elmett, 14th eiusdem
Robert Cooke the Londoner of Barwick in Elmett aforesaide, 21th eiusdem
Peter, the sonne of Stephen Shippen of Barwick in Elmett aforesaide, 3d October.
Anne, the daughter of Thomas Akid of Barwick in Elmett aforesaide, 10th eiusdem
John, the sonne of Samuell Stowen of Barwick in Elmett aforesaide, 6th Nouember
Symon Smyth of Wothersome, 8th December
John Smith of Wynne More, 29th eiusdem
Elizabeth, the daughter of John Gibsonne of Barwick in Elmett, 1st Januarie
Vrsula, the daughter of Samuell Crabtree of Barmebowe Carre, 6th eiusdem
Elias, the sonne of Elias Roberts of Shippen, 17th eiusdem
Willm, the sonne of John Burlande of Barwicke in Elmett aforesaide, 19th eiusdem
Anne, the daughter of Richard Taite of Scoles, 11th Februarie
Hellen, the daughter of George Handeley of Scoles aforesaide, 4th March
Elizabeth, the wife of Thomas Taite of Potterton, 6th eiusdem

Margarett, the wife of Thomas Tirrington of Shippen, 13th eiusdem
Francis, the sonne of Edwarde Benedict of Barmebow Carre, 17th eiusdem
Examinatur attestat. concordare cum Registro supra dicto, octano die mensis Aprilis, Anno Domini 1642. per W. Bridges, Minist. Ibid, Richard Tailor, Martin Weste, Robert Greenewood, Samuell Tayte, Church-wardens.

[FIRST REGISTER BOOK.]

The fifth day of November, 1653.

Richard Turner of Barwicke, in the Westryding of ye county of York, being elected was approved and sworne Register for Registring all mariages, Births and Burialls within the pish of Barwicke in Ellmett, Before me one of the Justices of peace for the sayde Ryding the day and yeare above written.

HEN. TEMPEST.

November, Anno Domini 1653.

Publication. The Bains of Matrimony betwixt Willm Mortimer of the towne and parish of Barwick in Elmett, husbandman, on the one partie, and Elizabeth Hickes of the same, spinster, on the other partie, weere published in the parish Church there on three severall Lords dayes to witt, 30th day of October last past and the 6th and 13th dayes of November after, 1653, without any cawse to the contrary obiected, being both of them of the full age of one and twentie yeares.

William Mortimer of Barwicke in Elmett, and Elizabethe Hickes of the same pish, were married together before me the fifteenth day of November one thousand six hundreth fify three, both of them beinge above the age of one and twenty yeares.

RO. BARWICKE.

John Hubye of Rhowndhey parke was buried the seaventeenth day of November aforesd.

Richard Vevers of the towne of Scoles was buried the 21th day of the same moneth.

Johan, the daughter of John Feather of Scoles aforesaid, was buried the 24th daye of the said moneth.

Publication. The marriage intended to be solemnized between Geo: Wright of the towne and parish of Kirke Dighton, in the countie of Yorke, yeoman, on the one partie, and Agnes Hopwood of Potterton Moreside, with in the parish of Barwick in Elmett, in the same County, widow, on the other party, being either of them above the age of one and twentie yeares, were published on three severall Lords dayes in the parish Church of Barwick in Elmett aforesaid, at the close of the Morneing Exercise there, with out any Exception obiected against either of them vizt, on the 27th day of November last past and on the 4th and 11th dayes of December instant in the yeare of our Lord 1653.

George Wright of the towne and parish of Kirke-Dighton, and Agnes Hopwood of Potterton Moreside, within the parish of

Barwick in Elmett, being both and either of them above the age of one and twentie yeares, were marrid togethr 13th day of December in the yeare of oure Lord one thousand six hundred fiftie three, before Robert Dicksonne, Thomas Spincke, John Manne and Willm Dawsonne, and before mee, Tho: Stockdale, Esqr, a Justice of the Peace within ye sd Westridd.

THO: STOCKDALE.

Edward, the sonne of Willm Glover of Rhowndhey, was buried 19th day of December, 1653.

January, 1653.

Abraham Rishforth of Barmebow, husbandman, and Ursula Harrison of the high Ash, widdow, being both of them with in the parish of Barwick in Elmett, and either of them above the age of one and twentie yeares, after the declaration of a marriage intended to be solemnized betweene them beeinge first published in the parish churche of Barwick in Elmett aforesaid according to the lait Act of Parliament made touching marriages, were married together the 4th day of Januarie in the yeare of our lord 1653, in the p'sence of Robert Armystead, Thomas Taylor, Thomas Terrington and Rich. Turner, before mee.

JOHN SAVILE.

Marie, the daughter of Richard Swaile of Potterton, was borne the Eighth day of the said moneth.

John, the sonne of Richard Andrew of Garforth moreside, was borne the nynth day of the same.

John, the sonne of Robert Prince youngr of Barwick in Elmett, borne 28th day of the same moneth.

Francis, the wife of Thomas Fletcher of Barwick in Elmett, was buried the 14th day of the said moneth.

Isabell Feather of Barwick in Elmett, widdowe, was buried the 26th day of the said moneth.

Anne, the daughter of Martine West of Rhowndehey, was buried the 27th day of the said moneth.

February, 1653.

Abraham, the sonne of Thomas Shippen of Barnebowe, was borne the 3d day of the said moneth.

Joseph, the sonne of John Haigh of Barwick in Elmett, was borne the 3d day of the said moneth.

Thomas, the sonne of Robert Scowthrop the youngr of Scoles, was borne the 18th day of the said moneth.

Samuell, the sonne of Richard Prince of Barwick in Elmett, was borne the 15th daye of the said moneth.

Anne, the daughter of Rich. Styham of Potterton More side, borne the 25th day of the said moneth.

Richard Crompton of Barmebow was buried the second day of February, 1653.

Margarett Atkinsonne of Potterton, widdowe, was buried the 15th day of the same moneth.

Mercy Butler of Rhowndehey, widdowe, was buried the said 15th day of the said moneth.

Samuell, the sonne of Samuell Younge of Rhowndehey, was buried the 18th day of the said moneth.

Mary, the daughter of the said Samuell Younge, was buried the 20th day of the said moneth.

Anne, the wife of George Haigh of Barwick in Elmett, buried the 21th day of the said moneth.

Samuel, the sonne of Rich. Prince of Barwick in Elmett, buried the 24th day of the said moneth.

Sara, the daughter of Richard Willsonne of Rhowndhey, buried the 25th day of the said moneth.

*Stephen Tempest of Barmebowe, Esquier, and Anne Gascoigne of the same, Gentlewoman, both of them of the parish of Barwick in Elmett, and either of them beeing above the age of one and twentie yeares, after the declaration of a marriage intended and agreed to be solemnized betweene them beeing first published three severall markett dayes at the Markett Crosse of Weatherby, according to the lait Act of Parliamt made touching Marriages, were married together the Eighth day of March in the yeare of our Lord one thousand six hundred fiftie three, in the p'sence of James Wright, John Tempest and Richard Turner, witnesses—Before mee.

JOHN SAVILE.

Marye, the daughter of Mathew Ingle of Barwicke, was borne 23th daye of Aprill, 1654.

Grace, the wife of Willm Wilcocke of Garforth Moreside, was buried 13th of Aprill, 1654.

Robert Shaw, labourer, and Susan Mounsey, widdowe, both of them of the towne and parish of Barwicke in Elmett, within the West riding of the countie of Yorke, and either of them being above the age of 21 yeares, after the declaration of a marriage intended and agreed to be solemnized between them beeing first published by the Register of the said parish 3 severall Lordes dayes in the said parish Church at the close of the morneing Exercise there, according to the lait Act of Parliamt made touching Marriages, were married together the 15th day of May in the yeare of our lord one thousand sixe hundred fiftie fower in the presence of John Ellis of Barwicke aforesaid, William Kitchingman and Nath. Baine of Tolston, and other witnesses. Before mee.

RO: BARWICKE.

Anne, the daughter of Thomas Blackburne of Morwicke, borne the 9th day of May.

Elizabeth, daughter of John Rodes of Wynmore, was borne the 10th day of ye same moneth.

Robert, the sonne of Jo. Burland of Barwicke, borne the 11th day of the said moneth.

Marke, the sonne of Matthew Mawe of Garforth Moreside, buried the 29th of Maye.

---

*His burial at Broughton in Craven, 14 March, 1672-3, is entered in this Register. His wife was the eldest daughter of Sir Thomas Gascoigne, and was buried 11 Sept., 1684. For pedigree see the Genealogist. vol. xi. N.S., page 152. The will of his father is printed in the Yorks. Record Series ix., page 45.

Thomas Thompsonne of Speigleys, Malster, and Elizabeth Hill of Stankes, spinster, in the parish of Barwick in Elmett, within the West rydeing of the County of Yorke, being either of them above the age of 21 yeares, after the publication of a marriage intended to be solemnized betweene them being first published by the Register of the said parish 3 severall lordes dayes in the said parish Church at the close of the morneing exercise there, according to the lait act of Parliam[t] made touching marriages, were married together the 24th day of June in the yeare of our lord 1654, in the p'sence of Henrye Wright and James Hurst and others, witnesses. Before mee

Jo: Warde.

Isabell Settle of Potterton, widdowe, was buried the 4th daye of June aforesaid.

Marie, the wife of John Hemsworth of Potterton aforesaid, buried the last day of June.

Oswald Harrison, labourer, and Margarett Turner, widdow, being both of Stanks, in the parish of Barwick in Elmett, within the West riding of the County of Yorke, and either of them above the age of one and twentie yeares, after the publication of a marriage intended to be solemnized betweene them being first made by the Register of the said parish 3 severall lordes dayes in the said parish Church at the close of the morning exercise there, according to the laite act of Parliament made touching marriages, were married together the last day of July in the yeare of our lord 1654, in the p'sence of Thomas Thompson and Robert Turner of Stanks aforesaid, and oth[rs], witnesses, before mee.

John Savile.

Marie, the daughter of John Taylor of Barwick, borne 4th daye of Julye.

Anne, the daughter of Isaac Wood of Potterton, borne 7th day of Julye.

John, the sonne of Thomas Varley of Garforth More, borne 14th day of Julye.

Anne, the wife of Geo. Wright of Potterton Moreside, buried 5th day of July.

Margarett, the wife of Thomas Knapton of Barwick, buried 9th day of July.

Robert Chambers of Grimesdike was buried the 23th day of July.

Stephen Turpin of the towne and parish of Sherburne, pinner, on the one partie, and francis Saundersonne of the towne and parish of Barwick in Elmett, spinster, on the other partie, being both of them within the west ryding of the Countie of Yorke, and either of them above the age of 21 yeares, after the declaration of a marriage intended to be solemnized betweene the said parties beeing first published by the Register of the said parish of Barwick in Elmett aforesaid 3 severall Lordes dayes in the parish Church of the said Parish at the close of the morneing Exercise there, according to the laite Act of Parliament made touching marriages, weere married together the 15th day of August in the yeare of or Lord 1654, in the p'sence of Thomas Wansley, Thomas Bird and John Gibsonne of Ba[r]wick in Elmett aforesaid, and others, witnesses, before mee.

Ro: Barwicke.

Joshua, the sonne of John Gibsonne of Barwick in Elmett, borne the 3d day of August.

Elizabeth, the daughter of Willm Taite of Potterton, borne the 9th day of the same.

Mary, the daughter of Matthew Haigh of Barwick in Elmett, borne 15th day of ye same.

Mary, daughter of Thomas Robinson of Garforth Moreside, buried 8th day of ye same.

Henry Nicholson of Barwick in Elmett buried the 14th day of the same

Anne, the daughter of John Mawe of Garforth Moreside, borne — day of 7ber.

Francis, daughter of Willm Cowper of Scoles, borne the 21th of the same moneth.

Samuel, the sonne of John Drurie of Barwick, borne 21th day of October

A still borne childe, sonne of Geo. Dicksonne of Wynmore, buried 26th Octobr.

Elizabeth, daughter of John Rhodes of Wynmore, buried 28th of October.

Mary, daughter of John Ellis of Barwick, gent., buried 29th of Octobr.

Elizabeth, daughter of Jo. Sayner of Potterton Moreside, borne 28th Novembr.

Robert Scowthrop of Scoles was buried the 11th day of November.

Isabell Thrash of Barwick, widdow, buried 25th day of Novembr.

John, the sonne of Robert Settle of Potterton, borne 3rd of December.

Christofer, sonne of Sam. Waterworth of Barwick, borne 23th Decembr.

Richard Willsonne of Rhowndhey was buried the 2d day of December.

Lydia, daughter of widdow Leighton of Barwick buried 20th Decembr

Joshua, sonne of Jo: Gibsonne of the same, buried 21th of ye same.

Christofer, sonne of Sam: Taite of Potterton, borne 7th of January.

Hellen, daughter of Robert Browne of Wynmore, borne 8th January.

Dorothy, daughter of Robt Taylor of Barwick borne 16th January.

Thomas, sonne of Robert Isott of ye same, borne the 21th January.

Willm, sonne of Willm Brough of Barwicke, buried 12th of January.

Mary, wife of Peter Slaiter of Wynmore, buried 16th day of January.

Thomas Knapton of the towne and parish of Barwick in Elmett, wheele wright, on the one party, and Mary Daniell of Potterton, in the same parish, spinster, on the other partie, beeing either of them above the age of 21 yeares, and both of them with in the West ryding of the County of Yorke, after the declaration of a marriage intended to be solemnized betweene the said parties beeing first published by the Register of the said parish 3 severall Lords dayes in the said parish Church at the close of the morneing exercise there, according to the lait act of Parliamt made touching marriages, weere married together the 12th day of February in the yeare of our Lord 1654, in the p'sence of Richard Daniell and John Settle of Potterton, and Sam. Knapton of Barwick in Emett aforesaid, and others wittnesses. Before me.

RO. BARWICKE.

Abigaile, daughter of Henry Shan of Barwick, borne 8th day of February.

Richard, the sonne of Thomas Thompson of Stankes, born the 12th day of February, 1655.

Anne, daughter of Anne Handley of Scoles, widdow, buried 2d of February, 1654.

Thomas Aked of Barwick in Elmett, Colyer, buried 15th of the same, 1654.

John Airey of the towne and parish of Barwick in Elmett, lynnen webster, on the one party, and Jane Prince of the same towne and parish, spinster, on the other party, being either of them above the age of 21 yeares, and both of them within the West Ryding of the County of Yorke, after the publication of a marriage intended, God willing, to be solemnized betweene the said parties being first openly made by the Register of the said parish three severall Lords dayes before in the said parish Church at the close of the morneing Exercise there, according to the Laite Act of Parliament made touching Marriages, were married together the 12th daye of March in the yeare of our Lord 1654, in the p'sence of Robert Greene, John Taylor and Thomas Taylor of Barwick in Elmett aforesaid, and others, witnesses, Before me.

RO. BARWICKE.

Christofer Ibbitsonne of Potterton, within the parish of Barwick in Elmett, labourer, on the one party, and Margarett Clement of the same towne and parish, widdow, on the other party, being [*as before*], were married together the 12th day of March in ye yeare of our Lord 1654, in the p'sence of Richard Ball, Thomas Taylor, Robert Matthew, and others, wittnesses.

Before mee, Ro: BARWICKE.

Robert, the sonne of Conan Hopkinsonne of Barwick in Elmett, borne 1st day of March.

Jane, ye daughter of George Wright of Grimesdike, buried the 25th day of March, 1655.

Elizabeth, daughter of Oswold Harrisonne of Stankes, borne 5th day of Aprill, 1655.

Willm, the sonne of Willm Deardon of Garforth More side, borne 12th day of Aprill.

Edith, daughter of John Clarke of Barwick in Elmett, borne 22th day of Aprill.

Mary, the Relict of John Huby of Rhowndheye, was buried the 13th day of Aprill.

Isaac, sonne of Martine Prince of Barwick in Elmett, buried 27th daye of April.

Mary, daughter of Tho: Beedehall of Barwick in Elmett, borne the 1st daye of Maye.

Samuell, the sonne of Richard Turner of the same towne, borne the 16th day of Maye.

Mary, the daughter of Willm Huby of Rhowndhey, was borne the 17th day of May.

Mary, the daughter of Thomas Dodshonne of the same, borne the 19th day of Maye.

[*Blank*], daughter of Richard Thompsonne of Speighleys, borne the second of June.

[*Blank*], of John Sharpehowse of Wynne More, borne the eighth day of June.

Jeremy, sonne of Alverey Vevers of Scoles, was buried the 5th daye of June.

Elizabeth, wife of John Haighe of Barwick, buried the 17th day of June.

*Phinehas, sonne of Mr. Nath. Jacksonne of the same, buried 29th day of June.

Robert, the sonne of Conon Hopkinsonne of the same, buried 30th day of June.

Robert Greene, the younger, of the towne and parish of Barwick in Elmett, howse-carpenter, on the one party, and Anne Wraye of the same towne and parish, spinster, on the other partye, being [*as before*], were married together the second daye of Julye in the yeare of our Lord 1655, in the p'sence of Robert Greene, the elder, Richard Turner and Thomas Cowpland of Barwick in Elmett aforesaid, and others, witnesses. Before mee JOHN SAVILE.

Thomas Settle of Potterton, in the parish of Barwick in Elmett, chandelour, on the one partye, and Elizabeth Sutton of the same towne and parish, spinster, on the other partie, being [*as before*], were marryed together the fourth day of Julye in the yeare of our Lord 1655, in the p'sence of Willm Settle and John Settle of Potterton aforesaid, and Richard Turner of Barwick in Elmett aforesaid, and others, witnesses. Before mee
JO: SLINGSEBY.

Richard, sonne of Richard Atkinsonne of Rhowndhey, borne 15th day of Julye.

Jeremy, the sonne of Robert Ball of Potterton, borne 23th day of the same.

Richard Settle of Potterton aforesaid buried the 15th daye of Julye.

---

*The Rev. Nathaniel Jackson was ordained deacon at Bishopthorpe, 8 June, 1623, being then A.B. of Christ's College, Cambridge, priest 22 Feb., 1623–4. In 1629 he became rector of Stonegrave. In 1648 he seems to have been living with his brother John at Barwick, and whom he may have succeeded as Puritan Minister there after his brother's death in Jan., 1648–9. He was buried in All Saints Pavement, York, 1 Nov., 1662, and by his will dated 18 Oct., 1662, he gave to the poor of Barwick £10 to be distributed by Mr. John Tayler and Thomas Vevers. His son Phineas was bapt. at Stonegrave 19 March, 1633–4. For his will, pedigree and an interesting account of the family see Canon Raine's Marske in Swaledale, Yorkshire Archaeological Journal, vol. vi., also Hunter's Familiae Minorum Gentium (Harleian Society), p. 1263.

Susanna, daughter of Thomas Prince of Scoles, borne 14th day of August.

John, sonne of Robert Knapton of Barwick, borne 2d day of September.

Wiffm, sonne of Wiffm Taite of Scoles, borne the 20th day of the same.

John Burnell of Rhowndehey Parke buried the 2d day of September.

Grace, the wife of Henry Shan of Barwick, buried the 24th day of the same, 1655.

Mary, the daughter of Thomas Thomeson of Stankes, born the 12 day of October, 1655 [entry erased].

Wiffm Wilcock of Garforth Moreside, in the parish of Barwick, labourer, on ye one party, and Jane Vaux of Wynmorside, of the same parish, widdow, on the other partye, being [*as before*], were married together the 22th of October instant, in the yeare of our Lord 1655. Before mee.

JOHN SAVILE.

Hellen, the daughter of Wiffm Ingle of Scoles, borne the 15th day of October.

Margaret, daughter of Geo. Bolland of Barwick, borne 20th daye of the same.

Marke the sonne of John Dennisonne of the same, borne the 30th day of the same.

Abigaile, daughter of Hen. Shan of Barwick, buried 2d day of October.

John Tym of Rhowndhey parke buried the 17th day of the same.

John, sonne of Thomas Sampsonne of Parlington, buried 19th of the same.

Andrew Hardecastle of Barwick in Elmett buried 21th day of the same.

Anne, daughter of Geo. Wright of Potterton, buried 24th day of the same.

Margarett, wife of Geo. Bolland of Barwick, buried 31th day of the same.

Thomas Cowpland of the towne and parish of Barwick in Elmett, Carpenter, on the one partie, and Anne Haigh of the same towne and Parish, spinster, on the [other] partie, being [*as before*], were married together the twelueth daye of November instant in the yeare of our Lord 1655, in the p'sence of Thomas Taylor and Joshua Turner and other witnesses. Before mee.

JOHN SAVILE.

Elizabeth, daughter of Richard Brough of Barwick, borne the 1st daye of November, 1655.

John, sonne of Geo. Dicksonne of Wynne more, the 3d day of the same.

Helen Willsonne of Rhowndehey parke, widdowe, buried the 5th daye of November.

Richard Kent of the towne and parish of Barwick in Elmett, sopemaker, on the one party, and Alice Burland, the younger, of the same towne and parish, spinster, on the other party, being [*as before*], were married together the tenth day of December in the yeare of our lord 1655, in the p'sence of Thomas Settle and Robert Matthew of Barwick in Elmett aforesaid, and Samuel Settle of Potterton, and other witnesses. Before mee—JOHN SAVILE.

Peter Slaiter of Win More, within the parish of Barwick in Elmett, Colyer, on the one party, and Mary Dikes of Stankes, within the said parish, spinster, on the other party, beeing [*as before*], were married together the 24th daye of December in the yeare of our Lorde, according to the computation of the Church of England, 1655. in the p'sence of Thomas Thompsonne and Francis Turner of Stankes aforesaid, and other witnesses. Before mee—JOHN SAVILE.

Thomas [*John* deleted], the sonne of Thomas Knapton of Barwick, borne the 8th daye of December.

Elizabeth, daughter of John Gibsonne of the same, borne 14th day of the same.

Jane, the wife of Willm Prince, Elder, of Barwick, buried 6th day of the same.

Elizabeth, daughter of Jo. Gibsonne of the same, buried 14th day of the same.

Mary Casse, widdowe, of Scoles, buried 25th daye of the same moneth.

Richard Jackson, the younger, of Scoles, of the parish of Barwick in Elmett, cloathmaker, on the one party, and Jane Greene of Stankes, of the same parish, spinster, on the other party, being [*as before*], were married together the 22th day of Januarye in the yeare of our Lord. according to the Computation of the Church of England, 1655, in the p'sence of Christopher Greene and Richard Jackson the elder, of the said pishe. Before JOHN SAVILE.

Richard, the son of Richard Jackson, younger, of Scoles, borne the 22th day of January.

Edward Knapton of Barwick was buried the 2^{d} day of January.

Anne, the daughter of Richard Swaile of Potterton, borne the 2^{d} daye of February.

Elizabeth, daughter of Stephen Eastburne of Wynmore, borne 14th of the same.

Rich., sonne of Rich. Jackson, younger, of Scoles, buried 14th day of February.

John, the sonne of John Ellis of Barwick in Elmett, buried 27th of the same.

Henrye, the sonne of John Ellis of Barwicke in Elmett, borne the 6th of Marche.

Richard, the sonne of Thomas Thompsonne of Stankes, borne the 8th day of the same.

Richard, the sonne of Richard Saunderson of Potterton, borne 17th of the same.

Willm Settle, the Elder, of Potterton, buried the 27th daye of March, 1656.

Robert, the sonne of Willm Taite of the same, buried the same daye, 1656.

[*Blank*], the wife of Richard Saundersonne of the same, buried the 30th of the same, 1656.

Katherine, the daughter of John Haighe, younger, of Barwicke, borne 28th of Aprill.

Willm Taite of Potterton was buried the 18th daye of Aprill.

Alice, the daughter of Christofer Ibbitson of the same, buried 22th of the same.

Katherine, the wife of Robert Vevers of Scoles, buried the 26th of the same.

Henry Shan of the towne and parishe of Barwick in Elmett, husbandman, on the one party, and Isabell Justice of Morwick, in the same Parish, spinster, on the other party, being [*as before*], were marryed together the 28th daye of Maye in the yeare of our lord, according to the computation and accompt now used in England, 1656, in the presence of Willm Vevers of Scoles and Ralph Collett, the Elder, of Barwick in Elmett aforesaid, and other wittnesses. Before mee.

JOHN DAWSONNE.

Abigaile, daughter of Willm Clarke of Kidhall more side, borne the 15th daye of Maye.

Robt, sonne of Willm Constable of Ladie growndes, buried the 12th daye of Maye.

John and Francis, sonnes of Jo. Hemsworth, younger, of Potterton, borne the 15th day of June.

Isabell, daughter of Thomas Settle of Barwicke in Elmett, borne the 11th day of June.

George, sonne of Rich. Hollings of the same, borne the 18th daye of the same.

John, the sonne of Mart. Prince of the same, borne the last daye of the same.

The still borne daughter of Hen. Haworth of Garforth-More-side buried the 9th of June, 1656.

Francis, sonne of Jo. Hemsworth, $young^{r}$, of Potterton, buried the 23th daye of the same.

John, sonne of the said John Hemsworth, younger, of Potterton, buried 24 daye of June.

Richard Prince of the towne and parish of Barwick in Elmett, Taylor, on the one partye, and Hellen Woodburne of the same towne and parish, spinster, on the other partye, being [*as before*], were marryed together the 16th daye of Julye in the yeare of our lorde, according to the Computation and accompt now used in Englande, 1656, in the p'sence of Thomas Settle and Robert Mathew of Barwick in Elmett aforesaid, and other witnesses. Before mee—JOHN SAVILE.

Mary, the wife of Willm Brough of Barwicke in Elmett, buried the 25th day of Julie.

Margaret, ye daughter of John Settle, ye Elder, of Potterton, borne the 25th day of August.

Willm, the sonne of Robert Taylor of Barwick in Elmett, borne the 9th day of September.

Joshuah [Timothy *written above*], sonne of John Smith of the same towne, borne the 15th day of the same moneth.

Richard, the sonne of John Taite of Potterton, borne the 16th day of the same.

Robert Bolland of Barmebow, in the parish of Barwick in Elmett, lynen-webster, on the one partye, and Anne Wardrop of the same town and parish, single-woman, on the other party, being [*as before*], being first openly published by the Register of the saide Parish three severall Markett dayes in 3 severall weekes at the markett Crosse of Weatherby, in the said County, to witt, on the 4th, the 11th and 25th dayes of September last past, 1656, according to the lait Act of Parliamt made touching Marriages, were married together the first day of October in the yeare of our lord 1656, in the p'sence of Francis Kendall and John Wright of the parish of Whitchurch, and other witnesses. Before mee.

John Savile.

Peter, the sonne of Peter Slaitor of Wynmore, borne the 1st day of October.

Mary, the daughter of John Taylor of Barwick in Elmett, buried the 6th day of October.

Willm Prince, the Elder, of the towne and parish of Barwick in Elmett, Taylor, on the one party, and Helen Beale of the Towne of Cliffourd and parish of Bramham, singlewoman, on the other partye, being either of them above the age of 21 years, and both of them within the west rydeing of the County of Yorke, after the declaration of the intention of a marriage, God willing, to be solemnized between the said partyes being first openly published by the Register of the saide parish in the said parish Church on 3 severall lords dayes at the close of the morning Exercise there in 3 severall weekes, being above 21 dayes since the noate of the Publication was delivered by the saide Willm Prince to the said Register were marryed together the 13th daye of October, 1656, in the p'sence of John Appleyard, Jur, Tho. Righton, both of Clifford, and other witnesses. Before mee—Hen. Fairfax.

John Johnsonne of Kiddall, within the parish of Barwick in Elmett, on the one party, and Alice Kirkeby of Potterton, of the same parish, on the other party, being [*as before*], were marryed together the 15th day of October in the yeare of our lord 1656, in the presence of Richard Knapton, the younger, of Barwicke in Elmett aforesaid, and Rich. Ellis of Potterton aforesaid, and other witnesses, before mee—John Savile.

Joseph Strickland of Scoles, within the parish of Barwick in Elmett, mill-wright, on the one party, and Hellen Haigh of the Towne and parish of Barwick in Elmett aforesaid, singlewoman, on the other party, being [*as before*], were married together the 28th daye of October in the yeare of our lord 1656, in the p'sence of Thomas Taylor and Robert Mathew of Barwick in Elmett aforesaid, and others, wittnesses. Before mee.

JO. WARDE.

Samuell Wright of the towne and parish of Barwick in Elmett, Howse Carpenter, on the one party, and Elizabeth Prince of the same towne and parish, spinster, of the other partye, with the full consents of theire parents of both sides, being both of them within the West ryding [*as before*], were married together the 10th day of November in the yeare of our lord 1656, in the p'sence of Samuell Shenton and Robert Shenton of Barwick in Elmet aforesaid, and other witnesses. Before mee.

JOHN SAVILE.

Margarett Wright, widdow, of Potterton, was buried the 22th day of November.

George Lofthowse of Osmondthorp, within the parish of Leedes, yeoman, on the one party, and Mary Taylor of Morwick, within the parish of Barwick in Elmett, singlewoman, on the other partye, with the full consents of the parents of both the saide parties, beeing both of them within the West ryding [*as before*], were married together the third day of December in the yeare of our lord 1656, in the p'sence of John Taylor of Morwick aforesaid, the brides father, and Richard Steade of Bardsey, in the said county, her uncle in lawe, and other wittnesses. Before mee—MARMA: HICKE, Ald'.

Thomas Wood of Barwick in Elmett the 2[d] day of December was buried.

Margaret, the dauter of John Settle of Potterton, buried 3[d] of the same.

Andreu Ellis of Barwick in Elmett buried the 8th day of the same.

John, the sonne of Samuel Wright of Barwick in Elmet, borne 16th of y[e] same.

George Hilton of Morwick was buried the 26th of January.

James, the sonne of Robert Prince of Barwick, borne the 24th of January.

Mary, the daughter of Richard Shippen of Barmebow, borne the last of the same.

Mary, the wife of Richard Knapton of Barwick buried 18th of February.

*George, the sonne of Nich. More of Kidhall, gent., borne the 3[d] day of March.

Rich., the sonne of Rich. Ferrar of Scoles, borne the 16th daye of March.

John, the sonne of Randall Constable of Wynmore, borne the last daye of March, 1657.

Johanna, the wife of Sam Waterworth of Barwick, buried the 2[d] daye of March, 1656.

Alice Burland of Barwick, widdowe, buried the 10th daye of March, 1656.

---

*See Dugdale's Visitation of Yorkshire, continued by Mr Clay in the *Genealogist*, vol. xii., page 43.

Sam. Knapton of Barwick buried the 23th daye of March, 1656.
Mrs Francis Hepworth of Scoles buried the 29th daye of March, 1657.
William, the sonne of Willm Marston of Morwicke, buried the same daye.
Stephen Walker of the Marsh layne, within the parish of Leedes, cloathier, on the one pty, and Elizabeth Waterhouse of the towne and pish of Barwicke in Elmett, singlewoman, on the other partye, with the full consentes of the parentes on both sides, after a noate of the publication [*as before*], were married together the [*blank*] day of [*blank*] in the yeare of our lord 1657, In the presence of John Taylor of Morwick, the brides uncle by the mothers side, and Rich. Steade, the brides uncle by the mothers side, and other witnesses. Before mee.

[*Not signed.*]

John, the sonne of Randall Constable of Wynne More, buried the fowerteenth day of Aprill, 1657.
Thomas Prince of Scoles buried the 22th daye of Aprill in the yeare of our lord 1657.
Thomas Smith of the towne and parish [of] Methley, on the one party, yeoman, and Isabell Reame of the towne of Shippen and parish of Barwick in Elmett, single woman, on the other party, being either of them above the age of 21 yeares [*as before*], were married together the [*blank*] daye of Maye in the yeare of our lord 1657, In the presence of John Errington of Barmebow, and John Scoley of Methley, yeoman, and other witnesses. Before mee.

JOHN SAVILE.

James Hopwood of the towne of Shippen and of the parish of Barwick in Elmett, Chandelor, on the one party, and Edith Collett of Barwick in Elmett, of the said parish, singlewoman, on the other party, being wth the full consent of the parents of both sides [*as before*], were married together the 28th day of May instant in the yeare of our lord 1657. In the p'sence of Mr John Erington of Barnbow, and Marke Hopwood of Micklefeild, and before me—JOHN SAVILE.
Mary, the daughter of John Burland of Barwick in Elmett, borne the first day of Maye.
William, sonne of Joseph Strickland of Barwick in Elmett, borne 15th daye of Maye.
Thomas, sonne of Chr: Shore of Barmbow, borne 19th daye of the same moneth.
Robert Sayner of Scoles buried the 10th daye of June, 1657.
Robert Prince of Barwick in Elmett buried the 15th daye of June.
Hellen, the wife of Alverey Vevers of Scoles, buried the 16th of June.
Thomas Bellas of Barw. in Elmett buried the 20th daye of June.
Willm Rhoidhouse of Shippen buried the 20th daye of June
[*Blank*], the sonne of Isaac Woode of Potterton, borne [*blank*] of June.
Ro., the sonne of Ro. Greene, younger, of Barwick, borne the 7th of July.

Willm, the sonne of Geo. Hunter of Wynnmore, borne the 12th of July.

Ruben, sonne of Rich. Prince of Barwick, borne the 13th of July.

Anne, daughter of Jo. Sayner of Grimesdike, borne the 14th of July.

Bridgitt, daughter of Martine West of Rhowndhay, buryed the 30th day of July.

Mary, illigitimate daughter of Mary More of Barwick, borne the 4th daye of August.

Henry, sonne of Geo. Dickonsonne of Wyn-more, borne the 10th daye of the same.

Tho., sonne of Tho. Varley of Garforth, borne the peenult daye of the same.

Leo. Thomson of Rhowndhay buried the 14th daye of August.

Margarett, daughter of Ro. Scowthrope of Scoles, borne the 4th daye of September.

Jonathan, sonne of Tho. Taite of the same, borne the [*blank*] daye of September.

Rebecca, daughter of Hen. Shanne of Barwick, borne the 20th day of September.

George Cowper of Barwick buried the 20th daye of September.

Tho: Hopwood and Anne Brough of the towne and parish of Barwick in Elmett, after publication of theire marriage published according to the laite Act of Parliamt, were married together by Mr Wright, Minister of Bardsey, the 26th daye of October.

Susan, daughter of Willm Constable of Wyn-more, borne the 6th daye of October.

John, the sonne of Jo. Johnson of Pottertonne, borne the 22th daye of October.

The still borne sonne of Jo. Airey of Barwick buried the 14th day of October.

Willm Clarke of Kidhall-more-side buried the 15th daye of October.

Francis Turner of Stankes buried the 28th daye of October.

Jo. Lee and Grace Baitesonne of the towne and parish of Barwick in Elmett, after the publication of theire marriage made according to the laite Act of Parliamt, were married together by Mr Smith, minister, the 2d daye of November.

Mary, the daughter of Thomas Thompson of Stankes, born the 12 of November.

Edward, sonne of Rich. Thompsonne of Speighley nooke, borne the 13th daye of November.

Eliz., daughter of Sam. Wright of Barwick, borne the 14th daye of November.

Marke Wright and Elizabeth Knapton of the towne and parish of Barwick, after publication made according to the lait Act of Parliament touching marriages, weere Married together by Mr Smith the 7th daye of December, 1657.

Anne, the wife of Jo: Beedhall of Scoles, was buried the 1st day of December.

Francis Jeffersone of Bramham was buried the 28th of December.

Richard, the son of Geo. Tildsley of Barmebowe, borne the 15th of January.

Samuell, the sonne of Ro: Knapton, borne the 15th daye of January.
Hanna, daughter of Tho. Settle of Barwick, borne the 18th daye of January.
Eliz., the wife of Jo. Gatenby of Barwick, was buried the 8th of January.
Anne Daniel, widdowe, of Barwick, was buried the 13th daye of January.
Anne Cooke, widdowe, of Barwick, was buried the 3d of February.
Christ. Shore of Barmebow buried the 19th daye of February.
Marg. Smith, widdowe, of Rhowndhey, buried 22th of February.
Michaell, the sonne of Rich. Atkinsonne of Rhowdhay, borne the 25th of February.
Rich., the sonne of Jo. Barker of Barwick, borne the 26th of the same.
Joseph, sonne of Ro. Ball of Potterton, borne the 5th day of March.
Mary, daughter of Jo. Hemsworth of Potterton, borne the 21th of March.
George Browne of Rhowdhay buried the first of March.
Christ. Shore of Barmebowe buried the 6th of March.

1658.

Jo: Kirkby of Potterton buried the 28th of March.
Eliz., daughter of Conon Hopkinson, borne in Barwick the 2d day of Aprill.
Willm, the sonne of Tho. Smith of Shippen, borne the 2d day of Aprill.
Mart. Procter of Barwick buried the 2d of Aprill.
John Greenwood of Scoles buried the 25th day of Aprill.
John, ye son of Joseph Strickland, was baptized ye 8th day of November, anno. Dom. 1658.
*Samuell Hallowes of Darby, Gent., and Elizabeth Jacksonne of Barwick in Elmett, Gentlewoman, after the publication of theire marriage before, were married together the 27th daye of May, 1658. Present at the marriage Mr Nathaneel Jackson, Thomas Charnells of Snarleston in Leicestershire, Esq., Mr Samuell Sleigh, Senr, and Samuel Sleigh, his sonne, of [*blank*] in Darbyshire, John Taylor of Morwick, and Thomas Hardcastle of Barwick parish, Willm Cooke of Sherburne, &c. They were married by Mr Rathband, Parson of Ripley.
Mary, daughter of Ro. Settle of Potterton, borne the 20th day of May.
Tho. Whaley, sonne of Tho. Whaley, borne the 2d daye of March, 1657.
Fra. Whaley, sonne of the sayed Thomas Whaley, borne the 1st day of August, 1658.

---

*Samuel Hallowes was the son of Samuel Hallowes, of Dethick, co. Derby, M.P. for the town of Derby. Elizabeth Jackson was the daughter of the Rev. Nathaniel Jackson, of Barwick, formerly of Richmond. Their son, Samuel Hallowes, born and baptized at Barwick in September, 1659, was of Dethick and Glapwell, married Elizabeth, sole daughter and heiress of Thomas Woolhouse, of Glapwell, and was the father of Thomas Hallowes, who married Lady Catherine Brabazon, daughter of Chambre, 5th Earl of Meath. *Hunter's Familiæ Minorum Gentium* (Harleian Society), p. 468.

1659.

Mary, the daughter of Thomas Cowpland, borne the 20th day of May.

A bond for the parish. Know all men by these presents that we, Robert Shore of Seacroft and County of Yorke, Taylor, and William Rishton of the same towne and County, yeoman, doe stand firmely bound and indebted unto Thomas Settle of Barwicke in Elmet, William Massie and William Settle of the same towne and parish, Churchwardens, or to the Churchwardens succeeding in the said office, in the summe of tenn pounds of good and lawfull currant money of England, to be paid unto them the said Thomas Settle, William Massie and William Settle, or to the Churchwardens succeeding, to the which payment well and truly to be paid satisfied and done, we the said Robert Shore and William Rishton doe bind us and both of us and either of us for both and the whole summe, our heires executors and administrators firmely by these prests. Sealed with our Seales, dated the sixth day of Aprill in the yeare of our Lord God one thousand six hundred fifty and nine.

Whereas George Heald late of Seacroft, deceased, did and hath done by his last Will and Testament give out of his copyhold lands lieing and being within the Mannor of Barwicke in Elmet, the summe of five shillings to be paid unto the Churchwardens of the said Barwicke yearely, and every yeare in or upon the foure and twentieth day of August of the same yeare, from yeare to yeare for ever for the use of the poore of the said Barwicke, soe long as he the said Robert Shore, his heires, executors, administrators and assignes, or any other person whatsoever, doe, may or claime title from by or under him or them.

The condition of this obligation is such that if the above bounden Robert Shore and William Rishton, they or either of them, their heires, executors, administrators and assigns, or any of them, doe well and truely pay or cause to be paid unto the abovesaid Churchwardens, and to the Churchwardens succeeding of Barwicke in Elmet, the inst summe of five shillings of currant English money yearely, and every yeare for ever at in or upon the fowre and twentieth day of August, being lawfully demanded that then this present obligation to be void frustrate and of none effect or else to stand remaine and be in full power, force, strength and vertue. Sealed and delivered in the presence of

This is a true copy of a bond sealed signed and delivered by Robert Shore and William Rishton In the presence of John Taylor and Leonard Winterburne, examined by us whose names are here underwritten.

George Spinke. Thomas Wansley.
Wm Vevers. John Taylor.

Samuell, the sonne of Samuell Hallowes, Gent., was borne the eighth day of September and baptized the eleventh day of September in the yeare of our Lord 1659.

Benjamin Pease of the parish of Whitchurch, on the one party, and Susan Tipling of Winmore-side, in the parish of Barwicke in Elmet, on the other party, after the publication of their marriage made according to the lait act of Parliament, were married together by Mr Jackson, Parson of Barwicke in Elmet, the 21 day of November.

Alice, the daughter of Thomas Thompson of the Stankes, born the 29 day of November.

Isabell, the wife of Thomas Potter of Potterton, buried the 1st day of December.

Elizabeth Ellis of the towne of Barwicke, widdow, buried the 4th day of December.

The still born child of Richard Daniel of Potterton buried the 8th day of December.

Ellis Robert of Shippon buried the 12th day of December.

Elizabeth, the wife of Henry Croft of Barwicke, buried the 21th of December.

Ellen Handley of Scoles, widdow, buried the 4th day of January.

Thomas Settle of the towne of Barwicke buried the 12th day of January.

Frances, the wife of Richard Daniel of Potterton, buried the 16th day of January.

Thomas, the sonne of Thomas Settle, deceased, born the 20th of January.

Thomas, the sonne of Widdow Shore of Barnbow, buried the 12th day of February.

Cathern, the daughter of William Constable of Winmoreside, borne the 22th day of February.

Jaine, the daughter of John Sayner of Potterton, born the 1st day of March.

[*Blank*], the daughter of Richard Swales of Potterton, buried the 10th of March.

Arthur, the sonne of Isaac Wood of Potterton, born the 10th day of March.

Mr John Gascoigne, Esqr, sonne of Sr Thom. Gascoigne of Barnbow, Baront, buried the 13th of March.

Edmond, the sonne of Isaacke Wood of Potterton, buried the 24th of March.

Henry, the sonne of Henry Shippen of Barnbow, born the 6th day of March.

1660.

William Prince of Barwicke, buried the first day of April.

John, the sonne of John Lee of Kidhall, born the second day of Aprill.

Mawd Potter of Potterton Buried the fourth day of Aprill.

Isabell Daniell, servant at Morwicke, Buried the 14th day of Aprill.

Samuell, the sonne of Thomas Knapton of Barwicke, buried the 29th of Aprill.

Cathern, the daughter of Willm Constable of Win-moreside, buried the 29th of Aprill.

William Constable of Win-more side, buried the 6th day of May.
William Haige of Barwicke buried the 12th day of May.
Alice, the daughter of Thomas Dodgson of Roundhey, born the 24th of May.
George Webster of the parish of More mountaine, on the one party, and Margaret Vevers of Scoles, in the parish of Barwicke in Elmet, on the other party, after the publication of the marriage on three severall Lords dayes, were married together by Mr Jackson, parson of Barwicke in Elmet, the 31 day of May.
John Hayworth of Garforth moreside, on the one partie, and Hellen Warrander of Shippon, on the other partie, both of the parish of Barwicke in Elmet, after the publication of their marriage on three severall Lords dayes, were married together by Mr Jacksonne, parson of Barwicke, the 11th of June.
Isabell, the wife of John Gouthwaite of Scoles, buried the 14th day of June.
Robert Scoughthrop of Scoles buried the 6th day of July.
Mary, the daughter of John Kirkby of Potterton, buried the 16th day of July.
John Hemsworth of Potterton buried 3^{d} day of August.
Jacob, ye son of Benjam' Pease of Worricke, was Baptised ye 11th day of October.
John Vevers of Scoles buried the 21 day of September.
Mary, the daughter of Marke Wright of Barwicke, borne the 20th day of September.

1661.

Willm, the sonn of Robert Shutleworth of Scoles, Baptiz., the 7th of Aprill.
Joseph, the sonn of Richard Swailes of Potterton, Baptized the 14th day of Aprill.
Alice, the wife of Willm Vevers of Potterton, Buried the 15th day of Aprill.
Margaret, the daughter of Rob. Johnson of Scoles, Buried the 17th day of Aprill.
Beniamen, ye sonn of Randall Briggs of Rondhey, was baptised the 14th day of April.
Ric., the sonn of Richard Shippon of Barmbow, Baptized the 5th of May.
Willm Renhold of Lynton, in the ꝑish of Spoforth, on the one ꝑtie, and Elizabeth Claton of the towne and ꝑish of Barwicke, on the other ꝑtie, after theire publication on several lords dayes, were married together by Mr Brigges, May the 6th.
Alice, the daughter of Robert Brooke of the Stankes, buried May the 10th.
Tho., the sonn of Tho: Tirington of Shippen, buried May the 13th.
George, the sonn of John Haige of Barwicke, Baptized May the 19th.
Fees to Mr Bridges 8^{d}, Clarke 10^{d}, besides Registering.
Richard, ye sonne of Samuell Stowin of Barwicke, Buried ye 2^{d} day of June.

Frances, ye daughter of Robert Johnson of Scoles, Buried ye 2d day of June.

Mary, the daughter of Thomas Knapton of Barwicke, was Baptized ye 9th of June.

*Anne, the wife of Sr Thomas Gascoigne Knight and Barot, was Buried ye 19th day of June, Anno Dom̄i 1661.

Robert Clough was Buried the 29th day of June.

Grace, ye Daughter of Solomon Jebson of Potterton Layne, was baptized ye 30th of June.

Elline, ye daughter of Henry Walton of Rowndhay, was buried ye 30th of June.

Marke, ye son of Hen. Walton of Rowndhey, was Baptized ye 28th of July.

William, son of Matthew Ingle of Barwicke, was Baptized ye 28th of July.

Robert, ye son of Wm Hardwicke of Grimesdicke, was borne ye 14th of July.

Rosamond Layton, Widdw, was Buried ye first of August.

Alice, ye wife of George Waite of Winmore, was buried ye 2d day of August.

Elizabeth Harrison, widdw, was buried ye seaven day of August.

John Rhoades was Buried ye eleventh day of August.

William, ye son of Robt Constable of Scholes, was Baptized ye eleventh day of August.

Catherine, ye Daughter of John Dawson of browne moore, was Baptized ye Last of Aug.

William, ye son of Richard Potter of Potterton, was baptized ye 22th of September.

Lawrence, ye son of Francis West of Roundhey, was Buried ye 27th of September.

Robert Taylor of Barwicke was Buried ye 28th of September.

Susanna, ye daughter of Thomas Varlow of Browne moore, was Baptized ye 29th Sepb.

Given to Henry Millington, an Inhabitant of greate Draton in Sallopp, being one of ye afores'd Towne appoynted for gathering of a Brieefe dated ye 21th day of January in ye Twelueth yeare of ye Reigne of King Charles ye second, and upon ye Tenth day of August in ye Third yeare of ye Reigne of King Charles 2 There happened a Greate fire, soe that it Burnt most pte of ye Towne, &c. Appoynted Treasuries for ye receaiuing of ye monies gathered, Tho. Cooke, cla' Minnister of Draton afores'id, and Mr Richard Walton, Bayliffe for ye time being, and others, which more playnly appeareth in ye s'd Briefe gathered upon ye 29th day of Septembr, 1661, By Tho: Taylor, one of ye Churchwardens of Barwicke in Elmett, in ye parrish Church ye sume of eighteen pence, and given by ye s'd Thomas to ye s'd Henry upon ye day of ye date above written.

Thomas, ye son of John Sharpous of ye Stankes, was Baptized ye 6th day of October.

---

*She was the daughter of John Symonds, of Brightwell, co. Oxon.

Mary, ye daughter of Cudbert Munsey, was Buryed ye 10th day of October.

Henry Wilson of Scoles Buried ye 24th day of October.

Jane, ye wife of William Massie, was buried ye 30th day of October.

John Halliday of Potterton, in ye pish of Barwicke in Elmett, and Alice Chambers of ye same, after ye baines of their publication 3 severall Lords days, was maryed together by Mr Bridges ye 29th day of October, Año Domi 1661.

Richard Ellis and Elizabeth Wilson, both of this parish, after ye baines of their publication on 3 severall Lords days, were married together by Mr Bridges ye 1st day of November.

George, ye son of John Haigue of Barwicke, was buried ye 3d day of Novembr.

Richard, ye son of John Smith of Barwicke, was Baptized ye 3d day of Novembr.

Jane Vevers of Scholes, widdw, was buried ye 3d day of December.

Sarah, ye Daughter of Richard Knapton of Potterton, was baptized ye 8th day of December.

Beniamine, the son of Randolph Briggs of Rhoundhey, was baptized Aprill 22th.

George Spincke and Anne Vevers of Scoles were marryed by licence June the 24th.

Robert Johnson of Scholes was Buried the 9th day of January.

William, son of Thomas Terrington, was buried ye 25th day of January.

Elizabeth, the wife of John Moore of Barwicke, was buried ye 3d day of February.

Francis, ye son of William Shillotoe, was buried ye 5th of February.

Wm, ye son of Randall Constable, was Baptized ye 9th day of February.

Richard Ball and Margeret Gouthwhaite, both of this parrissh, after their publisacone on severall Lord dayes, were maried by Mr Bridges on ye 10th day of February.

Jacob9, fili9 Jehosove Turner de Barwicke in Elmett, Baptizataus fuit Decimo septimo Februarij.

John Ingle of Scoles was Buried ye 2d day of March.

Elizabeth, ye daughter of Richard Atkinson of Rowndhey, was Baptized ye 2d day of March.

Elline, ye daughter of Thomas Thompson of ye Stanckes, was Baptized the 6th day of March.

Mary, ye Daughter of David Hopwood of Potterton, was Baptized the 14th of March.

1662.

John, ye son of Oswald Harrison, was Baptized ye 30th day of March.

Timothy, the son of John Leigh of Barwicke, was Baptized ye first day of Aprill.

Michael Turner of seacroft, in ye pish of Whitchurch, on ye one ptie, and Alice Constable of Grimesdicke, in this pish, on ye other ptie, after their publication on three severall Lords dayes, were Maried by Mr Bridges on ye 2d day of Aprill.

Robert, the son of William Cooper of Scoales, was Baptized ye 3d day of Aprill.

Jeremiah, the son of George Spincke of Scholes, was Baptized ye 22th day of March.

Henry Ellys of Barwicke, Gent', was Buried the 20th day of Aprill.

Thomas Wood of Abberforth, and Alice Calbecke of Potterton, after their publicac̄on, were maried by Mr Bridges ye 7th day of May.

Frances, ye Daughter of Thomas Dodgson of Rhoundhey Parke, was Bapt. ye 11th day of May.

Anne, ye Daughter of James Weardley of Winmore, was Baptized ye 22th day of June.

*Joseph, ye son of Randolph Briggs of Rowndhey Parke, was Baptized ye 21th day of June.

Thomas Akidd, ye son of Mary Akidd, widdow, of Barwicke, was buried the 10th day of July.

The still borne child of Thomas Coapland of Barwicke, buried ye 11th day of July.

Ann, ye daughter of Thomas Coapland aforesaid, was Buried ye 13th day of July.

Robert Idditson of Barwicke was Buried ye 21th of August.

William, ye son of George Haist of Barwicke, was Baptized ye 24th of Aug.

Anne, ye Daughter of Robert Brooke of ye Stanks, was Bapd ye 24th of Aug.

Mercie, ye daughter of Brian Bullacke, was Buried ye 25th August.

Anne, ye daughter of Robt G[r]een ye younger of Barwicke, was baptized ye Last of August.

John, ye son of William Lumbe of Morwicke, was baptized ye 7th day of Septr.

John Shippen had a Childe named Anne borne ye 15th day of September.

Mary, ye Daughter of Samuel Tate, was Baptized ye 21th of September.

John Bullocke had a still borne child Buried ye 2th.

Roger Gregson of Miglefield, in ye pish of Sheareborn, and Mary Taylor of Barwicke, wid', were maried ye 17th of September wth lycence.

William Jackson of Schooles, in this pish, and Grace Cash of ye same, after the Banns of Marriage asked on three severall Lord Days between both ye s'd pties, were maried the 24th of September.

Roger Spinke of Scholes, in this pish, and Alice Schofield of ye same, after the Banns of Marriage asked on three severall Lord days between both the s'd pties, were maried the 8th day of October.

Margett Prince of Barwicke was Buried ye 19th day of October.

John, ye son of William Lyster of Roundhey, was Baptized ye 26th Octobr.

---

*See Will of Brewen Briggs, of Roundhay, yeoman, ante page 44, also Thoresby's Ducatus 2nd Edition, pages 118a, 126, and Adel and Methley Registers (Thoresby Society), s. v. Brigg.

Mary, ye daughter of Richard Ellis of Barwicke, was Baptized ye 26th of Octob^{r}.

Elizabeth, ye wife of John Smith of Barwicke, was Buried the 31th of Octob^{r}.

Joseph Bollocke of Barwicke, and Martha Barraclough of ye same, after ye Banns of Marriage asked on three severrall Lords dayes, were maried the first day of November.

Elizabeth, ye wife of Richard Ellis of Barwicke, was Buried ye first of Nouember.

Richard Knapton of Barwicke was Buried the 29th of November.

October 31th, 1661.—Thomas Tate and Elizabeth Tempest, haveing first obteyned Lycense, were married according to Rites of ye Church of England in ye pish Church of St Michael, betwixt ye houres of Eight and twelve by Josiah Hunter, minister in Yorke.

Know all men whom it doth conserne that John Dodgson and Anne Tate were bond together in holy wedlock the sixt day of November in the parrish Church of Bishophill the younger, in Yorke, by Henry Mace, Minister.

Mary, ye Daugter of John Weatherall, was Buried ye 1st day of January.

Thomas, the sonne of William Braime of Barmbow carr, was buried ye 2^{d} day Feb.

Richard, the sonne of Robert Shuttleworth of Scoles, was Baptized the 16th of February

Thomas, the sonne of Richard Ball, was Baptized the 24th day of February.

Rosamand, ye Daughte^{r} of Richard Brough, was Baptized ye first Day of March.

William, the son of Marke Wright, was Baptized ye 5th day of March.

Anne, the Daughter of Cutbert Munsey, was Baptized ye 8th Day of March.

Hannah, the Daughter of Elizabeth Settle of Barwicke, widdow, was Buried ye 8th day of March.

Anne, ye Daughter of Joseph Bullocke, was Baptized ye 15th day of March.

Richard Turner of Barwicke, late Clarke, was buried the seventeenth of March, '62.

Daniel, the sonne [of] Edward Hudson of Leeds, now Clarke of Barwicke in Elmet, was Baptized the seventeenth Day of July in 1634.

May the 9th, 1666.—The Clark is to do all as to Reging, &c. Y^{e} Clark to allow p skinn 1^{s} 6^{d} p yeare, and to see it be done. Clar' fees, Buryall 10^{d}, Church 2^{d}, registring 4^{d}, wedings 1^{s}, cottage 4$\frac{1}{2}^{d}$.

Anne, y^{e} wife of Thomas Coapeland, was Buried y^{e} 20 day of March.

1663.

Robert, the sonne of Robert Ball of Potterton, was baptized y^{e} 29th of March.

Arthur Burton of Potterton was Buried y^{e} 11th day of Aprill.

Thomas, sonne of Joseph Stricland of Barwicke, was baptized April the 19th.
Matthew Haigue of Barwick was buried the 16th day of May, 1663.
George Spincke and Anne Vevers, both of Scoles, were marryed by licence June the 24th, 1661.
Robert Collet and Jennet Taylor, both of Barwicke, were marryed by licence November the 18th, 1661.
John Taylor of Barwicke, and Mary Vevers of Scoles, were marryed by licence February the 10th, 1661.
John Waugh of Leeds and Katherine Whalley of Roundhey, widdow, were marryed by licence December the first, 1662.
Thomas, the son of Thomas Taite of Barwicke, was borne, baptized and buried May the 29th, 1663.
Isaac, the son of Robert Butler of Roundhay, was baptized May the 31th, 1663.
Margaret, the daughter of Robert Sayner of Scoles, was baptized June the 14th, 1663.
Sarah, the daughter of Thomas Shippen of Barnebow, was buried July the 9th, 1663.
[*Blank*] Dinsdale of Barnbow, widdow, was buried July the 19th, 1663.
Francis Tim of Roundhay was baptized July the 29th, 1663.
William, son of Thomas Hopwood of Barwick, was baptized July the 26th, 1663.
Richard, son of George Spincke of Scholes, was baptized September the 4th, 1663.
James, son of Francis Sayner of Morwicke, was baptized August the 2d, 1663.
John, son of Thomas Stowen of Barwicke, was baptized October ye 11th, 1663.
Alice, ye daughtr of Henry Haworth of Garforth More side, baptized ye 11th of October, 1663.

1663. BAPTIZAT'.

Elizabeth, the daughter of John Weatherill of Barwicke, was baptized November the 21th.
Andrew, the son of William Jackson of Scoles, was baptized December the 6th.
Mercy, the daughter of Joshuah Turner of Barwicke, was baptized January the 1st.
Mary, the daughter of David Simpson of the white house by Potterton-moore, was baptized January the 8th.
Henry, the son of John Dawson of Browne-moore, was baptized Februa. the 7th.
Henry, the son of Peter Sclater of Spighleyes, was baptized February the 7th,
Richard, the son of Robert Collet of Barwicke, was baptized February the 21th.
Margaret, the Daughter of John Taite, senior, of Scoles, was baptized February the 28th.

1664 [BAPTISMS].

William, the son of John Hemsworth of Potterton, April the 12th

John, the son of John Bullocke of Barwicke, April the 17th
John, the son of Robert Browne of Winmoore side, April the 17th
Richard and Elizabeth the twins of John Sayner of Morwicke, May the 1st
William, the son of Joseph Bullocke of Barwicke, May the 15th
Richard, the son of Richard Knapton of Potterton lane, May the 15th
Jane, the daughter of James Wheateley of Winmoore side, May the 29th
Sarah, the daughter of Richard Jackson of Stankes, July the 17th
Mary, the daughter of John Holmes of Roundhay, July the 24th
Jennet, the daughter of David Hopwood of Potterton, August the 7th
Roebrt, the son of Martin Clough of Roundhay, August the 14th
John, the son of Richard Atkinson of Roundhay, August the 14th
Elizabeth, the Posthume daughter of Henry Walton of Winmoore side, October the 23th
Jane, the daughter of Richard Ellis, of Barwicke September ye 4th
John, the son of John Buck of Barwicke, October the 30th
Phinehas, the son of John Lee of Barwicke, November the 5th
George, the son of George Haist of Barwicke, November ye 13th
Anne, the daughter of Thomas Thompson of the Stankes, November the 24th
Alice, the daughter of Robert Brooke of the Stankes, November the 24th
Richard, the son of Thomas Wood of Barwicke, December the 18th
Elizabeth, the daughter of Marke Wright of Barwicke, December the 18th
Thomas, the son of Thomas Stowe[n] of Barwicke, December the 21th
Sarah, the daughter of Lawrence Hill of Stanks, December the 28th
John, the son of Richard Potter of Potterton, January the 8th
Michael, the son of Stephen Eastburne of Winmoore side, January the 15th
Anne, the daughter of Mr. John Ellis of Barwicke, January the 21th
Jane, the daughter of Henry Turner of the Stankes, February the 2d
Ralph, the son of Ralph Collet, junior, of Barwicke, February the 9th
Mary, the daughter of Thomas Varley of Garforth moore side, February the 12th
Thomas, the son of Robert Sayner of Scoles, February the 26th
Robert, the son of Solomon Jibson of Kidhall-lane-head, March the 3d
Frances, the daughter of Isaac Wood of Potterton lane, March the 3d

1665 [Baptisms].

Frances, the daughter of Richard Ball of Potterton, March the 26th
Anne, the daughter of Randolph Constable of Hurst moore, March the 27th
Benjamin, the son of Benjamin Pease of Morwicke, April the 2d
Sarah, the daughter of William Lumbe of Morwicke, April the 2d
Sarah, the daughter of Daniel Hudson of Barwicke, April the 8th
Elizabeth, the daughter of Bernard Turner of the Stankes, April the 9th
Sarah, the daughter of Cuthbert Munsey of Barwicke, May the 14th
Elizabeth, the daughter of Randolph Briggs of Roundhay, May the 17th

Joseph, the son of Joseph Strickland of Barwicke, May the 24th
Elizabeth, the daughter of Richard Swale of Potterton, May the 25th
Elizabeth, the daughter of Abraham Rishforth of the High Ash, June the 18th
John, the son of Robert Shaw of Brownemoore, June the 25th
Robert, the son of Richard Farrah of Scoles, June 25th
John, the son of Matthew Ingle of Barwicke, August the 2d
Mary, the daughter of Will. Thornton of Winmoore side, Octob. 22th
William, the son of Robert Greene, junior, of Barwicke, Novem. 19th
George, the son of Joshua Turner of Barwicke, December the 13th
Elizabeth, the daughter of John Dinnison, junior, of Barwicke, Decem. the 17th
Robert, the son of Robert Collet of Barwicke, Janua. the 9th
Anne, the daughter of Laurence Hill of the Stankes, Janu. the 25th
John, the son of James Wheateley of Winmooreside, Janu. the 28th
Isabell, the daughter of Henry Haworth of Garforth moor side, Janu. the 28th
Robert, the son of John Taite of Scoles, February the 11th
Anne, the daughter of George Spincke of Scoles, Februa. the 18th
Christopher, the son of David Hopwood of Potterton, March the 11th

1666.

John, the son of John Johnson of Potterton, was baptized April the 1st
Jane, the daughter of John Wetherall of Barwicke, April the 1st
William, the son of William Jackson of Scoles, April the 8th
George, the son of William Lister of Roundhay, April the 22th
Katherine, the daughter of Francis West of Roundhay, May the 17th
Elizabeth, the daughter of John Burnell of Roundhay, June ye 12th
John, the son of George Constable of Scoles, June the 24th
James, the son of John Bullock of Barwicke, July the 8th
William, the son of William Lumbe of Morwicke, July the 22th
Frances, the daughter of William Deardon of Garforth moore, Septem. 16th
Mary, the daughter of Richard Tait of Potterton, Septem. 23th
William, the son of William Ellis of Kidhall, Esq., Septem. ye 27th
Richard, the son of Richard Ellis of Barwicke, Octob. 7th
Miles, the son of Thomas Hopwood of Barwicke, Decem. the 9th
Jane, the Bastard daughter of Frances Thomson of Roundhay, Decem. the 16th
Thomas, the son of Martin Whitehead of Ollershaw lane head, January 13th
John, the son of John Coggan of Winmooreside, Jan. 20th
Ellenor, the daughter of John Buck of Barwicke, January ye 27th
Sarah, the daughter of John Aumbler of Winmoor side, Janu. ye 27th
William, the son of Thomas Stow of Barwicke, Janu. ye 30th
Richard, the son of Peter Sclater of Winmoore side, Febr. 3d
Elizabeth, the daughter of Robert Brooke of the Stankes, Feb. 6th
Samuel, the son of Marke Wright of Barwicke, February the 16th
James, the son of Thomas Dodgson of Roundhay, February the 17th
Frances, the daughter of Henry Wilkinson, a traveller, February the 24th

Susanna, the daughter of Cuthbert Munsey of Barwicke, March the 1st
James, the son of Luke Admergill of Potterton Lane head, March the 3d
Thomas, the son of Richard Knapton of Potterton lane, March the 11th
Samuel, the son of Joseph Bullocke of Barwicke, March the 17th

1667 [BAPTISMS].

Mary, the Bastard daughter of Elizabeth Watterworth of Barwicke, March ye 31th
Robert, the son of Henry Renton of Roundhay, April the 10th
John, the son of Randall Briggs of Roundhay, April the 10th
Anne, the Bastard daughter of Anne Tinsdall of Barwicke, May the 1st
Nathaneel, the son of John Lee of Barwicke, May the 5th
Robert, the son of Robert Browne of Winmoor side, May the 5th
William, the Bastard son of Katherine Moore of Barwicke, June ye 8th
Elizabeth, the daughter of James Wood of Potterton, June the 16th
[*Blank*] the [*Blank*] of Richard Jackson of the Stankes
Walter, the son of Joseph Strickland of Barwicke, June the 22th
Sarah, the daughter of William Thorneton of Winmoore, August the 11th
John, the son of John Taylor the younger of Barwicke, August the 27th
William, the son of Mr. John Ellis of Barwicke, August the 31th
Mary, the daughter of William Ellis of Kidhall, Esqr., Septem. the 11th
Margarett, the daughter of Robert Shaw of Barwicke, Septem. ye 14th
Richard, the son of Thomas Taite of Kidhall lane head, September the 29th
William, the son of Robert Collet of Barwicke, October the 2d
Sarah, the daughter of William Bridges, Curate of Barwicke, Octo. the 2d
Sarah, the daughter of Richard Slater of Winmoor, Octob. the 6th
John, the son of Laurence Hill of ye Stanke, October the 16th
Ellener, the daughter of Leonard Catton of Barwicke, October the 28th
James, the son of Oswald Harrison of the Stankes, Decem. the 22th
John, the son of Thomas Walker of Roundhay, Decem. the 22th
George, the son of George Haist of Barwicke, Decem. the 26th
Robert, the son of John Drury of Barwicke, January the 1st
Elizabeth, the daughter of Robert Saynor of Scoles, January the 12th
John, the son of Abraham Rishforth of the High Ash, February the 2d
Richard, the son of Richard Collet of Barwicke, February the 6th
Richard, the son of John Johnson of Potterton, March the 1st
Mary, the daughter of Henry Turner of the Stankes, March the 3d
Isabell, the daughter of David Hopwood of Potterton, March the 8th
Rosamund, the daughter of Thomas Watkinson [*since altered to* Atkinson] of Garforth moore, March the 12th
Richard, the son of Joshua Turner of Barwicke, March the 18th
Thomas, the son of Richard Potter of Potterton, March the 23th

[BAPTISMS] 1668.

Mary, the daughter of John Burnell of Roundhay, March the 29th
Samuel, the son of Samuel Taite of Kidhall lane head, April the 5th
Anne, the daughter of John Jackson, a traveller, April the 7th
Richard, the son of Joseph Turner of Potterton, April the 15th
Anne, the daughter of Wm. Taite, junior, of Scoles, April the 19th
Jane, the daughter of John Massy of Stocking, April the 23th
Anne, the daughter of John [? Dolphin] of Garforth moore side, May the 10th
Wm. the son of Ralph Collet, jun., of Barwicke, June the 3d
Thomas, the son of John Hemsworth of Potterton, June the 7th
William, the son of George Spincke of Scoles, June the 10th
Solomon, the son of Solomon Jibson of Kidhall lane head, June the 28th
Judith, the daughter of John Dodgeson of Kidhall lane head, Aug. ye 16th
William, the son of Richard Swale of Potterton, Septem. the 9th
John, the son of William Ellis of Kidhall, Esq'., Septem. the 10th
Sarah, the daughter of William Hodgeson of Potterton, Gentleman, Septem. the 15th
Jane, the daughter of John Bullock of Barwicke, Septem. the 20th
John, the son of William Jackson of Scoles, October the 18th
Frances, the daughter of John Aumbler of Winmoore side, Novem. ye 8th
William, the son of William Bridges, Curate of Barwicke, Nov. ye 18th
Richard, the son of Richard Taite of Potterton, Decem. the 20th
John, the son of Richard Ellis of Barwicke, December the 20th
Richard, the son of John Buck of Barwicke, Decem. the 29th
William, the son of James Clough of Roundhay, Decem. the 31th
Mary, the daughter of William Lumbe of Morwicke, Febru. the 7th
James, the son of John Saynor of Grimesdike, Febr. ye 14th
John, the son of William Lofthouse of Potterton, Febru. the 21th
Mary, the daughter of Matthew Norton of Roundhay, Febru. the 28th
John, the son of John Drury of Barwicke, March the 7th
Thomas, the son of Thomas Stowen, the elder, of Barwicke, March ye 15th

1669 [BAPTISMS].

Sarah, the daughter of Robert Brooke of ye Stankes, April ye 28th
Marke, the son of Marke Wright of Barwicke, May the 8th
William, the son of William Fawcett of Barwicke, May the 20th
Anne, the daughter of John Burnell of Roundhay, May the 20th
Henry, the son of Henry Turner of ye Stankes, May ye 23th
Alice, the daughter of Matthew Fox of Winmoor side, May ye 23th
Richard, the son of Richard Taylor of Barwicke, June the 25th
Richard, the son of Thomas Stowen, ye younger, of Barwicke, June the 27th
Ann, ye daughter of Joseph Strickland, 28th
Susanna, the daughter of Randolph Briggs of Roundhay, July ye 28th
Joseph, the son of Randolph Constable of Winmoore side, Septe. ye 5th

Alice, the daughter of John Browe, a traveller, Octob. ye 7th
Samuel, the son of Thomas Dodgeson of Roundhay, Octob. ye 10th
Anne, the daughter of Thomas Taite of Kidhall land head, Octob. ye 31th
Mary, the daughter of Peter Sclater of Winmoore-side, Octob. ye 31th
Anne, the daughter of Robert [? Greene] of Barwicke, Novem. ye 7th
[*Illegible*] the daughter of Thomas Thompson of the Stankes, Nov. ye 14th
[? Ellenor], the daughter of John Taite, junr., [? of Scoles] Novem. ye 21th
Richard, the son of William Bridges, Curate of Barwicke, Dece. ye 1st
John, the son of Robert Collet of Barwicke, Dec. ye 17th
Mary, the daughter of Mr. John Ellis of Barwicke, Dece. ye 29th
Mary, the daughter of Leonard Catton of Barwicke, Janu. ye 12th
Laurence, the posthume son of Laurence Hill of the Stanckes, Janu. ye 31th
Elizabeth, the daughter of David Hopwood of Potterton, Febru. ye 13th
Jane, the daughter of William Lumbe of Morwicke, Febr. ye 13th
Mary, the daughter of William Taite, junior, of Scoles, March ye 6th
Susanna, the daughter of Joshua Turner of Barwicke, March ye 7th
William, the son of Richard Vevers of Scoles, March ye 9th

1670 [BAPTISMS]

Anne, the daughter of Thomas Bakes of Scoles, April ye 10th
Richard, the son of Richard Sclater of Winmoore side, April ye 17th
Joseph, the son of John Shooesmith of Winmooreside, May ye 1st
Thomas, the son of John Massy of Stocking, May the 22th
Anne, the daughter of Richard Collet of Barwicke, May the 26th
Thomas, son of William Brame, junr., of Barnbow carre, June ye 12th
Elizabeth, the daughter of Philip Haist of Barwicke, June ye 19th
John, the son of George Haist of Barwicke, June ye 24th
Jane, the daughter of William Ellis of Kidhall, Esq., June ye 26th
William, the son of William Vevers of Scoles, July the 6th
Hannah, the daughter of Thomas Walker of Roundhay, August ye 21th
Joseph, the son of Joseph Bullocke of Barwicke, August ye 28th
Henry, the son of Christopher Aumbler of Winmooreside, Sept. ye 18th
Sarah, the daughter of William Twisleton of Potterton, Septe. ye 18th
Anne, the daughter of John Dunnell of Scoles, Octob. ye 21th
Elizabeth, the daughter of William Fawcett of Barwicke, Nove. ye 16th
Joshua, the son of William Lister of Roundhay, Novem. ye 20th
John, the son of George Browne of Barwicke, Novem. ye 21th
Mary, the daughter of William Bridges, Curate, Novem. ye 30th
Mary, the daughter of Richard Ball of Potterton, Decem. ye 17th
Elizabeth, the daughter of Richard Heslegrave of Scoles, Dece. ye 25th
George, the son of George Spincke of Scoles, Decem. ye 29th
Christina, the daughter of Thomas Stowing, senr., of Barwicke, Janu. ye 4th

William, the son of Richard Taylor of Barwicke, Januar. ye 5th
Mary, the daughter of Thomas Watkinson of Garforth Moore side Janu. ye 25th
Elizabeth, the Bastard daughter of Anne Tinsdall of Barwicke, Febru. ye 19th
Sarah, the daughter of Matthew Norton of Roundhay, Febru. ye 23th
Susanna, the daughter of George Hunter of Winmoore, Febru. ye 26th
Catherine, the daughter of James Clough of Roundhay, Februa. ye 27th.
Timothy, the son of Edward Hinchliffe of the Stanckes, March the 23th

1671 BAPTIZAT'.

Thomas, the son of Richard Ellis of Barwicke, March the 25th
Esther, the daughter of John Burnell of Roundhay, April ye 28th
Robert, the son of Richard Taite of Potterton, April the 30th
Mary, the daughter of William Oates of Winmoore, May the 29th
Thomas and Rebeccah, the children of Richard Prince of Barwicke, June ye 12th
Catherine, the daughter of William Briggs of Barwicke, June ye 22th
John, the son of John Aumbler of Winmoore-side, July the 9th
Joseph, the son of William Vevers, Junior, of Scoles, July the 13th
William, the son of Henry Beedall of Scoles, July the 19th
Francis, the son of Randall Briggs of Roundhay, July the 19th
Anne, the daughter of Abraham Rishforth of the High Ash, August ye 27th
George, the son of John Gibson of Barwicke, October the 28th
Thomas, the son of John Taylor, jun.', of Barwicke, Novem. the 16th
Richard, the son of John Dodgeson of Kidhall land head, Decem. ye 31th
Thomas, the son of John Outhwayt of Lazingcroft, Decem. ye 31th
Sarah, the daughter of Matthew Ingle of Barwicke, Janu. ye 25
John, the son of James Wood of Barwicke, February the 10th
Thomas, the son of John Buck of Barwicke, Febru. ye 29th
Anne, the daughter of Robert Collet of Barwicke, March ye 14th

1672 BAPTIZAT.

John, the son of William Hanley of Scoles, March the 31th
Mary, the daughter of Robert Brooke of ye Stanckes, April ye 14th
George, the son of William Ingle, jun'., of Scoles, April ye 24th
Esther, the daughter of John Massy of Stocking, May ye 1st
Henry, the son of William Ellis of Kidhall, Esq'., May ye 16th, being Ascension Day
Margarett, the daughter of Phillis Steele, a stranger, May the 29th
John, the son of John Dolphin of Garforth-moore-side, June the 9th
Ellenor, the daughter of David Hopwood of Potterton, July the 7th
Frances, the daughter of Richard Knapton of Potterton lane, July the 21th
Edward, the son of George Hunter of Winmoore-side, July the 28th
William, the son of John Bullock of Barwicke, July the 28th
William, the son of William Brame, jun., of Barnbow carre, July the 31th

William, the son of William Vevers, senr., of Scoles, August the 1st

Elizabeth, the daughter of John Clarke of Barwicke, August ye 4th

John, the son of Richard Hodgson of Winmoore side, August the 18th

Alice, the daughter of Leonard Catton of Barwicke, August ye 31th

Mary, the daughter of Thomas Taite of Kidhall lane-head, Septem. ye 8th

Elizabeth, the daughter of Joshua Turner of Barwicke, Septem. ye 25th

William, the son of William Taite, junr., of Scoles, Septem. 29th

John, the son of James Orton of Barwicke, October the 2d

William, the son of Matthew Fox of Winmoore, Novem. ye 21th

Martha, the daughter of Edward Hinchcliffe of Winmoore, Novem. ye 21th

Mary, the daughter of Benjamin Pease of Morwicke, Decem. ye 26th

Elizabeth, the daughter of George Haist of Barwicke, January ye 22th

Anne, the daughter of John Taylor, sen., of Barwicke, Febru. ye 2d

Jonathan, the son of Richard Taylor of Barnbow, February ye 5th

William, the son of William Deardon of Garforth Moore side, Feb. ye 7th

Paul, the son of Thomas Stowing, sen., of Barwicke, Feb. ye 10th

Thomas, ye son of Richard Braime of Barmbow carr, January 1st

Anne, the daughter of William Taite of Barwicke, March ye 18th

Jane, the daughter of William Bridges, Curate of Barwicke, March ye 19th

Thomas, the son of Randall Briggs, junior, of Rhoundhay, Febru. ye 9th

1673 [Baptisms].

Richard, the son of William Vevers of Potterton, April ye 7th

Elizabeth, the daughter of James Clough of Roundhay, April ye 29th

James, the son of William Fawcett of Barwicke, April ye 30th

Richard, the son of William Hanley of Scoles, May the 4th

Ralph, the son of Richard Collett of Barwicke, May the 7th

Jane, the daughter of John Marston of Morwicke, June ye 29th

Elizabeth, the daughter of John Thompson of Garforth Moore, June ye 29th

Anne, the daughter of George Browne of Barwicke, July the 1st

Christopher, the son of William Lumbe of Winmooreside, July the 13th

William, the son of William Baram of Roundhay, July the 20th

Elizabeth, the daughter of Richard Ellis of Barwicke, July the 21th

Elizabeth, the daughter of John Gibson of Barwicke, September ye 25th

Henry, the son of [*Blank*] of Winmooreside, Octob. ye 5th

Thomas, the son of Joseph Bullock of Barwicke, Octob. ye 12th

William, the son of John Norton of Barwicke, Octob. ye 13th

William, the son of John Taylor, Junr., of Barwicke, Octob. ye 15th

Helen, the daughter of Joseph Strickland of Barwicke, Octob. ye 29th

Frances, the daughter of John Aumbler of Winmoore, Novem. ye 2d

William, the son of Leonard Gayton of Winmoore, Novem. ye 2d

Richard, the Bastard son of Elizabeth Watterworth of Barwicke, Nov. 9th

Mary, the daughter of John Outhwayt of Scoles, Novem. ye 30th
Anne, the daughter of Thomas Taylor, Junr., of Barwicke, Decemb. ye 4th
Mary, the daughter of George Hay of Barwicke, January the 30th
Mary, the daughter of Henry Briggs of Potterton, Janu. the 30th
Mary, the daughter of Robert Collett of Barwick, February 23th
Ann, the daughter of Wm. Oates of Winmoor, the 26th ---
John, the son of John Ball of Potterton, March the 8th

1674 [Baptisms].

Margarett, the daughter of William Briggs of Barwicke, Mar. 25
Mary, the daughter of Robert Farrah of Penwell, Aprill the 12th
Sarah, the daughter of Marke Wright of Barwicke, May the 11th
Anne, the Bastard daughter of Anne Drury of Barwicke, May 31
Sarah, the bastard of Margarett Barker of Potterton, June xiiijth
Elizabeth, the daughter of Joshua Turner of Barwicke, July xixth
Cicilia, the daughter of Peter Slaytr of Winmoor, July xxvjth
Sarah, the daughter of John Massie of Stocking, Aug. 24th
Ann, the daughter of Richard Taite of Potterton, October 11th
James, the son of James Orton of Barwick, Octobr 21th
William, the son of William Taite of Barwicke, October the 30th
Anne, the daughter of Richard Burland of Barwicke, November the 12th
Sarah, the daughter of Wm. Braime of Barmbow carr, December the 2d
William, the son of William Handley of Scoles, Dec, 6th
Susanna, the daughter of Lawrence Andrew of Garforth moor side, December the 13th
Thomas, the son of Christopher Scott of Morwicke, the 10th of January
Sarah, the daughter of William Oates of Winmoore, near Kidall laine, January the 10th
Thomas, the son of Edward Hinchcliffe of ye Stanks, March ye 4th
John, the son of William Taite of Scoles, March 7th
Deborah, the daughter of Robert Hardcastle of Barwicke, the 6 day of June

1675 [Baptisms].

Thomas, the son of James Wood of Potterton, Apr. 4th
Anne, the daughter of William Jackson of Scoles, April 5th
Ledia, the daughter of William Twisleton of Potterton, May the 2d
William, the son of William Vevers of Potterton, May the 6th
Alice, the daughter of William Wilcocke of Garforth more, May the 9th
Roger, ye son of Richard Farrey of Scoles, May ye 30th
Richard, the son of Georg Hast of Barwick, June the 16th
Frances, the daughter of James Clough of Roundhey, Aug. ye 5th
Mary, the daughter of John Gibson of Barwicke, Aug. 8th
Richard, the son of Richard Braime of Barmbow-carr, August the 15th
Isabell, the daughter of George Rosse of Potterton, Septemb. ye 26th
Anne, the daughter of John Caluert of Barwicke, Octob. ye 6th
John, the son of William Vevers of Scoles, Octobr ye 15th
Martha, the daughter of Samuell Ryder of Leedes, October the 23th

William, the son of Henry Briggs of Potterton, November ye 21th
William, the son of Christopher Kelshaw of Roundhey, Decem. ye 9°
Sarah, the daughter of Thomas Taylor, iunior, of Barwick, Dec. ye 27th
John, the son of Robert Brooke of the Stanks, the 5th of Janua.
John, the son of Phineas Daniel of Barwicke, the 27th of January
Joseph, the son of George Spinck of Scoles, ye 7th of February
George, the son of Richard Green of Barwicke, Febru. ye 16th
Jane and Catherine, the children of William Allott of Barwicke, February ye xxth
Mary, the daughter of Richard Bollands of Barwicke, Feb. ye 27th
Thomas, the son of Leonard Catton of Barw., March ye 12th
George, ye son of George Hall of Barwicke, March the 24th

1676. BAPTIZAT.

Anne, the daughter of John Bullocke of Barwicke, was baptized March the 28th
John, the son of John Thompson of Garforth moorside, Aprill the 2
William, the son of John Aumbler of hurst moor, the same day
Dorothy, the daughter of Matthew Norton of Roundhey, was baptized att Chapple Allerton, Aprill the 16
Elizabeth, the daughter of John Ball of Potterton, Aprill the 23°
William, the son of William Briggs of Barwick, Ap. the 26°
Richard, the son of Richard Taylor of Barnbow carr, the same day
Thomas, the son of Robert Barker, a straunger in Roundhey, May ye 7th
Mary, the daughter of George Browne of Barwick, June the 10th
Susannah, the daughter of Leonard Gaceton on Win-moor, July the 2d
Elisabeth, the daughter of Thomas Tate of Kiddall Laine head, July the 30th
Jeremiah, the son of Richard Robinson of Scoles, August the xxvijth
Matthew, the son of Robert Collett of Barwick, was bapt. Sep. 6th
Robert, the son of John Burnel [*altered from* Burland] of Roundhey, October the 22th
Richard, the son of Richard Ball of Potterton, Dec. 3th
Anne, the daughter of John Wheelhouse of Scoles, Dec. 17°
William, the son of Richard Holmes of Roundhey, January the 3th
William, ye son of Robert Wilson of Roundhey, January the 10th
Anne, the daughter of Robert Farrer of Scoles, January the 10th
Matthew, the son of Thomas Clarkeson of Hopperley, January the 11th
John, the son of John Outhwaite of Scoles, Janu. ye 14th
Anne, the daughter of Henry Turner of Hurst moore, Jan. 20th
Richard, the son of Wm Vevers of Scoles, January the 25th.
Joseph, the son of Edward Hinchcliffe of Hirst more, Feb. the 8th
James, the son of James Prince of Barwicke, Febr. 18th
Mary, the daughter of James Clough of Roundhey, Feb. 25th.
Elisabeth, the daughter of John Marston of Morwick, March the 4th
Samuel, the son of Robert Green of Barwick, 17th of March
Joseph, ye son of James Orton of Barw., March 26th
Mary, the daughter of Christop. Scott of Morwicke, Apr. 1st

Rebeccah, the daughter of Richard Stiham of Kid. laine head, Aprill the 4th

1677 [Baptisms].

Jane, the daughter of Richard Norton of Penwell, Apr. 5th
Christopher, ye son of Christopher Kelshawe of Roundhey, Aprill ye 19th
Henry, ye son of William Brame of Barnbow carr, Aprill the 22th
John, the son of Richard Knapton of Potterton, May 16th
Anne, the daughter of John Taylor, iu^{r}, of Barwicke, May 23th
Easter, the daughter of Thomas Wright of Winmoore, June ye 14th
Mary, the Bastard Child of Elizab. Sawer of Abordford, ye same day
John, the son of Richard Ellis of Barwicke, June ye 20th
Daniel, ye son of Daniel Huitt of Scoles, June the 24
Elizabeth, the daughter of Richard Tate of Potterton, July the 1st
Anne, ye daughter of Laurence Andrew of Garthforth moore side, the sayme day
Richard, the son of William Vevers of Potterton, July 4th
William, the son of William Wilcock of Garthforth moore side, August the 19th
Elizabeth, the daughter of Joseph Bullocke of Barwicke, August the 26th
Alice, the daughter of Richard Haslegrave of Scoles, September ye 9th
William, the son of William Taite of Scoles, the youngest, September the 14th
Easter the daughter of Michael Rish of Hurstmoor end, or Allershawe laine, September the 23th
William, the son of Richard Burland of Barwick, Sept. 24th
Elisabeth, the daughter of Henry Briggs of Potterton, October the 14
Richard, ye son of Richd Green of Barwick, Octob^{r} ye 15°
Ann, ye daughter of Matthew Norton of Roundhay, November ye 22
Joseph, the son of Richard Braime of Barnbowe carr, January the 24th
William, the son of Richard Farrer of Scoles, Janu. 27
Sarah, the daughter of John Gibson of Barwicke, deceased, February ye 6th
John, the son of Thomas Tate of Barw., February the 28
Elizabeth, the daughter of James Wood of Potterton, March the 24th

Baptizat, 1678.

Elizabeth, the daughter of Willm Robinson of Garthforth moore, March the 24th
Elizabeth, the daughter of Richard Taylor of Barnbow carre, Aprill the 3^{d}
Francies, ye daughter of John Settle of Potterton, Aprill ye 9th
Elizabeth, the daughter of William Lumb of Winmoore, Aprill ye 14th
Marke, the son of John Aumbler of Hurstmoor, May ye 5th
Phillip, the son of George Haste of Barwicke, June the 19th
George, the son of Robert Barker of Roundhey Parke, June the 20th
[*Blank*], the son of W^{m}. Handley of Scoles, July the 14th
Katherine, the daughter of Robert Brooke of the Stanks, July the 24th
Robert, the son of Robert Oddy of Scoles, deceased, July ye 31th
Samuel, the son of John Scalvert of Barwicke, Aug. the 4th

Thomas, the son of Robert Collett of Barwicke, Aug. ye 7th
Mary, the daughter of Robert Wilson of Roundhey, August the 25th
Richard, the son of Richard Robinson of Scoales, Septembr 29th
James, the son of Leonard Gateton of Winmore, Sep. ye 6th
Sarah, the daughter of James Prince of Barwicke, Sep. 12th
John, the son of John Dawson of Brown moore, Octobr 13th
Richard, the son of William Halladay of Scoles, Octob. 20th
Abigaile, the daughter of William Smith of Barwicke, Octobr 23th
Grace, the daughter of George Bingley of Roundhey, Octobr 31
Joshua, the son of Joshua West and Eastr Thompson of Roundhey, Novembr ye 6th
John, the son of Christopher Kelshaw of Roundhey, November ye 6th
Francis, the son of Peter Varley of Browne moore, November ye 10th
Anne, the daughter of Robert Deardon of Brown moore, the same day
Martine, ye son of Jeremiah Ingle of Barwicke, Nov. ye 17th
Christopher, the son of Christ. Hill of the Stankes, Novembr ye 28th
Elisabeth, the daughter of Austin Nicholson of Barw., Dec. 22th
Anne, the daughter of Edward Hinchcliffe of the Stankes, on Hurstmoore, January 31th
Alice, ye daughter of Leonard Catton of Barwicke, February 22th
Anne, the daughter of Richd Holmes of Roundhey, February ye 27th

BAPTIZAT 1679.

Thomas, the son of Lawrance Andrew of Garthforth moreside, deceased Aprill ye 13th
Anne, the Bastard child of Rosamond Mawe of Garthforth more side, Ap. ye 18o
William, the son of Thomas Baker of Sheppen, Ap. ye 27
Elisabeth, the daughter of William Tate, the yeounger, of Scoles, May ye 7th
Isable, the daughter of James Clough of Roundhey Lodge, May ye 8th
Alice, the daughter of Thomas Walker of Roundhey, May the 15th
Sarah, the daughter of John Thompson of Garthforth more, June the 1st
John, the son of Thomas Popplewell of Barwicke, July the 2d
Sarah, the daughter of William Strickland of Barwicke, July the 16th
George, the son of Jo. Wheelhouse of Scoles, August the 7th
Elisabeth, the daughter of James Orton of Barwicke, August the 8th
Anne, the daughter of Christop. Leeds of Garthforth more side, Aug. 28th
Ann, the daughter of Thomas Brunton of Barnbow, Sep. ye 7th
William, the son of Thomas Taylor of Barw., the younger, Septembr ye 11th
Isable, the daughter of Thomas Smith of Barwicke, Sept. the 25th
Francis, the son of Thomas Clarkson of Hopperleay, October the 11th
Sara, the daughter of Aqualla Blackborne of Scoales, Octob. 19
Elisabeth, the daughter of Thomas Wright of Winmore, Novem. 23
Sarah, the daughter of George Browne of Barwicke, Novemb. 26
William, the son of Jeremiah Ingle of Barwicke, Dec. 3
Mary, the daughter of Daniel Huett of Scoles, Dec. 14th
Jane, the daughter of Christopher Hill of the Stanks, on Hurstmoore, December the 17th

George, the son of Elisabeth Burnell of Roundhey, February y[e] 11th
Elisabeth, the daughter of Matthew Norton, the same day
Margarett, the daughter of William Wilcocke of Garthforth more side, February y[e] 15th
Dorothy, the daughter of Edward Hinchcliffe of the Stanks, on Hurstmore, March the 18
Mary, the daughter of Richard Burland of Barwicke, March the 19th

BAPTIZAT' 1680.

Elisabeth, the daughter of John Outhwaite of Scoles, March 28th
Anne, the Bastard child of Elisabeth Killingbecke of Roundhey, April the 2[d]
Robert, the son of John Settle of Potterton, April y[e] 1st
Mary, the daughter of John Munsey of Winmoor head, April 14
William, the son of W[m] Lund of the Cross yeates, on Hurst more, April the 25th
Margaret and Martha, the children of Thomas Bradford, at Toloroug yate, May the 22th
Mary, the daughter of Richard Stiham of Potterton, June y[e] 18th
Isable, the daughter of Joshuah Lumbe, at the Cross yates, on the Hurst moor, July 18th
Elisabeth, the daughter of William Robinson on Garthforth mooreside, July the 25th
Sarah, the daughter of Henry Dickenson att Bull laine head on Winmoore, August the 15th
John, the son of Robert Pitts of Scoles, August the 22th
Elisabeth, y[e] daughter of John Stoaker of Scoles, September the 5th
Elinor, the daughter of George Smith of Grimesdike, the 3[d] day of October
John, the son of John Hunter of Hurst moore, the 15th day of October
Christopher, the son of John Hardisty of Barwicke, Octob[r] 21
John, the son of John Hopkinson of Barwicke, Novem. 25th
Hannah, the daughter of Thomas Batman of Garthforth more side, Novemb. 28th
Benjamine, the son of W[m] Lumbe of Winmore, Decemb. 13th
Mary, the daughter of James Prince of Barwicke, Decemb. y[e] 13th
Robert, the son of Robert Deardon of Brown moore, January the 16
John, the son of Richard Robinson of Scoles, the same day
Robert, the son [*altered from* Janet, the daughter] of Rob[t] Wilson of Roundhey, the same day
George, the son of George Bingley of Roundhey parke, the 20th day of January
Mary, the daughter of George Haste of Barwicke, January the 26th
Alice, the daughter of Christo. Hill of the Stanks on Hurst Moore, February the 2[d]
Robert, the son of William Knapton of Barwicke, February the 10th
Robert, the Bastard child of Mary Constable of Scoles, Feb. 13th
Bridgett, the daughter of Edward Walton of Morwick, Feb. the 13th
William, the son of W[m] Hallyday at the upper end of Hurst Moore, Feb. the 20th
Elisabeth, the daughter of James Wilcocke at the lower end of Hurst moore, February the 20th

Robert, the son of Richard Tate of Potterton, was baptized at Aberford, February the 21th
Samuel, the son of Christopher Kelshaw of Roundhey, March the 10th
Thomas, the son of Thomas Baker of Scoles, March the 20th

BAPTIZAT' 1681.

Francis, the son of Abraham Sheppen of Barnbow, March the 27th
Elisabeth, the daughter of Robert Green of Barwicke, March the 31th
Ruth, the daughter of John Marston of Morwicke, May the 1st
Sarah, the daughter of Samuell Robinson of Garthforth moor side, May the 13th
Anne, the daughter of John Frankland of Garthforth moor side, May 15th
Dorothy, the daughter of Martine Whitehead of Allershaw laine end on Hurst moor, the same day
Elisabeth, the daughter of Richard Farrer of Scoles, June the 3d
William, the son of Joseph Hague of Barwicke, June the 24th
Thomas, the son of Mr Thomas Atkenson of Barwicke, July the 21th
Sara, the daughter of Tho. Popplewell, Aug. 2
Anne, the daughter of Thom. Simpson of Garthforth moreside, October the 9th
Joseph, the son of Wm Strickland of Barwicke, 27th of October
Richard, the son of John Burland, junior, of Barw., November 5th
Anne, the daughter of John Munsey of Winmoor head, Novemb. 6th
Samuel, the son of Aqual Blackborne of Scoles, Novembr 27th
Anne, the daughter of Michael Rish at Allershaw laine end, the same day
Henritta, the daughter of Matthew Norton of Roundhey, December the 7th
Thomas, the son of Mr Gyles Hardwicke of Barwick, December the 22th
Jane, the daughter of Marke Cooper of Scoles, December the 28th
Alice, the daughter of Robert Maw of Garthforth more side, January the first
Thominsin, the daughter of Tho. Brunton of Sheppen, January the 15th
Wm, the son of James Orton of Barwicke, Jan 19th
Elisabeth, the daughter of Geo. Smith of Grimesdike, January the 30th
Thomas, the son of John Houlcroft of Scoles, February ye 5th
Jonathan, the son of Thomas Maud at Bull laine head, February ye 12
Sara, ye da. of Pet. Varley of Brown more, February the 19th
Mary, the daughter of John Bullock of Barwicke, February the 19th
William, the son of John Hunter of Winmore, March the 5th
Thomas, the son of John Thompson of Garthforth more side, Marche 12th

BAPTIZAT', 1682.

Cuthbert, the son of Wm Hemsworth of Scoles, Aprill the 2d
Alice, the daughter of William Smith of Barwick, April the 10th
Dorothy, the daughter of Robt Watkinson of Barwick, Aprill ye 13th
John, the son of Austin Nicholson of Barwick, Aprill ye 18th

John, the son of Robert Green of Barw., Aprill the 29th
Elisabeth, ye daughter of James Wilcock at Whitkirk laine end on Hurst moore, by lycence from Mr Hall, Curate at Whitkirk, May 7th
George, the son of Christopher Hill at the Stankes, May 10th
Jane, the daughter of Thomas Wright at the White Laith on Winmore, May the 17th
John, the son of Christopher Leeds of Garthforth more side, June the 11th
Elisabeth, the daughter of Rich. Robinson of Barwicke, June the 20th
Elisabeth, the daughter of John Moore of Barwicke, June the 20th
John, the son of John Settle of Potterton, July the 2d
Joseph, the son of George Haste of Barwick, Aug. 2d
Hellen, the daughter of Richard Settle of Potterton, born the 22th of July, and baptized the 19th of August
George, the son of Daniel Huett of Scoles, September 3d
William, the son of William Knapton of Barwick, the 28th of Septem.
Thomas, the son of Robert Thornes of Barwick, November the 1st
[*Illegible, altered from* Thomas], the son of Henry Dickenson at the Bull laine end on Winmore, November ye 5th
Mary, the daughter of Peter Slater at the Stanks on Hurstmore, November the 15th
Beatrix, the daughter of Leo. Catton of Barwick, November the 28th
Anne, the daughter of John Barker of Barwick 13 of December
Anne, the daughter of Robt Broon of Potterton, Dec. 20
Anne, the daughter of Katherine Moor of Barwicke, December 22th
aged
Elizabeth Bywater of Barwick, being about the age of Fifteen yeares, December the 26th
Myles, the son of Robert Wilson of Roundhey, January 21th
William and Sarah, the children of Thomas Walker of Roundhey, January the 25th
Elisabeth, the daughter of Wm Lister of the same, the same day
Wm, the son of George Browne of Barwick, Jan. the 26
Stephen, the son of William Watson of Barwick, January the 26
Christopher and Elisabeth, the children of Christop. Kelshaw of Roundhey, the first day of March

1683, BAPTIZAT.

William, the son of Wm Hardie of Scoles, the 22 of Aprill
William, the son of John Drury of Barwick, the same day
Benjamine, the son of Wm Eamorson of Roundhey, the 26 of Aprill
Thomas, the son of John Brown of Potterton, May the 23th
Grace, the daughter of John Offine of Scoles, June the 10th
Richard, the son of Mr Tho. Atkinson of Barwicke, June the 20th
William, the son of Francis Atkinson at the Bull lain head, June 24
Charity, the daughter of John Aumbler on Hurstmoore, the 17 of June
Charles, the son of Rich. Settle of Potterton, August the 25
John, the son of Elizabethe Burnell of Roundhey, September the 6
John, the son of Thomas Batman of Garthforth moore side, September the 30th

Anne, the daughter of Rich. Robinson of Scoles, the same day
Thomas, the son of John Taylor at the West End of Kiddall laine end, the 10 of October
John, the son of James Wetherall of Morwicke, the 14 of October
James, the son of James Hinley near Allersaw laine end, October the 21
Joseph, the son of Joseph Hague of Barwick, October the 22
Mary, the daughter of James Barker of Sheppen, Novemb. ye 18

1663, MARIT'.

Richard Ellis and Jane Abbott, after publication thrice made, November 18th
Richard Hanley of Scoles and Alice Potter of Barwicke, after publication thrice made, November the 26th
John Buck of Ribston in the parish of Spofforth and Elizabeth Croft of Barwicke, after publication thrice made, November the 30th
Daniel Hudson and Garthrid Ellis, both of Barwicke, after publication thrice made, December the 2d

1664 [MARRIAGES].

Henry Turner and Margery Chapman of the Stankes, after publication thrice made, August the 3d
Robert Shaw of Barwicke and Mary Moore of Browne more, after publication thrice made, September ye 1st
William Lockeland and Sarah Nickson of Leeds, by licence, September the 21th
John Johnson and Elizabeth Cryer of Potterton, after publication thrice made, November the 23th
Samuel Parish of Stainforth in the Parish of Hatfeild and Jane Bridges of Barwicke, by lycence, December the 13th
John Burnell and Elizabeth West, both of Roundhey, by lycence, February the 8th
*William Bridges, The son, Clerke, Master of Arts, entred to supply the Cure of Barwicke under Dr Dalton, upon Shrove Tuesday, 1660.

1665, MARIT.

Thomas Bakes of the Parish of Kirke-Fenton and Elizabeth Hardcastle of Scoles, after publication thrice made, November the 13th
William Lofthouse and Jennet Potter, both of Potterton, after publication thrice made, November the 15th
Thomas Walker and Anne Holmes, both of Roundhey, after publication thrice made, November the 22th
Matthew Fox of Heddingley in the parish of Leeds and Jane Aumbler of Hurst moore side, after publication thrice made, Februa. the 5th
William Howdill of Sheereburne and Sarah Massy of Stocking, after publication thrice made, Febru. the 14th

*William Bridges, St. John's Coll., Cambridge, M.A., 1661, married 3 Jan., 1664-5, Sarah, daughter of Richard Lodge of Red Hall. He was Rector of Castleford 1673-1696, where he was succeeded by his son William. See Elizabeth Thompson's Will, printed *ante* p. 71.

MARIT', 1666.

John Aumbler and Elizabeth Turner, both of Hurst Moore side, after publication thrice made, April the 16th

Thomas Casson of the Parish of Rothwell and Mary Massey of Stocking, after publication thrice made, July the 12th

Leonard Catton of the parish of Garforth and Betteris Stow of Barwicke, after publication thrice made, August the 22th

John Massy of Stocking and Sarah Turner of Weetwood in the parish of Leeds, after publication thrice made, September the 26th

John Taylor and Mary Collit, both of Barwicke, by Licence, in Garforth Church, November the 6th

Laurence Emerson of Seacroft in the parish of Whitekirke and Anne Taylor of Barwicke, after publication thrice made, November the 21th

Mr William Bridges, Curate of Barwicke, and Mrs Sarah Lodge of Winmore Hall, by Licence, in the Parish Church of Bardsey, Jan. 3rd

Henry Renton of the Parish of Barwicke and Elizabeth Prince of the parish of Leeds, after publication thrice made, January the 16th

Richard Sclater and Anne Walton of Winmoore side, both widdowes, after publication thrice made, February the 19th

1667 [MARRIAGES].

John Duffin of the parish of Abberforth and Mary Writer of Barnbow, after publication thrice made, June the 24th

Cuthbert Joy of the Parish of Garforth and Elizabeth Braham of Barnbow Carre, after publication thrice made, November the 20th

William Akid and Katherine Haigue of Barwicke, by licence, November the 21th

MARIT, 1668.

John Clarke and Elizabeth Norton, both of Barwicke, after publication thrice made, Septem. the 8th

Thomas Stowen the younger of Barwicke and Mary Wilson of Scoles, after publication thrice made, Septem. the 16th

John Dineley the elder of Barwicke, and Sarah Bateson of Roundhay, after publication thrice made, November the 28th

William Twisleton of Micklefeild in the parish of Sheerburne and Isabell Potter of Potterton, after publication thrice made, Novem. the 29th

1669, MARIT'.

John Ingle of the Parish of Garforth and Elizabeth Roote of this parish, after publication thrice made, May the 26th

Richard Kent and Dorothy Brawener, both of Barwicke, widdows, after publication thrice made, September the 22th

John Smith, junior, of Barwicke and Alice Hanley of Scoles, widdow, Febru. the 14th

John Dunnell and Anne Wilson of Scoles, widdows, February the 10th

Peter Bywater of Water Fryston and Anne Cash of Scoles, November ye [13th, or about that time, *added*]

MARIT', 1670.

Thomas Blackburne of Morwicke and Isabell Ingle of Grimesdyke, April ye 4th

Edward Hinchliffe and Ellen Walker, Widdow, of the Stanks, May the 23th

Edward Hoyle and Elizabeth Dickins of Leeds, by licence, August the 4th

Thomas Horbery of the parish of Leeds and Isabel Rakestraw of Barwicke, October the 4th

Joshua Lumb of Winmoore and Mary Dinefall of the parish of Bradford, January the 1st

1671, MARIT'.

Mr. Timothy Warwicke and Mrs. Susanna Netherwood of the parish of Leeds, by licence, April the 20th

Wm Johnson of the Parish of Garforth and Esther Blackburne of Barnbow-carre, Septem. 21th

Thomas Hurst of the Parish of Garforth and Mary Reedall of Barnbow, Novem' ye 1st

Richard Brame of Barnbow-carre and Mary Atkinson of Barwicke, February the 7th

John Clivinger of Leeds and Mary Ibbitson of Barwicke, by Lycence, March the 18th

1672 MARIT.

Thomas Stowing, Junior, and Frances Bullocke of Barwicke, April the 9th

John Thompson and Anne Fletcher of Garforth moore side, May the 8th

John Pitts and Elizabeth Clayton of Scoles, widdows, May ye 27th

William Baram of Rhoundhay hall and Mary Rishforth of Rhoundhay, widdow, May the 27th

James Orton and Anne Fentiman of Barwicke, by licence, June the 9th

Richard Fisher of the parish of Whitkirke and Elizabeth Settle of Potterton, July the 31th

Lancelot Aumbler and Jane Chamber, widdow, both of Winmoore, February ye 6th

*Richard Beresford, D.D., was inducted into the Rectory of Barwicke in Ellmett, February ye 5th

1673 MARIT.

Henry Briggs and Helen Settle of Potterton, April the 20th

George Rosse of Bickerton in the parish of Bilton and Frances Settle of Potterton, April ye 23th

George Hay of the parish of Bolton Percy and Mary Akid of Barwicke, May the 4th

John Milner of Seacroft in the parish of Whitkirke and Elizabeth Settle of Potterton, June the 11th

David Tuke of Thorner and Jane Collett of Barwicke, both Widdows, August the 6th

Richard Holmes and Mary West of Roundhay, September the 25th

*Rector 1672-1695. S.T.P. Cambridge, 1661, per Literas Regias.

Richard Taite and Jane Robinson of Scoles, November the 10th

John Bray of Leeds and Sarah Staveley, by licence, November the 22th

Lawrence Andrews of the parish of Featherstone and Elizabeth Deardon of this parish, January the 19th

John Robinson of the parish of Thorner and Frances Saynor of Potterton, February the 4th

William Bridges the son, clerke, Master of Arts, begun to supply this cure March the first, 1660, and gave over March the first, 1673, just thirteen yeares complete.

1674.

Roger Spincke and Rosomond Braime, both of this parish, August the 3d

William Hague and Elline Doughty, both of the parish of Fishlake, upon a Certificate from Mr. Mayon, vicar Ibedem, Novembr the 25th

MARIT', 1675.

William Allot of the parish of Addle and Katherine Akedd of this Parish, Aprill the 15th

Richard Robinson and Jane Hardwicke, both of this parish, November ye 17th

1676, MARIT.

Thomas Clarkson of Thorner and Elizabeth Stiham of Hopperley, by Licence, June the xjth

Robert Wilson and Frances Blackborne, both of this parish, July the 30th

Robert Green and Elisabeth Knapton, iunior, both of Barwicke, September the 20th

George Burton and Jane Cooke, both of Roundhey, Octob. the 25th

Thomas Foxcroft of the pish Harwood and Margaret Shoore of Barnbow, Novem. the 1th

MARIT. 1677.

John Prentice of ye Parish of Thorpparch and Ann Settle of Potterton in this parish, Aprill the 9

John Settle & Abigale Daniel of Potterton, June ye 20th

William Hemsworth of the parish of Garthforth & Isable Wheelhouse of Sheppen in this parish, July 4

William Hallyday of the parish of Spawforth & Anne Hunter of this parish, October the 24

Connon Hopkinson & Frances Tate, iunior, both of Scoles, Novembr the 19

Matthew Stiham of Hopperley in this parish and Elizabeth Hancocke of Seacroft wthin the parish of Whit Church, by licence, November ye 28th

William Morrice of the parish [of] Kippax and Anne Deardon of this parish, January the 16th

Richard Nouble of Walton in the pish of Thorpparch and Rebeckah Shan of this Parish, May the 1st, 1678.

MARIT, 1678.

William Strickeland and Mary Moore, both of this parish, June the 16th

Benjamin Birdsall of the parish of Kirkfenton and Elisabeth Taylor of this pish, July 4°

Aquala Blackeborn of the parish of Whitchurch and Elisabeth Tate of this parish, November the 6th

John Munsey and Hellen Brown, both of this pish, the same day

MARIT', 1679.

William Ingle of the pish of Garthforth and Elisab. Dawson of this parish, May the 8th

Thomas Pickering of the pish of Kirk Deighton and Elisabeth Jackson of this parish, June the 24th

Nathaniel Harrison of the parish of Garthforth and Margaret Evans of this parish, Aug. ye 3d

Thomas Batman and Anne Evans, both of this parish, Novem. 18th

Robert Green & Elisabeth Alleyson, both of this parish, Novem. 24th

William Knapton and Sara Turner, both of this pish, February the second 2d

MARIT, 1680.

Thomas Briggs and Anne Smith of Roundhey, both of this parish, the 17 day of Aprill

*Mr Gyles Hardwicke & Mrs Elisabeth Marsh, both of Barwicke, by Lycence, Aprill the 12th

James Wilcocke of the parrish of Whitkirke and Elisabethe Hopton of this parish, June the 21th

Francis Brunton & Anne Dawson, both of this pishe, June the 24th

MARIT, 1681.

Thomas Barker of the parish of Abborford and Isable Potter of this pish, after publication thrice made, were married by Mr. Hall, & the 1st that he married, July 13th

Robert Brown and Grace Burton, both of this pish after publication thrice made, were married by Mr Hall, February ye 22th

†Anno Domini 1681, May ye 11th day, Charles Hall, Clerke, Master of Arts, entred to supply the Cure of Barwicke in Elmett under Dr Beresforde, May ye Eleventh day.

MARIT, 1682.

Robert Johnson and Hannah Mawmond, both of this parish, after publication thrice made, May the 4th

William Witecarr of the parish of Leedes and Elisabeth Harrison of this parish, after publication thrice made, May the 31th

William Watson and Anne Thackerey, both of this parish, after publication thrice made, June the 6th

†Mr. Charles Hall, Curate of Barwicke in Elmett and Mrs Elizabeth Scholes of the same Towne, June the 29th, 1682, after publication thrice made in the parish church of Barwick in Elmett aforesaid

John Varley of the pish of Garthforth and Faith Walker of this pish after publication thrice made, October the 12th

Francis Atkinson and Sarah Dixon, both of this parish, after publication thrice made, Octobr ye 29

---

*Elizabeth Marsh was daughter of Henry, son of Dr. Richard Marsh, Dean of York. See Hardwick Pedigree, Thoresby's Ducatus, 2nd Edition, p. 121.

†Charles Hall, Christ's Coll., Cambridge, B.A. 1672, M.A. 1676. Married to Elizabeth Scholes 29 June, 1682.

Robert Wansley and Mary Tate, both of this parish, after publication thrice made January the 21th

James Prince and Alice Gibson both of this Parish, after publication thrice made, January the 31th, 1682

Thomas Burland & Sarah Smith, both of this pish, after Publication thrice made, February the 4th

1683, MARIT.

John Prince and Mary Hemsworth, both of this parish, after publication thrice made, April the 9°

Richard Varley and Francies Dineley, both of this parish, after publication twice made, June the 3°

Thomas Knapton, the yeo[n]ger & Mary Gibson, both this parish, after Publication thrice made, June the 5th

Richard Walker & Frances Ashton, both of the parish of Kippax, by a cirtificate from Mr Bainbridge, vicar, were married in our church, according to the cannon, July the 12th.

William Robinson & Deborah Watkinson, both of this parish, after Publication thrice made, July the 4th

John Coaxe and Isable Settle, both of this parish, by Lycence, in Saint Cuthbert Church, in the Cittie of Yorke, July the 30, by a Certificate from the Minister Ibidem

William Hopwood and Mary Wright, both of this parish, after publication thrice made, October the 28th

George Wright and Easter Smith, both of this parish, after publication thrice made, November the 12th

1663, SEPULT'.

Anne, ye daughter of Thomas Coapland of Barwick, October ye 30th

Mrs Janè Bridges of Barwicke, widdow, November the 21th

Alice, the wife of John Johnson of Potterton, December the 16th

Anne, the wife of Ralph Collett of Barwicke, January the 6th

Agnes Burnell of Roundhay, widdow, January the 14th

Samuel Turner of Barwicke, February the 1st

Margery, the daughter of Robert Settle of Potterton, February the 1st

Anne, the daughter of Thomas Dodgeson of Roundhay, February the 11th

Henry Shippen, the son of Widdow Shore of Barnebow, February the 19th

Elizabeth, the wife of Richard Sclater of Winmoore side, February the 23th

William Harrison of Garforth-moore-side, March the 24th

1664.

Henry Mullinax of Redhall, April the 3d

Henry Walton of Winmoore side, April the 10th

John Santon of Roundhay, April the 18th

Katherine Hague of Barwicke, widdow, May the 10th

Anne, the daughter of Cuthbert Munsey of Barwicke, June the 4th

John, the son of John Sharphouse of Sphigleyes, August the 7th

William, the son of Richard Potter of Potterton, August the 10th

Thomas, the son of John Sharphouse of Sphighleyes, August the 25th

Elline Prince of Barwicke, widdow, September the 23th
Henry, the son of Robert Shuttleworth of Scholes, October the 4th
Anne, the daughter of Robt. Greene, Junior, of Barwicke, October the 7th
Margaret, the daughter of John Taite, junior, of Scholes, October the 19th
Jennet, the daughter of David Hopwood of Potterton, October the 27th
Ursula, the wife of William Ingle of Scoles, November the 9th
Joane Crosland of Barwicke, widdow, November the 10th
Anne Taite of Kidhall lane Head, widdow, November the 13th
Edmond Clayton of Scoles, December the 5th
Elizabeth Bellaby of Winmoor side, widdow, December the 21th
Elizabeth, the wife of Thomas Taitt of Barwicke, December the 28
Margaret Hardcastle of Barwicke, December the 30th
John Gibson of Barwicke in Ellmett, January the 5th
Sarah, the daughter of Laurence Hill of the Stankes, January the 16th
Grace, the wife of Robert Greenewood of Scoles, January the 27th
*Robert Franke of Barwicke, Esquire, February the 14th
John Gaitenby of Barwicke, February the 22th

1665, Burials.

Anne, the wife of Richard Settle of Barwicke, April the 5th
Sarah, the Daughter of William Lumbe of Morwicke, April the 18th
Margaret Sayner of Scoles, widdow, April the 24th
Ellin Browne of Winmoore side, widdow, April the 29th
Michael Norton of Roundhay, May the 7th
Jane Kent of Barwicke, widdow, June the 21th
Frances Hardcastle of Barwicke, June the 23th
Samuel, the son of Robert Knapton of Barwicke, July the 13th
Luke Massey of Barwicke, September the 21th
Anne, the wife of William Munsey of Winmoore head, September the 23th
Grace, the Daughter of Solomon Jibson of Kidhall lane-head, Novem. the 15th
Arthur Snawden of Potterton, January the 1st
Edward, the son of Martin West of Roundhay, January the 21th
Jane, the wife of Rowland Ewans of Garforth moore side, Janua. the 31th
George Haigue of Barwicke, February the 4th
Peter Pearson of Osmond-thick house, February the 24th
Margaret Ingle of Scoles, March the 13th
John Heywood of Roundhay, March the 14th
Elizabeth Turner of Roundhay, March the 21th
John Dinnison, Jun^{9}, of Barwicke, March the 21th

1666, Burials.

John Tompson of Garforth Moore side, April the 11th
Jennet Clarke of Kidhall Lane head, widdow, May the 4th

*A pedigree of Frank of Alwoodley is in the Wilson MSS. in the Leeds Library.

Robert Knapton of Barwicke, May the 19th
Margaret, the wife of William Vevers of Scoles, May the 25th
Mary Holmes of Roundhay, widdow, June the 10th
William Vevers of Scoles, July the 2d
Peter Calbeck of Potterton, July the 5th
Thomas Robinson of Garforth-moore side, July the 29th
William, the infant of Thomas Watkinson of Garforth-moore, August the 18th
John Maw of Garforth moore, August the 20th
Robert Brawenor of Barwicke, October the 25th
Martin, the son of Martin West of Roundhay, November the 6th
Alverey Vevers of Scoles, November the 9th
Mistress Mary Robinson of Scoles, December the 14th
John Feather of Scoles, January the 5th
Jane, the daughter of Richard Ellis of Barwicke, January the 23th
Jenet Wansley of Barwicke, January 28th
Robert Fountains of Barwicke, January ye 30th
William Thorneton of Winmoore side, February the 1st
Dorothy Norton of Barwicke, widdow, February the 7th
Jennet Marston of Morwicke, widdow, March the 1st
Peter Nicholson of Barwicke, March the 7th

1667, Burials.

Mary, the wife of John Beedall of the Stankes, March the 31th
Henry Shuttleworth of Scholes, April the 1st
Elizabeth, the child of Richard Swale of Potterton, April the 5th
William Prince of Barwicke, April the 16th
Anthony Metcalfe of Garforth Moore side, May the 1st
Frances Thompson of Roundhay, June the 8th
Elizabeth, the child of Abraham Rishforth of high Ash, July the 14th
Thomas, the son of Joseph Strickland of Barwicke, July the 18th
Mr William Rishton of Barnbow, August the 16th
Thomas Walker of Winmoore side, August the 25th
Thomas, the son of Thomas Stowen of Barwicke, Septem. the 1st
Katherine Clough of Roundhay, September the 5th
Thomas, the son of Robert Saynor of Scoles, Septem. the 11th
Moses, the son of Mr William Hodgeson of Potterton, October the 5th
Anne, the daughter of Elizabeth Settle of Potterton, Octob. the 6th
Robert, the son of Martin Clough of Winmoore head, October the 29th
John, the son of Stephen Luck, a traveller, October the 31th
Anne Bellaby of Winmoore side, Novem. the 3d
Anne, the daughter of George Spincke of Scoles, Novem. the 4th
Alice, the wife of John Haigue, senior, of Barwicke, Decem. the 9th
Alice Feather of Scoles, widdow, December the 25th
Elizabeth Shippen of Barnbow Carre, widdow, January the 6th
Robert, the son of John Drury of Barwicke, January the 19th
Richard Hanley of Scoles, March the 18th

1668.

John Jowitt of Winmoore, March the 27th
Mary, the Daughter of Henry Turner of ye Stankes, April the 6th
Mary, the wife of Robert Shaw, the younger, of Barwicke, April the 7th
John Robinson, a Stranger, April the 13th
Katherine Nicholson of Barwicke, widdow, May the 6th
Isabell Walton of Winmoore side, widdow, June the 5th
Bridgett, the wife of George Hunter of Winmoore side, June the 6th
Elizabeth, the Daughter of Robert Brooke of the Stankes, June the 8th
Robert Greene of Barwicke, June the 13th
Prudence, the wife of John Clarke of Barwicke, June the 15th
Richard, the son of Peter Sclater of Winnemoore, June the 18th
Alice, the wife of Richard Kent of Barwicke, June the 19th
Richard Jackson of the Stanckes, June the 26th
John Maw of Garforth moore side, June the 28th
John Hardcastle, Junior, of Barwicke, July the 19th
Mary, the Daughter of John Burnell of Roundhay, July the 24th
John Smith, the younger, of Barwicke, August the 29th
Ellin Stowen of Barwicke, widdow, September the 9th
John Settle of Potterton, September the 23th
Margarett, the wife of William Brame, the younger, of Barnbow Carre, September the 30th
Matthew Barnby of Scoles, October the 2d
Robert Shaw of Barwicke, October the 8th
Mary, the wife of Thomas Hardwicke of Grimesdike, October the 30th
Katherine, the wife of Robert Saynor of Scoles, Novem: the 3d
Mary, the wife of Cuthbert Munsey of Barwicke, Novem: the 6th
Mary Vevers of Scoles, November the 22th
Eliza:, the wife of John Dunnell of Scoles, December the 10th
William Brough of Barwicke, January the 10th
William Burnell of Roundhay, February the 12th
Marÿ, the Daughter of William Lumbe of Morwicke, Februa: the 27th

1669, Burials.

John Thompson of Barwicke, April the 5th
Ralph Weare of Winmoore, April the 5th
Frances, the infant of Rowland Ewan of Garforth moore side, April ye 18th
Thomas Briggs of Roundhay, April the 21th
Mary, the Daughter of Richard Ellis of Barwicke, June ye 5th
Laurence Hill of the Stanckes, June the 10th
Jane, the wife of Robert Briggs of Barwicke, June the 12th
John Beedall of the Stanckes, June the 16th
Jane, the Daughter of James Wheateley of Winmooreside, June ye 30th
Alice, the wife of Richard Jackson of Scoles, July ye 26th

Robert Settle of Potterton, July the 26th
Ellen Ingle of Scoles, widdow, July the 29th
Agnes Briggs of Roundhay, widdow, August the 29th
Thomas Varley of Garforth moore side, Septem. ye 14th
Robert Holmes of Roundhay, September ye 19th
Isabell, the wife of John Saynor of Potterton, October ye 1st
Jane, the wife of Thomas Blackburne of Morwicke, Octob: ye 11th
Mr George Gascoigne of Shippen, October ye 15th
John Deardon of Browne moore, October ye 24th
Mary Harrison of Garforth-moore-side, widdow, October ye 26th
Richard, the son of William Bridges, Curate, Dece: ye 10th
Jane, the wife of Francis West of Roundhay, Decem. ye 16th
Alvarey Daniel of Barwicke, Dece. ye 23th
Wm Vevers of Potterton, January the 14th
Dorothy Norton of Roundhay, widdow, January ye 17th
Alice, the wife of Michael Turner of Penwell, Februa: ye 12th
Frances, the wife of Francis Saynor of Morwicke, March ye 1st

1670, Burials.

Frances, the daughter of Francis West of Roundhay, April ye 16th
John Taylor, senior, of Barwicke, April ye 28th
Robert Haigue of Barwicke, June ye 19th
Ralph Collet, Junior, of Barwicke, June ye 28th
William, the son of Katherine Moore of Barwicke, July ye 3^d
Sarah, the Daughter of Richard Sclater of Winmoore side, July the 17th
Ralph Bateman, July ye 23th
Anne, the wife of James Hunter of Winmooreside, August ye 18th
Ursula Andrews of Garforth moore side, widdow, August ye 23th
Anne, the wife of John Burland of Barwicke, August ye 25th
Grace Dineley of Barwicke, widdow, August ye 29th
Elizabeth Bruntõ of Garforth moore side, widdow, August ye 30th
Mary, the wife of Thomas Stowing, jun., of Barwicke, Sept. ye 9th
Dorothy, the wife of Richard Kent of Barwicke, Sept. ye 10th
Dorothy Fletcher of Garforth moore side, widdow, Septe. ye 10th
Randolph Briggs of Roundhay Hall, September the 12th
Katherine, the relict of Randolph Briggs, Sept. ye 14th
Jane Ingle, widdow, a sojourner at Grimesdyke, Sept. ye 18th
Sarah, the Daughter of Jane Jackson of the Stanckes, October the 5th
James Prince of Barwicke, October the 19th
Martine Hardcastle of Barwicke, October the 27th
William Kent of the Stanckes, October the 27th
Richard Taylor of Barnbow-carre, October ye 30th
Robert Ball of Potterton, November the 10th
Elizabeth, the wife of John Dawson of Browne-moore, Novr ye 10th
Elizabeth, the Daughter of Elizabeth Taite of Potterton, Nov: ye 15th
Ralph Collet of Barwicke, November the 24th
Mercy Taylor of Barwicke, December the 1st
Grace, the wife of John Lee of Barwicke, December the 15th

Richard Kent of Barwicke, December the 27th
William Huby of Roundhay, December the 27th
Jane Smith of Barwicke, widdow, Decem. ye 31th
Sarah, the Daughter of Richard Knapton of Potterton, Janua. ye 12th
John Rishforth of Roundhay, January the 13th
Anne, the wife of Thomas Watkinson of Garforth-moore-side, Janu. ye 25th
Thomas Terrington of Shippen, February the 6th
Ellin, the wife of Richard Prince of Barwicke, Februa: ye 23th
Esther Thompson of Garforth-moore-side, widdow, March the 2d
Frances, the Daughter of Isaac Wood of Potterton lane, March the 3d
Esther, the wife of John Pitts of Scoles, March the 13th
Margaret Varlow of Garforth-moore-side, widdow, March the 15th
Thomas Simpson of Potterton-moore, March the 20th
Rosamund Maw of Garforth-moore-side, widdow, March the 23th
Richard Potter of Potterton, March the 24th
William, the son of William Vevers, senior, of Scoles, March the 24th

1671, SEPULT.

Joseph, the son of Joseph Bullocke of Barwicke, March ye 29th
Elizabeth, the Daughter of Anne Tinsdall of Barwicke, March ye 30th
Mary, the Daughter of William Ellis of Kidhall, Esq., April the 11th
Thomas, the son of Christopher Leeds of Garforth-moore-side, April ye 13th
Rosamund, the Daughter of Richard Brough of Barwicke, April ye 18th
William, the son of James Clough of Roundhay, April the 20th
Michael Turner of Winmoore-side, April the 20th
Richard Sclater of Winmoore-side, April the 26th
John, the son of Richard Ellis of Barwicke, April the 27th
Elizabeth, the wife of Richard Farrand of Scoles, May the 14th
Gertrude Crumpton of Barnbow Carre, widdow, May the 17th
John Shippen of Barnbow, May the 20th
Deborah, the wife of Robert Hardcastle of Barwicke, May ye 22th
Stephen Eastburne, junr, of Winmoore, May the 29th
Susanna, the Daughter of Randall Briggs of Roundhay, August ye 17th
Deborah, the Daughter of Richard Daniell of Potterton lane, August ye 19th
Henry the Son of Henry Turner of ye Stanckes, Octob. ye 8th
Martin, the son of Robert Prince of Barwicke, Novem. ye 1st
William, the son of Mr Postgate of Rhoundhay, Novem. ye 2d
John Sharpus of Winmoore-side, Novem: ye 27th
Thomas Deardon of Scoles, December the 13th
Richard, the son of Richard Taylor of Barnbow carre, Decem: ye 29th
Solomon, the son of Solomon Jibson of Kidhall-lane-head, Janua: ye 27th

Elizabeth, the wife of Thomas Baker of Scoles, January the 28th
Jennet Constable of Scoles, February the 26th
Mr William Postgate of Rhoundhay, March the 14th

1672, SEPULT.

William Settle of Potterton-lane, April ye 22th
Rowland Ewans of Garforth-moore-side, April the 30th
George, the son of William Ingle, junior, of Scoles, May the 2d
Elizabeth, the wife of John Buck of Barwicke, May the 5th
Margarett, the wife of Robert Prince of Barwicke, May the 30th
Margaret, the child of Phillis Steele, June the 8th
Robert Greenewood of Scoles, June the 15th
John Dinnison of Barwicke, June the 22th
Thomas Gouthwayte, a sojourner at Potterton, June the 30th
Elizabeth Dinnison, widdow, of Barwicke, June the 30th
George, the son of Robert Browne of Winmoor-side, July the 8th
Grace Stephenson of Kidhall-lane head, August the 14th
Elizabeth, the wife of Robert Smith of Rhoundhay, August the 2d
Mary, the Daughter of Thomas Dodgeson of Rhoundhay August the 16th
Catherine Steward of Scoles, September the 11th
Stephen Smith of Scoles, October ye 7th
Elizabeth Simpson of Barwicke, widdow, November the 2d
Anne, the Daughter of William Taite, Junior, of Scoles, November the 4th
Obadiah Oddy of Scoles, Novem. ye 8th
Isabell, the wife of Richard Taite of Scoles, November the 13th
*Thomas Dalton, D.D., Rector of this church, dyed at the Falcon and Partridge in Leather lane in Hatton garden, London, November the 22th
Frances Shan of Potterton, widdow, December the 5th
Thomas Shippen of Barnbow, December the 28th
Matthew Maw of Shippen, December the 30th
Richard, the son of John Buck of Barwicke, January the 1st
Elizabeth, the wife of George Clarkson of Shippen, January the 23th
Anne, the Daughter of Robert Collet of Barwicke, January ye 26th
Anne, the daughter of John Taylor, sen', of Barwicke, Februa: ye 3d
Elizabeth Clough of Roundhay, widdow, February the 17th
Thomas Potter of Potterton, February the 18th
William, the son of William Deardon of Garforth more side, Febru: ye 22th
Rosamund, the Daughter of Tho: Watkinson of Garforth moore, Febr. 27
Mr John Errington of Barnbow, March the 2d
Frances, the wife of Thomas Stowing, jun., of Barwicke, March the 3d
Ellenor, the Daughter of David Hopwood of Potterton, March the 6th
Elizabeth, the Daughter of Connon Hopkinson of Barwicke, March the 10th
Paul, the son of Thomas Stowing, sen', of Barwicke, March the 11th
Sr Stephen Tempest of Barnbow, Knight, was buried at Broughton in Craven, March the 14th

*Rector (?)1660—1672.

Elizabeth Burnel of Roundhay, widdow, March the 18th
Anne, the wife of Richard Taite of Potterton, March the 23th

1673, Burials.

John, the son of Martin West of Rhoundhay, March ye 28th
Elizabeth, the Daughter of Joshua Turner of Barwicke, April ye 5th
Elizabeth, the wife of John Clarke of Barwicke, April the 6th
Robert, the son of Richard Taite of Potterton, April the 6th
Anne, the wife of Randall Briggs, jun., of Rhoundhay, April the 12th
Margarett Holmes of Rhoundhay, widdow, April the 13th
Isabell Drury of Barwicke, widdow, April the 19th
Mary Settle of Potterton, widdow, April the 19th
Mary, the wife of William Ellis of Kidhall, Esq., April the 26th
William Ingle of Scoles, May the 19th
John Clarke of Barwicke, May the 25th
Mary Taite of Barwicke, widdow, June the 20th
Robert Taylor of Barwicke, July the 18th
Sarah, the Daughter of John Aumbler of Winmoore side, July the 26th
John, the son of John Aumbler of Winmoore, July the 29th
Esther, the Daughter of John Massy of Stocking, August the 2d
Sarah, the Daughter of William Thorneton of Winmoore side, August the 21th
Barbara, the Daughter of Robert Shuttleworth of Scoles, September the 6th
Randall Briggs, senior, of Roundhay, September the 26th
Richard Atkinson of Roundhay, November the 10th
Elizabeth, the wife of Matthew Norton of Roundhay, November the 12th
Frances Atkinson of Rounday, widdow, November the 17th
One Child of Thomas Walker, another of William Baram, both of Roundhay, were buried at Chappelltowne
Christopher Kelshaw of Roundhay, December the 8th
Mary, the wife of George Hay of Barwicke, January the 30th
John Tayte, Junior, of Scoles, February the 2d
Anne Slater, widdow, and Elizabeth Slater, her Step-Daughter, both dyed together in one house on Winmoore, and were buryed in the same grave February the 3d
Mary, the daughter of John Outhwayt of Scoles, February the 3d
Elizabeth, the wife of Augustine Nicholson of Barwicke, Febru: ye 13th
Thomas, the son of John Buck of Barwick, deceased, March the 11th
Joseph Strickland of Barwick, March the 22th

1674, Burials.

Ann, the wife of James Wood of Barwicke, March the 29th
Alice, the wife of Roger Spincke of Scoles, Aprill the 11th
Ann, the basterd child of Ann Drury of Barwick, June the xivth
Mary, the wife of William Blaime of Roundhey, June the 4th
Elizabeth Walton of Winmoor, June the xxiijth
Widow Postgate of Roundhey, July the 1st
Aqual, the son of Richard Farrah of Scoles, the 8th
Jane, the daughter of James Wheatley of Winmoore, July the 12th

Sarah, the daughter of Margarett Barker of Potterton, July the xx^th^
Alice, the daughter of Leonard Catton of Barwick, Aug. the 16th
John Saynor of Potterton, September the 10th
Mr James Stead of Kings cross near Hallifax, died on Winmoore at Stocking, was buryed September the 11th
William Akedd of Barwicke Sept. 14th.
Benjamin Massie of Barwicke, October the xviijth
Richard, the son of William Vevers of Potterton, October the xixth
Richard, the basterd child of Elizabeth Watterworth of Barwick, October the xixth
Mary, the daughter of Henry Briggs of Potterton, October the 26th
John Robinson of Scoles, November the 3d
John Constable of Scoles, November the 20th
Ann, the wife of Robert Frankland of the new close spring, November the 24th
Mary, the daughter of Robert Brooke of the Stanks, Dec. the 19th
Dorothy Taylor of Barwicke, January the 17th
Robert Franckland of the spring, January the 23th
Susanna, the daughter of Thomas Walker of Roundhey, February the first
George Bollonds of Barwicke, February the 7th
Mr James Wright of Barwicke, aged 88 years, February 21th
William, the sonn of Richard Brough of Barwicke, Feb. the 26th

1675, BURIALS.

Michael, the son of Michael Rishe of Hirst moore, March the 26th
John, the son of Michael Rish of Hirst more, March 30th
Sarah, ye daughter of Robert Brooke of the Stancks, Mar. 31th
Katherine Browne of Roundhey, wid., Aprill the 26th
Cicilia, the daughter of Peter Slytor of Winmoore, May ye 4th
Robert Shenton of Barwick, May ye 25th
Elizabeth Watterworth of Barwicke, June ye xth
Grace, the wife of Joshuah Turner of Barwicke, June the 13th
Anne, the wife of Robert West of Rhoundhey, June the 14th
Elizabeth, the Daughter of Phillipp Haste of Barwick, June the 25th
Ellinor, the daughter of Ellinor Strickland of Barwicke, widow, July ye 4th
Elizabeth, the wife of John Drury of Barwicke, Augo 2d
Martha Bacckhous of Barwicke, Aug. the 8
Anne, the wife of Robert Green of Barwicke, August the 13th
A still borne Child of William Oates of Winmoore head near Kiddall laine, September the 5th
Thomas Walker, iunior, of Roundhey, Sept. 9th
Thomas Knapton, iu.', of Barwicke, October ye 3th
Thomas Saynor of Potterton, Octo. ye 23th
Elizabeth, the daughter of William Willcock of Garthforth moore November ye 14th
Joan Thompson of Garthforth moreside, widow, the 21th of No.
Susannah, the wife of Beniamin Pease of Morwicke, Nouember the 30th
A still borne childe of Thomas Taite of Barwicke, December the 16

Margaret, the wife of William Wilkocke, sen.', of Garthforth moor side, Dec. the 19th
Timothy Hopton of Hirst moor, Decemb^{r} the 19th
William Wilcocke the eld, of Garthforth more side, was buryed att Whitkirke, Dec: the 30th
Isable, the wife of William Taite the eld, of Scoles, January the 2^{d}
Richard Taite of Scoles, February the 6th
George, the son of Richard Green of Barw., February the 18th
Thomas Vevers of Barwicke, February the 27th

1676, SEPULT.

Mrs Isabell Irrington of Barnbow, widowe, Aprill the 1st
Frances Taylor of Barwicke, Aprill the 3^{d}
George, the son of George Hay, Aprill the 4th
Elizabeth Tate of Potterton, widow, May the 19
Susannah Shaw of Barwicke, widow, May the 21th
Edward, the son of George Hunter of Winmore, May the 29th
Isable, ye wife of Francis Johnson of ye Stank, June the 11th
Elizabeth Pickering of Barnbow, wid^{w}, July the 4th
Michael Hill of the stanks, July the 16th
William, the son of John Taylor, iu', of Barwicke, July ye 19°
Elisabeth Gibson of Barwicke, widow, July the 21
Richard Tate, iu', of Scoles, Sep. 1st
A s[t]ill born Child of Richard Burlands of Barwick, Sept. the 10th
A s[t]ill born Child [of] Michael Rish of Hirst moor, Septemb^{r} the 11th
Em Whitehead of Hirst moor, widow, was buried Septemb^{r} the 14th, at Whit Church
William, the son of William Deardon of Garthforth moor side, Sep. ye 19
Mary, the daughter of Mary Sharphurst of Hirstmoor, September the 26th
Elisabeth, the daughter of Joshua Turner of Barwick, Octob^{r} ye 8th
Oswald Harrison of Hirst moor, October 26th
William Briggs of Barwick, Octob^{r} 27th
Anne Deardon of Brown moore, Novemb^{r} ye 3th
Anne, the wife of Connon Hopkinson of Scoles, Nov. the 21th
Margarett, the wife of William Smith of Scoles, Nov. ye 25
John Settle of Potterton, the elder, was buried the same day.
Elisabeth, the wife of Richard Prince of Barwicke, Nouemb^{r} ye 29th
Richard Vevers of Potterton, Decemb^{r} the 9th
John, the son of William Vevers of Scoles, Dec. the 21th
Richard Jackeson of Scoles, January the 1
A still borne Child of William Lumbe of Winmoore, January the 1st
Anne Prince of Barwick, widow, Janua: ye 4th
Ann, the wife of William Tate of Scoles, Janua: the 14th
William Brame the eld^{r}, of Barnbowe carr, February ye 1st
Dorothy Spinke of Scoles, Widow, February ye xix.
John Gibson of Barwicke, March the 9th
William Crabtree of Barmbowe carr, March the 12th
John Johnson of Potterton, March the 21th

1677, BURIALS.

James, the son of William Fawcett of Barwicke, April x[th]
Elizabeth, the wife of Robert Green of Baıwicke, May the 6th
Richard, the son of William Vevers of Scoles, was buried y[e] same day
A still borne Child of Robert Prince of Barwicke, May 9th
Anne Strickland of Scoles, widow, May y[e] 13th
John, the son of Richard Knapton of Potterton, May y[e] 20th
W[m] Thornton of Bullaine head, June the 11th
John, the son of Richard Ellis of Barwicke, June the 27th
John Barker of Barwicke, July the 19th
Henry Shann of Potterton, August the 1st
Susannah, the wife of George Wright of Winmoore, August the 14th
Anne Robinson of Garforth moor side, wid[w], September the 6°
Katherin, the wife of Will'am Allott of Barwick, October y[e] 16
James, the son of Francis Grimes, a travilor, October the 24th
Hannah, the wife of Thomas Taylor, iu', of Barwick, Novemb[r] the 16th
Francis, the son of Francis Johnson of the Stanke, Decemb[r] y[e] 8th
Elinor, y[e] wife of William Munsey of Winmoore head, Dec. 10th
Anne Settle of Potterton, December the 27th
Robert Oddy of Scoles, December the 30th
Elizabeth Walker of Barnbow car, January 2[d]
Samuel, the son of Robert Green of Barwick, Janu. 12th
Nicholas Sheppen of Lasingcroft, March the First

1678, SEPULT.

Grace, the wife of Francis Saynor of Morwicke, March the 28th
Frances, the wife of John Tate of Scoles, April the 23th
Mary, the wife of Richard Braime of Barnbow carr, May the 15th
Sarah, the daughter of Robert Hardcastle of Barwicke, May the 17th
A still borne child of George Rosse of Potterton, June the 9
W[m] Tate of Scoles was Buryed in woollen, November the 5th
Thomas Hardwicke of Grimesdike was Buried in woollen, Novemb[r] y[e] 25th
*Mary Brooke, of the Stanks, widow, Nov: y[e] 27th
Isabell Tate of Potterton, widow, December the 5th
Jane Settle of Potterton, widow, Decemb. y[e] 22th
Ann Burton of Potterton, wid, Dec. the 25
Thomas Blackborn of Morwicke, Janu: 13th
Margary, y[e] wife of Henry Turner of Hurstmore, March the 5th
James Hunter of Winmore, March the xix[th]
A child of John Burland, the yeounger, of Barwicke, the same day
Robert Smith of Roundhey, March the 24th

SEPULT, 1679.

Martine, the son of Jeremiah Ingle of Barwicke, Aprill the 29th
Anne, the daughter of Edward Hinchcliffe of the Stanks on Hurstmore, May the 3[d]
Susannah Prince of the Lower end of Hurst more, May y[e] 12th
Hellen, the wife of M[r] Richard Vevers of Scoles, May the 17th

*All burials were expressed to be buried in woollen from here to the end of this register book, unless otherwise stated.

William Taylor of Scoles, June the 7th
Aqualla, the son of George Wright of Winmoore, July the 15
Mary Crabtree of Barnbow carr, widow, August the 7th
Katherine Stowen of Barwicke, widow, August the 9th
Thomas Jackeson of Barwick, August the 10th
George Hunter of Winmore was Buryed in woollen the same day
Anne, the wife of Christopher Leeds of Garforth more side, August the 28th
Anne, the daughter of Christopher Leeds of Garthforth moor side, September the 8th
Peter Sheppen of Scoles town end, September the 28th
Francis, the son of Thomas Clarkson of Hopperley, October the 12°
Rosomond Weare of Winmore, near Kidall laine end, October the 19th
Michael, the son of Martine Whitehead of Hurstmore, Octob: 22th
Alice Barker of Barwick, wid, No: 2
John, the son of Sam: Robinson of Garthforth more side, Nov. ye 8th
Robert, the son of Sam: Robinson of Garthforth more side, Novem: ye 22th
Anne, the daughter of Lawrence Andrew of the same, ye same day
Hellen, the daughter of John Frankland of Garthforth more side, November the 24th
Anne, the daughter of Rosomo[n]d Maw of the same, the same day
William, the son of John Taylor of Barwicke, the yeounger, Nov. 27th
Thomas Horsley of Garthforth more side, Dec. the 3th
Elinor, the wife of Peter Barker of Barwicke, Dec. 19th
A still born Child of Richard Robinson of Morwicke, Decr ye 27th
John Taite, the elder, of Scoles, January the 3th
Frances, the daughter of Francis West of Roundhey, February the 18th
Mary, the daughter of Thomas Blackburn of Morwicke, dec., March the 13th
Matthew, the son of Joshuah Lumb, at the cross Yeates on the Lower end on Hirst more, March 24th

SEPULT, 1680.

Mary Akedd of Barwicke, widow, March ye 30th
Mary Blackborne of Morwicke, widow, Aprill the 3d
Rebeckah, the daughter of Richard Prince of Barwicke, Aprill the 15th
Richard, the son of Samuel Robinson of Garforth more side, June the 8th
Mary Sheppen of Barnbow, widow, June the 16th
Samuell Fletcher of Barwicke, the 9th of July
Martha, the daughter of Thomas Bradford of Tolorough Yeates, the 15th day of July
Edward Hinchcliff of the Stanke on Hurstmoore, July the 24th
Richard Slator of Potterton, the 10th day of October
Mary, the wife of John Hardcastle of Barwicke, the 12th of October
Elisabeth, the wife of Martin West of Roundhey, October the 13th
Margarett Holmes of Roundhey, widow, was Buryed the same day
Mary, the wife of John Hunter of Hurstmore, died in childe birth, and was buried October the 15

Thomas Dodgson of Round[hey], October the 17th
Richard Settle of Barwick, was buried the same day
Richard Holmes of Roundhey, October the 21th
George Dawson of Sheppen, November the 11th
Isaac Wood of Potterton, Novembr the 12th
Richard Norton of the Penwell was Buryed at Whitchurch, November the 22th
Anne, the wife of Francis Brunton of Sheppen, the same day
Frances, the wife of Richard Stiham of Kidhall laine head, Novem: 24
Anne, the wife of William Lumbe of Winmore, December the 11th
A still born Child of William Tate of Scoles, Decembr ye 17th
Elizabethe, the wife of Roger Lund of Browne Moore, Dec. the xxviij
Thomas Tate of Scoles, the elder, the 30th of Dec.
Anne, the wife of Jeremiah Ingle of Barwick, Decembr ye 31st
The Abortive child of Thomas Clarkeson of Hopperley, January the 6th
Michaell Burton of Potterton, January the 14
Frances, the daughter of Richard Knapton of Potterton, January the 15th
Mary Sharphurst of Hurstmoore, widow, January the 18th
Mris Alice Hodgson of Potterton, widow, Janu: 24th
George Dickenson at the Bull Laine head on Winmoore, January the 26th
Anne, the wife of Richard Burland of Barwicke, January the 30th
Elisabeth Leadbeater of Barwicke, February ye 17th
Martha, the daughter of Thomas Maud at the Bull laine head on Winmore, Feb. the 19th
Samuel Shenton of Barwick, February ye 20th
Elizabeth, the daughter of Thomas Tate of Kidall laine head, March the 9th
Jane, the daughter of John Marston of Morwick, March the 9th
Mary, the daughter of Thomas Stowen of Whihill, March ye 19
A Bortive child of Thomas Briggs of Roundhey, March ye 6th

SEPULT, 1681.

Mary, the daughter of Richard Burland, Aprill the 17
Anne, the wife of Thomas Wansley of Barwick, March the 27th
Richard Knapton of Potterton, March the 30th
George Dickenson, iunior, of Bull laine head, March the 25
An Abortive child of Samuel Robinson of Garthforth moor side, May the 13th
A Child of Richard Robinson of Barwicke, May the 30th
Robert Strickland of Scholes, June the 1st
Anne Hills of the Stanks on Hurst moor, May the 22th
Elisabeth, the daughter of Rich Farrer of S[c]holes, June the 13th
John Dineley, the elder, of Barwicke, July ye 7th
John, the son of John Moore, the younger, of Barwicke, July the 10th
Thomas, the son of Joseph Bullock, July ye 13th
Elisabeth Dickenson at the Bull Laine head on winmoor, July the 18th
Francies Chambers of Grimesdicke, widow, Aug. 13th
George, the son of George Spinke of Scoles, Aug. the 22th

Mary, the daughter of George Haste of Barwicke, August the 23th
Sarah, the daughter of Robert Watkinson of Barwicke, September the 12th
Richard Ellis of Barwick, September the 15th
Robert, the son of William Knapton of Barwicke, September the 23th
Elisabeth Wright of Barwicke, October the 15
Elisabeth Settle of Potterton, wid., No: 4
Isabell Ingle of Scoles, widow, Novemb. 14
Sarah, the daughter of Samuel Robinson of Garthforth more side, November ye 22th
Benjamine, the son of Wm Lumbe of Winmore, November the [30]
[*Blank*] of Tho: Wright of Winmore, att Whitkirk by lycence from Mr Hall, the 17th day of February
Sara, the daughter of Geo. Browne of Barwicke, Dec. the 1st
Alexander Wood of Kidhall, Dec. 14th
Thomas Simpson of Garthforth more side, December the 29th
Isable, the daughter of James Clough of Roundhey Lodge, January the 12th
William, the son of Wm Lund at Cross Yates at the Lower end of Hurstmoor, January the 23th
George Gibson of Barwick, February the 7th
Mr Lever Wood of Barwicke, Feb. the 13th
Robt, the son [altered from Jane, the daughter] of Robt Wilson of Roundhey, February ye 18th
Elisabeth Ball of Potterton, wid^{w}, Feb. 19
John Chambers at the lower end of Hurst more near Whitkirke lane end, by licence from Mr Hall, at Whitkirk, Feb. ye 25
Sarah, the daughter of Thomas Maud at Bull laine head, March the 5th
Christopher, the son of Christop: Kelshaw of Roundhey, the same day
The Abortiue Child of John Brown of Potterton, March the 11th
Maiy, the daughter of Richard Bollands of Barwicke, March the 12th
Thomas Andrew of Garthforth more side, March the 13th
Anne Robinson of scoles, widow, March the 19th
Jane, the daughter of Leonard Gayton of Winmoore, March the 24th
Maike Cooper of Scoles, March the 25th
Margarett Harrison of the Stanks on Hurst moore, wid^{w}, the same day

SEPULT, 1682.

Marke Cooper of Scoles, March the 25th
Margaret Harrison of the stankes on Hurstmore, the same day
Michael, the son of Matthew Norton of Roundhey, March the 30th
John Burland, the eld^{r}, of Barwick, Aprill the 30th
Elisabeth, the wife of Martine Cash of Scoles, Aprill the 8
Helline Wilson of Scoles, Aprill the 9th
Eester Constable of Penwell, Aprill the 17th
William Wilcok of Garthforth more sd., Aprill 27
Roger Lund of Brown more, April 23
A Child of Mark Cooper, dec., Ap. 24

*Dorothy, the Daughter [of] Charles Engleby, Esquire, of Barnbow, Aprill the 27th
Timothy Hopton at Whitkirk lane end, May the 8th
Mary, the wife of James Prince of Barwicke, May the 12th
Peter Varley of the Brown more closes, May the 25
John, the son of Austine Nicholson of Barwick, June the 19th
Elisabeth, the wife of John Holmes of Roundhey, the 24th of July
William Walker of Scoles, July the 27th
John, the son of John Hunter of Hurstmore, July the 30th
Anne Maw of Garthforth more side, July the 31th
John, the son of Chr: Leeds of the same, the same day
Isable, the daughter of Wm Hair of Morwick, August the 8th
Anne, the wife of Thomas Tate of Barwick, August the 9th
Anne, ye wife of Wm Brame of Barnbow, Aug. the 10th
Helline, the daughter of Richard Settle of Potterton, September the 8th
The Abortiue Child of William Tate of Scoles, September the 25th
Richard Johnson of Scoles, September the 26th
Margarett, the wife of Wm Tate of Scoles, September the 27th
Elisabeth, the daughter of James Wilcocke at the Lower end of Huirst more near Allershaw laine end, Oc. 8
John Holmes of Roundhey, October the 15th
Beniamine Pease of Morwick, October the 31th
Thomas, the son of Robert Thornes of Barwicke in Elmett, November the 9th
George Gibson of Barwick, November the 27th
Beatrix, the daughter of Leo: Catton of Barwick, Nov: the 29th
Henry, the son of Francis Johnson of the Stank, Dec. 4
Robert Briggs of Barwick, December the 10th
Randolph Constable of Hurstmore, ye same day
Anne, the daughter of John Barker of Barwick, Dec. 20th
George, the son of John Wheelhouse of Scoles, Dec. the 28
Katherine, the Daughter [of] Mary Briggs of Barwick, widow, December the 31th
James Barker of Sheppen, January the 7th
Mary, the Daughter of James Prince of Barw:, January ye 18th
Robert Dinely of Barwicke, February the 3, and hath left the use of Ten pounds for ever to be distributed to the poor of Barwick Town after the Decease of Margarett, his wife.
John Robinson of Scoles, January the 25th
The Abortiue child of Mr Charles Hall of Barwick, March ye 4th
William Eskeritt of Scoles, March the 7th
Martin Hague of Barwick, March the 11th
James [? Prince] of Barwick, March the 15th
Mary, the wife of Roger Gregson of Barw:, March the 7th
[? Alice] Spinke of Scoles, March the 21th
Anne Hunter of Winmore, March the 22th

* Charles Engleby was probably Charles Ingleby, a Roman Catholic acquitted of complicity in the Gascoigne plot, 1680, made Baron of the Exchequer by James II., 1688, but dismissed by William III., knighted 1688, resumed practice. *Dictionary of National Biography*. For pedigree see Thoresby's Ducatus, 2nd Ed., p. 192.

1683, SEPULT.

John Dunnell of Scoles, March the 30th
Abraham Rishforth of the High Ash on Browne more, Aprill the 1st
Mary, the wife of Thomas Knapton of Barwick Aprill ye 12th
William, the son of Thomas Walker of Roundhey, the 1st of May
Anne, the wife of John Saynor of Grimesdike, the 3 of May
James Prince of Barwick, May the 20th
Grace, the wife of John Holcroft of Scoles, the 4th June
Susannah Hopton at the lower end of Hurst moore, June the 14
Mary, the wife of Austine Nicolson of Barwick, the 4 of July
Anne, the wife of Solomon Jibson at Kidall oake, August ye 18
Richard, the son of Mr Thomas Atkinsonne of Barwicke, Aug. ye 21
Robert Turner at Penwell, August the 26th
Martine West of Roundhey Parke, September the 5
Jonathan, the son of Thomas Maud at the Bull laine head on Winmore, was Buried the same day
Mary, the daughter of William Hague of Fishlake, the 26 of September
William, the son of Thomas Walker of Roundhey, Sep. 26
The Abortive child of Jeremiah Ingle of Barwick, October the 27
Christopher Scott of Morwick, November the 14th
Mary, ye wife of James Barker of Sheppen, November ye 18
James, ye son of Richard Farrer of Scoles, November ye 21th
Thomas Wansley of Barwick, November ye 23th
Mary Settle of Potterton, November the 24th
Christopher Ibbotson of the same, December the 1
Mary, the wife of Wm Handley of scols, Dec. 11th

Churchwardens for Barwicke in Ellmett.

1661

Barw: - - - Thomas Taylor
Scoles Division Robert Greenewood
Potterton - - Richard Daniel
Roundhay - - John Burnel

1662

Thomas Taylor
Robert Greenewood
Richard Daniel
Christopher Kelshaw

1663

Thomas Wansley
Michael Hill
Robert Settle
Randolph Briggs

1664

John Dineley
George Dickinson
Henry Shan
Martin West

Overseers of the Poore for Barwicke in Ellmett.

1661

Barw: - - John Taylor, junior
Scoles - - George Spincke
Potterton - Robert Ball

1662

William Jackson
Richard Thompson
Thomas Potter

1663

Thomas Bird
Richard Sheppen
John Settle

1664

John Haigue
Abraham Rishforth
Samuel Taite

Churchwardens—*continued.*

1665

John Taylor, senior
Henry Wright
John Settle
John Holmes

1666

Thomas Taylor
Thomas Blackeburne
Thomas Potter
Matthew Norton

1667

The last yeare Churchwardens executed the office againe this yeare.

Churchwardens 1668

Robt Dineley
Thomas Thompson
Samuel Taite
Robert Smith

1669

The last yeare Churchwardens elected againe this yeare.

1670

John Taylor, sen.
William Vevers, jun.
John Dodgeson
Randolph Briggs, sen.

1671

Bernard Mawmond
Robert Brooke
Richard Daniel
Thomas Walker

1672

John Taylor, junior
Mr Taylor of Morwicke
Henry Shan
Randolph Briggs, junior

1673

Robert Collett
Richard Taylor
Richard Settle
Thomas Dodgeson

1674

Thomas Taylor, sen'.
George Rosse
Benjamine Pease
Martine West

Overseers—*continued.*

1665

Thomas Knapton
Benjamin Pease
Thomas Taite

1666

John Burland
Robert Shore
Richard Daniel

1667

John Smith
Richard Vevers
Andrew Sclater

Overseers 1668

Thomas Taylor
Richard Vevers
John Dodgeson

1669

Roger Gregson
Robert Oddy
Henry Shan

1670

Thomas Stowing
Francis Johnson
Mr Hodgeson

1671

George Haist
William Vevers, sen.
William Settle

1672

William Briggs
Henry Wright
Thomas Potter

1673

Richard Collett
Martin Clough
Richard Ball

1674

Robert Hardcastle
Samll Fletcher
George Spincke
Richard Braime
William Vevers

Churchwardens—*continued.*

Churchwardens 1675

Robert Dineley
Richard Daniell
George Dickinson
Laurence Eamondsonne

1676

The last yeare Churchwardens chosen and elected againe this yeare

1677

John Taylor, senior
Samuel Taite
William Braime
Robert Lee

1678

George Haste
Christo: Hill
John Settle
Richard Holmes

1679

Jo: Smith, iunior
Jo: Massie
Jo: Dodgson
James Clough

1680

Marke Wright
Tho: Thompson
P. Daniell
Jo: Ball
Geo. Bingley

1681

John Taylor, iu.
John Marston
Ric: Settle
Matt. Norton

1682

John Hardisty
Rich: Sheppen
Rich. Danjell
Chr: Kelsha

1683

Wm Knapton
Wm Wood
Rich: Ball
Matt: Holmes

1684

William Taylor
Thomas Wright
William Featon
Richard Atkinson

Overseers—*continued.*

Oveiseers 1675

Bernard Mawmond
Richard Sheppen
Richard Thompson
William Vevers

1676

John Dineley
William Vevers
George Rosse

1677

John Smith, iu'.
Rich: Settle
William Taylor

1678

John Taylor, iu'.
Henry Wright
James Lee

1679

Tho: Tate
Ben Pease
Phineas Daniel

1680

John Hardisty
Mr Vevers, Scoles
Phi. Daniel

1681

Mr Gyles Hardwicke
Christo: Shore
John Settle

1682

Wm Strickland
Wm Braime
Sam: Tate
Rich: Aspenwald

1683

Marke Wright
John Massie
Geo: Rosse
Robt Lee

1684

Richard Varley
Chr: Hill
Hen: Briggs
Matthew Norton

Churchwardens—*continued.*

1685

Tho: Tate
Tho. Knapton to serve
H. Beedall
Wm Coapland
Tho: West

1686

Rob̄ Thornes
Wm Taylor, iu'.
John Ball
Wm Braime

1687

Ric. Varley
Tho. Rishforth
Geo. Rosse
Tho. Walker

1688

John Taylor
Roger Spinke
Henry Briggs
Peter Banks

1689

Rich: Robinson
Rich. Danjel
Rich. Thomson
Mathew Holmes

1690

Geo: Haste
Robt Brooke
Sam. Taite
Wm Lister

1691

Thomas Settle
Nathan Wright
John Settle
Wm Eamorson
Wm Lister to serve

Overseers—*continued.*

1685

Jos. Moore
Geo. Spinke
John Dodgson
Robt West

1686

Thomas Bird
Tho. Shepen
Wm Featon
Wm Eamorson

1687

Matt. Ingle
Tho: Shippen
Wm Coapland

1688

John Burland
Nicolas Sheppen
Mr Vevers of Pott'

1689

Rob̄t Collett
Mr Vevers of Pott'
Wm Tate

1690

Wm Knapton
Wm Braime
Rich. Settle
Richd Aspendwall

1691

Richd Smith
Wm Taylor of Scoles
Wm Featon
Robt Wilson

[SECOND BOOK.]

The Register off all thee Christinings, Marriages, and Burialls within the parish of Barwicke-in-Elmett, from the 25 Day of March, 1684.

BAPTIZAT', 1684.

Robert, the son of Robert Watkinson of Barwick, was bap. March the 26th
Matthew, the son of Matthew Norton of Roundhey, May the 20
John, the son of Tho. Knapton of Barwick, June the 6
Sarah, the daughter of Edmond Bland of Brownmoore, August the 6
Benjamine, the son of William Strickland of Barwicke, July the 24
Sarah, the daughter of William Hopwood of Barwick, August the 27
Joseph, the son of Thomas Maud of Bull laine end, September the 7th
Mary, the daughter of Robt. Wansley, the 15 of September
Thomas, the son of Thomas Popplewell of Bar., the 25 of September
Elisabeth, the daughter of Gascoigne Burnett of Scoles, the 29° of September
Helline, the daughter of John Hunter of Hirstmore, the 8th of October
Elizabeth, the daughter of John Taylor at ye West end of Kidall laine end, Oc. ye 15°
John, the son of Wm Smith of Barwick, the same day
Sarah, the daughter of John Marston of Morwicke, October the 23°
Henry, the son of Mr Giles Hardwick of Barwicke, Nov. 6
Grace, the daughter of Thomas Brunton of Barnbow, November the 23th
James, the son of John Prince of Potterton, November the 29th
John, the son of John Scalbert of Barwicke, Decemb. ye 3
William, the son of Aquall Blackborne of Scoles, December the 21
Thomisine the daughter of Peter Slator of the Stanks, January the 1st
Frances, the daughter of John Frankland of Garthforth-more side, January the 11
Anne, the daughter of William Coapland of Potterton, February ye 5th
Anne, the daughter of Samuel Tate of Barwick, February ye 22th
Matthias, the son of Daniel Huett of Scoales, March the 1st
Elinor, the daughter of Robert Brown of Potterton, the same day
Benjamen, the son of George Hast of Barwick, the 12 of March

BAPTIZAT', 1685.

John, the son of Richard Varley of Barwick, bapt. Apr. 13
Elizabet, daughter of William Knapton of Barwick, Ap. 20
Mary, the daughter of Will. Hardy of Scholes, Ap. 20
Mosses, the son [of] John Settle of Pott., Apl. 23
Hellen, the daughter of Robt. Wilson of Roundhey, Aprill 27
Sara, the daughter of Matthew Holmes of the same, May the 14
Sara, the daughter of Hen. Briggs of Potterton, August the 9
Easter, ye daughter of John Thompson of Garthforth more side, ye same day
Grace, the daughter of James Hineley of the Penwell, Aug. the 23

Anne, the daughter of Matthew Watkinson of Garthforth side, Octob. ye 11
Anne, the daughter [of] Christop. Hill of the Stank, 12
Anne, the daughter of Thomas Burland of Barwick, November the 26th
Matthew, the son of Jeremiah Ingle of the same, Dec. the 9th
Thomas, the son of Robt Wansley of Barwick, Dec. 16
Tho., ye son of Tho. Knapton, Dec. ye 26
Anne, the daug^{t} of Georg Smith of ye Cross yates, January ye 1st
Rosomond, the daughter of Robert Braime of Scoles, January the 17th
George, the son of William Handly of the same, January ye 24th
Anne, the daughter of Robt. Brown the yeounger of Winmore, February ye 28
David, the son of Rich^{r} Settle of Potterton, March 5
Elisabeth, the daughter of Joseph Hague of Barwick, March the 9
Thomas, the son of Matthew Issott of Barwick, March the 19

BAPTIZAT', 1686.

Mary, the daughter of Robert Thornes of Barwicke, was bapt. April the 19
Elisab., ye daughter of Richard Farrer of Scoles, May 2
Robert, the son of Andrew Duncan, Gent., of Spieghlys, the 20 of May
Elisabeth, the daughter of Rich. Atkinson of Roundhey, May the 24
William, the son of Jo^{n} Barker off Barwick, June ye 24
Isable, ye daughter of John Crabtree of Winmore head, June the 27
Sarah, the daughter of Thomas Wright at ye white layth on Winmore, July the 24.
[*Blank*] the daughter of Edmond Bland on Brown moore, July 29
Mary, ye daughter of Jo^{n} Frankland of Garthforth moor side, August the 8
Alice, the daughter of Robt Farrer of Penwell, August the 24
Robert, the son of Rich^{r} Smith of Barwick, Sept. the 24
Elisabeth, ye daughter of Tho. West of Roundhey, September 30
Barbarah, ye daughter of Solomon Jibson at Kidal laine end, Octob. 1st
Richard, ye son of John Smith, iunior, of Barwick, October the 8th
Elisabeth, the daughter of William Hopwood of Barwick, October the 22th
Rosomond, ye daughter of Gascoigne Burnett of Scoles, October the 25th
Elisab., the daughter of Henry Dickinson at the Bull laine end, Nov. the 21
Anne, the daughter of Richard Varley of Barwick, November the 29
Anne, daughter of Robertt Watkinson of Barwicke, December ye 2^{d}
Hellen, the daughter of Matt. Norton of Roundhey, December ye 9
Anne, ye daughter of Leonard Gaton on Winmore, Dec. the 19
Bridget, the daughter of John Hunter on Winmore, Jan. the 9th
Dorothy, ye daughter of Richard Lumb of ye same, Jan. ye 18th
Robert, the son of Robert Wansley of Barwick, January 21
Richard, ye son of Richard Robinson of Barwicke, January the 26
Anne, ye daughter of Thomas Maud of Winmore, January the 30
Thomas, the son of William Lister of Scoles, February the 6
W^{m} the son of Rosomond Mawe of Garthforth more side, February the 13

William, the son of Wm Smith of Barwicke, February the 24th
Anne, ye daughter of Humphrey Morrise of Hurstmore, March the 6
Robert, ye son of Robt. Pitts of Scoles, March the 14
Martine, the son of Saml West of the Penwell, March ye 20th

BAPTIZAT', 1687.

Benjamine the son of John Aumbler of the Hurstmore, was baptized Aprill ye 3th
Jane, daughter of James Wheatley on Winmore, July the 10th
Margarett, ye daughter of Chr. Hill of ye Stanks, July the 20th
Anne, the daughter of John Hardistye of Barwicke, July the 28
Sarah, the daughter of Robt Brame of S[c]oles, July the 31th
Aaron, the son of John Settle of Potterton, August the 20th
Thomas, the son of Richard Thompson of y^{e} Stanks, August y^{e} 28
John, y^{e} son of Alice Prince of Barwicke, widow, the same day
Robt, the son of Rich$_{d}$ Robinson of Scoles, Sept. 11
Sarah, the daughter of Leona$_{d}$ Catton of Barwicke, October y^{e} 6
Anne, the daughter of Daniel Huett of Garthforth more side, Oct. 24
Matthew, y^{e} son of Matthew Holmes of Roundhey, October 27
John, the son of William Haire of Morwick, October the 28
Matthew, the son of Wi$\hbar$m Hague of Barwicke, November 3
Mary, the daughter of Timo. Smith of Barwicke, Novem. y^{e} 24
Robert, the son of William Knapton of the same, Novemb. 30
Anne, y^{e} daughter of Thomas Poplewell of y^{e} same, Decemb. the 1st
Anne, the daughter of Wm Strickland of Barwicke, December the 18
Thomas, the son of Joshua Stringer of the same, December the 30
Joseph, the son of Matthew Issott of the same, Janu. ye 5th
*Anne, the daughter of William Eamorson of Roundhey, Jan. the 12
Sarah, ye daughter of Richard Settle of Potterton, January the 14th
Jane, ye daughter of John Taylor at the west end of Kidhall lane end, February the 1st
Mary, ye daughter of Rob. Wansley of Barwicke, Feb. ye 15
Elisabeth, the daughter of Richard Lumbe on Winemore, Feb. ye 26°
John, the son of Robt Brown of Potterton, March the 16
Peter, the son of Robert Wilson of Rhoundhey, March the 18th
†Samuel Dudson, clerke, Master of Arts, began to supply this Cure May the 10th, 1687.

BAPTIZAT, 1688.

George, the son of Richard Smith of Barwick, was baptized March 26
Anne, the daughter of Joseph Hague of the same, Aprill the 5th
Abraham, the son of Thomas Rishforth at ye High Ash on Brown more, Aprill the 12
Benjamine, the son of Jacob Pease of Morwicke, Aprill the 22
Elisabeth, the daughter of Michael Eastbourn on Hirstmore, May the 6
Frances, the daughter of Robert Thornes of Barw., May ye 10
Matthew, the son of Thomas West of Roundhey, June the 21
William, the son of William Lister of Scoles, August the 12
John, the son of Giles Hardwick of Barwicke, Gent, August the 21

*A pedigree of the Eamonson family is printed in Platt & Morkill's Whitkirk, page. 80. Ann Eamonson married Mr. Jeremiah Marshall of Guiseley, 21 Feb., 1731-2.

†Samuel Dudson, Christ's College, Cambridge, B.A., 1672.

Wm, the son of James Hinley at Penwell, August the 26
Thomas, the son of Matthew Watkinson of Garthforth more side, September the 9
Anne, the daughter of William Handley of Scoles, the same day
Matthew, the son of William Robinson of Garthforth more side, Sep. 23
Anne, the daughter of William Watson of Hopperley, October the 4
Michael the son of Jon Prince of Potterton, October the 8
Robert, the son of John Burland of Barwicke, October the 17th
Mary, the daughter of Edmond Bland of Brown more closes, November ye 8
William, ye son of Thomas Hewett of Potterton, November ye 10
Edmond, the son of James Clough on Winmore head, November ye 11
Peter, ye son of Peter Slaytor of the Stankes, the same day
Thomas, the son of Richard Varley of Barwicke, December the 3
Joane, the Bastard daughter of Alice Prince of Barwicke, January ye 6th
Sara, the daughter of Tho. Prince of the same, the same day
Jane, the daughter of Robert Watkinson of Barwicke, January the 14th
Elisabeth, the daughter of Samuel West of Penwell, January 16
Peter, the son of Robert Pitts of Scoles, the same day
Joseph, the son of Robert Oddy of the same, deceased, about 17 seveenthteen yeares of age, January the 17
Stephen, the son of John Aumbler, Junior, of Hurstmore, January the 20th
Elisabeth, the daughter of William Hemsworth of Potterton, January the 31
John, the son of John Saynor of Barwicke, February the 4th
Deborah, and Margaret the children of Robt Oddy, late of Scoles, deceased, the 14 day of Feb., being about the age of 15 and 13 yeares old, borne the 24 of June, 1673 and the other borne the 27 of March, 1676
Marke, the son of Thoms Cooper of Scoles, February the 21
Jane, ye daughter of Ralph Collett of Barwicke, March ye 20

BAPTIZAT, 1689.

Grace, the daughter of William Coapland of Potterton, was baptized March the 30
John, ye son of Jon Smith of Barwick, Apr. the 17
Mary, the daughter of Richd Atkinson of Roundhey, the same day
George, ye son of Richard Thompson of ye Stanks, ye 24 of Aprill
Thomas, the son of Wm Smith of Barwick, May ye 16
Debora, ye daughter of George Smith, July ye 11th, Near Cross yates
John, ye son of Henry Slaytor of Winmore, July ye 14
Grace, the daughter of Matthew Holmes of Roundhey, July the 17th
Matthew, the son of Gascoigne Burnett of Scoles, July the 25th
John, ye son of Thomas Hill of Barnbow, Aug. 4th
William, ye son of Robt Dodgson of Kidall laine end, August the 22
Elisabeth, the daughter of Chr. Hill of the Stankes, Aug. the 28
Charles, ye son of Robt Brame of Scoles, September the 1st
John, the son of Humphrey Morris of Hurstmore, October the 6

Jeremiah, the son of Thomas Huett of Potterton, October the 11
Anne, the daughter of John Hunter of Winmore, October the 13th
Elisabeth, ye daughter of Thomas Burland of Barwick, October the 31
Mary, the daughter of Andrew Jackson of Scoles, November the 20th
Mary, the daughter of Tho. Knapton of Barwick, Dec. ye 10
John, the Bastard Child of Hellen Walton of Winmore, January the 3d
Thomas, the son of John Settle of Potterton, January the 19
William, the son of Wm Hague of Barwick, Janu. the 27
Susannah, the daughter of Richard Settle of Potterton, ye same day
Thomas, ye son of Tho. West of Roundhey, January the 30
Alice, the daughter of Thomas Cooper of Scoles, February the 2
Elisabeth, ye daughter of Gyles Hardwicke of Barwick, Gentleman, deceased, the same day
Elisabeth, the daughter of Richd Smith of Barwicke, Feb. the 21
Richard, the son of Timothy Smith of the same, Feb. the 26th

BAPTIZAT, 1690.

Elisabeth, ye daughter of Willm Watson of Hopperley, was baptized Aprill 3
Anne, daughter of James Wheatly near Penwell, April 6
Roger, the son of John Southard of Brownemore, Ap. 8
Samuel the Bastard child of Elinor Thompson of the Stankes, the same day
John, the son of James Wilcocke at Allershawe laine end, Aprill the 13
Mary, the daughter of Jonath'n Eastwood at Bull laine head, Aprill the 21
George, the son of William Lister of Scoles, May the 4
Mary, ye daughter of Richd Robinson of the same, the same day
Thomas, ye son of Wm Handley of ye same, May ye 30
Joseph, the son of Thomas Rishforth at ye High Ash, June the 12
George, the son of Joseph Hague of Barwicke, June the 29
Mary, ye daughter of Wm Hopwood of ye same, ye same day
Matthew, ye son of Matthew Isott of Barwick, July ye 16
Samuel, ye son of Robert Wansley of ye same, ye same day
Mary, ye Bastard child of Mary Standley near Speighley, Aug. ye 10th
William, the son of Joshuah Stringer of Barwicke, Sept. the 3
Anne, ye daughtr of Henry Dickinson at Bull lane end, Sept. 21
John, the son of John Atkinson of Barwick, December ye 10
Thomas, the son of Tho. Knapton of the same, Dec. ye 17
Martin, ye son of John Prince of Potterton, December 20
Lucy, ye daughter of Martha Crosland, a traveller, at Sheppen, Decembr ye 27
Mary, ye daughter of Mr John Brooke of Leeds, was baptized at Stank house, the 8 day of January
Mary, ye daughter of Christo. Hill at ye Stankes, ye 14 of January
Anthony, ye son of John Massie of Grimesdike, ye 19 of January
Jane, ye daughter of John Smith, the 14 of January
James, ye son of James Bullock of Barw., Jan. 19
Anne, ye daughter of Daniel Jermaine of ye same, January 26
Thomas, ye son of Robt Browne of Potterton, January ye 29
Rowland, ye son of Robert Watkinson of Barwicke, Feb. ye 15

Mary, the daughter of Willm Eamorson of Roundhey, Marche the 19
Robt ye son of Micael Eastbourn of Speighleys, March the 17
Easter, ye daughter of Aqual Blackborn of Scoles, Ap. ye 10, 1691
[*Blank*] ye son of Richd Lumbe near Speighley nuke, May ye 9, 1691

BAPTIZAT 1691.

William, the son of Henry Slaytor of Hirstmore, was baptized March ye 29
Easter, the daughter of Robert Wilson of Roundhey, Aprill ye 12
Anne, the daughter of Wm Haire of Morwicke, Aprill 13
Robert, the son of Robert Dodg[s]on of Kidall laine end, deceased, Ap. 24
Thomas, ye son of Wm Knapton of Barwicke, Aprill ye 26
William, the son of Mr Samuel Dudson, Minister of Barwick, April ye 28
Mary, ye daughter of Richd Thompson, Junio^{r}, of ye Stanks, May the 6
Easter, ye daughter of Thomas Prince of Barwick, May ye 10th
Mary, the daughter of Willm Hemsworth of Potterton, ye same day
Robert, the son of Robt Thornes of Barwick, May the 12
Marke, ye son of Thomas Brunton of Sheppen, May ye 17
Mary, ye daughter of Ralph Collett of Barwicke, May ye 25
Anne, the daughter of William Dickinson of Winmore head, June ye 24
Mary, ye daughter of John Saynor of Barwicke, June ye 29
Edward, ye son of Tho^{m} West of Roundhey, July the 1st
John, the son of Peter Slator of ye Stankes, August the 9
Thomas, ye son of Thomas Tate of Scoles, Aug. the 16
Anne, ye daughter of John Aumbler on Hurst Moor, September the 6
Samuel the son of Thomas Hewett of Potterton, Sept. 13
Michael, the son of Thomas Settle of Barwicke, Octo. 14
William, ye son of Phillip Westerland, a strainger in Scoles, Octob^{r} ye 18
Mary, the daughter of Will Collett of Barwick, Octob^{r} 25
Anne, ye daughter of Thomas Cooper of Scoles, the 14th of November
George, ye son of Richd Smith of Barwick, November the 18th
Anne, the daughter of Robert Wansley of Barwick, December the 23th
Robert, ye son of Robt Brown near Penwell, Jan. 23
Thomas, ye son of Daniel Jermain of Barwicke, January ye 28th
Mary, ye daughter of Humphrey Morrice of Hurst more, at Whitkirk, by a note from our minist^{r}, Feb. ye 13
Jane, ye daughter of Richd Robinson of Barwicke, Feb. ye 12
Mathew, ye sonne of William Watson of Hopperley, February ye 18
Sara, ye daughter of Leonard Gaton of Bullane, Febr. ye 21
[*Blank*] y^{e} [*blank*] of Matthew Holmes of Roundhey, February ye 25
Alice, the daughter of William Shutleworth of Scoles, Mar. the 15
Robert, the son of Robt Brame of Scoles, March the 16
Hunt, the son of Daniel Hewett of Garthforth moorside, March the 13

BAPTIZAT, 1692.

William, the Bastard child of Elinor Munsey, widow, of Winmore head was bapt. June the 5
Mary, the daughter of Joshua Stringer of Barwicke, July ye 11th
Edward, the son of Richard Lumbe near Cross yates on hurst more, Aug. the 14°
Moses, the son of John Settle of Potterton, Aug. 28
Richard, the son of Robt Chambers of the same, Aug. 31

Matthew, the son of Matthew Issott of Barwick, Septembr ye 8
Marke, the son of James Bullocke of Barwicke, Sept. the 10th
Thomas, the son of John Potter of the same, Septembr ye 14
William, the son of Samuel Tate, iur, at Kidhall laine head, September ye 16
Dorothy, the Bastard child of Annie Tinsdall of Barwicke, Sept. the 29
Anne, the daughter of Gascoigne Burnett of Scoles, October the 2d day
Samuel, the son of John Massie near Penwell, October the 6
[*Blank*] of John Sothard near Allershaw laine end, at Whitkirk, by licence, Nov. 27
Charles, the son of William Ellis, iunior, Esqr, of Kidal Hall, November the 3d
James and John, the sons of James Wheatley nere Penwell on Hurstmoor, Novembr ye 21
Mary, ye daughter of Henry Briggs of Potterton, Novembr ye 30th
Anne, the daughter of Andrew Jackeson of Scoles, Decembr the 4
Anne, the daughter of Joseph Hague of Barwick, Dec. ye 18
Hellen, the daughter of Willm Sharphurst, at Speighleys, January ye 8th
Elizabeth, the daughter of Robt Watkinson of Barwick, Feb. the 2d
Jane, the daughter of William Collett of Barwick, February the 23th
Mary, the daughter of John Hardisty of the same, March the 16o
Mary, the daughter of Wm Coapeland of Potterton, March the 17th
John, ye son of Wm Hague of Barwick, Mar. 23

BAPTIZAT, 1693.

Anne, the daughter of Richd Atkinson of Roundhey Park, was baptized March 29th
Thomas, the son of Tho. Settle of Barwicke, April 18
John, ye son of John Prince of Potterton, the same day
John, the son of Daniel Jermaine of Barwick, the same day
John, the son of Wm Wright of Barwick, May the 3d
Isable, the daughter of Richard Robinson of ye same, May the 5
Mary, the daughter of John Barker of the same, May 10th
John, the son of Ralph Collett of the same, May ye 17th
Ruth, the daughter of William Hallyday near Bull laine, ye same day
Elizabeth, the daughter of John Ingle of Barwick, May the 24th
Elizabeth, the daughter of Jeremiah Ball of Barwicke, June the 9th
Edward, the son of Thomas Knapton of Barwicke, June the 25th
Grace, the daughter of Willm Hemsworth of Potterton, July the 30th
Rachel, the daughter of Robert Thornes of Barwick, August the 28th
George, the son of Mr Robert Walker of Barwick, September the 21th
Sarah, the daughter of Thomas Hill of Barnbow, Septembr the 24th
Elizabeth, the daughter of Rich. Robinson of Scoles, December the 1st
Elizabeth, the daughter of Wm Dickinson on Winmore head, Decembr the 14th
William, the son of William Ellis, junior, Esqr, of Kidall, February the 2d

*PAID TO A BRIEFFE, 10s

The 28th day of Augt', 1694 Receiued then of ye minister and Churchwardens of ye Parish of Barwick in Elmett in ye county of Yorke, the sum of Ten shillings, being collected on their

*See *Church Briefs* by W. A. Bewes, London, 1896.

Majesties Letters Patents for ye Relief of the Poor Protestants wch came forth of Franch, bearing Date the 31th of March, 1694. I say Receiued by me. Tho. Holmes.

BAPTIZAT, 1694.

Richard, the son of Henry Slator on Hurst more, was baptiz. March the 25th
William, the son of Thoms West of Roundhey, Aprill the 11th
Deborey, the daughter of William Middlebrooke of the Stanks, Aprill the 19th
Sarah, the daughter of Mattw Watkinson of Garforth more side, Aprill the 22th
Michael, the son of John Atkinson of Barwick, Aprill the 23th
Elizabeth, ye daughter of Timo. Smith of ye same, June ye 9th
Mary, ye daughter of John Potter of ye same, June ye 10th
Thomas, ye son of Tho. Brunton of Sheppen, June ye 17th
Samuel, the son of Samuel Tate of Kidal lainehead, the 29th day of June
Hannah, ye daughter of Matthew Holmes of Roundhey Parke, July the 4th
Elizabeth, ye daughter of Richd Smith of Barwick, July ye 18
Francis, the son of Richard Settle of Potterton laine, August the 6th
Edward, the son of James Bullock of Barwick, Sept. 2d
Jeremiah, the son of John Lumb of the Stanks, Sept. ye 19th
Daniel, the son of Thomas Walker of Roundhey, October the 4th
Elizabeth, the daughter of Mattw Issott of Barwick, Octob. ye 10th
Samuell, the son of Samuel Thornton of Grimes dike, the same day
Sarah, the daughter of William Knapton of Barwick, October ye 30th
Richard, the son of William Vevors of Scoles, November the 2
Joseph, the sonn of John Massie near Penwell, Novemb. ye 11
Moses, the sonn of Robt Bram of Barnbow carr, Nov. ye 18
Sarah, the daughter of John Jackeson of Brown more, December 8th
Sarah, the daughter of Robt Thornes of Barwick, Decemb. 16th
Isable, the daughter of John Saynor of the same, Dec. ye 20th
Martha, ye daughter of Andrew Jackson of Scoles, Dec. ye 30th
Margaret, ye daughter of Jos. Stringer of Barwicke, January 2d
[*Blank*] of Robert Wilson of Roundhey, Janu. the 9th
Anne, ye daughter of William Admergill of Potterton laine head, January the 11th
Thomas, the son of Richard Ellis of Stocking, January ye 12th
Wm, the son of Robert Brown of Potterton, February the 13th
Richard, the son of William Wright of Scoles, February ye 15th
Mary, ye daughter of Joseph Hague of Barwicke, Feb. ye 21th
Jane, the daughter of William Wood of Scoles, Feb. the 28th
Elizabeth, the daughter of Willm Morrett near Cross Yates, was bapt. at Whitkirk, by licence, March the 10th
William, the son of John Gilson of Lazingcroft, March the 14th
David, the son of Wm Ayre, at the West end of Kidal laine, March ye 15
Richard, the son of Richd Thompson of ye Stanks, March ye 20th
Edwa d, ye son of Anthony Lodge of Roundhey, July 17th

BAPTIZAT, 1695.

James, the son of James Wilcocke, at Allershaw laine end, was bapt. Aprill the 14th

Elizabeth and Jane, the children of Robert Wansley of Barwicke, April 27th
Susannah, ye daughter of Humphrey Morris of Hurstmore, May ye 26th
William, the son of William Vevers of Morwicke, May the 27th
William, the son of Henry Dickinson near Bull laine head, May the 28th
John, ye son of Phillip Westmerland of Scoles, June 14th
John, ye son of John Atkinson of Osmondthicke, July the 1st
*William, the son of William Collett of Barwicke, July ye 3th
William, ye son of Wm Butler of Speighley nuke, July ye 10th
Thomas, ye son of Richard Robinson of Barwicke, ye same day
Alice, ye daughter of Thomas Tate of Scoles, July the 14th
Robert, the son of Robt Cooper of the same, July the 28th
Elizabeth, the daughter of Wm Norton of Barwick, Aug. ye 5th
Matthew, the son of Ralph Collett of ye same, August the 20th
Isabella, the daughter of Wm Hague of the same, Aug. ye 21th
Joseph, the son of William Eamorson of Roundhay Park, Aug. ye 22th
Anne, ye daughter of Robt Brown near Penwell, September ye 1st
Robert, ye son of Matthew Hill, a stranger on Garforth Moor side, ye same day
Mary, ye daughter of Sam. Tate, iu, at Kidall laine head, Sept. the 17th
Margaret, the daughter of Wm Roebucke at Cross yates, September ye 25
Margarett, the daughter of Jeremiah Ball of Barwick, October ye 2d
Wm, the son of Wm Watson of Roundhey, was bapt about
Isabell, the daughter of Robert Chambers of Potterton, November ye 6th
Jane, the daughter of Richard Lumb on Hirstmore, Decemb. ye 1st
Richard, the son of Thomas Knapton of Barwicke, Decembr ye 22th
Abraham, the son of Abra. Sheppen of Barnbow, Janua. 2d
John, the son of Robt Watkinson of Barwicke, January the 5th
John, ye son of Wm Midlebrook of the Stanks, Jan. the 6th
Anne, the daughter of John Studdard near cross yates, Janua. the 12th
William, the son of Joshua Lister of Rounday, January the 26th
Samuel, ye son of Thomas West of Roundhey, January the 30th
Wm, the son of John Lister of Rounday, Janu. 26
Jane, ye daughter of John Jackson of Broon more, Janu the 29th
Josephus Filius Henrici Slater de Hirstmore, Febr. 23tio
Johñ, Filius Joannis Ambler de Winmore, Febr. 23tio
Sara, soboles Richi Atkinson de Roundhey, sacris intincta aquis erat decimo octavo die Martij 3

BAPTIZAT, 1696.

Jonathan, filius Willimi Hemsworth de Potterton, bapt. April 19no
Willielmus, filius Alexandri Thompson de Scholes, April vicesimo nono
Thomas, filius Tho. Hill de Barmbow, Maij 3tio

*Will of William Collet of Leeds, schoolmaster. Unto my son, Thomas C. of Berwick in Elmit, Butcher, £5. Unto my son, Richard C. of Nottingham, Framework Knitter, £5. Unto my daughter Sarah, the wife of Thomas Hebden of Leeds, butcher, £5 Unto my daughter, Elizabeth Pitt, widow, £8: all which legacies are to be paid out of money in the hands of Thomas Micklethwait of Leeds, Esq, and money owing to me by Henry Marsh of St Clements, London, cooper. Unto my son, Benjamin C. of the excise office in London, £5. Unto my daughter, Margaret C., servant to Sr. Basil Dixwell, £5. Unto my son, Arthur C. of Leeds, £4. and unto my said sons, Thomas C. and Richard C., £3 each further. Debt owing by Holyday, to children equally. Unto my daughter Elizabeth Pitt, my bed and all the rest of my household goods. Residue to my said dau hters, Sarah Hebden and Elizabeth Pitt. They exors. Dated 7 May, 1743. Witns., Wm. Turnerg Thos. Longley, John Lucas. Proved 17 June, 1749. William Collet o. Barwick and Margaret Berry of Featherstone Moor were married at Featherstone 7 Feb., 1696–7

Maria, filia Thom' Hacksop pochie de Aberford, Maij Decimo sept. die
Alicia, filia Thomæ Settle de Barwick, Junij 17mo
Martinus, filius Christo. Whitehead de Winmore, Junij 14to
Thomas filius Johan. Pearson de Kiddal lane, Junij 24to
Josephus, filius Gulielmi Wood de Scholes, Julij 5to
Samuel, filius Gulielmi Crossland, pochie de Thorner, July 19no
Thomas, filius Johan Smith de Barwick, Augusti 2do
Hestera, filia Roberti Thornes de Barwick, Augusti 4to
Dina, filia Rich. Settle de Barwick, eadem die
Gulielmus filius Guliet Dickinson de Winmoor-head, 5to
Maria, filia Dñi Gulielmi Ellis, iunioris, de Kiddal, August 6to
Johannes, filius Johan' Lumb de Stanks, Augusti 19no
Maria, filia Tho. Walker de Roundhay, Augusti 20mo
Richardus, spuria proles Marthæ Burrel et Jonathani Horner (ut aiunt) genitoris, Aug. 23^{tio}
Gulielmus, filius Guti Vevers de Scholes, Septembris 13^{tio}
Robertus, filius Tim' Smith de Barwick, Octobris 2do
Gracia, filia Guliel Air de Winmoor, Octobris 16to
Sara, filia Gulielmi Vevers de Morwicke, Octobris 20mo
Robertus, filius Josuae Stringer de Barwick, 8bris 22do
Hanna, filia Richardi Ellis de Barwick, Septembris 26to
Gulielmus, filius Johan' Atkinson de Kiddal lane, Octobris 2do
Gulielmus, filius Johan' Ingle de Barwick, Octobris 25to
Anna, filia Josephi Hague de Barwick, Novembris 15to
Jana, filia Johan' Prince de Potterton, Novembris 22do
Gulielmus, filius Danielis Germain de Barwick, Novembris 25to
Johannes, filius Johañis Massie de Winmoor, Novembris 29no
Elizabetha filia Zacħ Thorpe de Shippen, Decembris 2do
Thomas, filius Gascõ Burnet de Scholes, Decembris 13^{tio}
Anna, filia Samuelis Dodgson de Roundhey, Decembris 29no
Isabella, filia Micħ, Eastburn de Winmoor, Januarij 3^{tio}
Johannes, filius Richđi Thompson de Stanks, Februarij 12mo
Edvardus, filius Gulielmi Robinson, jun^{rs}, de Garthforth moor, Februarij 15to
Maria, filia Ricħdi Robinson de Barwick, Februarij 21mo
Johannes, filius Johan Gilson de Lazingcroft, Februarij 16to
Gulielmus, filius Samuelis Thornton de Grimsdike, Februarij 26to
Samuel, filius Thomae Knapton de Barwick, Februarij 28vo
Sara, filia Gulielmi Butler de Winmoor, Martii 5to
Maria, filia Guli Admergil de Potterton-lane, Martij 21mo

BAPTIZAT, 1697.

Susanna, filia Gulielmi Wright de Scoles, baptizata Martij 25to
Thomas, filius Thomae Cooper de Scoles, Aprilis 4to
Samuel, filius Philippi Westerland de Scoles, Aprilis 11mo
Debora, filia Matthei Watkinson de Garforth-moor, Maij 25to
Elizabetha, filia Nicholai Ball de Barwick, Junij 6to
Christopherus, filius Abrahami Shippen de Barmbow, Junij 20mo
Thomas, filius Thom' Hardisty de Potterton, Julij 25to
Jacobus, filius Gulielmi Norton de Barwick, Julij 26to

Josephus, filius Richardi Settle de Barwick, Julij 27mo
Thomas, filius Andreæ Jackson de Scoles, Septembris 5to
Johannes, filius Johãn Appleyard de Scoles, Octobris 24to
Alicia, spuria soboles Saræ Brownley et Georgij Stannyford, Novem. 17mo
Jana, filia Petri Slaytor de Winmoor, No. 7mo
Elizabetha, filia Johannis Saynor de Barwick, Novembris 21mo
Christopherus, filius Gulielmi Patteson de Barwick, $Novem^{is}$ 25to
Johannes, filius Thomæ Brunton de Shippen, Decembris 10mo
Elizabetha, filia Henrici Slaytor de Winmoor, Decembris 19no
Sara, filia Gulielmi Collet de Barwick, Decembris 23^{tio} die
Johannes, filius Johannis Collinwood, Januarij 25to
Johannes, filius Johan' Jackson de Brown-moor, Februarij 7mo
Johannes, filius Richardi Smith de Barwick, Martij 6to
Henricus, filius Humphridi Morisby de Winmoor, Martij 20mo
Georgius, fil' Jacob' Wilcock de Winmoor, Martij 23^{tio}

BAPTIZAT, 1698.

Joannes, filius Joannis Pearson de Potterton Lane, bap. Aprilis 14to
Elizabetha, filia Gulielmi Collet de Barwick, Aprilis 18vo
Joannes, filius Henrici Turner de Barmbow, Maij 6to
Anna, filia Thomæ West de Roundhey, Maij 14to
Maria, filia Richardi Hollings de Garforth, Junij 5to
Maria, filia Willielmi Vevers de Morwick, Julij 10mo
Thomas, filius $Chris^{ri}$ Whithead de Winmoor, Julij 20mo
Henricus, filius Nathanis Wright de Winmoor, Julij 20mo
Maria, Filia Stephani Hemsworth de Roundhey, Septemb' 22do
Johannes, Filius Gul. Dickenson de Winmoor, Junij 1mo
Richardus, Filius Richardi Atkinson de Roundhey, Oct'bris 6to
Elizabetha, Filia Johannis Lofthous de Potterton, Nov'bris 27mo
Maria, Filia Gulielmi Watson De Roundhey, Nov^{bris} 28vo
Thomas, Filius $Johan^{nis}$ Lumb De Stanks, Dec^{bris} 16to
Thomas, Filius Samuelis Dodgeson De Roundhay, Januarij 1mo
Sara, Filia Georgij Wilcock de Winmoor, Jan^{ij} 22do
Samuel, Filius Thomæ Hill De Barmbow, Jan^{ij} 29no
Johannes, Filius Jofinis Southward De Brown moor, Feb. 5to
Helena, Filia Gulielmi Eamerson De Roundhey, Feb^{ij} 20mo
Johannes, Filius Johannis Atkinson De Kiddal Lane, Martij 1mo
Maria, Filia Johannis Atkinson De Kiddall lane, Martij 1mo
Meurcia, Filia Gulielmi Hague De Barwick, Martij 8vo
Gulielmus, Filius Gulielmi Vevers De Potterton, Martij 19no

BAPTIZAT, 1699.

Christopherus, Filius Thomae Knapton De Barwick, Bapt. Martij 27mo
Sara, Filia Jeremie Ball De Barwick, Aprilis 10mo
Elizabetha, Filia Johannis Jackson De Garthforth moor, Aprilis 10mo
Maria, Filia Gulielmi Norton De Barwick, Aprilis 16to
Alicia, Filia Jos. Stringar de Barwick, Maij 14to
Guliel., Filius Guliel. Hargrave de Roundhay, Maij 4to
Elizabetha, Filia Josephi Hague De Barwick, Maij 14to
Georgius, filius Zachariæ Alsop De Shippen, Maij 14to
Maria, Filia Richardi Lumb De Winmore, Maij 21mo

Sara, filia Gulielmi Lister De Scholes, June 25to
Franciscus, Filius Gulielmi Air De Winmoor, July 9no
Timotheus, filius Timothei Smith De Barwick, July 19no
Josephus, Filius Thomae Settle De Barwick, July 19no
[? Maria] spuria soboles viduae England De Winmore et patris ignoti, July 30mo
Anna, Filia Thome Braim De Roundhay, Augusti 30mo
Jana, Filia Richardi Ellis de Barwick, $Sept^{bris}$ 9no
Sara, Filia Guliel' Tate de Scholes, Sep^{tbris} 25to
Margareta, Filia Gulielmi Collet De Barwick, Nov^{bris} 8vo
Edwardus, Filius Zacharie Thorp De Shippen, Nov^{bris} 9no
Sara, Filia Johannis Gilson De Lazingcroft, Nov^{bris} 12mo
Thomas, Filius Richardi Stead De Kiddall lane head, Dec^{bris} 2do
Richardus, Filius Roberti Chambers De Potterton, Dec^{bris} 5to
Anna, Filia Nathanis Wright De Winmoor, Dec^{bris} 8
Elizabetha, Filia Petri Slaytor De Winmoor, Dec^{bris} 17mo
Lydia, Filia Tho. Cooper de Scholes, Jan^{ij} 7mo
Johannes, Filius Jacobi Walker De Roundhay, Jan^{ij} 22do
Helena, Filia Matthei Watkinson De Garthforth moor, Feb^{ij} 11mo
Gulielmus, Filius Gulielmi Morrit de Winmoor, Feb^{rij} 18vo
Gulielmus, Filius Andree Jackson de Scholes, Feb^{ij} 18vo
Elizabetha, Filia Joh^{nij} Ambler de Winmoor
Jana, Filia Richardi Robinson De Barwick, Martij 4to
Anna, Filia Gulielmi Hemsworth De Potterton, Martij 10mo
Georgius, Filius Johannis Pearson De Kidhall lane, Martij 10mo
Guliel., Filius Gulielmi Robinson Jun^{ris} De Garthforth moor, Feb. 24to
Richardus, Filius Gulielmi Robinson de Garthforth moor, Feb. 24to
Maria, filia Henrici Slaytor De Winmoor, Martij 24to

BAPTIZAT, 1700.

Gulielmus, Filius Johannis Lofthouse De Potterton, Bapt. Apr. 3^{tio}
Sara, Filia Abrahami Shippen De Barmbow, Apr. 7mo
Sara, Filia Gulielmi Patteson De Barwick, Apr. 14to
Richardus, Filius Thome Potter De Potterton, Apr. 21mo
Anna, Filia Richardi Walton De Garthforth moore, Apr. 21mo
Gabriel, Filius Gulielmi Taylor, Jun^{ris}, De Barmbow Carr, Maij 1mo
Marcus, Filius Samuelis Thornton De Grimesdyke, Maij 15to
Elizabetha, Filia Matthei Eamerson De Scholes, Maij 21mo
Richardus, Filius Gulielmi Vevers De Potterton, Maij 25mo
Franciscus, Filius Gulielmi Vevers De Morwick, Junij 10mo
Richardus, Filius Joshuæ Lister De Roundhay, Junij 12mo
Anna, Filia Johannis Butcher De Scholes, Junij 29no
Gulielmus, Filius Johannis Massie De Winmoor, Junij 30mo
David, Filius Danielis Hewit De Winmoor, Junij 30mo
Johannes, Filius Gulielmi Coapland De Potterton, Aug^{ti} 1mo
Franciscus, Filius Thome Brunton De Shippen, Aug^{ti} 25to
Maria, Filia Thome Brunton De Shippen, Aug^{ti} 25to
Margareta, Filia Gulielmi Collet De Barwick, Aug^{ti} 28vo
Sara, Filia Joh^{nis} Potter De Barwick, $Sept^{bris}$ 8vo
Sara, Filia Gulielmi Admergill De Potterton, $Sept^{bris}$ 8vo
Anna, Filia Henrici Turner De Barmbow, Oct^{bris} 6to

Isabella, Filia Xtopheri Whitehead De Winmoor, Nov^{bris} 3^{tio}
Maria, Filia Gulielmi Air De Winmoor, Dec^{bris} 12mo
Nathan, Filius Nathanis Wright De Winmoor, Feb. 5to
Maria, Filia Richardi Vevers De Potterton, Feb^{ij} 20mo
Sara, Filia Stephani Hemsworth De Roundhay, Feb^{ij} 27mo

BAPTIZAT, 1701.

Lydia et Jana Gemellæ Filie Gulielmi Wood de Scholes, Bapt. Martij 30mo
Maria, Filia Zacharie Thorp De Shippen, Apr^{lis} 10mo
Margareta, Filia Nicholai Ball De Winmoor, Ap^{lis} 28vo
Charitas, Filia Humphridi Morrisby De Winmoor, Maij 18vo
Hanna, Filia Samuelis Nuby De Barwick, Junij 9no
Thomas, Filius Gulielmi Vevers De Scholes, Jul^{ij} 2do
Johannes, Filius Johannis Appleyard De Scholes, Julij 23^{tio}
Anna, Filia Joshue Stringar De Barwick, Julij 31mo
Thomas, Filius Danielis Germain De Barwick, Julij 20mo
Robertus, Filius Johannis Pearson De Kiddall Lane head, Sep^{bris} 3^{tio}
Samuel, Filius Georgij Haste, Jun' De Barwick, Sept^{bris} 10mo
Rogerus, Filius Gulielmi Norton De Barwick, Sept^{bris} 14to
Katherina, Filia Josephi Hague De Barwick, Sept^{bris} 17mo
Gulielmus, Filius Gul. Bullock de Scholes, Sept^{bris} 20mo
Maria, Filia Thome Hill De Barmbow, 8^{bris} 26to
Johannes, Filius Thome Settle De Barwick, Nov^{bris} 5to
Gulielmus, Filius Thome Knapton De Barwick, Nov^{bris} 20mo
Anna, Filia Roberti Chambers De Potterton, Nov^{bris} 23^{tio}
Elizabetha, spuria soboles incestuosi copulatus Francisci Lee de Garforth moor et Privigne ejus Eliz. Maw, Dec^{bris} 14to
Alicia, Filia Richardi Ellis de Barwick, Dec^{bris} 21mo
Anna, Filia Gulielmi Walton De Barwick, Dec^{bris} 27mo
Michael, Filius Michaelis Eastburn De Winmoor, Jan^{ij} 11mo
Johannes, Filius Richardi Stead De Kiddal lane head, Jan^{ij} 18vo
Johannes et Anna, Gemella Proles Gul. Shenton De Barwick, Jan^{ij} 29no
Josephus, Filius Tho. Braim De Roundhay, Jan^{ij} 1mo
Anna, Filia Marci Brunton de Brownmoor, nat: Jan. 18vo
Sara, Filia Joh^{nis} Sowthward de Brownmoor, Martij 1mo
Jacobus, Filius Jacobi Walker de Roundhay, Martij 12mo
Gulielmus, Filius Jos. Lister de Roundhay, Martij 12mo
Georgius, Filius Tim. Smith De Barwick, Martij 12mo
Maria, Filia Thome Potter de Potterton, Martij 15to
Dorothea, Filia Nathanis Wright de Winmoor, Martij 18vo

BAPTIZAT, 1702.

Maria, Filia Johannis Lumb de Winmoor, Bapt. Aprilis 6to
Maria, Filia Joh^{nis} Massie, Jun., de Winmoor, Aprilis 12mo
Sara, Filia Thomae Lightfoot de Brownmoor, Maij 3to
Elizabetha, Filia Humphridi Morisby de Winmoor, Maij 10mo
Thomas, Filius Gulielmi Hargrave de Roundhay, Maij —
Johannes, Filius Gulielmi Watson De Roundhay, Junij 24to
Maria, Filia Gulielmi Patteson de Kiddall Lane, Julij 5to
Johannes, Filius Johannis Sharphouse de Winmoor, Julij 6to

Johannes, Filius Gulielmi Taite de Scholes, Julij 15to
Maria, Filia Gulielmi Dickenson de Winmoor, Julij 16to
Gulielmus, Filius Gulielmi Air de Winmoor, Augusti 13^{tio}
Gulielmus, Filius Danielis Hewit de Winmoor, Aug^{sti} 9no
Johannes, Filius Joh̄nis Johnson de Scholes, Sept^{bris} 6to
Richardus, Filius Richardi Walton de Brownmoor, Sept^{bris} 6to
Richardus, Filius Richardi Smith de Barwick, Octo^{bris} 9no
Johannes, Filius Matthæi Watkinson de Garthforth moor, Nov^{bris} 15to
Thomas, Filius Gulielmi Harper de Winmoor, Nov^{bris} 22do
Henricus, Filius Abrahami Shippen De Barmbow, Nov^{bris} 29no
Anna, Filia Petri Slater de Winmoor, Dec^{bris} 6to
Isabella, spuria soboles Eliz. Sympson de Winmoor et Gul. Herd, Dec^{bris} 6to
Johannes, Filius Johannes Lister de Roundhay, Jan^{ij}. 11mo
Johannes, Filius Gulielmi Collet de Barwick, Jan^{ij} 13to
Helena, Filia Josephi Hague De Barwick, Jan^{ij} 14to
Thomas, Filius Richardi Vevers De Potterton, Martij 3^{tio}
Maria, filia Xtopheri Whitehead De Winmoor, Martij 7mo
Gulielmus Filius Johannis Appleyard De Scholes, Martij 10mo
Elizabetha spuria soboles Gulielmi Hopwood et Saræ Richardson De Barwick, Martij 10mo
Gulielmus, Filius Joh^{nis} Ambler De Winmoor, Martij 21mo

BAPTIZAT, 1703

Thomas et Anna, Proles Gemella Richardi [Johannis *erased*] Tarbotson de Barwick, Bapt. Ap. 6to
Robertus, Filius Jeremie Ball De Barwick, Maij 19no
Johannes, Filius Matthiæ Eamerson De Scholes, Maij 30mo
Elizabetha, Filia Gulielmi Wilson De Winmoor, Junij 9no
Maria, Filia Gulielmi Burland De Barwick, Aug^{ti} 4to
Johannes, Filius Gulielmi Beedall De Scholes, Augusti 7mo
Anna, Filia Gulielmi Vevers De Scholes, Aug^{sti} 7mo
Anna, Filia Johannis Orton De Barwick, Aug^{sti} 26to
Petrus, Filius Richardi Thompson De Winmoor, Aug^{sti} 26to
Sara, Filia Richardi Thomson De Winmoor, Aug^{sti} 26to
Sara, Filia Thome Mawd De Winmoor, Sept^{bris} 12mo
Carolus, Filius Joannis Howlcroft de Barwick, nat. Augusti 7mo
Michael, Filius Gulielmi Norton de Barwick, Oct^{bris} 10mo
Thomas, Filius Thome Potter de Potterton, Oct^{bris} 17mo
Joh^{nes}, Filius Joshuæ Lister de Roundhay, Maij 5to
Maria, Filia Sam. Dodgeson de Roundhay, Nov^{bris} 18vo
Henricus, Filius Hen. Turner de Barmbow, No. 21mo
Johannes, Filius [? Gul.] Hemsworth de Potterton, Dec. 5to

I, George Plaxton, Clerk, do declare my unfeigned Assent and Consent to all and every Thing conteined and p'scribed in and by the Book, Intituled ye Book of Common Prayer and Administrac̄on of the Sacraments and other Rites and Ceremonies of the Church, according to the use of the Church of England, together with the Psalter, or Psalms of David, pointed as they are to be said or sung in Churches, and the form and mann^{r} of makeing, ordaining and consecrateing of Bps., Priests and Deacons.

Memorandum upon Sunday, the Six and Twentieth day of September, in the yeare of our Lord 1703, George Plaxton, Clerk, Rector, or Parson of Berwick in Elmett, in the County, Diocesse and Province of York, did read ye Common prayers in ye Parish Church of Berwick afores^d^ both in the Forenoon and Afternoon, that is to say, the Morning and Evening service of and for the same Day, according to ye Form and Order p'scribed and directed by the Book, Intit. the Book of Common prayer and Administrac̄on of the Sacram^ts^ and other Rites and Ceremonyes of the Church according to ye use of the Church of England together wth the Psalter or Psalms of David, poynted as they are to be sung or said in Churches, and the Form and Mann^r^ of makeing, ordaining and consecrating of B^ps^, Priests and Deacons, and Immediately after his said Reading of ye same, made a declarac̄on of his unfeigned Assent and Consent to all the Matters and Things therein conteined according to ye form and in the words aboue written.

Memorandum, that ye s^d^ George Plaxton, Clerk, Rector or Parson of Berwick in Elmett, did upon the same day and yeare read the Nine and Thirty Articles of Religion [agreed upon by the Arch B^ps^ and Bishops of Both Provinces and the whole Clergy, in Convocation holden at London in ye yeare 1562, for the avoiding of Diversityes of Opinions, and for the Establishing of Consent, touching true Religion] in the Parish Church of Berwick in Elmett, aforesaid, dureing the time of Divine Service, and after his said Reading thereof did declare his unfeigned Assent and Consent to all Things therein conteined, in p'sence of us, who attest the same here under our hands, this 26 day of September, Anno Dom. 1703.

Jno Hemsworth John Gibson Will. Vevers
Tho. Brooke Wm Plaxton

Isabella, Filia Thome Settle De Barwick, Bapt: Dec^bris^ 20mo
Maria, Filia Johannis Johnson De Scholes, Dec^bris^ 26to
Stephanus, Filius Gulielmi Vevers De Morwick, Dec^bris^ 26to
Georgius, Filius Thome Brunton De Shippen, Dec^bris^ 27mo
Maria, Filia Thome Brunton de Shippen, Dec^bris^ 27mo
Johannes, Filius Jeremie Bolton De Barwick, Jan^ij^ 23^tio^
Henricus, Filius Nathanis Wright De Winmoor, Jan^ij^ 30mo
Thomas, Filius Jacobi Walker De Roundhay, Feb^ij^ 9no
Josephus, Filius Francisci Bateson De Plompton, in Par: de Spofforth Feb^ij^ 13
Mercia, Filia Richardi Stead De Kiddall Lane head, Feb^ij^ 19no
Gulielmus, Filius Richardi Lumb De Winmoor, Feb^ij^ 27mo
Franc: Filia Thome Hill de Barmbow, Feb^ij^ 27mo
Sara, Filia Samuelis Thornton De Grimesdyke, Martij 1mo
Margareta, Filia Georgij Hast, J^unis^, De Barwick, Martij 17mo
Johannes, Filius Richardi Tarbotson De Barwick, Martij 20mo

BAPTIZAT, 1704.

Jana, Filia Roberti Chambers De Potterton, Bapt. Apr^lis^ 2do
Susanna, Filia Gulielmi Air De Winmoor, Ap^lis^ 5to

Hanna, Filia Thome Sykes De Garthforth moor, Maij 7mo
Johannes, Filius Roberti Fenton De Potterton, Maij 9no
Johannes, Filius Johannis Burnley de Winmoor, Junij 7mo
Thomas, Filius Thomae Brown De Roundhay, Junij 24°
Maria, Filia Roberti Spencer De Barmbow, Junij 25to
Hanna, Filia Josephi Hague de Barwick, Julij 6to
Maria, Filia Francisci Rounthwait de Barwick, Julij 13^{tio}
Robertus, Filius Henrici Franck de Kirk Fenton, Julij 23^{tio}
Rachel, Filia Johannis Jackson de Brownmoor, $Octo^{bris}$ 1mo
Gulielmus, Filius Anthonij Saxton de Barwick, nat. $Sept^{bris}$ 11mo
[? Maria] Filia Johannis Appleyard de Scholes, Dec^{bris} 20mo
Maria, Filia Matthiæ Eamerson de Scholes, Dec^{bris} 30mo
Maria, Filia Gulielmi Beedall de Scholes, Janij 21mo
Margareta, Filia Danielis Hewit de Winmoor, Feb^{ij} 4to
Gulielmus, Filius Gulielmi Wilson de Winmoor, $Febr^{ij}$ 12mo
Maria, Filia Johannis Sharphouse de Winmoor, $Febr^{ij}$ 12mo
Thomas, Filius Thomae Robinson de Garthforth moor, Feb^{ij} 17mo

BAPTIZAT, 1705.

Jacobus, Filius Richardi Walton de Garthforth moor, bapt. Ap^{lis} 1mo
Edwardus, Filius Zacharie Thorp de Shippen, Ap^{lis} 1mo
Johannes, Filius Samuelis [? Nuby] de Barwick, Apr^{lis} 5to
Elizabetha, Filia Gulielmi Collet de Barwick, Ap^{lis} 14to
Esther, Filia Johannis Orton de Barwick, Apr^{lis} 22do
Richardus, Filius Richardi Vevers de Potterton, Apr^{lis} 25to
Maria, Filia Thome Sykes de Shippen, Maij 13^{tio}
Alicia, Filia Stephani Hemsworth de Roundhay, Maij 20mo
Thomas, Filius Thome Lightfoot de Brownmoor, Maij 20mo
William, the son [of] Wm Shenton and Mary, June 9th
Thomas, the son of Humph. Morrice and Mary, June the 24th, 2^{s}
Wyld, the son of Wm Norton and Mary his wife, August the 12th, 2^{s}
W^{m}, the son of William Taylor of Barmbow Car, Aug. 25, 2^{s}
Elizabeth, the daughter of Henry Turner and Eliz. his wife, Aug. 26, from Barmbow, 2^{s}, pauper
Georg, the son of George Willcox of Garfourth Moor side, Sep^{t} 2°, 2^{s}
Alice, y^{e} daughter of George Hast, jun., and $Marg^{t}$ his wife, $Sept^{r}$ 16°
Susanna, the daur. of John Johnson of Morwick, September y^{e} 19th
Anne, the daughter of Richard Tarbotson and Eliz. his wife, Sept. the 23°
Thomas, the son of Christo. Whitehead of Winmore, October 21, p.
Beatrix, daũr of Peter Slaytor, November the 4th, pauper
Robert, the son of Jos. Hague, Novemb. 14th
Mary, the daũr of John Southard, No. 20
Alice, daũr of John Atkinson of Roundhay or Barmbow, Nov. 21
John, the son of Thomas Owthwait, Decemb. 9th
Jennet, ye daũr of W^{m} and Mary Boardly, Jan. 30
Robert, ye son of John Appleyard of Scholes, Feb. 3°
Joshua, ye son of Josuah Lister of Roundhay, Feb. 27
Mary, the daũr of Wm Tait of Scholes, March 3°
W^{m}, the son of Thomas Settle of Berwick, March 13
Nathan, ye son of Nathan Wright, Nov. 13°
Samuel, ye son of Samuell Dodgson of Roundhay, March 24

Memorand there was a child born to Anthony Saxton, a papist, but where baptized I cannot tell, for no Notice of it hath been given to me.
Francis, the son of Francis Roundthwait, March the 6th

BAPTIZATI, 1706.

Elizabeth, ye daughter of Wm Burland and Eliz. his wife, was bapt. Aprill the 30th, 1706, 2s
John, the son of Rich Vevers and Mary his wife, May 1o, being Holy Thursday, 2s
Mary, the daughter of Godfrey Stonehouse and Ellen his wife, May 23, 2s Roundhay
Elizabeth, the daughter of Wm Vevers of Morwick and Mary his wife, May ye 20th
[*Blank*] the daughter of Lancelot Ambler and Grace his supposed wife, June the 2d
Joseph, the son of Jeremiah Bolton and Mary his wife, July 7th
Mary, the daūr of Rich. Stead of Potterton, 14 Aprill
Jane, the daūr of Tho. Mawd, May the 19
Christopher, son of Wm Renton and Mary his wife, July 14th
Eliz. the bastard daughter of one El. Clough, 4 Aug.
Joseph, the son of Daniell Jerman and Anne his wife, Sept. 1o
John, the son of John Daniel and Mary, Sept. 24
Anby, the son of Edwd Thomas and Eliz. his wife, 28o Septr
William, the son of Willm Hemsworth of Potterton, Septr 29
Thomas, son of John Dawson, Junr, Octob. 6th
Hannah, the daughter of Math. Watkinson and Margret, Octob. 6th
Thomas, son of James Walker of Roundhey, 13 Octob
Anne, ye daughter of Stephen Hemsworth of Roundhey, was born October the 5th and bapt Nov. 3d
Anne, the Bastard daū of Francis Lee and Alice Maw, his daughter in Law, Dec. 15th
Wm, the son of Tho. Braym, Decemb. 6
Andrew, the son of Robert Fenton, Dec. 27
Wm, the son of James Bolton on Windmore, 29 Decr
Mary, the daur. of Wm Sheynton, Jan. 26
Mary, the daur. of Thomas Scott, Feb. 13
Robert, ye son of John Jackson, Feb. 18
Margrett and Mary, the Twins of Matthias Hewit, 22o Feb.
Sarah, daughter of Richard Vevers, March 5th
Margret, daur. of John Lister of Roundhay, March 9th
Wm, the sonne of Tho. Braime of Roundhay, bapt. Decemb. 5o
Rachell, ye daughter of Wm Watson of Roundhay, March the 6th

1707 [BAPTISMS].

Wm, son of George Wilcock, March 28
John, son of Daniel Hewit, the same day
Elizabeth, daūr of John Orton, Apr 13
Mary, daūr of Wm Wilson, 14 of April
Wm, the son of William Beedall of Scoles, Aprill 20
Richard, the son of John Johnson of Morwick, June the 2d
Richard, the son of Andrew Jackson of Scholes, June 22

Thomas, son of Joseph Haigh, June 23
Joseph, son of John Appleyard of Scoles, June 27
Wm Ayres, a Bastard as we suppose, July 18th
Peter, son of William Emmetson of Roundhay, July 31
Ellen, daughter of Zach. Thorp, Aug. 9th
Thomas, ye son of Willm and Mary Collet, Aug. 22th
Mathew, son of John Upton, Sept. 7th
Thomas, son of Thomas Owthwait of Scoles, 28 Sept.
William, son of Samuel Thornton, October the 20th
Anne, the daughter of ye sd Samuel Thornton, October 21
Anne, ye daughter of William and Mary Bordley, Dec. 31
John, the Bastard Child of one Anne Robinson of the parish of Ryther, Jan. 25th
Wm, the son of John Sharphouse, January the 18th
Anne, daūr of Wm Dibb of Scoles, 15 Feb.
Anne, daūr of Francis Roundthwait of Barwick, March 3d
Wm, the son of Wm Walton of Barwick, March the 12
Anne, daūr of Christoph. Whitehead of Winmoor, March 7th
Eliz., daūr of John Dawson of Brown moor, Apl 18th, 1708.

BAPT., 1708.

Eliz., daūr of Rich. Tarbotton and Eliz. was bapt. June ye 15th
Samuell, son of Tho. Settle, Apr 25
Wm, son of Tho. Scott, May 24
Anne, daūr of John Varo, May 30
Abraham Abbot, June 23
Anne Elston, May the 28th
John, son of John Atkinson, July 30th
Eliz., daūr of Rich. Vevers of Potterton, June 30, and Mary
Tho., son of Francis Chapman, was bapt. Aug. 27
Jno, son of John Slater, Aug. 27, and Hannah, his wife
Susannah, daūr of Tho. Hill, Aug. 29, and Susanna, his wife
John, son of John Jordain of Scoles, Aug. 29
Rich. Hast, son of George Hast, Sept. 1o, and Margt his wife
Charles Walker of Roundhey, Octob. 14
Rich., son of Samuell Wright, Octob. 29, and Mary, his wife
Tho., son of Jo. Appleyard of Scoles, Nov. 10th
Anne, daūr of Godfrey Stonehouse, Nov. 18
Martha, daūr of Tho. Potter of Potterton, Dec. 5
[*Blank*] Sam Dodgson of Roundhay, [*blank*]
Eliz., daūr of Tho. Mawd, Jan 9th
John, son of Mr Vevers of Morwick, Jan. 19th
Sarah Hague, Feb. 2o
Wm, son of Nathan Wright, March 12
Richd, son of Wm Burland, March 15o

Ano 1709 [BAPTISMS].

Dorothy Lumb, Apr 8o
Anne Atkinson of Barnbow, Apr 17th
Judith, daughter of George Wilcox, Apr. 30th
Richard, the sonne of Mr. Thomas Perrot and Anastatia his wife, May the 12

Ann, daughter of William Emmotson, May 12
Thomas, son of William Dibbe, May the 30
Henry, sonne of Thomas Brayme, June the 8th
Phoebe, daughter of Tho. Hall, June 15th
Mary, daũr of Rob. Settle, July 11.
*Henry, son of Wm Beedall, Aug. 2
Mary, daũr of Richd Tate, Aug. 14
Thomas, son of Tho. Owthwait, Aug. 24
John, son of Tho. Popplewell, Sept. 11
Elizabeth, daũr of John Johnson, 8r 9th
John, the son of Andrew Byrdsall, Octob. 16
George, son of Dan. Hewitt, Octob. 16°
Tho., son of Tho. Thomson, Novemb. 6°
Joseph, son of John Daniel, Dec. 7th
John, son of Joseph Mawd, Dec. 7th
Rich., son of John Appleyard, Feb. 15
Jane, daũr of John Orton, Feb. 26
John, son of John Varo, March 19th

1710 [Baptisms].

Mark, son of John Ambler, Apr. 2°
Richard, son of Wiƚƚ Collet, May 1°
John, son of John Briggs, May 25°
†George, the son of Mr Tho. Perrot and Anastatia his wife, June 24
Eliz., Upton Aug. 13
Benjamin Pease, Aug. 16°
Benjamin, son of Tho. Settle, Sept. 5
Robert Walker, Sept. 13°
Samuel, the son of Sam. Wright, Sept. 20°
Sarah, dau. of Tho. Scot, Octo. 25
Eliz. Robinson, Nov. 15°
Eliz. Bolton, Nov. 19
Richd, son of Tho. Ball, Dec. 3
Mary, daũr of Wm Backhouse, Feb. 3°
John, son of Robert Settle, Feb. 7°
Mary Whitehead, Feb. 11
George, son of Benja. Hast, Feb. 19°
Wm, son of Wm Renton, March 11th
Edward, son of John Sharphouse, March 18

Anno 1711 [Baptisms].

Abraham Dodgson March 28
Sarah, daũr of Nathan Wright, Apr 10
Hester Dolphin, Apr 22
Mary Tarbotton, May 18
Chrispħ Lumb, May 20
Pentecoste Haigh, June 15
Benjamin Johnson, June 24

---

*Henry Beedal married at Methley (1) Mary Marler, and (2) Elizabeth Nicholson, and by her had several children baptised at Methley, where he was buried 11 May, 1781. His mother was Margaret, dau. of William Lund of Methley, married 4 Sept., 1701.

†George Perrot, Baron of the Exchequer 1763–75. Educated at Westminster School. Died 28 Jan., 1780. See Dictionary of National Biography.

George Dickenson of Scoles, 25°
Wm Renton, July 15°, of Barwick
Martha Tate of Scoles, July 19
Thomas, son of Rich Tate, — 22
Elizabeth Emmetson, July 26
James and John, twins of Wm Boardly, Aug. 12, of Kidhall Lane
John Vevers of Barwick, 24°
Wm Atkinson, Sept. 19
John Braym of Barmbow, Oct. 3
[*Blank*] Lister of Roundhay, Oct. 4
Eliz. Hast of Barwick, Oct. 24
Mary Lindly, Nov. 4
Thomas Poppewell, Decembr 30
Thomas, son of Tho. Wood, Jan. 25
Mary, daũr of Francis Chapman, Jan. 27
Grace, Owthwait Jan. 30, Scoles
Eliz., daũ of Benj. Hast, Feb. 20
John, son of Tho. Braym of Roundhay, Feb. 20
John Shay of Addle parish, Feb. 27
Sarah Mawd, March 16
Calisthenes Thomas, March 19, at Potterton
Willm, the [son of] Robt Eltson, June 11, 1710 [*an insertion*]

[Baptisms] 1712.

Ruth, daũr of Joseph Mawd, bap. Aprill 6°, 1712
Ester, daũr of Tho. Thompson, 6° Aprill
Henry, son of Joseph Binns, Apr 16
Peter, son of Peter Slator, Apr 13°
Mary, daũr of Rich. Vevers of Pottrton, Apr. 21
Samuel Appleyard, May 2°
John Atkinson of Barnbow, May 7th
Daniell, son of Dan. Hewit, May 11th
Mary, daũr of James Gayton, May 12
Mary, daũr of John Upton, June 9th
Mary Dibb of Scholes, June 11th
Anne Varo of Scoles, June 15th
Margret, daũr of Jos. Haigh, July 11th
Wm, sonn of Rich. Thomson, July 20°
Andrew Burstall of Barwick, Aug. 28
John, son of Samll Wright, Sept 3d
Benjamin, son of Wm Collet, Sept. 3d
Mary, daũr of Tho. Braym, Octob. 8°
Frances, daũr of James Walker of Roundhay, Nov. 16

Baptisms, 1713.

Alice, ye Dr of William Eamerson, Dec. ye 16th
Eliz., ye Dr of Wm Tait de Scoles, Decbr 30th
Sarah, ye Dr of Jos. Binns, Jan. 17th
Anne, ye Dr of John Sharphouse, Jan. 24th
Alice, ye Dr of Fran. Pool de Stockin, Jan. 29th
Martha, ye Dr of Thomas Braim, Feb. 3d
Wm, ye son of Rd Vevers de Barwk, Feb. 8th

James, ye son of Thomas Outhwait, Feb. 14th
Thomas, ye son of Jno Wood, March ye 10th

1714.

Eliz. Wood, March 29th
Jno, ye son of Jno Orton, March 28th
Joseph, ye son of Samuel Dodgson, Aprill 15th
Alice, ye Dr of Jo. Hague, April 23d
Jane, ye Dr of Fr. Chapman, May ye 2d
Mary, ye Dr of Wm Fenton, May ye 2nd
Elizabeth, ye Dr of Thos Warde, May 5th
Wm, ye son of Rob. Glover, May 31st
Elizabeth, ye Dr of Fr. Parker, June ye 20th
Richard, ye son of Thomas Braim, June 23d
Sarah, ye Dr of Jno Johnson, July 11th
Ralph, ye son of Ralph Watson, July 21st
Sarah, ye Dr of Jno Appleyard, Augt 25th
Richard, ye son of Jno Varley, Septbr 15th
Martha, ye Dr of Wm Dibb, Octobr 17th
Mary, ye Dr of Jno Mounsey, Octbr 22d
Mary, ye Dr of Martin Dawson, Novembr 7th
Grace, Dr of Mich. Sharp, Novembr 28th
Margarett, ye Dr of Richard Tarbotton, Decbr 1st
Martha, ye Dr of Benja. Haist, Decbr 13th
Wm, ye son of Wm Burland, Decembr 16th
Anne, ye Dr of Danll Huit, Jan. 16th
Elizabeth, ye Dr of Wm Vevers de Sco., Feb. 9th
Joseph, ye son of Joseph Maud, March ye 20th

BAPTISMS, 1715

Jno, ye son of Rd Tait, March ye 27th
Joseph, ye son of Rd Braim, March ye 30th
Thomas, ye son of Wm Benton, Aprill ye 3dth
Jno, ye son of Wm Bickers, Aprill ye 13th
Eliza., ye Dr of Wm Boardley, Aprill ye 20th
Esther, ye Dr of Thomas Outhwait, May ye 8th
Abigail, ye Dr of Tho. Settle, May ye 15th
Jo., ye son of Mattw Pool, June ye 4th
Thomas, ye son of Tho. Battey, June ye 22nd
John, ye son of Geo. Wilcox, July ye 17th
John, ye son of Edward Maxwell, July ye 24th
Joseph, ye son of Wm Collet, August ye 3d
Eleanor, ye Dr of Wm Eamerson of Roundey, August ye 8th
Anne, ye Dr of Robt Goodhall, Septembr ye 25th
Susannah, ye Dr of Robt Elston, Octobr ye 29th
Matthew and Anne, ye son and Dr of Mattw Jackson, Novembr 18th
James, ye son of Ja. Wilcox, November 24th
James, ye son of Richd Vevers de Potterton, Decbr 29th
James, ye son of Ben. Haist, February ye 1st
John, ye son of Jno Burland, February ye 12th
Susannah, ye Dr of Ralph Watson, February 17th
John, ye son of Robt Settle, February 26th

Joshua, ye son of Richard Vevers, February 27th
Valentine, ye son of Thomas Wood, March ye 2nd
James, ye son of John Atkinson, March 18th
Hannah, ye Dr of James Strodder, March 21st

Baptisms, 1716.

Mary, ye Dr of Jer. Bolton, April ye 22nd
Jacob, ye son of Jno Johnson, May ye 20th
John, ye son of Jno Varley, May the 25th
Elizabeth, ye Dr of William Adamson, May 27o
Marey, ye Dr of Jno Varey, May 27o
Hannah, ye Dr of Wm Prince, June 7th
William, ye son of William Dickinson, June ye 10th
Paul, ye son of Geo. Hinskip, June 13th
Alice, ye Dr of Tho. Outhwait, June 24th
Elizabeth, ye Dr of Richd Walton, July ye 15th
Joseph, ye son of Jo. Binns, July ye 18th
Richard, ye son of Richard Tarbotton, Septembr 12th
Elizabeth, ye Dr of George Dickinson, Octobr 7th
Mary, ye Dr of Tho. Thompson, Octobr 7th
Frances, ye Dr of Jo. Hague, Octobr 18o
Thos, ye son of Thos Braim de Barnbow, Decr 12o
Thos, ye son of Thos Braim de Roundey, Decr 13o
Jno, ye son of Jno Orton, Decr 16o
Jno, ye son of Jonas Hailey, January 9th
Elizabeth, ye Dr of Thomas Knapton, January 9th
Richd, ye son of Robert Goodhall, January 13th
Jno, ye son of Abra. Abbot, January 16th
Martin, ye son of Samuel Dodgson, January 17th
Wm, ye son of Geo. Thompson, January 17th
Elizabeth, ye Dr of Thomas Popplewell, February 17o
William, ye son of William Bickers, March ye 3d
John, ye son of Jno Fox, Mar. 24th

Baptisms, 1717.

Hannah, ye Dr of Jno Maud, Aprill 7th
David, ye son of Danl Huit, Aprill 14th
Anne, ye Dr of Wm Burland, May ye 19th
Wm, ye son of Wm Tait, May 22nd
Sarah, ye Dr of Wm Dibb, May 30th
Elizabeth, ye Dr of Jno Sharphouse, June 9th
Elizabeth, ye Dr of Richd Braim, July 14o
Thomas, ye son of Tho. Briggs, Augt 4o
Wm, ye son of Jno Wood, Augt 9o
Anne, ye Dr of Tho. Settle, Augt 9o
Wm, ye son of Wm Prince, Augt 11o
John, ye son of Matthew Pool, Septembr ye 8th
Mary, ye Dr of Matthew Jackson, Octobr 6th
Anne, ye Dr of Jo. Maud, Octobr 27th
Elizabeth, ye Dr of Tho. Walker, November 4th
James, ye son of James Bullock, Decbr 29th
Hannah, ye Dr of Tho. Powell, January 31st

Richard, ye son of James Wilcox, February 5th
John, ye son of Jno Dolphin, March ye 9th
Esther, ye Dr of Thomas Braim of Barnbow, March ye 12th
James, ye son of Jno Upton, March ye 19th

Baptisms, 1718.

George, ye son of Wm Lumb, Aprill 6th
Wm, the son of Wm Carver, Apl 23d
Elizabeth, ye Dr of Jane Bell, Apl 25th
Esther, ye Dr of Jno Atkinson, Apl 28th
Eleanor, ye Dr of Jno Briggs, May 18th
Susannah, ye Dr of Martin Dawson, May the 25th
Mark, ye son of Jno Ambler, June ye 2nd
Hannah, ye Dr of Jno Varley, June 9th
Wm, ye son of Jno Burland, June 12th
Thos, ye son of Rd Walton, June 29th
Frances, ye Dr of Thos Ball, July 13th
Christopr, ye son of Wm Dickinson, August ye 24th
Wm, ye son of Henry Atkinson, August 24th
Sarah, ye Dr of Jo. Hague, Septr ye 5th
Sarah, ye Bastard Child of Mary Barker of Barwick, Septr ye 5th
Jno, ye son of Tho. Wood, Septr ye 28th
Anne, ye Dr of Law. Milner, Octr 12th
Thos, ye son of Tho. Knapton, Novem. ye 16th
James, ye son of Ralph Watson, November ye 16th
Susannah, ye Dr of Tho. Preston, November ye 16th
Geo., the son of Geo. Longley, December ye 7th
Joseph, ye son of Rob. Settle, December ye 7th
Mary, the Dr of Richard Vevers, December the 27th
Francis, ye son of Fran. Walker, January the 25th
Joseph, ye son of Ja. Bullock, February the 1st
Wm, ye son of Richd Robinson, February the 4th
Susannah, ye Dr of Jos. Battey, February the 8th
Joseph, ye son of Francis Rounthwait, February 22nd
Paul, ye son of Jno Mounsey, February the 22nd
Mary, the Dr. of Wm Renton, March ye 8th

Baptisms, 1719.

Mary, the Dr of Tho. Popplewell, Aprill ye 19th
Jno, ye son of Joseph Dixon, Aprill the 22nd
Mary, ye Dr of Robt Goodhall, Apl 26th
Jane, ye Dr of Wm Hemsworth, Apl 26th
Thos, ye son of Tho. Maud, May ye 3d
Joseph, ye son of Tho. Outhwait, May ye 10th
Jno, ye son of Bryan Bradley, June ye 9th
Richd, ye son of Ja. Strodder, June ye 14th
Catherine, ye Dr of Benja Haist, July ye 8th
Robt, ye son of Robt Issot, July ye 15th
Eliza., the Dr of Richd Braim, July the 19th
Wm, ye son of Robt Knapton, July the 26
Mary, the Dr of Robt Brown, Augt ye 9th
Mary, ye Dr of Mattw Watson, Sept. ye 6th

Wm, ye son of Richd Slaytor, Septr ye 9th
Wm, ye son of Rich. Cook, Septr ye 10th
Richd, ye son of Tho. Braim, Septr 26th
Martha, ye Dr of Ja. Wilcox, Septr 20
Wm, ye son of Geo. Lister. Octr 14th
Hannah, ye Dr of Rd Vevers, Octr 14th
Jno, ye son of Jno Antoms, Oct. 25th
Wm, ye son of Jno Varey's, Novemr 8th
Jno, ye son of Wm Prince, Novemr ye 15th
Martha, ye Dr of Tho. Settle, Novemr 15th
Jno, ye son of Wm Carver, Decr 13th
Joseph, ye son of Jno Thompson, Decr 13th
Wm, ye son of Richd Tait, Decr 27th
Mary, ye Dr of Danl Huit, Decr ye 28th
Elizabeth, ye Dr of Robt Smith, January 6th
Sarah, ye Dr of Tho. Thompson, Jan. ye 24th
Richd, ye son of Rd Burland, Jan. ye 31st
Jno, ye son of Wm Hague, Feb. the 14th
Alice, ye Dr of Fran. Chapman, Feb. 14th
Anne, ye Dr of Jno Burland, Feb. 28th
Jno, ye son of Jno Thompson, March 6th
Sarah, ye Dr of Jno Maud, March 20th

BAPTISMS, 1720.

Dennis, the son of Tho. Smith, March 27th
Wm, the son of Wm Johnson, May 8th
John, ye son of Jo. Maud, May ye 15th
Margarett, the Dr of Mattw Jackson, June the 19th
Timothy, ye son of Saml Massie, July the 17th
John, the son of Henry Dunnel, July the 24
Mary, the Dr of Tho. Wood, October the 9th
Susannah, the Dr of Jos. Binns, December the 27th
Mary, the Dr of Robt Issott, December the 30th
Thomas, the son of Tho. Settle, February the 12th
Alice, ye Dr of Jno Sharphouse, February the 19th
Wm, the son of Tho. Thompson, February the 26th
Robt, the son of Robt Goodhall, March ye 19th

BAPTISMS, 1721.

Sarah, the Dr of Martin Whitehead, Aprill ye 2d
Mary, ye Dr of Rich̄ Clark, Aprill 11th
Rich̄, son of Thos Braim, Aprill 12th
Wm, ye son of Francis Walker, Aprill ye 16th
Wm, ye son of Wm Lumb, Aprll ye 30th
Diana, ye Dr of Martin Dawson, Aprill ye 30th
Thos, ye son of Jno Dolphin, May ye 28th
Thos, son of Jno Littlewood, June ye 5th
Mary, ye Dr of Jno Burland, June ye 11th
Eliza:, ye Dr of Jno Ball, June ye 25th
Jno, ye son of Richd Burland, July ye 9th
John, son of Thos Preston, July ye 16th
Edwund, [*sic*] ye son of Thos Littlewood, July 24th

Hannah, Dr of John Wood, August the 6th
Hannah, ye Dr of Willm Wardman, August ye 18th
Ann, the Dr of Matthw Coates, August ye 27th
Mary, the Dr of John Thompson, Septr ye 3d
Mary, the Dr of Saml1 Massie, Octbr the 4th
Rebekah, the Dr of Rich. Robinson, Octr ye 22d
Richd, ye son of Rich Cook, Novembr 16
Mary, ye Dr of Willm Dawson, Novembr the 23d
Ingram, the son of John Varley, Decembr the 10th
Mary, the Dr of George Thompson, Decembr ye 7th
Samll, the son of William Taite, December ye 17th
Robert, the son of Robrt Smith, Janry ye 14th
Ann, the Dr of James Bullock, January ye 21st
Stephen, the son of Lawrence Milner, Janry ye 21st
Joseph, the son of Henry Dunnell, Febry ye 4th
Catherine, the Dr of Benja Haist, Feb. ye 6th
Mary, ye Dr of Thos Morritt, Febry ye 11th
Martha, the Dr of Thos Shillitoe, Febry the 25th
William, the son of Mattw Watson, March the 4th

Baptisms, 1722.

Eliz., the Dr of Rich Robinson, March ye 26th
James, the son of Wm Prince, Aprill ye 30th
Eliz., the Dr of Robt Knapton, May the 8th
Sarah, the Dr of Jno Atkinson, May the 27th
Joseph, the son of Wm Carber, June the 24th
Eliz., the Dr of Tho. Braim, July the 18th
Mary, the Dr of Mattw Oddy, Augst the 12th
Hannah, the Dr of Matt. Jackson, Augst the 19th
Wm, the son of Wm Hague, Septr the 15th
Ann, the Dr of Rich Braim, Sepr the 18th
David, the son of Jno Wilson, Septr the 21st
Jno, the son of Jno Thompson, Septr the 30th
Jno, the son of Jno Bean, Septr the 30th
Mich, the son of Rich Taite, Octobr the 7th
Jno, the son of Wm Dickinson, Novembr the 25th
Christian, the Dr of Martin Whitehead, Jan. the 20th
Martha, the Dr of Jno Mounsey, Janry the 20th
Ann, the Dr of Tho. Wood, Febry the 17th
James, the son of Rich Vevers, Febry the 18th
Ann, the Dr of Chris. Teasdall, March the 17
Mary, the Dr of Rich Burland, March ye 17

Baptisms, 1723.

Thomas, ye son of Tho. Wildbore, Lenerich-hill, Apl. 29
Matw, the son of Robt Issot, March 27
Ann, Daughter of William Addiman, Aprill 8th
Samuel, the son of Samuel Liversiedge, April 21st
Willm, the son of Richard Clerk, Apl 29th
Willm, the son of Willm Johnson, May 5th
Sarah, the Dr of Robt. Brown, May 12th
Walter, the son of Thos Wildbore, May 28

Willm, The son of Willm Ward, June 2^{d}
Ann, Daug^{r} of Robt Knapton, June 16th
Mary, D^{r} of Wm Lumb, Jun: 30th
W^{m}, the son of J^{n} Wiate, June 30th
Jos^{p}, the son of Benjn Aier, Jun. 30th
John, ye son of Matt^{w} Watson, July 28
Christopher, the son of Robert Brown of Barnbow, August 7th
Jos^{p}, the son of Thos Braim, of Barnbow, Augt 14
George, the son of Mr John Plaxton, of Barwick, Augt 27
Ann, the daughter of John Bean of Barwick, Septr 1st
Rebekah, the Daughter of Richd Robinson of Barwick, the younger, Septr 19th
Johannah, the Daughter of J^{n} Dolbin, Septr 29
Thomas, the son of Hen. Wardle of Hubberley, Octr 2^{d}
Ellin, D^{r} of Jn. Tayte, Scholes, Oct. 12
Jane, the Daughter of Francis Walker of Barnbow, Octob^{r} 21
Rebekah, the Dau^{r} of Tho. Holmes of Barwick, Novr 8th
Saml, the son of Saml Massy of Stanks, Novr 10th
W^{m}, the Bastard child of Mary Pattison of Kiddal, November 17
Ellin, the Dau^{r} of Samuel Thornton of Hill Top, Novr 20
Ann, the Daughter of J^{n} Ambler of Winmore, Dec. 8th
Thomas, the son of Robt. Smith of Barwick, Decr 20th
Joseph, the son of Robert Goodall, Jany 19th, of Brown Moor
Willm, the son of John Varley of Barwick, Jany 24
Thos, the son of Thos Preston of Barwick, Jany 26
Mary, the D^{r} of Edwd Batty of Barwick, Feb. 2
Alice, the D^{r} of George Lister of Scholes, March 1st
*David Dawson, clerk, Vicar of Aberford, was admitted to the curacy of Barwick in Elmett, the 29th day of Sept^{r}, A. D. 1723

Baptisms, 1724.

Willm, the son of Thos Donwell of Barwick, Ap^{l} 7th
Ann, the Daugh^{r} of Henry Donwell of the Moor topp, Ap^{l} 5th
Thomas, the son of J^{n} Adkinson of the Stanks, Ap^{l} 12th
Betty, the Daug^{r} of Thomas Marrit of Cross gates, May 10th
Sarah, the Daug^{r} of J^{n} Ball of Potterton, May 15
Phebe, ye D^{r} of Jn. Rhodes of Bradford Parish, May 17
Mary, the Daugter of Jn. Hague of Stockhall, baptized June 5th
Michael, the son of Thom^{s} Wright of Scholes, Bapt. June 18
Hannah, Dau^{r} of James Worsman of Lazencroft, June 21
John, the son of Thomas Knapton, Jun: 28th
Francis, the son of Thos Wood of Winmore, July 5th
Jane, the Daug^{r} of Thos Poplewell of Winmorehead, July 12th
Lawrence, the son of Law^{ce} Milner of White Laith, July 19th
Thomas, the son of John Maud of Potterton, Augst 2
Augt 3^{d}. Dorathy, the Daught^{r} of Danl Rook of Barwick
Septr 20. Jane, the Daug^{r} of Henry Dõwell of Winm̃.
Sarah, D^{r} of David Goodall of B. Moor, Sep. 20
J^{n}, the son of John Bean of Barwick, Novr 29th

*St. John's, Cambridge, B.A., 1706. Married by licence 6 May, 1725 at Selby, to Mrs. Mary Baxter, spinster.

Elizth, the D^{r} of J^{n} Burland of Poterton, Decr 4th
Mary, the Posthumus Daughter of Wm Hague of Barwick, Jan. 10th
i. d. J^{n}, the son of J^{n} Dungworth of Barw^{k}
Thomas, the son of Richd Braim of Barwick, Jan. 14th
Elizth, Daugh^{r} of Martin Whitehead of Brown moor, Jany 24th
Issabell, the Daug^{r} of Thos Wildboar of Lenrick, Feb. 3
John, the son of Joseph Hague of Barw^{k}, Feby 6th
David, the son of Thos Wood of Barwick, March 5th
Elizth, the D^{r} of John Adkinson of Brown moor, Mãch 5th
Sarah, Daug^{r} of Thomas Shillato of Pott^{n}, March 29th

1725, Baptisms.

Thomas Issot, son of Robt Issot of Barwick, Ap^{l} 7th
Jane, the Daug^{r} of Mat^{w} Jackson of Barwick, Ap^{l} 11th
John Carter, son of John Carter of Scholes, Ap^{l} 17th
Mary, Daugh^{r} of Joseph Telford of Barwick, May 23^{d}
James, son of Mat^{w} Coates of Cross Gates, May 30th
Ann, the Daug^{r} of Fran^{s} Walker of Barnbow, Ju. 6th
John, the son of John Wate of Barwick, Jun. 8th
W^{m}, son of Wm Stanbank of Barwick, Jun. 9th
John, son of Wm Baccus of Scholes, Augs^{t} 1st
Thomas, son of Thomas Wood of Garforth Moor, Augst 1st
Mat^{w}, son of Mat^{w} Watson of Barwick, Augst 11th
J^{n}, the son of John Liversage of Barwick, Augst 15th
George, son of George Thompson of Scholes, Augst 25th
i. d. Bennoni, the Bastard child of Hannah Adams
John, the son of Willm Butler of Scholes, Sepr 5th
Thomas, son of Thomas Wright of Scholes, Oct. 1st
Thomas, son of Mark Thornton of Winmoor, Octob^{r} 17th
Ann, D^{r} of Wm Prince of Pot', Octr 22^{d}
Crispin, son of J^{n} Bean of Barwick, Oct. 27th
Novr 14. Thos, son of Thos Wilson of Leadsom
Ann, D^{r} of Jonas Haley of Scholes, Novr 17th
W^{m}, son of Henry Braim of Roundey, Dec. 15th
Dec. 30. Martha, Daughter of John Hague of Stockhill
Jan. 1. Robert, son of William Carburt of Potterton
Jan. 26. Thomas, son of Thomas Dunnell of Barwick
Jan. 30. Mary, Daughter of Thomas Maud of Penwell
Edward, son of Robert Brown of Barnbow, Jan^{ry} 30
Feb. 27th. Elizabeth, Daughter of Wm Mather of Cross-yates
David, son of Mr David Dawson, Curate of Barwick, was born Feb. 13th and baptiz'd Feb. 22^{d}, 1725/6
Rich^{d}, son of Robt Smith of Barwick, March 8th
Thos, son of Thos Holmes, 13 Feby.

1726, Baptisms.

Thos, son of J^{n} Carlin of Winmoor, Ap^{l} 23
Ann, D^{r} of Robt Brown, Jun., of Winmoor, Ap^{l} 23
Easter, D^{r} of Richd Clerk of Barwick, Ap^{l} 8th
Mary, Daug^{r} of James Bullock, jun', of Barwick, 11 May
Edwd, son of J^{n} Thompson of Stanks, May 30
Mary, daught^{r} of Christ^{o} Hargraue of Roundhey, June 1st

Wm, son of Francis Butterfield of Plumptõ in Knasbrough Par', June 8th
Mary, Daugr of Thos Adkinson of Winmoor, July 17th
Elizabeth, Daugr of Mr Willm Dawson of Kidhall, Augst 3d
Joseph, son of Joseph Huson, Augst 21
Christo, son of John Varey of Scholes, Augst 28th
Ann, Daugr of Robert Adkinson of Barwick, Septr 2d
Jane, Daugr of Thomas Preston of Barwick, Septr 12
Wm, son of Wm Lee of Scholes, Octobr 2d
Eliz., Daughr of James Worsman of Laz. Croft, Ocr 9
Eliz., Dr of Edwd Batty of Barwick, Novr 13
Eliz., Dr of Ge. Thompson, Ocr 16
Francis, son of Major Bradley of Stanks, Octr 30
Novr. 30. Thos, son of Jn Varley
I. d. Sarah, Dr of Jn Thompson of Stanks
Thomas, son of Joseph Braim of Roundhey, Jan. 1st
Chrispianus, son of John Bean of Barwick, Feb. 10th
Sarah, Daughter of John Adkinson of Barwk, Feb. 12th
i. d. Mary, Dr of John Carter of Scholes
Matw, son of Francis Walker of Barnbow, Mar. 7th
John, son of John Adkinson of Stanks, March 12th
i.d. Charles, son of Charles Hargraue of Scholes

BAPTISMS, 1727.

Edmund, son of Mr David Dawson, Curate of Barwick, was Born May 3d, Baptiz'd May 31st
Margret, Daughtr of John Smith of Garforth Mooreside, Born 16 Jany.
Christopher, son of Christr Ambler of Winmoor, Bap. Apl 9th
Jane, Dr of Jane Ambler of Winmoor, Baptiz'd Apll 23d
Thos, son of Jn Waite of Barwick, 7th May
Elizth, Daugr of George Smith of Barwick, May 24
Jn, son of Francis Wilson of Scholes, June 4th
Ruth, Dr of Joseph Hague of Barwick, June 28th
Thos, son of Matw Jackson of Barwick, July 2d
Martin, son of Martin Whithead of Garforth moorside, i.d.
Mary, Daugr of Jn Taite of Scholes, Augt 13th
Wm, son of Richd Braim of Barwick, Septr 17th
Robt, son of Robt Brown of Barnbow, Octr 22
Manasses, son of Wm Brook of Drinklington, in Burstal Parish, Octr 25
Issabel, Dr of Thos Wood of Brown Moor, Octr 29
Mary, Dr of Willm Appleyard of Barwick, Novr 2
James, son of James Orton of Barwick, Novr 28
Ann, Daughtr of William Hargrave of Roundhay, Decr 21st
Benjn, son of Joseph Tailford of Bar., Dr 27
Susannah, Daugr of Henry Blackburn of Brownm̃, Jan. 14
Richd, son of Jn Burland of Pott', Jany 18th
Frances, Dr of Wm Addiman of Maurick, Jany 28th
Jn, son of Thos Donwell of Barwick, Jan. 31th
James, son of Henry Donwell of the Hill top, March 3d
i.d. Sarah, Dr of Thos Settle of the Stanks

i. d. Thos, son of Matw Watson of Barw'
Benjn, son of Thos Wright, late of Scholes, Mar. 10th
Hannah, dr of William Dickinson of Scholes, March 17th

BAPTISMS, 1728.

Mercy, Dr of Jn Hague of Barw., Apl 5th
Joseph, son of Ricd Cook from Stanks, Apl 17
Jn, son of Jn Child of Winmoor top, Apl 19th
Edmund, son of Saml Liversage of Bar., Apl. 28th
John, son of Robert Knapton of Barwick, June 28th
Jn, son of Thomas Holmes of Barwick, July 5th
Saml, son of Adm Fleming, June 29
Ann, Daughter of Robt Brown of Penwell, July 21st
Wm, son of Lawrence Milner of Grimsdike, Augst 2d
John, son of James Robinson of Osmonthick, Octr 23
John, son of Robt Smith of Barwick, Augst 7
i. d. Edmond, son of Matw West of Roundhey
i. d. Thos, son of Tho. Shillito of Pot'
Ann, the Bastard child of Ester Thorns and Tho. Brown the reputed father, Octr 30
Ann, Dr of John Rooks of Wakefield, Novr 13
Ellin, Dr of Josh Batty, Decembr 1st
Mary Dorathy, Dr to Michl Easburn of Winmoor, Jany 5th
George, son of George Lister of Scholes, Jan. 12
Richd, son of Richd Wood of Potterton, Feb. 2d
Robt, son of Francis Wilson of Scholes, Feby 9
Paul, the Bastard child of Mary Dickinson, Feb. 17
Thomas, son of John Adkinson of Barwick, March 5th
Elizth, Daughter of John Thompson of Stanks, March 23

1729, BAPTISMS.

Saml, son of Saml Lumb of Stanks, March 30th
John, son of George Smith of Barwick, Apl 11th
Jn, son of Jn Bean of Barwick, May 9
Hannah, Dr of Mathew Tiplin of Stanks, May 30
Wm, son of James Norton of Barwick, May 28
Wm, son of Wm Abbot of Scholes, June 29
Elizabeth, Daugr of Richd Clerk of this Parish, July 6th
Samuel, son of Thomas Braim of Barnbow Carr, Augt 3d
Wm, son of Thomas Knapton of Barwick, Augst 10
Thomas, son of Wm Johnson of Leeds, Augst 17
Ruth, Daug' of John Thompson of Garforth moreside, Augst 24th
Thomas, son of Wm Johnson of Leeds, Augst 17
James, son of James Worsman, Octobr 5
Ann, Daughr of Thos Whitehead of Barwick, Octr 5
Hannah, Daughtr of Mr David Dawson, Curate of Barwick, was born the 9th and Baptized the 14th of September
Mary, Daughter of Richd. Lasinby of Winmoor, Octr 19
Elizabeth, Daugr of Wm Vevers of Scholes, Gentn, Octr 29
Jn, son of Jn Taite of Barwick, Novr the 12th
Wm, son of Mr Wm Dawson of Kidhall, Jany 2d
Saml, son of John Varley, Feby 6th

Mary, Daughtr of Mark Robinson of Pot', 8th Feb.
Hannah, Daghr of Henry Blackburn, Feby 15
Mary, Dr of John Atkinson of Stanks, Feb. 15th
Saml, son of Tho. Donwell of Barwick, Feby 18
Mary, Daughter of Barnard Blackburn of Barwick, Mar. 8
i. d. Hannah, Dr of Joseph Ward
Mary, Dr of Wm Holmes of Roundhey, March 15th

1730, Baptisms.

Elizth, Daugtr of Charles Wright of Sch̄, March 30
i. d. Ann, Dr of Jn Waite of Barwk
Willm, son of Timo Penny of Grimes Dike, April 12th
Rose, the Daugr of Thos Preston of Barwk, Apl 15th
Ann, Daughter of Robt Smith of Bark, May 6th
Richd, son of Gabriel Taylor of Barnbow Carr, May 10th
William, son of Willm Hargraue, junr, of Roundhey, Born April 16th
Martha, Daughter of Wm Appleyard of Barwick, May 29
Elizabeth, Daughter of Richd Taylor of Kidhall Lane End, Jun. 12th
Joseph, son of Josp Bins, o'th Hill Top, 4th June
i. d. Thos, son of Martin Whitehead of Garforth Moorside, June 14
Sarah, Dr of Robt. Knapton of Barwick, Augt 6th
James, son of Josh Braim of Roundhey, Born July 25th
Dorathy, Daughter of Thos Adkinson of Brown Mr, Augst 23
Ann, Daughter of Edward Batty of Barwick, Novr 1st
Joseph, son of Adã Fleeming of Tory-Lugg Gate, Novr 6th
Jn, son of James Norton of Barwick, Novembr 15
Elizabeth, the Daughr of Wm Thompson of Barnbow Carr, Novr 18
Joseph, son of Joseph Batty of Scholes, Novr 29
Martha, Daughr of James Robinson of Osmundthick, Jany 3d
Ann, Dr of Matw Watson of Barwick, Jany 6th
John, son of John Hague of Barwick, Jany 20
Joseph, son of Wm Reedall of Kidhall Laine End, Jan. 22
Edmund, son of Robt Ball of Barwick, Jany 29
Feby 13. John, son of Richd Wood of Potterton
Abrm, son of Robt Brown of Barnbow, Feby 28th

1731.

Jn, son of George Thompson of Penwel, Apl 4
An, Dr of Major Bradley of Sch̄, Ap. 19
Martha, Daugr of John Smith of Garforth More, Born Apl 25
James, son of John Thompson of Barnbow, Apl 25
Mary, Daughtr of George Smith of Barwk, Apl 20
Ann, Dr of John Sanor of Grimes Dike, May 2d
i. d. James, son of Matw Jackson of Barwick
John, ye son of Matw Tippling of Stanks, May 23
Sarah, Dr of Wm Brown of Penwell, May 30
Wm, son of Michael Graveley of Scholes, Jun' 16
John, son of Jn Benson of Winmoor head, July 24,
Stephen, the son of Richd Lazenby of Stanks, July 4
Jn, son of Caleb Selby of Potterton, July 18
Ann, Dr of Mr Stephẽ Vevers of Mawrick, July 28th

Hannah, Daug^{r} of J^{n} Dickinson of Winmoor, Aug. 8th
Rich^{d}, son of John Bean of Barwick, Septr 1st
Benjn, son of Thomas Braim of Barnbow Carr, Sept. 3^{d}
Ann, Daughter of James Bullock of Barwick, Septr 10th
Henrietta Maria, the Daught^{r} of J^{n} Tate of Barwick, Octr 24th
Ann, Daughter of Henry Donnel of the Hill Top, Novr 7th
Mary, Daug^{r} of Thos Lumb of Stanks, Decr 8th
Jane, D^{r} of J^{n} Wate of Barwick, Decr 27
Christ^{r}, son of Thomas Holmes, Jany 9
Sarah, D^{r} of Thos Whitehead of Barwick, Feb. 2
James, son of Wm Butler of Scholes, Feb. 6th
Ellin, ye D^{r} of Francis Roundthw^{t} of Sch̄, Feb. 13th
Sarah, D^{r} of Francis Wilson of Scholes, Feb. 21
Elizabth, D^{r} of James Worsman of Brown moor, March 5th
Mary, D^{r} of Richd Taylor from Kid hall Lane end, March 17th
George, the son of Wm Abbot of Sch̄, March 19
i. d. Mary, ye Daug^{r} of Willm Carbot of Pott^{n}
Eliz., Daug^{r} of Tho. Haist from Kidh̄l Lane End, March 24
George, son of William Abbot of Sch̄, March 19

1732.

William son of Wm Taylor of Barnbow Carr, April ye 16th
Elizth, D^{r} of Timothy Turnpenny of Grimesdike, Ap^{l} 23
Frances, Daug^{r} of Mark Robinson of Potterton, April 30th
Henry, son of Henry Blackbourn of Brown More, May 7th
W^{m}, son of Robt Smith of Barw^{k}, May 31st
Richard, son of Wm Vevers of Scholes, Gent., June 2
Sarah, ye Daug^{r} of Mathew Jackson of Barwick, June ye 11th
Charles, son of Charles Hargr[a]ve of Scholes, bap. May 26
Agnes, Dau^{r} of William Thompson of Barnbow, Decem^{r} ye 29°
William, son of Thos Smith of Potterton, January ye 19th, 1732/3
Benjamin, son of Thos Shillitto of Potterton, June 2^{d}
Eliz: Daugh^{r} of Gabriel Taylor of Barnbow, June 2^{d}
James, son of John Saynor of Grimesdike, July 16th
Sarah, Daughter of William Clarkson of Roundhay, July ye 16th
Ann, ye Daughter of Jno Atkinson of Barwick, bapt^{d} July ye 19th
Sarah, Daught^{r} of Christ^{r} Hargraue of Roundhey, born July 7th
Eliz., Daug^{r} of Wm Knapton, Septemb^{r} 3^{d}
Martha, Daug^{r} of James Robinson of Barwick, Ibid^{m}
John, son of John Atkinson of Roundhay, Octob^{r} 1st
Joseph, son of Jno Kirkham of Barnbow, Septr 27°
Ann, ye Daugh^{r} of Joshua Brown of Roundhay, Novemb^{r} 2^{d}
Mary, Daugh^{r} of Joseph Beck of Stanks, Novemb^{r} 12°
Thomas, son of Robert Knapton of Barwick, Novemb^{r} 15th
Joseph, son of Joseph Sympson of Winmoor Head, Novemb. 19
Ann, Daughter of William Appleyard of Barwick, Novemb^{r} ye 22^{d}
Elizabeth, Daughter of Adam Fleming of Turrilugg Gate, D^{r} 10th
Thos, son of John Bradley from the Top of Winmoor, D^{r} 10th
Ann, Daug^{r} of Benjn Haist of Barwick, D^{r} 10th
William, son of Thos Smith of Potterton, Feby 3
John, son of Robt Sympson of Barwick, March 2^{d}

Agnes, D^{r} of Benjn Rawden, Feby 21
Mary, the Daug^{r} of Richd Wood of Potterton, March 4th
Hannah, Daug^{r} of Martin Whitehead of Garforth Moorside, March 11th
Ibid^{m} Hannah, Daug^{r} of William Reedall of Kidhall Lane End
Ibid^{m} Joseph, son of Thomas Knapton of Barwick
Ibd. John, son of Barnard Blackbourn of Barwick

1733 BAPTISMS.

Mary, Daug^{r} of George Vevers of Barwick, March 25
Mathias, son of John Varley of Barwick, March 26th
W^{m}, the son of Jno Benson of Stanks, April 29th
Thos, son of Robt Barton of Barw^{k}, Ap^{l} 29
Ellin, D^{r} of Robt Land of Grimes Dike, Ap^{l} 29
Mary, Daught^{r} of John Waite of Barwick, May 2^{d}
Willm, son of Mr Steven Vevers of Mawrick, May 3^{d}
Mary, Daug^{r} of Matthew West of Roundhay, May ye 6th
Ann, ye Daug^{r} of Mr George Smith, Curate of Barwick, May ye 9th
Joseph and Cuthbert, the Twin sons of John Smith of Garforth Mooreside, Christ^{d} May 31
Mary, Daugt^{r} of Francis Wilson, June 3^{d}
Mary, Daught^{r} of Thos Robsha of Barwick, June 15th
Ann, Daughter of Thos Adkinson, Jun' 17th
John, son of Henry Wardell of Habberley, June 22^{d}
John, son of Joseph Dickinson of Barwick, July 8th
Ann, Daughter of Willm Vevers of Scholes, Gentu., July 12
Eliz., Daughter of George Lister of Scholes, July the 29th
Willm, son of Thos Whitehead of Garforth Moor side, Augt 26
Drusilla, Daughter of Wm Scot of Bar., Septr 9th
Mary, Daugh^{t} of Thos Donwell of Barwick, Septr 12th
Christopher, son of Thomas Haist from Kidhall Lane end, October the 7th
Sarah, Daug^{r} of George Smith of Barwick, Octr 21
Novr 11. Eliz., Daughter of Thos Preston
Sarah, Daug^{r} of Willm Limbard of Crossgates, Novr 25
Alice, Daug^{r} of John Bean of Barwick, Novemb^{r} 30th
Frances, Daughter of Thos Marshall of Seacroft, Feby 22
Joseph, son of Timothy Turnpenny of Grimesdike, March 3^{d}
J^{n}, son of Thomas Lumb of Stanks, Mar. 24th
i. d. Ann, Daughter of Francis Roundthwaite of Scholes

1734.

March 31. Thomas, son of Joseph Beck of Low moor
Ester, Daug^{r} of Thomas Settle of Barwick, April 7th
Mary, Daught^{r} of J^{n} Varey of Sch̄, Ap^{l} 21
Dorathy, Daugh^{r} of Willm Appleyard of Bar', Ap^{l} 28th
Saml, son of Saml Dodgion of Roundhay, May 8th
Jane, Daught^{r} of Joseph Maud of Winmoor, May 19th
Sarah, Daug^{tr} of William Abbot of Scholes, Jun. 3^{d}
Abrãm, son of Benjn Rawlinson, July 10th
Rich^{d}, son of Major Theaker of Scholes, Augt 25th
James, son of Wm Johnson of Osmundthick, Septr 1st
Hannah, Daught^{r} of Thomas Braim of Barnbow Carr, Septr 11^{h}

Mary, Daughter of Matt^{w} Tiplin of Stanks, Septr 22
Mary, Daug^{tr} of Willm Butler of Barwick, born Octr 6th
Rich^{d}, son of George Watson of Barwk., Octr 6
W^{m}, son of Willm Vevers of Scholes, Gent^{n}, Octr 17th
Jane, ye Daught^{r} of Tho. Whitehead of Bark, Octr 20th
Gabriel, son of Gabriel Taylor of Barnbow Carr, Octr 27
Thos, son of Tho. Whitehead of Garforth Moorside, Octr 27
Sarah, Daughter of Mr Stephen Vevers of Mawrick, Octr 27th
Mary, Daught^{r} of Wm Butler of Barwick, Novr 3^{d}
i. d. Rich^{d}, son of Geo. Watson of Barwick
Thos, son of Thos Sympsõ of Hebberley, Nov. 11th
i. d. Ann, D^{r} of Mark Robinson of Potterton
Sarah, Daughter of Robt Sympson of Barwick, Decr 26
Elizabeth, Daug^{r} of J^{n} Hague of Barw^{k}, Decr 27th
W^{m}, son of Thos Collet of Barwick, Decr 29th
Susannah, Daught^{r} of Richd Lumb of Barwick, Jany 22
John, son of Willm Taylor of Barnbow Carr, Jany 26th
George, son of Richd. Haist of Barwick, born the 16th of Jany Christ^{d} Feby 12th
Alice, D^{r} of J^{n} Waite of Barwick, born Feb. 5th, Christ^{d} March 23^{d}
Francis, son of Francis Holmes of Bar. and Rachel his wife, born Feby 10th, Christ^{d} Mar. 14
James and Alice, Twins, son and D^{r} of Thos Harper of Sch, Born the 5th of March, X^{td} the 7th Ap^{l}
J^{n}, son of John Thompson of Stanks, born Feb. 8th, Christ^{d} March 7th
*Willm, the son of Wm Lumb of Barwick, born March 7, Christ^{d} March 26th
Mary, the daughter of Thomas Haist of Kidhall Lain End, born March 9th
Mary, Daughter of Adam Fleeming, born Feb. 8, Christ. March 12th
Ellin, Daughter of Francis Wilson of Sch, born —, Christ^{d} Apl. 6th
Grace, the Daughter of Robert Appleyard, Labourer, of Scholes, bap. August ye 10th

BAPTISMS, 1735.

Ellin, Daught^{r} of J^{n} Varley of Barw^{k}, Yeoman, born —, Christ^{d} May 1st

---

*William Lumb, the father, was Constable in 1743, and Overseer of the Poor in 1747. William Lumb, the son, was married at Leeds, 1758, to Mary, daughter of Richard Dawson of Carr House, Garforth. He was schoolmaster at Barwick, and afterwards at Swillington, resided at Smeaton House, and died in 1801. He was also High Constable of the Upper Division of Skyrack, parish register, land agent, land surveyor for the Swillington and Rothwell Haigh Inclosure Acts, and he designed the Barwick (1765), Kippax and Garforth (1761) sundials. His son, Robert Lumb, J.P., removed to Lowther about 1800, and became Chief Agent for the Earl of Lonsdale, married, 1788, at Leeds, Mary, daughter of Henry Robinson of Ledsham. Their son, William Lumb of Brigham Hall, and grandson, James Lumb of Homewood, Whitehaven, were Deputy Lieutenants and High Sheriffs for Cumberland. William Lumb of Brigham Hall married Harriet, daughter of William Wilkin, M.D., of Appleby, and his brother, the Rev. Thomas Dawson Lumb, M.A., St. John's, Cambridge, Curate of Methley, married Priscilla, another daughter of Dr. Wilkin. It may be of interest to mention that Robert Lumb's daughter, Elizabeth, danced at the Duchess of Richmond's ball on the eve of Waterloo with the Duke of Brunswick. His grandson, the Revd. John Alfred Lumb Airey, M.A., Pembroke College, Cambridge, second Wrangler, 1846, is Rector of Great St. Helen's. Another grandson, the Rev. Canon J. G. Doman, was the well-known Vicar of St. Mark's, Bolton, and another, the Rev. Henry Lumb, M.A., University College, Durham, was Vicar of Kirkbride. Major Anthony Lumb, Somersetshire Light Infantry, who served in the Soudan campaign of 1884—5, and the North West Frontier campaign of 1897, where he was severely wounded, Captain Edward J. M. Lumb, Imperial Yeomanry, and James Lumb, M.A., Clare College, Cambridge, barrister at law, are his great grandsons. Richard Lumb (1775—1844), of Well Green, Swillington, succeeded his father, William Lumb, as High Constable. See Burke's *Landed Gentry*, 4th and 5th Editions, and "*Robinson of White House, Appleby*," page 20.

Edward, son of Edwd Batty of Barwick, Laber^{r}, baptiz'd May 26
Robt, son of Robert Barton of Barwick, House Carpinter, May 26
Frances, Daught^{r} of John Benson of Cross gates, Joyner, June 22^{d}
George, son of Willm Reedall of Kidhall Lain End, Lab^{r}, July 18
Penelope, the Daug^{r} of Henry Perkins, Rector of Barwick, Born and Bapt. July 4th
Joseph, son of Richd Jackson of Barwick, Chandler and Sope boyler, Augt 17
i. d. George, the son of J^{n} Adkinson of Barw^{k}, Linen Weaver
James, son of Thos Upton of Mawrick, Husbandman, Aug. 22
Ann, Daught^{r} of Joseph Stephenson of Crossgates, Lab^{r}, Aug. 22^{d}
Elizabeth, Daughter of Richd Wood of Potterton, Laber^{r}, Septr 28th
i. d. Mary, Daughter of J^{n} Adkinson of Winmore Top, Husbandman
Susannah, Daughter of Richd Wilson of Brown More, Lab^{r}, Octob^{r} 12th
James, son of James Robinson of Barwick, Lab^{r}, Octr 12th
John, son of John Varey of Scholes, Laber^{r}, Novr 2^{d}
James, son of James Norton of Barwick, Lab^{r}, Nov. 3^{d}
Benjamin, son of Benjn Haist of Barwick, Yeoman, Novr 3^{d}
Joseph, son of Saml Dodgion of Roundhay, Carpinter, Novr 28th
Sarah, Daughter of Matt^{w} Kirby on Winmoor top, Labour^{r}, Feb. 1st
Sarah, the Daughter of Richard Johnson, Tinker, July ye 20 Day
Rich^{d}, son of And^{w} Burdsal the Younger of Scholes, Buckle maker, Feby 7th
William, son of William Crummack of Winmoor-top, March ye 8th, Lab^{r}
Ann, the Daughter of Geo. Thompson of Penwell, Husbandman, March 19th

YEAR 1736, BAPTISMS.

Mary, the Daughter of John Bean of Barwick, Shoemaker, March 26th
Elizabeth, the Daughter of George Watson of Barwick, Labourer, March 28th
Sarah, Daughter of William Scot of Barwick, Joyner, April ye 4th
Ann, the Daughter of Thomas Whitehead of Garforth moor side, Collier, April ye 18th
Ellin, the Daughter of Jos^{h} Beck of Winmoor, Lab^{r}, May ye 9th
Alice, the Daughter of Thomas Settle of Barwick, Weaver, May ye 9th
[*Blank*] the Daughter of Thomas Collet of Barwick, May ye 16th
Joseph, son of Mathew Watson of Barwick, Carpenter, May ye 28th
Elizth, Daughter of Thomas Smith of Potterton, husbandman, June ye 14th
Timothy, son of Timothy Penny of Winmoor, Lab^{r}, June 20th
Martha, Daughter of William Thompson of Barnbow, Husbandman, Augt 12th
William, son of John Hewit of Garforth moor, Collier, Sepr 5th
Martha, the Daughter of Joseph Maud of Penwell, Labou^{r}, October ye 24th
Edmund, son of Thos Preston of Barwick, Taylor, Novr ye 21
Elizabeth, Daughter of James Strodder, Shoemaker, December ye 10th
Sarah, Daughter of Benjamin Rawlinson, Labo^{r}, December ye 27th
Sarah, Daughter of John Bradley, Lab^{r}, of Winmoor, January ye 30th
Sarah, the Daughter of Samuel Dodgson of Roundhay, Yeoman, Feby 16th
Thomas, son of John Upton, Jun', of Winmore, March ye 10th

1737, BAPTISMS.

William, the son of Joseph Dickinson of Barwick, Lab^{r}, Ap^{l} 3^{d}
George, the son of Jonath^{n} Bell of Barwick, Lab^{r}, April ye 10th
Sarah, Daughter of David Wright of Winmoor, Lab^{r}, April ye 24th
Elizabeth, the daughter of Thomas Asquith of Potterton, Lab^{r}, April ye 24th
Adam, the son of Adam Fleming of Turylug-gate, Yeoman, Ap^{l} 29th
Joseph, the son of Joseph Beck of Winmoor, Collier, May ye 8th
Thomas, the son of Robert Dawson of Shippen, Yeoman, May ye 15th
Eliz., the Daughter of John Varey of Scholes, Lab^{r}, May ye 29th
Abraham, son of John Waite of Barwick, Taylor, May ye 29th
Eliz., Daug^{r} of Gabriel Taylor of Barnbow, Lab^{r}, June 5th
John, ye son of Martin Whitehead of Garforth moor, Collier, June 12th
John, son of John Hemsworth of Potterton, Lab^{r}, June ye 19th
John, ye son of John Kirkham of Barnbow, Yeoman, June ye 24th
George, son of Thomas Haist, Inn-holder, from Kidhal Lane end, June y^{e} 26th
Samuel, son of Thomas Lumb of Stanks, Yeoman, July y^{e} 10th
Mary, daughter of Robt Simpson of Barwick, Lab^{r}, Augt y^{e} 7th
Andrew, the son of Richard Jackson of Barwick, Chandler, Augt 19th
Richard, the son of Richard Lumb of Bar$_{K}$, Husbandman, August y^{e} 31st
James, the son of Henry Wardle of Hubberley, Yeoman, Septr y^{e} 16th
Mary, Daughter of John Atkinson of Schõ, Lab^{r}, October y^{e} 16th
Richard, son of Richard Haist of Barwick, Yeoman, October y^{e} 20th
Eliz., Daughter of John Burland of Potterton, Lab^{r}, Octob. ye 23^{d}
Anthony, son of Thos Donwel of Barwick, Weaver, November ye 6th
John, son of Mark Robinson of Potterton, Husbandman, Novemb̄ ye 18th
John, son of Thomas Whitehead of Garforth moor, Collier, December ye 18th
Andrew, son of And^{w} Burdsal of Scholes, Buckle-Maker, December 27th
Hannah, the Daughter of James Strodder of Barwick, Shoemaker, January ye 31st
Thos, son of Richard Wood of Potterton, Lab^{r}, Febr'y ye 5th
Margret, Daughter of Michael Graveley, Yeoman, Febr'y ye 8th
James, the son of William Crummock of Winmoor, Lab^{r}, Febr'y 19th
John, the son of Step. Vevers, Gent., of Morwick, March the 9th

BAPTISMS, 1738.

Bersheba, the daughter of James Robinson of Barw^{k}, April ye 2^{d}
Martha, the daughter of Willm Taylor of Barnbow Carr, Dishturner, April ye 4th
James, the son of William Bell of Winmoor, Taylor, April ye 5th
Henry, the son of Thomas Simson of Winmoor, Lab^{r}, April ye 23
Eleanor, the Daughter of Mathew Golden of Barwick, Lab^{r}, May the 5th, 1738
Alice, the daughter of William Abbot of Barwick, Yeoman, June ye 4th

1684 MARIT.

John Smith, iu., and Elizabeth Pease, both of this parish, after publication thrice made according to Cannon, were married Octob^{r} the 26th

Edward Boulton and Frances Ball, both of the parish of Leeds, a Cirtificate from Mr Timo. Cookson, February the 22

1707. Surplice Fees to the Rr. Burialls, 12d. Churchings, 8d. Weddings, 2s 6d, Banns pub 1s 0d. Funerall sermons 10s and 1li plus and minus. Mar. wth Lycence, 10s. Registring, 6d. Mortuaries, 10s.

MARIT', 1685.

Richard Smith and Phillip [? Phillis] Marshall, both of this Parish, after publication thrice made according to Cannon, were married November the 9th

MARIT', 1686.

John Holcroft and Anne Foster, after Publication thrice made, were married April 8

Humphrey Morris and Mary Aumbler, August 28

Richard Lumb and Jane Thompson, October ye 14

Ralph Collett and Hannah Breatcliffe, Nov. 17

Robert Walton of ye pish. of Kippax and Elisab. Smith of this pish, Novemb. 24

MARIT, 1687.

Richard Hague of ye parish of Whitkirk and Anne Brooke of this parish, after Publication thrice made, were married Aprill the 28th

Jonathan Walsh of the parish of Kilwick and Elizab. Haworth of this p', May 25

William Hemsworth and Alice Birkes, both of this parish, September the 21th

John Saynor and Anne Lawe, both of this parish, Novembr ye 23

George Mawmond and Mary Anderson, both of this pish, February ye 12

MARIT, 1688.

Thomas Hewett and Elisabeth Featon, both of this parish, after publication thrice made, maried Aprill the 17

William Morret and Jane Foxe, both of this pish, the same day

George Wood of the parish of Abborford and Dorothy Lansdale of this parish, were married by licence, May the 30

Robert Dodgson of the parish of Bilton and Elisabeth Snawdon of this parish, June the 5th

BRIEFFS.

Aprill 30, 1688. Received then of ye Minister and Churchwarden of Barwick in Elmet the sume of seventeen shillings eight pence half penny, collected in that pish. upon a Brieff bearing date the 31 of January, 1687-8, and granted to the distressed Protestants of France. I say Recd the sume aforesaid by me.

A BRIEFE. T. Holmes.

Bealt in Comita Brecon Loss by fire 10780£

Thomas Hill of this parish and Susannah Munsey of the pish of Abborforth, after publication thrice made, were married February the 10th

Roger Tulip and Elisabeth Thornebrough, both of ye parish of Garthforth, by a cirtificate from Mr Witham, Rector, Ibidem, were married the 11 day of February

MARIT, 1689.

John Ingle and Anna Whitcroft, both of this parish, after publication thrice made, were married May the 16

July the 8, 1689. Received of the Ministr of Barwicke in Elmett the sume of Two pounds thirteen shillings seven pence halfe peñy, collected in that pish upon the Brieff for the Relieffe of the distressed protestants of Ireland. I say Reced the aforesaid sume p me. T. Holmes.

Mr Bateman rẽced for 2 mortuaries from Mr Dudson, i.e., for Tho. Tates 10s and for John Taylors, jun., 10s for ye use of Dr Beresford.

John Soothard and Sara Lund, both of this pish, after publicacõn thrice made, were married October the 6

William Wood of Scoles and Anne Green of this Towne, Novem. the 28th

Thomas Parker of the parish of Harwood and Rosamond Peell of this pish, Feb. the 3

Daniel Jarmayne and Jane Saynor, both of this parish, after publication thrice made, were married February the 24

Edward Wilson, Dr. Beresfords servant, received of Mr Dudson 10s for Hen. Rights Mortuary for ye Drs. use

1690. Mountsoryel in Lecesteshire, 520l loss by fire

Giuen to Mr Jon Clopton of ye citty of Norwich, who had a loss of stuff lost by ye sea, of 6000ls and upwards

Lykwise Morpeth in Northumberland, 3530l loss by fire

MARIT, 1690.

Dauid Hopwood of this parish and Anne Waudman of ye Parish of Leeds, after publicacõn thrice made, were married Dec. 11th

William Collett of the parish of Rodwell and Margarett Briggs of this pish were Marryed by Lycence, Decembr ye 18

Jan. 2do, 1690. Recd then of the Minister and Churchwardens of Berwick in Elmet for East Smithfields Brief, the sume of four shillings, by me. Tho. Critchley

RECEITS FOR BRIEFS.

Junij 2do, 1690. Received then of ye Minister and Churchwardens of ye Parish of Barwick in Elmet, the sume of sixteen shillings, being so much collected on ys M'ties 2d Brief for ye releif of ye new [? Milvers] Irish Protestants within ye Arch Deaconry of York. I say recd ye aforsd sume by me. Tho. Holmes

Junij 2do, 1690. Recd then of ye Churchwardens of Barwick in Elmet the sume of Six shillings, being money collected upon ye Brief for ye releif of ye inhabitants of new Alresford. I say received by me. Wm Richardson

Junij 2do. Recd of ye minister and Churchwardens of ye same parish the sume of fourteen shill. eleven pence half penny for ye poor sufferers of Bungay in Suffolk. I say rec'd by me. Wm Richardson

John Chambers of ye pish of Kippax and Mary Ingle of this pish, August ye 25

July ye 2d, '90. Collected wtin ye pish of Barwicke the sume of two shillings for ye poor sufferers of Stafford, and paid in ye 21 of Aug°

Collected wtin ye pish of Barwicke, June ye 23th, the sume of three shillings for ye poor sufferers of Bishop Lavington, and pd in at ye correction [*sic*], ye 21 of Aug.

Myles Hopwood and Mercy Tate, both of this parish, November the 12th

David Hopwood of this pish and Anne Waudman of the parish of Leeds, December ye 11

William Collett of ye pish of Rodwell and Margarett Briggs of this pish, were married by Licence, Dec. 18

William Sutleworth and Frances Cooper, both of this pish, Feb. 19

August the 10, 1691. Receiued then of the Minister and Church-wardens of Barwick in Elmet, the sum̃e of Two shillings and sixpence, beinge Collected towards the Briefe of Bealt in Wailes, p me, I say Recd 2s 6d J. Joanes, Collr.

Aug. ye 28. Recd. of ye Minister and Churchwãds the sum̃e of 4s for ye redeem of two Marchants out of Tunis in Turkey, their losses 8000l and their Ransum, 55l. Received by me.

Tho. Darell, Collector.

MARIT, 1691.

George Thompson of the parish of Kippax and Anne Watson of this pish, after publication thrice made, were marryed Aprill the 15

Richard Robinson of this parish and Alice Donfield of the parish of Garthforth, were marryed by Licence, May the 14th

Thomas Norfolke and Elizabeth Saynor, both of this parish, October the 21

Aug. 31, 1691. Recd. then of ye Ministr and Churchwardens of Barwick in Elmett in ye county of York, ye sum of Four shillings being Collected upon their Majesties Letters Patents for ye poor sufferers by fire at Thirske. p me, Wm Richardson, Coll.

John Potter of the Parish of Shearbourne and Alice Thompson of this pish, Nov. the 18th

John Sykes and Mary Dawson, both of this parrish, Nov. 23th

Daniel Jerman and Anne Massie, both of this pish, December ye 24th

MARIT, 1692

Richard Wilson of this parish and Susannah Fisher of the parish of Cawood, after publication thrice made, were married May ye 16

John Norhan and Mary Rasine, both of this pish, May ye 17

Jeremiah Ball and Elizabeth Wright, both of this Parish, June the 28th

William Ingle and Sarah Hudson, both of this Parish, August the 3° day

William Admergill of the Parish of More munckton and Elizab. Dodgson of this pish, October the 11th

John Santon and Anne Kelshawe, both of Roundhey in this Parish, October ye 23°

MARIT, 1693.

John Richardson of ye Parish of Bramham and Anne Strickland of this Parish, after Publication thrice made, were married together Aprill the 17th

Thomas Whitehead and Anne Dunnell, both of this Parish, May ye 11th

John Appleyard of ye Parish of Otley and Deborey Oddy of this Parish, May the 21th

John Wilson of the Parish of Garthforth and Elizabeth Johnson of this pish, June the 5th

Mr Francis Moseley and Mrs Jane Ellis of Kidhall were married by Lycence, June the 18th

Thomas Linley of the Parish of Whitkirk and Sara Thompson, after Publication thrice made, were married together July the 12th

William Midlebrooke and Margarett Hill, both of this Parish, Novembr the 1st

Samuel Thornton and Anne Webster, both of this parish, January the Tenth

John Gilson and Mary Heaton of Lazingcroft, both of this pish, February the Twentieth

MARIT, 1694.

George Waller and Mary Read of Kidall, were marryed by Lycence, April the 22th

William Nortõ and Mary Wild, both of this parish, after publication thrise made, were maried Nov. ye 13

William Ear ãd Elliner Brigs, both of this parish, Nov. 19

Samuel Dodgson and Sara Braime, both of Roundhey, January the 30th

MARIT, 1695.

John Longbothome of the Parish of Thorner and Mary Hearfield of Hopperley in this parish, after publicacon thrice made, were married together August ye 5th

John Firth of the Parish of Hallifax and Mary Joy of Scoles in this parish, August the 13th

John Atkinson and Mary Ellis, both of this parish, were married by Lycence, September the 25th

Henry Whittecars of the parish of Fenton and Sarah Ingle of this pish, October the 20th

*Jordanus Tancred, Clericus, M.A., Inductus fuit in hanc Rectoriam de Barwick in Elmet, 18vo die Junij, 1695

Guil. Bridges, Clericus, Art. Bacc., Admissus fuerit ad Peragendum officium Curati in hac Ecclesia per Johan Archiepisc Ebor., Sep. 22do, Quod quidem officium auspicabatur, 1mo die Octobris seq., 1695to

Richard Pate of the Parish of Wakefield and Anne Ellis of Kiddall were by Lyce[n]ce together [*sic*], Febr th. 2d

Danieli Hudson, Clerico Parochiali ad Plures abeunti successit in eodem munere Joannes Hemsworth, Febr 23tio, 1695to

MARIT, 1696.

Petrus Slayter et Jana Richinson, nupti fuerunt Jan. vicessimo

MARIT', 1697.

Thomas Turpen et Sara Massie, nupti fuere Aprilis 28vo

*Rector 1695—1703. Presentation dated 3 April, 1695. He was son of Charles Tancred of Arden. Christ Church, Oxon., B.A., 1685, M.A., 1687.—Foster's *Alumni Oxon.*

Robertus Brown et Helena Burken, Maij 25to
Rogerus Judson et Sara Wright, Junij vicessimo primo die
Johannes Lofthous et Jana Robinson, Novembris 17mo die

MARIT', 1698.

Johannes Butcher et Maria Tait, nupti fuerunt vicessimo tertio Junij
Samuel Nuby et Maria Slaytor, vicessimo septimo die Augusti
Josephus Moxon et Helena Munsy, Januarij 23^{tio}
Samuel Servant et Anna Tate, Januarij 29no

MARIT, 1699.

Josephus Sigston De Leeds et Elizabetha Hardcastle De Barwick, nupt. Maij 25to
Gulielmus Sare De Wetherby et Elizabetha Robinson de Barwick, Junij 18vo
Gulielmus Aire et Susanna Hodgeson, Jan'ij 31mo

MARIT, 1700.

Christopherus Wilson de Beckah et Maria Dixon De Potterton, Nupt. Junij 24to
Gulielmus Jewet De Ryther et Barbara Jebson De Potterton, Nov^{bris} 11mo
Anthonius Jackson de Walshford et Sara Wright de Barwick, Dec^{bris} 30mo
Johannes Wright et Anna Green de Barwick, Feb' 13^{tio}
Johannes Glover et Eliza. Burket, Nupt. ap. Ebór., Feb^{ij} 17mo

CONJUGAT, 1701.

Johannes Pearson et Maria Ellis, Nupt. May 1mo
Thomas Lightfoot de Whitkirke et Jana Doerdon de Brownmoor, Aug^{sti} 7mo
Johannes Johnson et Maria Pease, Nov^{bris} 2do
Gulielmus Middlebrooke et Anna Constable, Nov^{bris} 30mo
Josephus Hague et Helena Hardy, Jan^{ij} 29no

CONJUGAT, [1702].

Gulielmus Fawcet et Jana Robson de Barwick, nupt. Maij 5to
Richardus Tarbotson de Thorner et Elizabetha Ball de Potterton, Junij 7mo
Joshua Wait De Seacroft et Helena Westmorland De Scholes, Nov^{bris} 30mo
Andreus Backhouse de Shereburn et Tomisin Brunton De Shippen, Feb^{ij} 1mo
Jeremias Bolton et Eliz. Atkinson De Barwick, Nupt. —

*Georgius Plaxton, Clericus, A.M., Rector Eccliãrum de Donington et Kynnardsey in Agro Salopiensi, inductus erat in Realem actualem et Corporalem possionem Ecctiae et Rectoriæ de Berwick in Elmet, vicesimo quarto Die Mensis Septembris, Anno D'ni 1703.

Jo. Killingbeck	Will. Vevers
Cuthbt Witham	Tho. Brooke
Bright Dixon	Wm Plaxton
Witt Vevers	Jno Hemsworth

*Rector 1703—1721 St. John's College, Cambridge, B.A., 1669. He was an intimate friend of Ralph Thoresby. See D H. Atkinson's Ralph Thoresby, His Town and Times, and Thoresby's Diary and Correspondence, edited by Hunter.

Franciscus Rounthwait et Maria Lee de Barwick, Septembris 19no [1703]

CONJUGAT [1704].

Gulielmus Ambler De Leeds et Anna Orton De Barwick, Nupt. Jan^{ij} 14to
Samuel Eamondson et Ursilla Thurkill De Leeds, May 25to
Johannes Robinson et Elizabeth Orton De Barwick, Junij 7mo
Ezechiel Hopwood de Wakefield et Elizabetha Gayton de Scholes, Julij 16to
Gulielmus Robinson De Garthforth et Anna Jackson de Scholes, Nov^{bris} 15to
Gulielmus Boardley et Maria Atkinson de Kiddal Lane, Feb^{ij} 19no
Thomas Scott et Sara Ellison de Barwick, Feb. 19no

CONJUGAT [1705].

Godfrey Stonehouse and Ellen Burrough, both of Roundhey, were married July 30th, 1705. 2^{s} 6^{d} Due to ye Queen
William Robinson of Cawood and Anne Burland of Berwick, Novemb. 28th, 1705. 2^{s} 6^{d} to ye Queen
John Dawson of Brown Moor and Mary Ellijt, on St Andrews day, 2^{s} 6^{d}
Edward Thomson of ye parish of Kirkby over blows and Eliz. Briggs of Potterton, 20th of January. 2^{s} 6^{d} to the Queen
Wm Renton and Mary Daniel, Jan. 28th. 2^{s} 6^{d} to y^{e} Queen

NUPTIÆ, 1706.

Wm Emmetson of Roundhay and Alice Powell of the ꝑish of Bramham, were maryed at Barwick, August y^{e} 8th
Mr Thomas Simson of $Wakef^{d}$ and Mrs Mary Brook were maryed by Lycence, October the 3^{d}
James Story of Swillington and Mary Gibson, Jan. 16
Abraham Abbot and Sarah Gibson, the man of Swillington ꝑish, the woman of this parish, Feb. 12
Joseph Farnes and Marjory Gleadhall, both of Halyfax parish, were maried with a Lycence, March the 3^{d}

NUPTIÆ, 1707.

Mark Robinson of ye parish of Skipwith and Sarah Hopwood were maried May 22° by Banns
Jonathan Vincent of Swillington and Mary Thorns, July 10th
John Varo and Mary Harvy, Aug. 4th
Wm Dibb and Katherine Brook, October 6th
Anthony Turner of Collingham and Anne Tate, Decemƀ the 22
John Atkinson and Dorothy Fleming, both of Kydhall, November the 13th
Francis Chapman of Barwick and Jane Lightfoot of Whitkirk parish, January 21

WEDDINGS, 1708.

Wm Pickring of Parlington and Margrett Hewitt were maried Novemb. 8°
Wm Pickring, jun^{r}, and Jane Wheately, Novemb: 25
Tho. Popplewell and Anne Clough, Jan. 26th
Tho. Ball and Anne Tate, Feb. 18
*Tho. Perrot of York, Clerk, and Anastasia Plaxton, June the 17th

*See Perrot Pedigree in Thoresby's *Ducatus Leodiensis*, 2nd Edition, page 72.

Weddings, 1709.

James Jewit and Anne Robinson, married May 5°
George Johnson and Anne Shippen, Sept. 15°
George Dickenson and Anne Midlebrook, Novemb. 16th
George Hanly of Thorner and Sarah Briggs of Potterton, Feb. 2°

Marriages, 1710.

Henry Cowpland and Mary Scott were maried Jan. 16°
John Tasker and Anne Tate, Jan. 22

Marriages, 1711.

Godfrey Stonehouse and Mary Carrit, June 30, of Roundhay
Christophr Thornton and Bridgett Hunter, July 8
Wm, Yates of Bramham and Mary Smith, Nov. 28
Francis Parker of Leeds and Joanna Gibson als Prince, Decemb. 2°

Anno Domini 1712.

Edward Maxwell and Eliz. Hemsworth were maryed Apr 29
John Ball and Mary Jackson, May 13
Michael Prince and Elizabeth Brown, June 22

Marriages, 1713.

Jno Varley and Ellenr Demain, Octobr 29th
Martin Dawson of Seacroft and Anne Hunter, Jan: 5th
Michael Sharp of Kippax and Sarah Taylor, Jan. 26th

Marriages, 1714.

Wm Mounsey and Anne Dickinson, Novembr 1st
Wm Canfield and Grace Speight, Decr 1st
Mattw Jackson and Anne Robinson, Decr 5th
Geo. Hinskipp and Eliz. Backhouse, Feb. 7th
Abram Marshall and Anne Hardisty, Feb. 20th, wth a Licence

Marriages, 1715.

Joseph Cawwood and Elizabeth Sutherd, May ye 2nd
Ralph Collett and Anne Glover, August ye 3dth
Thomas Knapton and Mary Burton, August ye 31st
Jno Walton and Susannah Cryer, November ye 13th

Marriages, 1716.

Jno Sharp and Mary Beatson, June ye 18th, wth a Licence
Mattw Hanson and Eliza. Wilcock, July the 23d
James Bullock and Joan Brown, August ye 6th
Benja. Dawson and Eliza. Hill, Novembr ye 22nd

Marriages, 1717.

James Wilcox and Anne Bradford, Aprill 21st
Wm Carver and Mary Briggs, Aprill 25th
Edwd Balmforth and Isabel Dobson, July ye 8th
Wm Johnson and Mary Lee, Octobr 9th
Tho. Smith and Eliza. Denison, Octobr 20th
Robt Dodgson and Anne Walton, Novembr 26th
Tho. Preston and Anne Burnett, Decembr 23th
Richd Tarbotton and Alice Wilson, January 1st
Richd Robinson and Rosamond Appleyard, Feb. 20th

Marriages, 1718.

Robt Bateson and Rachel Thorns, Aprill ye 20th
Wm Hague and Mary Hardisty, August ye 4th

Robt Issot and Alice Tarbotton, August ye 13th
Richd Wilson and Susannah Oates, August 21st
those 3 Couple were married with a Lycence
Tho. Davy and Anne Wheatley, September ye 7th

MARRIAGES 1719.

Richd Slaytor and Eliza: Dickinson, Aprill the 12th
Joseph Hick and Elizabeth Hay, June the 30th
John Rook and Sarah Vevers, Septembr ye 1st, with a Lycence
Henry Dunnel and Anne Dickinson, Octobr 11th
John Wilson and Sarah Goodhall, October ye 29th
Tho. Shillitoe and Sarah Wood, November ye 8th
Wm Hague and Elizabeth Ball, November ye 9th
Richd Johnson and Susannah Walton, November ye 12th
James Hartley and Anne Ingam, January ye 7th, wth a Lycence

MARRIAGES, 1720.

John Easby of Rigton and Eliz. Pearson, June the 8th
Martin Whitehead and Elizabeth Lee, August ye 3d
Wm Bradford and Anne Wilcox, Sepr the 22nd
Wm Simpson of Whitkirk and Mary Stonear, Novembr ye 9th
Mattw Oddey and Mary Thompson, Decr ye 7th
Christopher Hargrave and Anne Atkinson, Decr ye 8th
Edmundus Barneby, Clericus, A.M., de Chelsey in Com. Middle., inductus erat in realem actualem et corporalem possessionem Ecclesiæ parochialis et Rectoriae de Barwick in Elmet, vicessimo octavo die mensis Martij, Anno Do. 1721. John Plaxton

MARRIAGES, 1721.

Rich̄ Robinson and Ann Dodgson, Both of this parish, Aprill ye 13th
Willm Heresie and Susanna Watson, Octbr ye 15th
Edward Batty and Elizabeth Watkinson, January ye 14th
Michael Dunn and Edith Stead, Febry ye 6th
John Hague and Mary Hebden, March the 8th, wth a Licence

MARRIAGES, 1722.

Thomas Brown of Saxton and Mary Hemsworth, March the 25th
Joseph Law of Kippax and Dorothy Watkinson, August the 1st
Thomas Holmes and Susanna Sykes, August the 27th
John Waite and Ann Abbott, September the 3d
Samuell Stead of Leeds and Alice Settle, October the 22nd
Christopher Teasdall and Ann Morresby, Octobr the 24th
Henry Braim and Ann Brittain of Saxton, Novembr the 28th
Charles Hargrave and Mary Jackson, January the 31st

MARRIAGES, 1723.

James Whittaker of Fenton and Elizabh Thornton of this Parh, April the 17th
Thos Bell and Mary Ambler, May 25
Willm Butler and Sarah Taite, July 29
Thos Knapton and Elizth Crowder, Septr 9th
Thomas Adkinson and Mary Lumb, Novr 17
James Ellis of Harwood and Jane Hebden of Roundhey, Novr 26th
Joseph Hague and Elisabeth Sharpra, Jany 15th

John Dungworth and Alice Stringer, Febry 17th

MARRIAGES, 1724.

John Carter of Pontefract and Sarah Lister of Scholes, Apl 6th
William Law of Leeds and Mary Hopwood of Barwick, Jun. 1st
Francis Walker and Ann Germai' of Barwick, Augst 13th
Joseph Telford and Rosimond Robinson of Barwick, Septr. 6
Willm Backhouse and Ann Cryer of Scholes, Sepr 27
Richd Tuke of Thorner and [*blank*] Clerkson of Hubberley, Novr 25th
Wm Lee and Ann Robinson of Scholes, Jan. 6th
Brian Thackwray of Roundhay, Elizth Mitchel of Sherburn, Jan. 20th
John Bean and Alice Ellis of Barwick, Jan. 20th
Mark Thornton of Barwick parish and Ellin Pepper of Parlinton, Jan. 27

1725.

David Dawson, Clerk, Vicar of Aberford and Curate of Barwick in Elmett; was married to Mrs Mary Baxter of Selby, Spinster, the sixth day of May, A.D. 1725
Robt Adkinson of Barwick and Issabella Sanor, August 8th
Richard Pennington and Ann Wright of the Parish of Tadcaster, Jan. 30th, 1725/6, Sunday.
Memdm. Mrs Eliz. Ellis, exectrx to Wm Ellis, Esqr, pd 10s for a Mortuary to D. Dawson, Cur.

MARRIAGES [1726].

Willm Aier and Eliz. Spencer of Barwick, May the 28th
Mr John Haigh of Selby and Mrs Frances Pickering of Wetherby, June 8th
Josep Maud and Ann Mounsey, Augst 22
Jn Wiglesworth of Rodwell Parish and Mary Gibson of Potterton, Ocr 16
Robert, son of John Pearson, pd 10s as a Mortuary for his Father to D. Dawson, Cur.

MARRIAGES [1727].

Daniel Huit and Grace Varley, Both of this Par̃, Novr 15
Willm Holmes and Martha Tiplin, both of this Par̃, 30 Nov.
Willm Dixon of Cowton in the Parsh of Whidchurch and Mary Robinson of this Parh, Decr 1st
Joseph Batty and Ann Jackson, both of this Parish, Decr 11
David Blackburn and Mary Burland, Decr 27
Saml Thompson and Ann Robson, both of this Parish, Jan. 30

MARRIAGES, 1728.

May 5th. George Bennet and Mary Waterworth, both of this Parish
Charles Wright and Margret Wright, both of this psh, July 3d
Gabriel Talor and Ann Bell, both of this Par.
Wm Johnson of Leeds and Judith Wilcock of Garforth Moorside, married wth License, Octr 17
Tho. Whithead and Mary Lumb, both this Parish, Novr 20th
Wm Cooper and Hannah Maud of Potterton, Decr 21
Wm Hebden the younger and Jane [*blank*], both of this Par., Apl 6th

1729, MARRIAGES.

George Thompson and Ann Butcher, after due publication, Both of this Parish, Mar. Apl. 6th

Thos Taylor and Mary Ball, both of this Par.
Richd Marshall and An Taite of this Parish, Jun' 24th
J^{n} Rishforth of Leeds parish and Dorathy Maud of this parish, June 25th
Joseph Ward of Tadcaster Parish and Sarah Robinson of this parish, July 6th
Richd Taylor and Ellin Thompson, both of this parish, Septr 7th
James Wilcock and Rebekah Tricket, both of this Parish, Octr 22
Richd Duffin of Brotherton parish and Mary Smith of this Parish, Novr 24th
Edwd Batty and Mary Barker, both of this parish, Jany. 27

1730, Marriages.

John Sanor of Whidchurch and Ann Wright of this Parish, May 6
Mat^{w} Jackson and Sarah Watson of this Parish, June 14th
Benjn Rawdẽ of Kippax parish and Mary Abbot of this Parish, July 23
Jn. Slater and Elizth Outhwaite, booth of this Parish, Augt 31
Wm Reedall and Grace Bateson, both of this parish, Octr 12th
John Dickinson of the Parish of Whidchurch and Mary Sharphouse of this Parish, Novr 2^{d}
Richd Lumb and Margret Ball, both of this Parish, Novr 29
Anthony Connel of the Parish of Whidchurch and Sarah Rowlinson of this Par^{h}, Feby 3^{d}
Thos Collet and Elizth Watkinson, both of this Par^{sh}, Feby 23

Marriages, 1731.

Thos Mirrit and Ann Sharphouse, both of this Parish, Ap^{l} 19th
Mr J^{n} Shacklet^{n} of Rippõ and Mrs Elizabth Vevers de Potter', Married wth Licence, Ap^{l} 28
i. d. Wm Clerkson and Jane Tipplin, both of this Par.
Josh Stephenson of the Parish of Whidchurch and Sarah Lightfoot of this Parish, Ap^{l} 29th
Richd Taylor and Sarah Scot, both of Barwick, May 24th
John Pickerin and Ellianor Backhouse, both of Abberforth
William Hardy and Mary Johnson, both of this Par:, Aug. 5th
Benjn Haist and Elizth Dawson, both of this Par., Married wth Licence, Octr 25th
Joshua Lisster and Mary Sympson, both of this Parish, Nov^{r}.—
Mr Jeremiah Marshall of the Par^{h} of Guisley and Mrs Ann Emanson of Roundhay, were married wth Licence, Feby 21
i. d. J^{n} Jordan and Margret Hemsworth from Roundhay, Feb. 21
Henricus Perkins, Clericus, A.M. Sacrista ecc. cath. de Lichfield, Inductus erat in Realem et Corporalem possessionem Ecclesiæ et Rectoriæ de Barwick in Elmet, vicesimo septimo die Martij, A.D. 1731

p^{r} D. Dawson.

Marriages, 1732.

Joseph Dickinson and Ann Atkinson, both of Barwick, April 20th
Thos Backhouse of Abberford and Mary Horner of Barwick, Apl. 26
David Carleton of Abberford and Ann Watkinson of Barwick, July ye 3
Robt Sympson and Mary Bell, both of this Parish, Septr 27th

Jonathan Bell and Ann Wood, both of this p'sh, Octob^{r} ye 9th
Ibid^{m}. Thomas Whitehead and Alice Brunton, both of this parish
Thos Donwell and Rebecca Hewson, both of this parish, ye 25° of October
Wm Scott of this parish and Mary Cawood of the parish of Swillington, Novem^{r} 6th
William Ward of the parish of Wooley and Mary Bradley of this parish, Decemb^{r} 1st
Richard Wilson and Ann Chapman of Brownmoor, both of this Parish, Decemb. 31

1733, MARRIAGES.

Joseph Maud and Deborah Middlebrough, both of this parish, married May ye 6th
Samuel Dodgion and Ann West, both of this parish, May ye 9th
Rich'd Lumb of Barwick and Hannah Atkinson of the Parish of Badsworth
J^{n} Prince of Kippax and Mary Varey of Scholes, Augs^{t} 11th
John Johnson of Thorner and Ann Prince of this Parish, August 19th
Robt Appley'd and Mary Wilson, both of this Parish, Novr 29
George Watson and Susannah Maxwell, both of this Parish, Decr 26
John Donwell and Elizth Broadley, both of this Par., Jan. 7th

MARRIAGES, 1734.

Jonathan Raper and Ann Amb^{r}, Ap^{l} 15th
James Higgins and Mary Orton, Both of this Par., Apl. 21
J^{n} Thompson and Sarah Cook, both of this Parish, May 4th
Willm Lumb and Martha Braim, both of this Parish, May 8th
[*Blank*] of the Parish of Abberford and Ann Walton of this Parish, Feb. 16
John Owin of the Parish of Rothwell and Ann Robinson of this Parish, Feb. 17
[*Blank*] of Abberfd and Ann Walton of Barwick, Feb. 17th
J^{n} Owen of Rodwell and Ann Robinson of Garforth Moor, Feb. 18
Andrew Burdsall and Elizabeth Cundal, Both of this Parish, Feb. 22^{d}

MARRIAGES, 1735.

Michael Settle, Labourer, and An Wilcock, Wid^{w}, Both of this parish, Octr 8th

1736, MARRIAGES.

James Strodder, Shoemaker, and Margret Eyre, were marry'd August 24th
Mathias Waite of the Parish of Harwood and Elizabeth Burland of this Parish, October ye 11th

1737, MARRIAGES.

Mathias Firth, Lab^{r}, and Jane Scalbert, Spinster, both of this Parish, were marry'd Apl. 11th

1684, SEPULT.

Alice, the wife of John Smith of Barwick, was Buried in woollen, June the 11th
Elisabeth, the wife of William Thompson of Hirstmoor, June ye 24
Mary, the wife of Joshua Lumb at Allershaw laine end, Aug. ye 3
The Laydy Anne Tempest of Barnbow, the 11th of September
Mary, the wife of Robert Wansley, the 15 of Sept.

Grace, the wife of Matthew Ingle of Barwick, the 22 of September
Richard, the son of Thomas Wood of Barwick, the 25 of Septem.
Christopher Kelshaw of Brandon, October the 15
Thomas Hopwood in Kidall lane, October the 17
Widow Shoosmith at the lower end of Hirstmore, October the 18
Anne Prince of Mounkey, wid', Nov. 1st
Elisabeth, the wife of Stephen Eastbourne of Spighleys, November 2
Christopher Shoore and Alice his wife, of Barnbow, both in one grave, Novem. the 19
A still borne child of Nicholas Sheppen of Sheppen, December the 16
A s[t]ill borne Child of John Moore of Barwick, December the 18
Richard, the son of Christopher Hill of the Stanks, Decemb. the 20
Elizabeth, the daughter of James Wilcocke at Allershaw laine end, was buried in woollen at Whitkirk, By lycence, the 19 of January
Frances, ye daughter of John Frankland of Garthforth moreside, February the 9
Thomas Knapton of Barwicke, Feb, ye 12
Alice Cooper of Scoles, February the 20
Mary, the daughter of Robert Wansley of Barwick, February the 23
*Mr Thomas Addyson of Barnbow, Gent., March the 12th

SEPULT, 1685.

James, the son of James Hinley of Penwel, was buried in wooll: Aprill ye 8
Mrs Mary Ellis of Barwicke, Aprill ye 27
Dorothy Oddy of Scoles, May the 15
William Lumb at the uper end on Hurstmore, August the 6
Elisabeth, the daughter of Mary Taylor of Barnbow carr, widow, Augo 16
Grace, the daughter of Thomas Brunton of Barnbow, August the 19
Anne, the wife of Richard Swals of Potterton, September ye 11th
Anne, the daughter of John [? Franland] of Garthforth more side, Octob. the 11, and the affidavit Brought the 18
Barbary Butler of Roundey, November ye 18
Jane Ellis of Barwick, Novemb. the 12
John Buck of the Stanks, Nov. the 13
Anne, the wife of John Dodgson, Nov. the 14
Robert Shuttleworth of Scoles, No. 22
Anne Turner of the Penwell, No. 27
William Ingle of Barwicke, No. 28
A still born Child of Richard Robinson of Barwick, December the 10
Margaret, the wife of Wm Wood of Scoles, Decemb. the 11
Samuel Waterworth of Barwicke, Dec. 13
Richard Hill of the Stanks, Dec. 16
Henry Hardwick of Barwick, Dec. 20
John Munsey of Winmore head, December the 28
Thomas, ye son of Tho. Knapton of Barwick, ye same day

---

*Lawrence Mowbray in his information respecting the Barnbow Plot, 1679 (printed 1680) mentions Mr. Thomas Addison, the priest to Mrs. Killingbeck, and the above is apparently the record of his burial.

William Munsey of Winmore head, Jan. 7
William Taylor of Barwick, January ye first
Barbary Shuttleworth of Scoles, Febr. the 23, and an Affidavitt broughte to me, 26
Mary Kelshawe of Roundhay, Febru. ye 28
Robert Shawe of Barwick, March 15
Cicilia, the wife of James Wheatley of Winmoor, March 24

SEPULT', 1686

Tho., the son of Samuel Robinson of Garthforth moor, was Buried in Woollen, April the 3, and Affidavitt Brought to me Ap. the 5
Elisabeth, the wife of Tho. Taylor of Barwick, Aprill the 14, Affida: brought the 15
John, ye son of Wm Smith of ye same, Aprill 16, Affedavit brought:
Anne, the wife of Wm Haire of Morwick, Ap. 26
Obidia, the son of Wm Handley of Scoles, Aprill the 10
Anne, the wife of Bernard Mawmond of Barwick, Ap. ye 11
Grace, ye daughter of James Hinley, at ye Penwell, May the 23, Affidav. brought the same day
Elisabeth Haslegrave of Scoles, May ye 25, And an affidavit brought to me ye 26
Ric. Sheppen of Barnbow, June ye 6th, And an affidavit brought ye 9
Richard Brough of Barwick, July ye 9
Francis Brunton of Garthforth more side, July the 13, and an affidavit Brought the same day, and slaine in a coal pitt. Ibid
Robert Knapton of Barwicke, July ye 22th, and an affidavit brought ye 28
Elisabeth, the daughter of Michael Rish at the lower end, on Hurstmore, was Buried at Whitkirk with lycence, Sept. the 22, from Mr Coope
Barbara, ye daughter of Solomon Jibson of Kidall laine end, October ye 4
Elisabeth, the wife of John Smith, iunior, of Barwick, October the 8th, and an affidavit Brought ye 10
Anne Burnel of Roundhey, Octob. 10, and an affidavit brought ye same day
John, the son of Christop. Leeds of Garthforth more sd, Nov. the 11, and an affidavitt brought 13
Beatrix, ye wife of Christ. Leeds of the same, Novemb. 16. Affida. brought ye 17
William Hardy of Scoles, November 23, and an Affidavit brought ye 27
Mercy Hague of Barwick, wid^{w}, Nov. 25, and an affidavitt brought ye 29
Magdaline, ye daughter of Nicolas Sheppen of Sheppen, Dec. the 7, and an affidavitt brought the 12
[*Blank*], the son of Abraham Sheppen of Barnbow, Decemb^{r} the 10, and an affidavitt brought the —
James, ye son of John Prince of Potterton, Dec. the 11, and an affidavit brought the 18 Instant
John Hardcastle of Barwicke, the 20 of Dec., and an affidavitt brought ye 24
Dorothy, ye daughter of Richard Lumbe on Winmoor, January the 26, and an affidavit brought the 28

Robert, ye son of Robt Wansley of Barwick, February the 5, and an affidavit brought ye 6 Instant

Thomas, ye son of Wm Lister of Scoles, Feb. 7, and an affidavitt brought ye —

Anne, ye wife of Thomas Walker of Roundhey, February ye 9, and an affidavitt brought ye 13th Instant

Elizabeth Crabtree of Roundhey, March the 9th, and an Affidavitt brought ye 12 Inst.

†Mr John Coope, Curate of this parish, March ye 21, and an affidavitt Brought the 27

SEPULT, 1687.

Alice Sheppen of Barnbow car was Buried in Woollen, May ye 2, and an affidavit Brought ye 9

Alice Hill of the Stanks, widow, July 2*

A still borne child of Aquall Blackeburn of Scoles, July ye 23*

John, the son of Alice Prince of Barwick, Septembr the 8*

William Briggs of Winmore, Decemb. the 9*

A still born child of Richard Atkinson of Roundhey, Decem. the 29*

Leonard Catton of Barw., Dec. the 31*

Elisabeth, ye wife of James Wilcock at ye lower end of Hirstmore, was Buried at Whitkirk by lycence, February the 6

This Letter following was directed thus for Mr Dudson, Curate of Barwick in Elmett.

These,

Sept. 28th, 1687.

Reverend Sir,

You are desired to receive five pounds from this bearer and to give it to your Churchwardens to distribute to your poor Parishioners as followeth, viz.: 50s to be equally divided to all the poor men which are 60 years of age or upward; and 50s to all the poor widdows which are of the same age, the wifes of one husband (widdows indeed). A proof for which Act of mine you may find in ye 1 Epis. to Timoth., 5 ch., 9 verse, and it is an example which I have learned from the right Reverend Father in God Dr Andrews, sometime Bishop of Winchester, as you may find in his life thus writt: A Prelate worthy of renown and a light of Charity fit for all men to imitate whom God has blessed with abilities. Sr, I have taken the freedom to trouble you upon this account, and if you think it a trouble I beg your Pardon for it; but upon second thoughts I conclude you think it an honour to be God's Almoner; thus desireing your fervent hearty prayers for me and mine, I rest Yours faithfull Lover in Christ, the unwilling to be Known, ANONYMUS.

SEPULT, 1688.

Mrs Dorothy Lodge of Roundhey was Buried in Woollen, April 7*

A still born child of John Thompson of Garthforth more side, Ap. 8*

Mary, ye Daughter of Robt Wansley of Barwicke, Aprill the 12*

Jane Bullocke of the same, widow, Aprill the 15*

Thomas Thompson of the Stanks, May the 9*

---

†John Coope, Magdalen College Cambridge, B.A., 1666; M.A., 1670.

*Signifies that an affidavit was brought.

Benjamine, the son of John Aumbler on Hurst moore, May 23*
Mr William Green of Potterton, May the 24*
William Ridley, a Norththumberland Man, was found dead on Cattle moor where we went our perambulation in the Rogation week ante on the 7 of June and an affidavit brought the 13 Instant Ju.
James, the son of James Wilcock at the lower end of Hurst moor near Whitkirk laine end, was Buried by lycence from Mr Dudson, curate, Whitkirk, on the 14 of June instant *
Connon Hopkinson of Scoles, June 28*
Beatrixe Catton of Barwick, the same day*
Edward Ingle of Barnbow was Buried by a Certificate at Whitkirk, July ye 26
A still born child of John Gascoigne of Parlington, Gent., the 4 of Aug.*
John, ye son of Gyles Hardwicke, Aug. ye 25*
John Drury of Barwicke, September the 6*
Anne, the Daughter of Wm Handly of Scoles, the 27 day of Sept.*
A still borne Child of Aqual Blackborne of Scoles, October the 20*
A still born Child of Richd Robinson of Barwicke, October the 22d*
Jane Snawden of Potterton, widw, November the 9*
William, the son of Thomas Hewet of Potterton, the 27 of Novemb.*
Martine Whitehead, iunior, of this pish, was buryed by lycence at Whitkirk, on the First day of December*
Elisabeth, the wife of William Sharphurst at the Speighleys, Janua. the First*
William Munsey on Winmore head, the 17 of January, and an affidavit brought the —. The Minister issued forth his Certifycate to the Churchwardens and overseers the 26 day Instant January for want of ye affidavitt
Rosomond Maw of Garthforth more side, the 23 day of Feb., and an affidavit brought the —. The Minister issued forth his Certificate to the Churchwardens and overseers the 4th of March, for want of the affidavitt
Marke, the son of Tho. Cooper of Scoles, March the 11*
Elisabeth, the wife of John Pitts of Scoles, March the 15*

Wes Riding Comt Ebor. } To all Bayliffs, Constables and other their Majties officers wthin ye sd Riding and especially to the Conble of Rigton.

Whereas Matthew Barnby, late of Scoles, left a House unto his Bror, Wm. Vevers, to pay unto ye poor ten shillings yearly, and yt ye sd. Wm. Vevers endeavours to defraud ye poor thereof to their damage and contrary to Lawes

These are therefore in their Majties name to Will and require you and Every of you That you or some of you do iñediately after your receipt hereof cause the said William Vevers to come before me or some other of their Majties Justices of the Peace for this Riding to shew cause why he refuses to pay ye poor the moneyes due to them, and you are also hereby further required to give the Churchwardens and oversers of the poor of Scoles aforesaid convenient

*Signifies that an affidavit was brought.

notice of the due execution hereof to the end that they may also appeare and be p'sent to make out this their Complaint and hereof ffaile not att your Perrills. Given under my hand and Seal at Preston, the 10th day of Aprill, 1691. Wm Lowther.

Geo. Hast, Robert Brooke, Churchwarden, Richard Braime, Overseer, William Knapton.

SEPULTIS, 1689.

Elisabeth Thompson of Barwick, widow, was Buried in Woollen, the 5 day of Aprill*
Mary, ye daughter of Tho. Walker of Roundhey, Aprill the 24*
John Thompson of Garthforth more side, May the 11*
John Dodgson, iu., of Kidall lane end, June the 4*
John Wright of Barwicke, June ye 6*
Richard Burland of Barwicke, June the 26*
Anne, ye wife of Tho. Poppleton of ye same, June ye 28*
Jane Fouston of Barwicke, July the 3*
Frances, the wife of William Smith of Barwicke, July the 10*
Anne, the daughter of Joseph Hague of Barwicke, July the 21
Mary, ye wife of George Mawmond and Isable his daughter, both was buried in woollen and laid in one grave, July the 27*
Thomas, the son of Thomas Knapton of the same, July 30*
George, the son of Richard Smith of the same, August the first*
Thomas Tate of Barwicke, August the 15*
John, ye son of Robert Browne of Potterton, August ye 18*
William Wilcocke of Garthforth more side, September the 5*
Gyles Hardwicke of Barwicke, Gent., Septembr the 12*
Mrs Elisabeth Massie of ye same, September the 14*
Henry Wright of ye Laydy grounds on Winmore, September the 16*
A still borne child of Robert West of Roundhey, Septembr 25, and no affidavit, ye cirtificate granted
Thomas Briggs of the same, Septembr 30*
William Watson of Barwicke, Octobr ye 4*
Hellen, the wife of William Taylor of Scoles, October the 22th*
A still born child of Robt Thornes of Barwicke, Dec. 7*
A still born child of Richard Robinson of ye same, Dec. 14*
Anne Briggs on Winmore, widw, Decembr ye 25*
Mary, ye daughter of Tho. Knapton of Barwicke, January ye 3d*
Mary, ye wife of David Hopwood of Potterton, January ye 6*
William Butler of Roundhey, Janu. the 11*
John Printice of Potterton, Janu. 15*
John Taylor, iunior, of Barwick, January the 16*
Two still born children of Jon Aumbler of Hirst more, the same day
A souldiers child of Potterton, January the 17
Austine Nicolson of Barwick, Janu. the 18*
Francis Johnson of ye Stanks, January ye 26*
Stephen Eastbourne of Hurst more, February the 23*
Moses, the son of John Settle of Potterton, February the 24*
John, the son of Wm Coapland of Potterton, March the 7*
John Burland of Barwicke, March the 11*

*Signifies that an affidavit was brought.

John Frankland of Garthforth more side, March ye 16*

SEPULT, 1690.

Elisabeth, ye daughter of Richard Smith of Barwick, was Buried in Woollen, Aprill ye 2*
Thomas Ellis, a serv^{t} at Kidall, Aprill the 7*
A still born child of Richard Lumb of Hurst more, Aprill the 26*
Anne, ye wife of Henry Haire at Kidhall laine end, April ye 30*
Thomas, ye son of Tho. West of Roundhey, May ye 15*
Margarett Ibbotson of Potterton, May ye 18*
Rich^{d}, ye son of John Smith of Barwicke, May ye 28*
Elisabeth, ye daughter of Willm Worfolk of Morwick, June ye 5*
Josuah Turner of Barwick, July ye 24*
Stephen, the son of Jo^{n} Lumbler, iu', of Hirstmore, ye 30, and no affidavitt brought, ye certifycate issued forth
John Hunter at ye uper end of Hurstmoore, August ye 13*
Grace Brough of Barwicke, Sept. the 4*
Elisabeth, ye wife of Abraham Sheppen of Barnbow, Sept. ye 9*
Charles Hardcastle of Roundhey, October the 23*
William Deardon of Garthforth more side, October ye 26*
Elisabeth, the wife of Robert Farrer at ye Bull lane head, Octob. ye 30*
Thomas Taylor of Barwicke, Nov. the 1st*
Christop., ye son of Jo^{n} Hardisty, Nov. the 7th*
Samuel, ye son of Robt Wansley of Barwick, Novemb. ye 20*
A still born child of Richd Robinson of Barwick, Dec. the 21*
Thomas, ye son of Robt Wansley of ye same, Decemb. ye 30*
A still born child of Richd Smith of ye same, January ye 7*
Robert Dodgson of Kidall laine head, the same day*
Grace, ye daughter of John Ingle of Barwick, January ye 13*
Elisabeth, ye daughter of Wm Knapton of Barwicke, Janu. 14*
Rebecca, ye wife of Richd Robinson of ye same, January ye 17*
Charles, ye son of Richd Settle of Potterton, Jan. 20*
Sara, ye daughter of Mat'. Watkinson, Garthforth moreside, ye same day*
A s[t]ill born child of Jo^{n} Offine of Scoles, ye 20 of Janu.*
John Hemsworth of Potterton, February ye 7*
Jane, ye wife of Daniel Jermaine of Barwicke, February ye 13*
Frances Sheppen of Scoles, widow, February the 20*
Elisabeth Issott of Barwick, widow, February ye 21*
Francis West of Roundhey, March the 4*

SEPPULTIS, 1691.

Margarett Barker of Potterton, widow, was Buried in Woollen, March the 31*
Anne Brown of Winmore, vi: Ap. 28*
Jane Thompson of Speighley, by lycense, at Whitkirk, May ye 1st
Rich^{d}, ye son of Richard Lumb of the same, May ye 11*
Tho., ye son of John Stoaker of Scoles, May 31*
Mary, ye daughter of Mr John Brooke of Leeds, June ye 29*
Christopher Hill of ye Stankes, July the 17*
Margaret Watson of Leeds was found dead at Cattle close head near

*Signifies that an affidavit was brought.

ye yate leading to Sheepen, and was Buryed in Woollen, Septemb. the 3d*

Elizabeth, the daughter of John Gascoigne, Esq. of Parlington, Octobr the 3d*

Elizab., ye daughter of Richard Atkinson of Roundhey Park, Decembr ye 20*

Anne, ye daughter of Thomas Cooper of Scoles, Janu. ye 22*

Elisabeth, ye daughter of Tho. Bradford of Tolerugg yate, January ye 28*

A still bourn child and Thomas, ye son of Danjel Jermaine of Barwicke, January ye 29*

Sara, ye daughter of Wm Hallyday at Bull laine end, February ye 28

Richard Glover at ye White laith was Buried at Whitkirk by a Certificate from our Minist., the 29 of February

Sara, the daughter of William Reedall, near Allershaw laine on Hurstmore, the 4 of March*

A still born Child of John Ingles of Barwick, March ye 5*

BRIEFFS.

The Tenth day of May, 1692. Received then of the Minister and Churchwardens of Barwicke in Elmett in the County of Yorke, for Clapton Brief the sume of Three shillings, and for Oswester Brief the sum̃e of Two shillings. Rec'd by me.

Abrah. Crowder, Coll

August the 31, 1691. Receiued then of ye Minister and Churchwardens of Barwicke in Elmett in the County of Yorke, the sum̃e of Four shillings for Thirske Brief. I say Received per me.

Willm Richardson, Collector.

SEPULTIS, 1692.

Mary Slaytor on Hurst moor were buried in woollen, Aprill the 2*

Mary Butcher of Barwick, Aprill the 20*

John Dodgson of Kidall laine end, May ye 17*

Jane, ye daughter of Richd Robinson of Barwick, May the 25*

Anne Holmes of Roundhey, June the 1st, for want of the Affidavitt the Minister granted forth his Certifycate to ye Churchwardens and overseers the 16o Instant

Elizabeth Knapton of Barwick, widow, July the 17*

Grace, the wife of Geo: Smith at Allershaw laine end on Hurst More, was Buried by lycense from Mr Dudson at Whitkirke, July the 25

William Lofthouse of Potterton, Aug: the 19th*

Thomas, the son of John Potter of Barwicke, Septemb. ye 15*

Easter, ye daughter of Aquall Blackborn of Scoles, Septembr the 22*

Thomas, the son of Robert Browne of Potterton, the same day

Anne, ye Daughter of John Aumbler, iu', on Hurst more, Octobr the 2d*

Richard Johnson of Lasingcroft was Buried in woollen at Garthforth by lycence, November the 25th

John, the son of Thomas Bradford of Tollerugg Yeate, November ye 27*

James, the son of James Wheatley on Hurstmore, the same day*

William, the son of Samuel Tate, iu', of Kidall laine head, Dec. the 25*

---

*Signifies that an affidavit was brought.

James Wheatley of Hurst more, near Penwell, Dec. the 28*
Robert Prince of Barwick, January the 3° day*
Easter, ye daughter of Tho. Prince of the same, Jan. the 8th
Hannah, the wife of ye sd Thoms Prince, January ye 14*
Edward, the son of Richd Aspenwald of Roundhey, Janu. the 25*
Anne Dodgson of Roundhey, widow, Janu. ye 25*
Thomas, the son of William Knapton of Barwick, February the 2d*
Elizabeth Settle of Potterton, widow, Feb. the 11th*
Frances Dodgson of Roundhey, March the 2d*
Richard Aspenwall, iu', of Roundhey, March the 6th*
Mary Standley, a Bastard at Speighley nuk, Mar. 21*

SEPULTIS, 1693.

Robert Saynor of Scoles was Buried in woollen, Aprill the 21th*
Faith Varley of Brown moore was Buried by lycence at Whitkirk, Aprill the 20th
Frances Butler of Barnbow, Aprill the 30th*
A still born child of John Lister of Roundhey, May the 15th
Dorothy Constable, widow, on Hurstmoore over against Speighley, May the 20th*
Peter Slaytor on Hurstmore, May the 21*
Anne Dunwell of Scoles, widow, June the 4th*
William, the son of Wm Handley of Scoles, June the 11*
Elinor, the wife of Anthony Wright of Grimesdike, July the 4*
George Smith near Allershaw laine end on Hurstmoore, was Buryed at Whitkirke by a Certificate and Lycence from Mr Dudson, curate, Aug. ye 16
George Wright on Winmore, near Lady ground, August the 23th*
Daniel Huett of Garthforth more side, Sept. the 23th*
Mary Hunter of Winmore, October the 5th*
Richard Prince of Barwick, October the 24th*
George Tinsdall of Parlington, Novr ye 2d*
Grace, the wife of William Hair at ye west end of Kidall laine end, November the 9th
Sarah, the wife of Wm Ingle of Barwicke, November the 11th*
William Smith of Scoles, December the 9*
Elizabeth, the wife of Richd Settle of Potterton, January the 19th*
Francis Saynor of Barwicke, January ye 20th*
Elizabeth Shenton of the same, widow, January the 21th*
Isable, the wife of Robert Carter at Allershall laine End on Hurst more, was Buryed by Licence from Mr Dudson, Curate at Whitkirk, February the 16th
John Smith of Barwicke, Febr. the 24*
Anne Smith of Scoles, widow, March the 2d*
Margarett, the wife of Wm Lister of Roundhey, March the 11th*

SEPULTIS, 1694.

Christopher Leedes of Garforth more side was Buryed April 7th*
Anne Hopwood, widw, in Kidhall laine, Aprill 10*
Frances, the wife of Thomas Bird of Barwick, Aprill the 11th*
Abigaile, ye wife of John Settle of Potterton, the same day*

*Signifies that an affidavit was brought.

Anne, the wife of George Spinke of Scoles, April the 17th*
Robert Hardcastle of Barwicke, the same day*
William Hopwood in Kidall laine, April the 23th*
Jane Prince of Barwick, May ye 18th*
Martin Prince of ye same, May ye 19*
Elizabeth Hopwood of ye same, May ye 20*
Elizabeth Fawcett of Barwicke, June ye 25*
Thomas More of Barwick, June ye 28*
Christop. Aumbler near ye cross yates on Hurst more, June ye 25*
A still born Child of John Lister of Roundhey, July ye 6*
John Saynor of Grimesdike, July ye 16*
Matthew Holmes of Roundhey, Aug. 6*
Easter Thompson of Garforth moreside, August the 24th
Anne Simpson of the same, the same day
Edmond Hunt of Lazincroft, was buried at Garforth, the 8th day of October
Grace, the wife of Thomas Brunton of Sheppen, October the 12th*
Matthew, ye son of Mattw Issott of Barwick, Octobr ye 29th*
Sara, the daughter of Jon Jackeson of Brownmoor, Dec. ye 18th*
Sara, ye daughter of Robt Thornes of Barwick, Dec. the 22th*
Mary, ye daughter of Richd Atkinson of Roundhey, Dec. ye 25th*
Moses, the son of Robert Brame of Barnbow carr, February the 20th*
Wm, ye son of Rob. Brown of Potterton, Feb. ye 22th
David, the son of Wm Ayre at the west end of Kidall laine, March the 17th

SEPULTIS, 1695.

James Orton, iu', of Barwicke, was Buried in woollen, Aprill the 3d day*
A still born Child of Tho. Settle of ye same, Aprill ye 10*
Richard Taite of Potterton, Aprill ye 11th*
William Barnett of Penwell, Aprill the 18th*
Jane, ye daughter of Robert Wansley of Barwick, Aprill ye 29th*
Elizabeth, his other daughter, May ye 1st*
Anne, ye wife of Robt Wansley of ye same, May ye 11th*
Sarah Prince of Potterton, May ye 14th*
Robert Mawe of Garforth moore side, May ye 15th*
Frances, ye wife of John Atkinson of Osmondthick, July ye 1st*
Alice Holmes of Roundhey, July ye 8th*
Robert Eastbourn near Speighleys nuke, July the 22th*
A Still Born-child of Jon Ingle of Barwick, July ye 29th*
John Westmerland of Scoles, July ye 30th
Thomas Holcroft of Barwick, Aug. the 25th
Anne, the daughter of Robt Wansley of Barwick, Sept. the 7th*
†Mr Myles Lodge of Redhall on Winmore head, Sept. the 8th*
Edward, son of Thomas Knapton of Barwick, Sept. ye 19th*
Alice, ye daughter of Thomas Tate of Scoles, September the 26th*
Jane, ye daughter of Wm Wood of ye same, October ye 1st*

---

*Signifies that an affidavit was brought.

†Red Hall was built by Mr. Richard Lodge, a Leeds Merchant. See Thoresby Society's vol. II. page 247, and for Pedigree see Thoresby's Ducatus, 2nd Edition, page 73.

Anne, the daughter of Joseph Hague of Barwick, October the 16th*
Francis, the son of Richard Settle of the same, October ye 19th*
Elizabeth, the daughter of Timothy Smith of the same, November the 1st*
Joan Frankland of Garforth more side, was buried in woollen Novembr ye 25th, and the Minister issued forth his Certificate to the Churchwardens and overseers for want of the Affidavitt
Wm, the son of William Butler of Speighley nuke, Dec. the 25th*
Richd, ye son of Thom. Knapton of Barwick, February the 11th
Daniel Hudson, qui per decursum 35 annorum Clerici Parochialis munus obivit in hac ecclesia sepultus fuit Februarij 20mo
Anthonius Wright de Grimesdyke, Februarij 29no
Elizabetha, uxor Aquillae Blackburn de Scholes, Martij 3tio

SEPULT., 1696.

Maria Bradford, Filia Thomæ Bradford de Potterton-moor, sepult' Octavo die Aprilis
Anna, uxor Petri Slater de Hirstmoor, Maij 14th
Johannes, Filius Johan. Atkinson de Kiddal Lane, Maij 27
Abrahamus, filius Abra. Shippen de Barmbow-carr, Julij 5to
Josephus Constable de Winmoor, Julij 10mo
Josephus, filius Gulielmi Wood de Scholes, Julij 12mo
Dina, filia Rich̄ Settle de Barwick, Augusti 16to
Jana, uxor Roberti Collet de Barwick, Novemb̄ris 12mo
Josephus filius Henrici Slayter de Winmoor, sepult Novembris 15to
Margareta Atkinson de Potterton-Lane, Novembris 23tio
Robertus Collet de Barwick, Novembris 29no
Elizabetha, uxor Zach̄ Thorp de Shippen, Decemb. 2do
Johannes, filius Radulphi Collet de Barwick, Decembris 16to
Elizabetha, uxor Johan' Ambler de Winmoor, Decembris 22do
Gulielmus Vevers de Potterton, Decembris 26to
Jonathan Taylor, filius Richardi Taylor de Barmbow carr, Januarij ult. die
Johannes, filius Joh̄an Lumb de Stanks, Februarij 3tio
Isabella Daniel de Potterton, Februarij duodecimo
Johannes, Filius Johañ Settle de Potterton, Februarij 18vo
Gulielmus Drury de Barwick, Februarij 24to
Henricus Hair de Potterton-Lane, Martij 4to
Samuel, filius Thomae Knapton de Barwick, Martij 12mo
Johannes, filius Joannis Prince de Potterton, eodem die
Matthew Barmby Gave by surrender unto Wiłł Vevers ye younger of Scholes, late of Rigton, one house and garth scituate in Scholes, and three Roods of arable lands (now in ye tenure and occupation of Wiłł Burman of Sturton, Gent.), Upon this condition, viz.: [That he, ye sd Wiłł Vevers and his heirs shall, out of ye sd premises pay ten shillings yearly and every year for ever upon ye one and twentieth day of December, unto ye poor of ye Towne of Scholes and Winmoor-side only and ye same to be distributed att ye time aboves̃d to ye s'd poor by ye said church-warden and overseer and their successors with ye assistance of

*Signifies that an affidavit was brought.

ye sd Will Vevers and his heirs for ever, paying likewise such rents and pforming such services as are thenceforth due and accustomed according to ye custom of ye sd Mannour]. As appears from ye copy of ye surrender among ye Court Rolls of Sr Thomas Gascoigne, Barnt, Lord of ye Mannor of Barwick and Scholes, made ye 4th of October, 1669, and examind ye 8th Jan., 1699, by me. Tho. Brooke, Curat' de Barwick.

SEPULT., 1697.

Alicia Shuttleworth de Scoles, inhumata erat Aprilis Octavo die
Johannes Lee de Potterton, morte praereptus repentina, sepultus Aprilis 27mo
Margareta, uxor Gulielmi Middlebrook de Stanks, Maij secundo
Maria Brown de Potterton, Maij decimo sexto
Maria, uxor Petri Shippen, Maij 24to
Robertus Horsley de Garforth moor, Junij 13tio
Maria Frankland de Garforth-moor, Junij 24to
Elizabetha, filia Josephi Hague de Barwick, Julij 17mo
Elizabetha, filia Jacobi Clough de Winmoor, Julij 21mo
Margareta Dineley, vidua de Barwick, Julij 27mo
Thomas Walker de Roundhey, Augusti 19no
Mattheus, filius Radulphi Collet de Barwick, Dec. 5to
Anna, filia Johannes Bullock de Barwick, Januarij 25to
Johannes, filius Johannis Jackson de Brownmoor, Februarij 10mo
Alicia, spuria proles Sarae Brownley et Georgij Stannyford, Februarij 25to
Maria, uxor Stephani Lodge de Roundhey, Feb. —
Alicia, uxor Gabrieli Robinson de Potterton, Februarij 25to
Anna, uxor Petri Banks de Roundhey, Martij 8vo
David Hopwood de Potterton, Martij 13tio
Sara, filia Gulielmi Morrit de Winmoor, Martij 15to
Jana Hardcastle de Barwick, Martij 19no die

SEPULT., 1698.

Josephus, filius Richardi Settle de Barwick, sep. Martij 25to
Robertus Green de Barwick, Decimo die Aprilis
Johannes Bullock de Barwick, vicessimo sexto Aprilis
Ursula Rushforth de Brown-moor, vicessimo octavo Aprilis
Anna Lund de Winmoor, Maij vicesimo quarto
Thomas Rushforth de Brown-moor, Julij Decimo quarto
Joannes, filius Johannis Appleyard de Scoles, Julij 29no
Jana, Filia Johannis Prince de Potterton, Septbris 27mo
Phoebe King de Barwick, Oct. 1mo
Thomas, Filius Christopri Whithead de Winmore, Octbris 3tio
Anna, Filia Johnis Holcroft de Barwick, Octrs 10mo
Thomas Taite de Kiddall Lane, Novbris 8vo
Will, Filius Hen. Slaytor de Winmoor, Novbris 17mo
Francisca Hopkinson de Barwick, Novbris 19mo
Gulielmus Sharphouse de Winmoor, Nov. 25to
Jana, Filia Petri Slaytor de Winmoor, Jan. 10mo
Jana Jackson De Stancks, Jan. 20mo
Robertus Watkinson De Barwick, Feb. jno

Edwardus, Filius Johannis Bullock De Barwick, Feb^{rij} 19no
Maria, Filia Thomae Tate De Kiddall Lane, Feb^{ij} 24to
Johannes West De Roundhay, Martij 3^{tio}
Gabriell Robinson de Potterton, Martij 12mo

SEPULT., 1699.

Gulielmus, Filius Henrici Dickenson de Winmoore, sep. Martij 30mo
Ursula, Filia Johannis More De Leeds, Aprilis 9no
Henricus Dickenson De Winmoore, May 1mo
Maria Turpen De Winmoore, Maij 28vo
Sara, Filia Zacharie Alsop De Shippen, Junij 12mo
Solomon Jebson De Potterton, Junij 14to
Margareta, Filia Thome Bradford De Munkhay, Junij 24to
Christopherus, Filius Thome Knapton De Barwick, Junij 28vo
Richardus Farrer De Scholes, Junij 30mo
Thomas, Filius Joĥnis Gascoigne de Parlington Armigeri, Julij 10mo
Maria Carter De Winmoor, 8^{bris} 26to
Maria, Filia Johannis Smith De Barwick, Nov^{bris} 6to
Richardus, Filius Roberti Chambers De Potterton, Dec^{bris} 6to
Sara Dineley de Barwick, vidua, Dec^{bris} 11mo
Barnardus Mawmond de Barwick, Dec^{bris} 16to
Martinus Clough de Winmoor, Dec^{bris} 25to
Jana, Filia Richardi Lumb De Winmoor, Dec^{bris} 25to
Gulielmus, Filius Samuelis Thornton De Grimesdike, Dec^{bris} 31mo
Gulielmus Tate De Scholes, Jan^{ij} 8vo
Anna Rushforth, vidua, De Brownmoor, Jan. 28vo
Hanna, uxor Thome Cooper de Scholes, Feb. 2do
Sara, uxor Roberti Doerdon de Brownmoor, Feb^{ij} 18vo
Elizabetha, Filia Johannis Ambler De Winmoor, Feb^{ij} 19no
Anna, vidua Tinsdale de Barwick, Feb^{ij} 19no
Anna, vidua Norton De Barwick, Feby 21mo
Susanna, vidua Ambler de Winmoor, Martij [? 6]
Georgius, Filius Johannis Pearson de Kidhall lane, Martij 12mo

SEPULT., 1700.

Robertus Brooke De Stancks, sep. Martij 30mo
Johannes Scalbert de Barwick, Aprilis 10mo
Johannes Kighley de Barwick, Apr. 12mo
Richardus Green de Barwick, Apr. 13^{tio}
Edvardus Filius Zacharie Thorp, Apr. 13^{tio}
Maria, uxor Johannis Pearson de Kidhall Lane head, Apr. 20mo
Anna, Filia Richardi Walton De Garthforth moor, Apr. 22do
Elizab., uxor Nich. Shippen de Barmbow, Maij 26to
Robertus Pickering de Potterton, Julij 2do
Phillippus Westerland De Scholes, Julij 6to
Maria More de Barwick, Julij 27mo
Franciscus, Filius Gulielmi Aire de Winmoor, Augusti 15to
Sara, Filia Gul. Admergill, $Sept^{bris}$ 30mo
Christophorus Ball, Oct^{bris} 18vo
Gertrud: Hudson, vidua de Barwick, Nov^{bris} 26to
Johannes Pitts De Scholes, $Decem^{bris}$ 6to
Alicia Tate De Scholes, $Decem^{bris}$ 17mo

Gulielmus Ingle De Barwick, Dec^{bris} 28vo
Josephus, Filius Thomæ Settle De Barwick, Janu^{ij} 2do
Thomas Bradford De Monckah, Jan^{ij} 10mo
Elizabetha, Filia Johannis Saynor De Barwick, Januarij 22do
Alicia, uxor Johannis Atkinson De Barwick, Feb. 7mo
Richardus, Filius Thome Potter De Potterton, Martij 9no
Elizabetha Bellhouse De Barwick, Martij 20mo

SEPULT., 1701.

Anna, uxor Gulielmi Wood De Scholes, sep. Martij 30mo
Gulielmus Lister De Roundhay, Apr^{lis} 6to
Nicholaus, Filius Nicholai Ball de Winmoor, Ap^{lis} 7mo
Anna Doerdon de Garthford moor, vid., Ap^{lis} 21mo
Gulielmus, Filius Andree Jackson De Scholes, Ap^{lis} 28vo
Anna, uxor Thome Mawd de Winmoor, Maij 16to
Richardus Robinson de Scholes, Maij 21mo
Elizabetha, uxor Radulphi Collet de Barwick, Junij 28vo
Thomas, fił Tho. Servant, ꝑciæ de Aberford, Julij 15to
Sara, Filia Jeremiæ Ball de Barwick, Julij 25to
Elizabetha, uxor Thome Briggs De Roundhay, Sept^{bris} 6to
Henricus Slaytor de Winmore, Sep^{bris} 30mo
Anna, uxor Josephi Hague de Barwick, Sept^{bris} 26to
Elizabetha, uxor Gulielmi Fawcett de Barwick, Oct^{bris} 1mo
Maria, filia Henrici Slaytor de Winmoor, Oct^{bris} 12mo
Sara, uxor Gulielmi Knapton de Barwick, Oct^{bris} 12mo
Rogerus Lunn de Brownmoore, Oct^{bris} 21mo
Elizabetha, uxor Johannis Glover de Winmoor, Nov^{bris} 20mo
Katharina, Filia Josephi Hague de Barwick, Dec^{bris} 9no
Johannes Lumb de Winmoor, Dec^{bris} 26to
[Johannes, *written in a different hand over an erasure*] Filius Johannis Gascoign de Parlington, Armigeri, Dec^{bris} 27mo
Johannes, Filius Johannis Atkinson de Kiddall lane, Jan^{ij} 25to
Anna, uxor Gul. Shenton de Barwick, Jan^{ij} 31mo
Anna, Filia Gul. Shenton de Barwick, Jan^{ij} 31mo
Maria, Filia Xtopheri Whitehead de Winmoor, Feb^{ij} 4to
Johannes, Filius Gulielmi Shenton de Barwick, Feb. 6to
Anna, uxor Johannis Wright de Barwick, Feb. 28vo
Maria Drury, vidua de Barwick, Martij 2do
Maria, uxor Gulielmi Hague de Barwick, Martij 3^{tio}

SEPULT., 1702.

Gulielmus, Filius Joshuæ Lister de Roundhey, sep. Aprilis 15to
Joannes, ffilius Joannis Howlcroft de Barwick, Aprilis 21mo
Anna, Filia Gulielmi Hemsworth de Potterton, Aprilis 22do
Maria, Filia Joannis Howlcroft de Barwick, Aprilis 23^{tio}
Henricus, Filius Nathanis Wright de Winmoor, Maij 1mo
Maria, uxor Gulielmi Vevers de Potterton, Maij 8vo
Anna, uxor Roberti Lee de Roundhey, Maij 8vo
Gulielmus Cobb, ꝑciae de Spoforth, Maij 9no
Charitas, Filia Joh^{nis} Ambler de Winmoor, Maij 27mo
[*Blank*] Black de Leeds, Junij 23^{tio}
Maria, uxor Johannis Hague De Barwick, Sept^{bris} 5to

Thomas Varley De Barwick, Sept^{bris} 8vo
Maria, uxor Gul. Winter, Sept^{bris} 16to
Maria, Filia Jacobi Barker de Shippen, Sep^{bris} 30
Maria, uxor Johannis Ellis De Barwick, Oct^{bris} 21mo
Joh^{nes}, Filius viduæ Crosland de Winmoor, Dec^{bris} 9no
Nathan, Filius Nathanis Wright De Winmoor, Feb^{ij} 8vo
Joanna, uxor Jeremiæ Ingle De Barwick, Jan^{ij} 26to
Marcus Brunton de Garthforth moor, Feb^{ij} 28vo

SEPULT., 1703.

Thomas, Filius Johannis Tarbotson de Barwick, sepult. Apr. 6to
Aña, Filia Johannis Tarbotson De Barwick, Ap. 6to
Richardus, Filius Richardi Walton De Brownmoor, Maij 18vo
Isabella, uxor Johannis Barker De Potterton, Maij 23^{tio}
Robertus Shore de Winmoor, Junij 22do
Josephus, Filius Jacobi Orton de Barwick, Julij 24to
Johannes, Filius Thomae Knapton de Barwick, Aug^{ti} 4to
Sara, Filia Richardi Thompson de Winmoor, Aug^{ti} 29no
Richardus Vevers de Scholes, Nov^{bris} 2do
Richardus, Filius Gulielmi Vevers de Scholes, Nov^{bris} 18vo
Petrus, Filius Richardi Thompson De Winmoor, Nov^{bris} 26to
Thomas, Filius Gulielmi Vevers de Scholes, Dec^{bris} 3^{tio}
Johannes, Filius Roberti Pitts De Scholes, Jan^{ij} 1mo
Georgius, Filius Thomæ Brunton De Shippen, Jan^{ij} 31mo
Maria, vidua Wilcock De Brownmoor, Feb^{ij} 5to
Elizabetha, uxor Michaelis Rush de Winmoor, Feb 20mo
Sara, Filia Samuelis Thornton De Grimesdyke, Martij 7mo
Anna, uxor Jacobi Orton De Barwick, Mar^{tij} 8vo

SEPULT., 1704.

Margareta, Filia Georgij Haste, Jun^{ris}, De Barwick, Martij 29no
Johannes Atkinson De Kiddall Lane, Maij 10mo
Jana Tate De Potterton, Junij 4to
Johannes Massey de Stocking, Junij 20mo
Juditha, Filia Stephani Hemsworth De Roundhay, Julij 12mo
Alicia Brunton, vidua, De Garthforth moor, Julij 19no
Gulielmus, Filius Johannis Ambler de Winmoor, Sept^{bris} 15to
Henricus, Filius Henrici Turner de Barmbow, Sept^{bris} 24to
Carolus, Filius Jo^{nis} Holecroft de Barwick, Sept^{bris} 27mo
Christopherus Rushton de Winmoor, Oct^{bris} 5to
Maria, uxor Georgij Wilcock de Garthforth moor, Oct^{bris} 6to
Johannes Taylor de Barwick, Oct^{bris} 15to
Michael, Filius Gulielmi Norton de Barwick, Oct^{bris} 18vo
Jacobus, Filius Johannis Holcroft de Barwick, Oct^{bris} 19no
Isabella, uxor Phinehæ Daniel de Potterton, Nov^{bris} 18vo
Eleanora, Filia Roberti Brown de Potterton, Dec^{bris} 18vo
Gulielmus, Filius Henrici Briggs de Potterton, Febr^{ij} 6to
Thomas, Filius Thomæ Robinson de Garthforth moor, Feb^{rij} 19no
Sara, uxor Thomæ Burland de Barwick, Feb^{rij} 20mo

SEPULT., 1705.

p. Susannah Ambler was buried Junij 10
4^{s} Margrett Cooper of Chappell Town was buried June the 12th

4^{s} Wm Shenton, an infant, June the 14th
4^{s} Alice, ye daughter of Stephen Hemsworth, July ye 12th, from Roundhey
4^{s} Elizab., the wife of Mark Wright of Barwick, July the 16th
4^{s} Mary Thomson, widow, from Barmbow, Aug. the 24th
John Dineley of Barwick, a poor blind man, September ye 12th
p. Elizab̄, ye wife of Robt Brown of Potterton, the same day, Sep^{t} 12°
4^{s} Mary Taylor, ye widow of John Taylor of Barwick, January 12th
4^{s} Katherine Shippen of Barmbow, Feb. ye 7th
4^{s} Sarah, the Daughter of Richard Atkinson of Roundhay, Feb. 19th
Mary Stotherd, an infant, March 18th, pauper
John Turner of Barmbow, March the 20th, pauper F.B.

SEPULTI, 1706.

Thomasin Slator of Windmore, was buried 29° Martij
Mary Hill of Barmbow, April the 19th, pauper
Elizabeth Turner of Barmbow, May ye 19th, a pauper
Sarah Dickenson of Wynmoor, May 26th
Margrett Hasslegrove, widow, June the 23, a pauper
Sam Tates wife of Kidhall Lane end, whose name was Jennet, was buryed at Barwick, August ye 25
A Child of Henry Turners, Sep^{t} the 4th, a pauper
Mary Norton, Aug. 31, a pauper
Richd Ball, Sept. 27
A child of the Widow Ayres, October 10th, pauper
Francis, the son of Tho. Brumpton, Novemb̄ 16th
Mary Eastwood, Dec. 1°
Robert Wilson of Winmoor, Dec. 8
Alice Massy, Windmore side, Dec. 29th
Mary, the Daur. of Wiłłm Sheyston, Jan. 28
Mark Wright of Barwick, Jan. the 28°
Tho. Lightfoot, Jan. 30
Robert Lee of Roundhay, Feb. 9th
[*Blank*] of John Jackson, 24th of February
George Spink of Scoles, 24 day of Feb.
Mary Scott, an infant, Feb. ye 25th
Mary Hewit, an Infant, Feb. 25
Marget, the daũr of Matt. Hewit, Feb. 28
Katherine, the wife of Wm Munsey, March 17
Alice Bullock, widow, was buryed March 21, pauper

[BURIALS], 1707.

Grace Jackson, Wid., Ap^{r}. 16
p. Frances Crosland, Ap^{r} 25
p. Anne Dawson, May 15th
Mary Waterworth, May the 16th
Frances Wilson, Widow, May 22th
Widow Wilson of Winmore was buryed May the 22, 1707
John Ambler was buryed May 25
John Ambler of Winmore, May 25
Mary, the wife of Wm Tate of Scoles, May 28th

A child of Thomas Mawe, 28 July
John Haigh, Aug. 10th, pauper
Andrew Slater, Aug. 21th
A child of Peter Slators of Windmore, 4 October
Wm, the son of Samuell Thornton, October 30th, a Twin
Thomas Owthwait, an infant, Octob. 22
Anne, the Daughter of Samuell Thornton, November the 4th
John, the son of Richard Vevers of Potterton, Novemb. 18th
John Shippen of Barmbow Carre, Feb. 22

BURYALLS, 1708.

Mary Turpin was buried June 8th
James Winter, —
Henry Turner and [*blank*] were buried, being killed in a Coale pit, 28° July. pp.
Wm Barker, Aug. 1
Anne Ayre, Aug. 14. p.
Tho. Watkinson, Spt 8
Richd. Braham, No. 27
Sam. Tate, Jan. 15
[*Blank*] Eire, Jan. 25
Mary Eastburn, Jan. 24
Anne Tinsdale, Feb. 8. p.
Wm Midlebrook, Feb. 9
Sam. Newby, Feb. 27th
Eliz. Hardisty, Feb. 28th
Eliz. Butcher, March 14th
Will Norton, March 19th. p.

[BURIALS], 1709.

George Hast, Ap. 8
John Southward, Apr 8. p.
Tho. Haigh, Apr 20
John Vevers, Apr 30
Mary, wife of Rich. Taylor, May 10th
John Dawson, May 15th
David Hewit, May 20
Humphry Morrisby, May 27
Alice Plaxton, the wife of Mr George Plaxton, Rector of Barwick, was buryed on the North side the Comunion Table in the Chancell, July 2°
Wm Knapton, July 18
A poor son of Morrisbys, Sept' 14
Henry Haworth, Octob. 3
Richard Perrot, an infant, December 9th
Susanna Hill, Dec. 21
James Clough of Winmoor, Dec, 29
Sybilla Lyster of Roundhay, Feb. 2°

[BURIALS], 1710.

Frances Battey of Scholes, Aprll 2°
John Byrdsall, 26 Feb., 1709
Anne Coupland, March 2°

Sarah Wilcock, March 8°
Bettreis Catton, Ap^{r} 13th
Alice Lyster of Scoles, May 12°
Mary, daughter of Jonathan Abbot, June 6°
Mark, son of John Ambler, June 11th
Mary, daūr of John Moorhouse of Kippax, July 7°
Wm Smith, Aug. 30°
Robert, son of James Walker, Sep^{t} 15
Elizabeth Settle, October 24
Mercy Hopwood, November 5th
John Smith, Feb. 1°
Frances, his wife, Feb. 3°
Issabella Slater, Feb. 26°
Alice Beedall, Feb. 28

[Burials], 1711.

Sarah, the wife of Nathan Wright, was buryed Apr. 19°
Jane Marshall, Ap^{r} 24
Eleanor Stonehouse of Roundhay, Ap^{r} 30
Wm Cowpland, Junr, of Pott^{r}ton, May 7th
Benjamin Pease, Juñ, June 17
Mary Stonehouse, June 23
Robert Deardon, July 27
Pentecost Haigh, July 31
Wm Blackburn, Aug. 10th, Scoles
Aquila Blackburn of Scoles, Sept. ye 5th
Elizabeth Emmerson, Oct. 1°
Rosamond Spink, Octo. 7°
Alice Prince ats Gibson, October 24
Mary Appleyard, Nov. 8°
Richd Appleyard, Nov. 16
Robert Pitts, jun., Nov. 18
Frances Shuttleworth, Novr 19
Jane Gayton, Nov. 21
Mary Backhouse, Decr 10
Roger Spink, Jan. 10
Phineas Daniel, Jan. 17
Will. Robinson, Jan. 25
Grace Owthwait, Feb. 2
Issabella Hayward, Feb. 2
Wm Mawlam, Feb. 5°
Anne Varo, Feb. 10°
John Mawd, Feb. 25

[Burials], 1712.

Widow Farrer, Ap^{r} 9th
Wm Ayre, a bastard, Ap^{r} 11th
Mary Gayton, May 12
Mary Tarbotton, May 23
Georg, son of Ben Hast, May 29
Hester Thomson, May 31°
Elizabeth Hast, June 2°

Ann Southward, June 17
Jeremiah Ball of Barwick, July 18o
Mary Vevers, July 24
Anne Stonehouse, July 27
Widd. Lee, Aug. 17th
Robert Chambers, Aug. 22
Margrett Knowles, Sept 5th
Hester Wright, Sept. 12th
Widow Pool, Decr 10
George Mawmond, Dec. 13
Frances Walker, Jan. 21
Ann Briggs, Jan. 24
Robert Ball of Barwick, Feb. 5th
Mary Fawcett, Feb. 17th
Martha Constable, March 22

BURIALS, 1713.

Anne Saynor, Decbr 3d
Ellenr Burland, Jan. 22nd
Mary Norton, Jan. 30th
Jane Taite, Feb. 4th
Esther Outhwait, Feb. 17th
Geo. Dickinson of Penwell, Feb. 10th
Geo. Dickinson of Scholes, Feb. 24th
John Hemsworth, Feb. 28

BURIALS, 1714.

Ellenr Tait, Aprill 17th
Mary, ye wife of Tho. Bradford, Ap. 25th
Jno Glover, May 3d
Frances, ye wife of Jno Dolphin, May ye 6th
Eliz. Briggs, May 21st
Sarah Hague, June 14th
Sarah Blackburn, June 15th
Martha Backhouse, June 26
Issabel Thompson, July 9th
Mary Fenton, Augt 22d
Phebe Hague, Augt 25th
Richard Thompson, Septbr 16th
Martha Jackson, Octobr 1st
Ellenr Whithead, Octbr 9th
Robert Briggs, Decbr 3d
Margarett Tarbotton, Decbr 3d
Martha Tait, Decbr 10th
Grace Sharp, Decbr 15th
Thomas Buzwick, Jan. 26th
Ralph Watson, March 5
Samuel Wright, March 7th
Jno Orton, March 17th

BURIALS, 1715.

Anne Varey, Aprill ye 5th
Anne Knowles, Aprill ye 9th

Phillis Shuttleworth, Aprill 10th
Jno Settle, Apll ye 14th
Anne Smith, Apll ye 18th
Jos. Shoosmith, Apll ye 30th
Tho. Cooper, June ye 7th
Esther Outhwait, June ye 24th
Sarah Appleyard, June ye 26th
Tho. Battey, Septembr ye 6th
Robt Brown, Septembr ye 18th
Mattw Ingle, Octobr ye 5th
Joseph Collet, Novembr ye 6th
James Outhwait, Novembr ye 7th
Eliz. Green, Decembr ye 10th
Jno. Dixon, Decembr ye 14th
Eliz. Vevers, January ye 9th
Wm Braim, January ye 23d
Ellen Walton, January ye 25th
Mary Tait, February ye 22nd
Mary Hespenall, February ye 25th
Fran. Dunnell, February ye 26th
Mary Bullock, February ye 27th

BURIALS, 1716.

Anne Brown, Aprill ye 12th
Anne, ye Dr of Jno Atkinson, May 5th
Anne Thompson, May ye 7th
Richd Bolland, May ye 12th
Richd Braim, June ye 8th
Jennet Lofthouse, Augt ye 6th
Tho. Brunton, Augt ye 13th
Wm Thompson, Augt ye 14th
Wm Thompson, Septembr ye 5th
Wm Hall, Septembr ye 9th
Jo. Binns, Septembr ye 13th
Elizabeth Gibson, Octobr 23d
Francis Shippen, Octobr 25th
Wm Wood, Decr 23d
Wm Constable, January 31st
Elizabeth Settle, February 5th
Tho. West, March ye 4th
Sarah Abbot, March 7th

BURIALS, 1717.

Wm Walton, Aprill 9th
Wm Shuttleworth, May 2nd
Elizabeth Tarbotton, June 17th
Jno, ye son of Jonas Hailey, July 7th
Geo. Dickinson, July 26th
Wm, ye Son of Wm Vevers de mor., July 29th
Mary Norton, July 29th
Alice Robinson, August 23d
Joshua, ye son of Richd Vevers, Septr 7th

Mary Scott, Septembr 15o
John Thompson, Septembr 25th
Jno Gilson, Octobr 15th
Wm Hague, Decr 17th
Mary Haist, January 18th
James, ye son of James Bullock, March ye 2nd

BURIALS, 1718.

Jane Brook of Stanks, March 27th
Richard Tarbotton hanged himself, March 29th
Anne, ye Dr of Wm Burland, June 7th
Wm, ye son of Jno Burland, July ye 1st
Sr Tho. Gascoigne, July ye 3d
Mich̄ Eastburne, July ye 7th
Tho., ye son of Jno Wood, July 26th
Esther, ye Dr of Tho. Braim, Augt 2nd
Jno, ye son of Jno Dolphin, Augt 15th
Eliza., ye Dr of Richd Braim, Augt 21st
Eliza., ye Dr of Wm Tait, Septr 22nd
Geo., ye son of Geo. Longley, Septr 23d
Hannah, ye Dr of Ja. Strodder, Octr 10th
Richd Atkinson, Octor ye 17th
Jno Stoker, November ye 12th
Hen. Briggs, November ye 24th
Wm, ye son of Geo. Thompson, Decr 10th
Lucy Sharphouse, Decr 24th
Richd Aspinwall, February the 5th
Tho. Walker, February the 25th
Geo., the son of Geo. Dickinson, March ye 8th
Godfrey Stonehouse, March 15th
Elizabeth Dickinson, March 24th
Francis Varley, Aprill ye 11th

BURIALS, 1719.

Hannah Newby, May the 14th
Elizabeth Bradley, June the 9th
Jno, ye son of Bryan Bradley, June 18th
Geo., ye son of Joseph Binns, Jũe. ye 23d
Mary, ye Dr of Richd Robinson, July 30th
John Holcroft, August the 8th
Gabriel Bradcliffe, August ye 15th
John Potter, August the 18th
John Walton, August the 20th
John Ball, Septbr the 8th
Catherine, ye Dr of Ben. Haist, Ocr 5th
Ellin Hill of Stanks, Novembr 6th
Wm Hopwood, November the 27th
Anne Powell, December the 2nd
Francis, ye son of Wm Vevers of Mork, Decr 14th
Tho. Wood, December the 24th
Alice Potter, January the 24th
Richd Settle, January the 29th

Ralph Watson, February the 9th
Elizabeth Bradford, February ye 21st
Sarah, ye D^{r} of Tho. Thompson, March 9th

BURIALLS, 1720.

Susannah, ye D^{r} of Ralph Watson, March 31st
Eliz., ye D^{r} of Geo. Wood, Aprill ye 3^{d}
Elizabeth Stoker, Aprill ye 8th
Eliza., ye D^{r} of Edwd Maxwell, Ap^{l} ye 8th
Rich^{d}, the son of Tho. Braim, Ap^{l} 16th
Matthew Norton of Roundhey, Ap^{l} 24th
Wm Vevers, Gent., of Scholes, May ye 1st
Ellin, the wife of Jo. Hague, May 2nd
Susannah, ye wife of Tho. Hill, June 9th
Jno, the son of Wm Hague, June ye 18th
Thos Knapton, July the 22nd
Ruth, the wife of Jos. Maud, Augt 23^{d}
Thos Eary, August ye 30th
Sarah, the wife of Step^{n} Hemsworth, Sep^{tr} ye 10th
Jno Jackson, Septemb^{r} the 10th
James, the son of Richard Vevers, September ye 21st
Richard, the son of Tho. Shillitoe, October the 9th
Catherine, the wife of Wm Dibb, October the 27th
John, the son of Jos. Maud, October the 30th
Mark Denison, Novemb^{r} 17th
Mary, the wife of Jos. Hague, Decr the 8th
Thomas Scott, Decem^{r} ye 11th
Elizabeth, ye wife of Richard Slaytor, Decem^{br} ye 27th
Wm Braim, January the 26th
Mary Huit, January the 29th
Tho. Popplewell, February ye 14th
Jno Fentiman, Clerk, February 15th
Benjn Telford, February ye 18th

BURIALLS, 1721.

Thos, ye son of Jno Littlewood, June ye 12th
Jane Clough, June ye 26th
Sarah Ambler, July the 10th
Sarah Holmes, August the 10th
Mary, the wife of Timothy Jackson, Augt ye 14th
William Scope, Septem^{br} ye 18th
Francis Lee, September the 21st
Mary Atkinson of Roundhey, Sep. 24th
Jane Lumb, October the 19th
John, the son of Richd Burland, Novem^{br} 17th
Amy, the wife of Dan. Huit, Novem^{br} 24th
Michael Rush, Decem^{br} the 3^{d}
Prudence Hardey, Decem^{br} ye 7th
Mary, D^{r} of George Thompson, Decem^{br} 11th
Willm, son of William Lumb, Jan^{ry} ye 28
Ann, D^{r} of James Bullock, Jan. ye 31st
Thos, ye son of Jno Dolphin, Feb^{ry} ye 7th

Barbara Jewett, Feb. the 18th
Samuell Robinson, Febry the 21st
Moses Settle, Febry the 26th
Stephen, the son of Lawrence Milner, February the 26th
William Heresie, March the 4th
John Abbot, March the 5th
Mary, Dr of John Mounsey, March 13th
Mary Brunton, March ye 16
Lady Mary Gascoigne, March ye 5th

BURIALLS, 1722.

Ann, the Dr of Jno Mounsey, March the 25th
Eliz., the Dr of Rich Robinson, Aprill the 1st
Catherine, the Dr of Benjn Haist, Aprill the 2nd
Wm, the son of Wm Johnson, Aprill the 27th
Eliz., the Dr of Rob. Knapton, May the 13th
Eliz., the Dr of Jno Burland, May the 19th
Mary, the Dr of Rich Clark, June the 24th
Wm, the son of Mattw Watson, July the 25th
Wm Massie, August the 20th
Wm Taylor, August the 29th
Rebekah, the Dr of Rich Robinson, Sep. the 16
Ann, the Dr of Jno Sharphouse, Septr the 17th
Ann, the wife of Wm Wardman, Sep. ye 23d
Mary, the wife of Tho. Knapton, Sep. ye 23d
Ellin Briggs, September the 26th
Jno, the son of Jno Bean, Octobr the 20th
Jno Ambler, November the 4th
Jos., the son of Henry Dunnell, Novem. 18th
Mary, the Dr of Mattw Watson, Novem. 29th
David, the son of Jno Wilson, Decembr the 29th
Rich Burland, Jan. the 26th
Martha, the wife of Jno Mounsey, Feb. the 9th
Ann, the Dr of Rich Braim, Feb. the 11th
Catherine, the wife of Rob. Elston, Feb. the 18th
Rich, the son of Jno Atkinson, March ye 13th
Fees belonging to the Clark in the parish of Barwick in Elmitt

	s.	d.
Licence, Wedding	5	0
Wedding by Banns	1	0
Burial	0	6
Churchings	0	4
Registring	0	6
Psalm at Funeral	0	6

BURIALS, 1723.

Elizabeth, the daughter of Robt Smith, March 25th
Mary Prince, Aprl 12th
Eliz., the Dr of Thos Braim, Apl 24th
Richd Shippen, Apl 30th
Thos Maud, June 14
Sr John Gascoigne, Bart, June 16th

Richd Andrews, Schoolmaster and Clerk, June 18th
Leonard Gayton, June 20th
Phebe, the wife of Thos Braim of Barnbow, Augt 14
James, the son of Mr Richard Vevers of Potterton, Augt 15
Willm Morrit, Augt 1st
George, the son of Mr John Plaxton, Septr 16th
Richd Robinson the younger, Septr 19th
Ann Ball of Potterton, Octob^{r} 14th
Jane, the wife [of] Francis Walker of Barnbow, Novr 3
Jane, ye daughter of Francis Walker of Barnbow, Oct. 31st
John, the son of Willm Cooper of Pontefract, Nov. 6th
Jane, the D^{r} of Willm Kneedson of Barn-Bow, Novr 9th
Thomas Outhwaite of Scholes, Novr 22^{d}
Thomas, the son of Willm Neeson of Barnbow, Novr 23
Elizabeth Thompson of Stanks, Novr 27th
John Jackson of Winmore, Decr 17th
Debora Robinson of Garforth-moor side, Decr 31
Mary, the Daughter of Richard Vevers of Potterton, Jany 21, 1723/4
Benjamin, the son of Thomas Braim of Roundhey, Jany 31st

BURIALS, 1724.

Richard Robinson, sen' of Barwick, Ap^{l} 19th
George Johnson of Barnbow, May 6th
Mary, the wife of John Tayte of Scholes, May 7th
Thomas Braim of Roundhay, Jun. 23
Mich^{l}, the son of Thos Wright of Scholes, July 25th
George, the son of Benjam. Haist of Barwick, July 29
Margret Watkinson of Garforth moorside, Septr 6th
Richd Varley of Barwick, Novr 1st
Elizth, the Daug^{r} of Mat^{w} West of Roundhey, Nov. 5
W^{m}, the son of J^{n} Thompsõ of Garforth-moor, Novr. 14
Robt Bremen of Brown Moor, Novr 18th
Mary, the Daug^{r} of Mat^{w} West of Roundhey, Novr 22^{d}
Jane Robinson of Scholes, Novr 27th
Frances Bean of Barwick, Novr 29th
Robt Nelson of Barwick, Decr 2^{d}
John, the son of J^{n} Bean, Decr 17th
Thos, the son of Dan. Germain of Barwick, Jan. 8th
Wm Mounsey of Winmoor Top, Feby 25th
Mary, D^{r} of J^{n} Briggs of Roundhey, March 2^{d}

BURIALS [1725].

Issabell Sympson of Garforth moor side, Ap^{l} 27th
Rich^{d}, son of Thos Ball of Potterton, May 19th
John Hardesty of Barw^{k}, May 28th
Ann Ball of Potterton, July 1st
Willm, son of Samuel Dodgion of Roundhay, Augt 30th
Thomas, the son of Thomas Wright of Scholes, Oc^{r} 16
Wm Lawson of Pot', Sep. 1
Thos, son of Thos Walker, Octob^{r} 29th
Ab^{m} Shippen of Barnbow, Novr 28th
Jan. 6. George, son of George Tompson of Scholes

Jan. 24. Jane, wife of Richard Ellis
Jan. 27. Thomas, son of Mark Thornton, Winmoor side
Feb. 26. Mr William Ellis of Kiddal
[*Blank*] son of Wm Carbut of Potterton, 1st Jany.
Richd Smith of Barwk, Feb. 21st
Richd Taite of Kidhall Laine End, March —

BURIALLS [1726].

Jn, son of Jn Adkinson of Barwick, Apl 8th
John Taite of Scholes, June 3d
Peter Shippen of Winmoor. Jun. 12
Paul Mounsey of Winmoor, son of Jn Mounsey, Jun. 22
Frances, Dr of late Peter Shippen of Winmoor, June 23
Ann Germain, wife of Danl Germain of Barwick, July 17
John Pearson of Kidhall Lain end, Augt 21
Jane Pattison of Kidhall Lain End, 16 Septr
Ann, wife of James Typling, Novr 11
John, son of Thos Wood of Garforth moorside, Ocr 22
Mary, Dr of Willm Prince of Potterton, Decr 2d
I. d. Alice Hemsworth of Pot'
John, son of Parcivel Baccas of Abberforth, Jany 25
Wm Benton of Garforth Moorside, Jan. 28
Saml, son of Wm Taite of Scholes, March 2d

BURIALS, 1727.

Thos, son of Robt Smith of Barwick, buried 30th Apl
Michl, son of Richd Taite late of Kidhall lain end, Apl 30
Wm, son of Jn Adkinson of Barwick, May 22d
Martha, Bastard daughtr of Jane Bell and of Michl Sharp, the supposed father, of Barwick, 22d May
Mary, daugr of Jn Adkinson of Barwick, May 27th
Edward West of Roundhey, June 1st
John Ambler of Hirst Moor, Jun. 14th
Willm, son of John Hague of Barwick, Jun. 17th
Rachel Batty of Stanks, Jun. 27th
Ester, Dr of Richd Clerk of Barwick, Jun. 30
An, Dr of Robt Brown Junr of Penwell, July 9th
Elizth, Daughr of late Richd Tarbotton of Barwick, July 20th
Sarah, Dr of Josh Bins of the Hill top, July 21
i: d: Sarah, Dr of Robt Brown, Jun', of Penwell
Christr, son of Christopher Ambler of the Hill top, Augst 11th
Thos Hill of Brown Mr., Augt 24th
Mary, wife of Willm Holmes of Roundhay, Augt. 28
Willm Renton of Bar., Septr 3
Ann, Daugr of Henry Donwell of the Hill top, Septr 5th
John Maud of Penwell, Septr 17.—Recd of Dor. Maud 10s for a Mortuary for her late Husband, by D. Dawson, Cur.
George Hardwick of Leeds, Octr 24
Ann, wife of Thos Thompson of Garforth moor, Octr 26th
Peter Slater of Winmoor, Novr 8th
Matw, son of Matw Watson of Barwick, Decr 7th
Wm Shenton of Barwick, Decr 8th

James, son of James Norton of Barwick, Decr 10
Ann, the Bastard child of Sarah Pattison of Kidhall lain End, Dr 10
Ann Teasdale of Winm̃ Decr 14th
Matw Robinson of Garforth-moor, Decr 15th
Richd Ellis of Barwick, Jany 7th
Ralph Collet of Barwick, Jany 9th
Mary Hague, widw, Relct of Wm Hague, late of Barw., Jan. 24th
Mary, Dr of Willm Hague late of Barw., Jan. 31st
Matw Coates of Cross-gates, Feby 14th
Jn Greenwood of Leeds, found dead upon Winmoor, Feby 26th
Thomas Wright of Scholes, March 10th

BURIALS, 1728.

John Butcher of Sch:, Apl 30th
John, son of Robt Fenton of Potterton, Apl 20th
Andw, son of Robt Fenton of Potterton, 23 Apl
Jn Maud of Potterton, Apl 28
Ellinor Wilson of Barwick, Apl 30th
Grace Chambers of Potterton, May 2d
Mary, Daugr of late Richd Taite of Kidhallain End, May 7
James Bullock of Barwick, May 8th
June, 1728. Recd of Mary Shenton of Barwick, Wid:, 10s for 1 Mortuary for her late Husband. E: B.
Mary Knapton of Barwick, May 11th
Michl Prince of Potterton, Jun. 3d
Dorathy Taite of Kidhall Lain End, July 13
Mr Jn Shippen of Winmoor, July 30th
Wm Nesham of Barnbow, Augt 15
Benjn son of late Thomas Wright of Scholes, Augt 20
Stephen Hemsworth of Roundhey, Augt 21
Mary Thorns of Barwick, Septr 2
Elizh Norfolk of Potterton, Sepr 9
Moses Bremin of Barnbow, Septr 17
Mary Becket, Octobr 17
Elizth, Dr of George Thompson of Scholes, Octr 21
Wm Boardley of Kidhall lain, Novr 2d
John Ball of Pott', Nov. 20
Francis Walkker of Barnb', Novr 22
i: d: Wm Settle of Potterton
i: d: Jn Adkinson of Barwick
John Sikes of Bar:, Novr 23
Jan: 13, Lanct Ambler oth Low moor
Mary Hebden of Stockall, Jany 19
Jn Settle of Potterton, Jan. 25
Jn Prince of Potterton, Jan: 26
Mrs Elizth Hespinal of Roundhay, Janr 30
Jane Thomspon [*sic*] of Sch̄, Feb. 4
Jn, son of Tho: Preston of Bar:, Feb. 9
i. d. Thos Settle from Seacroft
Ann, Wife of Wm Dickinson of Scholes, March 5
Francis, son of Major Bradley f[r]om Stanks, Mar: 16th

J^{n} Hemsworth from Parlinton, March 19th

1729, [BURIALS].

Richd Outhwaite of Scho', March 28th
Richd Lumb of Brownm̃, Ap^{l} 3
John Sharphouse, Ap. 12
Mary Admagill of Pot., Ap. 12
Roger Horsforth of Penwell, Ap^{l} 15
Abm. Abbot of Barwick, Ap. 17
Thos Maxfield of Partley Bridge, slain in a colepit, Ap. 19
Saml Thornton of Grimesdike, Ap. 20
Elizth, Daughter of James Worsman of Lazincroft, Ap. 23
W^{m}, son of Jos^{h} Brown of Roundhey, May 3^{d}
May 7, An Thornton of Grimsd.
Jacob Pease of Grimsdike, May 11th
i. d. Wm Dickinson of Scholes
John, son of Mark Robinson of Potterton, June 1st
W^{m}, son of James Norton, June 4th
Dorathy Wood of Barw^{k}., Jun. 16
June 20, Mat^{w}, son of Mat^{w} Norton of Roundhey
Susanna, Daughter of Henry Blackburn of Brown Moor, July 3^{d}
John, son of Thos Merrit of Cross Gates, Augst 14th
Elizth, wife of Edward Batty, Augst 16
Ann, wife of Mat^{w} Jackson, Augst 19th
Sarah, wife of Mr Wm Vevers of Mawrick, Sept. 24th
Agnes, Daughter of Wm Thompson of Barnbow Car, Octr 23^{d}
Martha Burrel of Barw^{k}, Novr 9
Sarah, the wife of Wm Clerkson of Roundhey, Novr. 20
Mary Sikes of Barwick, Novr 28
Elizth, D^{r} of Robert Land, January 21st
Mary, wife of Richd Vevers of Barwick, Decemb^{r} 12
Margaret, wife of late Jn. Earle of Weatherby, Decr. 23
Elizth, wife of Jn. Barker of Barwick, Decr 27
Ann, the wife of Joseph Mawd of Winmoor, Decr 28
Ellinor Sampson of Potterton, Jany 18
Edwd Sikes of Bar^{wk}, Jany 25
Robert, son of Robt. Land, Jany 30th
Mary Morrisby of the Low Moor, Feb. 2
I. d. Margaret, the wife of Christ. Whitehead of the Low Moor
Elizabeth, Daughter of Mr Wm Vevars of Scholes, was Bur^{d} Feb. 26th
*Mr Edmund Barneby, Rector of Barwick, dy'd at his own seat at Brockhampton, in Herefordshire, Mar. 9th, 17$\frac{29}{30}$

1730.

Robt Thorns of Barwick, May 4th
Margret, wife of John Slater of Low Moor, May 5
Mary, Daughter of Math^{w} Tipling of Stanks, May 27
Mary Donwell of Barwick, Augst 4th
Joseph Hague of Barw^{k}, Augs^{t} 4th
Wm Taylor of Barwick, Aug. 17th

*Rector 1721—1730. Son of William Barneby of London, gentleman. Wadham College, Oxford, B.A. 1710, M.A. 1713.—Foster's *Alumni Oxon.*

John Mounsey from The Topp of Winmoor, Augt 17th
Francis, son of James Walker of Roundhey, Septr 14th
John Tailford, buried the 5th of October
Esther, the wife of Thomas Settle of Barwick, Octob^{r} 14th
Jn. Massy of Penwell, Decr. 28
Joseph, son of John Appleyard of Scholes, Jany 22
Jane, D^{r} of John Ambler of Winmore, Feby 24
Hannah, wife of Benjamin Haist of Barwick, Feb. 27
Saml Dodgiõ of Roundhay, March 4th
Ann, wife of Richd Taylor of Barwick, March 24

1731, [BURIALS].

Sarah, wife of Thos Haist from Kidhall Lain End, March 30th
Mary, the wife of Joseph Braim of Roundhay, Ap^{l} 3^{d}
Mary, D^{r} of Mat^{w} Norton of Roundhay, Ap^{l} 9th
Mahitabel, wife of John Kirkam of Barnbow, Ap^{l} 14
Thos, son of John Adkinsõ of Barwick, May 29
Jane, Daughter of Francis Chapman of Brown-Moor, Jun. 13
Ann Tascard of Barwick, Jun. 21
Willm, son of Richd Vevers of Barwick, July 22
Mary, D^{r} of Thomas Haist of Kidhall Lain End, July 30th
Mary Shippen of Barnbow, July 30
Thomas, son of Mat^{w} Jackson of Barwick, Septr 3^{d}
Mary, D^{r} of James Bullock of Barwick, Septr 14th
William Dawson of Kiddal was B^{d} at Sherburn, June 30th
Ab^{m}, son of Robert Brown of Barnbow, Septr 19
Ann, Daughter of Edwd Batty of Barw^{k}, Septr 18th
Margaret, wife of Richd Lumb of Barwick, Octr 1st
Sarah, wife of Thos Smith of Brown Moor, Oc^{r} 13
John, son of Robt Smith of Barwick, Octob^{r} 19th

*I, Henry Perkins, Clerk, do declare my unfeigned Assent and Consent to all and every thing contained and p'scribed in the Book Intitled the Book of Common prayer and Administration of the Sacraments and other Rites and Ceremonies of the Church according to the use of the Church of England, Together with the Psalter or Psalms of David pointed as they are to be said or sung in Churches and the form and Manner of making, ordaining and Consecrating of Bishops, Priests, and Deacons.

Memorand^{m} upon Sunday, ye 28th day of March, 1731, Henry Perkins, Rector of Barwick in Elmett in the county of York, did read the Common prayers in the Parish of Barwick afores^{d}, both in the aforenoon and afternoon according to the form and order prescrib'd and directed by the book intitled the Book of Common prayer, &c. And immediately after his said reading of the same made a Declaration of his unfeigned Assent and consent to all the matters therein contained.

Memor^{dm}, That the s^{d} Henry Perkins did the same day and year read the 39 Articles of Religion (agreed upon by ye Archbishops and Bishops of both provinces and the whole Clergy in Convocation holden at London, A.D. 1562) in the Parish Church of

*Rector 1730—36. Son of Thomas Perkins of Hilmorton co. Warwick. Trinity Coll., Oxford; B.A. 1718, M.A. 1721.—Foster's *Alumni*

Barwick in Elmet aforesd during the time of Divine service, And after his sd reading thereof did declare his unfeigned Assent and Consent to all the things therein contained, In the presence of us, who attest the same here under our hands this 28th day of March, A. D. 1731.

David Dawson, Timothy Jackson, Clark
John Smeaton, } Churchwardens. Simon Wood
George Haist }

Ann, Dr of William Dickinson, late of Scho', Octr 19th
Jn Varey of Scholes, Octr 19th
Dorathy, Daughtr of Wm Neesham, late of Barnbow, Octr 20
George, son of Geo. Lyster of Sch., Novr 13
Sarah, Daugr of Willm Butler of Sch, Decr 13
Benj, son of Wm Neesham, late of Barnbow, Decr 15th
John, son of John Man of Hunslet, Decr 17th
Sarah, wife of Robt Brown of Barnbow, Dec. 21st
Mary, wife of Jonas Haley of Schs, Jan. 10
Richd Burrell of Barw., Feb. 14th
Elizth Lee of Garforth Mr, Feby 16
Joseph Cook of Stanks, Son of late Richd Cook, Feb. 19
Thos Robinson of Garforth Moor, Feby 29
Sarah, Dr of Francis Wilson of Scholes, March 2d
John Dolfin of Garforth moor side, March 15

1732, BURIALS.

Robert Brown of Stanks, April 28th
Thos Dawson from Lazincroft, Apr'l 14
Elizth, Daughr of Thos Merrit of Winmoor, Aprill ye 18
Mary, Dr of William Mather of Winmoor, April 24
Willm Harper of Stanks, 26 of Ap'l
Jn Baynes of Lazincroft, May ye 5th
Mary, ye Daughter of William Carbott of Potterton, May ye 11th
Sarah, Daughtr of Thos Haist from Kidhall Lane End, May —
Jn, son of Jno Benson of Stanks, May 30th
Mary, Bastard Child of Sarah Pattisson, June 2nd
Elizabeth, ye wife of Timo Smith of Barwick, July 19th
Mary, Daughter of Joseph Tailford of Barwick, July ye 22
Michael Thackwray of Barwick, July ye 22
Eliz:, wife of Robert Ball of Barwick, Sepr 2d
Mary, the wife of John Pearson, late of Kidhall Lane End, Octobr 12
James Wilcock of Barwick, 31 of October
John, son of Martin Wormills of Roundhay, ye 2d Day of Novembr
Ann, Daugr of William Appleyard of Barwick, November ye 28o
Joseph, son of Joseph Stephenson from Cross Gates, December 8th
Elizth, Daugr of Robert Land of Winmoor, Dr 10
Mary Brunton of Garforth Moorside, Decemr 13th
Mr David Dawson, Vicar of Abberford and Curate of Barwick, Decr 23
Mr Samuel Oates from Potterton, Decembr 24o
Ann, wife of Laurence Milner of Grimes Dike, Feby 11th
Richd Shittleworth of Scholes, Feb. 16
Laurence Milner of Grimes Dike and Lawrence his son, buried in one Grave, March 1st

Jane, the wife of Francis Chapman of Brown moor, the 18th of March

1733, Burials.

Agnes, the Daughter of Benjamin Rawlinson, buried April ye 9th
Margret, wife of George Haist of Barwick, May 11
Mary, the Daughter of Francis Wilson of Scholes, July the 16th
Ann West of Roundhey, July 21
Wm Shittleworth, July 28
Thos Shillito of Potterton, July 29
John, the son of Mathew Norton of Roundhay, August 19th
Thomas Settle of Barwick, Septemb^{r} 3^{d}
Anna, wife of Fra[n]cis Holmes of Barwick, Decr 14th
i. d. Alice Wilson of Barwick, wid^{w} woman
Mary, Daught^{r} of George Lister of Scholes, Decr 17th
Ann, wife of John Thompson of Stanks, Jan. 17th
[*blank*] of John Bradley of Winmoor head, Feby 28th
Ellin Moxon, Mar. 8th

Burials, 1734.

John Chetham of Pontefract, March 27th
Philip Smith, April 3
Mr Richd Vevers of Potterton, Ap^{l} 29
Crispin, the son of John Bean of Barwick, May 24th
Ann, Widow, Relict of John Pepper, late of Parlington, Jun. 4th
Mary Lambert of Winmoor, June 9th
Ann Knapton of Barwick, Jun. 12
Martha, D^{r} of Thos Settle, Jun., 12th
Ann Strother of Barwick, Jun. 14
Jonathan Bell of Scholes, July 5th
Ellin, Daught^{r} of Robt Land, Augt 11th
Mathew Issot, Septr 12
Rich^{d}, son of George Watson of Barwick, Novr 23^{d}
Willm, son of Willm Vevers of Scholes, Gent^{n}, Decr 29th
Nicholas, son of Nicolas Warrin of Barnbow, Jany 21st
Doratha Mather of Austhorp, slain in a sand Pitt upon the Low Moor, Buried March 6th
Susan Gullis of Barw.

Burials, 1735.

John Burland of Potterton, Householder, June 21
Frances, Daug^{r} of John Benson of Cross Gates, Joyner, June 26th
Mary, Daughter of Willm Johnson of Leeds, Paver, July 18
Timothy Smith of Barw^{k}, Blacksmith, July 31st
James, son of Wm Johnson of Kidhall Lain, Husbandman, Septr 12th
Penelope, Daughter of Mr Perkins, Rect^{r} of Barw^{k}., Novemb^{r} 12th
Mary, wife to Joshua Lyster of Roundhay, Husbandman, Novr 15th
John, son of John Varey of Scholes, Labor^{r}, Nov. 18
Ann, wife of Saml Dodgion of Roundhay, Carpinter, Novr 28th
Susan Gullis of Barwick, spinster, Decr 25th
Ann, Daughter of Thomas Adkinson of Hirst Moor, Lab^{r}, Decr. 28
Margret, Daughter of Willm Hemsworth of Garforth, Collier, Decem^{r} 31
Jonathan, son of Jonathn Bell of Barwick, Laber^{r}, Feby 2^{d}
Mary, wife of James Walker of Roundhey, Lab^{r}, Feb. 3^{d}

Saml Scafe of Grimsdike, Lab^{r}, Feby 11th
Mary, Daughter of Benjn Rawlinson of Barwick, Lab^{r}, Feby 11th
James, son of Thomas Wood of Brownmoor, Lab^{r}, Feby ye 28th
James Walker of Rounday, Labourer, March ye 18th

1736, Burials.

Elizabeth, Daughter of Gabriel Taylor of Barnbow, bury'd March 31st, Lab^{r}
Gabriel, the son of Gabriel Taylor of Barnbow, Lab^{r}, April ye 6th
Richard Taylor of Barwick, Husbandman, April 23
Eliz., wife of Thomas Knapton of Barwick, Carpenter, May 16th
Timothy Jackson of Barwick, Parish Clark and Schoolmaster, May ye 20th
Ellen, Daughter of Joseph Beck of Winmoor, Lab^{r}, May ye 30th
Benjamin, son of Benjamin Haist of Barwick, Yeoman, Augt 4th
Thomas Maud of Potterton, son of John Maud, 10th of August
Jane Slaytor, a poor Woman of Winmoor, bury'd August 17th
Richard Vevers of Barwick, Yeoman, August 26th
Mary, the Daughter of John Atkinson of Winmoor, Lab^{r}, September ye 14th
Margret Gibbon, a poor Woman from Lime Kiln Gate, near Hubberley, Septr 15th
Thomas, son of William Dixon of Scholes, Taylor, December ye 10th
Sarah, Daughter of Thomas Haist of Kidhall lane end, Inn-holder, Decemb̄ ye 15th
James, son of Charles Hargrave, Collier, December ye 22^{d}
John Holdsworth of Bramham, Labourer, slain by the fall of a Tree in Whittle Carr, buryed December ye 27
Mary, Daughter of Thomas Donwell, Weaver, January ye 3^{d}
William, son of John Taite of Barwick, Mason, January ye 4th
Mary Horsfield, a poor woman from Penwell, January ye 27th
Mary, the wife of late Richard Vevers of Potterton, Tanner, Feby ye 26th
Alice, the Daughter of John Waite of Barwick, Taylor, March ye 18th
Return'd at the Visitation at Tadcaster, June ye 30th, 1737. To John Crutchley, Col^{r}, Moneys collected upon ye sev^{l} Briefs within the Parish of Barwick (viz.):—

		s.	d.
For	Royston, ye summ	4	7
ditto	Mobberley	4	4¾
ditto	Swalsham Prior	3	2½
ditto	Cobham	4	4
d^{o}	Walton in ye Woulds Chu^{r}	3	0
ditto	S. John, Wapping	3	8
ditto	Houghton Regis	5	9
ditto	Castle Hays	3	0
ditto	Houghton Church	2	1
ditto	Pendle Chappel	4	0
		£1 18	0¼

Burials, 1737.

Mary Butcher of Scholes, widow, April ye 7th
Eliz^{h}, the wife of Alexander Thompson of Barnbow, Yeoman, May ye 6th
Edmund Lumb, Flax-dresser, May ye 24th

John, ye son of Martin Whitehead of Garforth moor, Collier, June ye 25th

Jane, the wife of Thomas Wood of Brown moor, Labr, July ye 6th

Sarah, the daughter of John Bradley of Winmoor, Labr, July ye 10th

Miriam Coates, a poor Woman from Winmoor, July ye 14th

Hanah, Daughter of Samuel Robinson of Garforth moor, Collier, August ye 8th

Isaac, son of Isaac Hall of Kidhall Lane end, Gelder, October ye 7th

Andrew Jackson of Scholes, Yeoman, October ye 8th

Richard Haist from Allerton in the Parish of Kippax, Yeoman, October ye 10th

Eliz., Daughter of William Burland of Barwick, Webster, Octob ye 28th

Mary, wife of Wm Appleyard of Barwick, Labr, Novr 12th

Ann Walsh of Garforth moor side, a poor Woman, Novr ye 18th

Elizh Jackson, a poor Widow of Brownmore, November ye 24th

Isabella Hague, a poor Woman, Decemr ye 29th

Susannah, the wife of the Revd Doctr Felton, Rectr of Barwick, Febry 10th

Michael, the son of Timothy Turnpenny of Winmoor, Labr, Febry 28th

Ann Graveley, a Widow Woman of Barwick, late of Halton, Mar. 18

BURIALS, 1738.

Samuel, the son of Samuel Dodgson of Roundhay, April ye 10th

Eliz. Wood of Potterton, Apl. 20

James, the son of Wm Bell of Winmoor, Taylor, April ye 23

James, the son of Thomas Popplewell of Winmoor, labr, May the 5th

Know all men by these presents that I, William Milner of Leeds in the county of York, Esqr, do hereby give, grant and convey unto John Daniel and John Bean, the present Churchwarden and Overseer of the Poor for the Township of Barwick in Elmet, and their Successors for ever, All those three Cottages lyeing in Potterton in the Parish of Barwick aforesaid, which I lately purchased of Mr William Vevers (that is to say) One Cottage and Garth, now in the possession of Widow Shillitoe, at the Rent of Seventeen shillings a year, One other Cottage in the possession of William Carbot, at the rent of ten shillings a year, And one other Cottage, lately in the possession of William Carver, at the rent of Eight shillings a year, The Rents of the whole amounting to one Pound fifteen shillings a year, with all my Right, Title, Interest and Property therein, yet nevertheless in Trust and for the use, Benefit and advantage of the Poor of the Township of Barwick aforesaid, either for some of the Poor of Barwick to live in, or the Rents and Profits of the said three Cottages to be received by the said Churchwarden and Overseer and distributed amongst such of the Poor of Barwick as are thought to be the greatest objects of Charity. Given under my hand and Seal, this Eleventh Day of May, 1735. William Milner

Sealed and Delivered in the presence of us, Benj. Haist Wm Read

Feb. ye 23d, 1707-8. Reced. then of the Minister and Churchwardens of Barwick in Ellmett For Spillsby Brieffe £00 09 07½

Item ffor Littleport Breiffe	00 09 08
Item ffor Southam Breiffe	00 08 00
Reced p me	£01 07 03½

W. Wilson, Collect[r]

November the 7th, 1708. Rec[d] then from the Minister of Barwick in Elmet the summe of Fiue shill and 4[d] for the Breif for Lisburn and Fower Shill and Two pence for the brief of Aconbury cum Weston Com Huntingd. I say rec[d] in the whole Nine shills and sixpence for the use of my M[r] William Wilson, of the Burrough of Stafford, Coll[r] of the said Breifs by mee. } 00 09 6

his Mark

Tho. T Myott

October 25th, 1719. In pursuance of an Agreem[t] made the 17th Day of July, in the Year 1716. I do by these presents give, grant and convey to Richard Taylor of Barwick in Elmet, a Seat in the fourth Stall from the Pulpit, lying and being on the North Side in the said Church, formerly in the Possession of Robert Oddy, to him and his heirs for ever, in lieu of a Seat w[ch] I have inclosed of the said Richard Taylors, to have, hold and possess as entirely, freely and Amply as I can convey away the said seat to all intents and purposes whatsoever, For which reason I have caused this declaration to be entered into the Register Book of the said Parish, to the intent y[t] no dispute or controversie for the future may ever ensue about the said seat. As witness my hand the day and year above written.

W[m] Vevers.

Witness to these presents, John Plaxton, Jos. Dixon.

October 25th, 1719. In pursuance of an Agreem[t] made the 17th Day of July, in the year 1716, I do by these presents give, grant and convey to W[m] Vevers, Gent., of Scholes, a seat in the third Stall from the Pulpit, lying and being on the North side in the Church of Barwick in Elmet, formerly in the Possession of Jn[o] Taylor, to him and his heirs for ever in lieu of another seat, w[ch] the said W[m] Vevers hath given me in the fourth Stall from the Pulpit, formerly in the Possession of Robert Oddy, to have, hold, and possess as entirely, freely and amply as I can convey away the said seat to all intents and purposes whatsoever, For which reason I have caused this declaration to be entered into the Register Book of the said parish, to the intent y[t] no disupte or controversie for the future may ever ensue about the said seat. As witness my hand the day and year above written. Rich. Taylor.

Witnesses to these presents, John Plaxton, Joseph Dixon.

Barwick in Elmet Churchwardens Elected and chosen on Easter Sunday, 1692.

W[m] Collett
W[m] Watson

The overseers of the poor, Chosen on Easter Sunday, 1692.

Barnard Mawmond
W[m] Worfolke

John Ball
Robt Lee

1693
Marke Wright
Richard Braime
Thomas Norfolke
Robert Wilsonne

1694
Jeremiah Ball
Thomas Ball
Benjamine Pease
Matt^{w} Norton

1695
William Knapton
John Lumbe
William Coapland
William Watson

1696
Jno Taylor
Tho. Hardisty
Will Dickinson
Will Braim

1697
Jno Hardisty
Jno Pearson
Zach Thorp
Rich Atkinson

1698
Rob Thorns
John Atkinson
Mat. Watkinson
Will Hargrave

1699
Wm Hague
Sam: Tait
Jno Massie
Sam. Dodgson

1700
Tho. Settle
Wm Vevers
Wm Middlebrook
Tho. West

Sam. Tate

1693
William Ingle
Willm Taylor
Willm Admergill

1694
Wm Hauge
Henry Beedall
Sam. Tate, iu.

1695
Rich. Robinson
Wm Vevers of Sco.
John Settle

1696
Jer. Ball
Zac. Thorp
Jno Ball

1697
Rob Wansley
Nath^{n} Wright
Tho. Ball

1698
Tho. Settle
Ben. Peas
Will Copland

1699
Geo. Haist
Jno Lofthouse
Tho. Brunton

1700
Rob Thorns
Phin: Daniel
Geo: Spink

Constables sworn at Micalmass Court in

1690
Robt. Thornes

1691.
Thomas Settle

1692
William Hague

1693
Richard Varley

1695
George Hast

1696
Richard Smith

1697
Willm Collet

1699 and 1700
Rich. Robinson

1694
William Ingle

Memorand that the Lease of the House upon London Bridge was lett to Mr Knapp of Haberdasher-hall, London. Edmund Barneby, Rector, Benjamin Haist, Richard Cook, John Burland, and John Briggs, Churchwardens for the present year one Thousand Seven Hundred and Twenty, at Eight pound ten shillings p annum.

On the front Cover.

The Stones in the Tyth Lath wall were found among the Rubbish and put there by Mr George Plaxton, Rector, June the 24th, 1705

Magister Richardus Burnham hanc domum hic fieri voluit anno Domini 1440. Merci Jesu.

The inscriptions under the 2 Statues at the West end of Barwick Church :—Orate pro Henrico Vavasour qui dedit Lapides. Orate pro Richardo Burnham qui dedit decem Marcas ad aedificandum hoc campanile.

In the West Window of the Church is the Picture of William Canon, in Glass. I supposed he glazed the Window, he was Rector here 1404 and dy'd about the year 1420, or resigns the Rectory

Memdm At the primary visitation of Lancelot Lord Archbishop of York, held at Leeds, August 4th, 1727, A Terrier was exhibited of all the Known Houses, & Edifices, Glebe Lands, Tythes, Easter Reckonings, surplice Fees, and other Ecclesiastical Dues of right belonging to the Rectory of Barwick in Elmet, and subscribed by Edmund Barneby, Rector.

David Dawson, Curate.
Samuel Wright of Barwick,
William Vevers of Morrick,
Richard Vevars of Potterton,
William Simpson of Rounday, } Church-wardens.

Barwick Church was Pew'd, a Gallery erected, and a new Pulpit made in the years 1725, 26, and 1727, towards wch Pulpit The Revnd Mr Barneby, Rector, gave ten pounds and ten shillings.

The monument in Barwick Xch was put up by Sr Edward Gascoign, Bartt, in the yr 1728.

T: D: D: C:

[THIRD BOOK.]

The Register of Baptisms, Marriages and Burials within the Parish of Barwick from May ye 7th, 1738.

Baptisms.

William, son of Thomas Thornton of Potterton, Lab^{r}, bapt^{d} June 11th
Rachel, the daughter of John Atkinson of Barwick, Webster, June ye 11th
Alvara, son of John Thompson of Stanks, Lab^{r}, June 25th
Peggy, daug^{r} of Benjamin Haist of Barwick, yeoman, June 28th
Keisilla, daug^{r} of William Reedal of Morwick, Lab^{r}, July 2^{d}
Jane, d^{r} of Thomas Smith of Potterton, Yeoman, July 7th
Catherine, the daughter of Thomas Robshaw of Barwick, Husbandman, July the 11th
James, the son of Mat^{w} Jackson of Barwick, Husbandman, Augt 13th
John, son of Richard Lazenby of Penwel, Lab^{r}, Octob. 1st
Sarah, daug^{r} of John Saynor of Mawrick, Husbandman, October ye 8th
Grace, d^{r} of Thomas Upton of Mawrick, Husbandman, Octob^{r} 15th
*Mary, y^{e} Bastard child of Elizth Bell of Barwick, Octo^{r} 27th
Jane, y^{e} daug^{r} of John Bean of Barwick, Shoemaker, November y^{e} 5th
Mary, d^{r} of William Scot of Barwick, Joyner, Novemb. 6th
Geo., son of Geo. Watson of Bar$_{k}$, Lab^{r}, Decemb. y^{e} 26th
Geo., son of Geo. Smith of Bar$_{k}$, Lab^{r}, Decemb. y^{e} 26th
Eliz., daug^{r} of Jacob Pease of Grimesdike, Lab^{r}, December y^{e} 27th
Richard, son of John Hewit of Garforth Moor, Collier, December y^{e} 31st
Richard, son of Richard Jackson of Barwick, Chandler, Febry. 23^{d}
John, son of Thomas Jackson of Scholes, Lab^{r}, March 18th
Betty, ye Daughter of Benjamin Rawlinson of Barwick, Lab^{r}, March 21st

1739, Baptisms.

Margret, daug^{r} of James Strodder of Barwick, shoemaker, baptiz^{d} April 14th
Elizabeth, Daughter of Step. Vevers of Morwick, Gent., Born May 7th
Sarah, daughter of William Bell of Penwell, Taylor, May 20th
Jeremy, son of Thomas Lumb of Stanks, Husbandman, May 27th
Mary, the Daug^{r} of John Taite of Barwick, Mason, May 27th
William, the son of Joseph Beck of Stanks, Lab^{r}, July ye 8th
Mary, ye daug^{r} of Thomas Harper of Barwick, Lab^{r}, July 22^{d}
Mary and Martha, daughters of David Wright of Stanks, Lab^{r}, August ye 5th
Isabella, the daughter of Robert Barton of Barwick, carpenter, August 12th
Ann, the daughter of Adam Fleming of Turry-lug-gate, Husbandman, Augt 17th
[*blank*], the son of John Mead, officer of Excise, Augt 21st
Sarah, the daug^{r} of Bernard Blackburn of Barwick, Lab^{r}, August 26th
Samuel, the son of Samuel Dodgson of Roundhay, Husbandman, Septemb^{r} 9th
Jane, the daughter of John Atkinson of Barwick, Webster, Septemb. 30th

---

*In the account of William Scott, Constable 1742:—"Paid for a Sheet for Eliz. Bell to do Pennance in 0—0—6."

Sarah, the daug^r^ of John Hemsworth of Potterton, Lab^r^, October ye 5th
[*blank*], the [*blank*] of Timothy Turnpenny of Winmoor, Lab^r^, Octob^r^ 14th
Thomas, the son of Thomas Robinson of Barnbow Carr, Carpenter, October 21st
William, the son of John Donwel of Mawrick, Lab^r^, Octob^r^ 24th
Gabriel, the son of Gabriel Taylor of Barnbow, Lab^r^, Octo^r^ 21st
Richard, son of Richard Haist of Barwick, Butcher, November ye 5th
Mary, Daughter of Robert Dawson of Shippen, Decemb. 12th
Sarah, daug^r^ of John Waite of Barwick, Taylor, Decemb. 26th
Thomas, son of Thomas Simpson of Roundhay, January ye 11th
Susannah, the daug^r^ of Geo. Watson of Potterton, Husbandman, Jany. 20th
Eliz^a^, the daug^r^ of Mathew Watson of Barwick, Carpenter, Feb'y 6th
Francis, son of Francis Wilson of Stanks, collier, March ye 16th

1740, BAPTISMS.

William, the son of Thomas Simpson of Winmoor, Lab^r^, bapt^d^ April ye 20th
William, son of William Thompson of Barnbow Carr, Husbandman, April ye 25th
Thomas, son of William Crummock of Winmoor, Lab^r^, April 27th
John, the son of Thomas Upton of Mawrick, Husbandman, May ye 11th
Samuel, the son of John Robinson of Barnbow, Lab^r^, May 11th
John, son of John Burland of Potterton, Lab^r^, June 1st
Jonathan, the son of Jonathan Bell of Barnbow, Lab^r^, June ye 1st
Sarah, the daug^r^ of Richard Wood of Potterton, Lab^r^, July ye 20th
John and Eliz^b^, the son and daughter of Thomas Taite of Barwick, Mason, July 26th
Mary, the daug^r^ of John Page of Winmoor, August 24th
James, the son of Thomas Collet of Barwick, Butcher, Augt 25th
Samuel, the son of Robert Simpson of Barwick, Lab^r^, Octob. 12th
Samuel, the son of James Robinson of Barwick, Lab^r^, Octob. 12th
John, son of Thomas Thornton of Potterton, Lab^r^, Novr ye 2^d^
George, the son of Jeremy Booth of Barwick, Novemb. ye 16th
Samuel, the son of Andrew Burdsal of Scholes, Bucklemaker, November ye 16th
Sarah, the daug^r^ of Thomas Batty of Barwick, shoemaker, Jan'ry 1st
Ann, the daug^r^ of John Atkinson of Scholes, Lab^r^, Jan'ry 25th
John, the son of Richard Jackson of Barwick, chandler, Feb'ry 6th
Ann, the daug^r^ of Mat^w^ Goldin of Barwick, Lab^r^, Febry. ye 20th
Betty, the daughter of John Saynor of Grimesdike, Husbandman, Mar. 4th
Thomas, the son of Mr Thomas Jackson of Barwick, Schoolmaster, was born Febry. 7th and baptized March ye 9th

1741, BAPTISMS.

Thomas, the Bastard Child of Mary Pattison, April ye 17th
Margret, the Daughter of John Bean of Barwick, shoemaker, April ye 24th
Mally, the Daughter of Benjamin Rawlinson of Barwick, Lab^r^, May 1st

John, son of Samuel Daniel of Barwick, Blacksmith, May ye 1st
John, son of Richard Slaytor of Stanks, May ye 21st
Martha, ye daugr of Thos Harper of Barwick, Labr, May 25th
John, the son of Richard Slaytor, June ye 19th
Ann, the daugr of Richard Varley of Barwick, Husbandman, July 17th
Benjamin, the son of Thomas Donwell of Barwick, Webster, Augt 2d
Hannah, the daughter of Thos Lumb of Stockhill, Augt 23d
Grace, the daughter of Richd Haist of Barwick, Yeoman, Aug. ye 27th
Ann, the daugr of Geo. Smith of Barwick, Labr, Augt 30th
Samuel, the son of Richard Shippen of Penwel, Husbandman, September ye 21st
Betty, daugr of Thomas Upton of Mawrick, September 27th
William, son of Robert Whitehead of Barwick, Labor, October ye 4th
Ann, the daugr of Gabl Taylor of Barnbow, Labr, Octobr 31st
Mary, the daughter of Joseph Beck of Stanks, Labr, Novr 8th
William, son of William Knapton of Barwick, smith, Novr 12th
William, son of William Scott of Barwick, Joyner, Novr 15th
William, son of Richard Burland of Barwick, Webster, Novr 22d
John, son of Richard Shackleton of Potterton, Tanner, Decembr 5th
Titus, son of Timothy Turnpenny of Winmoor, Decembr 6th
Ann, the daughter of Richd Lazenby of Penwel, Labr, December 20th
Joseph, the son of Joseph Lamb of Hobberley, January ye 7th
Sarah, the daughter of Geo. Thompson of Penwel, January ye 24th
Moses and Aaron, sons of William Reedal of Mawrick, Labr, Jan'ry 24th
Rebeckah, the daughter of Samuel Haist of Barwick, Yeoman, February 28th

Baptisms, 1742.

Richard, son of Thomas Taite of Barwick, mason, baptized April 2d
John, son of John Little of [*blank*], April ye 18th
Jonathan, son of James Robinson of Barwick, Labr, May 12th
Elizabeth, daughter of John Settle of Scholes, June ye 7th
David Wright, the son of David Wright of Stanks, June 11th
George, the son of William Bywater of Winmoor, Augt 22d
Ann, the daughter of George Watson of Potterton, Husbandman, Sepr 17th
Edmund, the son of William Crummack of Winmoor, Labr, Septr ye 24th
Mary, the daughter of Robert Appleyard of Scholes, October 10th
John, the son of Thomas Simpson of Winmoor, Novr ye 28th
Ann, the daughter of Benjamin Rawlinson of Barwick, Jan'ry 6th
William, the son of Jonathan Bell of Barnbow, Jan'ry 23d
Matthew, the son of Thos Upton of Mawrick, February ye 24th
James, the son of Richard Jackson of Barwick, Febry. 25th
Ann, the daughter of John Mountain of Barwick, Febry. 25th
William, the son of Luke Richardson of Potterton, shoemaker, Febry. 28th
William, the son of William Driver of Winmoor, March 13th
Thos, son of William Abbot of Barwick, March ye 16th
Thos, son of John Bean of Barwick, shoemaker, Marh 25th

Baptisms, 1743.

Thomas, son of Thomas Dodgson of Roundhay, Apl 4th

David, son of Joshua Brown of Roundhay, Apl 4th
Thomas, son of William Lumb of Barwick, Apl 15th
Richard, the son of Richard Waite of Barwick, May ye 1st
Ellen, the daughter of John Varey of Scholes, Labr, May 1st
John, the son of Andrew Burdsal of Scholes, Buckle maker, May 15th
Elizabeth, the daughter of Joseph Dickinson of Barwick, May ye 15th
Benjamin, son of John Waite of Barwick, Taylor, May 22d
John, son of Gabriel Taylor of Barnbow, May 22d
Hannah, daughter of Richard Shippen, of Stanks, May 26th
Mary, the daughter of Mr Stephen Vevers of Morwick, May ye 27th
Ann, the daughter of Thomas Thornton of Potterton, May 29th
Elizabeth, daughter of Sarah Whitaker, a travailing woman, June 23d
William, son of William Tipling of Scholes, June 24th
Samuel, son of Richard Haist of Barwick, June ye 27th
Isabel, daughr of Richard Wood of Potterton, July ye 3d
William, son of John Hemsworth of Potterton, July ye 6th
William, son of John Hemsworth of Potterton, Labr, July 31st
William, son of Matthew Goldin of Barwick, Labr, Septr 2d
Martha, daughter of Thomas Lumb of Stockhil, Septembr ye 7th
Mary, the wife of Isaac Hall of Kidhall Lane end, aged 40 years, October 30th
Hannah, the Posthume daughter of Samuel Haist of Barwick, November ye 16th
Betty, the daughter of Joseph Bargh of Potterton, Tanner, November 30th
George, the son of Francis Holmes of Barwick, Jan'y the 27th
Betty, the daughter of William Taylor of Barnbow Carr, Feb'ry. 1st
Alice, the daughter of Benjamin Rawlinson of Barwick, Febry. 2d
Elizabeth, daughter of William Bell of Penwell, Taylor, February ye 19th
Sarah, daughter of Robert Barton of Barwick, March 4th
Richard, the son of Richard Burland of Barwick, March ye 11th

BAPTISMS, 1744.

Mary, the daughter of William Waters of Knaresbrough, March 26th
Ann, the daughter of John Taite of Barwick, mason, March 28th
Eliza, the daughter of William Taylor of Barnbow Carr, March ye 28th
Elizabeth, daughter of Robt Whitehead, April ye 22d
David, son of David Wright, April 22d
Joseph, son of Joseph Outhwaite, Apl 22d
Thomas, the son of Robert Simpson of Barwick, May ye 4th
Mary, the daughter of Thomas Taite, June 3d
John, son of John Cleamshaw of Kidhall Lane, June 13th
John, son of Thomas Batty, June 17th
Sarah, daugr of James Strodder of Bark, July 8th
Nancy, daugr of Edmund Popplewel of Winmoor, August ye 12th
Faith, daughter of Joseph Broadbent of Stank House, Augt 22d
John, son of John Logg of Scholes, Augt 7th
Ann, the daughter of William Knapton of Barwick, Blacksmith, Augt 24
Grace, the daughter of Mary Hamilton, September ye 16th
Judith, daughter of Joseph Lamb of Winmoor, September 19th

Henry, son of Henry Wright of Winmoor, September 30th
Frances, daughter of Martin Whitehead of Garforth moor, ye 30th of September
Elizabeth, daughter of William Scot of Barwick, October 7th
Richard, the son of William Lumb of Barwick, October 19th
James, the son of Timothy Turnpenny of Winmoor, October 21st
Mary, the daugr of James Lambert of Hill Top, October 31st
Mary, daughter of Joseph Dawson of Potterton, November ye 11th
Martin, the son of Miles Hanshaw of Barwick, Novr ye 16th
Mary, daughter of William Abbot of Barwick, Novemr ye 16th
William, son of Robert Dawson of Potterton Lane, Novembr ye 28th
Samuel, son of Thomas Dodgson of Roundhay, December ye 5th
Stephen, the son of Mr Stephen Vevers of Morwick, December ye 7th
Martin, son of William Tipling of Schôles, ye 7th of December
John, son of John Thompson of Garforth moor, December ye 9th
Matthew, son of Thomas Upton of Mawrick, December ye 9th
John, son of John Atkinson of Ba[r]nbow, Jan'ry ye 20th
Ann, daugr of Thomas Jackson of Scholes, Febry. 10th
Frances, daugr of Willm Crummock of Winmoor, Febry. 10th
Benjamin, son of Richard Jackson of Barwick, Feby. 15th
Benjamin, son of Benjamin Rawlinson of Barwick, Feby. 22d
Richard, son of Richd Wilcock of Barwick, Febr'y 27th
Matthias, son of George Hewit of Barnbow, March 24th
Mary, daughter of John Saynor of Hill-Top, March 24th

BAPTISMS, 1745.

Mary, daughter of Thomas Simpson of Winmoor, April 7th
Sarah and Betty, daughters of Thomas Collet of Barwick, April 28th
Ann, daughter of Richard Shippen of Stanks, May 1st
Sarah, daughter of Richard Lazenby of Penwel, July 7th
Mary, daughter of James Scholefield of Barwick, Augt ye 8th
Betty, daughter of John Waite of Barwick, August 18th
Abraham, son of Roger Bell of Scholes, Blacksmith, September ye 8th
James, son of Thomas Harper of Bark, September 22d
William, son of Thomas Stead of Stanks, Taylor, September ye 22d
Jonathan, son of Gabriel Taylor of Barnbow, Labourer, September 28th
John, son of Richard Varley of Barwick, husbandman, October 16th
John, son of Christopher Scot of Barnbow, husbandman, November 1st
[*blank*], daughter of Joseph Broadbent of Stank House, October ye —
William, son of John Logg of Scholes, November 3d
Ann, the daughter of Thomas Lumb of Stockhill, Novr 22d
Fanny, daughter of James Lambert of Winmoor, Jan'ry 17th
Elizabeth, daughter of Miles Hamshaw, Jañry 22d
Elizabeth, daughter of Matthew Goldin of Barwick, Jan'y 24th
Bridget, bastard son [*sic*] of Jane Hopwood, Jany. 24th
Katherine, daughter of John Varey of Scholes, February 9th
Agnes, daughter of Joseph Holmes of Barwick, Febry. 16th
Benjamin, son of Richard Haist of Barwick, Feb'y 19th
Frances, daughter of Andrew Burdsal of Scholes, Feb'y 21st
Renton, the bastard son of Mary Haist of Barwick, March ye 5th
Joseph, son [of] John Bean of Barwick, March ye 7th

Baptisms 1746.

Mary Elizabeth, the daughter of John Braim of Barwick, carpenter, April 9th
Margret, daughter of Thomas Benton of Garforth moor side, April 20th
Jesse, the son of William Burrows of Hubberley, May 19th
William, son of Thomas Taite of Barwick, May ye 18th
Ann, daughter of Robert Simpson of Barwick, June 4th
Jinny, the daughter of Thomas Upton of Mawrick, June ye 8th
Hannah, daughter of William Tipling of Scholes, July ye 13th
Silvester, the son of John Petty of Winmoor, July 23d
James, son of John Cleamshaw of Kidhall Lane, Augt 22d
Alice, daughter of Thomas Thornton of Potterton, August 31st
Thomas, son of Richard Burland of Barwick, August 31st
Peggy, the bastard child of Elizabeth Whitehead of Garforth-moor-side, September ye 14th
William, son of Joseph Bargh of Potterton, Tanner, Octob. 1st
Mary, daughter of George Watson of Potterton, October 5th
Ann, daughter of William Abbot of Barwick, October 12th
William, the son of William Driver of Winmoor, October ye 19th
Susannah, daughter of William Taylor of Barnbow, November 2d
Elizabeth, daughter of Robert Barton of Barwick, 9ber 3d
Amabella, the bastard child of Mary England, December ye 7th
Elizabeth, daughter of Francis Holmes of Barwick, Decr 12th
Mark, son of Peter Brunton of Barnbow, March 1st

Baptisms, 1747.

John, son of Luke Richardson of Potterton, shoemaker, April 24th
Mary, daugr of Henry Wright of Winmoor, May ye 24th
William, the son of Richard Varley of Barwick, June 5th
William and Jeremiah, sons of Christopher Scot of Barnbow, July 20th
Sarah and Susannah, daugrs of Robert Whitehead of Barwick, July 20th
Sarah, daughter of Joseph Broadbent of Stankhouse, July 30th
Elizabeth, the bastard child of Hannah Varley of Barwick, July 30th
Sarah, daughter of Thomas Dodgson of Roundhay, August 9th
William, son of William Johnson of Barwick, Husbandman, Septr 3d
John, son of William Bell of Hill top, September 20th
Mary, the daughter of Thomas Jackson of Barwick, Schoolmaster, September ye 25th
Christopher, son of Christopher Dickinson, late of Barwick, Septr 27th
William, son of Thomas Lumb of Stockin, Novr 4th
Joseph, son of Joseph Outhwaite of Stanks, Novr 22d
James, son of John Logg of Scholes, November 27th
Roger, son of Roger Bell, December ye 2d
William, son of Joseph Holmes of Barwick, Taylor, December ye 20th
Ann, daughter of Thomas Smith of Scholes, Husbandman, Jan'ry 1st
Jane, the daughter of Thomas Upton of Morwick, Jan'ry ye 6th
Samuel, son of Timothy Turnpenny of Winmoor, Jan'ry 22d
Hannah, daughter of Joseph Bullock of Barwick, mason, Feb'y 23d
Thomas, son of William Scot of Barwick, joyner, March 2d
Samuel, son of John Thompson of Garforth-moor, March 13th
Reuben, son of William Burrows of Hubberley, March 13th

Thomas, son of Joseph Bargh of Potterton, Tanner, March 16th
Martha, daughter of Robt Dawson of Potterton, Lab^{r}, March ye 20th

BAPTISMS, 1748.

Elizabeth, daughter of Robert Smith ye younger of Barwick, March 27th
Sarah, daughter of Matthew Goldin of Barwick, April ye 10th
Richard and Elizabeth, son and daughter of Wm Knapton of Bar^{k}, blacksmith, April 11th
Mary, daughter of Samuel Liversedge of Barwick, April 11th
William, son of Benja^{n} Rawlinson of Barw^{k}, April 12th
Thomas, son of William Waite of Barw^{k}, May 1st
Samuel, son of Thomas Stead of Stanks, May 1st
William, the bastard child of Jane Hopwood of Barwick, May ye 15th
Alice, daughter of Stephen Vevers of Morwick, baptiz'd privately, March ye 20th, 1747, and receiv'd June ye 1th, 1748
Sarah, daughter of John Saynor of Winmoor, May 29th
Alice, the daughter of John Marshall of Barwick, June 26th
Joseph, the son of Jonathan Bell of Barwick, privately, July 15th
Sarah, the daughter of Thomas Haley of Scholes, July 20th
Sarah, daughter of Thos Tait of Barwick, September 11th
Thomas, son of Miles Hanch of Barwick, Octr 9th
Ann, daughter of Richard Burland of Barwick, Weaver, Decr 4th
William, son of William Slayter of Barwick, Decr 11th
Ann, daughter of John Vary of Scholes, Labourer, Feb. ye 5th
Hannah, daughter of William Abbott of Barwick, Feb. 12th
John, son of William Crummock of Scholes, Feb. 19th
George, son of George Watson of Potterton, March ye 13th
Ann, daughter of Christopher Scott of Scholes, March ye 22^{d}

BAPTISMS, 1749.

Betty, daughter of John Bean of Barwick, March ye 27th
Elizabeth, daughter of Andrew Berdsal of Scholes, April ye 7th
George, son of George Watson of Potterton, April ye 16th
Moses, son of Roger Bell of Barwick, April ye 23rd
Jane, daughter of Francis Holms, Linen Weaver, May ye 15th
Thomas, the bastard child of Elizabeth Bell, May ye 16th
Martha, daughter of Thomas Thornton of Potterton, May ye 28
Benj^{in}, son of Thomas Collet of Barwick, June ye 7th
Margret, daughter of Robert Simpson of Barwick, July ye 23rd
William, the son of William Eamonson of Lazincroft, Aug. 18
William, son of Will. and Frances Barker of Penwell, Aug. 20
Sarah, daughter of Henry Wright of Morwick and Sarah his wife, Sept. 8th
Mary, daughter of John Dickinson of Barnbow, Sept. 10
Richard, son of Richard Bowling of Turry-Lug-gate, September ye 28th
Joseph, son of Joseph Bargh of Potterton, October the 24th
Mary, daughter of Robert Smith, Junr, of Barwick, November ye 26th
Mary, daughter of Edward Poplewell of Winmoor, November ye 26th
Hannah, daughter of Thomas Poplewell of Winmoor, Decemb^{r} ye 3rd
Elizth, daughter of Willm Driver of Winmoor, Decemb^{r} ye 3rd
William, son of Thomas Upton of Morwick, December ye 8th
Elizth, daughter of John Clemishaw of Kidall Lane, Decemb^{r} ye 27th

Mary, daughter of John Gaggs of Barnbow, Decembr ye 27th
Mary, daughter of Thos Dogson of Roundhay, January ye 10th
Mary, daughter of Willm Johnson of Barwick, Feby ye 7th
Alice, daughter of Richd Street, Feb. ye 11th
Sarah, daughter of Saml Liversiege of Barwick, March ye 7th
Rebekah, daughter of Wm Burrow of Winmoor, March ye 11th
Ann Thompson, daughter of Thomas Thompson of Garforth Moor, baptiz'd at Garforth Church, February ye 22nd
Mary, daughter of John Logg of Scholes, baptiz'd at Garforth, March 2nd

Baptisms, 1750.

Benjamin, son of John Brambley of Potterton, April ye 11th
Ann, daughter of Joseph Bullock of Barwick, April ye 16th
Elizth, daughter of Thos Lumb of Stockin, May ye 2nd
Hannah, daughter of Matthew Golden of Barwick, May ye 16th
Charles, son of Charles Lawton of Potterton, Mason, June ye 20th
Elizabeth, daughter of Francis Wilson of Scholes, July ye 22nd
William, son of William Waite of Barwick, was privately baptiz'd July ye 24th
Peter, son of William Slaytor of Barwick, August ye 1st
Mary, the daughter of Joseph and Abigail Holmes of Barwick, Octobr ye 7th
Sarah, the daughter of Thomas Tayler of Barwick, November ye 4th
Sarah, the daughter of Christopher and Martha Varey of Barwick, Novr ye 18th
John, the son of Samuel and Frances Hindson of Scholes, November ye 21st
John, the son of Matthew and Ann Upton of Morwick, November the 23d
James, the son of James and Mary Lambert of Winmoor, February the 6th
Samuel, the son of Thomas and Jane Upton of Morwick, March the 10th

Baptisms, 1751.

Hannah, the daughter of William and Mary Littlewood of Potterton, March ye 31st
Hannah, the daughter of Thomas and Hannah Tate of Barwick, Aprill the 8th
Mary, the daughter of William and Ann Ward of Winmoor, Aprill ye 9th
Richard, son of Richard and Frances Green of Barwick, May the 19th
John, the son of George and Susanna Watson of Potterton, June the 9th
Sarah, the daughter of Edward and Sarah Thompson of Stanks, June the 16th
William, the son of Benj. and Eliz. Cook of Stanks, June the 23d
Priscilla, the daughter of Jno and Catherine Varey of Scholes, eodem die
Sarah, the daughter of James and Ann Perkin of Barwick, August the 4th
John, the son of Robert and Sarah Carbott of Potterton, August the 14th
James, the son of Joseph and Sarah Broadbent of Stank House, August the 21st
John, the son of William and Thomasin Burrow of Winmoor Head, August ye 25th

Elisabeth, the daughter of Abraham Baite of Potterton, September the 15th
Sarah, the daughter of Thomas Simpson of Roundhay, Septem^{r} the 25th
Ann, the daughter of John and Sarah Dickinson of Barnbow Carr, Octob^{r} the 6th
Ann, daughter of John Saynor of Winmoor, October the 13th
Joseph, the son of Willm and Ann Crummock of Barwick, Novemb^{r} the 10th
Alice, the daughter of Willm and Mary Slaytor of Barwick, eodem die
Mary, the daughter of Robert and Martha Whitehead of Barwick, eodem die
Jane, the daughter of Andrew and Eliz. Burdsall of Scholes, November the 15th
Joseph, the son of Willm and Hannah Tiplin of Barwick, Decemb^{r} ye 23^{d}
Joseph, the son of Thos and Mary Taylor of Barwick, Decemb^{r} the 26th
Willm, the son of John Bramly of Potterton Lane, January the 5th
Mary, the daughter of Joseph and Ann Daniel of Potterton Lane January the 8th
Sarah, the daughter of William Barker of Grimesdike, January the 19th
Mary, the daughter of Abraham and Cressy Wormhill of Barwick, February 12th
John, the son of John Dungwith of Barwick, February the 23^{d}
William, son of William and Frances Brown of Winmoor, March the 8th
Sarah, the daughter of Robert and Mary Smith of Barwick, March the 8th
Elisabeth, the daughter of John and Ann Logg of Scholes, March the 8th
John, the son of John and Margaret Gaggs of Barnbow, March the 15th
Alice and Sarah, twin-daughters of Roger and Alice Bell of Barwick, March 22^{d}

Baptisms, 1752.

Martha, the daughter of Willm and Catharine Abbott of Barwick, March 30th
William, the son of William and Mary Bell of Winmoor, Aprill the 26th
Maria, the daught^{r} of Thos and Mary Thornton of Potterton Lane, Aprill the 26th
John, the son of Richard and Sarah Bowling of Turrylug-gate, May the 24th
William, the son of John and Mearcy Ellis of Kippax, June the 21st
*Carr, the son of Sr Henry Ibbetson, Bart., of Red Hall, July the 30th
Frances, daughter of Richard and Frances Green of Barwick, born July the 30th and baptized August the 27th
Mary, the daughter of Joseph and Mary Bullock of Barwick, Septemb^{r} the 17th
John, the son of Major and Mary Dickinson of Roundhay, October the 8th

*"Sir Henry was High Sheriff of Yorkshire 1746, when above 20 were hanged and about 90 transported for Rebellion. He caused the Pope, Cardinal Tencin, the young chevalier and his associate to be hanged in Effigie in Leedes" *Wilson MS.* *Burke's Peerage* states that having raised a corps of a hundred men at his own expense during the rebellion of 1745 he was in consideration thereof created a Baronet 12 May, 1748. He married 2ndly 1741, Isabella, dau. of Ralph Carr of Cocken. His son was a Captain of Dragoons and married Miss Fletcher, niece of Sir Hugh Palliser, Bart.

Jane the daughter of Edmund Popplewell of Winmoor-head, October the 15th

Sarah, the daughter of Charles and Ann Lawton of Potterton, Novembr the 12th

BAPTISMS, 1753.

Ann, the daughter of Luke and Elisabeth Richardson of Potterton, January ye 6th

Rebecca, the daughtr of Joseph and Rebecca Chappel of Potterton, February the 4th

Thomas, the son of John and Ellen Cawood of Scholes, February the 23d

Joseph, the son of Thomas and Jane Upton of Morwick, February the 25th

William and Jane, son and daughter of William and Ann Ward of Winmoor, Aprill the 1st

Thomas, the son of Matthew and Hannah Golden of Barwick, April 15th

Thomas, the son of William and Elisabeth Johnson of Barwick, April 15th

Moses, the son of Francis and Ann Wilson of Scholes, April 15th

Thomas, the son of Joseph and Abigail Holmes of Barwick, May 6th

Mary, the daughter of Abraham and Sarah Baite of Potterton, May 6th

Elizabeth, the daughter of Christopr and Elis. Demesne of Winmoor-head, May 27th

Peter, the son of David and Mary Buchan of Winmoor head, June 10th

Thomas, the son of James and Ann Perkin of Barwick, July 1st

Sarah, the daughtr of Edward and Mary Day of Potterton, July 8th

Martha, the bastard daughter of Mary Haist of Barwick, July the 25th

Benjamin, son of Peter and Ellen Eamonson of Roundhay, July the 26th

Mary, the daughter of Samuel and Sarah Braim of Barwick, August 8th

George, the son of Willm and Sarah Driver of Winmoor, August the 12th

Nancy, the daughtr of Willm and Ann Waite of Barwick, August the 26th

Benjamin, the son of James and Hannah Strother of Barwick, Octobr 8th

Alice, the daughtr of John and Elisabeth Dungwith of Barwick, Octobr 14th

Betty, the daughtr of Willm and Hannah Tiplin of Barwick, Octobr 19th

John, the son of Joseph and Ann Daniel of Potterton-lane, Novembr 1st

Betty, the daughtr of Abram and Cressy Wormhill of Barwick, Novembr 9th

William, the son of John and Sarah Dickinson of Barnbow-Carr, December 2d

Martha, the daughr of Miles and Mary Hampshaw of Barwick, Decemr 16

BAPTISMS, 1754.

Mary, the daughtr of Christopher and Martha Varey of Stanks, January 1st

William, the son of Charles and Ann Lawton of Potterton, January the 20th

John, the son of William and Sarah Knapton of Barwick, February the 20th

James, the son of Thomas and Margaret Whitehead of Barwick, March the 1st

Carmi, the son of Willm and Thomasin Burrow of Winmoor head, March 31st
Martha, the daught^{r} of Thos and Hannah Tate of Barwick, April the 16th
William, the son of William and Mary Slaytor of Barwick, May the 5th
Isaac, the son of Roger and Alice Bell of Barwick, May the 26th
John, the son of Joseph and Sarah Broadbent of Stank-house, June the 13th
Sarah, the daughter of John and Mary Batley of Scholes, June the 21st
Benjamin, the son of Willm and Ann Crummock of Barwick, June the 30th
Edward Higgin, the bastard son of Sarah Powell of Potterton, July 7th
Robert, the son of Robert and Martha Whitehead of Barwick, July the 28th
Sarah, the daughter of John and Ann Logg of Scholes, August the 25th
John, the son of Robert and Ann Dixon of Barwick, September the 8th
Betty, the daughter of John and Elisth Clemishaw of Kiddal-lane, Septr 27th
Susanna, the daughter of Rich^{d} and Susanna Jackson of Barwick, Septem^{r} 27th
Sarah, the daughter of Benjamin and Elis. Cook of Barwick, October the 6th
Ruth, the daughter of John and Sarah Butler of Scholes, October the 23^{d}
William, the son of Robert and Mary Smith of Barwick, November the 5th
Samuel, the son of John and Ellen Cawood of Scholes, November ye 6th
Robert, the son of Willm and Frances Brown of Winmoor, December the 1st
Elis. the daug^{r} of Willm and Frances Barker of Grimes-Dike, Decemb^{r} the 1st
William, the son of Andrew and Elis. Burdsall of Scholes, Decem^{r} 27th

BAPTISMS, 1755.

Hannah, the daughter of Joseph and Mary Bullock of Barwick, baptized January the 26th
James, the son of Thomas and Elisabeth Shillitoe of Barwick, February the 2^{d}
William, the son of William and Deborah Wright of Scholes, March the 7th
Hannah, the daughter of Samuel and Sarah Braim of Barwick, April the 2^{d}
William, the son of Thomas and Mary Thornton of Potterton-lane, April the 6th
Ann, the daughter of Thomas and Susanna Bailey of Winmoor, April the 27th
Abraham, the son of Thomas and Margaret Whitehead of Barwick, May the 1st
Joseph, the son of Joseph and Ann Daniel of Potterton lane, May the 19th
Thomas, the son of Edmund and Mary Popplewell of Winmoor-head, June the 1st

Sarah, the daughter of Willm and Ann Ward of Winmoor, June the 29th
Benjn, the son of John and Rose Bramley of Potterton lane, July the 6th
James, the son of Joseph and Rebecca Chappel of Potterton, July the 6th
Elisabeth, the daughter of Willm and Elisabeth Eamonson of Lazincroft, August the 14th
William, the son of James and Mary Butler of Scholes, August the 24th
John, the son of Edward and Mary Day of Potterton, August the 31st
John, the son of Abraham and Sarah Baite of Potterton, September the 28th
John, the son of John and Ann Robinson of Barwick, October the 17th
Patience, the daughter of Edward and Ann Thompson of Scholes, Novem^{r} the 2^{d}
Matthew, the son of William and Hannah Tiplin of Barwick, November 5th
Isabella, the daughter of James and Mary Brennand of Barwick, born October the 18th, baptized November the 14th
Ann, the daughter of Abraham and Cressy Wormald of Barwick, November the 16th
Robert, the son of Robert and Elisabeth Ellott of Barnbow-hall, December the 7th

BAPTISMS, 1756.

Elisabeth, the daughter of Richard and Frances Green of Barwick, bapt: Feby the 7th
Thomas, the son of John and Elisabeth Dungwith of Barwick, February the 8th
Grace, the daughter of Robert and Ann Dixon of Barwick, February the 22^{d}
William, the son of Willm and Deborah Wright of Scholes, February the 26th
William, the son of William and Hannah Smith of Barnbow Carr, March 14th
Elisabeth, the daughter of John and Elis. Norton of Barwick, April the 20th
Sarah, the daughter of John and Eliz. Clemishaw of Kiddal lane, April the 30th
Betty, the daug^{r} of Thos and Martha Saunderson of Moor-mountain, June the 6th
Roger, the son of Roger and Alice Bell of Barwick, July the 18th
Francis, the son of Willm and Sarah Driver of Winmoor, July the 25th
John, the son of John and Ellen Cawood of Scholes, August the 20th
Mary, the daug^{r} of Thomas and Susanna Bailey of Winmoor, August 29th
Josiah, the son of Robert and Martha Whitehead of Barwick, Septem^{r} 19th
Samuel, the son of Samuel and Sarah Braim of Barwick, September the 27th
James, the son of Joseph and Hannah Dawson of Potterton, October the 3^{d}

Sarah, the daug^{r} of David and Mary Buchan of Winmoor-head, October the 3^{d}
Hannah, the daug^{r} of Thos and Margaret Whitehead of Barwick, October the 20th
Sarah, the daughter of Willm and Sarah Knapton of Barwick, November 5th
James, the son of James and Ann Perkin of Barwick, December the 28th

BAPTISMS, 1757.

David, the son of James and Hannah Strother of Barwick, bapt: January the 9th
Nathanael, the son of Willm and Susanna Gill of Potterton, January the 23^{d}
John, the son of Robert and Mary Smith of Barwick, March the 6th
Richard, the son of Benj. and Elisabeth Cook of Stanks, March the 6th
Ann, the daug^{r} of Joseph and Ann Daniel of Potterton lane, March the 9th
James and Joseph, Twins, sons of Joseph and Mary Bullock of Barwick, March the 20th
Thomas, the son of Thomas and Elisabeth Shillito of Barwick, March the 20th
John, the son of John and Sarah Dickinson of Barnbow carr, March the 27th
Alice, the daughter of Thomas and Mary Taylor of Barwick, April the 3^{d}
Ann, the daughter of Christopher and Martha Varey of Scholes, April the 3^{d}
Mary, the daughter of Willm and Frances Barker of Grimesdike, April the 11th
Thomas, the son of John and Ann Logg of Scholes, May the 1st
Michael, the son of Joseph and Mary Settle of Barwick, May the 8th
Thomas, the son of William and Mary Lumb of Barwick, May the 12th
James, the son of James and Mary Butler of Scholes, May the 15th
William, the son of Willm and Ann Waite of Barwick, May the 15th
Sarah, the daughter of John and Sarah Lyster of Potterton, June the 5th
Alice, the daughter of Willm and Elisabeth Eamonson of Lazincroft, June the 20th
Mary, the daughter of Willm and Frances Brown of Winmoor, July the 10th
Timothy, the son of Willm Smith of Barwick, July the 17th
James, the son of John and Ann Robinson of Barwick, July the 17th
Mary, the daug^{r} of Thomas and Hannah Tate of Barwick, July the 17th
William, the son of Benjn and Susanna Watson of Barwick, August the 14th
James, the son of James and Esther Horsfield of Potterton, September the 4th
Ann, the daug^{r} of Benjn and Mary Stringer of Winmoor, September the 4th
Hannah, the daughter of Edward and Mary Day of Potterton, September the 19th
Thomas, the son of William and Ann Ward of Winmoor, September the 25th
Mary, the daughter of William and Mary Slaytor of Barwick, September the 25th

Mary, the daughter of John and Sarah Tate of Barwick, October the 2d
Matthew, the son of Matthew and Ann Upton of Morwick, October the 23d
Edmund, the son of Willm and Ann Crummock of Barwick, November the 20th
Mary, the daugr of Joseph and Abigail Holmes of Barwick, December the 11th
Mary, the daugr of Robert and Sarah Smith of Barnbow-carr, December the 18th
John, the son of John and Sarah Butler of Scholes, December the 27th
William, the son of William and Henrietta Maria Smith was Born October 24th

BAPTISMS, 1758.

Thomas, the son of Abraham and Cressy Wormald of Barwick, January the 6th
Mary, the daughter of John and Elisabeth Robinson of Winmoor-Stile, March the 2d
Alice, the daughter of Roger and Alice Bell of Barwick, March the 26th
Joseph, the son of William and Deborah Wright of Scholes, March the 31st
William, the son of James and Mary Brennand of Barwick, born March the 13th, and baptized April the 6th
Betty, the daughter of John and Elisabeth Norton of Barwick, May the 7th
Mary, the daughter of Samuel and Sarah Varley of Barwick, May the 16th
Elisabeth, the daughter of Edward and Elis. Monks of Potterton, June the 18th
William, the son [of] John and Elisabeth Dungwith of Barwick, June the 25th
Samuel, the son of Samuel and Dorothy Thompson of Stanks, June the 30th
Jane, the daughter of David and Mary Buchan of Winmoor-head, July the 2d
William, the son of William and Mary Lumb of Shippen, July the 23d
Ann, the daughter of Robert and Ann Dixon of Barnbow, August the 13th
Elizabeth, daughter of Joseph and Ann Daniel of Potterton-lane, October the 12th
Margret and Mary, Twins, daughters of Thomas and Margret Whitehead, October the 13th
Sarah, daughter of Samuel and Sarah Braim, October the 22d
Joseph, son of Joshua White of Potterton, October the 22d
John, son of Robt Leach of Potterton, October the 29th
Michael, son of Wm Watson of Barwick, October 12th
William, the son of James Parkin of Barwick, Decer 26

BAPTISMS, 1759.

Thomas, the son of William Tipling of Barwick, bapd January 6th
Betty, the daughter of Luke Richardson of Potterton, Jany 16
John, the son of Chrisr Varey of Schooles, March 4th
John, the son of John Lumb of Stanks, April 16th
William, the son of Benj. Shillitoe of Scholes, April 22d

Thus fare Posted and sent into the Court at York.

Thomas, the son of William and Martha Calvert, blacksmith, of Barwick, May the 4th

Hannah, the daughter of Thomas Handson, Lab^{r}, of Barwick, May the 13th

Sarah, the daughter of James and Mary Butler of Scholes, Pipe maker, May the 27

Mary, the daughter of the Rever^{d} Mr Bains, Curate of Barwick, June the 3^{d}

Henry, the son of John and Elizth Cawood of Scholes, Blacksmith, June 15th

Mary, the daughter of Benj. and Elizabeth Braim of Barnbow Carr, July the 15th

Margret and Mary, twins, daughters of John and Mary Bean of Barwick, shoemaker, July the 24

Mary, the daughter of William and Mary Lumb of Barwick, husbandman, June ye 24

Mary, the daughter of John Peart, clogger, of Barwick in Elmett, July ye 6

Thomas, the son of William Driver of Winmoor, Lab^{r}, July ye 22

Ann, the daughter of Robt and Sarah Smith of Barnbow Carr, collier, Augt 12

Isaac, son of William Barker of Winmoor, Labourer, Sepr the 2

John and Nanny, twins, son and daughter of William and Sarah Knapton of Barwick, Blacksmith, September ye 14th

John, son of John Robinson of Winmoor stile, Yeoman, September the 19th

Isabella, the daughter of Benj. Watson of Barwick, wheelright, Septem^{br} the 30th

Hannah, the daughter of Benj. Stringer of Winmoor, October the 3^{d}

Martha, the daughter of Willm and Mary Lumb of Barwick, Schoolmaster, was born October the 7, betwixt 4 and 5 o'th Clock in the evening, and Baptizd Novem^{r} the 5th

BAPTISMS, 1760.

Roger, the son of Roger Bell of Barwick, baptized January the 1st

Thomas, the son of Thomas Bailey of Winn Moor, Jan. 13th

Sarah, the daughter of Thomas and Elisabeth Shilitoe of Barwick, Taylor, was born Jan. the 26, betwixt 5 and 6 o'clock in the evening, and baptiz^{d} Mar. 2nd

Abraham, the son of Abraham and Cressy Wormald of Barwick, Blacksmith, Feb. ye 17th

John, the son of John and Ann Linley of Turry lug Gate, February the 22nd

Frances, the daughter of Robert Brown of Penwell, March the 16th

William, the son of Robert and Mary Smith of Barwick, Labourer, March the 23^{d}

Mary, d^{r} of John and Sarah Lyster of Barwick (Husbandman), April 6th

Martha, d^{r} of John and Mary Lunn of Barnbow, collier, April 7th

Sarah, d^{r} of John Hardgrave of Winmoor (sadler), April 7th

Sarah, d^r of William and Ann Waite of Barwick (Labourer), April 27th
Ann, d^r of Edward and Ann Monks of Bramham-Moor (Labourer), May 12th
Ann, d^r of William and Mary Slator of Berwick, July 6th
Mary, d^r of James and Ann Perkins of Barwick, July 16th
Joseph, son of Samuel and Crisse Simpson of Barnbow Carr (Collier), July 27
Henrietta Maria, d^r of Joseph and Mary Bullock of Berwick (Mason), Augt 24th
Elizabeth, d^r of William and Eliz. Wilson of Bramham-moor (Labourer), Augt 24th
Frances, d^r of Robert and Frances Brown of Winmoor (Labourer), Au^t 28
Abraham, son of John and Ann Logg of Scholes (Labourer), Sepr 14th
Richard, son of Thomas Ellar and Mary (of Kidhall Lane, Horse Jockey), 14 October
Octr 27. John, son of Samuel and Sarah Braim, Berwick, Joiner
Novr 3. John, son of John and Mary Norton of Berwick, Labourer
6. Nancy, dau^r of Robert and Elizabeth Ellis, Potterton, Blacksmith
13. Mary, dau^r of John and Grace Vevers, Berwick, Joiner
16. William, son of Henry and Mary Simpson, Winmoor, Labourer
30. John, son of Edmund and Grace Popplewell, Winmoor, Labourer

1761.

Jan^r 28. George, base-born son of Susan Littlewood, Potterton
28. Elizabeth [daughter] of Joshua White and Martha, Potterton, Waggoner
29. Isabella, d^r of Robert and Ann Dixon, Barnbow, Labourer
Jan^r 30. Mary, d^r of John and Ellen Cawwood, Winmoor, Blacksmith
Feby 3. George, son of John and Elizabeth Dungwith, Berwick, Labourer
13. Elizabeth, d^r of John and Ann Robinson, Berwick, Wheelwright
Mar. 18. William, son of Edward and Mary Day, Potterton, Mason
April 5. Joseph, son of George and Mary Scoles, Barnbow, Collier
9. Thomas, son of John [Thomas *erased*] and Elizabeth Robinson, Winmoor, Farmer
*May 9. John, son of William and Mary Lumb, Berwick, School master
19. Mary, dau^r of Richard and Mary Lumb, Berwick, Farmer
22. Sarah, dau^r of Thomas and Margaret Whitehead, Berwick, Farmer
31. Ann, baseborn dau^r of Hannah Hill, Barwick
June 7. Ann, dau^r of John and Ann Lumb, Stanks, Husbandman
July 29. Martha, dau^r of Benjamin and Mary Shillitoe, Barnbow, Labourer
Aug. 9. James, son of John and Mary Bean, Berwick, shoemaker
Octr 18. Mary, dau^r of James and Mary Butler, Scholes, Pipe-maker
30. Hannah, dau^r of Christopher and Martha Varey, Scholes, Labourer
Novr 2. Matthew, son of Samuel and Sarah Varley, Berwick, Farmer

*John Lumb died 1 August, 1796, at Duke Street, London, "an eminent clock and watch maker."

2. Isaac, son of Roger and Alice Bell, Barnbow, Labourer
Dec[r] 20. Dinah, dau[r] of James and Tomasin Norton, Berwick, Labourer
1761 Baptisms, 21. F. Wray, Curate of Berwick.

BAPTISMS, 1762.

Jan[r] 10. John, son of Thomas and Susanna Baly, Winmoor, Labourer
31. Ann, dau[r] of Richard Smith and Ann, Berwick, Farmer
Feb[y] 7. Thomas, son of Thomas and Margaret Hanson, Berwick, Labourer
March 28. John, son of Abraham and Crissy Wormald, Berwick, Blacks[m]
28. Titus, bastard son of Susanna Watson, Potterton
April 3. William, son of Edward and Mary Day, Potterton, Mason
12. John, son of John and Mary Lunn, Barnbow-Carr, Collier
12. Thomas, son of Robert and Sarah Smith, Berwick, Collier
12. Richard, son of Richard and Elizabeth Hewitt, Barnbow Carr, Collier
13. Thomas, son of Henry and Mary Simpson, Roundhay, Labourer
13. Joseph, son of Robert and Elizabeth Ellis, Potterton, Blacks[m]
May 31. James, son of Henry and Sarah Perkins, Winmoor, Labourer
31. Mary, dau[r] of William and Frances Barker, Winmoor, Labourer
June 1. Benjamin, son of Benjamin and Elizabeth Braim, Barnbow-Carr, Wright
14. Robert, son of William and Frances Smith, Winmoor, Labourer
21. John, son of Francis and Ann Hawkins, Bram. moor, Waggoner
July 21. Mercy, dau[r] of John and Elizabeth Robinson, Winmoor, Farmer
Aug[t] 8. Susanna, dau[r] of Thomas and Mary Parker, Winmoor
13. Elizabeth, dau[r] of William and Hannah Waite, Berwick, Tailor
29. James, son of John and [*blank*] Bramley, Winmoor, Labourer
Sep[r] 18. John, son of Richard and Mary Wright, Kiddal Lane, Labourer
18. Martha, d[r] of Thomas and Elizabeth Shillitoe, Berwick, Tailor
Oct[r] 10. John, son of Edward and Elizabeth Monk, Berwick, Lab[r]
15. John, son of Joshua and Martha White, Bram. moor, Waggoner
16. Elizabeth, dau[r] of Abraham and Eliz. Rawlinson, Berwick, Lime-burner
Nov[r] 21. Joseph, son of Joshua White, Potterton, Waggoner
28. Rachel, dau[r] of Joseph and Hannah Kirkem, Barwick
30. Jane, dau[r] of Benj[n] and Mary Stringer, Winmoor
Dec[r] 10. Hannah, dau[r] of Joseph and Ann Daniel, Potterton Lane
26. George, son of Joseph and Mary Reedal, Scholes

BAPTISMS, 1763.

Jan[y] 24th. Betty, daughter of John and Ellin Cawood, Blacksmith, Winmoor
Jan[y] 26th. Mary, the daughter of Mark and Rose Toppin, Skinner, Barwick
Feb[y] 2nd. Rich[d], the son of James and Ann Parkin, Farmer, D[o]

March 25th. Mary, daughter of Robt and Elizth Barton, Junr, Joiner, Do
April 10th. Martha, of Willm and Mary Lumb, Farmer, Do
April 7th. Mary, daur [of] Georg and Mary Scholes, Barnbow [*Inserted*]
*May 5th. Willm, son of John and Sarah Nelson, Whitesmith, Leeds
7th. Sarah, daughter of Thos and Mary Ellar, Jocky, Kiddal Lane End
15th. Mary, daughter of Thos and Sarah Hewit, Labourer, Barwick
June 8th. Mary, daughter of Anthony and Sarah Dunwell, Weaver, Do
July 15th. Willm, son of Thos and Margaret Whitehead, Farmer, Do
Augst 14th. William, son of Matthew Hill, Labourer, Do
James Brooke, Curate, August 18, 1763.
Sepr 18th. Richd, son of John and Elizth Dungwith, Labourer, Do
21st. Robert, son of John and Elizth Robinson, Farmer, Winmoor
25th. Willm, son of Jonathan and Hannah Hodgson, Labourer, Barnbow
Ocr 2nd. John, son of Thos and Ann Bennet, Potmaker, Barwick
9th. Ann, daughter of John and Ann Robinson, Wheelwright, Do
18th. Sarah, daughter of Saml and Sarah Varley, Farmer, Do
Novr 20th. Phebe, daughter of Saml and Sarah Braim, Joiner, Do
27th. Simon, son of James Butler and Mary his wife, Pipemaker, Scholes
Decr 7th. Richd, son of Richd and Elizth Lumb, Farmer, Barwick
9th. Mary, daughter of Willm and Elizth Challinger, Limeburner, Do
11th William, son of Willm and Hannah Waite, Tailor, Do
18th. Susanna, daughter of Thos and Susanna Bayley, Labourer, Winmoor
26th. John, son of Thos and Elizth Hewit, Collier, Barwick

BAPTISMS, 1764.

Janry 4th. Thos, son of John & Ann Lumb, Stanks, Labourer
18th. Richard, son of John and Elizth Norton, Barwick, Labourer
Febry 19th. Ann, daughter of Roger and Alice Bell, Barwick, Blacksmith
April 1st. Margaret, daughter of Thos and Sarah Pitt, Barwick, Farmer
22nd. Sarah, daughter of Benjn and Susanna Watson, Barwick, Wheelwright
23rd. Ann, daughter of John and Mary Lunn, Barnbow Cr, Collier
23rd. William, son of Samuel and Cressy Simpson, Barnbow Carr, Collier
May 7th. Benjamin, son of Benjamin and Mary Shillitoe, Barnbow, Labourer
27th. Joannah, dr of John and Mary Lazenby, Scholes, Labourer
June 5th. George, son of Thomas and Mary Parker, Barwick, Potmaker

---

*John Nelson, of Kirkgate, Leeds, whitesmith, died 21 March, 1802, aged 62 years. Sarah his wife, died 19 June, 1800 aged 60 years. Their son William, died 5 June, 1789, aged 26 years. They are buried at St. John's Churchyard, Leeds. John Nelson was the father of James Nelson, of Briggate, Leeds, ironmonger, died 1844, aged 79, who was the father of Henry Nelson, of Leeds, solicitor, died 1899, aged 84, and grandfather of Captain Robert Henry Nelson of Methuen's Horse, who accompanied Stanley in his expedition across Africa, and of whom Stanley said there was "merit on his very face."

21st. Hannah, daughter of Richard and Ann Smith, Barwick, Farmer

23rd. Hannah, daughter of Henry and Sarah Perkin, Bram. moor, Waggoner

August 24th. John, son of William and Deborah Wright, Scholes, Farmer

Sepr 2nd. Ann, daughter of Henry and Mary Simpson, Winmoor, Labourer

2nd. Sarah, daughter of Abraham and Crissy Wormald, Barwick, Blacksmith

14. Ann, bastard daughter of Sarah Hunton, Barwick

30. Robert, son of Joseph Goodall, Brown moor, Collier

Octr 7. Mary, daughter of Thomas and Margaret Hanson, Barwick, Labourer

14. Sarah, daughter of Samuel and Elisabeth Mawkin, Barwick, Potmaker

Novr 7. Thomas, bastard son of Mary Hammond

Decr 23. John, son of William and Dorothy Varey, Scholes, Labourer

23. William, son of Benjamin and Ann Rawlinson, Barwick, Labourer

BAPTISMS, 1765.

Jan. 9. Rebekah, daughter of Joseph and Ann Daniel, Potterton Lane, Farmer

18. Mary, daughter of Edward and Mary Day, Potterton, Mason

27. John, son of John and Frances Bramley, Potterton, Labourer

Feby. 17. John, son of William and Frances Brown, Penwell, Labourer

17. Betty, daughter of Benjamin and Hannah Stringer, Winmoor, Tailor

March 3. Mary, daughter of Benjamin and Elizabeth Ellison, Morwick, Labourer

27. James, son of John and Mary Strodder, Barwick, Wheelwright

April 3. Timothy, son of John and Elizabeth Robinson, Winmoor, Farmer

April 8. Sarah, daughter of Edward and Elizabeth Monk, Barwick, Labourer

21. Mary, daughter of Thomas and Elizabeth Shillitoe, Barwick, Tailor

June 9. Hannah, daughter of William and Ann Waite, Barwick, Labourer

9. Henry, son of William and Esther Hodgson, Barnbow, Labourer

12. James, son of James and Tomasin Norton, Barwick, Labourer

16. Mark, son of Mark and Rose Toppin, Barwick, Skinner

Augst 4. Deborah, daughter of Willm and Margaret Dawson, Born July 15, Barwick, Clerk

Octr 27. Thomas, son of Robert and Elizabeth Barton, Junior, Barwick, Joiner

Novr 3. Jonathan, son of Jonathan and Hannah Hodgson, Barnbow Labourer

9. Sarah, dr of Anthony and Sarah Dunwell, Barwick, Weaver

11. William, son of Robert and Ann Dixon, Barnbow, Labourer
Decem^r 15. Hannah, daughter of Thomas and Ann Benton, Brown moor
15. Abraham, son of Richard and Hannah Nailer, Garf^h moorside
18. John, son of John and Sarah Lyster, Barwick

BAPTISMS, 1766.

Feby 4. John, son of William and Elizabeth Challinger, Limeburner, Barwick
23. Martha, daughter of Christopher and Martha Varey, Scholes, Labourer
March 9. Richard, son of Richard and Elizabeth Lumb, Barwick, Farmer
27. John, son of Thomas and Jane Todd, Scholes, Labourer
April 6. Margaret, daughter of James and Ann Bean, Barwick, Farmer
May 12. Peter, son of Peter and Frances Stephenson, Cross Gates, Labourer
13. Michael and Elizabeth, son and dau^r of William and Ann Rooke, Kid-Hall
28. Phebe, daughter of Thomas and Susanna Bayley, Winmoor, Labourer
June 15. Joseph, son of George and Mary Scoles, Barnbow, collier
29. Thomas, son of William and Mary Simpson, Scholes, Labourer
Augt 3. John, son of William and Mary Lumb, Barwick, Farmer
Sepr 7. Benjamin, son of Samuel and Crissy Simpson, Barnbow Carr, Collier
7. Mary, daughter of John and Mary Lunn, Barnbow Carr, Collier
7. Ann, daughter of John and Elizabeth Dungwith, Barwick, Labourer
7. Benjamin, son of Benjamin and Ann Rawlinson, Barwick, Labourer
20. Hannah, daughter of Abraham and Crissy Wormald, Barwick, Blacksmith
Octr 19. Ann, daughter of John and Mary Lazenby, Barnbow, Labourer
Octr 19. Hannah, daughter of Richard and Ann Smith, Barwick, Farmer
Decr 3. Nancy, daughter of Thomas and Mary Parker, Barwick, Potmaker
21. Mary, daughter of Benjamin and Mary Shillitoe, Barnbow, Labourer
28. Hannah, daughter of Henry and Mary Simpson, Winmoor, Labourer

BAPTISMS, 1767.

Jany 4. Mary, daughter of John and Elizabeth Norton, Fire Engine, Collier
Feby 9. Joseph, son of George and Mary Reedal, Scholes, Farmer
6. Thomas, son of Thomas and Margaret Whitehead, Barwick, Farmer
March 1. Susanna, daughter of Richard and Elizabeth Lee, Barwick, Labourer

Feby 27. Leah daughter of Joseph and Ann Daniel, Potterton Lane, Farmer
March 22. Thomas, son of William and Hannah Waite, Barwick, Tailor
April 12. Hannah, daughter of William and Dorothy Varey, Scholes, Labourer
19. Lyddy, daughter of Benjamin and Hannah Stringer, Winmoor, Tailor
19. Matthew, son of Benjamin and Susanna Watson, Barwick, Wheelwright
21. James, son of James and Sarah Ayre, Winmoor, Collier
21. Sarah, daughter of Thomas and Margaret Hanson, Barwick, Labourer
29. John, son of Samuel and Sarah Varley, Barwick, Farmer
29. Hannah, daughter of Thomas and Sarah Hewit, Barwick, Labourer
29. Ellen, daughter of Roger and Alice Bell, Barwick, Blacksmith
29. William, son of John and Frances Bramley, Potterton, Labourer
May 1. Hannah, daughter of Edward and Elizabeth Monk, Barwick, Labourer
3. Betty, daughter of Thomas and Sarah Granger, Barnbow Car, Groom
17. Elizabeth, daughter of John and Ann Lumb, Stanks, Labourer
June 15. Hannah, daughter of John and Mary Strodder, Barwick, Labourer
19. John, son of William and Mary Clapham, Kid Hall Lane, Farmer
21. Nelly, daughter of John and Ellin Cawood, Winmoor, Blacksmith
27. William, son of James and Bathsheba Wright, Barwick, Labourer
Novem. 1. William, son of Abraham and Crissy Wormald, Barwick, Blacksmith
8. Elizabeth, daughter of William and Ann Dufton, Barwick, Labourer
11. William, son of John and Alice Batty, Barwick, shoemaker
Decr 6. Richard, son of Thomas and Elizabeth Shillitoe, Barwick, Tailor
18. Thomas, son of William and Ann Rooke, Kid-Hall

BAPTISMS, 1768.

Jany 10. Elizabeth, bastard daughter of Elizabeth Gowling, Barwick
31. Mary, daughter of John and Izabella Harrison, Potterton, Labourer
Feby 10. Elizabeth, daughter of Robert and Elizabeth Barton, Barwick, Joiner
21. John, son of James and Ann Perkins, Barwick, Farmer
March 4. Elizabeth, daughter of John and Grace Vevers, Barwick, Joiner
25. Sarah, daughter of John and Sarah Tate, Barwick, Farmer
30. Betty, daughter of William and Esther Hodgson, Barnbow Cr, Labourer

April 2nd. Mary, daughter of Thomas and Ann Hargrave, Roundhay, Farmer
April 24. Ann, daughter of Richard and Elizabeth Lumb, Barwick, Farmer
May 1. James, son of James and Ann Bean, Barwick, Farmer
1. Thomas, son of Anthony and Sarah Dunwell, Barwick, Weaver
13. Ann, daughter of Thomas and Margaret Laureman, Fire Engine, Labourer
June 19. William, son of William and Elizabeth Challinger, Barwick, Labourer
26. Ann, daughter of Thomas and Jane Todd, Scholes, Labourer
July 9. James, son of William and Frances Brown, Penwell, Labourer
9. Jonathan, son of Jonathan and Mary Dineson, Stanks, Labourer
10. Jane, daughter of Francis and Ann Hawkins, Scholes, Labourer
10. John, bastard son of Elizabeth Watson, Barwick
24. Sarah, daughter of William and Mary Lumb, Barwick, Farmer
27. William, son of John and Elizabeth Robinson, Winmoor, Farmer
Augst 14. James, son of Joseph and Sarah Holmes, Barwick, Tailor
14. Mary, daughter of Thomas and Mary Stephenson, Stanks, Labourer
28. Mary, daughter of William and Dorothy Scott, Barwick, Joiner
28. Dorothy, daughter of William and Mary Simpson, Barnbow Carr, Collier
Septr 9. Thomas, son of Benjamin and Elizabeth Collet, Barwick, Butcher
11. Nanny, dr of Abraham and Mary Bell, Potterton, Labourer
October 9. Benjamin, son of John and Mary Rawden, Winmoor, Labourer
Novr 20. Dinah, daughter of William and Mary Clayton, Fire Engine, Blacksmith
20. Ann, daughter of James and Tomasin Norton, Barwick, Labourer
22. Lucy, daughter of John and Hannah Thompson, Barnbow Carr, Collier
27. Margaret, daughter of William and Alice Robshaw, Barwick, Labourer
Decr 4. John, son of John and Catharine Barker, Barwick, Tailor
28. Adiman, son of William and Frances Barker, Winmoor, Labourer

BAPTISMS, 1769.

Jany 8. Frances, daughter of Bartholomew and Elizabeth Glover, Fire Engine, Labourer
24. Joseph, son of William and Elizabeth Eamonson, Lazincroft
Feby 8. Betty, daughter of John and Mary Lunn, Barnbow Carr, Collier
March 25. Martha, daughter of Edward and Mary Day, Potterton, Mason
Hannah, daughter of Thomas and Ann Hargrave, Roundhay, Farmer

28. Richard, son of Richard and Ann Smith, Barwick, Farmer
31. Ann, daughter of William and Mary Clapham, Kid-Hall Lane, Farmer
April 2. John, son of John and Alice Batty, Barwick, Shoemaker
16. John, son of Joseph and Hannah Kirkham, Barwick, Labourer
16. Mary, daughter of William and Elizabeth Hardington, Scholes, Labourer
16. Thomas and William, Twins, sons of Samuel and Sarah Varley, Barwick, Farmer
23. Jonathan, son of James and Bersheba Wright, Barwick, Labourer
May 9. Edmund, son of Thomas and Mary Parker, Barwick, Labourer
7. Christopher, son of Christopher and Martha Varey, Scholes, Labourer
10. William, son of John and Mary Strodder, Barwick, Labourer
11. David, son of Jonathan and Hannah Hodgson, Scholes, Labourer
28. Sarah, daughter of Benjamin and Hannah Stringer, Winmoor, Tailor
28. JonathanWilkinson, bastardson of Widow Horstfield, Potterton
June 4. William and George, Twins, sons of Renton and Hannah Haist, Crossgates, Labourer
4. Anna, daughter of William and Margaret Dawson, Barwick, Clerk
25. Sarah, daughter of Alvara and Sarah Thompson, Winmoor, Labourer
July 16. John, son of Gabriel and Mary Tomlinson, Scholes, Labourer
16. George, son of George and Mary Scoles, Barnbow, Collier
16. Sarah, daughter of Benjamin and Mary Shillitoe, Barnbow, Labourer
23. John, bastard son of Martha Lumb, Stocking
25. Margaret, daughter of William and Dinah Sherriff, Potterton, Gardiner
30. Isaac, son of Thomas and Sarah Granger, Barnbow Carr, Groom
Aug^st 27. Susy, daughter of Thomas and Susanna Bayley, Winmoor, Labourer
Septem^r 6. Jane, daughter of Edward and Elizabeth Monk, Barwick, Labourer
10. Mary, daughter of William and Ann Hemsworth, Kidhall Lane, Labourer
Octr 8. Ann, daughter of John and Izabella Harrison, Potterton, Labourer
*25. Samuel, son of Samuel and Hannah Lumb, Stanks, Farmer

*Samuel Lumb, whose baptism is here recorded, married, 1797, at Kippax, Mary, dau. of John Poynton, died 16 Feb., 1826, and was buried at St. John's, Leeds. He was an auctioneer and valuer, and with John Smallpage had the privilege of issuing silver tokens at Leeds in 1812. Two of his sons were Charles Poynton Lumb (1798—1868) of Leeds, and Edward Lumb (1804—1872) of Buenos Ayres, merchant, who married there 1825, Elizabeth Yates, and entertained Charles Darwin when on his tour in the Beagle. Edward Lumb was father of Charles Poynton Lumb of Buenos Ayres, merchant, Alfred Overton Lumb, Consul at London for Argentina, Edward Henry Lumb of Guaranins Hall, Ann, wife of The Right Hon. Sir Hugh Guion Macdonell, G.C.M.G., C.B., British Minister at Lisbon, and Harriet Blake Armstrong, the first wife of the 11th Baron Napier and Ettrick. Samuel Lumb (1729—1801) the father, was Overseer of the Highways at Barwick in 1740, of the Poor 1741, Churchwarden 1746, and was married to Hannah Wood, 1767, at Barwick.

27. Betty, daughter of John and Frances Clark, Winmoor, Farmer
29. William, son of Thomas and Judith Pickersgill, Grimes dyke, Labourer
Nov[r] 5. Betty, daughter of William and Sarah Richardson, Barwick, shoemaker
12. Elizabeth, daughter of John and Jane Milner, Winmoor, Labourer
24. Hannah, daughter of George and Hannah Reedal, Scholes, Farmer
Dec[r] 8. Thomas, son of Richard and Elizabeth Lee, Barwick, Labourer
10. John, son of Richard and Alice Waite, Barwick, Tailor
10. Joseph, son of John and Frances Bramley, Potterton, Labourer
24. Benjamin, son of William and Sarah Rawlinson, Barwick, Labourer

BAPTISMS, 1770.

Feb[y] 4. John, son of Bartholomew and Elizabeth Glover, Fire Engine, Labourer
4. Susanna, daughter of Benjamin and Susanna Watson, Barwick, Wheelwright
7. Mary, daughter of Thomas and Mary Haley, Scholes, Farmer
March 11. Jonathan and Martha, Twins, son and dau[r] of James and Bersheba Wright, Barwick, Labourer
14. Betty, daughter of Abraham and Cressy Wormald, Barwick, Blacksmith
14. William, son of John and Mary Bean, Barwick, Cordwainer
27. Mary, bastard daughter of Ann Thornton, Potterton Lane
April 3. Ann, daughter of Thomas and Elizabeth Abbot, Barwick, Labourer
17. Thomas, son of Thomas and Sarah Tilney, Scholes, Labourer
May 13. John, son of Thomas and Margaret Hanson, Potterton, Labourer
20. Thomas, son of John and Alice Batty, Barwick, Shoemaker
24. Henry and Thomas, Twins, sons of William and Elizabeth Challinger, Barwick, Labourer
June 20. Thomas, son of Tho[s] and Ann Hargrave, Roundhay, Farmer
July 27. James, bastard son of Margaret Dean, Hill Top
Aug[t] 5. Sarah, daughter of Jeremiah and Ellin Lumb, Stanks, Labourer
19. Ann, daughter of Thomas and Margaret Hampshaw, Barwick, Labourer
26. Mary, daughter of Richard and Mary Wright, Kidhall Lane End, Labourer
Sep[r] 2. Thomas, son of John and Hannah Thompson, Barnbow Carr, Collier
9. James, son of William and Mary Lumb, Barwick, Farmer
Nov[r] 2. Mary, daughter of James and Sarah Hare, Stanks, Labourer
25. Mary, daughter of Jonas and Jane Vince, Garforth M. side Collier

Dec[r] 2. Ann, daughter of John and Mary Rawden, Winmoor, Labourer
2. William, son of Anthony and Sarah Dunwell, Barwick, Weaver
16. Betty, daughter of William and Dorothy Varey, Barnbow Carr, Labourer
25. Benjamin, son of John and Mary Lunn, Barnbow Carr, Collier
25. Rebekah, daughter of William and Mary Simpson, Barnbow Carr, Collier

BAPTISMS, 1771.

Jan[y] 20. Mary, daughter of James and Ann Bean, Barwick, Farmer
Feb[y] 17. Elizabeth, daughter of Thomas and Jane Todd, Scholes, Labourer
17. Betty, daughter of Francis and Ann Hawkins, Scholes, Labourer
March 15. Martha, the daughter of Thomas and Elizabeth Shillitoe, Potterton, Tailor
27. Ann, the daughter of William and Sarah Richardson, Barwick, Shoemaker
April 1. Thomas, the son of William and Frances Brown, Penwell, Labourer
21st. Richard, the son of James and Mary Jackson, Barwick, Farmer
28. Lyddy, daughter of Henry and Mary Simpson, Redhall, Labourer
May 2nd. Hannah, daughter of William and Sarah Lumb, Barwick, Labourer
12th. Robert, the son of Robert and Elizabeth Barton, Barwick, Joiner
June 2nd. John, the son of Thomas and Abby Bean, Barwick, Cordwainer
2nd. William, the son of Samuel and Hannah Lumb, Jun[r], Stanks, Farmer
2. Alvara, son of Thomas and Sarah Thompson, Stanks, Labourer
16. Elizabeth, the daughter of Edward and Mary Day, Potterton, Mason
23. Hannah, dau[r] of James and Bathsheba Wright, Berwick, Labourer
July 21. John, son of Michael and Magdalene Atkinson, Winmoor, Farmer
Aug[t] 11. Mary, dau[r] of Roger and Ann Brownrigg, Scholes, Taylor
Sep[r] 1. Job, son of Jonathan and Hannah Hodgson, Stanks, Labourer
1. Nanny, dau[r] of Jonathan and Mary Dennison, Stanks, Brickmaker
6. Ann, dau[r] of Joseph and Sarah Holmes, Berwick, Taylor
22. Christopher, son of Tho[s] and Susanna Bailey, Hill-top, Labourer
30. Ann, dau[r] of John and Alice Batty, Berwick, Shoemaker
*Oct[r] 4. James, son of Richard and Elizabeth Lumb, Berwick, Farmer
6. Rachel, dau[r] of Christopher and Martha Varey, Scholes, Labourer

---

*James Lumb (1771—1842) of Grove House, Barwick, married Tabitha Turner, had eight children who have all died without issue. He was buried in Barwick Churchyard. M.I.

9. Elizabeth, daur of William and Ann Hemsworth, Bram. moor, Labourer
13. Joseph, son of Joseph and Ann Mather, Grimsdike, Labourer
Novr 3. William, son of Benjamin and Eliz: Collet, Berwick, Butcher
3. William, son of William and Judith Waite, Berwick, Labr
17. Thomas son of Benjamin and Mary Shillitoe, Barnbow, Labr
24. David, son of David and Ann Carter, Stanks, Labr
24. Ann, daur of Richard and Ann Stead, Berwick, Labr
Decr 5. William, son of William and Dinah Sheriff, Potterton, Gardiner
8. David, bastard son of Gezaiah Riddle, Scholes
26. Richard, son of Richard and Alice Waite, Berwick, Tailor

Baptisms, 34. F. Wray, Curate.

BAPTISMS, 1772.

Janr 1. Henry, son of Richard and Ester Parke, Winmoor, Farmer
1. Thomas, son of Thomas and Mary Parker, Berwick, Labr
19. Ann, daur of Gabriel and Mary Tomlinson, Scholes, Collier
Feb. 5. William, son of Peter and Ann Newby, Berwick, Joiner
9. Elizabeth, daur of David and Elizabeth Hodgson, Berwick, Labr
26. Mary, daur of Richard and Ann Smith, Berwick, Farmer
Mar. 15. Benjamin, son of John and Frances Bramley, Potterton, Labr
25. Samuel, son of John and Hannah Thompson, Barnbw Carr, Collier
April 12. Hannah, daur of Thomas and Elizabeth Abbott, Berwick, Labr
29. John, son of George and Mary Scholes, Barnbow, Collier
June 21. Mary, bastard daur of Margaret Dean, Winmoor
26. Ann, daur of William and Mary Simpson, Barnbow, Collier
July 12. John, son of Joshua and Hannah Atkinson, Berwick, Travellers
12. Sarah, daur of Joshua and Hannah Atkinson (8 years old), Do Do
26. John, son of Thomas and Margaret Whitehead, Berwick, Farmer
Aug. 30. Benjamin, son of Benjamin and Hannah Stringer, Hill top, Taylor
Sepr 20. Phillippa, daur of Edward and Elizabeth Monk, Berwick, Labr
29. Margaret, daur of James and Elizabeth Whitehead, Berwick, Labr
Oct. 4. John, son of Benjamin and Susanna Watson, Berwick, Wright
4. William, son of William and Sarah Stringer, Winmoor, Taylor
12. Joseph, son of Joseph and Hannah Kirkham, Berwick, Labr
23. William, bastard son of Mary Pease (baptised by Revd Mr Baxtor), Moorhouse, Garforth
25. William, son of Samuel and Susanna Thompson, Barnbow, Collier
Novr 1. Helen, daur of William and Dorothy Varey, Scholes, Labr
1. Richard, son of William and Elizabeth Challinger, Barnbow, Labr
2. Mary, daur of Thomas and Sarah Pitts, Berwick, Farmer

8. James, son of William and Martha Derrick, Winmoor, Lab^r^
Decr 6. Jane, dau^r^ of Henry and Mary Simpson, Winmoor, Lab^r^
13. John, son of Robert and Sarah Jordan, Stanks, Lab^r^
28. Luke, son of William and Sarah Richardson, Berwick, Shoem^r^
Baptisms, 30. F. Wray, Curate.

BAPTISMS, 1773.

Jany 17. Thomas, son of William and Alice Robshaw, Berwick, Lab^r^
31. John son of Robert and Elizabeth Barton, Berwick, Carp^r^
Feby 7. John, son of William and Sarah Lumb, Winm^r^, Lab^r^
7. William, son of Henry and Elizabeth Greenwood [*erased*], Berwick
21. Mary, dau^r^ of Peter and Frances Stephenson, Crossgates, Lab^r^
23. Thomas, son of Henry and Elizabeth Greenwood, Berwick, Lab^r^
28. Grace, dau^r^ of John and Jane Milner, Winm^r^, Lab^r^
28. William, son of Thomas and Sarah Grainger, Barnb^w^ Carr, Huntsman
March 2. Mary dau^r^ of Abraham and Mary Rawlinson, Berwick, Lime-man
3. Mary, dau^r^ of John and Mary Rawden, Winmoor, Lab^r^
14. Richard, son of Thomas and Margaret Hamshaw, Berwick, Lab^r^
25. John-spooner, son of Mr Benjamin and Martha Rookes, Kidhall, Farmer
28. William, bastard son of Mary Barrett (Capt. Wood reputed Father), Berwick
30. James, son of James and Mary Jackson, Berwick, Lab^r^
Ap^l^ 10. Elizabeth, dau^r^ of Jeremiah and Helen Lumb, Bramhm^r^, Lab^r^
19. Benjamin, son of John and Alice Batty, Berwick, shoemaker
20. John, son of James and Bathsheba Wright, Berwick, Lab^r^
May 3. George, bastard son of Sally Waite, Berwick
5. Sarah, dau^r^ of John and Catharine Barker, Engine, Banksm^n^
9. Mary, dau^r^ of Alvary and Sarah Thompson, Winmoor, Lab^r^
16. William, son of Richard and Ann Lee (half a year old) Berwick, Lab^r^
(2^d^) 30. Richard, son of Thomas and Abigail Bean, Berwick, Farmer
(1st) 16. William, son of Francis Hawkins and Ann his wife, Scholes, Lab^r^
July 6. Mary, dau^r^ of Thomas and Jane Todd, Scholes, Lab^r^
6. William, son of David and Mary Buchanan, Scholes, Lab^r^
18. Ann, dau^r^ of Richard and Esther Parke, Winmoor, Farmer
18. Mary, bastard dau^r^ of Mary Simpson, Barnb: Carr.
25. Hannah, dau^r^ of Jonathan and Hannah Hodgson, Stanks, Lab^r^
Augt 23. Elizabeth, dau^r^ of William and Elizabeth Ardington, Berwick, Lab^r^
Sepr 12. William, son of William and Elizabeth Deighton, Berwick, Lab^r^
20. Peter, son of Peter and Ester Higgins, Berwick, Lab^r^
Octr 3. Benjamin, son of Antony and Sarah Dunwell, Berwick, Lab^r^
17. Sarah, dau^r^ of Thomas and Elizabeth Smith, Scholes, Lab^r^
Novr 7. Elizabeth, dau^r^ of Richard and Elizabeth Lumb, Berwick Farmer

21. Elizabeth, daur of Richard and Ann Stead, Berwick, Labr
Decr 5. Jacob, son of William and Frances Brown, Penwell, Labr
18. Thomas, son of James and Ann Bean, Berwick, Farmer
18. Benjamin, bastard son of Elizabeth Cockshaw, Berwick
26. William, son of David and Ann Carter, Stanks, Labr
28. Ann, daur of William and Ann Hemsworth, Bram: Moor, Labr

Baptisms, 39. F. Wray, curate.

BAPTISMS, 1774.

Janr 2. Mary, daur of Joseph and Ann Mather, Grimesdike, Labr
16. John, son of William and Dinah Sheriff, Potterton, Gardiner
Feb. 8. Sarah, daur of William and Sarah Richardson, Berwick, Shoemr
11. Thomas, son of Thomas and Mary Clapham, Bramh: Moor Publican
13. John, son of John and Sarah Lidster, Berwick, Farmer
20. Sarah, daur of George and Grace Hopton, Scholes, Collier
27. William, son of Thomas and Sarah Tilney, Scholes, Mason
March 27. Joseph, son of Joseph and Ann Cawthorn, Berwick, Labr
27. Ann, daur of Mr Benjn and Martha Rookes, Kidhall, Farmer
May 8. Benjamin, son of John and Hannah Thompson, Barnbow Carr, Collier
8. William, son of William and Mary Simpson, Scholes, Collier
8. David, son of James and Mary Jolley, Scholes, Labourer
18th. Ann, the daughter of Thomas and Elizabeth Buckle, Born May 7th, Scholes, Bricklayer
June 17th. Sarah, the daughter of Richard and Alce Waite, Barwick, Tailor
19. Dorathy, daughter of William and Julia Waite, Barwick, Labourer
July 3rd. Sarah, daughter of Thomas and Sarah Huit, Barwick, Farmer
David, son of Benjamin and Mary Shillitoe, Baptized July 24th, Barnbow hall, Labr
July 24th. Joseph, son of Bartholomew and Elizabeth Glover, Fire Engine, Labourer
25th. Hannah, the daughter of Luke and Ann Dawson, Barnbow Farmer
Augst 21th. Elizabeth, the daughter of Benjamin and Elizth Collet, Barwick, Butcher
Sepr 6th. Sarah, daughter of William and Ann Hemsworth, Kiddal Lane, Labourer
25th. Rachel, the daughter of John and Mary Strother, Scholes, Wheelwright
Octr 4th. Mary and Martha, Twins, daughters of Henry and Mary Simpson, Redhall, Labourer
24th. Frances, daughter of William and Hannah Barker, of Wetherby, Waggoner
Novr 7th. Nancy, the daughter of Thomas and Elizabeth Shillitoe, Potterton, Tailor
7th. Ann, the daughter of Michael and Magdalene Atkinson, Redhall, Farmer

27th. Mary, the daughter of Thomas and Mary Parker, Barwick, Labourer

Decr 4th. David, son of William and Elizabeth Challinger, Scholes, Labourer

BAPTISMS, 1775.

Jany 1st. Thomas, son of Thomas and Abigail Bean, Barwick, Shoemaker

6. William, son of Robert and Sarah Jordan, Stanks, Labourer

13th. Thomas, son of Thomas and Sarah Pitt, Barwick, Farmer

20th. Martha, daughter of Thomas and Judith Pickersgill, Grimesdike, Farmer

22n. Stephen, son of John and Sarah Slaytor, Winmoor, Labourer

29th. Cressey, daughter of Samuell and Susannah Thompson, Barnbow Carr, Collier

29th. Christopher, son of Thomas and Frances Simpson, Barnbow Cr, Collier

Febry 12. William, son of William and Alice Robshaw, Barwick, Collier

19. Edward, son of John and Catherine Barker, Engine, Banksman

March 5th. Martha, daughter of Henry and Elizth Greenwood, Barwick, Laboror

5th. Mally, bastard daughter of Hannah Wilkinson of Holbeck, Barwick, spinster

April 9th. Mary, daughter of John and Alice Batty, Barwick, shoemaker

16. Jeremiah, son of Jonathan and Hannah Hodgson, Stanks, Labourer

16. Richard, son of Alvara and Sarah Thomson, Winmoor, Labourer

19th. Sarah, daughter of William and Alce Carr, Kiddal lane, Inkeeper

23. Elizabeth, daughter of Joseph and Sarah Lister, Barnbow, Labourer

May 7th. Benjamin, son of Abraham and Mary Rawlinson, Barwick, Lime Man

7th. Samuel, son of William and Jane Thompson, Barnbow, Collier

14th. Sarah, bastard daughter of Elizabeth Cockshaw, Barwick, Spinster

21st. Joseph, son of James and Bathsheba Wright, Barwick, Labourer

June 4th. Sarah, daughter of John and Mary Rawden, Winmore, Labourer

4th. Ann, daughter of Benjamin and Susanah Watson, Barwick, Wright

5th. Elizabath, daughter of Peter and Ann Newby, Barwick, Carpenter

*26th. Mary, daughter of Luke and Ann Dawson, Barnbow, Farmer

---

*William Dawson, the celebrated Wesleyan Local Preacher, was their eldest child, being born at Garforth, 30 March, 1773, died 4 July, 1841, and was buried at Barwick. See his memoirs by Everitt, and the Dictionary of National Biography.

July 16th. Matthew, son of James and Mary Jackson, Barwick, Labr
16th. Betty, daughter of Gabril and Mary Tomlinson, Scholes, Collier
16th. Richard, son of Jonothan and Mary Dinison, Stanks, Carpenter
August 6th. Thomas, son of Richard and Mary Thompson, Crosgates Labourer
6th. John, son of John and Jane Milner, Winmoor, Labourer
6th. Pally, daughter of James and Mary Jolley, Scholes, Labourer
13th. William, son of Thomas and Ann Whitead, Potterton, Farmer
27th. Ann, daughter of Roger and Ann Brownrig, Scholes, Taylor
27th. John, son of William and Elizabeth Carter, Penwell, Blacksmith
27th. Mary,daughter of Renton and Sarah Haist,Barwick,Labourer
Septem. 8th. Benjamin, son of Samuel and Sarah Harrison, Potterton, Labourer
17th. Joshua, son of William and Mary Britaine, Barnbow, Bricklayer
October 1st. Thomas, son of Samuel and Ann Simpson, Scholes, Collier
November 5th. William, son of William and Sarah Robshaw, Barwick, Labourer
5th. Michael, son of Thomas and Jane Todd, Scholes, Labourer
5th. George, son of Richard and Elizabeth Lee, Barwick, Labor
5th. Mary, daughter of William and Sarah Lumb, Winmoor, Labourer
5th. Dinah, daughter of William and Mary Clayton, Engine, Blacksmith
27th. James, son of William and Sarah Bell, hiltop, Labourer
December 17th. Francis, son of Francis and Ann Hawkins, Scholes, Labourer

BAPTISMS, 1776.

January 7th. Ann, daughter of Thomas and Sarah Tilney, Scholes, Mason
February 18th. William, son of John and Hannah Thompson, Barnbow, Collier
28. John, son of John and Ann Greenwood, Crosgates, Carpinter
March 7th. Thomas, son of James and Jane Pawson, Roundhay, Farmer
10th. Samuel, son of Antoney and Sarah Dunwell, Barwick, Weaver
17th. Jane, daughter of Bartholomew and Elisabeth Glover, Engine, Labourer
29. Elizabeth, daughter of William and Ann Vevers, Kiddalhall, Farmer
31st. Samuel, son of John and Mary Lunn, Barnbow, Collier
April. 5th Thomas, son of John and Ellen Wright, Winmoor, Labourer
7th. William, son of William and Sarah Rawlinson, Barwick, Labourer
14th. Richard, son of Robert and Sarah Jordon, Stanks, Labourer
May 8th. Ann, daughter of Richard and Elizabeth Lumb, Barwick, Farmer

26th. Mary, daughter of Peter and Easter Higgens, Barwick, Labourer
June 23d. John, son of Thomas and Ann Benton, Born May 11th, Brownmoor, Collier
July 7th. Hannah, daughter of David and Hannah Carter, Stanks, Labourer
26. John,son of William and Alice Carr, Kiddall Lane End,Inkeper
28th. Elizabeth, daughter of Thomas and Elizabeth Hewitt, Barwick, Collier
August 7th. Grace, daughter of Joseph and Mary White, Scholes, Farmer
Sept' 15th. James, son of Matthew and Jane Miller, Kidhall lane End
October 6th. James, son of James and Mary Plowright, Barwick, shopkeeper
6th. Hannah,daughter of Richard and Alice Waite,Barwick,Taylor
13th. Thomas, son of John and Maria Cullingworth, Potterton, Shoemaker
November 3d. Richard, son of Luke and Ann Dawson, Barnbow, Farmer
3d. Joseph,son of Thomas and Abbigal Bean, Barwick,Shoemaker
24th. John, son of Thomas and Julea Waite, Barwick, Labourer
December 1st. William, son of John and Grace Vevers, Barwick, Joiner
1st. Joseph, son of James and Mary Jackson, Barwick, Labourer
8th. Sarah,daughter of William and Elizabeth Hardinton,Barwick, Labourer
15th. Beniamin, son of Joseph and Mary Thackerhey, Barwick, Labourer
18th. John, son of Robert and Ann Bickerdike, Potterton, Farmer
25th. Sarah, bastard daughter of Ann Dufton, Barwick
25th. Ann, bastard daughter of Elizabeth Norton, Barwick
26th. Betty, daughter of Thomas and Frances Simpson, Barnbow, collier

BAPTISMS, 1777. Place Business

February 2nd. James, son of John and Alice Batty, Barwick, Shoemaker
9th. Andrew, son of John and Jane Blackburn, Garforth moor, collier
16th. Ann, daughter of Thomas and Sarah Tinley, Scholes, Mason
22. Martha, daughter of Thomas and Hannah Morritt, Winmoor, Labourer
March 2d. Fanny, bastard daughter of Hannah Lunn, Barnbow
7th. William,sonofSamuelandSarahHarrison,Potterton,Labourer
23d. Thomas, son of Thomas and Margrit Ampshaw, Barwick Labourer
31st. James, son of John and Sarah Slayter, Winmoor, Labourer
April 27th. John, son of Renton and Sarah Haist, Barwick, Labourer
John Simpson, son of Henrey Simpson of Hiltop in the parish of Barwick in Elmett, Labourer, Desended from Thomas and Mary Simpson of the said parish and of Martha Simpson, descended

from Joseph and Deborah Maud of the said parish, born on Friday, the 21st of March, baptzed on Sunday, the eleventh of May.

Samuel Thompson, son of Richard Thompson of Crosgates in the parish of Barwick in Elmet, Labourer, decended from Richard and Mary Thompson of Seacroft, in the parish of Witkirke, and of Mary Thompson decended from Samuel and Chrissey Simpson of the parish of Barwick, Born on Thursday the 6th of March, baptized on the Monday, the 19th of May

Mary Barker, daughter of John Barker of the Ingine, in the parish of Barwick in Elmet, Banksman, Decended from John and Sarah Barker of Garforth and of Catherine Barker, decended from Thomas and Catherine Robshaw of Barwick in Elmet, born Friday, the 2d of May, Btized May 25th

Elizabeth Thompson, daugr of Samuel Thompson of Barnbow, Collier, Descended from John and Frances Thompson of Garforth, and of Susannah Thompson, descended from William and Susannah Taylor, Barnbow, Born Friday, 9th of May, Bap. Sunday, 8th of June

Mary Lidster, daugr of Joseph Lidster of Scholes, shoemaker, [descended] from William and Mary Lidster of Garforth, and of Sarah Lidster, Descended from Samuel and Chrissey Simpson, Barnbow, [born] Setterday, 29 of March, [bap.] Sunday, 8 of June

John Robshaw, son of William Robshaw of Barwick, Labourer, from Thomas and Catherine Robshaw, Barwick, and of Alice Robshaw, Descended from Wm and Margrit Rothmell, Knaisborough, [born] Munday, 12th of May, [bap.] Sunday, 8 of June

Henry Sherriff, son of Willm Sherriff, Potterton, Gardiner, from George and Margrit Sherriff, Lancashire, and of Dina Sherriff, descended from Hery and Margrit Foster, Lancashire, [born] Setterday, the 3d of May, [bap.] Sunday, the 15th of June

Sarah Wright, daughter of James Wright, Barwick, Labourer, descended from Henry and Sarah Wright, Bilbrif, and Bathsheba Wright, descended from James and Martha Robinson, Barwick, [born] Sunday, 4 of May, [bap.] Sunday, 22th of June

John Park, son of Richard Park of Winmoor, Farmer, descended from Willm and Mary Park, Ludtherton, Farmer, and of Easter Park, descended from Robert & Maudland Bardon, Kirkby-over-blows, born Monday, the 2d of June, baptised Sunday, the 6th of July

Elizabeth Pickersgill, daugr of Thomas Pickergill, Winmoor, Farmer, [descended from] George and Martha Pickersgill, Kirstall, and of Judith Pickersgill, [descended from] John and Elizabeth Stead, Farmer, [born] Sunday, the 29th of June, [bapt.] Sunday the 13 of July

Ann Thompson, daugr of Wm Thompson, Barnbow, Collier, descended from Thomas and Ann Thompson, Garforth, and of Jane Thompson, des. from Thomas and Mary Pickerin, Purston, [born] Munday, the 9th of June, [bap.] Sunday, the 13th of July

John Collet, son of Benj[n] Collet, Barwick, Bucher, descended from Thomas and Elizabeth Collet, Barwick, and of Elizabeth Collet, descended from William and Sarah Knapton, Barwick, [born] Tuesday the 10 of June, [bap.] Sunday, the 13 of July

Benjamin Shillito, son of Thomas Shillito, Potterton, Taylor, descended from Thomas and Sarah Shillito, Potterton and of Betty Shillito, descended from Richard and Betty Dalby, Seacroft [born] Thursday, the 6th of June, [bap.] Sunday, the 20th of July

Ann Scholes, daug[r] of George Scholes, Barnbow, collier, des[d] from John and Ann Scholes, Rothwell, and of Mary Scholes, des[d] from John and Mary Atkinson, Barnbow, [born] Stterday, the 28th of June, [bap.] Sunday, the 3[d] of Aug.

James Jolly, son of James Jolly, Scholes, Labourer, des. from Matthew and Mary Jolly, Newsom Green, and Mary Jolly, des. from Christopher and Martha Vary, Schol, [born] Friday, 25 July [bap.] Sunday, the 10 of Aug.

Elizabeth Jawit, daug[r] of Willm. Jawit, Barwick, Labourer, des. from John and Susannah Jawet, Shadwell, and of Alice Jawit, descended from Jn[o] and Eliz[th] Dangwith, Barw., [born] Monday, the 16 August, [bap.] Sunday, the 14 of September.

Hannah Green, dau. of Richard Green, Scholes, collier, bap. Wednesday the 24 of Sept.

William Wood, son of John Wood, Potterton, Farmer, des. from Richard and Mary Wood, Potterton, and of Elizabeth Wood, des. from Timothy [&] Eliz[th] Waite, Thorner, [born] Setter [day], the 23 August, [bap.] Sunday, the 24 September

Joseph Denison, son of Jonathan Dinison, Stanks, Carpinter, des. from Joseph and Alice Dinison, Coulton, and of Mary Dinison, des. from Richard and [*blank*] Beardshaw, Monkfryston, [born] Setter., the 16 August, [bap.] Sunday, the 28 September

Peter Jordan, son of Tho[s] Jordan, Scholes, Labourer, des. from Thomas and Elizabeth Jordan, Seacroft, and of Sarah Jordan, des. from David and Mary Buchanan, Scholes, [born] Tused., the 2[d] Septem., [bap.] Sunday, the 5th October

Sarah Thorns, basdard d. of Mary Thorns, Potterton, [born] Monday, the 11th of August, [bapt.] Monday the 6th of October

Mary Bell, dau. of W[m] Bell, Hiltop, des. from William and Mary Bell, Hiltop, and of Sarah Bell, des. from Thomas and Sarah Shilburn, Seacroft, [born] Friday, the 13 October [bap.] Sun., the 9 Nov.

Samuel Simpson, son of Samuel Simpson, Barnbow, Collier, des[d] from Samuel and Crissey Simpson, Barnbow, and of Ann Simpson, des. from Tho[s] and Ann Thompson, Garforth moor, [born] Monday, 27th October, [bap.] Sunday the 23[d] of November

Mary Burland, d. of Will[m] Burland, Barwick, Labourer, des. from Elizabeth Burland, Seacroft, and of Sarah Burland, des. from Robert and Mary Smith, Barwick. [bn.] Thursday, 17th Oct. [bp.] Sunday the 30th of Nov.

BAPTISMS, 1778.

William Moss, son of Francis Moss, Kiddall Lane, Farmer, des. from Francis & Susannah Moss, Heasselwood, and of Sarah Moss, des. from Thos & Elizabeth Addiman, Scholes, [bn.] Thurs., Dec. 6, [bp.] Sun. 18 Jan.

Hannah Thompson, d. of John Thompson, Barnbow, Collier, des. from John & Frances Thompson, Garforth, and of Hannah Thompson, desd. Thos & Ann Thompson, Garforth, [bn.] Wed., Dec. 24, [bp.] Sun. 25 Jan.

Martha Youdan, d. of Miles Youdan, Barwick, Farmer, des. from John and Frances Youdan, Woodhouse, and Ann Youdan, des. from Joseph & Martha Youdan, Woodhouse, [bn.] Weds., 4 Dec., [bap.] Sun., 25 Jan.

John Cawthorn, son of Joseph Cawthorn, Barwick, Labourer, des. from Benjamin & Elizabeth Cawthorn, Britaine and of Ann Cawthorn, des. from John and Sarah Dickison, Bar', [bn.] Tues., 30 Dec., [bp.] Sun., 25 Jan.

William Rawlinson, son of Abraham Rawlinson, Barwick, Farmer, des. from Benjamin and Mary Rawlinson, Barwick, and Mary Rawlinson, des. from Wm and Mary Scott Barwick, [bn.] Mon., 19 Jan., [bp.] Sun., 22 Feb.

Elizabeth Dawson, d. of Luke Dawson, Barnbow, Farmer, des. from Richard and Mary Dawson, Garforth, and of Ann Dawson, des. from Wm. and Sarah Peas, Gar., [bn.] Mon., 26 Jan., [bp.] Sun., 1 Mar.

John Richardson, son of Wm Richardson, Potterton, shoemaker, des. from Luke and Elizabeth Richardson, Potterton, and of Mary Richardson, des. from John and Mary Richardson, Wortley, [bn.] Tues., 27 Jan., [bp.] Tues. 3 March

Elizabeth Thompson, dr of Alvara Thompson, Winmoor, Labourer, des. from John and Sarah Thompson, Stanks, and of Sarah Thompson, des. from Richard & Ann Lazenby, Winmoor, [bn.] Fri. 13 Feb., [bp.] Sun., 15 March

Martha Jordan, d. of Robert Jordan, Stanks, Labourer, des. from Thomas & Elizabeth Jordan, Seacroft, and of Sarah Jordan, des. from Thos and Elizabeth Lightfoot, Brownm., [bn.] Thurs., 19 Feb., [bp.] Sun., 29 March

John Hodgson, son of Jonathan Hodgson, Winmoor, Labourer, des. from Wm and Ellin Hodgson, Kezrick, and of Hannah Hodgson, des. from Thos and Martha Lumb, Stockhill, [bn.] Thurs., 22 Jan., [bp.] Sun., 5 April

Ann Glover, d. of Bartholomew Glover, Ingene, Labourer, des. from Cornee and Jane Glover, Garforth, and of Elizabeth Glover, des. from John and Frances Thompson, Garforth, [bn.] Setterday, 21 Feb., [bp.] Sun., 5 April

Benjamin Watson, son of Benjamin Watson, Carpinter, Barwick, des. from Matthew & Erabella Watson, Barwick, and of Suannah Watson, des. from John and Mary Pollard, Bradford, Clothyer, [bn.] Thurs., 26 March, [bp.] Sun., 12 April

*William Lumb, son of Richard Lumb, Barwick, Farmer, des. from Richard and Ann Lumb, Barwick, and of Elizabeth Lumb, des. from W^m^ and Ann Carew, Lisbon, in Portugle, [bn.] Tues., 17 March, [bp.] Thurs., 16 April

Mary Mackontrout, d. of John Mackontrout, Barwick, Labourer, des. from John and Ann Mackontrout, Kippax, and of Martha Mackontrout, des. f. Miles and Mary Ampshaw, Barwick, [bn.] Setterd., 31 Jan., [bp.] Mon., 20 April

James Bean, son of Thomas Bean, Barwick, shoemaker, des. from John and Alice Bean, Barwick, and of Abigal Bean, des. from John and Ellin Harrison, Ecup, [bn.] Tues., 24 March, [bp.] Sun., 26 April

Joseph White, son of Joseph White, Scholes, Farmer, des. from John and Grace White, Akaster Malbess, and of Mary White, des. from Georg and Elisabeth Barker, Hensaul, [bn.] Tues., 31 March, [bp.] Wed., 13 May

James Carr, son of Willm Carr, Kiddall lane end, Inkeeper, des. from John and Elizabeth Carr, Doncaster and of Alice Carr, des. from Willm and Ann Mason, Eastby, [bn.] Setterday, 4 April, [bp.] Fri., 15 May

Mary Deane, d. of Jeremiah Deane, Whinmoor, Carpenter, des. from Jerimiah and Elizabeth Deane, Seacroft, and of Elizabeth Deane, des. from Gabril and Elizabeth Thompson, Watkert, [bn.] Tues., 17 March, [bp.] Sun., 17 May

Harry Milner, son of John Milner, Winmoor, Labourer, des. from John and Elizabeth Milner, Halton, and of Jane Milner, des. from Jane Horsman, Seacroft, [bn.] Tues., 28 April, [bp.] Sun., 7 June

John Whitehead, son of Thomas Whitehead, Potterton, farmer, des. from Thomas and Alice Whitehead, Garforth, and of Ann Whitehead, des. from William and Ann Ward, Abberford, [bn.] Fri., 29 May, [bap.] Sun., 28 June

Sarah Higgins, d. of Peter Higgins, Barwick, Labourer, des. from James & Mary Higgens, Wheton, and of Easter Higgens, des. from Robert and Isabella Poppleton, Abberford, [bn.] Tues., 23 June, [bp.] Sun., 2 August

William Abbot, son of Thomas Abbot, Barwick, Labourer, des. from Willm and Catherine Abbot, Barwick, and of Elizabeth Abbot, des. from Matthew [&] Elizabeth Pickering, Sherburn, [bn.] Sun., 12 July, [bp.] Sun., 23 August

Ann Newby, d. of Peter Newby, Barwick, Carpenter, des. from Peter & Elizabeth Newby, Margit Weton, and of Ann Newby, des. from Richard and Doratha Burland, Barwick, [bn.] Sun., 26 July, [bp.] Wed., 26 August

Joseph Benton, son of Thomas Benton, Brownmoor, collier, des. from Thomas and Margret Benton, Garforth,and of Ann Benton,

---

*William Lumb was of St Agnes Gate, Ripon, married 30 March, 1805, Martha, dau of John Rawson, Mayor of Ripon, 1808—9. He died 18 May, 1831, & was buried in the Minster yard. Their only child William Eedson Lumb, Trinity Coll., Camb., B.A, 1830, M A., 1834, Vicar of Halford & Sibdon, married at St. Margaret's, Lynn, 17 June, 1830, Emily, dau. of Lieut. James Dillon, R.N., died 1885, & was buried at Halford, leaving 5 children.

des. from John and Mary Appleton, Plumpton, [bn.] Fri., 17 July, [bp.] Sun., 13 Sep.

Mary Plowright, d. of James Plowright, Barwick, shopkeeper, des. from Edward and Mary Plowright, Houghton, and of Mary Plowright, des. from Thomas and Elizabeth Addiman, Scholes, [bn.] Sun., 30 Aug., [bp.] Sun., 4 Oct.

Thomas Todd, son of Thomas Todd, Scholes, Farmer, des. from Thomas and Mary Todd, Newby, and of Jane Todd, des. from Thomas and Elizabeth Smith, Potterton, [bn.] Wed., 19 Aug., [bp.] Sun., 11 Oct.

Betty Brittain, d. of William Brittain, Barnbow, Bricklayer, des. from Joseph and Betty Brittain, Rothwell, and of Mary Brittain, des. from John and Margret Geggs, Barnbow, [bn.] Fri., the 16 Oct., [bp.] Sun., 1 Nov.

Elizabeth Cullingworth, d. of Jno Cullingworth, Barwick, shoemaker, des. from Joseph and Elizabeth Cullingworth, Abberford, and of Maria Cullingworth, des. from Thomas and Mary Thornton, Potterton, [bn.] Mon., 12 Oct., [bp.] Sun., 6 Dec.

Simon Blackburn, son of John Blackburn, Garforth moor, collier, des. from Henry and Mary Blackburn, Garforth moor, and of Jane Blackburn, des. from W^m and Hannah Smith, Garforth moor, [bn.] Wed., 4 Nov., [bp.] Sun., 13 Dec.

George Lorriman, son of Thomas Lorriman, Iingine, Collier, des. from George and Margret Lorriman, Garforth, and of Elizabeth Lorriman, des. from James and Elizabeth Tillotson, Ingine, [bn.] Fri., 6 Nov., [bp.] Sun., 13 Dec.

Christanah Simpson, bastard, d. of Christanah Simpson, Barnbow, [bn.] Thurs., 3 Dec., [bp.] Sun., 20 Dec.

James Whitehead, son of James Whitehead, Barwick, Marriner, des. from Thomas and Margret Whitehead, Barwick, and of Elizabeth Whitehead, des. from Robert and Martha Whitehead, Barwick, [bn.] Mon., Nov. 30, [bp.] Sun., 27 Dec.

BAPTISMS, 1779.

John Forster, son of Henry Forster, Potterton, Labourer, des. from Henry and Margret Forster, Bishope Wilton, and of Zilpha Forster, des. from John and Ellin Cauwood, Winmoor, [bn.] Wed., 2 Dec., [bp.] Fri., 1 Jan.

Hannah Simpson, d. of Thomas Simpson, Barnbow, collier, des. from Samuel and Chrisanah Simpson, Barnbow, and of Frances Simpson, des. from Rich^d and Easter Claburn, Garforth, [bn]. Sun., 29 Dec., [bp.] Sun., 24 Jan.

Thomas Harrison, son of Samuel Harrison, Potterton, Labourer, des. from Benjamin and Ann Harrison, Metley and of Sarah Harrison from Robert and Isabella Poppelton, Aberford, [bn.] Mon., 21 Dec., [bp.] Sun., 7 Feb.

Mary Milner, d. of Matthew Milner, Kiddall Lane, Groom, des. from James and Rachel Miller, Richmond, and of Jane Milner, des. from Moses and Mary Pawson, Kiddall Lane [bn.] Fri., 15 Jan., [bp.] Sun., 21 Feb.

Elizabeth Carter, d. of David Carter, Stanks, Labourer, des. from George and Elizabeth Carter, Kippax, and of Hannah Carter, des. from Willm and Hannah Tipling, Barwick, [bn.] Sun., 13 Dec., [bp.] Sun., 21 Feb.

Sarah Tinley, d. of Thomas Tinley, Scholes, mason, des. from Nicolas and Sarah Tinley, Ingine, and of Sarah Tinley, des. from Thomas and Mary Haley, Scholes, [bn.] Fri., 15 Jan., [bp.] Sun., 28 Feb.

Samuel Leach, bastard son of Elizabeth Leach, Barwick, [bn.] Mon., 1 Feb., [bp.], Sun., 28 Feb.

Mary Hewit, d. of Thomas Hewit, Barwick, collier, des. from George and Frances Hewit, Crosgates, and of Elizabeth Hewit, des. from Thomas and Margret Hemsworth, Swil^{n}, [bn.] Sun., 17 Jan., [bp.] Sun., 7 March

Christanah Lidster, d. of Joseph Lidster, Scholes, Shoemaker, des. from William and Mary Lidster, Garforth, and of Sarah Lidster, des. from Samuel and Chrissey Simpson, Barnbow, [bn.] Fri., 19 Feb., [bp.] Sun., 21 March

Ann Waite, d. of Thos Waite, Barwick, Labourer, des. from W^{m} and Ann Waite, Barwick, and of Julia Waite, des. from W^{m} & Dorotha Sinyard, Brotherton, [bn.] Tues., 12 Jan., [bp.] Sun., 21 Mar.

John Waite, dr. [*sic*] of Richard Waite, Barwick, Tayler, des. from Richard and Suseannah Waite, Barwick, and of Alice Waite, des. from W^{m} and Sarah Barker, Barwick, [bn.] Thurs., 25 Feb., [bp.] Sun., 4 April

Elizabeth Dunwell, d. of Antoney Dunwell, Barwick, weaver, des. from Thomas and Rebecka Dunwell, Barwick, and of Sarah Dunwell, des. from W^{m} and Mary Scott, Barwick, [bn.] Wed., 28 Jan., [bp.] Sun., 4 April

Grace Carolina Brook, d. of Richard Brook, Scholes, Captain, des. from James and Mary Brook, Killingbeck, and of Fra[n]ces Brook, des. from Richard and Frances Brook, York, [bn.] Thurs., 18 Feb., [bp.] Tues., 6 April.

Sarah Robshaw, d. of Willm Robshaw, Barwick, Labourer, des. from Thos. and Ellin Robshaw, Hosbon, and of Sarah Robshaw, des. from W^{m} and Sarah Knapton, Barwick, [bn.] Setterday, 3 April, [bp.] Sun., 25 April

Sarah Pitt, d. of Thomas Pitt, Barwick, Farmer, des. from John and Elizabeth Pitt, Leeds, and of Sarah Pitt, des. from Richard and [*blank*] Wood, Potterton, [bn.] Tues., 4 May, [bp.] Sun., 23 May

Peter Brownrig, son of Roger Browrig, Scholes, Taylor, des. from Peter and Martha Brownrig, Spofforth, and of Ann Brownrig, des. from John and Catherine Vary, Scholes, [bn.] Fri., 28 April, [bp.] Sunday, 23 May

Hannah Slayter, bastard, d. of Margret Slayter, Winmoor, [bp]. Sun., 30 May

Mary Gibson, d. of John Gibson, Hambleton, Farmer, des. from John and Hannah Gibson, Hambleton, and of Elizabeth Gibson, des. from Robert and Mary Smith, Barwick, [bn.] Sun., 10 April, [bp.] Sun., 17 April

Hannah Clayton, d. of William Clayton, Ingine, Blacksmith, des. from John and Grace Clayton, West harchley, and of Mary Clayton, des. from Thomas and Ellin Bellouse, Garforth, [bn.] Fri., 14 May, [bp.] Sun., 6 June

Ann Braim, d. of Thomas Braim, Barnbow, Farmer, des. from Thomas and Hannah Braim, Barnbow, and of Ann Braim, des. from John and Mary Atkinson, Barnbow, [bn.] Mon., 24 May, [bp.] Sun., 27 June

Hannah Simpson, d. of Samuel Simpson, Barnbow, Collier, des. from Samuel and Christanah Simpson, Barnbow, and of Ann Simpson, des. from Thomas and Ann Thompson, Garforth, [bn.] Setterday, 12 June, [bp.] Sunday, 11 July

William Burland, son of William Burland, Barwick, Labourer, des. from Elizabeth Burland, Seacroft, and of Sarah Burland, des. from Robert and Mary Smith, Barwick, [bn.] Wed., 16 June, [bp.] Sun., 1 Aug.

Elizabeth Pirkin, d. of Thomas Pirkin, Barwick, Labourer, des. from James and Ann Pirkin, Barwick, and of Mary Pirkin, des. from Robert and Elizabeth Thorns, Parlington, [bn.] Sun., 20 June, [bp.] Sun., 8 Aug.

Hannah Slayter, d. of Peter Slayter, Barwick, Farmer, des. from William and Mary Slayter, Barwick, and of Mary Slayter, des. from Joseph and Mary Bullock, Barwick, [bn.] Sun., 27 June, [bp.] Sun., 8 Aug.

Robert Carr, son of William Carr, Kiddall Lane end, Inkeeper, des. from John and Elizabeth Carr, Doncaster, and of Alice Carr, des. from Willm and Ann Mason, Eastby, [bn.] Mon., 2 Aug., [bp.] Setteday, 11 Sept.

Samuel Richardson, son of Willm Richardson, Potterton, shoemaker, des. from Luke and Elzath Richardson, Potterton, and of Mary Richardson, des. from Jno & Mary Richardson, Wortley, [bn.] Fri., 13 Aug., [bp.] Sun., 12 Sept.

Easter Dawson, d. of Luke Dawson, Barnbow, Farmer, des. from Richard and Mary Dawson, Garforth, and of Ann Dawson, des. from William and Sarah Pease, Garforth, [bn.] Wed., 13 Oct., [bp.] Thurs., 14 Oct.

John Greenwood, son of Samuel Greenwood, Kiddall lane end, Labourer, des. from John and Ann Greenwood, Mickelfield, and of Ann Greenwood, des. from Benjamin and Ann Harrison, Methley, [bn.] Wed., 22 Sept., [bp.] Sun., 31 Oct.

Hannah Pawson, d. of James Pawson, Roundhay, Farmer, des. from Thos and Alice Pawson, Brandon, and of Jane Pawson, des. from Thomas and Mary Dodgson, Roundhay, [bn.] Fri. 24 Sep., [bp.] Wed., 27 Oct.

John and Ellen Dunwell, son and d^{r}. of William Dunwell, Winmoor, Labourer, des. from John and Elizath Dunwell, Winmoor, and of Margret Dunwell, des. from Thomas & Hannah Dean, Potternewton, [bn.] Tues., 14 Sept., [bp.] Wed., 3 Nov.

Frances Dean, d. of John Dean, Winmoor, Labourer, des. from Thomas and Hannah Dean, Potternewton, and of Ann Dean, des. from Henry and Elizabeth Mills, Aketoun, [bn.] Fri., 8 Oct., [bp.] Wed., the 3 Nov.

Martha Lofthouse, d. of Mark Lofthouse, Potterton, Farmer, des. from Mark and Martha Lofthouse, Netherton, and of Charlotta Lofthouse, des. from William [&] Dorotha Sunyard, Brotherton, [bp.] Sun., 7 Nov.

Mary Jackson, d. of James Jackson, Barwick, Farmer, des. from Matthew and Sarah Jackson, Barwick, and of Mary Jack., des. from Joseph and Easter Atkinson, Witley, [bn.] Fri., 15 Oct., [bp.] Sunday, 7 Nov.

Abigal Thompson, d. of James Thompson, Barwick, Labourer, des. from John and Ann Thompson, Seacroft, and of Mary Thompson, des. from Joseph and Abigal Holmes, Barwick, [bn.] Tues., 19 Oct., [bp.] Mon., 8 Nov.

Mary Jordan, d. of Robert Jordan, Stanks, Labourer, des. from Thomas and Elizabeth Jordan, Seacroft, [and of] Sarah Jordan, des. from Thomas and Elizabeth Lightfoot, Brownmoor, [bn.] Fri. 5 Nov. [bp.] Fri., 26 Nov.

Sarah Bell, d. of William Bell, Hiltop, Labourer, des. from William and Mary Bell, Hiltop, and of Sarah Bell, des. from Thomas and Sarah Shilburn, Seacroft, [bn.] Mon., 18 Oct., [bp.] Sun., 28 Nov.

Ann Stubs, d. of John Stubs, Barwick, des. from Jno and Ann Stubs, Tadcaster, and of Elizabeth Stubs, des. from John and Ann Robinson, Barwick, [bn.] Sun., 7 Nov., [bp.] Sun., 5 Dec.

BAPTISMS, 1780.

Thomas Goodall, son of Thomas Goodall, Ingine, Collier, des. from W^m^ and Elizabeth Goodall, Garforth, and of Ann Goodall, des. from John and Ann Tillotson, Garforth, [bn.] Tues., 14 Dec., [bp.] Sun., 9 Jan.

Sarah Logg, d. of James Logg, Scholes, Labourer, des. from John and Ann Logg, Scholes, and of Mary Logg, des. from John and Sarah Horton, Askham, [bn.] Mon., 20 Dec., [bp.] Sun., 23 Jan.

Sarah Haist, d. of Renton Haist, Barwick, Labourer, des. from Mary Haist, Barwick, and of Sarah Haist, des. from Willm and Ann Ward, Barwick, [bn.] Set^y^., 11 Dec., [bp.] Sun., 23 Jan.

John Sherrif, son of William Sherrif, Potterton, Gardiner, des. from George and Sarah Sherrif, Abberwaite, and of Dina Sherrif, des. from Henry and Margret Forster, Bishop Wilton, [bn.] Fri., 21 Jan., [bp.] Sun., 20 Feb.

Hannah Bell, d. of Benj. Bell, Scholes, Labourer, des. from Jonathan and Ann Bell, Scholes, and of Frances Bell, des. from Thomas and Margret Burrall, Leeds, [bn.] Sun., 8 Feb., [bp.] Sun., the 26 March

James Jordan, son of Thomas Jordan, Stanks, Labour., des. from Thomas and Elizabeth Jordan, Seacroft, and of Sarah Jordan, des. from David and Mary Buchanan, Scholes, [bn.] Fri., 25 Feb., [bp.] Sun., 2 April.

Ann White, d. of Joseph White, Scholes, Farmer, des. from John and Grace White, Akaster Malbles, and of Mary White, des. from George and Elizabeth Barker, Hensaul, [bn.] Tues. the 15, Feb. [bp.] Mon., 3 April

Richard Lumb, son of Richard Lumb, Barwick, Inkeper, des. from Will[m] and Martha Lumb, Barwick, and of Bridget Lumb, des. from William and Ann Cuningham, Wakefield, [bn.] Sun., 12 Mar., [bp.] Sun., 16 Apr.

John Moss, son of Francis Moss, Kidall lane, Farmer, des. from Francis and Susannah Moss, Heaselwood, and of Sarah Moss, des. from Tho[s] and Elizabeth Addiman, Scholes, [bn.] Fri., 10 Mar., [bp.] Sunday 16 April

Fanny Clark, d. of John Clark, Whinmoor, Farmer, des. from Christopher and Su[s]annah Clark, Bardsey, and of Fanny Clark, des. from James and Mary Lambart, Whinmoor, [bn.] Sun., 20 Feb., [bp.] Wed. 19 Apr.

Fanny Thompson, d. of Samuel Thompson, Barnbow, collier, des. from John and Fanny Thompson, Garforth, and Suannah Thompson, des. from William and Suannah Taylor, Barnbow, [bn.] Fri., 24 Mar., [bp.] Sun., 2 Apr.

John Robinson, son of John Robinson, Stanks, Collier, des. from John and Elizabeth Robinson, Garforth, and of Alice Robinson, des. from Thomas and Mary Taylor, Barwick, [bn.] Fri., 31 Mar., [bp.] Sun., 30 Apr.

John Thompson, son of Alvrey Thompson, Stanks, Labourer, des. from John and Sarah Thompson, Stanks, and of Sarah Thompson, des. from Richard and Ann Lazenby, Penwell, [bn.] Thurs., 30 Mar., [bp.] Sun., the 14 May

Joseph Rawlinson, son of Abraham Rawlinson, Barwick, farmer, des. from Benj[n] and Mary Rawlinson, Barwick, and of Mary Rawlinson, des. from William and Mary Scott, Barwick, [bn.] Wed., 12 Apr., [bp.] Sun., 14 May

John Mackon, des. from John Mackontrout, Barwick, Lab., des. from John and Ann Mackontrout, Kippax, and of Martha Mackontrout, des. from Miles and Mary Ampshaw, Barwick, [bn.] Mon., 27 Mar., [bp.] Mon., 15 May

Joseph Lunn, son of John Lunn, Barnbow, Collier, des. from John and Ann Lunn, Porston, and of Mary Lunn, des. from John and Martha Hopton, Kippax, [bn.] Thurs., 20 Apr., [bp.] Mon., 22 May

*Thomas Lumb, of Richard Lumb, Barwick, Farmer, des. from Richard and Ann Lumb, Barwick, and of Elizabeth Lumb, des. from W[m] and Ann Carew, Lisbon, in Portugal, [bn.] Fri., 28 Apr., [bp.] Wed., 31 May

George Blackburn, son of Henry Black[n], Coalpitts, Collier, des. from Henry and Hannah Blackburn, Garforth, and of Elizabeth Blackburn, des. from W[m] and Hannah Ingle, Sturton, [bn.] Thur., 4 May, [bp.] Sun., 4 June

Hannah Watson, d. of Michel Watson, Barwick, Wright, des. from W[m] and Hannah Watson, Barwick, and of Hannah Watson, des. from John and Martha Dodsworth, Cawwood, [bn.] Fri., the 14 Apr., [bp.] Sun., 4 June.

---

*Thomas Lumb, of Leeds, auctioneer, married 1806 at Leeds, Charlotte, dau. of Richard Clayton of Blackman Lane, Leeds, cloth merchant, and had issue 2 children, Richard and Elizabeth. He died 1843 and is buried at Barwick,

Thos Hodshon, son of Jonathan Hodson, Scholes, Labourer, des. from William and Ellin Hodgson, Barnbow, and of Hannah Hodgson, des. from Thomas and Hannah Lumb, Stockhil, [bn.] Fri., 17 Mar., [bp.] Sun., 11 June

Sarah Othick, d. of Benjamin Othick, Harmley, Labourer, des. from John and Sarah Othick, Harmley, Lab., and of Mary Othick, des. from Edward and Elizabeth Monks, Barwick, [bn.] Sat., 13 May, [bp.] Sun., 11 June

John Shillito, son of Benjn Shillito, Barnbow, Labourer, des. from Thomas and Sarah Shillito, Potterton, and of Mary Shillito, des. from John and Catherine Vary, Scholes, [bn.] Fri., 30 June, [bp.] Sun., 30 July

Hannah Lumb, d. of Jerimiah Lumb, Stockhill, Farmer, des. from Thomas and Hannah Lumb, Stockhill, and of Ellin Lumb, des. from Robert and Ellin Vevers, Potterton, [bn.] Tuesday, 11 July, [bp.] Sun., 6 Aug.

Elizabeth Watson, d. of Richard Watson, Whinmoor, Lab^{r}, des. from Willm and Ann Watson, Thorner, and of Mary Watson, des. from Thos and Mary Simpson, Whinmoor, [bn.] Fri., 21 July, [bp.] Sun., 20 Aug.

Richard Newby, son of Peter Newby, Barwick, Carpinter, des. from Peter & Elizabeth Newby, Margit weton, and of Ann Newby, des. from Richard and Dorotha Burland, Barwick, [bn.] Wed., 26 July, [bp.] Fri., 25 Aug.

Mary Denison, d. of Jonathon Denison, Stanks, Carpinter, des. from Joseph and Alice Dinison, Coulton, and of Mary Dinison, des. from Richard and Mary Beardshaw, Monkfriston, [bn.] Tues., 18 July, [bp.] Sun., 10 Sept.

William Cawthorn, son of Joseph Cawthorn, Barwick, Labour', from Benjn and Elizabeth Cawthorn, Brittain, and of Mary Cawthorn, des. from John and Sarah Dickinson, Barwick, [bn.] Tuesday, 22 Aug., [bp.] Sun., 22 Oct.

Mary Thompson, d. of Willm Thompson, Barnbow, Collier, des. from Thos and Ann Thompson, Garforth, and of Jane Thompson, des. from Thomas and Mary Pickering, Purston, [bn.] Mon., 30 Oct., [bp.] Sun., 29 Nov.

Samuel Pickersgill, son of Thomas Pickersgill, Whinmoor, Farmer, des. from George and Martha Pickersgill, Kirstall, and of Judith Pickersgill, des. from John and Elizabeth Stead, Thorner, [bn.] Sat., 21 Oct., [bp.] Sun., 29 Nov.

Frances Catherine Brook, d. of Richard Brook, Scholes, Major, des. from James and Mary Brook, Killingbeck, and of Frances Brook, des. from Richard and Frances Brook, York, [bn.] Wed., 8 Nov., [bp.] Fri., 8 Dec.

Mary Jackson, d. of John Jackson, Barwick, Shoemaker, des. from John and Ann Jackson, Wistow, and of Mary Jackson, des. from William and Mary Lumb, Barwick, [bn.] Mon., 27 Nov., [bn.] Sun., 10 Dec.

Ellin Blackburn, d. of John Blackburn, Garforth, Collier, des. from Henry and Mary Blackburn, Garforth, and of Jane Blackburn, des. from William and Hannah Smith, Garforth, [bn.] Mon., 20 Nov., [bp.] Sun., 17 Dec.

William Watson, son of William Watson, Barwick, Wellright, des. from Benjamin and Suseannah Watson, Barwick, and of Jane Watson, des. from Jane Barker, Garforth, [bn.] Wed., 6 Dec., [bp.] Sun., 24 Dec.

Baptisms, 1781.

Mary Simpson, d. of Thomas Simpson, Brownmoor, Lab^{r}, des. from John and Mary Simpson, Austhorp, and of Mary Simpson, des. from Richard and Jane Screaton, Minsgip, [bp.] Sun., 4 Jan.

William Lazenby, bastard son of Mary Lazenby, Bradford house, [bp.] Sun., 11 Feb.

Alice Carr, d. of Willm Carr, Kidall lanend, Inkeeper, des. from John and Elizabeth Carr, Doncaster, and of Alice Carr, des. from William and Ann Mason, Eastby, [bn.] Sun., 7 Jan., [bp.] Fri., 23 Feb.

Elizabeth Tinley, d. of Thomas Tinley of Scholes, Mason, des. from Nicolas and Sarah Tinley, Ingine, and of Sarah Tinley, des. from Thomas and Mary Haley, Scholes, [bn.] Mon., 15 Jan., [bp.] Sun., 4 March

Richard Lowriman, son of Thomas Lowriman, Ingine, Labourer, des. from Richard and Sarah Lowriman, Garforth, and of Mary Lowriman, des. from James and Mary Tillotson, Ingine, [bn.] Mon., 28 Jan., [bp.] Sun., 11 Mar.

William [Joseph *erased*] Thackray, son of Joseph Thackray, Barwick, Labourer, des. from John and Ann Thackray, Spofforth, and of Mary Thackray, des. John and Elizabeth Chambers, Dun Kessick, [bn.] Mon., 26 Mar., [bp.] 8 April

*John Waite, son of Richard Waite, Barwick, Taylor, des. from Richard and Susannah Waite, Barwick, and of Alice Waite, des. from William and Sarah Barker, Barwick, [bn.] Sat., 3 Feb., [bp.] Sun., 15 April

Jane Miller, d. of Matthew Miller, Kidall lane end, groom, des. from James and Rachil Miller, Richmond, and of Jane Miller, des. from Moses and Mary Pawson, Kidall lane end, [bn.] Wed., 14 Mar., [bp.] Sun., 15 April

Mary Whitehead, d. of James Whitehead, Barwick, Labourer, des. from Thomas and Margret Whitehead, Barwick, and of Elizabeth Whitehead, des. from Robert and Martha Whitehead, Barwick, [bn.] Fri., 9 Mar., [bp.] Sun., 22 April

Benjamin Robshaw, son of William Robshaw, Barwick, Labourer, des. from Thomas and Catherine Robshaw, Bar^{k}, and of Alice Robshaw, des. from W^{m} and Margret Rothmell, Knaisbrough, [bn.] Thurs., 22 Mar., [bp.] Sun., 29 April

Joseph Robinson, son of John Robinson, Stanks, Collier, des. from John and Elizabeth Robinson, Garforth, and of Alice Robinson, des. from Thomas and Mary Tayler, Barwick, [bn.] Sun., 1 Apr., [bp.] Sun., 6 May.

---

* "Mr. Waite, late of Barwick-in-Elmet, but now of St. John's College, Cambridge, was on Saturday, se'nnight admitted Bachelor of Arts." *Leeds Mercury*, 5 Feb., 1803. Admitted M.A., 1806.

Joseph Lister, son of Joseph Lister, Scholes, Labourer, des. from Willm and Mary Lidster, Garforth and of Sarah Lidster, des. from Samuel and Chrissey Simpson, Barnbow, [Garforth *erased*], [bn.] Wed., 11 April, [bp.] Sun., 20 May.

Richard Carter, son of David Carter, Stanks, Labourer, des. from George and Mary Carter, Kippax, and of Hannah Carter, des. from William & Hannah Tipling, Barwick, [bn.] Fri., 30 Mar., [bp.] Sun., 20 May

Hannah & Lewcy Lofthouse, drs. of Mark Lofthouse, Potterton, farmer, des. from Mark and Martha Lofthouse, Netherton, and of Charlotte Lofthouse, des. from William & Dorotha Sinyard, Brotherton, [bn.] Wed., 28 Mar., [bp.] Sun., 27 May

Michel Waltan, son of John Waltan, Barwick, Lab., des. from John and Ann Walton, Barwick, and of Mary Walton, des. from John and Elizabeth Nettleton, Mickelfield, [bn.] Thur., 10 May, [bp.] Sun., 3 June

Ann Perkin, d. of Thomas Perkin, Barwick, Lab., des. from James and Ann Perkin, Barwick, and of Mary Perkin, des. from Robert and Elizabeth Thorns, Parlington, [bn.] Fri., 1 June, [bp.] Sun., 1 July

Susannah Sparling, d. of Joseph Sparling, Potterton, Lab., des. from Joseph and Ann Sparling, Abberford, and of Mary Sparling, des. from George [&] Susannah Watson, Potterton, [bp.] Sun., 1 July

Frances Simpson, d. of Thos Simpson, Barnbow, Collier, des. from Samuel and Chrissey Simpson, Barnbow, and of Frances Simpson, des. from Richard and Easter Claburn, Garforth, [bn.] Mon., 11 June, [bp.] Sun., 8 July

Thomas Rhumbo, son of Christopher Rhumbo, Saxton, Labour, des. from Thomas and Elizabeth Rhumbo, Newton, and of Sarah Rhumbo, des. from Isack and Jane Dodgshon, Whinmoor, [bn.] Thurs., 7 June, [bp.] Sun., 15 July

Elizabeth Abbot, d. of Thos Abbot, Barwick, Labourer, des. from Wm and Catherine Abbot, Barwick, and of Elizabeth Abbot, des. from Mathew and Elizabeth Pickering, Sherburn, [bp.] Sun., 22 July

Thomas Thompson, son of Willm Thompson, Morwick, Labourer, des. from John and Frances Thompson, Garforth, and of Catherine Thompson, des. from Henry and Mary Pickard, Kippax, [bn.] Sat., 30 June, [bp.] Sun., 5th August

William Cullingworth, son of John Cullingworth, Barwick, Shoemaker, des. from Joseph and Elizabeth Cullingworth, Abberford, and of Maria Cullingworth, des. from Thomas and Mary Thornton, Potterton, [bn.] Thur., 28 June, [bp.] Sun., 5 Aug.

David Hewitt, son of Thomas Hewitt, Barwick, Collier, des. from George and Frances Hewitt, Ingine, and of Elizabeth Hewitt, from Thomas and Margret Hemsworth, Swillington, [bn.] Thurs., 28 June, [bp.] Sun., 12 Aug.

Martha and Milly Benton, twins, drs. of John Benton, Stanks, Collier, des. from Thos [&] Margret Benton, Garforth, and of

Milly Benton, des. from David and Ellin Hurst, Pogmoor, [bn.] Wed., 18 Aug., [bp.] Sun., 2 Sept.

Mary Goodall, d. of Thos Goodall, Ingine, Collier, des. from Wm & Elizabeth Goodall, Garforth, and of Ann Goodall, des. from John and Ann Tillotson, Garforth, [bn.] Fri., 24 Aug., [bp.] Sun., 16 Sept.

Easter Thompson, bastard d. of Mary Thompson, Barwick, [bn.] Wed., 22 Aug., [bp.] Sun., 23 Sep.

William Smith, son of William Smith, Barwick, Farmer, des. from Wm & Herietta Maria Smith, Barwick, and of Ann Smith, des. from William and Sarah Knapton, Barwick, [bn.] Tues., 4 Sept., [bp.] Sun., 30 Sept.

John Thompson, son of Richard Thompson, Crosgates, Labourer, des. from Thos and Elizabeth Thompson, Seacroft, and of Sarah Thompson, from Samuel and Chrissey Simpson, Barnbow, [bn.] Mon., 10 Sept., [bp.] Sun., 17 Sep.

Sarah Robinson, d. of William Robinson, Crosgates, Labourer, des. from William and Sarah Robinson, Rigton, and of Elizabeth Robinson, des. from Thos and Mary Thompson, Seacroft, [bn.] Wed., 26 Aug., [bp.] Sun., 17 Sept.

William Richardson, son of William Richardson, Potterton, shoemaker, des. from Luke and Elizabeth Richardson, Potterton, and of Mary Richardson, des. from John and Mary Richardson, Wortley, [bn.] Sat., 18 Aug., [bp.] Sun., 7 Oct.

Joseph Simpson, son of Samuel Simpson, Barnbow, Collier, des. from Samuel and Crissey Simpson, Barnbow, and of Ann Simpson, des. from Thomas and Ann Thompson, Garforth, [bn.] Tues., 4 Sept., [bp.] Sun., 7 Oct.

John Britaine, son of William Britaine, Barnbow, Bricklayer, des. from John and Betty Britain, Rothwell, and of Mary Britain, des. from John and Margret Geggs, Barnbow, [bp.] Sun., 7 Oct.

John Stubs, son of John Stubs, Barwick, des. from John and Ann Stubs, Tadcaster, and of Elizabeth Stubs, des. from John and Ann Robinson Barwick, [bn.] Mon., 24 Sept., [bp.] Sun., 21 Oct.

Susannah Herring, d. of George Herring, Kidall-lane-end, Groom, des. John and Jane Herring, Highionton, and of Alice Herring, des. from William and Mary Waller, Bramham Park, [bn.] Sat., 18 Aug., [bp.] Thurs., 25 Oct.

William Jackson, son of James Jackson, Barwick, farmer, des. from Matthew and Sarah Jackson, Barwick, and of Mary Jackson, des. from Joseph and Easter Atkinson, Witley, [bp.] Sun., 4 Nov.

Sarah Linley, d. of Joseph Linley, Inkeeper, Whinmor, des. from Tamer Linley, Seacroft, and of Sarah Linley, des. from Robert and Isabella Poppleton, Abberford, [bp.] Sun., 18 Nov.

John Collet, son of Ralph Collet, Barwick, Farmer, des. from Thomas and Elizabeth Collet, Wighton, and of Mary Collet, des. from William and Batricks Nickelson, Weardley, [bn.] Sat., 3 Nov., [bp.] Fri., 30 Nov.

Ann Robshaw, d. of William Robshaw, Barwick, Labr, des. from Thomas and Ellin Robshaw, Hosbon, and of Sarah Robshaw, des. from William and Sarah Knapton, Barwick, [bn.] Fri., 9 Nov., [bp.] Sun., 2 Dec.

Mary Haist, d. of Renton Haist, Barwick, Labourer, des. from Mary Haist, Barwick, and of Sarah Haist, des. from William and Ann Ward, Barwick, [bn.] Fri., 9 Nov., [bp.] Sun., 9 Dec.

James Pawson, son of James Pawson, Roundhay, farmer, des. from Thomas and Alice Pawson, Brandon, and of Jane Pawson, des. from Thomas and Mary Dodgson, Roundhay, [bn.] Mon., 19 Nov., [bp.] Wed., 26 Dec.

Ann Greenwood, d. of Samuel Greenwood, Potterton, Labourer, des. from John and Ann Greenwod, Mickelfield, and of Ann Greenwood, des. from Benjamin and Ann Harrison, Methley, [bn.] Sun., 4 Nov., [bp.] Wed., 26 Dec.

BAPTISMS, 1782.

Elizabeth Bell, d. of William Bell, Hiltop, Lab^r, des. from William and Mary Bell, Hiltop, and of Sarah Bell, from Thomas and Sarah Shilburn, Seacroft, [bn.] Wed., 12 Dec., [bp.] Sun. 13 Jan.

William Hodgson, son of Jonathan Hodgson, Scholes, Lab^r, des. from William and Easter Hodgson, Barnbow, and of Hannah Hodgson, des. from Thomas and Martha Lumb, Stockhill, [bp.] Sun., the 6 Jan.

Elizabeth Hodgson, bastard d. of Ellin Hodgson, Barnbow, [bp.] Sun., 20 Jan.

Thomas Dunwell, son of Anthoney Dunwell, Barwick, Weaver, from Thomas and Rebecka Dunwel, Barwick, and of Sarah Dunwell, from William and Mary Scott, Barwick, [bn.] 4th Decem., Mon., [bp.] Sun., 10 Mar.

Mary Thompson, d. of James Thompson, Barwick, Lab^r, des. from John and Ann Thompson, Seacroft, and of Mary Thompson, des. from Joseph and Abigal Holmes, Barwick, [bn.] Fri., Feb. 17, [bp.] Sun., March 24

Elizabeth Goodall, d. of Edward Goodall, Stanks, Collier, des. from Edward and Sarah Goodall, Garforth, and of Sarah Goodall, des. from Benjamin and Elizabeth Cook, Stanks, [bn.] Wed., 25 Feb., [bp.] Sun., 31 Mar.

Joseph Todd, son of Thos Todd, Scholes, Labourer, des. from Thomas and Mary Todd, Newby, and of Jane Todd, from Thomas and Elizabeth Smith, Potterton, [bn.] Thurs., 26 Feb., [bp.] Sun., 7 April

Hannah Braim, d. of Thomas Braim, Bar[n]bow, Farmer, des. from Thomas and Hannah Braim, Branbow, and of Ann Braim, des. from John and Mary Atkinson, Barnbow, [bn.] Sat., 16 Mar., [bp.] Sun., 14 April

Sarah Robinson, d. of John Robinson, Stanks, Collier, des. from John and Elizabeth Robinson, Garforth, and of Alice Robinson, des. from Thomas & Mary Tayler, Barwick, [bn.] Wed., 17 April, [bp.] Sun., 19 May

Richard Wheater, son of Robert Wheater, Barwick, Labourer, des. from John and Frances Wheater, Templehirst, and of Jane Wheater, des. from John [&] Isabella Mossaby, Templehirst, [bn.] Sun., 17 Mar., [bp.] Sun., 19 May

*Richard Lumb, son of Richard Lumb, Barwick, Farmer, des. from Richard and Ann Lumb, Barwick, and of Elizabeth Lumb, des. from William and Ann Carew, Lisbon, Portugle, [bn.] Mon., 22 April, [bp.] Wednesday, 29 May

Benjamin Bell, son of Benjamin Bell, Scholes, Lab^{r}., des. from Jonathan and Ann Bell, Barnbow, and of Frances Bell, from Thomas and Margret Burrall, Leeds, [bn.] Setterday, 20 April, [bp.] Sunday, 9 June

Mary Dodgson, bastard daughter of Mary Dodgson, Whinmoor, [bp.] Sun., 16 June

Abigal Bean, d. of Thos Bean, Barwick, shoemaker, from John and Alice Bean, Barwick, and of Abigal Bean, from John and Ellin Harrison, Ecupt, [bn.] Mon., 10 June, [bp.] Wed., 19 June

William Armitage, son of Thomas Armitage, Collier, Whinmoor, from Joseph and Elizabeth Armitage, Porston, and of Mary Armitage from John and Judith Carlin, Garforth, [bn.] Tues., 4 June, [bp.] Sun., 7 July

Elizabeth Jordan, d. of Robert Jordon, Stanks, Lab^{r}, from Thomas and Elizabeth Jordon, Seacroft, and of Sarah Jordon, from Thomas and Elizabeth Lightfoot, Brownmoor, [bn.] Sat., 8 June, [bp.] Sun., 7 July

William Sparling, son of Joseph Sparling, Potterton, Lab^{r}, from John and Ellin Sparling, Parlington, and of Mary Sparling from George and Susannah Watson, Potterton, [bn.] Wed., 12 June, [bp.] Sun., 14 July

Matthew Miller, son of Matthew Miller, Kidall lane end, Groom, from James and Mary Miller, Richmond, and of Jane Miller, from Moses and Mary Pawson, Kidall lane end, [bn.] Wed., 19 June, [bp.] Sund., 21 July

Sarah, d. of Richard Lumb, Barwick, Inkeeper, from William and Martha Lumb, Barwick, and of Bridget Lumb, from William and Ann Cunningam, Wakefield, born Fri., 21 June, bap. Sun., 21 July

Miles, son of John Mackontrought, Barwick, Labourer, from John and Ann Mackontrout, Kippax, and of Martha Mackontrought, from Miles and Mary Ampshaw, Barwick, [bn.] Mon., Aug. 5, [bp.] Sun., Sep. 15

Sarah, daughter of Luke Dawson, Barnbow, Farmer, from Richard and Mary Dawson, Garforth, and of Ann Dawson, from William and Sarah Pease, Garforth, [bn.] Sun., 11 Aug., [bp.] Sept. 15

William, son of Joseph Kitcheman, Barwick, Lab^{r}, from James and Martha Kitcheman, Chapeltown, and of Martha Kitcheman, from William and Mary Lumb, Barwick, [bn.] Mon., 26 Aug., [bp.] Sun., 22 Sep.

John son of John Connell, Scholes, Lab^{r}, from Anthoney and Sarah Connell, Halton, and of Sarah Connell, from Samuel and Hannah Farrah, Bramley, [bn.] Sat., 24 Aug., [bp.] Sun., 3 Nov.

---

*Richard Lumb, the son, was married 1808, at Leeds by licence, to Beatrice, dau. of Joseph Wilkinson, of Aberford, and Mary his wife, dau. of Henry Sampson. He had issue two sons, George Lumb, of Swillington, and Richard Lumb, of Leeds, and four children died young. He died 1860, and was buried at Garforth.

Mary, d. of William Goodall, Brownmoor, Collier, from Joseph and Mary Goodall, Barnbow, and of Ann Goodall, from John and Ann Backhouse, Swillington, bn. Fri., 11 Oct., [bp.] Sun., 3 Nov.

Ann, d. of Gregory Lofthouse, Potterton, La^r, from Mark and Martha Lofthouse, Netherton, and of Elizabeth Lofthouse, from John and Abigal Hissot, Brodsworth, [bn.] Tues., 8 Oct., [bp.] Mon., 4 Nov.

Mary Ann, d. of Richard Brooke, Scholes, Major, from James and Mary Brookes, Killingbeck, and of Frances Brooke, from Richard and Frances Brooke, York, [bn.] Mon., 14 Oct., [bp.] Fri., 15 Nov.

Samuel, son of Samuel Harrison, Potterton, Labourer, from Benjamin and Ann Harrison, Methley, and of Sarah Harrison, from Thomas and Isabella Poppleton, Abberford, [bn.] Sun., 20 Oct., [bp.] Sun., 8 Dec.

Frances, d. of Jonathan Dinison, Stanks, Carpinter, from Joseph and Alice Denison, Colton, and of Mary Denison, from Richard and Mary Beardshaw, Monck friseton, [bn.] Tues., 12 Nov., [bp.] Sunday, 22 Dec.

BAPTISMS, 1783.

Benjamin, bastard son of Mary Barrett, Barwick, [bp.] Sun., 5 Jan.

James, son of Francis Moss, Kidall-lane, Farmer, from Francis and Susanna Moss, Heaselwood, and of Sarah Moss, from Thomas and Elizabeth Addeman, Scholes, [bn.] Tues., 19 Dec., [bp.] Sun., 12 Jan.

Isabella, d. of Richard Watson, Whinmoor, Labourer, from William and Ann Watson, Thorner, and of Mary Watson, from Thomas and Mary Simpson, Whinmoor, [bn.] Tues., 3 Dec., [bp.] Sun., 19 Jan.

Ruth, the d. of Thomas Tilney, Scholes, mason, from Nicolas and Sarah Tilney, Ingine, and of Sarah Tilney, from Thomas and Mary Haley, Scholes, [bn.] Sat., 7 Dec., [bp.] Sun., 2 Feb.

John, son of Michell Watson, Barwick, Carpinter, from William and Hannah Watson, Barwick, and of Hannah Watson, from John and Martha Dodsworth, Cauwood, [bn.] Tues., 24 Dec., [bp.] Sun., 23 Feb.

William, bastard son of Elizabeth Norton, Barwick, [bp.] Sun., 2 Mar.

Frances, daughter of William Dunwell, hiltop, Labour[er] from William and Elizabeth Dunwell, Whinmoor, and of Margret Dunwell, from Thomas and Hannah Deane, Potternewton, [bp.] Sun., 2 March

Hannah, d. of Joseph Lidster, Scholes, Labourer, from William and Mary Lidster, Garforth, and of Sarah Lidster, from Samuel and Chrissey Simpson, Barnbow, [bn.] Sat., 1 Feb., [bp.] Sun., 23 Mar.

John, son of Roger Brownrig, Scholes, Taylor, from Peter and Martha Brownrig, Spofforth, and of Ann Brownrig, from John and Catherine Vary, Scholes, [bn.] Fri., 7 Feb., [bp.] Sun., 23 Mar.

Mary, d. of William Slayter, Barwick, Labourer, from William and Mary Slayter, Barwick, and of Ann Slayter, from William and Mary Hargrave, Hoberley, [bn.] Sun., 16 Feb., [bp.] Sun., 23 Mar.

Elizabeth, d. of John Walton, Barwick, Labourer, from John and Ann Walton, Barwick, and of Mary Walton, from John and

Elizabeth Nettleton, Mickelfield, [bn.] Wed., 12 Feb., [bp.] Sun., 30 Mar.

James, son of John Flockton, Barwick, Labourer, from James and Ruth Flockton, Leeds, and of Mary Flockton, from Benjn and Susannah Watson, Barwick, [bn.] Fri., 14 Feb., [bp.] Sun., 30 Mar.

Thomas, son of Abraham Wormald, Barwick, Blacksmith, from Abraham and Chrissey Wormald, Barwick, and of Sarah Wormald, f. Richard and [*blank*] Naylor, Aberford, [bp.] Sun., 20 Apr.

Jane, d. of William Jackson, Kidall lane-end, Lab^{r}, from William and Hannah Jackson, Ecup, and of Ann Jackson, from Richard and Jane Laburn, Stanford Bridge, [bn.] Tues., 25 Mar., [bp.] Sun., 20 Apr.

John, son of John Blackburn, Garforth moor, Collier, from Henry and Mary Blackburn, Brownmoor, and of Jane Blackburn, from William and Hannah Smith, Garforth Moor, [bn.] Sun., 6 Apr., [bp.] Sun., 4 May

Henry, son of William Thompson, Morwick, Labourer, from John and Frances Thompson, Garforth, and of Catherine Thompson, from Henry and Mary Pickhard, Kippax, [bn.] Fri., 21 Mar., [bp.] Sun., 11 May

Elizabeth, d. of John Anderson, Potterton, farmer, from John and Jane Anderson, Marton, and of Mary Anderson, from William and Mary Clifforth, Sandhutton, [bn.] Thurs., 20 Mar., [bp.] Sun., 11 May

John Thompson Hawking, bastard son of Ann Hawkin, Scholes, [bp.] Sun., 25 May

Elizabeth, d. of Thomas Lowriman, Ingine, Collier, from Richard and Sarah Lowriman, Garforth, and Mary Lowriman, from James and Mary Tillotson, Ingine, [bn.] Fri., 16 May, [bp.] Thurs., 9 May

Sarah, bastard d. of Elizabeth Tipling, Stanks, [bp.] Sun., 8 June

John, son of Samuel Thompson, Barnbow, Collier, from John and Frances Thompson, Garforth, and of Suseanah Thompson, from William and Suseannah Tayler, Barnbow, [bn.] Sun., 18 May, [bp.] Sun., 22 June

Ann, d. of Jonothan Tayler of Stanks, collier, from Gabril and Mary Tayler, Sturton, and of Ellin Tayler, from William and Mary Jefroy, Tholthorp, [bn.] June 9, [bp.] July 13

Mary, d. of Jeremiah Lumb of Stockhil, Farmer, from Thomas and Hannah Lumb, Stockhill, and of Ellin Lumb, from Robert and Mary Vevers, Potterton, [bn.] June 14, [bp.] July 20

Ellin, d. of John Goodall, Barnbow, Collier, from Joseph and Mary Goodall, Barnbow, and of Ellin Goodall, from Richard and Ellin Goodall, Coulton, [bn.] June 1, [bp.] July 20

Henry, son of Henry Blackburn, Coalpits, Sinderburner, from Henry and Hannah Blackburn, Brownmoor, and of Elizabeth Blackburn, from William and Hannah Ingle, Sturton, [bn.] July 4, [bp.] August 3

Elizabeth, d. of Joseph Cawthorn, Ba[r]wick, Labourer, from Benjamin and Elizabeth Cawthorn, Britaine, and of Ann

Cawthorn, from John and Sarah Dickinson, Barwick, [bp.] June 4, [bp.] August 3

Thomas, son of Thomas Abbot, Barwick, Labourer, from William and Catherine Abbot, Barwick, and of Elizabeth Abbot, from Matthew and Elizabeth Pickring, Sherburn, [bn.] June 18, [bp.] August 3

Hannah, d. of William Thompson, Barnbow, Collier, from Thomas and Ann Thompson, Garforth, and of Jane Thompson, from Thomas and Mary Pickring, Purston, [bn.] July 8, [bp.] Aug. 10

Thomas, son of Thomas Pickersgill, Whinmoor, Farmer, from George and Martha Pickersgill, Karstall, and of Judith Pickersgill, from John and Elizabeth Stead, Thorner, [bn.] July 13, [bp.] Aug. 31

William and Peter, twins, sons of Peter Slayter, Barwick, Farmer, from William and Mary Slayter, Barwick, and of Mary Slayter, from Joseph and Mary Bullock, Barwick, [bn.] Aug. 17, [bp.] Aug. 17

Elizabeth, d. of Thomas Goodall, Ingine, Collier, from William and Elizabeth Goodall, Garforth, and of Ann Goodall, from John and Ann Tillotson, Garforth, [bn.] Aug. 11, [bp.] Sept. 7

Martha, d. of David Carter, Stanley, Labourer, from George and Elizabeth Carter, Kippax, and of Hannah [Ann *erased*] Carter, from William and Hannah Tipling, Barwick, [bn.] Aug. 5, [bp.] Sept. 14

William, son of James Whitehead, Barwick, Lab^r, from Thomas and Margret Whitehead, Barwick, and of Elizabeth Whitehead, from Robert and Martha Whitehead, Barwick, [bn.] Aug. 19, [bp.] Sept. 14

Edmund, son of Benjamin Rawlinson, Barwick, Lab^r, from Benjamin and Mary Rawlinson, Barwick, and of Frances Rawlinson, from William and Ann Cromek, Barwick, [bp.] Sept. 14

Mary, d. of Thomas Simpson, Barnbow, Collier, from Samuel and Cressey Simpson, Barnbow, and of Frances Simpson, from Ester Claburn, Garforth, [bn.] Aug. 16, [bp.] Sept. 21

Julca, d. of Thomas Waite, Barwick, Lab^r, from William and Ann Waite, Barwick, and of Julca Waite, from William and Dorotha Sinyard, Brotherton, [bn.] August 11, [bp.] Sept. 21

Mary, d. of Mary Turpin, Crossgates, [bn.] Aug. 2, [bp.] Sept. 28

Mary, d. of William Richardson, Potterton, Shoemaker, from Luke and Elizabeth Richardson, Potterton, and of Mary Richardson, from John and Mary Richardson, Wortley, [bn.] Aug. 6, [bp.] Sep. 28

Ann, d. of Richard Hornby, Burniston, Lab^r, from Richard and Mary Hornby, Burniston, and of Henry Hornby, from Isaac and Jane Dodgshon, Whinmoor, [bn.] Aug. 30, [bp.] Sept. 28

Isaiah, son of Robert Aveson, Scholes, Weaver, from Henry and Elizabeth Aveson, Bardsaw, and of Mary Aveson, from Benjamin and Grace Hill, Scholes, [bn.] Sept. 13, [bp.] Oct. 19

William, son of George Herring, Kidall-lane-end, Groome, from John and Jane Herring, Highianton, and of Alice Herring, from

William and Mary Whaller, Bramham park, [bn.] Aug. 13, [bp.] Oct. 24

James, son of John Mather, Garforth Moor, Lab^r^, from John and Ann Mather, Brownmoor, from Mary Mather, from Richard and Hannah Naylor, Garforth Moor, [bn.] Sept. 28, [bp.] Oct. 26

Ann, d. of John Robinson, Stanks, Collier, from John and Elizabeth Robinson, Garforth, and of Alice Robinson, from Thomas and Mary Tayler, Barwick, [bn.] Sept. 26, [bp.] Nov. 2

Mary, d. of William Watson, Barwick, Weelwright, from Benjamin and Susannah Watson, Barwick, and of Jane Watson, from Jane Barker, Garforth, [bn.] Oct. 14, [bp.] Nov. 2

Thomas, son of William Smith, Barwick, Farmer, from William and Henrietta Maria Smith, Barwick, and of Ann Smith, from William and Sarah Knapton, Barwick, [bn.] Nov. 2, [bp.] Nov.30

Hannah, d. of John Benton, Stanks, Collier, from Thomas and Margret Benton, Garforth, and of Milly Benton, from David and Ellin Hurst, Pogmoor, [bn.] Nov. 25, [bp.] Dec. 7

Joseph, son of William Carr, Kidall-lane-end, Inkeeper, from John and Elizabeth Carr, Doncaster, and of Alice Carr, from William and Ann Mason, Eastby, [bn.] Oct. 16, [bp.] Dec. 8

Ann, d. of Mark Lofthouse, Potterton, Blacksmith, from Mark and Martha Lofthouse, Netherton, and of Charlotte Lofthouse, from William and Dorotha Sinyard, Brotherton, [bn.] Oct. 19, [bp.] Dec. 14

Liddy. d. of Samuel Simpson. Barnbow, Collier, from Samuel and Christiana Simpson, Barnbow, and of Frances Simpson, from Richard and Easter Claburn, Garforth, [bn.] Nov. 25, [bp.] Dec. 21

James, son of Thomas Perkin, Barwick, Lab^r^, from James and Ann Perkin, Barwick, and of Mary Perkin, from Robert and Elizabeth Thorns, Partington, [bn.] Nov. 22, [bp.] Dec. 26

Ann, d. of Richard Winson, Leeds, from Thomas and Jane Whinsor, Littondale, and of Grace Whinsor, from Robert and Ann Dixon, Barnbow, [bn.] Nov. 28, [bp.] Dec. 27

James, son of Jonathan Hodgson, Scholes, Lab^r^, from William and Easter Hodgson, Barnbow, and of Hannah Hodgson, from Thomas and Hannah Lumb, Stockhil, [bn.] Sept. 6, [bp.] Dec. 31

BAPTISMS, 1784.

Susannah, d^r^ of Richard Lumb, Barwick, Farmer, from Richard and Ann Lumb, Barwick, and of Elizabeth Lumb, from William and Ann Carew, Lisbon, in Portugal, [bp.] Jan. 1

George, son of Joseph White, Scholes, from John and Grace White, Akaster Malbles, and of Mary White, from George and Elizabeth Barker, Hensaul, [bn.] Nov. 19, [bp.] Jan. 5

Thomas, son of Thomas Green, Whinmoor, from James and Elizabeth Green, Whinmoor, and of Mary Green, from Peter and Mary Park, Strensal, [bn.] Dec. 17, [bp.] Jan. 29

John, son of John Cullingworth, Barwick, Shoemaker, from Joseph and Elizabeth Cullingworth, Aberford, and of Maria Cullingworth, from Thomas and Mary Thornton, Potterton, [bp.] Feb. 1

William, son [of] Alvray Thompson, Penwell, Lab^{r}, from John and Sarah Thompson, Stanks, and of Sarah Thompson, from Richard and Ann Lazenby, Penwell, [bn.] Dec. 27, [bp.] Feb. 8

Hannah, d. of George Darton, Barwick, Lab^{r}, from George and Susannah Darton, Calverley, and of Ann Darton, from John and Elizabeth Dungwith, Barwick, [bn.] Dec. 21, [bp.] Feb. 22

Ann, d. of William Bell, Hill-top, from William and Mary Bell, Hiltop, and of Sarah Bell, from Thomas and Sarah Shilburn, Seacroft, [bn.] Jan. 21, [bp.] Feb. 29

Henry, son of Henry Frank, Scholes, Labourer, from Henry and Jane Frank, Wikill, and of Mary Frank, from James and Jane Laboura, Akester, [bn.] Feb. 5, [bp.] Mar. 14

Henrietta Maria and Mary, Twins, ds. of David Heaton, Barwick, Lab^{r}., from James and [? Rose] Heaton, West Hardsley, and of Maria Heaton, from Joseph and Mary Bullock, Barwick, [bn.] Feb. 23, [bp.] Mar. 28

Benjamin, son of Edward Goodall, Stanks, from Edward and Sarah Goodall, Garforth, and of Sarah Goodall, from Benjamin and Elizabeth Coocke, Stanks, [bn.] Mar. 1, [bp.] April 4

William, son of Samuel Greenwood, Potterton, from John and Ann Greenwood, Mickelfield, and of Ann Greenwood, from Benjamin and Ann Harrison, Methley, [bn.] Jan. 19, [bp.] April 4

Frances, d. of Benjamin Bell, Scholes, Lab^{r}, from Jonathan and Ann Bell, Barnbow, and of Frances Bell, from Thomas and Margret Burwell, Leeds, [bn.] March 13, [bp.] April 11

Elisabeth, d. of Joseph Walton, Barwick, Farmer, from John and Ann Walton, Barwick, and of Sarah Walton, from Edward and Mary Day, Potterton, [bn.] March 13, [bp.] April 18

James, son of James Thompson, Barwick, Lab^{r}, from John and Ann Thompson, Seacroft, and of Mary Thompson, from Joseph and Abigal Holms, Barwick, [bn.] May 6, [bp.] May 30

Matthew, son of Gregory Lofthouse, Potterton, Lab^{r}, from Mark and Martha Lofthouse, Netherton, and of Elizabeth Lofthouse, from John and Abigal Hisot, Brodsworth, [bn.] April 18, [bp.] May 30

Edward Maxfield, son of Joseph Sparling, Potterton, Lab^{r}, from John and Ellin Sparling, Abberford, and of Mary Sparling, from George and Susannah Watson, Potterton, [bn.] April 22, [bp.] June 6

George Charles, son of Richard Brooke, Scholes, Major, from James and Mary Brooke, Killinbeck, and of Frances Brooke, from Richard and Frances Brooke, York, [bn.] May 23, [bp.] June 18

Ann, d. of Renton Haist, Barwick, Labourer, from Mary Haist, Barwick, and of Sarah Haist, from William and Ann Ward, Barwick, [bn.] April 19, [bp.] June 20

Henry, son of John Forster, Barwick, Labourer, from Thomas and Elizabeth Forster, Sherburn, and of Sarah Forster, from Benjamin and Susannah Watson, Barwick, [bn.] May 24, [bp.] June 20

Catherine, d. of William Robshaw, Barwick, Labourer, from Thomas and Catherine Robshaw, Barwick, and of Alice Robshaw, from William and Margret Rothmell, Knazebrough, [bn.] May 17, [bp.] June 27

Mary, d. of Francis Linley, Hiltop, Lab^{r}, from William and Mary Linley, Seacroft, and of Ann Linley, from Thomas and Susannah Baley, Hiltop, [bn.] June 1, [bp.] June 27

Elizabeth, d. of John Stubs, Barwick, from John and Ann Stubs, Tadcaster, and of Elizabeth Stubs, from John and Ann Robinson, Barwick, [bn.] June 1, [bp.] July 4

Barnard, son of Thomas Hewitt, Barwick, Collier, from George and Frances Hewitt, Ingine, and of Elizabeth Hewitt, from Thomas and Margret Hemsworth, Swillington, [bn.] June 22, [bp.] Aug. 8

Mary, d. of William Burland, Barwick, Lab^{r}, from [*blank*] Burland, Seacroft, and of Sarah Burland, from Robert and Mary Smith, Barwick, [bn.] July 20, [bp.] Aug. 22

Isabella, d. of Robert Wheater, Barwick, Labourer, from John and Frances Wheater, Templehirst, and of Jane Wheater, from John and Isabella Mossaby, Temple hirst, [bn.] July 29, [bp.] Sept. 12

Ann, bastard d. of Mary Craggs, Barwick, [bp.] Sept. 16

Elizabeth, d. of Thomas Brook, Kidall hall, [bp.] Sept. 22

Peter Powell, son of Benjamin Eamonson, Lazencroft, from Peter and Elianor Eamondson, Roundhay, and of Elianor Eamonson, from Joseph and Elianor Powel, Bramham, [bn.] August 23, [bp.] Sept. 29

Ruth, d. of John Butler, Scholes, pipemaker, from John and Sarah Butler, Scholes, and of Hannah Butler, from John and Ann North, Newbery, Barkshire, [bn.] Sept. 7, [bp.] Oct. 10

Hannah, d. [of] Thomas Armatage, Whinmoor, Collier, from Joseph and Elizabeth Armatage, Purston, and of Mary Armatage, from John and Judith Carlin, Garforth, [bn.] Sept. 4, [bp.] Oct. 10

Ann, bastard d. of Elizabeth Horsfield, Barwick, [bp.] Nov. 7

John, son of John Monks, Barwick, Labourer, from Edward and Elizabeth Monks, Barwick, and of Elizabeth Monks, from William and Jane Wadington, Otley, [bn.] Oct. 17, [bp.] Nov. 7

Thomas, son of John Cauwood, Coalpits, Collier, from Josuah and Elizabeth Cauwood, Garforth, and of Ann Cauwood, from Andrew and Elizabeth Joy, Sherburn, [bn.] Nov. 29, [bp.] Dec. 5

Sarah, d. of John Connell, Scholes, labourer, from Anthoney and Sarah Connell, Halton, and of Sarah Connell, from Samuel and Hannah Farrah, Bramley, [bn.] Oct. 26, [bp.] Dec. 5

Mary, d. of Joseph Cawthorn, Barwick, Lab^{r}, from Benjamin and Elisabeth Cawthorn, Britaine, and of Ann Cawthorn, from John and Sarah Dickinson, Barwick, [bn.] Oct. 23, [bp.] Dec. 5

Rachel, d. of Thomas Tilney, Scholes, Mason, from Nicolas and Sarah Tilney, Ingine, and of Sarah Tilney, from Thomas and Mary Haley, Scholes, [bn.] Nov. 4, [bp.] Dec. 19

Joseph, son of William Goodall, Barnbow, Collier, from Joseph and Mary Goodall, Barnbow, and of Ann Goodall, from John and Ann Bachouse, Swillington, [bn.] Nov. 9, [bp.] Dec. 26

BAPTISMS, 1785.

Martha, d. of Matthew Miller, Kidall-lane-end, from James and Mary Miller, Richmond, and of Jane Miller, from Moses and Mary Pawson, Kidall-lane-end, [bn.] Nov. 26, [bp.] Jan. 2

Ann, d. of Robert Jordan, Stanks, Lab[r], from Thomas and Elizabeth Jordan, Seacroft, and of Sarah Jordan, from Thomas and Elizabeth Lightfoot, Brownmoor, [bn.] Dec. 8, [bp.] Jan. 9

Sarah, d. of Benjamin Collett, Barwick, Butcher, from Thomas and Elizabeth Collett, Barwick, and of Elizabeth Collett, from William and Sarah Knapton, Barwick, [bn.] Dec. 31, [bp.] Jan. 23

Christiana, d. of William Walton, Barwick, Labourer, from John and Ann Walton, Barwick, and of Elizabeth Walton, from Joseph and Elizabeth Pearson, Waleworth, [bn.] Jan. 5, [bp.] Feb. 13

William, son of William Dunwell, Hiltop, Lab[r], from William and Elizabeth Dunwell, hiltop, and of Margaret Dunwell, from Thomas and Hannah Deane, Potternewton, [bn.] Jan., 6 [bp.] Feb. 13

Richard, son of William Jackson, Kidall lane end, Lab[r], from William and Hannah Jackson, Ecup, and of Ann Jackson, from Richard and Jane Laburn, Stamford Bridge, [bn.] Jan. 14, [bp.] Feb. 20

Samuel, son of John Robinson, Stanks, Collier, from John and Elizabeth Robinson, Garforth, and of Alice Robinson, from Thomas and Mary [Elizabeth *erased*] Taylor, Barwick, [bn.] Jan. 21, [bp.] Feb. 27

Hannah, d. of William Richardson, Potterton, shoemaker, from Luke and Elizabeth Richardson, Potterton, and of Mary Richardson, from John and Mary Richardson, Wortley, [bn.] Jan., 18 [bp.] February 27

William, son of John Anderson, Potterton, Farmer, from John and Jane Anderson, Marton, and of Mary Anderson, from William and Mary Clifforth, Sandhutton, [bn.] Feb. 2, [bp.] Mar. 27

Hannah, d. of William Slayter, Barwick, Lab[r]. from William and Mary Slayter, and of Ann Slayter, from William and Mary Hargrave, Hoberley, [bn.] Feb. 27, [bp.] Mar. 27

William, son of Jonathan Tayler, Stanks, Collier, from Gabril and Mary Tayler, Sturton, and of Ellin Tayler, from William and Mary Jefray, Tholthorp, [bn.] Feb. 3, [bp.] April 3

Joseph, son of Abraham Wormald, Barwick, Blacksmith, from Abraham and Chrissy Wormald, Barwick, and of Sarah Wormald, from Richard and Sarah Naylor, Abberford, [bn.] Mar. 2, [bp.] Apr. 10

Henry, son of James Goodall, Barnbow, Collier, from Joseph and Mary Goodall, Barnbow, and of Ellin Goodall, from William and Hester Hodgson, Barnbow, [bn.] Feb. 27, [bp.] April 10

William, son of John Mackontrout, Barwick, Lab[r], from John and Ann Mackontrout, Kippax, and of Martha Mackontrout, from Miles and Mary Ampshaw, Barwick, [bn.] Feb. 24, [bp.] Apr. 17

Benjamin, bastard son of Elizabeth Cockshaw, five years and two months old, [bp.] April 17

Samuel, son of Joseph Lidster, Barnbow, Lab[r], from William and Mary Lidster, Garforth, and of Sarah Lidster, from Samuel and Chrissey Simpson, Barnbow, [bn.] Mar. 20, [bp.] April 24

Hannah, d. of Henry Blackburn, Coalpits, Sinderburner, from Henry and Hannah Blackburn, Brownmoor, and of Elizabeth Blackburn, from William and Hannah Ingle, Sturton, [bn.] Mar. 26, [bp.] April 24

Sarah, d. of George Scholes, Barnbow, Collier, from John and Ann Scholes, Rothwell, and of Mary Scholes, from John and Mary Atkinson, Barnbow, [bn.] Mar. 24, [bp.] April 24

Mary, d. of William Robshaw, Barwick, Lab^r^, from Thomas and Ellin Robshaw, Hosbon, and of Sarah Robshaw, from William and Sarah Knapton, Barwick, [bn.] April 20, [bp.] May 15

William, bastard son of Ann Hawkin, Scholes, [bp.] May 16

Richard, son of John Goodall, Barnbow, Collier, from Joseph and Mary Goodall, Barnbow, and of Ellin Goodall, from Richard and Ellin Goodall, Coulton, [bn.] May 28, [bp.] May 29

William, son of Samuel Womack, Barwick, from Samuel and Sarah Womack, Heath, and of Ann Womack, from Richard and Ann Smith, Barwick, [bn.] May 3, [bp.] July 3

Ann, d. of Arthur Turner, Roundhay, from William and Ellin Turner, Shadwell, and of Isabella Turner, from John and Elizabeth Simpson, Roundhay Grange, [bn.] July 2, [bp.] Aug. 12

John Clarkson, son of Richard Brooke, Scholes, Major, from James and Mary Brooke, Killingbeck, and of Frances Brooke, from Richard and Frances Brooke, York, [bn.] June 22, [bp.] Sept. 2

Thomas, son of William Tipling, Stanks, Lab^r^, from William and Hannah Tipling, Barwick, and of Elizabeth Tipling, from John and Elizabeth Settle, Scholes, [bn.] July 1, [bp.] Aug. 28

Thomas, son of Richard Watson, Whinmoor, Lab^r^, from William and Ann Watson, Thorner, and of Mary Watson, from Thomas and Mary Simpson, Whinmoor, [bn.] Aug. 21, [bp.] Sept. 18

Richard Tottie, son of Thomas Brook, Kidall-hall, Farmer, from Thomas and Martha Brook, Glasshoughton, and of Mary Brook, from John and Elizabeth [Sarah *erased*] Tottie, Moor Town, [bn.] Aug. 16, [bp.] Oct. 2

Frances, bastard d. of Mary Brown, Whinmoor, [bn.] Aug. 27, [bp.] Oct. 2

Susannah, d. of Joseph Johnson, Brownmoor, Collier, from James and Mary Johnson, Austhorp, and of Susannah Johnson, from Joseph and Grace Hanson, Halton, [bn.] July 21, [bp.] Oct. 2

Matthew, son of Thomas Abbot, Barwick, Lab^er^, from William and Catherine Abbot, Barwick, and of Elizabeth Abbot, from Matthew and Elizabeth Pickring, Sherburn, [bn.] Oct. 8, [bp.] Nov. 6

Mary, d. of George Darton, Barwick, Lab^r^, from George and Susannah Darton, Calverly, and of Ann Darton, from John and Elizabeth Dungwith, Barwick, [bp.] Nov. 6

William, son of Thomas Todd, Scholes, Farmer, from Thomas and Mary Todd, Newby, and of Jane Todd, from Thomas and Elizabeth Smith, Potterton, [bn.] Sept. 17, [bp.] Nov. 6

Sarah, d. of James Jackson, Barwick, Farmer, from Matthew and Sarah Jackson, Barwick, and of Mary Jackson, from Joseph and Easter Atkinson, Witley, [bn.] Sept. 16, [bp.] Nov. 6

Luke, son of Mark Lofthouse, Potterton, Farmer, from Mark and Martha Lofthouse, Netherton, and of Charlotta Lofthouse, from William [and] Dorotha Sinyard, Brotherton, [bn.] Oct. 18, [bp.] Nov. 6

Sarah, d. of Thomas Simpson, Barnbow, Collier, from Samuel and Chrissey Simpson, Barnbow, and of Frances Simpson, from Easter and John Claburn, Garforth, [bp.] Nov. 6

Ann, d. of John Flockton, Barwick, Labourer, from James and Ruth Flockton, Leeds, and of Mary Flockton, from Benjamin and Susannah Watson, Barwick, [bn.] Oct. 24, [bp.] Nov. 6

Susannah, d. of Francis Linley, Hiltop, Labourer, from William and Mary Linley, Seacroft, and of Sarah Linley, from Thomas and Ann Baley, Hiltop, [bn.] Nov. 11th, [bp.] Dec. 11

John, son of John Loder, Kidall lane end, [bp.] Dec. 9

BAPTISMS, 1786.

Joseph, son of Joseph Simpson, Brownmoor, Collier, from Samuel and Chrissey Simpson, Barnbow, and of Sarah Simpson, from Henry and Sarah Clarkson, Abberford, [bn.] Dec. 18, [bp.] Jan. 15

Roger, son of John Foster, Barwick, Labr, from Thomas and Elizabeth Foster, Sherburn, and of Sarah Foster, from Benjamin and Susannah Watson, Barwick, [bn.] Jan. 12, [bp.] Feb. 5

Martha and Mary, twins, ds. of Thomas Waite, Barwick, Labr, from William and Ann Waite, Barwick, and of Julca Waite, from William and Dorotha Sinyard, Brotherton, [bn.] Jan. 5, [bp.] Feb. 12

Mary, d. of Samuel Simpson, Barnbow, Collier, from Samuel and Chrissy Simpson, Barnbow, and of Ann Simpson, from Thomas and Ann Thompson, Garforth, [bn.] Feb. 11, [bp.] Feb. 11

Joseph, son of David Heaton, Barwick, Labr, from James and Roose Heaton, West Hardsley, and of Maria Heaton, from Joseph and Mary Bullock, Barwick, [bn.] Jan. 15, [bp.] Feb. 19

Mary, d. of Francis Ciburry, Barwick, Labr, from Francis and Elizabeth Syburry, Brininton, and of Ann [Mary *erased*] Syburry, from Thomas and Mary Taite, Barwick, [bn.] Jan. 16, [bp.] Feb. 26

John, son of Joseph Walton, Barwick, Farmer, from John and Ann Walton, Barwick, and of Sarah Walton, from Edward and Mary Day, Potterton, [bn.] Jan. 29, [bp.] March 5

Elizabeth, d. of Gregory Lofthouse, Potterton, Labr, from Mark and Martha Lofthouse, Netherton, and of Elizabeth Lofthouse, from John and Abigal Isot, Brodsworth, [bn.] Jan. 19, [bp.] Mar. 5

John, son of Thomas Goodall, Ingine, Collier, from William and Elizabeth Goodall, Garforth, and of Ann Goodall, from John and Ann Tillotson, Garforth, [bn.] Feb. 10, [bp.] March 12

Frances, d. of Thomas Lowreman, Ingine, Collier, from Richard and Sarah Lowreman, Garforth, and of Mary Lowriman, from James and Mary Tillitson, Ingine, [bn.] Feb. 17, [bp.] March 19

Martha, d. of Samuel Thompson, Barnbow, Collier, from John and Frances Thompson, Garforth, and of Susannah Thompson, from William and Susannah Tayler, Barnbow, [bn.] Feb. 26, [bp.] Apr. 2d

Elizabeth, bastard d. of Ann Marshall, Barwick, [bp.] Apr. 9th
Thomas, son of Thomas Perkin, Barwick, Labr, from James and Ann Perkin, Barwick, and of Mary Perkin, from Robert and Elizabeth Thorns, Parlington, [bn.] Mar. 2, [bp.] Apr. 16th
Mary, bastard daughter of [*blank*] Parkin, Workhouse, [bp.] Apr. 16
William, son of William Bell, Hiltop, Labr, from William and Mary Bell, Hiltop, and of Sarah Bell, from Thomas and Sarah Shilburn, Seacroft, [bn.] Mar. 14, [bp.] Apr. 23
John, son of Thomas Pickersgill, Whinmoor, Farmer, from George and Martha Pickersgill, Karstall, and of Judith Pickersgil from John and Elizabeth Stead, Thorner, [bn.] March 7, [bp.] Apr. 30
Sarah, d. of Edward Goodall, Stanks, Collier, from Edward and Sarah Goodall, Garforth, and of Sarah Goodall, from Benjamin and Elizabeth Coock, Stanks, [bn.] Apr. 6, [bp.] Apr. 30
Elianor Anne, d. of Benjamin Eamonson, Lazencroft, from Peter and Elianor Eamonson, Roundhay, and Elianor Eamonson, from Joseph and Elianor Powell, Bramham, [bn.] Apr. 3, [bp.] May 4
Elizabeth, d. of William Thompson, Morwick, Jober, from John and Ann [Frances *erased*] Thompson, Garforth, and of Catherine Thompson, from Henry and Mary Pickhard, Kippax, [bn.] May 8, [bp.] May 25
Hannah, d. of John Goodall, Barnbow, collier, from Joseph and Mary Goodall, Barnbow, and of Ellin Goodall, from Richard and Ellin Goodall, Coulton, [bn.] Apr. 28, [bp.] May 25
Thomas, son of John Butler, Scholes, Pipemaker, from John and Sarah Butler, Scholes, and of Hannah Butler, from John and Ann North, Newberry, Birkshire, [bn.] April 26, [bp.] June 4
Thomas, son of David Carter, Stanks, Labourer, from George and Elizabeth Carter, Kippax, and of Hannah Carter, from William and Hannah Tipling, Barwick, [bn.] April 30, [bp.] June 25
Mary, d. of Jonathan Hodgson, Scholes, Labr, from William and Easter Hodgson, Barnbow, and of Hannah Hodgson, from Thomas and Hannah Lumb, Stockhill ,[bn.] May 5, [bp.] July 2
Hannah, d. of Renton Haist, Barwick, Labr, from Mary Haist, Barwick, and of Sarah Haist, from William and Ann Ward, Barwick, [bn.] June 1, [bp.] July 9
*John, son of Thomas Shepley, Barwick, from Thomas and Ann Shepley, Leeds, and of Ann Shepley, from Francis and Ann Iles, Tadcaster, [bn.] June 19, [bp.] July 21
Sarah, d. of Matthew Varley, Barwick, Farmer, from Samuel and Sarah Varley, Barwick, and of Sarah Varley, from Thomas and Margret Whitehead, Barwick, [bn.] July 5, [bp.] July 25
James, bastard son of Hannah Mountaine, Barwick Workhouse, Pauper, [bp.] July 23
William, son of Roger Brownrig, Scholes, Taylor, from Peter and Martha Brownrig, Spofforth, and of Ann Brownrig, from John and Catherine Vary, Scholes, [bn.] June 26, [bp.] July 30

*For pedigree of and notes on the Shepley family see the Northern Genealogist 1896, p. 199. According to tradition, Thomas Shepley the elder resided at Barwick Rectory as lessee, which is corroborated by Jeffery's Map of Yorkshire, 1771. Thomas Shepley the younger resided at an old house in "The Boyle" now partly pulled down.

Matthew, son of William Watson, Barwick, Weelwright, from Benjamin and Susanna Watson, Barwick, and of Jane Watson, from Jane Barker, Garforth, [bn.] July 15, [bp.] Aug. 13

James, son of James Barker, Whinmoor, Labourer, from William and Frances Barker, Penwell, and of Frances Barker, from William and Elizabeth Morret, Coulton, [bn.] July 25, [bp.] Aug. 27

Ann, d. of William Jackson, Kidhall lane end, Lab^r, from William and Hannah Jackson, Ecup, and of Ann Jackson, from Richard and Jane Laburn, Stamford Bridge, [bn.] Aug. 8, [bp.] Sept. 3

Joseph, son of William Smith, Barwick, Farmer, from William and Henrietta Maria Smith, Barwick, and of Ann Smith, from William and Sarah Knapton, Barwick, [bn.] Aug. 30, [bp.] Sept. 24

Mary, d. of Thomas Wriglesworth, Rothwell, Lab^r, from John and Mearcy Wrigelsworth, Hollorton, and of Hannah Wrigelsworth, from Joseph and Hannah Kirkham, Barwick, [bn.] Aug. 11, [bp.] Oct. 1

John, son of John Benton, Stanks, collier, [from] Thomas and Margret Benton, Garforth, and of Milly Benton, from David and Ellin Hirst, Pogmoor, [bn.] Sept. 2, [bp.] Oct. 1

Richard, son of Richard Thompson, Crosgates, Lab^r, [bn.] Sept., [bp.] Nov. 5

Elizabeth, d. of William Gough, Barwick, farmer, from William and Mary Gough, Brownmoor, and of Ann Gough, from John and Ann Carrot, Headingley, [bp.] Nov. 5

Joseph, son of John Cullingworth, Barwick, Shoemaker, from Joseph and Elizabeth Cullingworth, Abberford, and of Maria Cullingworth, from Thomas and Mary Thornton, Potterton, [bn.] June 28, [bp.] Nov. 5

William, son of John Walton, Barwick, Lab^r, from John and Ann Walton, Barwick, and of Mary Walton, from John and Elizabeth Nettleton, Mickelfield, [bn.] Nov. 10, [bp.] Dec. 10

Mary, bastard d. of Martha Haist, Barwick Workhouse, Pauper, [bn.] Oct. 29, [bp.] Dec. 10

John, son of Thomas Tilney, Scholes, mason, from Nicolas and Sarah Tilney, Ingine, and of Sarah Tilney, from Thomas and Mary Haley, Scholes, [bn.] Oct. 4, [bp.] Dec. 15

Elizabeth, d. of William Burland, Barwick, Lab^r, from Ann Burland, Seacroft, and of Sarah Burland, from Robert and Mary Smith, Barwick, [bn.] Oct. 31, [bp.] Dec. 27

John, son of John Loder, Kidall lane end, Groom, from John and Ann Loder, Marston, and of Sarah Loder, from Henry and Sarah Apott, Hasdon, Suffolk, [bn.] Oct. 29, [bp.] Dec. 29

Sarah, d. of Robert Greenwood, Leeds, from William and Mary Greenwood, Abberford, and of Sarah Greenwood, from Anthoney and Sarah Dunwell, Barwick, [bn.] Dec. 6, [bp.] Dec. 31

Baptisms, 1787.

George, son of George Hopton, Stanks, collier, from George and Sarah Hopton, Garforth, and of Grace Hopton, from John and Martha Boys, Shelf, [bp.] Jan. 14

Susannah, d. of William Dunwell, Hiltop, Lab^{r}, from John and Elizabeth Dunwell, Hiltop, and of Margret Dunwell, from Thomas and Frances Deane, Seacroft, [bn.] Nov. 29, [bp.] Jan. 21

Edward, son of John Monks, Barwick, Lab^{r}, from Edward & Elizabeth Monks, Barwick, and of Elizabeth Monks, from William and Jane Wadington, Otley, [bn.] Nov. 28, [bp.] Jan. 28

Thomas, son of Thomas Clapham, Potterton, Farmer, from Thomas & Rebecca Clapham, Learley, and of Elizabeth Clapham, from Thomas and Mary Robinson, Asqueth, [bn.] Dec. 21, [bp.] Feb. 4

Mary, d. of John Robinson, Stanks, collier, from John and Elizabeth Robinson, Garforth, and of Alice Robinson, from Thomas and Mary Tayler, Barwick, [bn.] Jan. 10, [bp.] Feb. 4

Thomas, son of Joseph Sparling, Potterton, Lab^{r}, from John and Elizabeth Sparling, Parlington, and of Mary Sparlıng, from George and Susannah Watson, Potterton, [bn.] Jan. 5, [bp.] Feb. 11

Jane, d. of Robert Jordan, Stanks, Labourer, from Thomas and Elizabeth Jordan, Seacroft, and of Sarah Jordan from Thomas and Elizabeth Lightfoot, Brownmoor, [bn.] Jan. 24, [bp.] Mar. 4

Ann, d. of Samuel Simpson, Barnbob, collier, from Samuel and Chrissy Simpson, Barnbow, and of Ann Simpson, from Thomas and Ann Thompson, Barnbow, [bn.] Feb. 8, [bp.] Mar. 11

John, son of William Slayter, Barwick, Lab^{r}, from William and Mary Slayter, Barwick, an[d] of Ann Slayter, from William and Mary Hargrave, Hoberley, [bn.] Jan. 9, [bp.] Mar. 11

Mary, bastard d. of Mary Barret, Barwick, Pauper, [bp.] Mar. 11

James, son of James Goodall, Barnbow, collier, from Joseph and Mary Goodall, Barnbow, and of Ellin Goodall, from William and Easter Hodgson, Barnbow, [bn.] Feb. 13, [bp.] Mar. 25

William, son of John Connell, Barwick, Farmer, from Anthoney and Sarah Connell, Halton, and of Sarah Connell, from Samuel and Hannah Farrah, Bramley, [bn.] Jan. 5, [bp.] Apr. 1

Sarah, d. of Thomas Collet, Brownmor, wright, from William and Elizabeth Collet, Kippax, and of Ann Collet, from Matthew and Mary Wilson, Halton, [bn.] March 12, [bp.] Apr. 8

Mary, d. of William Robshaw, Barwick, Lab^{r}, from Thomas & Catherine Robshaw, Barwick, and of Alice Robshaw, from William and Margret Rothmell, Knazebrough, [bn.] Apr. 25, [bp.] May 27

Joseph, son of Thomas Armatage, Winmoor, collier, from Joseph and Elizabeth Armatage, Purston, and of Mary Armatage, from John and Judith Carling, Garforth, [bn.] May 29, [bp.] June 24

Robert Bentley Brooke, son of Richard Brooke, Scholes, Major, from James and Mary Brooke, Killinbeck, and of Frances Brook, from Richard and Frances Brook, York, [bn.] May 25, [bp.] June 29

Thomas, son of Luke Dawson, Barnbow, Farmer, from Richard and Mary Dawson, Garforth, and of Ann Dawson, from William and Sarah Pease, Garforth, [bn.] May 28, [bp.] July 8

Elizabeth, d. of Thomas Hewitt, Barwick, collier, [bp.] June 5

William, son of William Jowet, Barwick, Lab^{r}, from William and

Susannah Jowet, Shadwell, and of Alice Jowet, from John and Elisabeth Dungwith, Barwick, [bn.] June 27, [bp.] July 22

Elianor, d. of Jonothan Taylor, Stanks, collier, from Gabril and Mary Tayler, Storton, and of Ellin Tayler, from William and Mary Jefray, Tholthorp, [bn.] July 6, [bp.] July 29

Mary, d. of John Liley, Barwick, Lab^r, [bp.] Aug. 2

George, son of Gregory Lofthouse, Potterton, Labourer, from Mark and Marth Lofthouse, Netherton, and of Elizabeth Lofthouse, from John and Abigal Hisot, Brodsworth, [bn.] June 11, [bp.] Aug. 12

Thomas, son of Francis Linley, Hiltop, Lab^r, from William and Mary Linley, Seacroft, and of Sarah Linley, from Thomas and Ann Baley, Hiltop, [bn.] Aug. 10, [bp.] Sept. 2

Ann, d. of George Hill, Winmoor, farmer, from Joseph and Hannah Hill, Winmoor, and of Elizabeth Hill, from John and Ann Deane, Winmoor, [bn.] July 30, [bp.] Sept. 2

Thomas, son of Joseph Simpson, Brownmoor, collier, from Samuel and Cressey Simpson, Barnbob, and of Sarah Simpson, from Henry and Sarah Clarkson, Abberford, [bn.] Aug. 26, [bp.] Sept. 23

Jane, d. of William Richardson, Potterton, Shoemaker, from Luke and Elizabeth Richardson, Potterton, and of Mary Richardson. from John and Mary Richardson, Wortley, [bn.] Sept. 9, [bp.] Oct. 5

Elizabeth, d. of John Burrow, Roundhay, from William & Thomas Burrow, Roundhay, and of Sarah Burrow, from Edward and Elizabeth Monks, Barwick, [bn.] Sept. 14, [bp]. Nov. 4

Mary, bastard d. of Sarah Lunn, Brownmoor, [bp.] Dec. 2

John, son of John Hewitt, Barwick, Collier, from Thomas & Elizabeth Hewitt, Barwick, and of Elizabeth Hewitt, from Robert & Elizabeth Barton, Barwick, [bn.] Oct. 26, [bp.] Dec. 9

Rebecca, d. of Jerimiah Lumb, Stockhill, farmer, from Thomas and Hannah Lumb, Stockhill, and of Elianor Lumb, from Robert and Mary Vevers, Potterton, [bn.] Nov. 25, [bp.] Dec. 23

John, son of Mark Lofthouse, Potterton, farmer, from Mark & Martha Lofthouse, Netherton, and of Charlotta Lofthouse, from William & Dorotha Sinyard, Brotherton, [bn.] Nov. 2, [bp.] Dec. 25

Thomas, son of John Mackontrout, Barwick, Lab^r, from John & Ann Mackontrout, Kippax, and of Martha Mackontrout, from Miles and Mary Ampshaw, Barwick, [bn.] Nov. 6, [bp.] Dec. 30

Hannah, d of James Thompson, Barwick, Lab^r, from John & Hannah Thompson, Seacroft, and of Mary Thompson, from Joseph and Abigal Holmes, Barwick, [bn.] Nov. 30, [bp.] Dec. 30

BAPTISMS, 1788.

John, son of George Dawgill, Barwick, Labourer, from George and Susannah Daugill, Calverley, and of Ann Dawgill, from John and Elizabeth Dungwith, Barwick, [bn.] Dec. 25, [bp.] Jan. 1

Sarah, d. of James Tillotson, Brownmoor, collier, from John and Ann Tillotson, Garforth, and of Sarah Tillotson, from John and Mary Hewitt, Swillington, [bn.] Dec. 22, [bp.] Jan. 27

Cilicia, d. of John Foster, Barwick, Labourer, from Thomas & Elizabeth Foster, Sherburn, and of Sarah Foster, from Benjamin and Susannah Watson, Barwick, [bn.] Jan. 1, [bp.] Jan. 27

Jonothan, son of Benjamin Bell, Scholes, Labourer, from Jonothan & Ann Bell, Barnbow, and of Frances Bell, from Thomas & Margret Burwell, Leeds, [bn.] Jan. 4, [bp.] Feb. 24

Abia, d. of Thomas Lowriman, Ingine, Collier, from Richard & Sarah Lowreman, Garforth, and of Mary Lowreman, from James & Mary Tillotson, Ingine, [bn.] Feb. 6, [bp.] Mar. 16

Richard, son of John Tillotson, Garforth moor, collier, from John & Ann Tillotson, Garforth, and of Margret Tillotson, from Thomas and Elizabeth Hewitt, Barwick, [bn.] Feb. 15, [bp.] Mar. 23

Mary, d. of John Wright, Whinmoor, Labourer, [bn.] Feb. 22, [bp.] March 23

Grace, d. of William Bell, Hiltop, Lab^{r}, from William & Mary Bell, Hiltop, and of Sarah Bell, from Thomas and Sarah Shilburn, Seacroft, [bn.] Feb. 1, [bp.] Mar. 23

Hannah, d. of Thomas Goodall, Ingine, Collier, from William & Elizabeth Goodall, Garforth, and of Ann Goodall, from John and Ann Tillotson, Garforth, [bn.] Mar. 16, [bp.] Apr. 13

Mary, d. of John Brogden, Woodhouse, Farmer, from Edward and Ann Brogdin, Rigton, and of Sarah Brogden, from Samuel and Mary Marshall, Rawden, [bn.] March 14, [bp.] April 13

James, son of David Heaton, Barwick, Farmer, from James & Rosse Heaton, West Hardsley, and of Maria Heaton, from Joseph and Mary Bullock, Barwick, [bn.] Mar. 30, [bp.] May 11

Sarah, d. of William Watson, Barwick, weelwright, from Benjamin & Susannah Watson, Barwick, and of Jane Watson, from Jane Barker, Garforth, [bn.] April 17, [bp.] May 11

Ann, d. of William Knapton, Barwick, Blacksmith, from William and Sarah Knapton, Barwick, and of Sarah Knapton, from William and Mary Lumb, Barwick, [bn.] April 5, [bp.] May 13

William, son of James Barker, Winmoor, Labourer, from William and Frances Barker, Winmoor, and of Frances Barker, from William and Elizabeth Morritt, Coulton, [bn.] Apr. 6, [bp.] May 18

Benjamin, son of Benjamin Eamonson, Lazincroft, from Peter and Elianor Eamonson, Roundhay, and of Elianor Eamonson, from Joseph and Elianor Powell, Bramham, [bn.] May 5, [bp.] June 4

John, son of Jonathan Richardson, Winmoor, Lab^{r}, from James & Sarah Richardson, Moor-Town, and of Mary Richardson, from John and Sarah Prince, Seacroft, [bn.] May 31, [bp.] July 13

George, son of Thomas Tilney, Scholes, Mason, from Nicolas and Sarah Tilney, Ingine, and of Sarah Tilney, from Thomas & Mary Haley, Scholes, [bn.] June 7, [bp.] July 27

Sarah, d. of Joseph Cauthorn, Barwick, from Benjamin and Elizabeth Cawthorn, Brittain, and of Ann Cauthorn, from John and Sarah Dickinson, Barwick, [bp.] Aug. 3

John, son of James Lowrance, Winmoor, from George and Pations Lowrance, Wetherby, and of Ellin Lowrance, from John and Ann Stanbank, Windgate hill, [bn.] July 14, [bp.] Aug. 16

Sarah, d. of John Benton, Stanks, from Thomas and Margret Benton, Garforth, and of Milly Benton, from David and Ellin Hirst, Pogmoor, [bn.] Aug. 13, [bp.] Aug. 31

Benjamin, son of Joseph Simpson, Brownmoor, from Samuel and Chrissey Simpson, Barnbow, and of Sarah Simpson, from Henrey and Sarah Clarkson, Aberford, [bn.] Aug. 7, [bp.] Sept. 7

Jane, d. of Renton Haist, Barwick, from Mary Haist, Barwick, and of Sarah Haist, from William and Ann Ward Barwick, [bn.] August 12, [bp.] Sept. 14

MARRIAGES, 1738.

Henry Slaytor, collier, & Elizabeth Parker, spinster, both of this parish, marry'd May ye 22^d^

Thomas Thompson and Susannah Shepherd, both of this parish, were marry'd November 14th

Thomas Simpson of this parish, Husbandman, & Mary Ainsley of the parish of Leeds, spinster, were marry'd by Licence Decemb. 26

[*The words "were marry'd" are omitted hereafter.*]

1739, MARRIAGES.

Samuel Haist of Barwick, Husbandman, and Rebekah Clough of Barwick, spinster July ye 23^d^

Jeremy Booth, Lab^r^, & Mary Bolton, spinster, both of this parish, July ye 25th

John Abbot, butcher, & Mary Mead, both of this parish, July ye 29th

William Burton of Barwick, husbandman, and Alice Dungwith, Aug. 1

Thomas Taite of Barwick, Mason, & Hannah Westerman of Barwick, spinster, Septr 3^d^

Tho. Batty of Barwick, shoemaker, & Ann Cook of Barwick, spinster, Novr 8th

Thomas Goodal of the parish of Whitkirk, Lab^r^, and Elizabeth Upton of this parish, Novr ye 29th

1740, MARRIAGES.

John Wood of Abberford, pinner, & Ellen Balmer of this parish, spinster, April ye 7th

Thomas Thornton & Ann Parker, both of this parish, Augt 17th

Abraham Dodgson of the parish of Kippax, & Hannah Wright of this parish, Augt 18th

Richard Varley of Barwick, Husbandman, and Ann Graveley, w^w^, October 7th

Thomas Warbutton of West Aukland in the county of Durham, & Rebekah Jackson of Pannel, in the county of York, by Licence, October ye 25th

Richard Burland of Barwick, Webster, & Dorothy Evers of the parish of Sherburn, Nov. 13th

Peter Eamonson, yeoman, & Elizabeth Eamonson, spinster, both of this parish, by License, January ye 28th

Richard Shackleton of Potterton, Tanner, & Mary Dawson of Barwick, spinster, Febry ye 10th

1741, MARRIAGES.

John Settle & Elizabeth Bradeley, both of this parish, ye 18th of May

William Knapton of Barwick, Blacksmith, & Sarah Graveley of Barw^{k}, by License, August ye 1st

Thomas Whitehead & Hannah Day, both of this parish, Nov. 12th

William Bywater of Thorner & Mary Popplewell of this par., Nov. 23^{d}

William Butler of the parish of Whitkirk & Mary Johnson of this parish, Decemb. 14th

William Thompson of the parish of Spoforth & Hannah Maud of this parish, February ye 28th

1742 MARRIAGES.

John Wainman of the parish of Leeds & Dorothy Lumb of this parish, June ye 14th

William Tipling & Hannah Wright, both of this parish, Augt 22^{d}

Joseph Braim of the parish of Methley, Joyner, & Sarah Knapton of this parish, August 30th

William Abbot & Catherine Fearnelagh, both of this parish, Oct. 25

William Coates of the parish of Hunsingore & Sarah Atkinson of this parish, December ye 22^{d}

Richard Townsley of Castleford & Elizabeth Anderson of this parish, December ye 23^{d}

MARRIAGES, 1743.

William Norton & Alice Burton, both of this parish, June ye 2^{d}

John Atkinson & Mary Smith, both of this parish, ye 12th day of June

Joseph Outhwaite & Ann Ambler, both of this parish, July 3^{d}

Richard Wilcock and Mary Abbot, both of this par., ye 31st day of Oct.

John Logg & Ann Lambert, both of this parish, Novr 9th

John Backhouse of the parish of Brotherton, & Hannah Wilcock of this parish, Febry. 6th

MARRIAGES, 1744.

Miles Hampshaw and Mary Braim, both of this parish, July 9th

Joseph Hudson and Ann Walker, both of this parish, July 29th

Anthony Green and Ann Hudson, both of this parish, Novemb^{r} ye 25

George Stead of the parish of Newton and Jane Forster of Clifford, by License, December ye 29th

MARRIAGE, 1745.

John Marshal & Esther Atkinson, both of this parish, April 25th

MARRIAGES, 1746.

*John Atkinson of Leeds, Esq., & Mrs Priscilla Vevers, by Licence, October ye 3^{d}

Christopher Dickinson & Fanney Dixon, both of this parish, Novr 13th

Henry Paver of the Parish of Sherburn, & Ann Braim of this Parish, December ye 10th

1747, MARRIAGES.

Robert Smith and Mary Renton, both of Barwick, May ye 13th

Francis Wilson and Ann Jackson, both of this parish, July 27th

William Dickinson & Alice Outhwaite, both of this parish, August 9th

Thomas Turr and Esther Clayburn, both of this parish, October ye 1st

Henry Smith and Margret Braithwaite, both of this par., Dec. ye 21st

MARRIAGES, 1748.

William Barker & Frances Addyman, both of this parish, May ye 9th

* See Platt & Morkill's Whitkirk, p. 97.

John Pickering and Sarah Whitehead, both of this parish, July 28th
Thomas Popplewell & Elizabeth Johnson, both of this par., Sept. 29th
William Morritt & Ann Butler, both of this parish, Nov. 13th
Joshua Cawood & Elizabeth Higginbottom, both of this par., Nov. 15
John Holiday of ye par. of Selby & Mary Brown of this par., Decr 13th
Joseph Carbutt & Ann Jakeman, both in this parish, Decr 25th
Joseph Strodder & Mary Atkinson, both of this parish, Jan. ye 17th
John Laycon of ye parish of Leeds & Mary Outerbridge of this parish, Feb. 2d
Isaac Barker & Ann Wood, both of this parish, Feb. ye 13th

Marriages, 1749.

Robert Jefferson & Ann Toppin, both in this parish, April ye 10th
Thomas Taylor of ye parish of Leeds & Mary Settle of this parish, August ye first
Benjamin Woodhead of ye parish of Ackworth, and Abigail Jowett of this parish, November ye second
Christopher Varey & Martha Smith, both of this parish, Nov. ye 21st
Jonathan Hopwood of ye parish of St. Peters, York, & Margt Batty of ye parish of Whit Church, December ye 3rd, by License
James Perkin & Ann Smith, both of this parish, December ye 24th
Matthew Upton & Ann Taite, both in this parish, Feby ye 5th
Thos Pouter in ye parish of Bardsey & Eliz. Smith of this par., Feb. 26
John Appleyard in ye parish of Kirby Wharf & Sarah Chapman of this parish, Feby ye 26th

Marriages, 1750.

William Cowper & Jane Dickinson, both of this parish, April ye 16th
Thomas Teasdale and Marget Swinglehorss, both of this par., May 1st
Samuel Nickleson in the parish of Sherburn & Jane Preston in this parish, May ye 13th
Hearsey Morton & Ann Smith, both of this parish, May ye 16th
William Booth & Mary Hague, both of this parish, Novembr the 6th
Robert Gibson of the parish of Sherburn & Ellen Lofthouse of this parish, Novembr ye 7th
James Lun & Elizabeth Walker, both of this parish, November ye 11th
William Brown & Frances Dean, both of this parish, November ye 14
John Orton & Elisabeth Binns, both of this parish, December the 3d
Abraham Wormhill of this parish & Cressy Shirkley of the parish of Batley, February the 3d

Marriages, 1751.

John Knubley of the Parish of Leeds and Eliz. Dawson of this parish, married by Licence, Aprill the 10th
Mark Sawer & Ann Hope both of this parish, Aprill the 14th
Jonathan Park of the parish of Leeds and Mary Hargraves of this parish, May the 1st
John Dungwith and Elisabeth Smith, both of this parish, May 24th
William Bannister and Sarah Moorhouse, both of this parish, July 28
Thomas Crofts of the parish of Whitchurch and Rebecca Wilcock of this parish, Septembr the 19th
John Hackshup of the parish of Fenton & Jane Hopwood of this parish, by Licence, Octr the 9th

Major Dickinson and Mary Hudson, both of this parish, October 21st
Richard Nelson of the parish of Leeds & Ellen Dixon of this parish, Novembr the 11th
Willm Goodhall of the parish of Garforth and Eliz. Hardwicke of this parish, November the 24th
William Walker & Hannah Robinson, both of this parish, Dec. 15th

MARRIAGES, 1752.

Edward Day & Mary Robinson, both of this parish, July 26th
*George Lumley of Leeds, Gent., & Susanna Maud of Wakefield, spinster, married by Licence, August the 9th
John Wetherhead of the parish of Abberford and Frances Dickinson of this parish, August the 24th
John Colturd & Sarah Lutey, both of this parish, August the 31st
Samuel Braim and Sarah Tate, both of this parish, October the 9th

MARRIAGES, 1753.

David Buchan of the parish of Thorner and Mary Yates of this parish, Aprill 23rd
Mark Poskitt of this parish, and Ann Felwell of the parish of Wistow, married by Licence, May the 8th
John Tillison and Ann Dean, both of this parish, May the 28th
Richard Jackson and Susanna Lumb, both of this parish, May 29th
John Walker of the parish of Sexton & Elisabeth Knapton of this parish, Novembr ye 19th
Stephen Sharp and Mary Clarkson, both of this parish, Novembr 27th
William Stancliff & Mary Holmes, both of this parish, Dec. the 12th
John Tate & Sarah Whitehead, both of this parish, December the 20th

MARRIAGE, 1754.

Richard Braim and Susanna Waite, both of this parish, Feb. the 10th

BURIALS, 1738.

Mathew Watkinson of Garforth moorside, Butcher, bury'd May ye 7th
Timothy, son of Timo Turnpenny of Winmoor, Labr, bury'd May 22d
John Dungwith of Barwick, Labr, bury'd June 11th
Rachel, daugr of John Atkinson of Barwick, webster, bury'd June 14
Mary, wife of Gervas Harrison of Barwick, Labr, bury'd July 3d
Geo. Wilcock of Garforth moorside, Collier, bury'd July ye 19th
Mary, wife of John Kirkham of Barnbow, husbandman, bury'd Augt ye 6th
Geo., son of Francis Holmes of Barwick, Yeoman, bury'd Sept. ye 21st
Wm Vevers, late of Mawrick, Gent., bury'd Octobr 20th
Peggy, daugr of Benjamin Haist of Barwick, Yeoman, Jan. 12th
Nathan Wright of Winmoor, Yeoman, bury'd Jan'ry 25th
Mary, wife of William Pattison of Kidhall lane end, bury'd Feb. ye 1st
Mary, daugr of John Taite of Barwick, Mason, bury'd Febr'y 4th
George, son of Geo: Watson of Barwick, Labr, bury'd Febr'y 4th
Hannah, ye daugr of Robert Land of Cross Gates, Collier, bury'd Febr'y 13th
Robt Goodal of Brownmoor, collier, bury'd Febr'y 14th
Wm Holmes of Roundhay, husbandman, bury'd Febr'y 14th
Wm Hebden of Barwick, pipemaker, bury'd Febr'y 14th
Mary Ball of Potterton, bury'd March 18th

*See Hunter's Familiæ Minorum Gentium.—*Harleian Society*, p. 622.

Jane Brown of Winmoor, bury'd March 21st

1739, Burials.

Thomas Norfolk of Potterton, April ye 14th
Edward Maxfield of Potterton, Husbandman, April ye 7th
Grace Ambler, a poor woman of Winmoor, April 29th
Eliz., the wife of Richard Slaytor of Winmoor, Labr, May 6th
Thomas, son of Thomas Braim of Barnbow Carr, Carpenter, May ye 7
Ann, ye daugr of Richard Lazenby of Penwel, Labr, May ye 23d
Ann, the daugr of Geo. Smith of Barwick, Labr, May 24th
Sarah, the daugr of Geo. Smith of Barwick, Labr, May 31st
Dorothy Eastburn of Winmoor, July ye 8th
John, the son of Robt Appleyard of Scholes, July ye 9th
Michael Graveley of Barwick, Yeoman, July ye 28th
Frances, the daugr of Mark Robinson of Potterton, husbandman, Septr 5th
Ann Tinsdale of Barwick, Sept. 6th
John, son of Mark Robinson of Potterton, husbandman, Sept. ye 9th
Jane, the daugr of Tho. Smith of Potterton, husbandman, Octob. ye 3
Thomas, son of Mark Robinson of Pott., husbandman, October 15th
Sarah Sharp of Barnbow Carr, Labr, January ye 2d
Alice Harper of Barwick, Widow, Febr'y 16
Michael Sharp of Barnbow Carr, Labr, Febr'y 23d
Mary Rounthwaite of Scholes, Febr'y 23d
*The Revd Henry Felton, Doctr of Divinity, Rectr of Barwick in Elmet, March ye 5th
Thomas Thompson of Garforth moor, Collier, March ye 7th
Mary, wife of William Abbot of Barwick, husbandman March ye 14th
Ann, the daugr of Adam Fleming of Turrylug-gate, husbandman, Mar. 17th

1740, Burials.

William Carbot of Potterton, Labr, April ye 8th
Thomas Haist of Kidhall Lane-end, April ye 8th
Daniel Germain of Barwick, Shoemaker, April ye 19th
Elizabeth Jordan of Garforth-moor, April ye 29th
Mary, wife of Samuel Donwell of Barwick, Taylor, May ye 2d
Ann, the daugr of James Bullock of Barwick, Mason, May ye 11th
Thomas Morrit of Stanks, collier, July ye 26th
James, the son of Thomas Collet of Barwick, Butcher, October ye 9th
Joseph, the son of Richard Slaytor of Penwel, Labr, December ye 18th
John, son of John Atkinson of Scholes, Labr, December ye 18th
Jane, the wife of William Calvert of Stockhill, Husbandman Jan. 4th
William Johnson of Scholes, Husbandman, Febr'y ye 27th
Gabriel, the son of Gabriel Taylor of Barnbow, Labr, March 4th

1741, Burials.

John Appleyard of Scholes, April 19th
Mary Gayton of Winmoor, Apl. 29th

---

* Henry Felton (1679-1740) M.A., 1702, domestic chaplain to the three dukes of Rutland; D D., 1712; controverted Locke's theory of personality and identity, 1725 —*Dictionary of National Biography.* In the Account of Robert Smith, Churchwarden for the year 1737 :—"Ringing for Madam Felton when she came 0 1 0; Candles at the same time 0 0 2." She was buried at Barwick, 10 Feb., 1737—8. He was Rector, 1736—1740.

Katherine Donwel of Barwick, July 20th
John Hall, a poor man from Turry-Lugg-gate Augt 23^{d}
Joseph, the son of Joseph Stephenson of Winmoor, Lab^{r}, Sept. 1st
Richard, the bastard child of Elizabeth Bell of Barwick, Septr 7th
John Saynor of Grimesdike, husbandman, Octob^{r} 19th
Ann, the daug^{r} of Gabriel Taylor of Barnbow, Novr 1st
Ann, the wife of Michael Settle of Barwick, Lab^{r}, Novr 12th
Mary, the wife of Thomas Whitehead of Barwick, Husbandman Novr 28th
John Abbot of Barwick, Novr 29th
Eliz^{h}, wife of John Upton of Morwick, Decemb. ye 5th
Robert Knapton of Barwick, blacksmith, December ye 29th
Mally, ye daughter of Benjamin Rawden of Barwick, Lab^{r}, Dec. ye 29
Moses & Aaron, sons of William Reedal of Mawrick, Lab^{r}, Jan'ry 25th
John Upton of Morwick, Febr'y 13th
Robt Fenton of Potterton, Febr'y 27th
Rebekah, thc daughter of Samuel Haist of Barwick, March ye 1st
John Slaytor of Winmoor, March 8th
Margaret Beedal of Scholes, March 12th

1742, Burials.

William, the son of Joseph Dickinson of Barwick, Lab^{r}, June 1st
Matthew, the son of James Westerholm of Brownmoor, bricklayer, June 22^{d}
David, the son of David Wright of Stanks, Lab^{r}, June 27th
Samuel, the son of James Robinson of Barwick, Lab^{r}, June 28th
Ann, the wife of Joseph Beck of Stanks, July 9th
James, the son of Henry Donwel of Winmoor, Augt 11th
William Slaytor of Barwick, Augt 28th
William Dibb of Kirkby, Augt 29th
Rosamond, the wife of Joseph Tailford of Barwick, September ye 8th
Matthew, the son of [*blank*] Jordan of Garforth moor, October 11th
Martha, the daughter of David Wright of Stanks, Lab^{r}, Octob^{r} 20th
John Wood of Winmoor, shoemaker, Novr 13th
William, the son of Richard Cook late of Stanks, Novr ye 28th
Alexander Thompson of Barnbow, December ye 23rd
John, son of Thomas Popplewel of Winmoor, February ye 6th
Richard Braim of Barwick, Febr'y 13th
Eliz^{a}, wife of John Thompson of Garforth, Febr'y 22
William Burton of Barwick, Febr'y 23^{d}

Burials, 1743.

Robert Dodgson of Barw^{k}, Ap^{l} 15th
Ann, the daughter of John Mountain, Ap^{l} 23^{d}
George Haist of Barw^{k}, Ap^{l} 25th
Samuel Haist of Barwick, April 26th
Ann Dodgson of Barwick, May 1st
Mary, the wife of Thos Atkinson, May 15th
Ann, the wife of Joseph Dickinson, May 15
Eliz^{a}, the wife of Thos Whitehead, June 8th
Mrs Ann Vevers of Scholes, widow, June y^{e} 24th
Jeremy Booth of Barwick, July y^{e} 5th

Elizabeth, dau. of Sarah Whitaker a travailing woman, July y^e 6th
Esther Thorns of Barwick, $Sept^r$ 12th
Thomas, the son of Thomas Thompson of Garforth moor side, Sep. 30
William, the son of John Wood of $Barw^k$, November 17th
Adam, the son of Adam Fleming of Turry-lug-gate, December 3^d
Elizabeth, the wife of Adam Fleming of Turrylug-gate, December 15th
John Atkinson of Winmoor, Janr'y 8th
Elizabeth, the daughter of Joseph Dickinson of Barwick, Febr'y 20th

BURIALS, 1744.

Alice, the d. of Mr William Eamonson of Lazincroft, April ye 9th
Mary Akaster of Parlington, April 22^d
Ann, the daughter of John Taite of Barwick, May 1st
William Taite of Scholes, May y^e 12th
Thomas, son of Thomas Jackson of Scholes, June 13th
Joseph, son of Joseph Outhwaite, June 20th
John Logg, son of John Logg, Augt 27th
Martin, son of Martin Hanshaw of $Barw^k$, Decr 25th
Joseph Lamb of Hubberley, January y^e 12th
John Appleyard of Barwick, $Janu^{ry}$ 22th
Mr William Vevers of Scholes, Feb'y 4th
Richard, son of Richard Wilcock of Barwick, Febr'y y^e 28th

BURIALS, 1745.

Mary Taylor of Barnbow, April 23^d
George Smith of Barwick, May y^e 21st
Samuel Wright from York, June 1st
Michael, son of William Gough, Potter, Augt 10th
Lucy, d. of Thomas Thompson of Garforth moorside, August 24th
[*blank*] of John Robinson of Garforth moorside, September ye 26th
Henry Holmes, October ye 8th
Joseph Batty of Scholes, Lab^r, October ye 10th
Ellen Dickinson of Winmoor, October ye 13th
Mary Pattinson of Kidhill lane End, October 17th
John, son of Richard Varley of Barwick, 8ber 21st
[*blank*] daughter of Joseph Broadbent of Stankhouse November y^e—
Elizabeth, d. of Thomas Knapton of Barwick, Carpenter, Nov. 3^d
George Clarkson, December ye 6th
Robert Doughty of Barwick, December ye 7th
Mary, wife of Thomas Taylor of Potterton, December ye 31st
Agnes, ye wife of Joseph Brown of Roundhay, January y^e 24th
Hannah, daughter of Samuel Malkil of Brownmoor, Jan'y 30th
Johanna Bullock of Barwick, Feb'y 23^d
Sarah, daughter of Thomas Collet of Barwick, March y^e 20th
John Johnson of the Hill Top, March 21st

BURIALS, 1746.

Betty, daughter of Thomas Collet of $Barw^k$, March 26th
Hannah, daughter of Thomas Benton of Garforth, Ap^l 5th
Robert Brown of Barnbow, April y^e 8th
Sarah, daughter of Joseph Stephenson of Crossgates, April 13th
William Pattinson of Kidhall, May y^e 1st
Thomas Jackson of Scholes, May 13th

Margret, wife of James Strodder of Barwick, June 1st
William Lambert of Winmoor, June 16th
Sarah Taylor of Barwick, July 24th
Ann, the daughter of Thomas Lumb of Stockhil, August ye 12th
Samuel, son of Richard Haist of Barwick, August ye 14th
Thomas, son of Richard Burland of Barwick, September ye 3d
Ann, daughter of Matthew Golden of Barwick, September ye 6th
Richard, son of George Smith of Barwick, September ye 11th
Ann, the wife of Thomas Popplewell of Winmoor, October 12th
Bridget, the Bastard child of Jane Hopwood of Barwick, October 13th
Peggy, ye daughter of Thomas Benton of Garforth moor, October 16th
Richard, son of Richard Burland of Barwick, October ye 25th
Lucy, d. of Thomas Thompson of Garforth moor, November 22d
Agnes, daughter of Joseph Holmes of Barwick, December ye 6th
Thomas, son of John Thompson of Garforth moor, January ye 3d.

BURIALS, 1747.

Frances Burdsal of Scholes, April 21st, 1747
Elizabeth Ellis of Barwick, April 25th
John, son of Matthew Watson of Barwick, May 10th
Sarah, daugr of Thomas Robshaw of Barwk, May ye 12th
Mary Johnson of Penwel, May 17th
Ellen, wife of Francis Wilson of Stanks, May ye 26th
Mark, son of Thomas Lightfoot of Brownmoor, Labr, June ye 24th
Thomas, son of Thomas Wood of Brownmoor, July 13th
William & Jeremiah, sons of Christopher Scot of Barnbow, July 20th
Sarah, daughter of Robert Whitehead of Barwick, August 9th
Christopher Dickinson of Barwick, slain in the Quarry, bury'd Sep. 6
Lydia Massey of Barwick, Septr 18th
William the [son of] John Logg of Scholes, September 21st
Mary, d. of John Robinson of Garforth-moor-side, Septemb. 30th
Elizabeth, daugr of John Waite, Novr 9th
Joseph Tailford of Barwick, Decr ye 15th
Elizabeth, the daughter of James Lambert of Winmoor, February 18
George Thompson of Scholes, Febr'y 25th
Roger, son of Roger Bell of Barwick, March 2d

BURIALS, 1748.

Thomas Smith of Potterton, Apl 10th
Isabella, daugr of Robert Barton of Barwk, May 6th
Ann Thompson of Barnbow, July 15th
John Atkinson of Barnbow, July 27th
Mary, daughtr of William Tomlin of Garforth Moor, August 14th
Thomas Jackson, Clerk and Schoolmaster of this parish, August 16th
Sarah, wife of Isaac Barker of Winmoor, Septr 10th
Thomas Knapton, Novr 1st
Deborah Appleyard, widow from Scholes, Novr 23d
Joseph Dickinson of Barwick, Labourer, Jan. 8th
Mary, the daughter of Matthew Tipling of Stanks, January 22nd
Sarah, the wife of John Hemsworth of Potterton, Febry ye 12th

BURIALS, 1749.

Samuel Liversiege of Barwick, April ye 11th

Mary, wife of Mr William Steel of Roundhay, April ye 15th
Elizabeth, wife of Charles Lawton of Skelmonthorp in ye parish of Embley, April ye 28
*Mr Willm Harper, Rector of Barwick, May ye 16th, 1749
Richard, son of Willm Knapton of Barwick, Blacksmith, May ye 18th
Esther, wife of John Marshal of Barwick, July ye 9th
John, son of John Daniel of Potterton, July ye 25th
William, son of William Barker of Shippen, Sept. 19, 1749
Michael Settle of Barwick, October ye 25th

BURIALS, 1750.

Ann, ye wife of Isaac Barker of Winmoor, June ye 2nd
Mary, ye wife of Jerry Bolton of Barwick, June ye 5th
Mary, ye wife of Richd Wood of Potterton, June ye 13th
Grace Eamonson of Barwick, widow, June ye 16th
Ellen Jackson of Scholes, widow, June ye 24th
William, son of William Waite of Barwick, July ye 25th
John Thompson of Barnbow, August ye 1st
Mary, ye wife of Edward Batty of Barwick, October ye 2d
Thomas, the son of William Lumb of Barwick, Octobr ye 5th
Jeremiah Bolton of Barwick, November the 11th
Elizabeth Appleyard of Barwick, January the 27th
Mary, the d. of Robert Simpson of Barwick, February the 11th
John, the son of Luke Richardson of Potterton, March the 6th

BURIALS, 1751.

John Moorhouse of Kiddal-Lane, Aprill the 28th
Elisabeth, the wife of Matthew Norton of Roundhay, June the 5th
Margaret, the wife of John Jordan of Scholes, July ye 5th
Isaac Barker of Winmoor, July the 19th
Elisabeth, the wife of William Burland of Barwick, July the 23d
John Hudson of Roundhay, September the 2d
Richard Johnson of Barnbow, September the 12th
Alice, the wife of Willm Eamonson from Austrop in the parish of Whitchurch, September ye 17th
Ann, the daughter of Joseph Bullock of Barwick, Octobr 4th
John Wood of Barwick, October the 27th
Elisabeth Dodgson of Potterton, December the 10th
Elisabeth, the wife of Benj. Haist of Barwick, January the 5th
Ann, the wife of Hearsy Morton of Barwick, February ye 1st
Ann, the wife of Michael Eastburn of Winmoor, February the 2d
Mary Shenton of Barwick, wid., February the 12th
Ann Collett, widow, of Barwick, March the 22d

BURIALS, 1752.

Garvas Harrison, of Barwick, Aprill the 19th
Elisabeth, the d. of Abraham Baite of Potterton, Aprill the 19th
Thomas Wood of Brownmoor, May the 5th
Mearsy, the wife of John Robinson of Winmoor stile, May 7th
Joseph, the son of Thomas Taylor of Barwick, June the 6th
Mary, the daughter of Thomas Tate of Barwick, June the 11th
Sarah, the daughter of Thomas Tate of Barwick, June the 12th

* Rector 1740-49. St. John's Coll., Cam., B.A. 1732, M.A. 1749.

Mary, the daughter of Joseph Holmes of Barwick, June the 21st
William the son of Willm Slaytor of Barwick, July the 1st
Hannah, the daughter of Joseph Bullock of Barwick, July 12th
Benjamin, the son of John Bramley of Potterton Lane, August the 22
Sarah Dodgson, widow of Roundhay, Octobr the 22d
Eleanor, the daughter of Mr William Eamonson of Austhroph Hall in the parish of Whitchurch, November the 17th

BURIALS, 1753.

Jonah, the son of Samuel Malkin of Brown-moor, January ye 6th
Ann, the d. of Willm Knapton, blacksmith of Barwick, January the 14
Sarah Pease, widow, of Grimes-dike, January the 15th
Ann Hebden, widow, of Barwick, April the 14th
Sarah, the daughter of Roger Bell of Barwick, May the 5th
Alice, the daughtr of Roger Bell of Barwick, May the 6th
Christopher Bustard of Barwick, May the 17th
Francis Chapman of Brownmoor, May the 21st
William, the son of William Ward of Winmoor, June 9th
William Hardy of Scholes, June the 26th
Peter, the son of Jno Thompson of Garforth-moor, July 5th
Ann, the wife of John Waite of Barwick, July the 22d
Benjamin Haist of Barwick, July the 24th
Hannah, the d. of James Worstman of Brown-moor, August the 4th
Mary, the wife of Benjamin Rawlinson of Barwick, August the 6th
James Bullock of Barwick, August the 7th
Ann, the wife of the above James Bullock, August 9th
Martha, the wife of Willm Lumb of Barwick, August 11th
Richard Waite of Barwick, August the 15th
*Richard Lumb of Barwick, September the 3d
Thomas Ball of Potterton, September the 14th
John Thompson of Garforth Moor, October the 25th
Martin Whitehead of Garforth moor, November the 28th
William Lamb of Scholes, November the 30th
Isaac Hall of Kiddal-lane end, December the 18

BURIALS, 1754.

Jane, the wife of Willm Cooper of Barwick, January 16
William Clark of Barwick, January the 31st
Susanna, the wife of George Watson of Potterton, Feby 10th
Mary Newby, widow, of Barwick, March the 4th
Mary, the wife of Saml Robinson of Garforth moor, April 23d
Richard Holmes of Roundhay, May the 2d
Mark Robinson of Potterton, May the 3d

---

* He was probably the son of Richard Lumb of Barwick [? 1659-1729], being baptized there 14 August, 1692, and registered "Edward," of which name there is afterwards no record. His first wife Margaret [1695-1731] was a dau. of Jeremiah Ball of Barwick, and his second wife Anne [1693-1781] was a dau. of Richard Atkinson of Roundhay Park His son Richard married Elizabeth dau. of William Carew. He was Constable, 1735, Overseer of the Poor, 1737, and Churchwarden, 1741-2, and he and his brother William [1704-1790] signed the minutes of a parish meeting held 10 May, 1747, here reproduced. A silver cream jug bearing his initials is still in the possession of a descendant.

The occurrence of the name of Richard in the family is of some interest. In records of 1277-1290. Richard Lomb of Lynn occurs, and in a subsidy of 1301 Richard Lom of Yafforth near Northallerton. In the Poll Tax for 1379, Richard Lome was taxed at Barwick-in-Elmet, and also Agnes and Alice Lome.

In the Subsidy of 1598, Richard Lome of Wakefield paid 8/-, and in more recent times Richard Lumb [1726-1807], a Wakefield merchant, resided there and at Ackton Hall near Pontefract.

Mary, the wife of Jn° Daniel of Potterton, May the 9th
Widow Dolphin of Garforth moor, May the 22d
Mary, the wife of Thos Bean, Junr, of Barwick July the 25th
Margaret Hodgson of Barwick, July the 31st
Elisabeth, the wife of John Tasker of Barwick, Augst 28th
John, the son of Willm Knapton, Blacksmith, of Barwick, September the 19th
William Burland of Barwick, September the 22d
Susanna, the wife of Richd Jackson of Barwick, September the 27th
Susanna, the daughter of Richd Jackson of Barwick, Octr 27th
Robert Pearson of Kidhall-lane-end, Novemr the 22d

BURIALS, 1755.

Ruth, the d. of John Thompson of Garforth-moor, February the 21st
Joseph Binns of Winmoor, March the 16th
Willm, son of Willm Wright of Scholes, March the 23d
John Daniel of Potterton-lane, March 27th
Ann Brown of Winmoor, May 17th
Thos, son of Willm Ward of Winmoor, June 22d
Hearsey Morton of Barwick, June 25th
Richard Clark of Barwick, July 9th
Ann, the wife of William Gough of Lazincroft, September the 9th
Willm Prince of Potterton, October 6th
Elisabeth, the wife of Thomas Popplewell of Winmoor-head, Oct. 19th
John Slaytor of Winmoor, October 21st
John, the son of John Walker of Sexton, December the 3d
Mary, the wife of Robert Simpson of Barwick, December the 5th
Robert Ellot of Barnbow-hall, Decemr 29

BURIALS, 1756.

Ann, the wife of Richard Lazenby of Winmoor, January the 11th 1756
William, the son of Robert Smith of Barwick, January the 15th
Susanna, the d. of Wm Tomlinson of Garforth-moor, January the 22d
William Eamonson of Austrop in the parish of Whitchurch, Feby 1st
Samuel Robinson of Garforth moor, February the 21st
Robert, the son of Robert Brown of Winmoor, February the 29th
Elisabeth Plumpton, of Frickley in the parish of Clayton, March 1st
Willm Bakehouse of Barwick, March the 5th
Benj. Ambler of Winmoor, March 11th
Agnes, the daughter of Jonathan Bell of Barnbow, March 27th
John Robinson of Winmoor stile, April the 22d
Hannah, the daughter of Benj. Rawlinson of Barwick, Augst 25th
Alice, the daughter of Thomas Settle of Barwick, September the 2d
Mary, the wife of Edmund Popplewell of Winmoor-head, Septemr 13
James, the son of Peter Brumpton of Brown-moor, September the 16
Sarah, the wife of Matthew Jackson of Barwick, October the 12th
Betty, the d. of Abram Wormald of Barwick, December the 26th

BURIALS, 1757.

Samuel Lumb of Stanks, January the 14th
Elisabeth, the wife of John Robinson of Garforth-moor, Jan. the 14th
Edmund, the son of Willm Crummock of Barwick, February the 7th
James, the son of Joseph Bullock of Barwick, April the 6th

Joseph Lamb of Scholes, April the 24th
Elisabeth, the daughter of John Norton of Barwick, May the 2d
Jane, the wife of John Anderson of Winmoor head, May the 9th
Martha Tate, widow, May the 9th
Widow Slaytor of Barwick, July the 18th
Widow Bramley of Potterton lane, July 19th
Ann, the daugr of Christopher Varey of Scholes, July the 24th
Willm Dickinson of Barwick, Augst 21
Timothy, the son of Willm Smith of Barwick, August the 22d
Willm Appleyard of Barwick, Septemr 9th
Willm Butler of Scholes, October the 8th
Francis, the son of Willm Driver of Winmoor, November the 2d

BURIALS, 1758.

John, the son of Benjamin Shillito of Scholes, January the 1st
Mary, the wife of John Atkinson of Barwick, January the 4th
Mary Colley of Winmoor, Jany 26th
Thos Bateson of Scholes, January the 31st
Ann Morritt of Barwick, February 6th
Abigail Danby of Barwick, February 15th
John Anderson of Winmoor, Feby the 23d
Margarett, the wife of Thos Benton of Garforth-moor, March the 19th
Isaac, the son of Roger Bell of Barwick, March the 24th
Samuel, the son of Samuel Braim of Barwick, March the 31st
Roger, son of Roger Bell of Barwick, April the 11th
Thomas, son of Benjamin Braim of Barnbow Carr, April the 20th
Sarah, the daughter of William Calvert of Barwick, April the 26th
Isabella, the d. of James Brennand of Barwick, April the 29th
Willm Scott, of Barwick, May the 29th
Mary, the daughter of Thomas Tate of Barwick, May the 30th
Thomas & Mary, son and d. of Wm Ward of Winmoor, June the 21st
Ann, the daughter of Benjn Stringer of Winmoor, July the 21st
Mary Brunton of Brownmoor, July 28th
Hannah, the wife of Matthew Tiplin of Stanks, July the 31st
Elizabeth Liversiege of Barwick, October the 1st
William Smith of Barwick, October the 8th
Ann, the daughter of Michl Topham of Leeds, Novr 29th

BURIALS, 1759.

David Wright of Barnbow, January the 4th, 1759
John Wray of Lazincroft, Feb. the 19th
Thus fare Posted and sent into the Court at York
Hannah, the wife of Matthew Golden, July the 7th
James Horsefield, July the 22th
Margret and Mary, twins, daughters of John and Mary Bean of Barwick, shoemr, July the 26th
Mary, daughter of Thos Whitehead, September the 9th
The Daughter of John Saynor of Winmoor, November the 9th

1760.

Richard, the son of Richd Shippen of Stanks, Jan. the 25
Matthew Tipling of Stanks, February the 8th
William, the son of Stephen Vevers of Morwick, March the 8th

A Militia Man who Dy'd on Winmoor, was buried March the 14th
Catharine Briggs, March the 22d, but no Cerimony said over her
Francis Wilson of Scholes (Labourer) May 12th
Robert Brown of Penwell, July 3d
Mary, dr of James & Ann Parkins of Barwick, Inft, July 16th
John Tasker of Addle, Augt 1st
John, son of John Bean of Barwick (shoemaker), Augt 8th
Alice, wife of John Bean of Barwick, Augt 12th
Abraham, son of John Waite of Barwick (Tailor), Sepr 7th
John Hague of Barwick, October 21st
Samuel, son of Robert Simpson of Barwick, Labourer, Sepr 21
Sarah, dr of Robert Jefferson of Tadcaster, Novr 7th
John, son of John Dickenson of Barwick, Labourer, Novr 9th

BURIALS, 1761. Place Business Age

Feby 7. Mary, wife of James Norton senr of Berwick, Labourer, 66
17. Susanna Kirkham, Widow, Berwick
24. Alice [Ann *erased*], wife of Thomas Whitehead of Garfh Moor side, Farmer
March 1st. Frances Settle, widow, Potterton, 78
12. Jane Bell, Widow, Berwick, 87
16. Ann, daur of William & Mary Sclater, Berwick, Farmer
19. William, son of Edward & Mary Day, Potterton, Mason
May 5. John, son of Thomas [John *erased*] & Margaret Hanson, Berwick, Husbandman
28. Agnes Wilcox, widow, Garf. Moorside, 88
June 29. Richard Jackson, son of Richard, Berwick, Labourer, 22
July 5. Matthew Fowler of Kid-hall-Lane, 15
11. Thomas Settle, Berwick, Weaver, 69.
13. Hannah, daur of Richard & Mary Wright, Kidhall Lane, Inft
Sepr. 19. Elizabeth Taitt, wife of William, Berwick, Builder
Novr 25. William Driver, Winmoor, Labourer
Decr 12. Thomas, son of John & Elizabeth Robinson, Kidhall Lane, Inft
25. Mary, wife of Peter Yates, Winmoor
29. Hannah, wife of Thomas Taitt, Berwick, Mason, 50

BURIALS, 1762.

Jany 28. Robert Briggs, Berwick, Tailor, 75
30. William, son of Thomas & Hannah Taitt, Berwick, Mason, 14
Feby 4. John, son of Edmund & Grace Popplewell, Winmoor, Inft
21. Mary Neeson (Papist), interred in ye Church yard, Berwick
28. Sarah Wilson, Berwick, 55
March 2. Michael Eastburne, Winmoor, Labourer, 61
17. Francis Holmes, Berwick, Weaver, 81
31. Susanna Heresy, Widow, Berwick, 81
April 20. Ann Roper, wife of Jonathan (Killed by a Cart), Low-moor, Potseller, 72
May 7. Joseph Wetherhead (Papist), interred in ye Church-yard, Berwick, Farmer, 27
16. Mary, wife of Richard Lumb, Berwick, Farmer, 30.
July 12. Abigail, wife of Joseph Holmes, Berwick, Tailor, 48
20. William Bannister, of a Dropsy, Kidhall Lane, Jockey, 54

26. James Whitehead (of a Mortification in his Foot), Addle Parish, Farmer, 60
Aug[t] 17. Elizabeth, dau[r] of William & Hannah Waite, Berwick, Tailor, Inf[t]
Nov[r] 30. Ann Ambler, Winmore, Widow, 78
Ann, daughter of John & Eliz[th] Norton, Barwick, Inf[t]

BURIALS, 1763.

Jan[ry] 2. Susanna Johnson, wid[w], Barnbow, Widow
March 18th Ann Burland, Barwick, Old Maid
April 2. Francis, son of Rachel Holmes, Barwick
May 14. Elizabeth, daughter of Rachel Holmes, Barwick
April 9th. Margaret, the wife of Tho[s] Bean, Barwick, Farmer
July 7th. John, the son of Matthew Upton, Morwick, Farmer
July 8th. William Knapton, Barwick, Sexton
July 17th. Ellin, the wife of Rob[t] Land, Crosgates, Labourer
July 27th. John, the son of Abraham Wormald, Barwick, Blacksmith
Aug[st] 17th. Mary, the wife of Tho[s] Benton, Garforth moor, Collier
Sep[r] 8th. John Varley, Barwick, Farmer
24th. Mary, the [*sic*] of Benj[n] Stringer, Winmoor, Taylor
Oct[r] 27th. Martha, the wife of Rob[t] Whitehead, Barwick, Labourer
Nov[r] 7th. Tho[s], the son of Mary Scot, Barwick, Joyner
8. Ann, the daughter of Henry Dunwell, Hilltop, Labourer
27. Tho[s] Braim, Barnbow, Carpenter
Dec[r] 3rd. Rich[d], the son of Rich[d] Lumb, Barwick, Farmer, Inf[t]

BURIALS, 1764.

*Jan[ry] 18th. Lady Gascoigne, Parlington, Papist
29. Ann Batty, Scholes, Widow
March 2nd. Elizabeth, the wife of Abraham Rawlinson, Barwick, Limeburner
14. Michael, the son of John Walton, at the Engine, Collier
April 29th. Elizabeth, d. of Abraham Rawlingson, Barwick, Limeburner
June 1st. Matthew Watson, Barwick
June 24. Hannah, daughter of Richard & Ann Smith, Barwick, Farmer, Inf[t]
Sep[r] 21. Ann, wife of Thomas Preston, Barwick, Tailor
28. William, son of William Firth
Nov[r] 17. Ann, bastard daughter of Sarah Hunton, Barwick
Dec[r] 17. John, son of Godfrey & Mary Gough, Barwick, Potmaker

BURIALS, 1765.

Feb[y] 3. Mary, daughter of Joseph & Ann Outhwaite, Low Moor, Labourer
June 12. Godfrey, son of Godfrey & Mary Gough, Barwick, Potmaker
23. Thomas Benton, Garf. Moor side, Collier
July 14. John, son of Samuel & Sarah Braim, Barwick, Joiner
14. Mary, daughter of Thomas & Mary Taitt, Barwick, Farmer
18. Mercy, d. of John & Elizabeth Robinson, Winmoor, Farmer
20. John, son of John & Margaret Gaggs, Barnbow, Farmer

---

* Mary, Lady Gascoigne died at York 14 January. She was the daughter and heiress of Sir Francis Hungate, Bart., of Huddleston Hall, and the widow of Sir Edward Gascoigne, 6th Baronet.

21. Phebe, daughter of Samuel & Sarah Braim, Barwick, Joiner
25. John, son of John & Ann Lumb, Stanks, Labourer
26. Ann, daughter of William & Deborah Wright, Scholes, Farmer
Augst 14. Richard, son of Richard & Catharine Collet, Soldier
Sepr 3. Mary, daughter of Edward & Mary Day, Potterton, Mason
11. James, son of John Bramley Junr, Potterton, Labourer
14. Ann, daughter of Luke & Elizabeth Richardson, Potterton, Shoemaker
Octr 20. Isaac, son of Roger & Alice Bell, Kidhall Lane
21. Joseph, son of George & Mary Scoles, Barnbow, Collier
27. Roger, son of Roger & Alice Bell, Kidhall Lane

BURIALS, 1766.

Feby 4. James Marshall, Winmoor, Labourer
11. John Oxley, Scholes
17. Mary Prince, widow, Scholes
26. Mary Wood, Spofforth
27. Thomas Wildbore
March 18. Robert Walker, Scholes, Carpenter
22. Isabella Watson, widow, Barwick
30. John, son of John & Sarah Lyster, Barwick, Husbandman
April 6. Elizabeth, wife of William Parkin, Winmoor, Farmer
May 30. Phebe, daughter of Thomas & Susanna Bayley, Winmoor Labourer
June 6. Stephen Vevers, Gent, Morwick
15. Susanna, d. of Thomas & Susanna Bayley, Winmoor, Labourer
July 15. Mary, the wife of Thomas Harper, Barwick, Labourer
Augst 5. Ellin, daughter of Robert Walker, late of Scholes
Octr 1. Jane, daughter of Edmund Popplewell, Winmoor, Tailor
23. Hannah, daughter of Abraham & Crissy Wormald, Barwick, Blacksmith
29. Elizabeth Wilson, Scholes
31. Mary, daughter of Peter Yates, Winmoor, Labourer
Decr 15. Ann Prince, from the Workhouse, Barwick
Decr 31. Thomas Whitehead, Garf. Moor-side

BURIALS, 1767.

Jany 17. Richard Vevers, Esqr., Scholes
Feby 3. George Hill, Stanks
7. Alice, wife of William Norton, Barwick, Farmer
14. Ann, daughter of Robert Simpson, Barwick, Labourer
March 24. Mary, daughter of John & Elizabeth Robinson, Winmoor, Farmer
May 10. William, son of John & Elizabeth Wainwright, Brown-Moor Labourer
31. Richard Cawood of the parish of Whitkirk, Labourer
June 1. Izabella Tipling
8. James Norton, Barwick, Labourer
24. Richard Cox, Potterton, Farrier
28. William, son of James & Bersheba Wright, Barwick, Labourer
July 26. Mary Hague, Widow, Barwick
Augst 21. Susanna Binns, Winmoor

Sepr 26. John, son of John & Mary Lunn, Barnbow-Car, Collier
Octr 3. Barnard, son of James & Elizabeth Wilcock, Cross Gates Labourer
5. Richard, son of Richard & Elizabeth Lumb, Barwick, Farmer
9. Hannah, d. of William Varey, Scholes, Labourer
18. Mary, wife of Thomas Ellar, Kidhall Lane, Jockey
Decr 13. Mary Vevers, Morwick
27. Mary, d. of Benjamin & Mary Shillitoe, Barnbow, Labourer

BURIALS, 1768.

Jany 1. John Johnson from the Workhouse, Barwick
4. Mary Robinson, widow, Potterton
10. William Waite, Barwick, Tailor
30. Thomas Whitehead, Barwick, Farmer
31. Thomas Atkinson, Brownmoor
Feby. 10. Mary Brown, Widow, Penwell
21. Sarah, d. of Renton & Hannah Haste, Winmoor, Labourer
28. Mary, daughter of Michael & Sarah Toppin, Leedes, Glover
March 6. Elizabeth Worsman, widow, Brown-moor
7. William Forest, drowned in Grimesdike, Shadwell
25. James Perkins, Barwick, Farmer
April 2. Mary Renton, widow, Barwick
14. [*blank*] Michel, a Foreigner, at Blue Boar, Kid Hall Lane
20. Rachel Holmes, widow, Barwick
May 21. William, son of Joseph & Ann Outhwaite, Low Moor, Labourer
June 16. Hannah, d. of John & Mary Strodder, Barwick, Labourer
Aug^st 14. William Robinson, bastard son of Ann Webster, Scholes
Novr 30. Betty, daughter of William & Esther Hodgson, Barnbow Carr, Labourer

BURIALS, 1769.

Jany 2. William Norton, Barwick, Farmer
Feby 19. George Nicholson from the Workhouse, Barwick
March 12. Sarah Stephenson, Stanks
18. James Lambert, Winmoor
20. Mary Lightfoot (Papist), interred in the Church Yard, Brown-moor
May 12. William, son of John & Mary Strodder, Barwick, Labourer
29. Priscilla, wife of John Atkinson, Esqr, Scholes
June 4. James Butler, Scholes, Pipe Maker
5. George, son of Renton & Hannah Haist, Crossgates, Labourer
10. Jonathan, son of James & Bersheba Wright, Barwick, Labourer
20. William, son of Renton & Hannah Haist, Crossgates, Ditto
Augt 27. Anthony Dawson, Barwick, Farmer
Septr 3. William Cowper from the Work-house, Barwick
6. Beatrix Atkinson, Barnbow Carr
Septr 10. Joseph Eamonson, York
Octr 17. Hannah, wife of Joseph Dawson, Scholes
Decr 23. Dinah, daughter of William & Mary Clayton, Fire Engine, Blacksmith

BURIALS, 1770.

March 1. Ann, d. of Abraham & Mary Bell, Abberford parish
3. Ann, d. of Joseph & Izabella Batty, Cross Gates, Labourer
8. James Worsman, Brown-Moor
16. William Addimon, Grimesdike
17. Jonathan, son of James & Bersheba Wright, Barwick, Labourer
27. Sarah, wife of Richard Kingsley, Kidhall Lane End
April 3. Catharine, wife of Wm Gough (Papist), Brown-Moor, Potmaker
4. Ann, wife of Jonathan Bell (Papist), Scholes
8. Martha, d. of James & Bersheba Wright, Barwick, Labourer
22. Henry Dunwell, Winmoor, Labourer
May 1. Thomas Popplewell, Red-Hall, Labourer
22. Mary, daughter of Edward & Mary Day, Potterton, Mason
July 15. Elizabeth, daughter of Robert & Mary Raingill, Scholes
22. George Hewit, Fire Engine, Collier
Augt 8. Matthew, son of Thomas & Jane Upton, Morwick, Farmer
Sepr 16. John Bean, Barwick
Octr 1. Deborah, wife of Joseph Maud, Hill Top, Labourer
7. Thomas, son of William & Elizabeth Challinger, Barwick, Labourer
14. Jeremiah Lumb, Stanks
Novr 30. Elizabeth Binns, Hill Top
Decr 2. Sarah Shillitoe, Barwick
5. Ann Dunwell, Hill-Top.
15. Thomas Whitehead, Garforth M. Side, Farmer

BURIALS, 1771.

Jany 26. Ann Bacchus from the Workhouse, Barwick
Feby 6. John, bastard son of Elizabeth Watson, Barwick
March 4. Thomas, the son of Thomas Dodgson, Roundhay, Farmer
April 7. James Midgley, Winmoor, Husbandman
March 31. Mary, the wife of Benjamin Cook
April 16th. William Ellis, Esqr, Belonging Kiddal hall, Dyed at Leeds, Buried at Barwick, Leeds, Gentleman
Apr. 21st. Susanna, the wife of Richd Brain, Barwick
May 16. Margaret, the wife of Thomas Hanson, Potterton, Spinster
May 26. Thomas, son of William & Elizabeth Johnson, Barwick
May 29. Catharine, d. of Godfrey Gough, papist, Barwick, Potmaker
July 22. Elizabeth, dau' of Joseph & Isabella Battey, Cross Gates, Labourer
Augt 12. Ann, wife of William Tipling, Winmoor, Farmer
Augt 30. John Slack, servant to Mr Stephen Vevers, Morwick, servant, 23.
Sepr 5. Mary, dau^r^ of Henry & Sarah Wright, Morwick, Farmer, 24
16. Thomas, son of Thomas Hanson, Potterton, Lab^r^, 10
Octr 7. Mary Barker, widow, Shippen, 71
Decr 8. Sarah, dau^r^ of Thomas Hanson, Potterton, Lab^r^

BURIALS, 1772. Place business age

Feb. 14. Elizabeth, dau^r^ of Thomas Hanson, Potterton, Lab^r^, 17

16. William Slater, Berwick, Farmer, 75.
16. Thomas Dodgson, Roundhay, Wheelwright, 73
Mar. 8. Judith Addimon, Winmoor, widow, 84
20. Helen, wife of Mark Thornton, Brown Moor, 76
28. Luke Richardson, Potterton, Shoemaker, 65
Ap^{l} 12. Rachel, dau^{r} of Christopher & Martha Varey, Scholes, Inf^{t}
13. William Hopwood, Berwick, 26
26. Mary Fowler, Kidhall Lane, Widow, 73
June 4. Henry, son of Richard & Ester Parke, Winmoor, Farmer, Inf^{t}
July 12. Jonathan Dennison, Cross-gates, Brickmak^{r}, 57
31. Henry Wright, Winmoor, Yeoman, 70.
Aug. 30. Benjamin, son of John & [*blank*] Wainwright, Brownmoor, Lab^{r}, Inf^{t}
Sepr 8. Alice, dau^{r} of Mary Slater, Berwick, Widow, 21
Octr 28. Hannah, wife of Benjamin Stringer, Winmoor, Taylor, 45
Novr 5. Mary, dau^{r} of Thomas & Mary Taitt (Papist), Throstle Nest, Gelder, Inf^{t}
Decr 19. Elizabeth, dau^{r} of Mr. William & Elizabeth Eamonson, Lazincroft, 17

BURIALS, 1773.

Jan^{r} 2. Hannah, dau^{r} of William & Mary Simpson, Barnb. Carr, Collier, Inf^{t}
Feb. 13. Elizabeth, dau^{r} of William & Margaret Dawson, Berwick, Schoolm^{r}, 21
28. John, son of Joseph & Ann Cawthorn, Berwick, Lab^{r}
Ap^{l} 4. Joseph Maud, Winmoor, Lab^{r}, 90.
4. Ann, dau^{r} of Richard & Elizabeth Lumb, Berwick, Farmer, 5
18. Mary, dau^{r} of Thomas & Sarah Hewitt, Berwick, Badger, 10
May 1. Mary, dau^{r} of Samuel & Sarah Varley, Berwick, Publican, 15
7. George, bastard son of Salley Waite, Berwick, Inf^{t}
12. John Dungwith, Berwick, Labourer, 48
June 15. Mary, dau^{r} of William & Margaret Dawson, Berwick, School M^{r}, 19
19. Elizabeth, dau^{r} of Thomas & Ann Foster, Scholes, Brickm^{r}
20. Ann, dau^{r} of Joseph & Sarah Holmes, Berwick, Taylor, Inf^{t}
July 22. Dickey, son of William & [*blank*] Hargrave, by redhall, 7
30. Elizabeth, dau^{r} of William & Dorothy Varey, Scholes, Lab^{r}, 3
Augt 22. Thomas Battey, Berwick, Shoem^{r}, 59.
Sepr 12. Mary, wife of John Hemsworth, Bramh'm^{r}, Labourer, 75
26. Mary, dau^{r} of Thomas & Sarah Pitt, Berwick, Farmer, Inf^{t}
Novr 4. William Ward, Berwick, Lab^{r}
30. Martha, dau^{r} of Thomas & Elizabeth Shillitoe, Pottert^{n}, Taylor, 3
Decr 4. William Taylor, Barnb. Carr, Wheelw^{t}, 68
18. Mary, wife of William Butler, Berwick, Lab^{r}, 84
27. Benjamin, bastard son of Elizabeth Cockshaw, Berwick, Inf^{t}
30. Ann, dau^{r} of William & Ann Hemsworth, Bram. moor, Lab^{r}, Inft.
June 22. John, son of Thomas Hanson, Potterton, Lab^{r}, 3

July 12. Mosley, son of William & Margaret Dawson, Berwick, schoolm^r, 17

BURIALS, 1774. Place Business Age

Jany 3. Richard, son of William & Elizabeth Challinger, Berwick, Labourer, Inf^t

4. Robert Barton, Berwick, Carpenter

24. Charles, son of Edward & Elizabeth Randall (papist), Morwick, Farmer, Inf^t

28. Hannah, wife of James Strother, Berwick, Shoemaker, 30

Feb. 8. Sarah, wife of William Richardson, Berwick, Shoem^r, 30

Mar. 21. Thomas, son of John & Mary Barrett, Berwick, Clothier, 22

April 10. John, son of John & Sarah Lidster, Berwick, Farmer, Inf^t

23. Mary, wife of Miles Hampshaw, Berwick, Farmer, 62

26. William Gough from Pa[r]lington Hall, Parlinton, Papist, 87

26. Henry, the son of William & Elizabeth Challinger, Berwick, Labourer, 3

May 17. Elizabeth, daughter of William & Elizabeth Arthington, Berwick, Labourer, 7

21. David, the son of James & Mary Jolley, Berwick, Labourer

22. Eliz^th, the d. of Willm & Ann Dufton, Berwick, soldier, 6

June 11. Mary, d. of Mary Slaytor, widow, Berwick, spinster, 17

14. John, son of William & Dinah Sheriff, Potterton, Gardener

15. Margaret, the daughter of William Tiplin at Whitelares, Winmoor, spinster, 27

July 25th John, the son of William Waite, Barwick, Husbandman, 28

Aug^st 10th. Thomas, son of Edmund Popplewell, Redhall, Weaver, 19

10. Ann, daughter of John Watson in the Ratten Row, Hirst moor, Labourer, 17

12. Thomas Thornton, Potterton lane, Thatcher, 67

14. Jane, the wife of William Clarkson, Roundhay, spinster, 73 [*sic*]

21st Mary, widow of Thos Thornton, Potterton lane, spinster, 64

Sepr 9th. Sarah, daughter of William and Ann Hemsworth, Kiddal lane, Labourer

Ann, the wife of Joshua Lamb, Winmoor, Spinster [*sic*], 70

Sepr 18th. Thomas, son of Anthony & Sarah Dunwell, Barwick, Weaver, 6

Octr 24th. Mary, the wife of John Barret, Barwick, spinster, 70

Novr 22. William Bell, Hill Top, Tailor, 68

Decr 2nd. Joshua Lamb, Winmoor, Blankit weaver, 73

BURIALS, 1775.

Jan^ry 9th. William, son of Robert Jordon, Stanks, Labourer

9th. Widow Scalbut, belonging Rothwel parish, Scholes, spinster, 70

29th. Jonas Doughty, Barwick, Farmer, 67

30th. Rose Harrison, belonging to the parish of Ecope, died at Barwick, spinster

Feb. 8. John, son of John & Ann Robinson, Barwick, Carpenter

March 29. Elizabeth, wife of Jacob Pease, Grimesdike, spinster, 68

April 17. Jane, daughter of Andrew Burdsal of Scholes, spinster, 23

May 11th. William Dawson, Barwick, Parish Clark, 46

June 26. Ann, daughter of Luke Dawson, Barnbow, Farmer, Inf^t

July 9th. Rebekah, wife of Thomas Dunwell, Barwick, Weaver, 80
30th. Joseph Daniel, Potterton, Farmer, 66
Sepr 3d. Hannah, d. of William Abbot, Barwick, Labour[er], 27
14th. Sarah, d. of Antoney Dunwell, Barwick, Weaver, 10
October 22d. Betty, daughter of Gabril and Mary Tomlinson, Scholes, Collier, Infant
26th. Elizabeth Watson, Barwick, Spinster, 35
November 25th. Frances, wife of John Thompson, Garforth, Collier, 38
29th. Matthew, son of James and Mary Jackson, Barwick, Labourer, Infant

BURIALS, 1776. Place Business Age

January 9th. Ann, d. of Thomas & Sarah Tilney, Scholes, Mason, Infant
13th. Mark Thornton, Winmore, Labourer, 75
24th. Samuel Braim from Abberford, Carpinter, 46
March 1st. John, son of John and Ann Greenwood, Crosgates, Carpinter, Infant
9th. Hannah Braim, Barnbow, widdow, 78
24th. Mary, wife of William Booth from Leeds Parish, 51
May 3rd. Elizabeth, wife of Andrew Bordsil, Scholes, Basket maker, 65
24th. Joseph Baitson, Scholes, Labourer, 75
Sepbr 29. William Demaind, Barwick, 86
October 1st. Rebekah, wife of Peter Deane, Barwick, 50
November 10th. Mary Scott, widow, Barwick, 66
23d. William Renton, Barwick, Farmer, 66

BURIALS, 1777. place business age

January 12th. Grace Reder, widow, Scholes, 79
February 20th. William Thompson, Barwick, Farmer, 81
22th. Thomas Morritt, Winmoor, Labourer, 37
22th. Sarar, d. of Abraham Wormald, Barwick, Blacksmith, 12
March 11th. Mary, daughter of Robert Smith, Barwick, Labr, 27
12th. Ann Hill, widow, Garforth moorside, 76
22th. Sarah Walker, widow, Scholes, 61
April 6th. Thomas Dunwell, Barwick, Weaver, 80.
23d. Robert, son of Robert Whitead, Barwick, Labourer, 22
May 2d. John Thompson, Stanks, Labourer, 84
Richard Jordan, Stanks, son of Robert Jordan of Stanks, Labourer, by Sarah his wife, died 15 of May, buried 16 of May, Churchyard, Age 1. Distemper, Smallpox.
Matthew Norton, Roundhay, son of Matthew Norton of Roundhay, Farmer, by Elizabeth is wife, died 20th of May, buried 22 of May, Churchyard, Age 93
Mary Thackerey, Barwick, daugr of Joseph Thackerey of Barwick, Labourer, by Mary is wife [died] 22th of May, [buried] 25th of May, Churchyard, age 3
Samuel Varley, Barwick, son of John Varley of Barwick, Farmer, by Ellin is wife, [died] 30th of May, [buried] 1st of June, Churchyard, [age] 47. Complant of is Brest

Easter Hodgson, Barnbow, [died] 11th of June, [buried] 13th of June, Churchyard, 50. Dropsy.

Joseph Bean, Barwick, son of Thomas Bean, Barwick, shoemaker, by Abigal his wife, [died] 11th of June, [buried] 13th of June, Churchyard, Infant

Willm Butler, Barwick, [died] August the 30th, [buried] August 31st, Churchyard

Sarah Renton, Barwick, daughter of Edward Batty, Snaw-hill, by Sarah his wife, [died] August the 29th, [buried] August 31st, Churchyard, 68

Sarah Lam, Seacroft, [died] August 29th, [buried] August 31st, Churchyard, 77

Thos Wadington, Whinmoor, son of Richard Wadington, Whinmoor, Labr, [died] September the 14, [buried] Sepr 15th, Churchyard, Infant

Hannah Green, Scholes, daughter of Richard Green, Scholes, Collier, by [*blank*] his wife, [died] September the 24th, [buried] Sepr 25, Churchyard, Infant

Thos Beane, Barwick, son of Jefferah Bean, Bramman, by [*blank*] is wife, [died] October the 20th [buried] Octor 22d, Churchyard, 82

Jno Lorriman, Ingine, son of Thomas Lorriman, Ingine, Labourer, by Margret his wife, [died] October the 20th, [buried] Octr 22d, Churchyard, 8. Convulshon fits.

Elizabeth Maxfield, Potterton, daughter of William Hemsworth, Potterton, Labourer, by Alice his wife, [died] October the 30, [buried] Novr 1st, Churchyard, 90

Edmund Cromek, Barwick, son of William Cromek, Barwick, Labourer, by Ann his wife, [died] November the 3d, [buried] Novr 5th, Churchyard, 20. Consumption.

Sarah Blackburn, Barwick, daughter of Barnard Blackburn, Barwick, Labourer, by Mary, his wife, [died] December the 17, [buried] December the 19th, Churchyard, 38. Consumption.

John Cheatam, Winmoor, [died] December the 25th, [buried] December the 27th, Churchyard, 59

BURIALS, 1778. Died. Buried. Age. Distemper.

John Atkinson, Barwick, son of Michel Atkinson, Barwick, Labourer, by Margret his wife, [died] January the 5th, [buried] January the 7th. 6. Worm fever.

Elizabeth Norton, Barwick, daughter of Richard Taylor, Braham, Labourer, by Sarah his wife, [died] January the 30th, [buried] February the 1st, Churchyard, 48

Joseph Bullock, Barwick, son of Joseph Bullock, Barwick, Mason, by Mary, his wife, [died] February the 3d, [buried] February the 5th, Churchyard, 21

Mary Appleyard, Scholes, daughter of John Wilson, Clifton, Milner, by Dorotha, his wife,[died] February the 13th,[buried] Fe[b]ruary the 15th, Churchyard, 69

Thomas Preston, Barwick, son of John Preston, Scipton, Labourer, by Mary his wife, [died] March the 30th, [buried] April the 1st, Churchyard, 94

John Beane, Barwick, son of Thomas Bean, Barwick, Farmer, by Jane his wife, died April the 19th, buried April the 21st, Churchyard, Age 47

Easter Claburn, Barnbow, daughter of John Dolphin, Garforth, Labourer, by Alice his wife, [died] April the 23d, [buried] April the 25th, Churchyard, 70

Bello Dixon, Barnbow, daughter of Robert Dixon, Barnbow, Labourer, by Ann his wife, [died] April 26th, [buried] April 28, Churchyard, 17. Consumption.

William Robshaw, Barwick, son of William Robshaw, Barwick, Labourer, by Sarah his wife, [died] June the 20th, [buried] June the 21st, 3. Wormfever.

Thomas Poulter, Potterton, [died] June the 28th, [buried] June the 30, 60

Edward Batty, Barwick, [died] June the 28th, [buried] June 30th, 80

William Abbot, Barwick, son of Abraham Abbot, Barwick, Labourer, by [*blank*] his wife, [died] July the 14th, [buried] July the 16th, 79. Kild by a fall from a Cart.

Catherine Greenwood, daughter of Robert Greenwood, Shippen, Labourer, by Mary, his wife, [died] July 20, [buried] July the 22, Infant

James Tillison, Ingine, [died] July 23d, [buried] July 25th, 80

Alice Bell, Barwick, [died] July 30th, [buried] Augt 1st, 59. Dropsy

Elizabeth Hewitt, daughter of Thomas Hewitt, Barwick, Collier, by Elizabeth his wife, [died] August the 7th, [buried] August the 8th, 2. Smallpox.

Sarah Burland, daughter of William Burland, Barwick, Labourer, by Sarah, his wife [died] August the 7th, [buried] August the 9th, Infant. Smallpox.

Robert Youdan, son of Miles Youdan, Barwick, Farmer, by Ann his wife, [died August] the 12th, [buried] the 13th, 3. Smallpox

Sarah Hewitt, daughter of Benjamin Rawlinson, Barwick, Farmer, by Mary his wife, [died August] the 17th, [buried] the 19th, 42. Canser

Thomas Cullingworth, son of John Cullingworth, Barwick, Shoemaker, by Maria his wife, [died] September the 8th, [buried] Sepr the 9th, 2. Smallpox

William Lee, Potterton, Labourer, [died] Sepr 18, [buried] Sepr 20th, 79

Benjamin Thackerhey, son of Joseph Thackerhey, Barwick, Labourer, by Mary his wife, [died] October the 14, [buried] October the 15th, 2. Smallpox

Alice Batty, Barwick, daughter of Benjamin Rawlinson, Barwick, Farmer, by Mary his wife, [died Octr.] the 22d, [buried] the 24th, 35. Childbed

Catherine Vary, Scholes, Dyed Octr 25, Bured Octr 27, Age 72

Thomas Robshaw, Barwick, [died] Novr 3d, [buried] Novr 5th, [age] 73

Benjamin Shillito, son of Thomas Shillito, Potterton, Tayler, by Elizabeth his wife, [died Nov.] the 21st, [bur.] the 22d, [age] 1, Smallpox

BURIALS, 1779. Died. Buried. Age. Distemper.

Ann Watson, Potterton, daughter of George Watson, Potterton, farmer, by Mary his wife [died] January the 7th [bur.] January the 7th. 36. Child Bed.

Catherine Robshaw, Barwick, [died Jan.] the 16th [buried] the 18th. 73

*Edward Gray, Esqr, Kippax, son of [*blank* died] April 1st [bur.] April 6th. 80

Thomas Wood, Potterton, son of John Wood, Potterton, by Sarah h. wife [died] April 13th [bur.] Apl 15. 12

Catherine Popplewell, Whinmoor [died Apr.] 20th [bur.] 21st. 93

Richard Cass, Barwick, Farmer, [died Apr.] 30th [bur.] May 2d. 39 Dropsy

Sarah Smith, Barwick, [died] May 3 [bur.] May 5th. 86

Mary Clayton, Ingine, daughter of Willm Clayton, Garforth, by Mary his wife [died May] the 11th [bur.] the 13th. 20

John Waite, Barwick, son of Richard Waite, Barwick, Taylor, by Alice his wife [died] June 15th [bur.] June 17. Infant.

Fanny Piper, daughter of Andrew Bordsil, Scholes, by Elizabeth his wife [died] July 23 [bur.] July 25. 33. Consumption.

Jacob Pease, Morwick, [died] August 7, [bur.] August 9. 69

James Plowright, Barwick, [died Aug.] 24th, [bur.] 25th. 33

Mary Taitt, Barwick, [died Aug.] 25th, [bur.] 26th. 45

Thomas Harper, Barwick, [died] Sep. 11th, [bur.] Sep. 13th. 77

Easter Dawson, daugter of Luke Dawson, Barnbow, Farmer, by Ann his wife, [died] October 22, [bur.] Octr 24. Infant.

John Dunwell, son of William Dunwell, Winmoor, Labr, by Margret his wife, [died] Novr 11, [bur.] Novr 13. Infant.

Sarah Smith, daughter of Richard Smith, Barwick, Farmer, by Ann his wife, [died] Novr 14, [bur.] Nov. 16. 26

John Dungwith, son of John Dungwith, Barwick, Labr, by Elizth his wife, [died Nov.] 25th [buried] 27th. 27

Henrietta Maria Cass, daughter of John Taitt, Barwick, Farmer, by Mary his wife, [died Nov.] 27th, [bur.] 29th. 47

Hannah Watson, daughter of Matthew Jackson, Barwick, by Sarah his wife, [died] Dec. 11th, [bur.] Dec. 13. 52

BURIALS, 1780. Died. Buried. Age. Distemper.

Mary Strother, Barnbow, Jan. 3, Jan. 5. 75

Sarah Fletcher, dr. of James Fletcher, Halton, by Sarah his wife, [died Jan.] 17, [bur.] 19. 1

James Robinson, Barwick, [died Jan.] 25, [bur.] 27. 78

Thomas Taitt, Barwick, [died] Feby 19, [bur.] Feb. 20th 66

Sarah Thompson, Stanks, [died] April 16, [bur.] A. 18. 87

Mary Boldwin, dr. of Robert Whitehead, Barwick, by Martha his wife [died Apr.] 25, [bur.] 26. 24. Childbed.

Su[s]annah Tayler, Barnbow, [died Apr.] 30, [bur]. May 2. 80

Hannah Lumb, Stockhill, [died] May 13th, [bur.] 16. 77

Andrew Jackson, son of Richard Jackson, Barwick, by Mary his wife [died May] 20th, [bur.] 21st. 42

---

*Edward Gray, Mayor of Leeds 1749 and 1768, built Morwick Hall, and died unmarried. For pedigree and account of the family see *Platt and Morkill's Whitkirk*, p. 92.

Ann Lunn, dr. of John Lunn, Barnbow, by Mary his wife [died May] 21, [bur.] 22. 17
Thomas Addiman, son of Thos Addiman, Scholes, by Elizabeth his wife, [died May] 23, [bur.] 25. 45
Thomas Addiman, Scholes, [died May] 25, [bur.] 27. 75
Elizabeth Jonson, Barwick, [died May] 31, [bur.] June 2. 60
Henry Doughty, Barwick, Kild with a Cart, [died] June 6, [bur.] 8. 68
Elizabeth Poulter, Potterton, [died] June 18, [bur.] 20. 82
William Hodgson, son of Jonothan Hodgson, Scholes, by Hannah his wife, [died June] 19, [bur.] 21. 16
Elizabeth Vevers, dr. of John Vevers, Scholes, by Grace his wife [died] July 31, [bur.] Aug. 1st. 12
Mary Hambleton, Barwick, [died] Augt 14, [bur.] 15
Ann Haist, dr. of Renton Haist, Barwick, by Sarah his wife [died] Octr 6, [bur.] Octr 8. 1
Richard Waller, Barwick, [died Oct.] 15, [bur.] 16
Thos Hodgson, son of Jonothan Hodgson, Scholes, by Hannah his wife, [died Oct.] 18, [bur.] 19. Infant.
Hannah Waite, daughter of Thomas Braim, Barnbow, by Hannah his wife, [died Oct.] 27, [bur.] 29. 48

BURIALS, 1781. Died. Buried. Age. Distemper.

Ann Lumb, [died] Jan. 26, [bur.] 29. [Age] 87
Ann Glover, dr. of Bartholomew Glover, Ingine, by Elizabeth his wife, [died] Feby 18, [bur.] Feb. 18. 3. Small pox
Mary Haist, dr. of Renton Haist, Barwick, by Sarah his wife, [died Feb.] 19, [bur.] 20. 5. Measels
Sarah Wood, Garforth Moor [died Feb.] 22, [bur.] 24. 11
William Eamonson, Lazincroft, [died] Marh 6, [bur.] March 8 61
Thomas Fox, Stanks, [died March] 26, [bur.] 28. 29
Grace Wood, Brownmoor, [died March] 30, [bur.] April 1st. 73
Helen Varley, York, [died] May 1st, [bur.] M. 4th. 96
Christopher Dickinson, Lowmoor, Kild in Seacroft Coolpitts, [died May] 16, [bur.] 17. 33
Ann Dawson, Ledsum, dr. of William Dawson, Barwick, by Margret his wife, [died May] 21, [bur.] 23. 12. Consumption.
Elizabeth Cockshaw, Barwick, [died] July 2, [bur.] July 3.
Susannah Sparling, dr. of Joseph Sparling, Potterton, by Mary his wife, died July 11, buried July 13. Infant.
Ann Cromek, Barwick, [died July] 11, [bur.] 13. 66
Sarah Wright, Barnbow, [died] Septr 28, [bur.] Septr 30. 79
Sarah Vary, dr. of Christopher Vary, Scholes, by Martha his wife, [died Sept.] 30, [bur.] Octr 2. 30. Consumption.
Robert Dawson, Barnbow, [died] Octr 18, [bur.] 21. 70
Robert Appleyard, Scholes, [died Oct.] 24, [bur.] 26. 76
John Kirkham, son of Joseph Kirkham, Barwick, by Hannah his wife, [died] Dec. 6, [bur.] Dec. 8. 12
Sarah Haist, Kidall-lane-end, [died Dec.] 24, [bur.] 26. 88

BURIALS, 1782.

Alice Waite, Barwick, [died] Jan. 31, [bur.] Feb. 1st, [age] 36 Childbed.

Elizabeth Collet, Barwick, [died] Feby 2, [bur.] 4. 79

Grace Vary, Scholes, [died] March 13, [bur.] March 15 62

John Robinson, Garforth Moorside, [died] April 1st, [bur.] Ap^{l} 3. 69

Thomas Taylor, Barwick, [died April] 6, [bur.] 8. 82

Ralph, son of Ralph Collet, Barwick, [died] April 8, [bur.] 10. 7

Ann Cheethem, Whinmoor, [died] April 9, [bur.] 10. 80

Thomas Simpson, Whinmoor, [died] May 8, [bur.] May 11. 83

Ann Rawlinson, Barwick, [died May] 18, [bur.] 20. 49

Robert Dixon, Barnbow, [died May] 16, [bur.] 18. 53

Mary Greenwood, Shippen, [died May] 19, [bur.] 21. 5

Thomas Simpson, Barnbow, [died May] 19, [bur.] 21. 6

William Brown, Whinmoor, [died May] 24, [bur.] 26. 69

Martha Potter, Barwick, [died] June 14, [bur.] June 15. 69

Mary Sparling, Potterton, [died June] 17, [bur.] 18. 8

Margret Tillotson, Ingine, [died June] 21, [bur.] 23. 80

Robert Greenwood, Shippen, [died June] 23, [bur.] 24. Infant

Samuel, son of John Lunn, Barnbow, [died] July 2, [bur.] July 4. 6

Mary Bullock, Barwick, [died] Augt 5, [bur.] Au^{t} 7. 64

Mary Lee, Potterton, [died] Octr 15, [bur.] Octr 17. 61

Sarah Batty, Barwick, [died] Novr 19, [bur.] N. 21. 81

William Knapton, Barwick, [died] Decr 8, [bur.] Decr 10. 66

Jane Carlin, Wood House, [died] Dec. 10, [bur.] Dec. 12. 88

Robert Whitehead, Barwick, [died] Dec. 29, [bur.] Dec. 31. 76

BURIALS, 1783. Died. Buried. Age.

Mary Maud, Hiltop, [died] March 4, [bur.] March 6. 75

Milly Benton, dr. of John Benton, Stanks, [died Mar.] 23, [bur. March] 25. 1

Sarah Hardington, Barwick, [died] April 8, [bur.] April 9. 6

Elizabeth, daughter of Peter Newby, Barwick, [died April] 18, [bur.] 19. 8

Elizabeth Whitehead, Barwick, [died] May 2, [bur.] May 4. 78

Mary, daughter of James Thompson, Barwick, [died] June 11, [bur.] June 13. 1

Mary Gough, Barwick, [died June] 16th, [bur.] 18th. 45

Sarah Varley, Barwick, [died] July 20th, [bur.] July 21st. 54

Mary Taite, Barwick, [died July] 27th [bur.] 28th. 81

Ellin Bell, Barwick, [died July] 28, [bur.] 29. 16

Mary Ann, daughter of Richard Brooke, Scholes, Major, [died] August 3^{d}, [bur.] August 5th. 9 months

Ann Horner, Bramham Park, [died August] 28th, [bur.] 29. 51

Peter, son of Peter Slayter, Barwick, [died] Septr 6, [bur.] Septr 7. Infant

Mary, daughter of James Whitehead, Barwick, [died Sept.] 15th, [bur.] 16. 2

Mary Lambert, Whinmoor, [died Sept.] 16, [bur.] 18. 63

Elizabeth, daughter of Joseph Cawthorn, Barwick [died] Octr 12th, [bur.] 14. 4 months

William, son of James Jackson, Barwick, [died Oct.] 15, [bur.] 16th 2

Ann, daughter of Thomas Perkin, Barwick, [died] Octr 30th, [bur.] 31st. 2

Sarah, daughter of Thomas Pitt, Barwick, [died] Novr 2^{d}, [bur.] Novr 3^{d}. 4
Ann, daughter of John Stubs, Barwick, [died Nov.] 13th, [bur.] 14th. 4
Mary, daughter of Mary Turpin, Crosgates, [died Nov.] 28, [bur.] 29th. Infant
Abigal, daughter of James Thompson, Barwick, [died] Decr 11th, [bur.] Decr 12th. 4
Bridget Simpson, Potterton, [died Dec^{r}] 14, [bur.] 15. 79
Francis, son of Francis Hawking, Scholes, [died Dec.] 21, [bur.] 22. 7
Isaiah, son of Robert Aveson, Scholes, [died Dec.] 24, [bur.] 25. Infant
Elizabeth Hurry, Kidall-lane-end, [died Dec.] 24, [bur.] 26. 54
John Thompson Hawking, bastard son of Ann Hawking, Scholes, [died Dec.] 29, [bur.] 31. Infant

BURIALS, 1784. Died. Buried. Age.

William Barker, Shippen, [died] January 2^{d}, [bur.] January 4th. 84
Robert, son of William Carr, Kidall-lane end, [died Jan.] 16th, [bur.] 17th. 4
Jane, daughter of William Jackson, Kidall lane end, [died Jan.] 22, [bur.] 23. 9 months
Richard Waite, Barwick, [died Jan.] 23, [bur.] 25. 40
John, son of William Sherriff, Potterton, [died Jan.] 23, [bur.] 25. 4
Mary, daughter of William Goodall, Barnbow, [died Jan.] 30, [bur.] February 1st. 1
Elizabeth, daughter of John Anderson, Potterton, [died] February 2, [bur.] 3. 9 months
Benjamin Harrison, Kidall lane end, [died Feb.] 18, [bur.] 20. 66
Jane Upton, Morwick, [died Feb.] 29th, [bur.] March 3^{d}. 74
Richard Lazenby, Penwell, mentain'd by the Parish, [died] March 6th, [bur.] 8th. 83
Richard Wright, Kidall-lane-end, [died Mar.] 7th, [bur.] 10th. 50
Elizabeth, daughter of Thomas Goodall, Ingine, [died Mar.] 13th, [bur.] 14th. 9 months
Mary Blackburn, Barwick, Mentain'd by the Parish, [died] April 12th, [bur.] April 14th. 80
Sarah Green, Potterton, [died April] 14th, [bur.] 16th. 14
Anne Maw, Barwick, Mentaind by the Parish, [died] May 14th, [bur.] May 16. 84
William Parkin, Seacroft, [died May] 28th, [bur.] 30th. 79
Ann Dawson, Stanks, [died] June 10th, [bur.] June 12. 85
Ann Thompson, Garforth moor, [died June] 22^{d}, [bur.] 24th. 77
Thomas Upton, Morwick, [died] July 30th, [bur.] August 4th. 81
Frances Thompson, Barwick, [died] Aug. 11th, [bur.] August 14th. 84
John Thompson, Garforth moor, [died] Septr 13th, [bur.] Septr 15th. 65
Elizabeth, daughter of Thomas Brooke, Kidall hall, [died Sept.] 27th, [bur] 28th. Infant
Elizabeth Richardson, Abberford, [died] Octr 9, [bur.] Octr 11. 71

BURIALS, 1785. Died. Buried. Age

Julea, daughter of William Thompson, Garforth Moor, [died] Jan. 1st, [bur.] Jany 2^{d}, 14
Thomas Lumb, Stockhill, maintained by the Parish, [died] Feb. 5th, [bur.] Feb. 9th. 87

Joseph Cromek, Barwick, Schoolmaster, [died Feb.] 6th, [bur.] 9th. 33
Martha Robinson, Barwick, maintained by the Parish, [died] March 27, [bur.] March 29. 88
Mary Simpson, Whinmoor, [died] May 27, [bur.] May 29. 83
Richard, son of John Goodall, Barnbow, [died] June 6, [bur.] June 6. Infant
Ann, daughter of Richard Lumb, Barwick, [died June] 22d, [bur.] 25th. 9
Mary Bell, Hiltop, [died] Octr 8th, [bur.] Octr 10th. 79
Matthew, son of Richard Whanewright, Appleton, [died Oct.] 14th, [bur.] 16. 3
Richard Wood, Potterton, maintained by the Parish, [died] Novr 12, [bur.] Novr 14. 85
Elizabeth Dunwell, Grimesdike, [died Novr] 18th, [bur.] 20th. 71
John, son of John Loder, Kidall-lane-end, [died] Decr 28, [bur.] Decr. 29. Infant

BURIALS, 1786.

Frances Bell, Potterton, maintain'd by the Parish, [died] Jan. 4th, [bur.] Jan. 5th. 66
Sarah Rawlinson, Barwick, [died Jan.] 11th, [bur.] 13th. 35
*Dame Mary Gascoigne, Parlington, [died] Feby 1st, [bur.] Feb. 8. 34
Ann Vevers, Scholes Park, [died Feb.] 8, [bur.] 11. 79
Mary, daughter of Samuel Simpson, Barnbow, [died Feb.] 12,[bur.] 12. Infant
Henrietta Maria, daughter of David Heaton, Barwick, [died] March 16, [bur.] March 18. 2
Thomas Wilcock, Garforth Moor side, [died] Mar. 19th, [bur.] 21st. 75
John Brooke, Brownmoor, [died] May 31st, [bur.] June 1st
Susannah Brook, Brownmoor, [died] June 5th, [bur.] June 7th. 63
Sarah Butler, Prestwhich, Lancashire, [died] July 14th, [bur.] July 18th. 87
Frances Pickring, Ingine, maintained by the Parish, [died July] 22d, [bur.] 23. 79
Sarah Varley, Barwick, [died July] 23d, [bur.] 25th. 25
Francis Moss, Kidall lane, [died] Augt 8, [bur.] August 10th. 86
Benjamin Rawlinson, Barwick, [died Aug.] 16, [bur.] 18. 83
John, son of John Anderson, Barwick, [died] Septr 19, [bur.] Septr 20. 11
John, son of Robert Arnton, York, [died] Octr 9, [bur.] Octr 11. 1
Sarah Dickinson, Barwick, [died Oct.] 29th, [bur.] Novr 1st. 69
Timothy Waite, Potterton, Paupor [died] Novr 3rd, [bur.] 5. 99
Isaac, son of Isaac Hunter, Garforth moor, [died Nov.] 14th, [bur.] 16th. Infant
Elizabeth Monks, Barwick, [died Nov.] 18, [bur.] 20. 59
Edward, son of Thomas Parker, Barwick, [died] Novr 26, [bur.] Novr 28th. 17
John Settle, Stanks, [died Novr] 26, [bur.] 30. 87
Thomas, son of Thomas Ampshaw, Barwick, [died] Decr 29, [bur.] Decr 31st. 10

*Dame Mary was the wife of Sir Thomas Gascoigne, eighth baronet, and daughter of James Shuttleworth. Esq., of Gawthorp, Forcett, and Barton Lodge, Co. York, and widow of Sir Charles Turner, of Kirkleatham, baronet. By her, Sir Thomas Gascoigne had an only child, Thomas Charles Gascoigne, died 1809.

BURIALS, 1787.

Thomas Simpson, Barnbow, [died] Decr 30th, [bur.] Jany 1st. 41
Sarah Hare, Lowmoor, [died] Feb. 19th, [bur.] Feb. 21st. 55
Sarah, daughter of Matthew Varley, Barwick, [died] March 24th, [bur.] March 25. Infant
John Waite, Barwick, Paupor, [died] April 24th, [bur.] April 26. 92
Susannah Moss, Heaslewood, [died] June 21st, [bur.] June 23. 84
Elizabeth, daughter of Thomas Hewitt, Barwick, [died] July 10, [bur.] July 11. Infant
John Taite, Thostlenest, [died July] 15, [bur.] 17. 86
Mary, daughter of John Liley, Barwick, [bur.] August 3. Infant
Elizabeth Leach, Barwick Workhouse, Paupor, [bur.] Aug. 18. 84
Joseph Boulton, Barwick, [bur. Aug.] 22. 81
Thomas, son of Joseph Simpson, Brownmoor, [bur.] Octr 2d. Infant
James Beane, Barwick, [bur. Oct.] 17. 53
Elizabeth, daughter of William Orton, Roundhay, [bur.] Novr 22d. Infant
Elizabeth Tophin, Barwick, [bur. Nov.] 24th. 67
Jane Gill, Kidall lane End, [bur.] Decr 6th. 58
William Taite, Barwick, [bur. Dec^r^] 7th. 70

1778.

Alice Robinson, Stanks, [bur.] Jany 15. 30
Ann, daughter of John Robinson, Stanks, [bur.] Feb. 1st. 4
Ann, daughter of John Harrison, Potterton, [bur. Feb.] 22d. 18
Thomas Thompson, Garforth Moor side, paupor, [bur.] March 2d. 78
Mary, daughter of John Robinson, Stanks, [bur.] April 4th. 1
Edmund Popplewell, Winmoor, [bur. Apr.] 10th. 67
Mary Lumb, Poorhouse, [bur.] May 2d. 52
Francis Hewitt, Ingine, Paupor, [bur. May] 3d. 80
Elizabeth Strother, Barwick, [bur. May] 11th. 25
William Cromek, Barwick, Paupor, [bur.] May 29. 84

[*Here follow copies of deeds, court rolls, appointments of parish clerks and other memoranda*]

[FOURTH BOOK.]

Baptisms, 1788.

Ann Elizabeth, daughter of Thomas Shepley, Barwick, from Thomas and Ann Shepley, Leeds, and of Ann Shepley from Francis and Ann Iles, Tadcaster, Born July 2d, Baptised Septr 18th

Mary, daughter of Joseph Simpson, York, from William and Mary Simpson, York, and of Margret Simpson from William and Mary Clayton, Ingine, [born] August 23d, [bapt.] Octr 5th

Benjamin, son of Thomas Pickersgill, Winmoor, from George and Martha Pickersgill, Kirstall, and of Judith Pickersgill, from John and Elizabeth Stead, Thorner, [born] Septr 10th, [bapt.] Octr 12th

Robert, son of Luke Dawson, Barnbow, from Richard and Easter Dawson, Garforth, and of Ann Dawson, from William and Sarah Pease, Garforth, [born] August 30th, [bapt.] Novr 2d

Elizabeth, daughter of Thomas Hewitt, Barwick, from George and Frances Hewitt, Barwick, and of Elizabeth Hewitt, from Thomas and Mary Hemsworth, Swillington, [born] July 30th [bapt.] Novr 2nd

Thomas, son of John Cullingworth, Barwick, from Joseph and Elizabeth Cullingworth, Aberford, and of Maria Cullingworth from Thomas and Mary Thornton, Potterton, [born] August 20th, [bapt.] Novr 2nd

William, son of William Vincent, Coalpits, from Jonas and Jane Vincent, Garforth Moor, and of Mary Vincent from George and Mary Scholes, Barnbow, [born] Octr 30th, [bapt.] Novr 30th

Baptisms, 1789.

Sarah, daughter of David Carter, Stanks, from George and Elizabeth Carter, Kippax, and of Hannah Carter from William and Hannah Tipling, Barwick, [born] Octr 9th, [bapt.] Jany 11th

Hannah, daughter of Edward Goodall, Stanks, from Edward and Easter Goodall, Garforth, and of Sarah Goodall from Benjamin and Elizabeth Coock, Stanks, [born] Decr 14, [bapt.] Jany 11th

James, Bastard son of Liddia Simpson, Hiltop, [bapt.] Jan. 26th

Elizabeth, daughter of John Liley, Barwick, from Stephen and Elizabeth Liley, Birstle, and of Elizabeth Liley from John and Elizabeth Norton, Barwick, [born] Novr 25th, [bapt.] Feb. 8th

Elizabeth, daughter of John Goodall, Barnbow, from Joseph and Mary Goodall, Barnbow, and of Ellin Goodall from Richard and Ellin Goodall, Colton, [born] Jany 11th, [bapt.] March 8th

Ann, daughter of Thomas Perkin, Barwick, from James and Ann Perkin, Barwick, and of Mary Perkin, from Robert and Elizabeth Thorns, Parlington, [born] Feby 9th, [bapt.] March 15th

Hannah, bastard daughter of Ann Norton, Barwick, Born at Tadcaster, Febr 4th, [bapt.] March 15th

Sarah & Maria, Twins, daughters of William Smith, Barwick, from William & Henney Smith, Barwick, and of Ann Smith, from William and Sarah Knapton, Barwick, [born] Feby 23d, [bapt] March 22d

Mary, daughter of Abraham Wormald, Barwick, from Abraham and Cressey Wormald, Barwick, and of Sarah Wormald from Richard and Sarah Naylor, Aberford, [born] March 9th, [bapt.] March 29th

Thomas, son of William Robshaw, Barwick, from Thomas and Ellin Robshaw, Osburn, and of Sarah Robshaw from William and Sarah Knapton, Barwick, [born] March 15th, [bapt.] April 13th

William Hargrave, son of William Slaytor, Barwick, from William and Mary Slayter, Barwick, and of Ann Slayter from William and Mary Hargrave, Hoberly, [bapt.] April 19th

Joseph, son of Joseph Walton, Barwick, from John and Ann Walton, Barwick, and of Sarah Walton from Edward and Mary Day, Potterton, [born] March 24th, [bapt.] April 26th

Catherine Elizabeth, daughter of Richard Brooke, Scholes, from James & Mary Brooke, Killinbeck, and of Frances Brooke from Richard and Frances Brooke, York, [born] April 20th, [bapt.] April 27th

Samuel, son of John Braithwaite, Barwick, from William [&] Jane Braithwaite, Aberford, and of Elizabeth Braithwaite from John and Elizabeth Soudon, Righcroft, [born] March 26th, [bapt.] May 3^{d}

	Born	Bap.
Mary Thekston, bastard dau. of Sarah Wilkinson, Barnbow	May 15	May 22
Joseph, son of William and Rebecca Bullock, Potterton, Farmer	Apl. 22	24
Frances, dau. of George and Grace Hopton, Stanks, Collier	30	31
Millia, dau. of Robert and Sarah Jordan, Stanks, Labourer	8	31
William, son of William and Hannah Thompson, Barwick, Farmer	7	Jun. 7
Mary, dau. of Joseph and Mary White, Scholes, Farmer	19	13
Matthew, son of George and Sarah Mallam, Garforth Moor, Lab.	March 8	21
John, son of Matthew and Elizabeth Upton, Morwick, Farmer	May 26	24
Susannah, dau. of Samuel and Susannah Thompson, Barnbow, Lab^{r}	26	28
George, son of John and Elizabeth Monks, Barwick, Labourer	Feb. 28	Aug. 2
William, son of Francis and Sarah Linley, Hiltop, Labourer	Jun. 13	9
Ann, dau. of John and Mary Cullingworth, Stank House, Farmer	10	9
Martha, dau. of Roger and Ann Brownrig, Scholes, Taylor	Jul. 5	16
Sarah, dau. of Thomas and Julea Waite, Barwick, Labourer	May 23	23
Isaac and Jacob, Twins, sons of William and Margaret Dunwell, Hiltop, Lab^{r}	Aug. 10	30
Frances, dau. of James and Frances Barker, Penwell, Labourer	Jun. 11	30
Willam, son of William and Jane Thompson, Garforth Moor, Collier	Jul. 24	30
Richard, son of Richard and Mary Watson, Winmoor, Labourer	Aug. 15	Sep. 13
Mary, dau. of Benjamin and Elianor Eamonson, Lazencroft	13	16

Thomas, son of Thomas & Mary Tillotson. Garforth Moor, collier	Aug. 26	Sep. 20
William, son of William and Sarah Knapton, Barwick, Blacksmith	31	20
John, son of James and Ellin Goodall, Barnbow, collier	8	27
Martha, dau. of John and Martha Reed, Lutherton, Labourer		27
Henry, son of John and Jane Blackburn, Garforth Moor, Collier	Sep. 15	Oct. 18
Richard, son of John and Sarah Connell, Barwick, Farmer	Apl. 5	Nov. 1
John, son of Thomas and Ann Collet, Brownmoor, Weelright	Sep. 16	Nov. 1
Charls, son of James and Mary Norton, Barwick, Labourer	Sep. 1	1
William, son of John and Susannah Robinson, Stanks, collier	27	8
James, son of William and Mary Richardson, Potterton, shoemaker		Dec. 6
Edward, son of John and Sarah Brogdin, Woodhouse, farmer	Nov. 2	27

Baptisms, 1790.	Born	Bap.
Robert, son of John & Sarah Loder, Kidhall lane end, Groom	Mar. 7	Jan. 1
Susannah, dau. of William & Alice Jowitt, Barwick, Labourer	Dec. 19	17
Mary, dau. of John & Margret Tillotson, Ingine, collier	Jan. 12	Feb. 7
Thomas and Rachal, Twins, son and dau. of Samuel and Ann Simpson, Barnbow, collier	Jan. 25	Mar. 7
Mary, dau. of Matthew and Ann Varley, Barwick, Farmer	Feb. 3	7
George, son of John & Elizabeth Hewitt, Barwick, collier		7
Frances, bastard dau. of Ruth Buckel, Barwick	Mar. 14	28
William, son of William & Elizabeth Walton, Barwick, Labourer	Feb. 11	Apl. 4
John, son of Thomas & Mary Armatage, Lowmoor, collier	24	4
Ann, dau. of James & Sarah Tillotson, Brownmoor, collier	Mar. 5	4
Ann, dau. of James & Mary Denhil, Winmoor, Labourer	21	18
Sarah, dau. of George & Ann Dawgill, Barwick, Labourer	Apl. 6	May 2
John, son of William and Mary Vincent, Coalpts, collier	18	23
Mary, dau. of Joseph and Mary Johnson, Brownmoor, collier		23
George, son of Jeremiah and Ellin Lumb, Stockhill, Farmer	23	24
Ann, dau. of John & Sarah Gough, Potterton, Gardiner		Jun. 2
Christopher, Bastard son of Mary Crags, Barwick	May 16	6
James, son of Renton and Sarah Haist, Barwick, Labourer	5	20
Sarah, dau. of John and Elizabeth Stubs, Barwick, Lab^{r}	Jun. 8	Aug. 8
William, son of Thomas and Ann Goodall, Ingine, Collier	21	8
Joseph, son of James and Mary Thompson, Barwick, Labourer	Jul. 28	22
Elizabeth, dau. of John and Elizabeth Tomlinson, Brownmoor, Labourer	29	22
Ann, dau. of William and Rebecca Bullock, Potterton, Farmer	Aug. 17	Sep. 26

Mary, dau of John & Millea Benton, Stanks, collier	Aug. 30	Oct. 3
Jane, dau. of John & Elizabeth Monks, Barwick, Labourer	May 30	3
Isabella, dau. of William & Jane Watson, Barwick, Weelwright	Sep. 2	3
Mary, dau. of Mark & Hannah Benton, Garforth moor, collier	22	24
Hannah, bastard dau. of Mary Hunter, Barwick	25	24
Mary, dau. of Matthew & Elizabeth Upton, Morwick, Farmer	Oct. 6	Nov. 7
Charls, son of John & Martha Mackontosh, Barwick, Labourer	8	7
Robert, son of Robert and Jane Wheater, Barwick, Farmer	12	7
John, son of John and Elizabeth Liley, Barwick, Labourer	25	7
Richard, son of John and Maria Cullingworth, Barwick, Shoemaker	20	7
David, son of Joseph and Ellin Scott, Barwick, Miller	18	9
Judith, dau. of Thomas and Judith Pickersgill, Winmoor, farmer	Nov. 6	Dec. 3
Ann, dau. of Peter and Mary Slayter, Barwick, Farmer		Nov. 13
Baptisms, 1791.	Born	Bap.
Matthew, son of Mark and Charlotta Lofthouse, Potterton, Farmer	21	Jan. 2
*Caroline, dau. of Edward & Anne Wilkinson of Potterton Lodge	Dec. 15	Jan. 21
Mary, dau. of William and Sarah Knapton, Barwick, Blacksmith	Jan. 8	Feb. 6
Ann, dau. of Joseph and Ann Cawthorn, Barwick, Labourer	Dec. 18	13
Ann, bastard dau. of Jane Dufton, Poorhouse, p.		25
Nicolas, son of Thomas and Sarah Tilney, Scholes, mason	Jan. 26	27
Thomas, son of David and Mary Whin, Scholes, Labourer	26	27
Elizabeth, dau. of Benjamin and Elianor Eamonson, Lazincroft	Feb. 1	Mar. 3
John, son of John and Hannah Butler, Scholes, pipemaker	Jan. 31	6
Mary, dau. of William and Mary Starfford, Barwick, Blacksmith	9	6
Elizabeth, dau. of John and Elizabeth Braithwaite, Barwick, farmer	Feb. 14	6
John, son of John and Ellin Goodall, Barnbow, collier		6
William, son of Joseph and Sarah Simpson, Brownmoor, collier	16	13
Richard, son of Edward & Sarah Goodall, Stanks, collier	Mar. 10	Apl. 17
Timothy, son of William & Ann Smith, Barwick, Farmer	11	17
Ann, dau. of William & Mary Batty, Bramham, Shoemaker	Apl. 22	May 22
John, son of David & Maria Heaton, Barwick, Farmer	13	22
Richard, son of Abraham & Sarah Wormald, Barwick, Blacksmith	13	22
George, son of John & Mary Cullingworth, Stank House, Farmer	Apl. 24	Jun. 5

*Edward Wilkinson was the son of John Wilkinson, of Potterton Lodge, by Anne, his wife daughter of John Denison, of Great Woodhouse, Leeds. John Wilkinson succeeded his brother-in-law, Robert Denison, of Leeds and Ossington (Notts.), merchant, as owner of Potterton.

Mary, dau. of John & Sarah Gough, Potterton, Gardiner	May 9	Jun. 5
Sarah, dau. of William & Elizabeth Dickinson, Barwick, Butcher	13	12
James, son of Jon[a]than and Mary Richardson, Winmoor Lime leather	Apl. 10	19
Ann, dau. of Jonathan and Ellin Tayler, Stanks, collier	Jun. 9	Jul. 17
John, son of James and Mary Barker, Penwell, Farmer	Jun. 21	Jul. 17
John, son of Thomas and Mary Tillotson, Garforth Moor, collier	Jun. 24	Jul. 17
Maria, bastard dau. of Mary Barton, Barwick		28
Ann, bastard dau. of Mary Goodall, Barnbow	Jul. 10	31
Hannah, dau. of John and Margret Tillotson, Ingine, collier	Jun. 17	31
Alice, dau. of William and Ann Slayter, Barwick, Labourer	Jul. 9	Aug. 14
Sarah, bastard dau. of Sarah Dickinson, poorhouse, p.		14
Joseph, son of Robert and Sarah Jordon, Stanks, Labourer	18	28
Joseph, son of William and Margret Gough, Barwick, Joyner	Aug. 17	Sep. 11
Samuel, son of Matthew and Ann Varley, Barwick, Farmer	12	25
Hannah, dau. of Peter and Elizabeth Benson, Scholes, Labourer	26	Nov. 6
Richard, bastard son of Ann Hawking, Scholes		6
George, son of John and Elizabeth Hewitt, Barwick, collier	Oct. 10	6
John, son of John and Ann Thompson, Barwick, Collier	27	6
James, son of Joseph and Sarah Walton, Barwick, Farmer	Nov. 5	Dec. 4
John Baines, son of Revd John Graham and Dorothy his wife	Nov. 6	Dec. 9
Thomas & Elizabeth, Twins, son and dau. of Thomas and Martha Marshall, Winmoor, Farmer		Dec. 14
BAPTISMS, 1792.	Born	Bap.
David, son of William and Jane Thompson, Garforth moor, collier	[Nov.] 21	Jan. 1
Jane, dau. of John and Jane Blackburn, Garforth moor, collier	23	Jan. 1
Mary, dau. of John and Sarah Clapham, Barwick, Labourer	Jan. 1	Feb. 5
Ann, dau. of Seath and Hannah Stacha Brista, Winmoor, Labr	19	12
Mary, dau. of William and Mary Vincent, Coalpits, collier	25	26
Elizabeth, dau. of John and Sarah Loder, Kiddall lane end		27
George, son of Renton and Sarah Haist, Barwick, Labourer	Feb. 3	Mar. 4
Mary, dau. of Richard and Ann Perkin, Barwick, Farmer	Jan. 23	18
Easter, dau. of James and Ellin Goodall, Barnbow, collier	Jan. 24	Apl. 8
Benjamin, son of William and Rebecca Bullock, Potterton, farmer	Mar. 31	29
John, son of John and Sarah Brogden, Woodhouse, Farmer	Apl. 17	May 27
Joseph, son of Joseph and Susannah Johnson, Brownmoor, Collier	May 11	Jun. 10
Benjamin, son of Thomas and Mary Armatage, Lowmoor, collier	Jun. 27	Jul. 22

Sarah, dau. of Thomas and Ann Goodall, Ingine, collier	15	29
Catherine, dau. of John and Sarah Gough, Potterton, gardiner	Jul. 8	Aug. 5
John, son of John and Ann Auchtertownie, Barwick, gardiner	21	19
James, son of Thomas and Hannah Lowreman, Ingine, collier	2	26
Maria, dau. of George and Ann Darton, Barwick, Labourer	Aug. 5	Sep. 2
Mary, dau. of John and Ann Baley, Brownmoor, Laburer	7	9
Benjamin, son of John and Mary Barber, Stanks, Collier	29	23
Elizabeth, dau. of Samuel and Catherine Thompson, Barwick, collier	Sep. 12	Nov. 4
William, son of William & Sarah Robshaw, Barwick, Labourer	6	4
Hannah, dau. of John & Ann Atkinson, Stanks, Labourer	22	11
George, son of Leonard & Mary Cauwood, Winmoor, Shoemaker	15	23
Thomas, son of William & Sarah Knapton, Barwick, Blacksmith	Nov. 12	25
Mary, dau. of Joseph & Mary Upton, Morwick, Farmer	Oct. 7	28
BAPTISMS, 1793.	Born	Bapt.
Joseph & Johannah, twins, son [&] dau. of William and Hannah Beanley, Barwick, Taylor		Jan. 5
Thomas, son of John & Emelley Benton, Stanks, collier	Dec. 3	13
James, son of Thomas and Mary Tillotson, Garforth moor, collier	30	27
Ann, dau. of John & Ann Thompson, Barwick, collier	27	27
John, son of John and Hannah Wetherill, Woodhouse, Farmer	Jan. 15	Feb. 10
Roger, son of Roger and Ann Brownrig, Scholes, Taylor	3	10
William, son of William and Elizabeth Robinson, Barwick	30	13
Ann, dau. of David & Maria Heaton, Barwick, Farmer	5	Mar. 3
Abigal, dau. of James & Mary Thompson, Barwick, Labourer	Jan. 29	3
James, son of William and Mary Batty, Bramham, Shoemaker	Feb. 14	10
William, son of Thomas and Martha Marshall, Whinmoor, Farmer	Dº 6	Dº 18
John, son of Joseph and Sarah Simpson, Brownmoor, collier	Dº 21	Dº 24
Martha, dau. of John and Martha Mackontosh, Barwick, Labr		22
James, son of John and Maria Cullingworth, Barwick, shoemaker	3	24
Charles, son of David and Mary Win, Scholes, collier	Feb. 4	Mar. 31
Jane, dau. of John and Elizabeth Scholes, Barnbow, collier	Mar. 20	Apl. 2
Elizabeth, dau. of Matthew and Ann Varley, Barwick, Farmer	Feb. 11	7
Thomas, son of Thomas and Julea Waite, Barwick, Labourer	Mar. 6	7
George, son of William and Ellin Rawlinson, Barwick	17	May 5

William, son of William and Margret Gough, Barwick, Joyner	Apl. 18	19
Sarah, dau. of John and Mary Cullingworth, Stankhouse	Jul. 15	29
Robert, son of Peter and Elizabeth Benson, Scholes, Labourer	Apl. 2	Jun. 9
Mary, dau. of William and Ann Goodall, Barnbow, collier	Mar. 19	9
Ann, dau. of John and Sarah Clapham, Barwick, Labourer	May 23	23
Abraham, son of Abraham and Sarah Wormald, Barwick, Blacksmith	7	30
Ann, dau. of Francis & Sarah Buck of York, Petergate, servant	Jul. 1	Do
Hewley, son of John Graham, clerk, & Dorothy, his wife, of Barwick	May 3	Jul. 11
Peter, son of John and Sarah Gough, Potterton, gardiner	Jun. 14	14
Rebecca, dau. of Thomas and Sarah Tilney, Scholes, mason	May 31	28
John, son of John and Ann Braithwaite, Barwick, Farmer	Jul. 14	Aug. 18
Mary & Martha, Twins, daus. of Thomas and Mary Perkin, Barwick, Labourer	Sep. 20	Sep. 20
Thomas, son of Thomas & Ann Lowreman, Brownmoor, collier	28	Nov. 3
William, son of William & Mary Pickersgill, Potterton, Farmer	Oct. 11	3
Hannah, dau. of Richard & Ann Perkin, Barwick, Farmer	Jul. 2	3
Joseph, son of William and Ann Smith, Barwick, Farmer	Oct. 31	3
Mary, dau. of Joseph and Hellen Scott, Scholes, Millwright	8	3
Matthew, bastard son of Ann Norton, Barwick, p.		3
Richard, son of Jonathan and Ellin Tayler, Stanks, collier	24	Dec. 1

Baptisms, 1794.	Born	Bap.
Ann, dau. of James and Ellin Heaton, Potterton, servant	Nov. 30	Jan. 5
Jane, dau. of William and Mary Vincent, Barnbow, collier	Dec. 23	12
Ann, dau. of Thomas and Ann Goodall, Ingine, collier	9	12
Rebecca, dau. of William and Jane Watson, Barwick	Jan. 1	12
Elizabeth, dau. of Matthew and Elizabeth Upton, Scholes	Dec. 31	27
Mary, dau. of Edward and Sarah Goodall, Stanks, collier	Jan. 19	Feb. 16
Elizabeth, dau. of John and Martha Mackontosh, Barwick, Labourer	Jan. 17	Feb. 23
Sarah, dau. of John and Hannah Butler, Scholes, Pipe maker	Feb, 9	Mar. 2
James, son of John and Margret Tillotson, Barwick, Collier	4	30
Elizabeth, dau. of Renton and Sarah Haist, Barwick, Labourer	Mar. 10	Apl. 6
Jane, dau. of John and Sarah Burrow, Farmer, Roundhay	Dec. 19	20
Sarah, dau. of John and Elizabeth Hewitt, Barwick, collier	Mar. 27	27
Charls, son of William and Ellin Rawlinson, Barwick,	Apl. 24	30
William, son of William and Hannah Beanley, Barwick, Taylor	Mar. 30	May 11
Hannah, dau. of Isaac and Mary Hunter, Stanks, collier	27	11
Harriot, bastard dau. of Mary Green, Scholes	Apl. 8	Jun. 1

*David, son of Thomas and Ann Stoner, Barwick, miller	6	10
Ann, dau. of Thomas and Hannah Waite, Barwick, Taylor	May 16	10
Alice, dau. of George and Ann Daughill, Barwick, Labourer	6	15
Jane, dau. of John and Jane Goodall, Barnbow, Collier	Apl. 22	15
John, son of Robert and Mary Greenwood, Barwick	Jun. 5	22
James, son of John and Elizabeth Stubs, Barwick, servant	May 18	29
Elizabeth, dau. of William and Sarah Knapton, Barwick, blacksmth	Jun. 18	Jul. 6
Mary, dau. of Jonothan and Mary Richardson, Winmoor, Labourer	May 12	6
Barnard, son of John and Sarah Gough, Potterton, Gardiner	Jun. 24	20
Susanna Barwicke, a Foundling (name unknown) taken up on the Common, p.		Aug. 17
Mary, dau. of Benjamin and Frances Bell, Winmoor, Labourer	Aug. 5	31
John, son of William and Rebecca Bullock, Potterton, Farmer	9	Sep. 7
Mary, dau. of Thomas and Martha Collet, Barwick, Lab^{r}	11	7
Martha, dau. of Richard and Elizabeth Shillito, Kidhall-lane End, Taylor	9	Oct. 5
Elizabeth, dau. of John and Ann Thompson, Barwick, Collier	Sep. 27	26
Ann, dau. of John and Sarah Brogden, Morwick, Farmer	Oct. 1	Nov. 2
Mary, dau. of Richard and Elianor Pease, Barwick, collier	23	2
Mary, dau. of Richard and Elizabeth Dungwith, Barwick, Lab^{r}	3	2
Harriot, dau. of Samuel and Catherine Thompson, Barnbow, collier	26	23
John, son of Jacob and Sarah Brown, Winmoor, Labourer	30	30
Mary, dau. of Thomas and Mary Tillotson, Garforth moor, collier	Nov. 14	Dec. 7
Sarah, dau. of William and Sarah Smith, Bramham park	4	28

BAPTISMS, 1795.

Benjamin, son of John and Maria Cullingworth, Barwick, Shoemaker	Nov. 12	Jan. 11
Hannah, dau. of John and Jane Atkinson, Winmoor, Labourer	Dec. 21	25
Elizabeth Jackson, dau. of John and Mary Kettlewell, Barnbow	17	Feb. 8
Sarah, dau. of Matthew and Sarah Varley, Barwick, Farmer	..	22
John, son of William and Margret Gough, Barwick, Joyner	Jan. 28	Mar. 1
George, son of John and Elizabeth Scholes, Barnbow, collier	Feb. 17	15
Frances, dau. of John and Emelia Benton, Garforth moor, collier	17	29
John, son of David and Mary Whin, Scholes, collier	Mar. 6	Apl. 5

*David Stoner was a zealous preacher in the Wesleyan Ministry. Appointed to the Leeds Circuit 1814, afterwards to Huddersfield, Bradford, Bristol, York, and Liverpool where he died 23 October, 1826. See *Memoir of David Stoner* by William Dawson and Dr. John Hannah, New York, 1853, and Stevens's *History of Methodism*, Vol. III.

William, son of David and Maria Heaton, Barwick, Farmer	Jan. 25	[Apr]. 5
Hannah, dau. of John and Hannah Wetherill, Woodhouse, Farmer		6
John, son of Thomas and Martha Marshall, Winmoor, Farmer	Mar. 10	6
Charlotta, dau. of Joseph and Susannah Johnson, Stanks, collier	13	19
John, son of John and Sarah Clapham, Ba[r]wick, Farmer	25	26
Dinah, dau. of William and Ann Clayton, Ingine, Collier	25	26
George, son of Benjamin and Ann Rawden, Stanks, Labourer	Feb. 25	26
James, son of John and Mary Barber, Scholes, collier	Mar. 30	May 3
Sarah, dau. of Richard and Ann Perkin, Barwick, Farmer	Feb. 17	10
John, son of Revd William Hodgson, clerk, and Catharine, his wife, of Barwick	Feb. 8	Mar. 21
Ann, dau. of Revd William Hodgson, clerk, and Catharine, his wife, of Barwick	Feb. 8	Mar. 21
Ann, dau. of William and Ellin Rawlinson, Barwick	Apl. 22	May 31
Mary, dau. of Thomas and Elizabeth Barton, Barwick, Butcher	May 6	Jun. 7
John, son of Leonard and Mary Cauwood, Winmoor, shoemaker		7
Henrey, son of Joseph and Sarah Simpson, Brownmoor, collier	27	21
James, son of Thomas and Mary Armatage, Winmoor, Collier	30	28
David, son of Joseph and Ann Cawthorn, Barwick, Labourer	2	28
Hannah, dau. of John and Mary Smith, Ingine, Labourer	Jun. 24	Jul. 12
Henry, son of John & Dorothy Graham, clerk, Barwick	Jun. 4	Jun. 24
John, son of Jonothan & Ellin Taylor, Stanks, collier	Jul. 13	Jul. 26
Henrey, son of Thomas & Ann Goodall, Ingine, collier	22	Aug. 23
James, son of John and Sarah Gough, Potterton, gardiner	Sep. 30	Oct. 25
Thomas, son of Thomas and Mary Morritt, Barwick, Labr	23	Nov. 1
Joseph, son of William and Hannah Beanley, Barwick, Taylor	10	
William, son of John and Ann Braithwaite, Barwick, Farmer	Jul. 4	1
John, son of William and Mary Clough, Barwick, Farmer	Sep. 12	1
Elizabeth, dau. of William and Sarah Knapton, Barwick, Blacksmith	Oct. 7	1
Hannah, dau. of William and Mary Pickersgill, Winmoor		Nov. 22
William, son of Thomas and Hannah Waite, Barwick, Taylor	Nov. 17	Dec. 13
James, son of William and Jane Thompson, Garforth Moor, collier	Oct. 30	13
Hannah, dau. of Richard and Mary Waite, Barwick, Butcher	Nov. 21	27

Baptisms, 1796.	Born	Bap.
John, son of John and Elizabeth Holmes, Winmoor, Labourer		Jan. 24

George, son of William and Isabella Simpson, Stank, collier		31
William, son of Job and Sarah Hodgson, Scholes, Labourer		31
Elizabeth, dau. of John and Jane Atkinson, Crosgates, Labourer	Jan. 14	Feb. 7
John, son of William and Sarah Robshaw, Barwick, Labourer		14
Matthew, son of William and Jane Watson, Barwick, Woodfeller	Feb. 4	21
Jane, dau. of Joseph and Mary Upton, Morwick, Farmer	Dec. 23	24
Alice, dau. of Thomas and Ann Stoner, Barwick, Miller	Jan. 6	26
Christopher William, son of Edward and Ann Wilkinson, Potterton Lodge		22
Elizabeth, dau. of John and Ellin Smith, Barwick, Labourer	Mar. 6	Apl. 3
Sarah, dau. of John and Sarah Groves, Barwick, Carpinter		3
John, son of James and Mary Thompson, Barwick, Labourer	Apl. 1	May 1
Charls, son of Foljombe and Mary Hall, Potterton	Mar. 20	2
Ann, dau. of Richard and Elizabeth Shillito, Kidhall lane, Taylor	31	6
John, son of John and Mary Groves, Potterton, Farmer	Feb. 24	15
Thomas, son of Leonard and Mary Canwood, Winmoor, shoemaker	Mar. 30	15
Robart, son of John and Elizabeth Stubs, Barwick	Jan. 13	22
Thomas, son of Thomas and Mary Wood, Potterton, Labourer		29
William, son of Richard and Mary Hewitt, Barwick, collier	May 8	Jun. 19
Ann, dau. of Matthew and Elizabeth Upton, Scholes, Labourer	6	19
Faith, dau. of Joseph and Elizabeth Turner, Stanks, collier	30	Jul. 17
James, son of John and Martha Mackontosh, Barwick, Labourer		31
George, son of William and Hannah Carr, Kidhall lane end, Carpinter	Jul. 1	Aug. 1
Mary, dau. of James and Tabitha Lumb, Barwick, Farmer		3
George, son of George and Ann Daughill, Barwick, Labourer		7
George and Sarah, twins, son and dau. of William and Mary Vince, coalpitts, collier	12	14
Elizabeth, dau. of Richard and Elizabeth Dungwith, Barwick, Labourer	15	14
Isaac, son of Abraham and Sarah Wormald, Barwick, Blacksmith	2	Sep. 4
Samuel, son of Thomas and Hannah Thompson, Garforth moor, collier	Aug. 13	18
John, bastard son of Ann Newhouse, poorhouse		25
Sarah, dau. of John and Jane Hunter, Stanks, collier	15	Oct. 2
David, son of David and Mary Winn, Scholes, collier	27	2
Pheabe, dau. of John and Elizabeth Monks, Barwick, Labourer	Apl. 13	16
Mary, dau. of Thomas and Sarah Tilney, Scholes, Mason	Oct. 3	Nov. 6

John, son of William and Ann Copley, Barwick, Labourer	Sep. 22	6
John, son of William and Mary Heaton, Barwick, Labourer	Aug. 23	6
Hannah, dau. of Thomas and Mary Simpson, Stanks, Lab^{r}	Oct. 13	20
BAPTISMS, 1797.	Born	Bap.
Henrey, son of James and Ellin Goodall, Barnbow, collier		Jan. 15
Mary Ann, dau. of John and Jane Goodall, Barnbow, collier		22
Hannah, dau. of Thomas and Mary Morritt, Barwick, Labourer	Dec. 2	22
John, son of Benjamin and Martha Stringer, Hilltop, Taylor	Jan. 17	Feb. 5
Mary, dau. of William and Margret Gough, Barwick, Joiner	Jan. 11	5
Richard, son of John and Elizabeth Hewitt, Barwick, collier	Dec. 20	5
Sarah, dau. of John and Sarah Clapham, Barwick, Labourer	Jan. 11	12
Sarah, dau. of Thomas and Elizabeth Barton, Barwick, Farmer	12	12
George, son of Samuel and Cathrine Thompson, Barwick, collier	19	26
Ann, dau. of Matthew and Ann Varley, Barwick, Farmer,	Dec. 19	26
Elizabeth, dau. of Thomas and Martha Collet, Barwick, Labourer	Jan. 29	Mar. 5
John, son of John and Elizabeth Scholes, Barnbow, Collier	Feb. 7	12
William, son of John and Hannah Butler, Scholes, pipe Maker	Mar. 11	Apl. 16
John, son of Sam^{ll} & Catherine Robinson, Garforth Moorside, collier	Apl. 4	23
Ann, daug^{tr} of John & Hannah Wetherill, Winmoor stile, Farmer	Mar. 26	May 7
John, son of John & Margaret Tillotson, Barwick, Collier	Apl. 15	D^{o} 21
William, son of John & Elizabeth Bean, Barwick, Shoemaker	May 20	Jun. 18
Edward, son of Edward & Sarah Goodall, Stanks, collier	May 21	Jun. 18
Elizabeth, d^{r} of George & Elizth Pickersgill, Grimsdike, Cartdriver	Jun. 18	Jun. 25
Elizabeth, d^{r} of William & Eleanor Rawlinson, Barwick, Labourer	May 26	Jul. 9
Sarah, d^{r} of John & Sarah Brogdin, Morwick, Labourer	Jul. 8	Aug. 13
Thomas, son of Thomas & Ann Stoner, Barwick, Miller	Jul. 8	Sep. 1
Mary, d^{r} of William & Rebecca Bullock, Potterton, Farmer	Aug. 31	Oct. 1
Sarah, d^{r} of William & Sarah Knapton, Barwick, Blacksmith	Aug. 24	Oct. 1
Richard, son of Richard & Elizabeth Pease, Barwick, collier	Oct. 11	Nov. 5
Samuel, son of William & Hannah Beanley, Barwick, Tailor	Sep. 4	Nov. 5
Sarah, d^{r} of William & Mary Linley, Barnbow, Labourer	Oct. 1	Nov. 5
Elizabeth, d^{r} of Richard & Ann Perkin, Barwick, Farmer	Jun. 21	Nov. 5
Matthew, son of John & Elizabeth Braithwaite, Barwick, Farmer	Sep. 2	Nov. 5

David, son of David & Hannah Maria Heaton, Barwick, Farmer	Jul. 18	Nov. 5
Hannah, dr of Thomas & Hannah Waite, Barwick, Tailor	Oct. 21	Nov. 6
Elizabeth, dr of James & Tabitha Lumb, Barwick, Farmer	Oct. 5	Nov. 6
Sarah, dr of John & Ann Johnson, Stanks, collier	Nov. 8	Dec. 3
Charlotte, bastard dau. of Hannah Hodgson, Scholes	Nov. 9	Dec. 10
Robert, son of Jonathan & Elizabeth Taylor, Stanks, collier	Nov. 4	Dec. 17

BAPTISMS, 1798.	Born	Bap. 1798
John, son of William & Frances Collet, Potterton lane, Blacksmith	Dec. 12	Jan. 7
Hannah, dr of Joseph & Sarah Simpson, Brown Moor, collier	Dec. 11	Jan. 7
William, son of Thomas & Mary Tillotson, Barrowby lane end, collier	Dec. 6	Jan. 14
Alice, dr of Richard & Mary Waite, Barwick, Butcher	Nov. 17	Jan. 21
Elizabeth, dr of James & Frances Barker, Penwell, Labourer	Jan. 2	Feb. 4
Thomas, son of Peter & Catherine Higgins, Bradford bottom, Labourer	Jan. 4	Feb. 4
John, son of Wm & Mary Atkinson, Barwick, Labourer	Jan. 17	Feb. 11
James, son of Thomas & Mary Parker, Barwick, Labourer	Nov. 20	Feb. 18
Mary, dr of James & Eleanor Heaton, Barwick, Labourer	Dec. 31	Feb. 25
Frances, dr of Thomas & Martha Marshall, Winmoor, Farmer	Jan. 13	Feb. 26
Elizabeth, dr of John & Elizabeth Dean, Winmoor, Huckster	Jan. 24	Mar. 4
Hannah, dr of Richard & Mary Hewitt, Barwick, collier	Feb. 1	Mar. 11
Richard, son of John & Eleanor Smith, Barwick, Labourer	Feb. 19	Mar. 25
Benjamin, son of Benjamin & Jane Thompson, Barwick, collier	Jan. 23	Mar. 25
Jane, dr of John & Mary Smith, Engine, Waggoner	Jan. 20	Apl. 8
Mary, daughter of the Revd William Hodgson, clerk, & Catharine, his wife, of Berwick	Feb. 19	Mar. 25
James, son of Peter & Elizabeth Benson, Scholes, collier	Feb. 22	Apl. 15
Mary, dr of John & Mary Barber, Scholes, collier	Apl. 14	May 13
Hannah, daur of William & Ann Copley, Barwick, Labourer	May 3	May 27
Robert, son of William & Mary Heaton, Barwick, Labourer	Apl. 6	May 27
John, son of Richard & Elizabeth Dungwith, Barwick, Labourer	May 9	Jun. 3
Thomas, son of Thomas & Martha Robuck, Potterton lane, Farmer	May 11	Jun. 10
Ann, daur of William & Jane Watson, Barwick, Labourer	Apl. 7	Jun. 7
George, son of William & Elizabeth Walton, Barwick, Labourer	Jun. 3	Jun. 10
Elizabeth, daur of Richard & Sarah Jackson, Barwick, Waiter at an Inn	Jun. 2	Jul. 1
George, son of John & Ann Thompson, Garforth-moor-side, collier	Jun. 7	Jul. 1

Mary, daur of Thomas & Mary Armatage, Lowmoor, collier	Jun. 4	Jul. 8
Catherine, daur of William & Mary Pickersgill, Potterton, Farmer	Jun. 10	Jul. 15
Sarah, daur of Jonathan & Mary Richardson, Winmoor, Labourer	May 30	Jul. 22
Sarah, daur of John & Sarah Gough, Potterton, Gardener	Jun. 20	Jul. 22
Grace, daur of John & Jane Goodall, Barnbow, collier	Jun. 9	Jul. 22
William, son of James & Mary Thompson, Barwick, Labourer	Jun. 24	Aug. 5
John, Bastard son of Hannah Carter, Roundhay, Maid-servant	Jul. 21	Aug. 26
William (born at Stanks), son of John & Jane Hunter, Garforth, collier	Sep. 1	Sep. 23
Elizabeth, daur of Thomas & Mary Morritt, Barwick, Labourer	Aug. 21	Oct. 7
John, son of John & Ann Todd, Barwick, Labourer	Oct. 4	Nov. 4
Thomas, son of Christopher & Faith Simpson, Barnbow, collier	Sep. 15	Nov. 4
William, son of John & Elizabeth Monk, Stanks, Labourer	May 1	Nov. 4
James, son of John & Hannah Butler, Scholes, Pipemaker	Oct. 12	Nov. 4
Sarah, daur of Abraham & Sarah Wormald, Barwick, Blacksmith	Sep. 11	Nov. 4
Patience, daur of John & Ann Atkinson, Winmoor, Labourer	Oct. 6	Nov. 11
Richard, son of William & Mary Vincent, Green Lane, Collier	Oct. 25	Nov. 25
James, son of Joseph & Mary Sparling, Kidhall Lane end, Labourer	Oct. 26	Nov. 25
Thomas, son of John & Sarah Whitehead, Barwick, Farmer	Oct. 28	Nov. 28
Mary-Ann, daur of Thomas & Mary Balance, Scholes, collier	Nov. 27	Dec. 23
Benjamin, son of Benjamin & Martha Stringer, Hill-top, Taylor	Dec. 5	Dec. 23
Joseph, son of John & Sarah Clapham, Barwick, Farmer	Nov. 22	Dec. 23
Hannah, daur of William & Hannah Carr, Kid Hall Lane end, Joiner	Nov. 22	Dec. 25
William, son of George & Ann Daughill, Barwick, Labourer	Dec. 5	Dec. 30

Baptisms, 1799.	Born	Bap.
William, son of John & Elizabeth Holmes, Grimsdike, Labourer	Nov. 27	Jan. 13
Hannah, daur of Samuel & Catherine Tompson, Barwick, Collier	Dec. 13	Jan. 13
Bella, daur of John & Mary Cawthorne, Scholes, Shoemaker	Dec. 22	Jan. 20
John, bastard son of Hannah Stead, Barwick	Jan. 20	Feb. 10
Mary, daur of Thomas & Elizabeth Robshaw, Barwick, Woodman	Jan. 29	Feb. 24
Hannah, daur of Richard & Elizabeth Pease, Barwick, collier	Dec. 27	Feb. 24
James, son of William & Ann Clayton, Engine, Collier	Jan. 1	Mar. 3

Elizabeth, daur of Thomas & Ann Goodall, Engine, collier	Jan. 5	Mar. 3
George, son of Thomas & Elizabeth Barton, Barwick, Farmer	Jan. 24	Mar. 3
John, son of Joseph & Martha Kirkham, Barwick, Labourer	Mar. 7	Mar. 7
Jane, daur of William & Margaret Gough, Barwick, Carpenter	Feb. 16	Mar. 24
Benjamin, son of Leonard & Mary Cauwood, Grimsdike, Publican	Feb. 1	Mar. 25
Harriet, bastard daur of Hannah Wright, Poor-house	Feb. 19	Mar. 31
John, son of Matthew & Ann Varley, Barwick, Farmer	Jan. 19	Apl. 14
Sarah, daur of John & Elizabeth Scholes, Barnbow, collier	Mar. 1	Apl. 21
Hannah, daur of William & Sarah Knapton, Barwick, Blacksmith	Apl. 5	May 5
Joseph, son of Thomas & Ann Stoner, Barwick, Miller	Mar. 29	May 13
William, son of George & Sarah Simpson, Barwick, Labourer	Apl. 19	May 12
James, son of William & Eleanor Buckanan, Scholes, Labourer	Jun. 10	Jun. 12
Joshua, son of John & Ann Eastwood, Stanks, collier	Apl. 14	Jun. 16
Sarah, daur of John & Grace Hemsworth, Barwick, collier	May 5	Jun. 23
Ann, daur of John & Sarah Groves, Barwick, Carpenter	Jun. 12	Jul. 7
Ann, daur of John & Amelia Benton, Barrowby-lane-end, Collier	May 21	Jul. 7
James, son of James & Mary Dodd, a private in ye Warwickshire Cavalry	Mar. 12	Jul. 19
George, son of James & Mary Hirst, Barwick, Labourer	Jul. 3	Aug. 11
James, son of John & Elizabeth Bean, Barwick, Shoemaker	Jul. 9	Aug. 18
Thomas, son of Thomas & Sarah Tilney, Scholes, Mason,	Aug 19.	Sep. 8
Elizabeth, daur of Thomas & Mary Todd, Barwick, Man-servant	Aug. 4	Sep. 15
Thomas, son of Thomas & Hannah Waite, Barwick, Tailor	Aug. 23	Oct. 11
Sarah, daur of Joseph & Sarah Simpson, Brown-moor, collier	Sep. 10	Oct. 13
James, son of John & Elizabeth Monk, Stanks, Labourer	Jul. 1	Oct. 20
Thomas, son of Joseph & Ann Speight, Scholes, Labourer	Oct. 8	Nov. 3
Richard, son of Richard & Ann Perkin, Barwick, Farmer	Jul. 10	Nov. 3
Richard, son of Richard & Mary Hewitt, Barwick, collier	Sep. 18	Nov. 3
Mary, daur of John & Elizabeth Braithwaite, Barwick, Farmer	Sep. 14	Nov. 3
Hannah, daur of John & Elizabeth Hewitt, Barwick, Collier	Jul. 12	Nov. 3
Thomas, son of Thomas & Martha Collet, Barwick, Labourer	Sep. 24	Nov. 3
Jonathan, son of Samuel & Frances Pickard, Terraloggate, Gamekeeper	Sep. 13	Nov. 24
William, son of William & Frances Collet, Potterton lane, Blacksmith	Nov. 5	Dec. 1
Sarah, daur of John & Elizabeth Dean, Winmoor, Huckster	Nov. 5	Dec. 8
James, son of John & Hannah Johnson, Stanks, Collier	Nov. 27	Dec. 25

Baptisms, 1800.	Born	Bap.
Elizabeth, dau^{r} of William & Mary Linley, Barnbow, Labourer	Dec. 19, 1799	Jan. 10
Seth, son of Peter & Catherine Higgins, Bradford bottom, Labourer	Aug. 20, 1799	Feb. 2
Mary, dau^{r} of James & Jane Batty, Barwick, Shoemaker	Feb. 10	Mar. 16
Abraham, son of Matthew & Elizabeth Riley, Barnbow, Labourer	Feb. 20	Mar. 23
Richard, son of William & Elizabeth Dickinson, Barnbow, Labourer	Feb. 27	Mar. 30
Benjamin, son of William & Hannah Beanley, Barwick, Tailor	Mar. 13	Apl. 13
Sarah, dau^{r} of William & Eleanor Rawlinson, Barwick, Labourer	Feb. 22	Apl. 20
Edward, bastard son of Eleanor Nettleton, Poorhouse	Mar. 20	Apl. 20
Abraham, son of John & Sarah Whitehead, Barwick, Farmer	Mar. 23	Apl. 27
Thomas & Hannah, son & dau^{r} of John & Ann Todd, Barwick, Labourer	Apl. 28	Apl. 29
Thomas, son of James & Tabitha Lumb, Barwick, Farmer	Mar. 27	May 2
Thomas, son of William & Ann Burnill, Woodhouse, Farmer	Feb. 19	May 11
Isaac, son of James & Frances Barker, Penwell, Farmer	Apl. 19	May 11
Thomas, son of Thomas and Hannah Thompson, Barnbow, Collier	Mar. 24	May 11
Elizabeth, dau^{r} of Thomas & Martha Marshall, Winmoor, Farmer	Apl. 14	May 19
William, son of Richard & Elizabeth Pease, Barwick, collier	Apl. 22	May 25
James, son of Benjamin & Jane Thompson, Barwick, collier	Apl. 4	Jun. 1
Richard, son of Richard & Margaret Goodall, Stanks, collier	Nov. 16	Jun. 1
Peter, son of William & Eleanor Buckanan, Scholes, Labourer	May 11	Jun. 8
William, son of Jonathan & Mary Richardson, Winmoor, Labourer	May 18	Jun. 29
John, son of John & Eleanor Smith, Barwick, Labourer,	May 8	Jul. 6
Elizabeth, dau^{r} of John & Mary Smith, Engine, Waggoner	Jun, 14	Jul. 13
Joseph, son of John & Mary Cawthorne, Scholes, Shoemaker	Jun. 29	Jul. 27
Jane, dau^{r} of William & Elizabeth Batty, Barwick, Shoemaker	Jul. 30	Aug. 31
Hannah, dau^{r} of William & Mary Heaton, Barwick, Labourer	Apl. 29	Sep. 14
John, son of Job & Sarah Hodgson, Scholes, Labourer	Sep. 10	Sep. 21
William, bastard son of Elizabeth Linley, Engine	Aug. 20	Sep. 21
Hannah, dau^{r} of William & Hannah Wainwright, Morwick, Labourer	Aug. 28	Sep. 28
Lydia, dau^{r} of John & Ann Thompson, Potterton, Shepherd	Aug. 17	Oct. 5

William, bastard son of Ann Maud, Rounday	Oct. 13	Oct. 23
Ann, daur of John & Elizabeth Thompson, Potterton, Labourer	Oct. 7	Nov. 2
William, son of William & Ann Copley, Barwick, Labourer	Oct. 1	Nov. 2
William, son of James & Eleanor Goodall, Barnbow, collier	Sep. 8	Nov. 2
Thomas, son of Samuel & Catherine Thompson, Barwick, collier	Sep. 18	Nov. 2
Mary-ann, daur of John & Ann Carr, Barwick, Joiner	Nov. 8	Dec. 14
Thomas, son of Joseph & Mary Sparling, Kidhall Lane-end, Labourer	Nov. 16	Dec. 21

BAPTISMS, 1801.	Born	Bap.
William, son of William & Mary Atkinson, Barwick, Labourer	Jan. 3	Feb. 8
Sarah, daur of Thomas & Mary Hudson, Potterton, Labourer	Jan. 19	Feb. 15
Thomas & Sarah, twin son & daur of Thomas & Eliz. Robshaw, Barwick, Farmer	Feb. 7	Feb. 7
Ann, daur of William & Margaret Gough, Barwick, Carpenter	Feb. 13	Mar. 8
Sarah, daur of Peter & Elizabeth Benson, Scholes, Labourer	Dec. 13, 1800	Mar. 15
Mary, daur of Joseph & Martha Kirkham, Barwick, Labourer	Feb. 3	Apl. 5
William, son of John & Mary Robshaw, Barwick, Labourer	Mar. 5	Apl. 5
Ann, daur of Thomas & Mary Morritt, Barwick, Labourer	Jan. 6	Apl. 5
Robert, son of John & Jane Goodall, Barnbow, collier	Jan. 31	Apl. 5
Henry, son of Leonard & Mary Cauwood, Grimsdike, Publican	Feb. 7	Apl. 6
Mary, bastard daur of Margaret Dearlove, Poorhouse	Mar. 9	Apl. 12
James, son of Richard & Ann Perkin, Barwick, Farmer	Dec. 8, 1800	Apl. 19
Benjamin, son of John & Elizabeth Holmes, Grimsdike, Laborer	Mar. 3	Apl. 26
Joseph, son of William & Susanna Lidster, Brownmoor, Laborer	Apl. 13	May 3
George, son of Bennet & Mary Johnson, Barwick, Laborer	Mar. 31	May 10
Elizabeth, daur of John & Ann Todd, Barwick, Laborer	Apl. 6	May 10
Robert, son of Thomas & Elizabeth Barton, Barwick, Farmer	Mar. 20	May 24
Elizabeth, daur of Christopher & Faith Simpson, Barnbow, collier	Mar. 25	May 24
Jane, daur of George & Ann Daughill, Barwick, Laborer	May 12	Jun. 7
Ruth, daur of Abraham & Sarah Wormald, Barwick, Blacksmith	Apl. 23	Jun. 7
Ann, bastard daur of Martha Morritt, Winmoor	Jun. 9	Jun. 28
James, son of James & Mary Hirst, Barwick, Laborer	Jun. 14	Jul. 12
Mary, daur of Richard & Elizabeth Dungwith, Barwick, Laborer	Jun. 16	Jul. 19
Richard, son of Matthew & Mary Johnson, Scholes, collier	Jun. 4	Jul. 19
William, son of Thomas & Mary Todd, Barwick, Laborer	Jun. 10	Jul. 26

Ann, daur of Stephen & Elizabeth Flowet, Barwick, Laborer — Jun. 28 Aug. 2
Thomas, son of William & Mary Vincent, Green lane, collier — Jun. 23 Aug, 16
Ruth, daur of Thomas & Sarah Tilney, Scholes, Mason — Jul. 12 Aug. 16
Hannah, daur of Thomas & Elizabeth Ward, Barwick, Laborer — Jun. 28 Sep. 13
Richard, son of William & Sarah Knapton, Barwick, Blacksmith — Jun. 28 Sep. 27
Grace, daur of Ephraim & Mary Jolly, Barwick, Laborer — Sep. 11 Sep. 26
Grace, daur of John & Sarah Clapham, Barwick, Farmer — Sep. 5 Oct. 4
Susanna and Sophia, twin daughters of the Reverend William Hodgson and Catharine, his wife, of Berwick in Elmet, born 5th, baptized 26th of Aug.
Thomas, son of Samuel & Abigal Watson, Kidhall lane end, Laborer — Sep. 24 Oct. 18
Ann, daur of Francis & Jane Wilkinson, Potterton, Farmer — Aug. 22 Oct. 30
Elizabeth, daur of John & Elizabeth Scholes, Barnbow, collier — Jul. 23 Nov. 1
William, son of James & Mary Smith, Austhorp, Laborer — Sep. 6 Nov. 20
Richard, bastard son of Lydia Hewitt, Barwick — Nov. 2 Nov. 22
Joseph, bastard son of Hannah Harrison, Poorhouse — Nov. 2 Nov. 22
Sarah, daur of William & Elizabeth Batty, Barwick Shoemaker — Nov. 10 Dec. 13

BAPTISMS, 1802. — Born Bap.

George, son of Richard and Frances Baker, Stanks, Labourer — Oct. 2, 1801 Jan. 1
Sarah, dau. of George & Ann Connell, Barwick, Labourer — Dec. 15 Jan. 19
Sarah, daugr of Thomas & Hannah Waite, Barwick, Tailor — Nov. 17 Jan. 31
Elizabeth, daugr of Peter & Catherine Higgins, Bradford Bottom, Labourer — Nov. 27 Feb. 7
John, son of Richd & Elizabeth Pease, Barwick, collier — Feb. 6 Feb. 12
Thomas, son of John & Elizabeth Braithwaite, Barwick, Farmer — Jan. 1 Feb. 19
Maria, daugr of Saml & Catherine Robinson, Green Lane collier — Jan. 17 Feb. 21
James, son of Richd & Ann Perkins, Barwick, Farmer — Nov. 25, 1801 Feb. 21
Hannah, daugr of Mattw & Dinah Watson, Barwick, Labourer — Dec. 21, 1801 Feb. 28
Sarah, daugr of John and Mary Cawthorne, Scholes, Shoemaker — Mar. 20 Apl. 18
William, son of John and Sarah Gough, Potterton, Gardener — Feb. 21 Apl. 18
Ann, daugr of William & Mary Linley, Barnbow, Labourer — Apl. 14 May 9
Sarah, daugr of John & Mary Robshaw, Barwick, Labourer — May 8 May 14
Ann, daugr of Richd & Mary Rooke, Halifax, born at Barnbow — Apl. 18 May 16
William, son of Thomas & Ann Thompson, Barnbow, collier — Apl. 13 May 16
William, son of John & Hannah Johnson, Stanks, collier — May 8 Jun. 6

John, son of William & Ann Burnell, Woodhouse, Farmer	May 30	Jul. 18
Elizabeth, daug^{r} of Thomas & Mary Hudson, Potterton, Labourer	Jun. 14	Jul. 18
Sarah, daug^{r} of Benjamin & Jane Thompson, Berwick, collier	May 13	Jul. 18
William, son of Joseph & Ann Speight, Scholes, Labourer	Jul. 6	Aug. 1
Ann, daug^{r} of William & Elizabeth Bramley, Potterton, Labourer	Jun. 22	Aug. 8
Robert, son of George & Elizabeth Pickersgill, Grimsdike, Huckster	Aug. 2	Aug. 4
Elizabeth, dau. of Richard & Mary Hewitt, Barwick, collier	Jul. 12	Aug. 5
John, son of William & Ann Jackson, Barwick, Labourer		Sep. 19
William, son of William & Hannah Wainwright, Garforth-moor-side, Lab^{r}	Aug. 22	Sep. 19
Ann Elizabeth, dau. of Revd James & Winifred Hodgson, Barwick Rectory	May 29	Sep. 21
Joseph, son of William & Hannah Beanland, Barwick, Tailor	Aug. 20	Aug. 23
Ann, daug^{r} of John & Jane Crosland, Scholes, Gent^{n}		Oct. 18
George, son of David & Maria Heaton, Barwick, Farmer	Oct. 7	Nov. 7
Ann, daug^{r} of William and Mary Heaton, Barwick, Labourer	Oct. 6	Nov. 7
Elizabeth, daug^{r} of John & Elizabeth Hewit, Barwick, collier	Sep. 10	Nov. 7
Sarah, daug^{r} of John & Mary Wheater, Barwick, Tailor	Sep. 12	Nov. 7
Hannah, daug^{r} of Henry & Hannah Clayton, Engine, Labourer	Nov. 9	Nov. 28
Mary, daug^{r} of W^{m} & Christiana Watson, Limekiln Gate, Lab^{r}	Nov. 24	Dec. 26
Ellen, daug^{r} of Jeremiah & Ann Maud, Potterton, Labourer	Dec. 4	Dec. 26
Ann, daug^{r} of James & Jane Batty, Barwick, Shoemaker	Nov. 13	Dec. 26
Sarah, daug^{r} of John & Hannah Carr, Barwick, Innkeeper	Nov. 27	Dec. 30

BAPTISMS, 1803.	Born	Bap.
Thomas, son of James & Frances Barker, Penwell, Labourer	Dec. 1, 1802	Jan. 16
John, son of Thomas & Mary Morrit, Barwick, Labourer	Dec. 17	Jan. 20
Mary Ann, daug^{r} of James & Mary Dodd, Barwick, shoemaker	Nov. 2	Jan. 23
Martha, daug^{r} of James & Mary Dodd, Barwick, shoemaker	Nov. 17	Jan. 23
Ann, daug^{r} of Benjamin & Betty Watson, Barwick, carpenter	Dec. 22	Jan. 23
Mary, daug^{r} of Willm & Elizabeth Batty, Barwick, shoemaker	Dec. 18	Jan. 23
Joseph, son of Christopher & Faith Simpson, Barnbow, collier	Dec. 24	Feb. 6
Ann, daughter of Samuel & Catherine Thompson, Barwick, collier	Dec. 11	Feb. 6

William, son of Thomas & Elizabeth Robshaw, Barwick, Labourer	Jan. 29, 1803	Feb. 20
James, son of William & Sarah Knapton, Barwick, Blacksmith	Jan. —	Mar. 3
Elizabeth, dau. of John & Hannah Wood, Scholes, Labourer	Dec. 7, 1802	Mar. 13
Ellen, dau. of Leonard & Mary Cawood, Grimesdike, Shoemaker	Jan. 21, 1803	Apl. 11
Martha, daug^{r} of John & Mary Smith, Laverack, Labourer	Feb. 24	Apl. 3
Richard, son of James & Tabitha Lumb, Barwick, Farmer	Feb. 26	Apl. 15
Ann, daug^{r} of Joseph & Mary Sparling, Kidhall Lane, Labourer	Mar. 22	Apl. 24
John, son of Thomas & Martha Collet, Barwick, Labourer	Mar. 30	May 1
Sarah, daug^{r} of William & Mary Pickersgill, Barwick, Farmer	Mar. 31	May 15
Sarah, daug^{r} of Thomas & Sarah Tilney, Scholes, Mason	Apl. 28	May 29
Thomas, son of John & Elizabeth Holmes, Grimsdike, Labourer	Mar. 24	May 29
Ann, dau. of Richard & Ann Perkin, Barwick, Farmer	Jan. 8	Jun. 12
John, son of James and Mary Hirst, Barwick, Labourer	May 11	Jun. 12
Elizabeth, daug^{r} of Thomas & Mary Armitage, Whinmoor, collier	May 24	Jun. 26
James, son of John & Sarah Clapham, Barwick, Farmer	Jun. 14	Jul. 10
John, son of Thomas & Elizabeth Barton, Barwick, Farmer	May 16	Jul. 17
George, son of James & Ann Gill, Barwick, Miller	Jun. 27	Jul. 24
Thomas, son of John & Eleanor Simpson, Hilltop, Labourer	Jun. 5	Jul. 31
Thomas, son of Bennet & Mary Johnson, Barwick, Labourer	Apl. 23	Jul. 31
Joseph, son of Joseph & Martha Kirkham, Barwick, Labourer	Jul. 1	Jul. 31
Elizabeth, daug^{r} of Stephen & Elizabeth Flawett, Barwick, Labourer	Jun. 24	Aug. 7
Jane, daug^{r} of Thomas & Mary Todd, Barwick, Labourer	Jun. 28	Aug. 7
Charles, son of William & Susan Lidster, Brownmoor, Labourer	Jul. 12	Aug. 14
Hannah, daug^{r} of Matthew & Ann Varley, Barwick, Farmer	Jul. 19	Aug. 21
Jane, bastard daug^{r} of Ann Hawkins, Scholes	Jul. 11	Aug. 28
Sarah, daugh^{r} of Samuel & Abigail Watson, Kiddal Lane, Lab^{r}	Aug; 7	Aug. 28
Thomas, bastard son of Elizabeth Wood, Barwick		Sep. 3
John, son of James & Elizabeth Tomlinson, Barwick, Farmer	Aug. 27	same day
Sarah, daugh^{r} of William & Margaret Gough, Barwick, Carpenter	Aug. 13	Sep. 11
Mary, daug^{r} of Jeremiah & Ellen Beck, Barwick, Weaver	Aug. 19	Sep. 18
James, son of William & Hannah Varley, Kiddal Lane, Inn-keeper	Jul. 12	Sep. 21
Jonathan, son of Matthew & Mary Johnson, Scholes, Labourer	Aug. 29	Sep. 13
John, son of William & Hannah Beanland, Barwick, Tailor	Aug. 3	Sep. 25
James, son of George & Ann Daughill, Barwick, Labourer	Aug. 27	Sep. 25

Ann, dau. of William & Elizabeth Cullingworth, Barnbow, Labourer	Sep. 4	Oct. 9
Joseph, son of John & Elizabeth Scholes, Barnbow, collier	Oct. 16	Nov. 6
William, son of William and Mary Lindley, Barnbow, Labourer	Sep. 23	Nov. 6
Ellen, daug[r] of James & Elizabeth Furness, Winmoorside, Labourer	Oct. 12	Nov. 6
Ann, daug[r] of Benjamin & Ann Hill, Scholes, Labourer	Jun. 7	Nov. 6
James, son of John & Elizabeth Braithwait, Barwick, Farmer	Sep. 30	Nov. 6
Benjamin, son of George & Hannah Blackburn, Stanks, collier	Oct. 31	Nov. 27
William, son of George & Ann Connell, Barwick, Labourer	Nov. 18	Dec. 18

BAPTISMS, 1804.	Born	Bapt.
Richard, son of William & Mary Atkinson, Barwick, Labourer	Dec. 11, 1803	Jan. 8
William, son of Thomas & Mary Hudson, Stanks, Labourer	Nov. 7, 1803	Jan. 8
Benjamin, son of William & Elizab[h] Batty, Barwick, shoemaker	Dec. 19, 1803	Jan. 15
Benjamin, son of William & Sarah Rawlinson, Barwick, Labourer	Dec. 14, 1803	Jan. 15
George, son of John and Frances Hampshire, Brownmoor, Labourer	Dec. 28, 1803	Jan. 29
Ann, bastard dau. of George Holmes & Ann Cowell, Poor-house	Jan. 5	Feb. 5
Alice, dau. of the Rev[d] William Hodgson and Catharine, his wife	Dec. 27, 1803	Feb. 5
Thomas, son of Benj[n] and Martha Stringer, Hill Top, Tailor	Jan. 23	Feb. 19
Joseph, son of John and Jane Goodall, Barnbow, collier	Nov. 17, 1803	Feb. 19
John, son of William and Ann Jackson, Barwick, Labourer	Feb. 13	Mar. 18
Alice, dau. of Peter & Catherine Higgins, Bradford bottom, Labourer	Jan. 3	Mar. 25
Hannah, daug[r] of Thomas & Hannah Thompson, Barnbow, collier	Feb. 29	Mar. 30
James, son of Thomas & Mary Morritt, Barwick, Labourer	Jan. 20	Apl. 1
Harriet, daug[r] of Nathan[l] & Hannah Ward, Scholes, Shoemaker	Mar. 8	Apl. 1
John, son of John & Mary Cawthorne, Barwick, Shoemaker	Mar. 1	Apl. 3
Jane, daug[r] of Thomas & Elizabeth Waid, Barwick, Labourer	Mar. 15	Apl. 15
Elizabeth, daug[r] of William & Ann Burnell, Barwick, Farmer	Mar. 21	Apl. 22
Mary, daug[r] of Matthew & Dinah Watson, Barwick, Labourer	Mar. 22	Apl. 29
Harriet, bastard dau. of Ann Atkinson, Poorhouse	Apl. 28	May 18
Jane, dau. of Joseph & Mary Newis, Scholes, Labourer	Feb. 28	May 20
William, son of William & Hannah Malham, Stanks, a soldier	May 3	Jun. 3

Ann, daug^{r} of Thomas & Ann Stoner, Barwick, Miller	May 7	Jun. 8
Ann, daug^{r} of William & Ann Copley, Barwick, Labourer	Apl. 30	Jun. 10
Hannah, daug^{r} of Robert & Ann Lenox, Kidhall, Labourer	Mar. 25	Jun. 10
John, son of Thomas & Mary Wright, Scholes, Labourer	Apl. 5	Jun. 10
Samuel, son of Joseph & Sarah Simpson, collier, Brownmoor	Jun. 13	Jul. 8
William, son of William & Elizabeth Bramley, Labourer, Potterton	May 29	Jul. 22
William, son of William & Rose Kitchinman, shoemaker, Kilwick	Jan. 24	Jul. 29
Sarah, daug^{r} of John & Elizabeth Bean, shoemaker, Barwick	Jul. 25	Aug. 19
Mary, daug^{r} of Richard & Mary Hewet, collier, Barwick	Jun. 27	Aug. 19
John, bastard son of Ellen Nettleton, Barwick	Jul. 27	Aug. 19
John, son of John & Hannah Carr, carpenter, Barwick	Aug. 5	Aug. 24
George, son of James & Elizabeth Tomlinson, Farmer, Barwick	Aug. 5	Aug. 24
John, son of Joseph & Ann Speight, Labourer, Scholes	Aug. 2	Aug. 24
Ann, daug^{r} of George & Sarah Johnson, Labourer, Kidhall	Aug. 7	Sep. 2
Betty, daug^{r} of William & Martha Jenkinson, Labourer, Grimsdike	Jul. 4	Sep. 2
Charles, son of Richard & Frances Baker, Labourer, Stanks	Mar. 15	Sep. 2
Mary, daug^{r} of Thomas & Martha Marshall, Farmer, Winmoor	Jul. 27	Sep. 3
Thomas, son of John & Elizabeth Smith, Labourer, Barnbow	Jul. 19	Sep. 30
Martha Duncan, daug^{r} of John & Ann Cullingworth, Stanks, born at Leeds	Aug. 26	Oct. 5
John, son of John & Jane Crossland, Gent^{n}, Scholes	Feb. 1	Oct. 26
Mary, daug^{r} of Benjamin & Jane Thompson, collier, Barwick	Sep. 13	Nov. 4
James, son of Thomas & Frances Eastwood, Labourer, Scholes	Jul. 19	Nov. 4
William, son of William & Hannah Varley, Kidhall lane, Farmer	Sep. 15	Nov. 18
Judith, daug^{r} of George & Elizabeth Pickersgill, Farmer, Grimesdike	Oct. 26	Nov. 26
William, son of John & Ellen Simpson, Hill Top, Labourer	Oct. 24	Dec. 16
George, son of Stephen & Sarah Warrington, Roundhay, Labourer	Nov. 21	Dec. 23

Baptisms, 1805.	Born	Bapt.
Martha and Mary, twin daug^{rs} of Samuel & Catherine Thompson, Barwick, collier	Oct. 29, 1804	Jan. 6
George, son of James & Ellen Goodall, Stanks, collier	Oct. 18, 1804	Jan. 27
Hannah, daug^{r} of William & Elizabeth Batty, Berwick, shoemaker	Dec. 27, 1804	Feb. 24
Richard, son of John & Elizabeth Jackson, Barwick, Chandler	Jan. 8	Feb. 24
James, son of John & Hannah Cullingworth, Barwick, shoemaker	Jan. 4	Feb. 24

Ann, daug^{r} of John & Mary Wheater, Barwick, Tailor	Dec. 30, 1804	Feb. 24
John, son of Christop^{r} & Faith Simpson, Barnbow, collier	Jan. 5	Mar. 3
Thomas, son of Thos & Elizabeth Barton, Barwick, Farmer	Feb. 15	Mar. 24
Ann, daug^{r} of Thomas & Mary Hudson, Stanks, Labourer	Feb. 25	Mar. 31
William, son of William & Mary Heaton, Barwick, Labourer	Feb. 21	Apl. 7
Barnabas, son of John & Elizabeth Hewitt, Barwick, collier	Mar. 24	Apl. 14
Jane, daug^{r} of William & Sarah Knapton, Barwick, Farmer	Jan. 3	Apl. 14
Thomas, son of James & Mary Dodd, Barwick, Labourer	Jan. 12	Apl. 14
John, son of John & Hannah Wood, Scholes, Labourer	Jan. 9	Apl. 14
Abraham, son of Matt^{w} & Mary Johnson, Scholes, collier	Jan. 8	Apl. 14
Thomas, son of Thomas & Elizabeth Carr, Kidhall, Innkeeper	Feb. 7	Apl. 15
Ann, daug^{r} of Leonard & Mary Cawood, Grimsdike, Shoemaker	Mar. 19	Apl. 15
Harriet, daug^{r} of John & Mary Smith, Engine, Labourer	Apl. 3	Apl. 28
James, son of John & Ann Todd, Barwick, Labourer	May 1	[May] 26
Hannah, daug^{r} of Joseph & Martha Kirkham, Barwick, Labourer	Jun. 9	[Jun.] 14
Thomas, son of Jeremiah & Ann Maud, Potterton, Labourer	May 13	Jun. 30
Elizabeth, daug^{r} of Rich^{d} & Eliz. Oxley, Barwick, Servant	Jun. 4	30
Amelia, daug^{r} of James & Alice Whitehead, Kidhall Lane, Malster	Apl. 26	Jul. 7
Benjamin, son of Saml & Abigail Watson, Kidhall Lane, Labourer	Jun. 11	Jul. 7
Jane, dau. of John & Sarah Clapham, Barwick, Farmer	Jun. 20	Jul. 14
Richard, son of Thomas & Margaret Waterton, Engine, Blacksmith	Jul. 10	Jul. 21
Thomas, son of John and Ann Johnson, Stanks, collier	Jul. 2	Jul. 28
Ann, daug^{r} of Thomas & Sarah Tilney, Scholes, Mason	Jun. 6	Aug. 4
Hannah, daug^{r} of James & Mary Hirst, Barwick, Labourer	Jul. 6	Aug. 4
Thomas, son of William & Mary Lindley, Barnbow, Labourer	May 21	Aug. 4
Mary & Martha, twin daug^{rs} of Saml & Sarah Hardesty, Winmoor, Labourer	[*blank*]	[*blank*]
George, son of James & Elizabeth Furness, Winmoor, Labourer	Jul. 24	Aug. 11
Elizabeth, daug^{r} of John & Eliz^{h} Thompson, Barwick, Labourer	Jul. 21	Aug. 11
Mary, daug^{r} of Joseph & Mary Wright, Barwick, Labourer	Jul. 9	Aug. 11
Elizabth, dau. of Thomas & Martha Collet, Barwick, Labourer	Jul. 19	Aug. 18
Mary, daug^{r} of Wm Wait & Martha Turner, Morwick, Labourer	Jul. 23	Sep. 1
John, son of Stephen & Elizth Flowett, Barwick, Labourer	Aug. 2	Sep. 8
Maria, bastard daug^{r} of Mary Hodgson, Scholes	Aug. 16	Sep. 29
Thomas, son of William & Christiana Watson, Lime kiln gate	Sep. 25	Oct. 20
John, son of Rich^{d} & Eliz^{h} Pease, Barwick, Collier	Jun. 13	Nov. 3

John, son of Matthew & Ann Varley, Barwick, Farmer	Aug. 20	Nov. 3
Ann, daug^{r} of Richard & Ellen Newby, Barwick, Farmer	Aug. 31	Nov. 3
Joseph Jenkinson, son of Isaac & Rebecca Ward, Scholes, Labourer	Oct. 11	Nov. 3
James, son of James & Tabitha Lumb, Barwick, Farmer	Sep. 28	Nov. 4
John, son of John & Mary Batty, Throstle nest in Aberford Parish	Sep. 10	Nov. 8
Peter, son of Francis & Betty Mountain, Morwick, Labourer	Oct. 12	Nov. 10
Mary, daug^{r} of James & Frances Barker, Penwell, Labourer	Oct. 7	Nov. 24
Joseph, son of Joseph & Mary Sparling, Kidhall Lane, Labourer	Oct. 10	Nov. 24
Ann, daug^{r} of George & Ann Connell, Barwick, Labourer	Nov. 6	Nov. 24
Maria, daug^{r} of William & Elizth Cullingworth, Barnbow, Labourer	Oct. 10	Dec. 1
James, son of James & Phebe Jackson, Barwick, Farmer	Oct. 25	Dec. 15

Baptisms, 1806.	Born	Bapt.
Thomas, son of Thos & Mary Parker, Barwick, Labourer	Nov. 18, 1805	Jan. 12, 1806
William, son of Willm & Martha Jenkinson, Grimesdike, Labourer	Jan. 4	Jan. 26
Alice, daug^{r} of Benjn & Mary Robshaw, Barwick, Labourer	Jan. 11	Feb. 16
Mary, daug^{r} of George & Sarah Johnson, Barwick, Labourer	Jan. 6	Feb. 23
James, son of James & Elizabeth Tomlinson, Barwick, Farmer	Dec. 15	Mar. 2
Sarah, daug^{r} of Thomas & Elizth Robshaw, Barwick, Labourer	Feb. 6	Mar. 9
James, son of Thos & Hannah Thompson, Barnbow, Collier	Mar. 2	Mar. 30
Elizabeth, daug^{r} of Willm & Mary Pickersgill, Barwick, Farmer	Jan. 22	Apl. 6
Sarah, daug^{r} of Benjn & Martha Stringer, Hilltop, Tailor	Feb. 22	Apl. 6
Maria, daug^{r} of James & Grace Derrick, Winmoor, Labourer	Feb. 23	Apl. 6
Rich^{d}, son of Joseph & Ann Turpin, Brownmoor, Labourer	Dec. 18, 1805	Apl. 13
William, son of William & Ann Burnell, Barwick, Farmer	Mar. 11	13
Joseph, son of Thos and Mary Todd, Barwick, Labourer	Mar. 29	Apl. 27
Rose, daug^{r} of Willm & Sarah Hudson, Barwick, Mill-wright	Mar. 18	Apl. 27
Ellen, daug^{r} of Thomas & Mary Wright, Scholes, Labourer	Jan. 9	May 4
Ann, daug^{r} of Thos & Elizabeth Cawood, Barnbow, Collier	Apl. 26	May 25
Richard, son of Richard & Ann Smith, Barwick, Farmer	May 11	May 25
Elizabeth, daug^{r} of William & Elizth Dickinson, Barwick, Labourer	May 2	Jun. 15
Thomas, son of William & Hannah Varley, Kidhall Lane, Farmer	May 17	Jun. 29
William, son of John & Sarah Whitehead, Barwick, Farmer	Jun. 3	Jul. 6
Ann, daug^{r} of John & Elizth Clemishaw, Winmoor, Farmer	May 27	Jul. 6

Ann, daugr of William & Elizth Haines, Barwick, Labourer	Mar. 7	Jul. 13
Richard and Robert, twin sons of Peter & Cathe Higgins, Bradford bottom, Labourer		Jul. 27
Ann, daugr of Joseph and Ann Speight, Scholes, Labourer	June 26	Jul. 27
Mary daugr of Willm & Mary Linley, Barnbow, Labourer,	May 13	Jul. 27
Elizabeth, daugr of Bennet & Mary Johnson, Barwick, Labourer		Aug. 3
Joseph, son of William & Hannah Beanland, Barwick, Tailor	Jun. 30	Aug. 8
Elizabeth, daugr of John & Elizabth Darby, Barnbow, Labour.	Jul. 10	Aug. 17
Susannah, daugr of Mattw & Dinah Watson, Barwick, Labourer	Jun. 17	Aug. 17
Sarah, daugr of James & Hannah Thompson, Barwick, Labourer	Aug. 1	Aug. 31
Ann, daugr of Willm and Ann Eastwood, Winmoor, Labourer	Jul. 18	Aug 31
John, son of Wm & Elizabeth Batty, Barwick, Shoemaker,	Aug. 17	Aug. 31
Martha, daugr of John & Ellen Simpson, Hilltop, Labourer	Sep. 5	Oct. 5
Mark Skelton, son of Nathan & Hannah Ward, Scholes, Shoemaker	Sep. 27	Nov. 2
Charlotte, daugr of Willm & Margaret Gough, Barwick, Carpenter	Oct. 20	Nov. 2
Ann, daugr of William & Hannah Robinson, Barnbow, Farmer	Oct. 7	Nov. 2
James, bastard son of Jane Osborn, Barwick	Oct. 20	Nov. 2
George, son of Robert & Elizth Dutton, Woodhouse, Farmer		Nov. 5
Sarah, daugh of John & Mary Batty of Throstle Nest in the Parish of Aberford, Farmer		Dec. 26
James, son of James and Ann Gill, Barwick, Labourer	Nov. 30	Dec. 28

1807.	Born	Bapt.
Benjamin, son of Thomas & Mary Morritt, Barwick, Labourer	Nov. 12, 1806	Jan. 11
William, son of John & Hannah Carr, Barwick, Inn-keeper	Nov. 17	Jan. 18
Ann, daugr of John & Hannah Cullingworth, Barwick, shoemaker	Nov. 1	Jan. 18
David, son of John & Elizabth Scholes, Barnbow, collier	Dec. 1	Jan. 25
Jane, daugr of John & Mary Wheater, Barwick, Tailor	Jan. 5	Feb. 1
Sarah, daugr of Wm & Elizabth Atak, Stanks, collier	Jan. 8	Feb. 1
Mary, daugr of Thos & Mary Hudson, Grimesdike, Labr	Jan. 18	Feb. 15
James, son of Wm & Mary Heaton, Barwick, Labourer	Dec. 19, 1806	Feb. 22
Henry Aaron, son of John & Sarah Gough, Potterton, Gardener	Jan. 21	Mar. 22
John, son of Joseph & Mary Lodge, Winmoor, Labourer	Jan. 30	Mar. 22
William and Jane, twin son & daugr of Benjn & Jane Thompson, Barwick, Collier	Feb. 13	Mar. 22
Thomas, son of John & Ann Richardson, Potterton, Shoemaker	Jan. 22	Mar. 30

John, son of Thomas & Ruth Sotheron, Potterton, Farmer Dec. 29, 1806 May 3
William Henry, son of W^m^ & Grace Salmon, Hilltop, Labourer Apl. 18 May 17
Ellen, dau. of Thos & Ann Stoner, Barwick, Miller Apl. 3 May 18
James, son of Josh & Sarah Wright, Barwick, Labourer May 6 Jun. 7
Elizabeth, dau. of Wm & Elizh Bramley, Barwick, Labourer Mar. 7 Jun. 14
Jane, dau. of Stephen & Elh Flowet, Barwick, Labourer May 1 Jun. 14
Mary, dau. of Saml & Sarah Hardisty, Winmoor, Labourer Aug. 16, 1806 Jun. 21
Mary, daughr of Richd & Eleanor Newby, Barwick, Farmer May 12 Jul. 5
Thomas, son of John & Elizh Hewitt, Barwick, Miner May 25 Jul. 5
Nanny, daughr of Richd & Mary Hewitt, Barwick, Miner May 13 Jul. 5
William, son of James & Mary Hirst, Barwick, Labourer Jun. 1 Jul. 12
Elizabeth, daughr of James & Phoebe Jackson, Barwick, Farmer Jun. 28 Aug. 16
Thomas, bastard son of Ann Robshaw, Barwick Jul. 14 Aug. 16
Benjamin, son of Geo. & Elizh Pickersgill, Grimesdike Jul. 11 Aug. 30
Ann, dau. of James & Elizh Furness, Labourer Aug. 30
John, son of Leonard & Mary Cawood, Grimesdike, Shoemaker Aug. 31
William, son of Wm & Chrissy Watson, Limekiln Gate, Labourer Aug. 16 Sep. 13
George, son of Thos & Sarah Tilney, Scholes, Mason May 31 Sep. 20
Ann, daughr of John & Hannah Wood, Scholes, Labourer Aug. 30 Sep. 27
Sarah, daughr of Thos & Elizh Wormald, Barwick, Blacksmith Oct. 9 Nov. 1
Joseph, son of James & Mary Mouncy, Youlton in ye Parish of Horn, Labourer Aug. 18 Nov. 1
William, son of James & Tabitha Lumb, Barwick, Farmer Oct. 26 Nov. 2
Ann, daughr of Bennet & Mary Johnson, Barwick, Labourer Nov. 10 Dec. 25
Jane, daughr of Henry & Sarah Thompson, Barwick, Labourer Nov. 10 Dec. 28

BAPTISMS, 1808. Born Bapt.

James, son of Wm & Rose Kitchingman, Colne, Shoemaker Dec. 10, 1805 Jan. 15, 1808
Eliza, daughr of Wm & Mary Linley, Engine, Labourer Dec. 19 Jan. 17
William, son of Wm & Elizh Batty, Barwick, shoemaker Nov. 28 Jan. 22
Sarah, daughr of Jas & Francis Barker, Penwell, Labourer Dec. 24 Jan. 24
John, son of Michael & Ann Walton, Barwick, Labourer Dec. 19 Jan. 24
Mary Ann, daughr of Isaac & Rebekah Ward, Scholes, Labourer Dec. 13 Jan. 24
Ruth, daughr of Matthew & Mary Johnson, Scholes, collier Aug. 29 Jan. 24
Harriet, daughr of John & Sarah Bleasby, Barwick, Carpenter Dec. 6 Jan. 31
Robert Hancock Stead, bastard son of Dinah Stead, Barwick Jan. 16 Jan. 31
Mary, daughr of Josh & Hannah Simpson, Brownmoor Jan. 8 Feb. 7

Sarah, daugh^{r} of Rich^{d} & Eliz^{h} Pease, Barwick, collier Jan. 11 Feb. 13
Mary, daugh^{r} of W^{m} & Sarah Hudson, Barwick, Millwright Nov. 15 Mar. 20
George, son of John & Ann Johnson, Stanks, Collier Mar. 4 Apl. 3
Sarah, daugh^{r} of Thos & Martha Marshall, Winmoor, Farmer Jan. 30 Apl. 11
Frances, daugh^{r} of Wm Waite Turner & Martha, his wife, Morwick, Labourer Feb. 29 Apl. 17
Mary, daugh^{r} of W^{m} & Eliz^{h} Cullingworth, Barwick, Labourer Mar. 28 Apl. 24
George, son of Geo. & Sarah Johnson, Barwick, Labourer Feb. 17 Apl. 24
Ruth, daugh^{r} of John & Eliz^{h} Clemishaw, Winmoor, Farmer Mar. 16 Apl. 24
Thomas Cowper, bastard son of Hannah Stead Apl. 9 May 1
Mary, daugh^{r} of George & Ann Connell, Barwick, Farmer Mar. 30 May 1
John, son of Thomas & Elizabeth Robshaw, Barwick, Woodman Apl. 16 May 15
Ann, daugh^{r} of John & Mary Jakeman, Potterton, Labourer Apl. 16 May 29
Abraham, son of W^{m} & Sarah Rawlinson, Barwick, Labourer May 3 Jun. 5
William, bastard son of Ann Atkinson, Poor-house May 5 Jun. 5
Ann, bastard daugh^{r} of Ellen Nettleton, Poor-house Apl. 24 Jun. 5
Isaac, son of Samuel & Sarah Hardisty, Winmoor, Labourer Feb. 26 Jun. 19
William & Sarah, Twin son & daugh^{r} of Thos & Eliz^{h} Barton, Barwick, Farmer Mar. 3 Jun. 19
Dinah, daugh^{r} of John & Mary Smith, Engine, Labourer May 16 Jun. 26
Matthew, son of Matthew & Ann Varley, Barwick, Farmer Apl. 2 Jul. 3
William, son of William & Sarah Turner, Stanks, Miner Aug. 27 Sep. 25
Elizabeth, daugh^{r} of John & Mary Batty, Throstle Nest, Parish of Aberford Sep. 30
Andrew, son of Thos & Elizth Cawood, Barnbow, Miner Oct. 5 Nov. 6
Ann, daugh^{r} of Thos & Mary Todd, Barwick, Labourer Sep. 16 Nov. 6
John, son of Roger & Mary Foster, Barwick, Tailor Aug. 15 Nov. 6
John, son of John & Eliz^{h} Thompson, Barwick, Labourer Aug. 31 Nov. 6
William, son of Rich^{d} & Ellen Newby, Barwick, Farmer Oct. 3 Nov. 6
Elizabeth, daugh^{r} of Ja^{s} & Hannah Thompson, Barwick, Labourer Oct. 2 Nov. 6
Elizabeth, daugh^{r} of John & Eliz^{h} Scholes, Barnbow, Labourer Sep. 3 Nov. 6
William, son of Rich^{d} & Ann Perkin, Barwick, Farmer Jun. 20 Nov. 6
Selina, daugh^{r} of Edmund & Ann Rawlinson, Barwick, Schoolmaster Jul. 21 Nov. 6
Mary, daugh^{r} of John & Ellen Simpson, Hilltop, Labourer Oct. 12 Nov. 27

BAPTISMS, 1809. Born Bapt.

John, son of William & Sarah Taylor, Stanks, Labourer Dec. 12, 1808 Jan. 8
Sarah, daug^{r} of Samuel & Sarah Lumb (or Thompson), Stanks, Lab^{r} Nov. 28 Jan. 15
John, son of John & Elizth Darby, Barnbow, Lab^{r} Dec. 24 Jan. 22
Fanny, daug^{r} of Nathan & Hannah Ward, Scholes, Shoemaker Jan. 2 22

Joseph, son of John & Hannah Carr, Barwick, Innkeeper Jan. 28 Feb. 8
Mary, daug^{r} of Joseph & Mary Sparling, Kidhall Lane, Lab^{r} Dec. 29 Feb. 19
George, son of Benjam^{n} & Mary Robshaw, Barwick, Lab^{r} Jan. 20 Feb. 26
Richard, son of William & Ann Wilson, Barwick, Lab^{r} Mar. 4 Mar. 4
Thos, son of John & Eliz^{h} Bean, Barwick, Shoemak^{r} Feb. 12 Mar. 12
Ann, daug^{r} of Thos & Ruth Sotheron, Potterton, Farmer Aug. 30, 1808 Mar. 19
George, son of W^{m} & Hannah Beanland, Barwick, Tailor Jan. 3 Apl. 2
George, son of George & Mary Gomersall, Barwick, Laborer Feb. 24 Apl. 2
Ann, daug^{r} of John and Ann Todd, Barwick, Labourer Dec. 28 Apl. 2
Ann, daug^{r} of George & Elizab^{h} Pickersgill, Grimsdike, Farmer Jan. 13 Apl. 2
Mary, daug^{r} of Robt & Ann Lenox, Potterton, Labourer Feb. 19 Apl. 2
Elizab^{h}, daug^{r} of Joseph & Ann Speight, Scholes, Labourer Apl. 17 Apl. 30
William, son of Thomas & Martha Collett, Barwick, Labourer Mar. 22 May 7
George, son of Joseph & Sarah Simpson, Brownmoor, collier Apl. 7 May 7
Ruth, daug^{r} of Thomas and Elizab^{h} Wormald, Barwick, Blacksmith Apl. 21 May 21
Ann, daug^{r} of Joseph & Ann Turpin, Brownmoor, Labourer Apl. 26 May 21
Thomas, son of James & Ann Gill, Barwick, Labourer Mar. 16 May 21
Hannah, daug^{r} of Joseph & —— Reader, Scholes, Labourer May 9 May 16
Hannah, daugh^{r} of Thomas & Mary Hudson, Grimsdike, Lab^{r} Apl. 28 May 28
Elizabeth, daugh^{r} of William & Hannah Robinson, Barnbow, Farmer Jun. 4 Jul. 16
Hannah, daugh^{r} of John & Sarah Clapham, Barwick, Lab^{r} Jun. 26 Aug. 6
George, son of John & Hannah Cullingworth, Barwick, Lab^{r} Apl. 26 Aug. 13
Thomas, son of Stephen & Eliz^{h} Flowet, Barwick, Lab^{r} Jul. 9 Aug. 27
Elizabeth, daugh^{r} of W^{m} & Mary Cheesebrough, Engine, Carpenter Aug. 15 Sep. 3
Mary, daugh^{r} of William & Mary Heaton, Barwick, Lab^{r} Aug. 9 Sep. 10
Jane, daugh^{r} of Thomas & Sarah Tilney, Scholes, Mason Apl. 9 Nov. 5
Thomas, son of Thos & Eliz^{h} Varley, Winmoor, Farmer Apl. 24 Nov. 5
Eliz^{h}, daugh^{r} of Rich^{d} & Beatrice Lumb, Barwick, Farmer Oct. 3 Nov. 5
Mary, daugh^{r} of W^{m} & Hannah Varley, Kidhall Lane, Farmer Feb. 23 Nov. 6
Richard, son of the Revd Thos Pullan, clerk, & Sarah, his wife, Barwick Sep. 21 Nov. 6
William, son of James & Phoebe Jackson, Barwick, Farmer Sep. 17 Dec. 22
David, son of John & Eliz^{h} Scholes, Barnbow, collier Nov. 12 Dec. 24
Mary, daugh^{r} of W^{m} & Mary Pickersgill, Barwick, Farmer Nov. 5 Dec. 25

1810. Born Bapt.

Mary, daugh^{r} of W^{m} & Ellen Scott, Stanks, Miller Dec. 16, 1809 Jan. 14
Thomas, son of Matthew & Ann Varley, Barwick, Farmer Dec. 11 Jan. 14

Peter, son of Saml & Sarah Lumb (or Thompson), Stanks, Lab^{r}	Dec. 23	Jan. 21
Mary, daugh^{r} of Jos$_{h}$ & Jane Jowet, Kidhall Lane, Lab^{r}	Dec. 27	Jan. 21
Mary, daugh^{r} of Henry & Sarah Thompson, Barwick, Lab^{r}	Dec. 28	Feb. 18
William, son of John & Hannah Wood, Scholes, Lab^{r}	Feb. 27	Mar. 31
John, son of James & Tabitha Lumb, Barwick, Farmer	Mar. 20	Apl. 8
Henry, son of Saml & Sarah Hardisty, Winmoor, Lab^{r}	Mar. 10	Apl. 15
Emma, daugh^{r} of John & Eliz^{h} Clemishaw, Winmoor, Farmer	Jan. 30	Apl. 29
George, son of George & Ann Connell, Barwick, Farmer	Mar. 16	Apl. 29
James, son of Thos & Eliz^{h} Robshaw, Barwick, Woodman	Apl. 7	Apl. 29
Jos$_{h}$, son of Matthew & Martha Hanley, Barnby in y^{e} Parish of Embrough	Nov. 26	May 20
Elizabeth, daugh^{r} of Nathl & Eliz^{h} Hanks, Potterton, Farmer		Jun. 3
Ruth, daugh^{r} of Thos & Ruth Sotheron, Potterton, Farmer	Mar. 17	Jun. 10
Ann, daugh^{r} of John & Eliz^{h} Hewitt, Barwick, Miner	Feb. 25	Jun. 12
John, son of John & Ann Richardson, Potterton, Shoemaker.	Jun. 14	Jul. 22
John, son of Benjn & Jane Thompson, Barwick, Miner	Mar. 22	Jul. 30
Charles, son of Bennet & Mary Johnson, Barwick, Lab^{r}	Jun. 6	Aug. 12
George, son of Joseph & Martha Scholes, Barnbow, Farmer	Jul. 4	Aug. 26
Elizabeth, daugh^{r} of W^{m} & Eliz^{h} Cullingworth, Barwick, Lab^{r}	Jul. 29	Aug. 26
Rachel, daugh^{r} of James & —— Barker, Penwell, Lab^{r}	Jul. 16	Sep. 2
Samuel, son of Thos & Martha Marshall, Winmoor, Farmer	Jul. 24	Sep. 2
Ann, daugh^{r} of Thos & Ann Teal, Grimesdike, Lab^{r}	Jul. 12	Sep. 2
Elizabeth, daugh^{r} of Jos$_{h}$ & Mary Richardson, Aberford, Shoemaker	Aug. 6	Sep. 2
William, son of Leonard & Mary Cawood, Grimesdike, Shoemaker	Sep. 16	Sep. 30
Ann, daugh^{r} of Joseph & Sarah Wright, Barwick, Lab^{l}	Aug. 30	Sep. 30
John Bell, son of James & Grace Derrick, Winmoor, Lab^{r}	Aug. 28	Oct. 14
Thomas, bastard son of Sarah Simpson, Barnbow	Sep. 12	Oct. 14
Ann, daugh^{r} of John & Ann Johnson, Seacroft in ye Parish of Whitkirk	Aug. 30	Oct. 14
Sarah, daugh^{r} of John & Alice Scruton, Barwick, Labr	Sep. 14	Oct. 14
Esther, daugh^{r} of George & Sarah Johnson, Barwick, Lab^{r}	Apl. 21	Oct. 28
Thomas, son of William & Ann Wilson, Barwick, Lab^{r}	Sep. 1	Nov. 4
Ruth & Rachel, twin daugh^{rs} of Thos & Eliz^{h} Barton, Barwick, Farmer	Oct. 3	Nov. 4
Beatrice, daugh^{r} of John & Sarah Bleazby, Barwick, Carpenter	Aug. 21	Nov. 4
Sarah, daugh^{r} of Rich$_{d}$ & Eliz^{h} Pease, Barwick, Collier	Jul. 13	Nov. 4
William, son of W^{m} & Eliz^{h} Bramley, Barwick, Lab^{r}	Aug. 23	Nov. 4
Sarah, daugh^{r} of Benjn & Mary Robshaw, Barwick, Lab^{r}	Sep. 26	Nov. 5
Mary, daugh^{r} of Robt & Eliz^{h} Dutton, Woodhouse, Farmer	Oct. 8	Nov. 11
Matthew, son of Matthew & Mary Johnson, Scholes, collier	Sep. 2	Nov. 11
Ann, daugh^{r} of W^{m} & Sarah Taylor, Stanks, Lab^{r}	Oct. 5	Nov. 25
William, son of W^{m} & Ellen Buchanan, Scholes, Lab^{r}	Nov. 5	Dec. 23

Baptisms, 1811.	Born	Bapt.
Thomas, son of John & Jane Crossland, Scholes, Gent.	Jun. 4 1807	Jan. 14
Elizh, daughr of John & Jane Crossland, Scholes, Gent.	Dec. 26 1808	Jan. 14
Mary, daughr of John & Jane Crossland, Scholes, Gent.	Aug. 11 1810	Jan. 14
Benjamin, Bastard son of Ann Thowley, Barwick	Jan. 10	Feb. 4
William, son of Josh & Mary Lodge, Winmoor, Labourer	Jan. 23	Feb. 24
John, son of Willm Waite & Martha Turner, Winmoor	Jan. 2	Feb. 25
Sarah, daughr of John & Ellen Simpson, Hill-top, Labr	Jan. 27	Mar. 10
Elizabeth, daughr of Edward & Betty Burley, Morwick, Dancing Master	Feb. 19	Mar. 10
Richard, son of Richd & Ellen Newby, Barwick, Farmer	Feb. 7	Mar. 10
Martha, daughr of Thos & Mary Hudson, Grimesdike, Labr	Jan. 6	Mar. 10
Elizabeth, daughr of John & Sarah Robshaw, Barwick, Labr	Feb. 11	Mar. 24
Joseph, son of John & Elizh Thompson, Barwick, Labr	Mar. 13	Apl. 21
William, son of Josh & Ann Simpson, Stanks, Miner	Apl. 14	May 12
George, son of William & Chrissy Watson, Limekiln Gates, Labr	May 6	Jun. 2
George, son of Richd & Beatrice Lumb, Barwick, Farmer	Mar. 17	Jun. 2
Nicholas, son of Thos & Sarah Tilney, Scholes, Mason	Jan. 24	Jun. 2
Charlotte, daughr of John & Mary Batty, Throstle Nest, parh of Aberford, Farmer	Feb. 11	Jun. 4
Ann, daughr of Wm & Rachel Goodall, Engine, Miner	Jun. 6	Jun. 23
Sarah, daughr of Geo. & Elizh Pickersgill, Grimesdike, Farmer	May 5	Jun. 30
William, son of Thos & Mary Todd, Barwick, Labr	Jun. 20	Aug. 4
Ann, daughr of Geo. & Mary Gomersall, Barwick, Labr	Jul. 11	Aug. 4
John, son of Edward & Mary Kilnar, Engine, Paper Maker	Jul. 18	Aug. 11
Mary, daughr of John Rothery & Martha Thompson, Hunslet, parh of Leeds, Cloth-maker	Nov. 13	Aug. 25
William, son of Thos & Sarah Linley, Hill-top, Labr	Aug. 22	Sep. 1
Sarah, daughr of Wm & Mary Heaton, Barwick, Labr	Aug. 19	Sep. 8
Hannah, daughr of Josh & Martha Kirkham, Barwick, Labr	Sep. 14	Nov. 3
George, son of Josh & Ann Reader, Scholes, Labr	May 23	Nov. 3
Thomas, son of Thos & Mary Wright, Scholes, Labr	Mar. 6	Nov. 3
Thomas, son of Wm & Elizh Batty, Barwick, Shoemaker	Aug. 30	Nov. 3
William, son of Roger & Mary Foster, Barwick, Taylor	May 26	Nov. 3
Hannah, daughr of John & Hannah Cullingworth, Barwick, Shoemaker	Oct. 10	Dec. 1
Mary, daughr of Stephen & Elizh Flowett, Barwick, Labr	Oct. 11	Dec. 29

Baptisms, 1812.	Born	Bapt.
Elizabeth, daughr of Thos & Margt Perkin, Barwick, Labr	Sep. 22	Jan. 5
William, son of Henry & Sarah Thompson, Barwick, Labr	Nov. 29	Jan. 26
Mary, daughr of Josh & Elizabeth Thompson, Barnbow, shoemaker	Nov. 26	Feb. 2
Elizabeth, daughr of William & Hannah Varley, Kidhall lane, Farmer	Jan. 4	Mar. 12

Joseph & Mary, twin son & daugh^{r} of Jos^{h} & Ann Turpin, Brownmoor, Lab^{r}	Mar. 27	Mar. 31
Fanny, daugh^{r} of Edwd & Susannah Farrar, Stanks, miner	Jan. 19	Apl. 19
Sarah, daugh^{r} of John & Sarah Whitehead, Barwick, Farmer	Feb. 21	Apl. 23
Eliza, daugh^{r} of Nathan^{l} & Eliz^{h} Hanks, Potterton, Farmer	Apl. 4	Apl. 27
Barnabas, son of Thos & Eliz^{h} Robshaw, Barwick, woodman	Jun. 13	Jul. 5
George, bastard son of Ann Teal, Green lane	Jun. 22	Jul. 5
Hannah, bastard daugh^{r} of Alice Slater, Barwick	Jun. 15	Jul. 19
Hannah, daugh^{r} of Rich^{d} & Eliz^{h} Oxley, Barwick, Lab^{r}	Jun. 6	Jul. 26
John, son of John & Hannah Wood, Scholes, Lab^{r}	May 13	Aug. 2
John, son of Thos & Eliz^{h} Cawood, Barnbow, Miner	Jul. 10	Aug. 9
Jane, daugh^{r} of Saml & Eliz^{h} Oates, Kidhall Lane, Joiner	Jun. 5	Aug. 9
James, son of Jos^{h} & Jane Jowett, Kidhall Lane, Lab^{r}	Jul. 19	Aug. 23
John, son of John & Hannah Pickersgill, Grimesdike, Lab^{r}	Jun. 23	Aug. 30
Jennet, daugh^{r} of John & Jane Crossland, Scholes, Gent.	Mar. 15	Sep. 6
Mary, daugh^{r} of Jos^{h} & Ann Speight, Scholes, Lab^{r}	Aug. 27	Sep. 13
Hannah, daugh^{r} of James & Frances Barker, Penwell, Farmer	Aug. 30	Oct. 18
John, son of Thos & Frances Eastwood, Scholes, Farmer	Mar. 16	Nov. 1
Peter, son of Rich^{d} & Ellen Newby, Barwick, Farmer	Sep. 21	Nov. 1
Charles, son of Rich^{d} & Eliz^{h} Pease, Barwick, Miner	Sep. 28	Nov. 1
Richard, son of William & Hannah Vincent, Barwick, Mason	Sep. 15	Nov. 1
Frances, daugh^{r} of Matthew & Ann Varley, Barwick, Farmer		Nov. 1
William, son of Jos^{h} & Martha Scholes, Barnbow, Farmer	Nov. 2	Nov. 12
Hannah, daugh^{r} of John & Sarah Roberts, Stanks, Lab^{r}	Oct. 31	Nov. 29
Phoebe, daugh^{r} of James & Phoebe Jackson, Barwick, Farmer	Aug. 15	Nov. 29
Faith, daugh^{r} of Charles & Eliz^{h} Turner, Barwick, Miner		Dec. 21
John, son of George & Sarah Johnson, Barwick, Lab^{r}	Nov. 24	Dec. 27

BURIALS, 1788.	Age.
William, son of Peter Nuby, Barwick, Octr 22.	16
John Barret, Poorhouse, Pauper, Octr 26.	92
James Bean, Barwick, Novr 5.	20
Mary Wilcock, Garforth Moorside, Decr 2^{d}.	81
Edward Monks, Barwick, Decr 10th.	62
Thomas Lowreman, Ingine, Decr 10th.	40
John Gaggs, Barnbow, pauper, Decr 11th	73
Elizabeth Doughty, Barwick, Decr 16th	74
Frances Barker, Penwell, Decr 25th.	61
William Brogdin, Poorhouse, pauper, Decr 30th	75
Sarah Barton, Leeds, Decr 31st	78

1789. Buried.	Age.
William, son of James Barker, Winmoor, Jany 23^{d}.	Infant
Elizabeth, daughter of Alvara Thompson, Winmoor, Jany 23.	11
Robert Smith, Barwick, Jany 31st.	92
James, bastard son of Lidia Simpson, Hiltop, Feby 1st.	Infant

Susannah, d^r of Thos Collet, Brownmoor, Feby 11th.	6
Sarah, d^r of Thos Collet, Brownmoor, Feby 11th.	2
William Norton, Barwick, Feby 15th.	6
John Forster, Barwick, Paupor, Feby 18.	27
John Challinger, Scholes, Feby 21st.	22
Chrissey Wormald, Barwick, March 5.	59
Robert, son of Luke Dawson, Barnbow, March 12.	Infant
Elizabeth, daughter of Thos Hewitt, Barwick, March 19.	Infant
Matthew Goulding, Poorhouse, pauper, March 27.	84
Martha Taylor, Barnbow, April 6th.	51
Joseph, son of William Smith, Barwick, April 24.	2
Frances Brooke, Scholes, April 27th.	34
Ann Boys, Thorner, pauper, May 1st.	
Sarah, d^r of Joseph Cauthorn, Barwick, May 6th.	1
Hannah, d^r of James Thompson, Barwick, May 26.	1
Matthew, son of Wm Watson, Barwick, May 30th.	2
Robert Poppleton, Barwick, pauper, June 13th.	80
George Sherrif, Barwick, June 20th.	23
Mary, daughter of Wm Robshaw, Barwick, June 29th.	2
Thos, son of John Cullingworth, Barwick, July 19.	1
Robert, son of Richard Brooke, Scholes, Ot^r 6.	2
Jane Miller, Kiddall lane, Nov. 7.	34
Matthew Upton, Morwick, Nov. 25th.	86
Richard Lowriman, Ingine, Decr 5.	9
Richard, son of John Connell, Barwick, Decr 9.	Infant
1790.	
Joseph Outhwaite, Lowmoor, pauper, February 2.	73
Henrey Green, Potterton, February 12.	23
Elizabeth Lumb, Barwick, February 19.	17
Thomas Moss, Kid-hall lane, February 20.	14
Hannah, da^r of Edward Goodall, Stanks, March 5.	1
George, son of John Hewitt, Barwick, March 12.	Infant
George Dungwith, Barwick, March 30.	29
Sarah, daughter of David Carter, Stanks, Apr. 3.	1
Elizabeth, daughter of Jonathan Taylor, Stanks, Apr. 24th.	7
Robert, son of John Loder, Kidall lane end, May 15th.	1
Richard Wood, Potterton, p., May 21.	25
Ann, daughter of John Gough, Potterton, June 3.	Infant
Frances Lowreman, Ingine, p., June 29.	4
Mary Connell, Kiddall-lane, July 6.	7
Ann Simpson, Poor House, p., July 12th	85
Abraham Logg, Scholes, p., July 13th	29
Abia. Lowreman, Ingine, p., July 16.	2
Mary, daughter of John Tillotson, Ingine, July 24.	Infant
William Smith, Barwick, July 25.	30
Frances, d^r of Major Brooke, Scholes, July 25.	9
William Lumb, Barwick, August 18.	89
Margret Ampshaw, Barwick, August 26.	49
John Logg, Scholes, p., August 30.	76
Alvara Thompson, Winmoor, Septr 3^d.	19

John Lidster, Barwick, Septr 27.	69
Richard Burland, Barwick, Octr 5.	82
Ann Haley, Scholes, p., Octr 24.	67
James Strother, Barwick, p., Octr 27.	82
Mary Beane, Barwick, Novr 21st.	64
Henrey Binns, Hiltop, p., Novr 27.	82
Ann, dr of Peter Slayter, Barwick, Decr 19.	Infant
Sarah Hawking, Scholes, Decr 19.	2
William Thompson, Winmoor, Decr 31.	7
1791.	
Mary Day, Potterton, March 5th.	61
John Thompson, Garforth moor, p., March 6.	79
John, son of John Goodall, Barnbow, March 10.	In.
Richard Jackson, Barwick, March 14th.	84
Grace Popplewell, Winmoor, March 21st.	71
Sarah Tilney, Ingine, March 27.	82
John Thompson, Lowmoor, March 29.	11
Mary Beedle, Poor House, p., April 29.	85
Mary Brown, Winmoor, April 29.	33
Thomas Smith, Huskhill, June 26.	62
Maria, dr of Mary Barton, July 12th.	Infant
Luke Dawson, Barnbow, August 8th.	50
Elizabeth Broadbent, poorhouse, Sep. 16th.	
Margret Bean, Barwick, Sept. 18.	25
Alice Outhwaite, Lowmoor, p., Octr 14th.	69
Thomas Lightfoot, Brownmoor, p., Octr 23.	89
William Slayter, Barwick, November 13th.	37
Mary Benton, Garforth moor, Decr 1st.	27
1792.	Age.
William Jowet, Barwick, Jan. 3d.	40
Elizabeth Whitehead, Garforth moor, p., Jany 23d.	100
Thomas Collet, Barwick, p., January 29th.	85
William, son of David Winn, Scholes, March 8.	3
Sarah Butler, Scholes, March 13th.	73
John, son of James Tillotson, Brownmoor, May 6th.	6
William, son of William Dunwell, Hiltop, May 17th.	7
Joseph Bullock, Barwick, May 26th	74
Peter Slayter, Barwick, June 25.	41
John Wood, Potterton, July 8th.	35
Benjamin Braim, Ingine, August 13th.	61
John Vary, Scholes, August 15.	85
Sarah, daughter of Thos Waite, Barwick, Septr 2d.	3
William Waite, Barwick, October 16th.	28
William Barker, Penwell, October 30th	43
Sarah Thompson, Penwell, Novr 18th	
Sarah Wright, poorhouse, p., Novr 26th	
Margret Dawson, Thorner, p., Nov. 27.	69
Ann Daniel, Barwick, Novr 30.	62
Sarah, dr of George Scholes, Barnbow, Decr 9.	7
Isabella Todd, Scholes, Decr 18th.	51
Thomas Kettlewell, Barnbow, Decr 23d.	6

1793.	Age.
Joseph, son of William Beanley, Barwick, Jan. 6.	Inf.
Johannah, dr of William Beanley, Jan. 6.	Infant
Susannah, dr of Samuel Thompson, Barnbow, Jan. 13th.	3
John, son of James Goodall, Barnbow, Jan. 27.	3
James Tillotson, Garforth moor, March 5th.	32
William Clarkson, Roundhay, March 6th.	102
Elizabeth, dr of William Burland, Barwick, March 9th.	6
George Smith, Barwick, March 13th.	53
Mary, dr of William Burland, Barwick, March 17th.	8
Deborah Robinson, Garforth moor, March 20th.	78
Martha, dr of John Mackontosh, Barwick, Mar. 23.	Infant
Sarah Thompson, Lowmoor, March 24th.	23
Hannah Norton, Barwick, April 8th.	4
Maria, dr of George Darton, Barwick, April 22d.	Infant
Ellin Goodall, Barnbow, April 24th.	33
William Wright, Winmoor, April 26.	21
Ann Shillito, Potterton, May 18th.	19
Richard Thompson, Lowmoor, June 2d.	18
James Lumb, Parlington, June 16th.	23
William, son of John Blackburn, Garforth moor, June 20th.	Infant
Elizabeth Goodall, Stanks, June 21st.	11
John Maxfield, Potterton, July 2d.	79
Ann Johnson, Barnbow, August 19th.	52
Martha Perkin, Barwick, October 14.	Infant
Leah Peurey, Aberford, October 19.	26
Elizabeth Tipling, Winmoor, October 30th.	78
Mary Perkin, Barwick, Decr 11th.	Infant
William Hodgson, Barnbow, Decr 17.	89
Matthew Norton, Barwick, Decr 19.	Infant
1794.	Age.
Elizabeth Shillito, Potterton, Jan. 11th.	61
Thomas Collet, Garforth, Jan. 15th.	57
George Watson, Barwick, Jany 21st.	88
Sarah Taite, Barwick, Jany 28th.	61
Thomas Thompson, poor House, March 4.	
Mary Lofthouse, Winmoor, March 9.	21
George Lowreman, Barwick, March 29.	15
Joseph Mather, Roundhay, April 15.	53
Charls Rawlinson, May 16th.	Infant
Hannah Hutton, Brownmoor, June 1st.	28
Jane Daniel, Potterton, June 7th.	50
Dorothay Burland, Barwick, June 8th.	83
William Haist, Roundhay, June 17th.	68
A Traviling Woman, July 14th.	
John Lumb, York, July 22d.	28
Richard Brooke, Scholes, July 31st.	18
Elizabeth, daughter of Wm Knapton, Barwick, August 3d.	Infant
William Smith, Barwick, August 6th.	35
Robert Simpson, Poorhouse, Septr 14.	92
Elizabeth Wood, Potterton, Decr 9th.	60

1795.	Age.
Ann Watson, Barwick, Jan. 5th.	19
John Benton, Brownmoor, Jan. 21st.	18
Willm Tillotson, Garforth moor, Feb. 5th.	23
Margret Tillotson, Garforth moor, Feb. 5th.	25
David Carter, Stanks, March 9.	43
Willm, son of Willm Beanley, Barwick, March 11.	Infant
Andrew Burdsill, Scholes, March 19.	82
Willm Barker, Penwell, March 23.	79
Martha, dr of Richard Shillito, March 29.	In.
Richard Tillotson, Barwick, April 1st.	7
Hannah Benton, Garforth moor, May 14th.	12
Ann Thompson, Garforth moor, May 24.	17
Martha Varey, Barwick, June 3d	
Edward Ellerker, Roundhay, June 7th.	72
John Cauwood, Winmoor, June 17th.	Infant
Sarah Dean, Kidall-lane end, June 23.	15
John Pickard, Potterton, June 24t.	13
Christopher Varey, Barwick, Augt 2.	69
John, son of David Whin, Scholes, Angut 11th.	Infant
Sarah Waite, Barwick, August 19.	55
Mary, dar of Richard Dungwith, Barwick, August 20.	Infant
Ann Braim, Barwick, Septr 22	
Isabella Harrison, poorhouse, Septr 27.	70
Henrey Goodall, Barnbow, Octr 14th.	12
William Staincliff, Lowmoor, Octr 18th.	70
Mary Watson, Barwick, Octr 31st.	88
BURIALS, 1796.	
Nicolas Tilney, Scholes, Jany 29th.	75
Mary Hanson, Seacroft, Febr 5.	22
David, son of Joseph Cawthorn, Barwick, March 3d.	Infant
Hester Higgens, Barwick, March 9th.	63
Hannah Popplewell, Winmoor, April 7th.	47
Sarah, dr of John Groves, Barwick, April 12th.	Infant
Ann Linley, Ingine, April 15.	16
William Wood, Potterton, May 6th.	18
Rachael Hutchinson, Barwick, May 12,	54
William, son of Wm Clough, Barwick, June 8.	Infant
William Watson, Thorner, June 25.	72
Harriet Green, Scholes, July 18th.	2
Elizabeth Shillito, Kidhall lane, July 23d.	27
John Tayler, Stanks, July 28.	1
Ann Shillito, Kidhall lane end, August 8.	Infant
Jane Upton, Scholes, August 15th.	Infant
Ann Rawlinson, Barwick, August 21st.	1
George Haist, Barwick, August 22.	5
Jonothan Bell, Thorner, Septr 15th.	95
Mary Lumb, Barwick, Septr 28th.	Infant
William Brown, Scholes park, Octr 16	10
Ann Logg, Poorhouse, Octr 17.	86

1797.	Age.
Elizabeth Helsworth, Thorner, Jan. 3.	
[*blank*] Carter, Stanks, January 22d.	18
John Copley, Barwick, January 22d.	Infant
Ann Hemsworth, Kidall lane end, Jan. 27.	53
John Hague, Knazebrough, Jan. 28.	67
Thomas Shillito, Potterton, January 29.	69
Ann Dixon, Barnbow, February 7.	
Ellin Wright, Winmoor, March 1st	
Hannah Goodall, Stanks, March 9th.	1
William Settle, Barwick, April 5th.	26
James Thompson, Barwick, April 8th.	1
Mary Ann Goodall, Barnbow, April 12th.	Infant
John Batty (clerk), Barwick, April 13th.	53
Jane Moss, Kiddle lane, April 17th.	31
Elizabeth Goodall, Barnbow, April 21th.	8
Ann, dr of Widow Slayter, Barwick, April 29th.	12
Elizth, dr of John Smith, Barwick, May 21th.	1
James, son of John Mackintosh, Barwick, May 18th.	1
Eleanor, dr of Joseph Scott, Aberford, June 25.	Infant
Elizabeth, wife of George Pickersgill, Grimsdike, June 25.	21
John, son of John Tillotson, Barwick, July 10.	Infant
Mary Jackson, Barwick, July 14th.	101
Joseph, son of Wm Beanley, Barwick, July 16th.	2
Mary, wife of Wm Simpson, Manston, Aug. 15.	58
Samuel, son of Saml Simpson, Barnbow, Sepr 5.	19
Mary-Anne, dr of Wm & Mary Collet, Garforth, Sepr 13.	Infant
Edward, son of Edward Goodall, Stanks, Sepr 24.	Infant
John Tillotson, Barwick, Octr 3.	35
James Bean, Leeds, Novr 27.	36
Mary, wife of William Batty, Barwick, Novr 30.	26
Ann Upton, Scholes, Decr 5.	85
Thomas Benton, Brown Moor, Decr 13.	58
Mary Dogshon, Seacroft, Decr 17.	90
Rebecca, wife of Matthew Watson, Barwick, Decr 17	

Burials, 1798.	Age.
William Clapham, Poor house, Jany 18.	64
Sarah, dr of Peter Hanson, Seacroft, Feb. 18.	2
Hannah, dr of Saml & Ann Simpson, Barnbow, March 2.	18
Alice, dr of Thos & Ann Stoner, Barwick, Mar. 6.	2
John Norton, Barwick, Mar. 8.	68
Ann Tillotson, Barrowby lane end, Mar. 25.	65
Robert, son of Jonathan Taylor, Stanks, April 1.	Infant
Thomas, son of Thomas Goodall, Engine, April 4.	18
Joseph Todd, Scholes, May 1	55
John Clarkson, son of Col. Richard Brooke, Scholes, May 8.	12
Joseph, son of John & Maria Cullingworth, Barwick, Shoemaker, May 22.	12
Elizabeth, dr of George Pickersgill, Grimsdike, cart driver, May 22.	Inf.

Benjamin, son of Edward Goodall, Stanks, May 27. 14
Mark Carew, Barwick, May 30. 46
George, son of William Walton, Barwick, June 14. Infant
Frances, dau^{r} of William Dunwell, Hill-top, June 24. 15
George, son of William Rawlinson, Barwick, June 25. 5
Elizabeth, dau^{r} of Joseph Walton, Barwick, July 4. 14
Joseph Settle, Barwick, July 13. 70
Joanna Horner, Barwick, Augt 5. 67
Henry Simpson, Hill-top, Augt 9. 60
John Tillotson, Barrowby-lane-end, Augt 30. 64
Elizabeth (run over by a cart), D^{r} of Thos Collet, Barwick, Sepr 24. 1
Hannah, wife of Samuel Lumb, Stanks, Octr 25. 74
Mary, wife of John Rawden, Hilltop, Novr 24th. 63

BURIALS, 1799. Age.

James Jackson, Barwick, Feby 5. 60
Elizabeth, dau^{r} of John Dean, Grimsdike, Feby 7. 1
*The Revd Robt Deane, B.D., late Rector of y^{s} Parish, Feby 9. 63
Hannah, dau^{r} of John Dean, Grimsdike, Feby 10. 3
Joseph Dawson, Scholes, Feby 22. 82
Sarah, dau^{r} of Francis Moss, Kidhall lane, Feby 28. 25
Ann, wife of Roger Brownrigg, Scholes, March 3. 51
Hannah, dau^{r} of Thomas Waite, Barwick, March 3. 1
Roger Bell, Barwick, March 13. 81
John, son of Joseph Kirkham, Barwick, March 16. Infant
Sarah, dau^{r} of Jonathan Richardson, Winmoor, March 22. Infant
Elizabeth Varley, Poorhouse, April 19. 51
Joseph Jaques, Poorhouse, April 30. 53
Ann Varley, Barwick, May 10. 80
John, son of Matthew Varley, Barwick, May 22. Infant
Mary, wife of John Barker, Barrowby lane end, June 10. 32
James, son of William Buchanan, Scholes, June 12. Infant
Ann, wife of Matthew Varley, Barwick, June 17. 31
Hannah, wife of John Butler, Scholes, June 19. 42
Mary, dau^{r} of Joseph Goodall, Barnbow, July 19. 38
†Richard Brooke, Esqr, Scholes, Lieutenant Colonel of the 3rd regiment of dragoon Guards, July 20. 55
Christiana Simpson, Scholes, Aug. 15. 20
James, son of John Barker, Barrowby lane end, Aug. 25. 1
Mary Hirst, Barnbow, Octr. 27 50
Samuel Simpson, Scholes, Novr 14. 76

*Rector 1772-99 St. John's College, Camb, B A, 1756, M A, 1759, S T.B, 1767. Presented to Barwick 13 March, 1772, and to Castleford 14 March, 1772 "On Wednesday last died, at his Rectory at Barwick in-Elmet, the Rev. Rob. Deane, B D, the humane and benevolent Rector of Barwick and of Kirkbramwith, in the Deanery of Doncaster He was formerly Fellow of St. John's College in Cambridge, and Preceptor to the present Earl of Clarendon and his Brothers; to whose father, the late Earl, when Chancellor of the Dutchy Court of Lancaster, he owed his preferments. He married Miss Marriot, daughter of the Rev Dr. Marriot, late Rector of Darfield, near Barnsley, who survives him His upright conduct, and mild conciliating manners, deserved and secured to him the friendship and affection of a very numerous list of respectable characters; by whom, and by his parishioners (particularly the poor), he will be much lamented." *Leeds Intelligencer*, 11 Feb. 1799.

†Colonel Brooke (1742-1799), was the son of James Brooke of Killingbeck, (1712-1766) He married first, Frances, dau. of the Rev Richard Brooke, by whom he had George Charles Brooke, Lieutenant 20th Regiment of Foot, killed in the battle of Vimiera, 21 August, 1808, James Croft Brooke, of Littlethorpe, near Ripon, and 6 other children, and secondly, Jane Marcella, dau. of the Rev. Dr. Drake. See Platt & Morkill's *Whitkirk*, p. 84.

Elizabeth Addeman, Scholes, Dec. 6.	87
Elizabeth, daur of John Walton, Barwick, Decr 19.	16
Catherine Abbott, Barwick, Decr 26.	91

Burials, 1800.	Age.
Mary Taite, Poorhouse, Jany 24.	85
Susanna, daur of Thomas Bailey, Lazingcroft, Feby 9.	30
Hannah, daur of William Copley, Barwick, Feby 22.	1
Martha Patterson, Winmoor, Feby 23.	82
Hannah, daur of Thomas Goodall, Engine, April 28.	12
Thomas & Hannah, son & daur of John Todd, Barwick, April 30.	Infants
James, son of William Clayton, Engine, May 2.	1
John Butler, Scholes, May 17.	76
Renton Haist, Barwick, June 23.	55
Elizabeth, daur of Richard Watson, Winmoor, July 1.	20
John Walton, Barwick, July 18.	84
Mary, wife of James Mallory, Rounday, July 21.	84
Joseph Holmes, Barwick, July 25.	84
Charles Pickard, Barwick, July 25.	15
Martha Wilcock, Poorhouse, Aug. 1.	60
Jonathan, son of John Hemsworth, Barwick, Aug. 13.	15
Matthew Riley, Brownmoor, Aug. 24.	33
Miles Hampshaw, Barwick, Sep. 26.	86
Margaret, wife of William Dunwell, Hill-top, Octr 2.	55
William, son of Richard Lumb, Barwick, Octr 25.	23
William, son of Ann Maud, Rounday, Octr 26.	Infant
Ann, wife of John Robinson, Barwick, Octr 28.	81
*Richard Lumb, Barwick, Decr 11.	63

Burials, 1801.	
Samuel Lumb, Stanks, Feby 18.	71
Sarah, daur of Thomas Robshaw, Barwick, Feby 26.	Infant
Elizabeth Dungwith, Barwick, March 16.	75
William, son of William Copley, Barwick, March 20.	Infant
Ann Norton, Rounday, April 29.	65
Sarah, wife of John Connell, Barwick, May 9.	53
George Reder, Scholes, May 10.	67
Ruth, daur of Joseph Scott, Aberford, May 27.	5
Sarah Taite, Barwick, May 29.	80
James, son of Richard Perkin, Barwick, June 1.	Infant
Richard Smith, Barwick, June 14.	75
William, son of John Robshaw, Barwick, July 5.	Infant
John Rawlinson, Seacroft, July 18.	60
Benjamin Hill, Scholes, July 23.	87
James, son of Thomas Parker, Barwick, Aug. 7.	3
Mary, wife of Thomas Haily, Scholes, Aug. 8.	77
Dorothy Allen, Knaresborough, Octr 3.	70
Francis Moss, Womersley, Oct. 4.	64
Grace, daur of Ephraim Jolly, Barwick, Oct. 5.	Infant

*On Monday last died, aged 63, Mr. Richard Lumb, of Barwick-in-Elmet, near this town; a man universally regretted by all who knew him *Leeds Intelligencer*, 15 Dec., 1800

William Carr, Kidhall lane, Oct. 26.	69
Richard Green, Scholes, Dec. 11.	52

BURIALS, 1802.	Age.
Margaret Stancliff, Winmoor, Jany 6.	76
Mary, wife of Abraham Bell, Langwith, Jany 6.	56
Thomas Haley, Scholes, Jany 14.	81
William Tipling, Stanks, Jany 29.	83
Sarah, daug^{r} of Willm Batty, Barwick, Feby 1st	Infant
Abraham Bell, Langwith, Feby 24.	59
Ann Benson, Barwick, March 1st	36
John Taite, Barwick, March 13.	72
Richard Braim, Barnbow Car, March 15.	82
Mary Jackson, Barwick, April 29.	21
Sarah, daug^{r} of John Robshaw, Barwick, May 16^{h}	Infant
Mary, wife of John Robshaw, Berwick, June 18.	22
Beatrice Wrigglesworth, Berwick, June 18.	58
Thomas Whitehead, Berwick, June 26.	79
Robert Gray, Amstead, July 19.	37
Jeremiah Lumb, Scholes, July 23^{d}	62
William, son of Thos Tillotson, Barrowby Lane end, July 24.	4
William Richardson, Potterton, July 25.	59
Robt, son of George Pickersgill, Grimesdike, Augt 13.	Infant
George Scholes, Barnbow, Augt 14.	69
Joseph Kirkham, Barwick, Augt 15.	75
Dorothy Lumb, Stanks, Augt 15.	73
Martha Simpson, Hill Top, Sepr 2^{d}	28
James, son of Ja^{s} Hirst, Barwick, Octr 11.	1
Joseph, son of Willm Beanland, Barwick, Octr 16.	Infant
Elizth, daug^{r} of John Scholes, Barnbow, Octr 25.	1
Hannah Atkinson, Barwick, Octr 27.	60
Hannah Kirkham, Barwick, Novem^{r} 22.	73
Elizab^{h}, daug^{r} of Chr: Simpson, Barnbow, Novr 22^{d}	1

BURIALS, 1803.	Age.
Benjamin Stringer, Hill Top, January 9^{h}.	85
John, son of Thos Morritt, Barwick, January 25th.	Infant
Mary, wife of Thomas Taylor, Barwick, March 4.	85
James, son of William Knapton, Barwick, March 7.	Infant
Robert Stubbs, Barwick, March 10.	74
Sarah, wife of John Loder, Kiddall Lane, March 20.	50
Anthony Dunwell, Barwick, March 23.	65
Grace Hill, Scholes, March 27.	90
John, son of William Jackson, Barwick, March 27.	Infant
Richard Shippen, Speakley-Nook, April 6.	91
William Dunwith, Barwick, Poor House, April 10.	45
Mary Eastburn, Speakley Nook, April 12.	76
Judith, wife of Thos Pickersgill, Grimesdike, April 17.	57
John, son of Richard Pease, Barwick, April 19.	1
Hannah, wife of Thos Waite, Barwick, April 24.	36
Elizabeth, wife of Willm Whitehead, Leeds, April 27.	42
James, son of John Butler, Scholes, Augt 13.	4

Mary, wife of Joseph Upton, Grimesdike, Augt 25.	55
Mary, daugh^{r} of James Batty, Barwick, Augt 30.	3
John, son of James Tomlinson, Barwick, Augt 31.	Infant
Ann, daug^{h} of Willm Bell, Hill-top, Sepr 2^{d}.	19
Jonathan, son of Matt^{w} Johnson, Scholes, Sep^{br} 21.	Infant
Jane, wife of Robt Wheater from York, Septr 24.	54
Mary, wife of James Thompson, Barwick, Septr 30.	49
Richard, son of William Knapton, Barwick, Octr 8.	2
Thomas Parker, Barwick, Octr 23^{d}.	65
Alice Jowet, Barwick, Novr 7.	51
George Gill, Kiddall Lane end, Novr 10.	73
Elizabeth, wife of Richard Pease, Barwick, Decr 22^{d}.	30

BURIALS, 1804.	Age.
Sarah Knapton, Barwick, Jany 27.	82
Elizabeth, daug^{r} of Richd Dungwith, Barwick, Jany 29.	7
Benjamin, son of George Blackburn, Stanks, Jany 30.	Inf^{t}
Benjamin, son of William Batty, Barwick, March 15.	Infant
John Cawthorn, Barwick, April 3^{d}.	26
Joseph Thackeray, Barwick, April 12.	64
John, son of Richard Dungwith, Barwick, April 25.	5
Ann, wife of George Daughill, Barwick, June 5.	38
Bennet Johnson, Barnbow, 14th June.	70
Mary, daug^{r} of Joseph Upton, Grimsdike, 18th July.	11
John Thompson, Barwick, 7th Sept^{r}.	60
Ellen, daug^{r} of James Furness, Winmoor, 23^{d} Sept^{r}.	Infant
Benjamin Cook, Stanks, 21st Oct^{r}.	81
Sarah, daug^{r} of John Wheater, Barwick, 16th Dec^{r}.	2

N.B.—The Revd William Hodgson, School Master of Barwick, died accidentally on Tuesday night the 27th of Novr in a Field near Roundhay, the body was not found till Thursday afternoon the 29th of Novr 1804. Buried at Aberford. [*Note on fly leaf.*]

BURIALS, 1805.	Age.
James, son of George Daughill, Barwick, 11th Jan^{y}.	1
Mary Scholes, Barnbow, 12 Jan^{y}.	68
David Buchanan, Scholes, 12^{h} February.	84
Alice Chippendale, Kidhall, 17^{h} Feb^{y}.	79
Martha, daug^{r} of Saml Thompson, Barwick, 4th March	Infant
Thomas Wait, Barwick, 8^{h} March.	39
William, son of John Thompson, Barwick, 31st March.	2
Ann, daug^{r} of James Batty, Barwick, 7^{h} April.	2
Mary, wife of John Walton, Barwick, 2^{d} May.	60
William, son of Thos Todd, Barwick, 7^{h} May.	3
James, son of John Cullingworth, Barwick, June 5.	12
Sarah Wright, Morwick, June 19.	89
Hannah, daug^{r} of Joseph Kirkham, Barwick, June 21.	Infant
Ruth, daug^{r} of John Butler, Scholes, June 26.	20
Mary & Martha, twin daug^{rs} of Saml Hardesty, Winmoor, Augt 7	Infants
Hannah, daug^{r} of John Hewitt, Barwick, Augt 23.	6
Robert Brown, Winmoor, Septr 3.	42

Rich^{d}, son of Mary Simpson, Barnbow, Septr 14.	Infant
John, son of Joseph Speight, Scholes, Septr 27.	1
*George Holmes, Barwick, Octr 6.	62
Faith, wife of Christ^{r} Simpson, Barnbow, Octr 11.	24
Mary, daug^{r} of Thos Tilney, Scholes, Novr 17.	4
BURIALS, 1806.	Age.
Mary, wife of Robt Smith, Barwick, Jany 5.	88
Thos Taite, Barwick, Jany 10.	71
Mary, wife of Robt Greenwood, Shippen, Jany 12.	65
John, son of John Batty, Throstle nest, Jany 19.	Infant
Francis Linley, Hill top, Feby 11.	45
Thomas Roebuck, Potterton, Feby 25.	40
Joseph, son of Thos Todd, Scholes, Feby 27.	25
Martha Roebuck, Potterton, Feby 28.	40
James Fletcher, Garforth, March 14.	56
Thomas Thompson, Barnbow, March 30.	33
John Hutchinson, Barwick, April 2.	74
John Loder, Kidhall Lane, April 4.	61
Willm, son of Ja^{s} Thompson, Barwick, Ap^{l} 6.	7
Joseph Strother, Barnbow, April 7.	87
William Thompson, Syke House, April 20.	31
Thos Milner, Roundhay, May 11.	22
Ann Smith, Barwick, May 24.	78
Samuel Lumb, Stanks, May 28.	69
Samuel Thompson, Barnbow, June 9^{h}.	60
James Tomlinson, Barwick, June 23^{d}.	39
Gabriel Tomlinson, Scholes, June 24^{h}.	77
John Walton, Barwick, July 2^{d}.	58
Sarah, wife of Job Hodgson, Scholes, July 6.	52
Joseph, son of Benjn Stringer, Hill-top, July 17.	9
John, son of John Wood, Scholes, July 20.	1
William Chaloner, Scholes, July 23.	70
Ann Batty, Barwick, August 9.	97
Dorothy Dean, Winmoor, Septr 6.	78
John, son of Wm Batty, Barwick, Septr 11.	Infant
Eliz^{h}, daug^{r} of Bennet Johnson, Barwick, 25^{h}.	Infant
John Clark, Seacroft, Octr 22.	70
—— Clark, Seacroft, Novr 1st.	60
John, son of John Wilson, Roundhay, Novr 9.	Infant
Hannah, daug^{r} of Saml Thompson, Garforth moorside, Novr 9.	7
James Wright, Barwick, Novr 30.	70
William Addeman, Barwick, Decr 2.	63
Mary, daughter of John Crossland, Scholes, Decr 4.	1
John, son of Matt^{w} Varley, Barwick, Decr 8.	1
Joseph, son of Joseph Pease, Barwick. ——	Infant

*By his will proved 29 Sept. 1805, he gave to his sister Jane, the wife of William Addiman, three closes, then in one, called Beckhay Bridge Closes, late the estate of his sister, Anne Horner. Real estate in Barwick, unto his wife, Elizabeth, for life, and after her decease unto Thomas Wood and John Clayton the younger, both of Kippax, gentlemen, upon trust to sell and divide the proceeds in ninths between his cousins, George Atkinson, George Clarkson and his sister, William Prince of York, William Fentiman of York, Stephen Gant of Tockwith, Thomas Gant his brother, George Ellingworth of Beal, Jane Ellingworth his sister, and Sarah Slaytor of Leeds.

Burials, 1807.	Age.
Charles Wood, Barwick, Jany 17.	32
Hannah Reader, Scholes, February 22.	83
William Clough, Barwick, March 19.	42
Ann, daug^{r} of Thos Goodall, Engine, March 22.	13
William Clayton, Engine, March 25.	81
Edward Day, Barwick, April 2.	78
Sarah, daug^{r} of Ben^{n} Stringer, Hilltop, April 5.	1
William Atkinson, Barwick, April 7.	41
Willm, son of Thos Todd, Scholes, April 23.	21
Frances, daugh^{r} of James Barker, Penwell, June 5.	18
Mary Clarkson, daugh^{r} of Grace Hemsworth, Barwick, July 5.	26
Ann Lumb, Barwick, Ang^{t} 19.	50
Mary, wife of Geo. Gummersall, Barwick, Augt 21.	81
Mary, wife of Benjn Shillito, Stanks, Sept. 11.	74
Henry Pickard, Barwick, Octo. 6.	84
David, son of John Scholes, Barnbow, Octo. 15.	Infant
Rich$_{d}$ Dungwith, Barwick, Octo. 20.	44
Joseph, son of John Goodall, Barnbow, Nov. 5.	4
Martha, wife of Benjn Stringer, Hill top, Nov. 7.	30
Mary Clayton, Engine, Nov. 19.	70
Mary Lunn, Brown-moor-bottom, Nov. 21.	20
John Goodall, Barnbow, Nov. 22.	50
William Woolley, Barnbow, Nov. 25.	2
William, son of Wm Burland, Aberford, Dec. 6.	2
Mary, wife of John Robshaw, Barwick, Decr 8.	27
Beersheba Wright, Barwick, Decr 9.	70
Burials, 1808.	**Age.**
William, son of Wm Bramley, Barwick, Jany 15	3
Robert Avison, Scholes, Jany 20.	61
Eliz^{h}, wife of Peter Porter, Old Staith, Par^{h} of Aberford, Jany 22.	76
John, son of John Mawkin, Garforth, March 1.	1
Benjn, son of Geo. Pickersgill, Grimesdike, March 6.	Inf^{t}
El^{h}, daugh^{r} of Wm Linley, Engine, May 4.	Inf^{t}
William Waite, Barwick, May 10.	90
Samuel Shippen, Speakley Nook, June 7.	66
Mary, wife of Jos^{h} Goodall, Barnbow, July 4.	84
Benjn Jackson, Barwick, July 10.	
John Wood, Potterton, July 30.	78
Sarah Vevers, Scholes Park, Sept. 9.	74
Joseph, son of Jos$_{h}$ Jowet, Kidhall Lane, Octo. 12.	Infant
Mary, daugh^{r} of Jos$_{h}$ Simpson, Brownmoor, Octo. 16.	Infant
Ruth, daugh^{r} of Abr^{m} Wormald, Barwick, Nov. 15.	7
Thomas Carr, Kidhall Lane, Dec. 3.	36
Sarah, daugh^{r} of John Brogden, Scholes, Dec. 8.	11
1809.	**Age.**
Robert Smith, Barwick, Jany 11.	88
Elizab^{h}, wife of James Furniss, Winmoor, Jany 15.	30
George, son of James Gill, Barwick, Jany 27.	5
Sarah, d^{r} of Saml Lumb or Thompson, Stanks, Feby 12.	Inf^{t}
Eliz^{h}, d^{r} of Joseph Speight, Kidhall Bar, Feby 15.	18

Elizab^{h}, wife of Peter Benson, Scholes, February 22.	43
Rich^{d}, son of Willm Wilson, Barwick, March 5.	Inf^{t}
William Womack, Barwick, April 16.	23
Hannah Thompson, Barwick, April 19.	63
George Dickinson. Barwick, April 23.	38
Alice, wife of Wm Robshaw, Barwick, May 2.	63
Hannah, wife of Thos Hargrave, Roundhay, May 5.	76
Hannah, daug^{r} of Joseph Reader, Scholes, May 25.	Infant
Mary, daug^{r} of Hannah Hodgson, Scholes, June 9.	3
Jane, daugh^{r} of John Monks, Stanks, June 26.	19
William, son of Roger Brownrigg, Scholes, July 6.	22
Ann Linley, Hilltop, Augt 5.	54
John, son of John Gough, Potterton, Augt 7.	20
W^{m}, son of Mary Bramham, Barwick, Augt 25.	Inf^{t}
John, son of John Thompson, Barwick, Augt 27.	Inf^{t}
Joseph Upton, Grimesdike, Septr 8.	56
James, son of Eliz^{h} Tomlinson, Barwick, Sept. 24.	3
Alice Kemp, Kidhall, Octo. 3.	70
Eliz^{h}, daugh^{r} of Ja^{s} Thompson, Barwick, Octo. 4.	1
Jane, wife of Jos$_{h}$ Simpson, Stanks, Octo. 6.	23
Sarah, daugh^{r} of Rich$_{d}$ Pease, Barwick, Octo. 24.	1
Mary, wife of Jos^{h} Sparling, Kidhall lane, Octo. 25.	35
*Thomas Charles Gascoigne, Esqre, son of Sir Thos Gascoigne, Bar^{t}, Parlington, Octo. 28.	23
Mary Tomlinson, Scholes, Octo. 31.	77
James, son of Jos$_{h}$ Sparling, Kidhall-Lane, Nov. 14.	11
Mary Jackson, Barwick, Dec. 6.	67
1810.	Age.
Ann Waite, Barwick, Jan. 7.	88
Thos Taylor, Barwick, Jan. 11.	88
John Jackson, Scholes, Jan. 22.	71
Joseph Goodall, Barnbow. Jan. 23.	86
Ann, wife of Wm Copley, Barwick, Feb. 11.	43
William, son of Thos Morritt, Barwick, Feb. 12.	Inf^{t}
†Sir Thos Gascoigne, Bar^{t}, Parlington, Feb. 17.	65

*His death was caused by an accident in hunting, and he expired 20th October, at Walling Wells Notts., the seat of Sir Thomas White, Bart.

"About a mile from cover, the hounds passed the village of Woodset, near Worksop, near which are many small inclosures, the fences abound with timber. Mr Gascoigne was unfortunately first, Lord Scarbro's whipper-in next, but very near, and seeing Mr. Gascoigne about to leap the fence, on the other side of which was a bog, he exclaimed *a bog! a bog!* On hearing this, Mr. Gascoigne suddenly stopped his horse, and went a little distance in search of a more favourable situation, but alas! unfortunately for him, he pitched upon one, over which hung the bough of a stubborn oak, and against which he struck a little above the shoulders, and so injured the spine as to cause his death. The height of the bough from the ground was 7 feet nine inches, that of the fence 3 feet 6 inches, so that the space between the fence and the bough was only 4 feet 3 inches. The remains of this lamented youth were interred on Friday in the family vault at Barwick. We understand that a drawing of the tree is taken by a gentleman of Worksop (not an artist), and the tree is now cut down."

Leeds Intelligencer, 30 October, 1809.

†On the 9 January, 1780, Sir Thomas read his recantation from the errors of the Church of Rome before the Archbishop of Canterbury. He married in 1784, Mary, daughter of James Shuttleworth, Esq, of Gawthorp, and widow of Sir Charles Turner, of Kirkleatham, by whom she had issue—Mary Turner, married Richard Oliver, Esq, of Castle Oliver, who, on succeeding by devise to the Parlington Estates, assumed the surname and arms of Gascoigne, and had issue, Mary Isabella Oliver Gascoigne, married 1850, Frederick Charles Trench, Esq, Thomas Oliver Gascoigne died unmarried, Richard Silver Gascoigne died unmarried, and Elizabeth Gascoigne married, 1852, Frederick Mason Trench, 2nd Baron Ashtown.

'Early yesterday morning, at his seat at Parlington, near Aberford, Sir Thomas Gascoigne, Bart. The melancholy event which recently occurred in his family (the death of his only child), has indeed, as he himself prophesied on that afflicting occasion "brought his grey hairs in sorrow to the grave."'

Leeds Intelligencer, 12 February, 1810.

Sarah, wife of Josh Lister, Coalpits, Feb. 21. 66
Barbara, wife of David Strother, Barwick, March 11. 56
William Whitehead, Leeds, April 9. 47
Eliz^{h}, wife of John Wainwright, Brownmoor, April 12. 77
William, son of Ja^{s} Jackson, Barwick, June 9. Inf^{t}
Anne, wife of Francis Hawkin, Scholes, June 15. 80
Benjn Shillito, Stanks, Augt 5. 79
Mary, daugh^{r} of Ann Slater, Barwick, Augt 26. 27
*The Revd James Hodgson, M.A., late Rector of y^{s} Parish, Octo. 15. 61
Eliz^{h}, daugh^{r} of Nathl Hanks, Potterton, Octo. 18. Inf^{t}
Susannah, wife of Thos Bailey, Scholes, Nov. 5. 80
John Gray, Carlton, Nov. 22. 53
William, son of Wm Whitehead, Leeds, Dec. 5. 11
John Johnson, apprentice to John Clemishaw, Winmoor, ran over by a Cart, Dec. 22. 13

BURIALS, 1811. Age.

Samuel, son of Joseph Simpson, Brownmoor, Feb. 10. 6
Sarah, daugh^{r} of John Butler, Scholes, Feb. 17. 17
James Goodall, Stanks, Feb. 17. 50
Thomas Thornton, Potterton, March 16. 76
Edwd, son of Jos^{h} Sparling, Potterton, March 17. 26
John Cawood, Coalpits, Ap^{l} 19. 63
Thos Perkin, Barwick, Ap^{l} 25. 57
Abigail, wife of Thos Bean, Barwick, Ap^{l} 28. 67
Eliz^{h}, wife of Benjn Collet, Barwick, May 12. 63
John, son of Ja^{s} Barker, Penwell, May 14. 19
Mary, wife of John Batty, Throstle Nest in ye Parish of Aberford, June 26th. 41
Ann Taylor, Poor House, June 29th. 60
William, son of John Kirby, Leeds, July 24. Inf^{t}
Eliz^{h}, wife of Benjn Stringer, Hilltop, Augt 8. 36
William, son of John Bean, Barwick, Augt 27. 14
Mary, daugh^{r} of Hannah Thompson, Barnbow, Septr 8. 13
Abraham Rawlinson, Barwick, Sept. 21. 79
Martha Simpson, Hill-top, Sept. 25. 76
Rachel, daugh^{r} of Ja^{s} Barker, Penwell, Nov. 17. 1
Frances Simpson, Barnbow, Dec. 10. 68

BURIALS, 1812. Age.

John Atkinson, Stanks, Jany 2. 68
Mary Simpson, Hill-top, Jan. 7. 39

---

*Rector 1799—1810. Son of James Hodgson of Leominster; Christ Church, Oxford, B A., 1770; M A., 1773.—Foster's *Alumni Oxon.* In 1801 he presented Silver Communion Vessels to Barwick Church.

On Wednesday, the Rev. James Hodgson, M A, Rector of Barwick-in-Elmet, near this town, and one of His Majesty's Justices of the Peace for this Riding. The worthy minister and active magistrate had been, the day preceding his death, attending to his magisterial duties, as usual, at this place He returned home to dinner, and shortly after was attacked with violent spasms, which gave way to the remedies applied Retiring to bed at the usual hour, he was again attacked in a similar way; he arose about one o'clock in the morning, calling for relief, at the same time saying that he could not long survive; and he expired very soon afterwards. These particulars we are requested to publish, in consequence of a very erroneous statement having made its appearance in a neighbouring paper.—The valuable living of Barwick, thus vacant, is in the gift of Mr Perceval, as Chancellor of the Duchy of Lancaster. *Leeds Intelligencer*, 15 October, 1810.

James Eyre, Stanks, Jan. 11.	70
Richd Watson, Limekiln Gate, Feb. 27.	72
Catharine, wife of John Bell, Winmoor, Mar. 10.	70
Mary, daughr of Josh Turpin, Brownmoor, Apl 7.	Inft
Josh son of Josh Turpin, Brownmoor, Apl 14.	Inft
Hannah, daughr of John Cullingworth, Barwick, June 2.	Inft
John Lunn, Brownmoor Bottom, June 5.	82
Josh Kitchingman, Barwick, June 8.	52
Peter Newby, Barwick, June 21.	68
James, son of Jas Derrick, Winmoor, July 19.	Inft
Samuel, son of Jas Lumb, Barwick, July 30.	Inft
Ann Whitehead, Poor-house, Augt 23.	73
Hannah, daughr of Alice Slater, Barwick, Augt 26.	Inft
Jane, wife of Thos Burton, Scholes, Augt 28.	80
Charlotte, daughr of Ephrm Jolly, Barwick, Sept. 1.	16
John, son of Josh Simpson, Brownmoor, Sept. 29.	19
Alice Tillotson, Barnbow, Octo. 11.	81
Hannah, daughr of Wm Pickersgill, Barwick, Oct. 27.	16
William, son of Josh Simpson, Brownmoor, Dec. 10.	21
Elianor Gray, Carlton, Dec. 26.	55

[FIFTH BOOK.]

A Register Book of Marriages belonging the Parish of Barwick in Elmett, begun March the 25th, 1754.

No 1, Banns of Marriage between John Hemsworth and Mary Hall, both of this Parish, were published April the 21st, the 28th, and the 5th of May in the Year 1754. The said John Hemsworth Yeoman, and the sd Mary Hall, widow, both of this parish in the Diocese of York, were married in this Church by Banns this eight day of May in the Year One Thousand seven hundred & fifty four, by me, Levett Harris, Curate of Barwick. This marriage was solemnized by us, John Hemsworth, his × mark, Mary Hall, her × mark, in the presence of J. Brennand, William Knapton.

[*The following entries are abstracted. The marriages were by Levett Harris, Curate of Barwick, from here to the 7 February, 1758, and by Banns, unless otherwise stated.*]

1754, May 12. James Butler, pipemaker, and Mary Lumb, spinster, both of Barwick. Witns., William Taite, John Lumb.

1754, July 22. John Waites of Barston, in the parish of Sherborn, Yeoman, and Mary Haist, of Barwick, by Licence from Edwd Cookson, Surrogate. Witns., James Brennand, William Knapton.

1754; Oct. 22. John Robinson, yeoman, and Ann Dobson, spinster, both of Barwick, by John Boardman. Witns., John Varley, James Brennand.

1754, Nov. 25. Benjamin Shillito, of Whitchurch, yeoman, and Mary Varey, spinster, of Barwick, by John Boardman. Witns., Tomas Shillito, James Brennand.

1754, Dec. 26. James Brennand, parish-clerk, and Mary Butler, spinster, both of Barwick. Witns., William Taite, William Marshall.

1755, April 10. William Brown, of Garforth, yeoman, and Ann Whitehead, spinster, of Barwick. Witns., Alice Hurst, John Pitt.

1755, June 15. Joseph Batty, of Abberford, yeoman, and Isabella Hudson, of Barwick, spinster. Witns., William Knapton, William Lumb.

1755, June 17. Thomas Sanderson, of Moor mountain, yeoman, and Martha Robinson, of Barwick, spinster. Witns., Jas Robinson, James Brennand.

1755, Oct. 1. Robert Robinson, of Rothwell, yeoman, and Sarah Thompson, of Barwick, spinster. Witns., John Taite, James Brennand.

1755, Oct. 5. Eli Musgrave, of Leeds, stuffmaker, and Mary Blackburn, of Barwick, spinster. Licence. Witns., Bernard Blackburn, James Brennand.

1755, Oct. 23. Thomas Naylor, of Leeds, yeoman, and Dorothy Appleyard, of Barwick, spinster. Witns., Jeremiah Lister, James Lambert.

1755, Nov. 2. William Smith, yeoman, and Henrietta Maria Taitt, spinster, both of Barwick. Witns., Richard Smith, Timothy Smith.

1755, Nov. 4. Richard Abbey, yeoman, of Tadcaster, and Sarah Simpson, of Barwick, spinster. Witns., Roger Bell, James Brennand.

1756, Jan. 7. John Tiplin, of Barwick, and Elisabeth Smith, of Abberford, spinster, by T. Bentham. Witns., William Knapton, James Bean.

1756, Feb. 7. John Hirst, of Carlton, in the parish of Rothwell, stuffweaver, and Johanna Dolphin, of this parish, spinster. Licence. Witns., Richard Lumb, Richd Burland.

1756, June 7. Michael Topham, yeoman, and Sarah Knapton, spinster, both of Barwick, by T. Bentham. Witns., William Knapton, Benjamin Watson.

1756, Sept. 21. Thomas Popplewell, yeoman, of Barwick, and Catherine Batty, spinster, of Thorner. Witns., Jno Fleming, Richard Lumb.

1756, Nov. 8. Thomas Barton, of Kippax, yeoman, and Nancy Rawlinson, of Barwick, spinster. Witns., Willm Lumb, Nancy Byfield

1756, Nov. 29th. William Wales, of Brotherton, yeoman, and Joanna Burton, of Barwick, spinster. Witns., Richard Lumb, James Brennand

1756, Dec. 5. James Horsfield, yeoman, and Esther Poppleton, spinster, both of Barwick. Witns., Robert Popleton, James Brennand.

1756, Dec. 7. Benj: Watson, yeoman, and Susanna Pollard, spinster, both of Barwick, by T. Bentham, Vicar of Abberford. Witns., Michael Topham, William Smith.

1756, Dec. 29. Willm Lumb, yeoman, and Mary Hill, spinster, both of Barwick. Witns., William Knapton, James Brennand

1757, Feb. 21. Thomas Collett, butcher, and Agnes Thompson, spinster, both of Barwick, Witns., Thos Bean, Richard Lumb.

1757, July 2. Benjamin Braim, of Barwick, Carpenter, and Elisabeth Turnpenny, of Leeds. Licence from Edward Cookson. Witns., James Brennand, Joseph Settle

1757, July 7. William Varey, yeoman, and Ann Thompson, widow, both of Barwick. Witns., John Taitt, Thomas Collet

1757, Aug. 9. John Almond, yeoman, of Castleford, and Margt Clark, spinster, of Barwick. Witns., Joseph Settle, Jas Brennand

1757, Sept. 6. Bennett Johnson, yeoman, and Ann Smith, spinster, both of Barwick. Witns., Godfrey Gough, James Brennand

1757, Nov. 7. Edmund Popplewell, yeoman, and Grace Stead, spinster, both of Barwick, by T. Bentham. Witns., James Butler, William Knapton

1757, Nov. 24. William Watson, yeoman, and Joanna Watson, spinster, both of Barwick. Witns., John Robinson, Jas Brennand

1757, Dec. 1. William Calvert, yeoman, and Martha Thompson, spinster, both of Barwick. Witns., J. Wilkinson, Henry Robinson

1757, Dec. 26. Godfrey Gough, yeoman, and Mary Taitt, spinster, both of Barwick. Witns., Wm Smith, Samuel Braim

1758, Jan. 9. George Aughty, yeoman, and Alice Dickinson, widow, both of Barwick. Witns., Joseph Settle, Wm Smith

1758, Feb. 7. Samuel Thompson, yeoman, and Dorothy Atkinson, both of Barwick. Licence from William Campey, proctor. Witns., Thomas Atkinson, Jas Brennand

1758, June 11. John Wainwright, yeoman, of Whitkirk, and Elisabeth Woolstenholme, spinster, of Barwick, by H. Baines. Witns., Nathan Waddington, William Knapton

1759, Feb. 21. John Linley, yeoman, of Whitkirk, and Ann Bowling, spinster, of Barwick, by H. Baines, curate. Witns., Wm Procter, Samuel Bowling

1759, April 16. Chr Aumbler, yeoman, and Eliz. Athuck, spinster, both of Barwick, by H. Baines, curate. Witns., Wm Procter, Mark Topham

1759, May 7. Richard Stead, and Ann Wilson, both of Barwick, by H. Baines, cure. Witns., Ingram Grant, Willm Lumb

1759, June 10. Thomas Whitehead, husbandman, and Susanna Darnbrough, spinster, both of Barwick, by H. Baines, curate. Witns., Willm Lumb, James Bean

1759, July 10. Matthew Tipling, yeoman, in Barwick, and Izabella Akid, widow, of Abberford, by H. Baines, cure. Witns., Willm Lumb, John Dungwith

1759, Nov. 5. Joseph Weatherhead, yeoman, of Abberford, and Henrietta Maria Smith, widow, of Barwick, by H. Baines, curate. Witns., William Lumb, John Taitt

1759, Nov. 26. Joseph Kirkham, yeoman, and Hannah Smith, spinster, both of Barwick, by H. Baines, cure. Witns., Will Lumb, Joseph Watson

1760, Jan. 8. John Vevers, carpenter, and Grace Appleyard, spinster, both of Barwick, by H. Baines, cure. Witns., Willm Lumb, Samuel Braim

1760, Sept. 15. David Kellet, of Yeadon in the parish of Guisley, & Martha Hague, in this parish, by Edm: Baxter. Witns., Thom. Marshall, James Parkin

1760, Oct. 8. William Morrit and Betty Slater, both in Barwick, by Edm: Baxter. Witns., John Tipling, Wm Thompson

[*All marriages were by T. Wray, curate, from here to the* 25 *October,* 1762, *and by Banns, unless otherwise stated.*]

1760, Oct. 21. William Waite & Hannah Braim, both of Barwick. Witns., Samuel Braim & William Knapton

1760, Nov. 16. Matthew Higgins & Ann Bland, both of Barwick. Witns., Edmund Popplewell, William Knapton

1760, Nov. 24. Francis Carbut, of Bolton Piercy, & Helen Batty, of Scholes, in this parish. Witns., Thos Hartley, William Knapton

1761, Jan. 15. John Birkinshaw, of Garforth (Farmer), & Jane Whitehead, of Barwick, spinster. Licence. Witns., John Taitt, William Birkinshaw

1761, April 13. William Goodall, of Whitkirke, & Mary Hardy, of Barwick. Witns., David Scholes, John Varley

1761, June 1. Thomas Whitehead, of Otley, Gentleman, & Isabella Eamonson, of Roundhay in this Parish. Licence. Witns., Mary Whitehead, Nancy Marshall

1761, July 9. Abraham Rawlinson, batchelor, & Elizabeth Pitt, spinster, both of Barwick. Witns., William Pitt, Joseph Watson

1761, Sept. 17. John Gould, of Bradfild parish, and Ellen Gould, of Barwick parish, by Cha: Wighton, Rector of Garforth. Witns., Thomas Taitt, Thom: Oneal

1761, Sept. 24. James Norton and Thomasin Sissons, both of Barwick, by T. Bentham, vicar of Abberford. Witns., William Knapton, William Johnston

1761, Sept. 28. Joseph Watson, of Barwick, & Mary Hodgson, by T. Bentham, vicar of Abberford. Witns., Abraham Rawlinson, Benjamin Watson

1761, Oct. 1. Thomas Taitt and Mary Gough, both in Barwick, by C. Wighton, Rector of Garforth. Witns., Godfrey Gough, Francis Holmes

1761, Dec. 3. Anthony Dawson and Esther Settle, both of Barwick, by T. Bentham, vic[r] of Abberford. Witns., Joseph Settle, Abram Rawden

1761, Dec. 23. Thomas Hewett, batchelor, & Sarah Rawlinson, spinster, both of Barwick. Witns., Thomas Pitt, Cornelius Toft

1761, December 24. Robert Plows, of Scholes in this parish, Malster, & Margaret Beann, of this Town. Licence. Witns., James Parkin, James Bean

1762, Jan. 27. Henry Parkins & Sarah Bell, both of Winmore in this parish. Witns., James Lambert, Joseph Hill

1762, Feb. 7. Joseph Reedall & Mary Appleyard, both of Scholes in this parish. Witns., John Vevers, Thomas Pitt

1762, Feb. 8. John Bramley, of Methley, & Frances Parkin, of Potterton in this parish. Witns., William Knapton, John Batty.

1762, June 20. Anthony Dunwell & Sarah Scott. Witns., W[m] Norton, Cornelius Toft

1762, July 5. John Nelson, of Leeds, & Sarah Batty, of this parish. Witns., John Batty, Robert Plowes

1762, July 19. Thomas Pitt & Sarah Wood, of Potterton, both in this parish. Witns., John Batty, Benjamin Rawlinson

1762, Aug. 3. Robert Barton, batchelor, & Elizabeth Bradley, widow, both of this parish. Witn., Will Knapton

1762, Sept. 16. William Taite, of this parish, & Sarah Tatam, of Kippax, by Tho[s] Clarke, curate of Kippax. Licence. Witns., John Porter, Joseph Taite

1762, Oct. 25. John Jones & Phyllis Hering, both of this parish. Witns., William Walker, William Knapton

1762, Nov. 25. Jonathan Hodgson & Hannah Lumb, both of this parish, by W. Wighton, curate. Witns., William Knapton, Tho[s] Collet

1762, Nov. 28. Thomas Benton, of Garforth, & Ann Appleton, of Barwick, by W. Wighton, curate. Witns., Godfrey Gough, Peter Appelton

1762, Dec. 30. W[m] Chalinger, of Thorner, & Eliz[th] Hayge, of Barwick, by W. Wighton, curate. Witns., Andrew Jackson, James Parkin

1763, Jan. 6. Richard Kingsley, of Barwick in Elmitt, Farmer, & Sarah Banister, of the said parish, widow, by W. Wighton, curate. Licence. Witns., Tho. Shillito, William Knapton

1763, Feb. 23. Richd Lumb, of Barwick in Elmitt, Farmer, & *Elizabeth Carew, of the said town & parish, by W. Wighton, curate. Licence. Witns., Thos Shepley, Martha Carew

1763, May 12. Thos Tate & Mary Boueth, both of Barwick, by Thos Eglin, curate of Thorner. Witns., Robert Labron, Wm Knapton

1764, Jan. 2. Robert Wright, of Collingham, & Jane Daniel, of Barwick, by J. Brooke, curate. Witns., Robert Wright, Jane Danell

1764, March 5. Thomas Smales, of Kippax, & Mary Bell, of Barwick, by J. Brooke, curate. Witns., Willm Dawson, John Batty.

1764, June 5. James Mathers, of Leedes, & Mary Foster, in Berwick in Elmit, by Thos Eglin, curate of Thorner. Witns., Wm Dawson, R. Burland.

1764, July 25. John Brooke and Susanna Atkinson, both of Barwick by Thomas Eglin. Witns., Willm Dawson, John Dungwith.

1764, Aug. 14. Benjamin Dickinson, of Kippax, & Mary Brown, of Barwick, by James Brooke, curate. Witns., Willm Dawson, Thomas Collet.

1764, Aug. 15. Benjamin Rawlinson & Anne Littlewood, both of Barwick, by James Brooke, curate. Witns., John Batty, Thomas Hewett.

1764, Sept. 2. William Wainwright, of Whitkirke, & Martha Lumb, of Barwick, by James Brooke, curate. Witns., John Greenwood Willm Dawson.

1764, Sept. 7. John Atkinson & Ann Wilson, both of Barwick, by James Brooke, curate. Witns., Richd Lumb, Jonathan Bell.

1764, Nov. 26. Joseph Madther & Ann Lazenby, both of Barwick, by James Brooke, curate. Witns., William Dawson, John Lazenby.

1766, Dec. 11. John Lowden, of Whinmoor in this parish, Farmer, and Mary Denison, of the same, singlewoman, by Edm: Baxter, assistant. Licence. Witns., Willm Dawson, Thomas Pitt.

---

*Elizabeth Carew, was the eldest daughter of William Carew, of Lisbon, Merchant, was born there 31 May, 1742, aud died at Barwick, 19 Nov., 1818. William Carew was killed in the earthquake at Lisbon, 1 Nov, 1755 He was son of Thomas Carew, of Cork, by Susanna Frankland, and was married at Lisbon, 1741, to Anne, daughter of Marmaduke Shepley, of Wakefield. See *Collectanea Topographica et Genealogica*, Vol V., p 93: *Miscellanea Genealogica*, second series, Vol IV., p. 321, and third series, Vol I, p 28 Cussans's *History of Hertfordshire*, (Hundred of Cashio), p. 187; *Notes and Queries*, fourth series, X., pp 296 and 397; *Northern Genealogist* 1896, p. 199. For notes on the family of Richard Lumb see *Miscellanea Genealogica*, third series, Vol. I., p 132.

[SIXTH BOOK.]

[*All marriages were by James Brooke, curate, and by Banns unless otherwise specified from here to the* 1st *day of April,* 1771.]

No. 1. James Bean & Ann Wheatherill, of this Parish, married in this Church by Banns this thirteenth day of August in the Year One Thousand seven Hundred and sixty-five, by me, Richard Capstick, Curate of Bardsey. This marriage was solemnized between us, James Bean, Ann × Wheatherill's mark. In the Presence of William Dawson, William Thompson.

1765, Nov. 25. Barthow Glover & Elizabeth Thompson, of Barwick. Witns., John Smith, William Dawson.

1765, Dec. 25. James Eare & Sarah Morrit, of Barwick. Witns., Thos Haley, Mary Scott.

1766, Jan. 13. Christopher Topham, of Leedes, & Ann Shippen, of Barwick. Licence. Witns., Saml Wroe, Mary Veuers.

1766, Feb. 27. James Mallorie & Mary Hargrave, of Barwick, by Peter Simon, Vicar of Whitkirke. Licence. Witns., Willm Dawson, Richd Lumb.

1766, March 31. John Thompson & Hannah Thompson, of Barwick, by Edm: Baxter, Assistant Curate. Wits., Willm Dawson, John Smith.

1766, May 20. John Greenwood, of Whitkirke, & Ann Lumb, of Barwick. Witns., William Warnwright, William Booth.

1766, June 16. William Harrison, of Leedes, and Elizabeth Rawlinson, of Barwick. Wits., John Batty, William Knapton.

1766, August 10. John Tarboton, of Thorner, & Anne Marshall, of Barwick, by Edm: Baxter, assistant curate. Witns., Willm Dawson, Edword Tarboton.

1766, Aug. 18. Jeremiah Lumb & Elen Vevers, both of Barwick. Wits., Willm Dawson, Robt Vevers.

1766, Oct. 19. James Wright & Bersheba Robinson, of Barwick. Wits., Willm Dawson, Abraham Wormald.

1766, Nov. 26. William Clapam & Mary Fowler, of Barwick. Wits., Thos Cooper, William Richardson.

1766, Dec. 24. John Harreson, of Bradford, & Izabella Wood, of Barwick. Wits., Thomas Pitt, Georg Holmes.

1767, Jan. 12. John Rawden, of Whitkirke, & Mary Webster, of Barwick. Wits., Abram Rowlinson, William Dawson.

1767, March 15. Joseph Holmes & Sarah Hunton, of Barwick. Wits., James Norton, Thomas Bean.

1767, May 24. William Donwell, of Ledsom, & Catherine Varey, of Barwick. Wits., Jer Thompson, John Butler.

1767, Aug. 3. Samuel Lumb & Hannah Wood, of Barwick. Wits., Daniel Wood, Willm Dawson.

1767, Oct. 12. John Batty & Alice Rawlinson, of Barwick. Wits., Thomas Hewett, William Knapton.

1767, Oct. 19. William Robshaw & Alice Rothmil, of Barwick. Witns., Richd Lumb, Bengam Collt.

1767, Nov. 24. Joseph Sparling, of Abberford, & Mary Watson, of Barwick. Wits., Richard Waite, William Knapton.

1768, Feb. 28. Robert Stephenson, of Wighill, & Elizabeth Pease, of Barwick. Licence. Wits., Thomas Blackburn, William Dawson.

1768, May 2. Benjamin Collete & Elizabeth Knapton, of Barwick. Wits., John Taitt, jun[r], William Knapton.

1768, July 19. Alvara Thompson & Sarah Lazenby, of Barwick. Wits., John Batty, Benjamin Rawlinson.

1768, Nov. 14. Stephen Ballance & Mary Harper, of Barwick. Wits., Charles Goodall, William Dawson.

1768, Nov. 23. John Stead & Elizabeth Dunwell, of Barwick. Wits., Thomas Wright, William Dawson.

1768, Dec. 5. John Clark & Fanny Lambert, of Barwick. Wits., John Marshall, James Lambert.

1768, Dec. 8. Thomas Pickersgill & Judith Stead, of Barwick. Wits., Rich[d] Lumb, John Stead.

1769, Jan. 5. Thomas Tilney & Sarah Haley, of Barwick. Wits., Ponsonby, Richard Pike.

1769, Feb. 20. Richard Waite & Alice Barker, of Barwick. Wits., Rich[d] Lumb, William Knapton.

1769, March 12. Richard Watson, of Thorner, and Mary Simpson, of Barwick. Wits., John Dungwith, William Dawson.

1769. March 27. David Wood, of Leedes, & Sarah Popplewell, of Barwick. Wits., William Dawson, Tho[s] Batty.

1769, May 17. William Rawlinson, of Barwick, and Sarah Perkin, of the same, by Edm: Baxter, Assistant Curate. Wits., John Batty, Abram Rawlinson.

1769, June 8. John Holmes, of the parish of St. Mary le Strand, in the county of Middlesex, & Sarah Broadbent, of this parish, by Miles Atkinson. Licence, John Clough, sur. Wits., Faith Broadbent, Faith Eastburn, Elizabeth Wilkinson, John Wilton.

1769, Dec. 20. Joseph Barmby, of Thorner, and Jane Upton, of Barwick. Wits., George Upton, Joseph Upton.

1770, June 4. John Slayter, of Sherburn, and Sarah Peart, of Barwick, by Edm: Baxter, assistant Curate. Wits., Rich[d] Lumb, Matt. Bullock.

1770, Sept. 19. John Overind, of Rothwell, and Margaret Gaggs, of Barwick. Witns., John Atkinson, Mary Gaggs.

1770, Nov. 5. John Mortan and Esther Dawson, both of Barwick, by T. Wilson. Wits., Joseph Settle, William Dawson.

1770, Nov. 6. Joseph Cawthorn, of Coulton of the parish of Whitchurch, & Ann Dickinson, of Barwick, by T. Wilson. Licence. Wits., Rich[d] Lumb, Thomas Pitt.

1770, Dec. 13. Henry Greenwood & Elizabeth Johnson, of Barwick. Wits., Benjamin Watson, Will[m] Dawson.

1770, Dec. 24. David Hotchson & Elizabeth Lumb, of Barwick. Wits., Ann burland, William Knapton.

1771, Feb. 11. William Derrick & Martha Maud, both of Barwick. Witns., An Sayner, [?Hany Binn].

1771, April 1. Peter Newby, of Sherburn, and Ann Burland, of Barwick. Witns., Tho[s] Richardson, Thomas Ward.

1771, May 2. Robert Plows, of Whitkirk, and Martha Lumb, of Barwick, by E. Carne, Vicar of Aberford. Licence. Witns., William Lumb, Samuel Lumb.

1771, June 17. Jonathan Bell, of Barwick, Labourer, and Hannah Ould, spinster, of Barwick, by F. Wray, curate. Wits., Richd Lumb, Thomas Pitt.

[*All marriages were by F. Wray, curate, and by banns from here to the 4th April, 1774, unless otherwise specified.*]

1771, August 1. James Banks, of Leeds, Linnen Draper, & Rebecca Rooke, of Barwick, spinster. Licence by consent of her Father. Witns., Wm Rooke, Susanna Fretwell, Mary Vevers.

1771, Sept. 30. Henry Hall, of Leeds, Stuff maker, & Elizabeth Broadbent, of Barwick, spinster. Licence. Witns., Ann Calloway, Wm Broadbent.

1771, Oct. 14. William Cryer, batchelor, and Mary Wilson, spinster, both of Barwick. Wits., Thomas Hargrave, Abram Rawden.

1771, Oct. 14. John Linlay, of Whitkirk, batchelor, and Hannah Perkin, of Barwick, spinster. Witns., Sarah Vevers, Abram Rawden.

1771, Nov. 4. Thomas Harper, labourer, and Ann Pollard, spinster, both of Barwick, by James Brooke. Witns., Thomas Pitt, William Robshaw.

1771, Nov. 25. Robert Smith, singleman, & Mary Marshal, spinster, both of Barwick. Witns., Thos Burton, William Dawson.

1771, Nov. 25. Francis Steel, of Walton, in the parish of Thorp Arch, singleman, & Martha Thornton, of Barwick. Witns., Thos Thornton, Sarah Gibbons.

1771, Dec. 9. James Fletcher, of Garforth, collier, & Sarah Taylor, of Barwick, spinster. Witns., May Scott, Richd Lumb.

1771, Dec. 30. William Staincliff, of Barwick, Husbandman, and Margaret Bullock, widow. Witns., Jacob Pease, William Dawson.

1772, Jan. 6. Samuel Shippen, yeoman, and Mary Dawson, spinster, both of Barwick. Witns., Marey Gaggs, Samuel Wright.

1772, May 19. Samuel Thompson & Susanna Taylor, both of Barwick. Witns., Thomas Braim, Wm Knapton.

1772, July 20. Abraham Rawlinson & Mary Scott, both of Barwick. Witns., Richd Lumb, Wm Thompson.

1772, Nov. 23. Peter Higgins, singleman, and Esther Horsfield, widow, both of Barwick. Witns., Richard Smith, William Dawson.

1772, Nov. 24 Thomas Simpson, of Barwick, batchelor, and Frances Claybourn, spinster. Witns., Lawrance Milner, William Dawson.

1773, March 31. George Hopton, batchelor, and Grace Boyse, spinster, both of Barwick. Licence. Witns., Benjamin Collite, Mary Taitt.

1773, April 25. William Tipling, widower, and Elizabeth Rowland, widow, both of Barwick. Witns., John Dungwith, William Dawson.

1773 July 7. Elias Fletcher, of Walton in this county, batchelor, & Sarah Barker, spinster. Witns., William Dawson, Elizabeth Fletcher.

1773, July 13. John Steuart, of Abberford, brickmaker, and Mary Elley, in Barwick, spinster. Witns., Thos Elley, Thos Shillito.

1773, Aug. 18. Thos Buckle & Elizabeth Logg, both of Barwick, by Wm Swaine, Vicar of Bramham. Witns., John Buckle, James Logg.

1773, Sept. 15. Richard Thompson, of Overhelmsley, batchelor, & Mary Simpson, of Barwick. Witns., Saml. Varley, John Batty.

1773, Sept. 22. Joseph Todd, batchelor, & Elizabeth Bradley, spinster, both of Barwick. Witns., Richard Park, William Dawson.

1773, Sept. 27. Henry Stainburn, of Whitkirke, batchelor, & Helen Dunwell, of Barwick, spinster. Witn., William Dawson.

1773, Nov. 22. Robert Greenwood, of Saxton, batchelor, and Mary Barker, of Barwick, spinster. Witns., Robt Dawson, William Greenwood.

1774, March 9. James Pawson, of Harwood, and Jane Dodgshon, of Barwick, spinster, by E: Carne, Vicar of Aberford. Witns., John Pawson, Abram Rawdon.

1774, April 4. Samuel Mawson, batchelor, and Ruth Clarkson, spinster, both of Barwick. Witns., John Hewett, Benjamin Jackson.

1774, Aug. 11. William Gough, Husbandman & Potmaker, and Ann Carritt, spinster, both of Barwick, by Robt Deane. Witns., Godfrey Gough, Wm Dawson.

1774, Sept. 11. Thomas Hargraves, of Whitkirke, and Hannah Clarkson, of Barwick, by J. Thompson, minister. Witns., Benjamin Jackson, Francies Beecroft.

1774, Sept. 14. Joseph Dawson and Anne Varey, both of Barwick, by E: Carne, Vicar of Aberford. Licence. Witns., Benjamin Jackson, John Batty.

1774, Nov. 22. William Turpin, of Halton, in the parish of Whitkirk, & Mary Atkinson, of Barwick, by Guy Fairfax, Rector of Newton Kyme. Licence. Witns., Matt. Smith, William Dawson.

1774, Nov. 23. Thomas Paxton, batchelor, & Margaret Harford, spinster, both of Barwick, by John Metcalfe, curate. Witns., Christopher Flower, John Walton.

1774, Nov. 24. Samuel Simpson, batchelor, and Ann Thompson, spinster, both of Barwick, by John Metcalfe, curate. Witns., William Thompson, William Dawson.

[*All marriages were by Robt Deane, rector, and by banns from here to the* 31 *day of March*, 1791, *unless otherwise stated.*]

1775, Jan. 12. William Brittain, of Abberford, and Mary Gaggs, of Barwick, spinster. Witns., Richard Smith, John Batty.

1775, Feb. 5. William Vevers, batchelor, and Ann Rooke, spinster, both of Barwick. Licence. Witns., Benjamin Rooke, William Vevers.

1775, Mar. 2. Samuel Harrison, batchelor, and Sarah Poppleton, spinster, both of Barwick. Licence. Witns., William Sheariffe, Matthew Hardwick.

1775, Mar. 31. Ralph Brotherton, of Kirby Overblows, batchelor, and Ann Vevers, ot Barwick, spinster. Licence. Witns., Wm Vevers, Peter Newbey.

1775, April 5. Renton Haist, laborher, and Sarah Ward, spinster, both of Barwick. Witns., William Thompson, Richard Waite.

1775, April 9. John Boys, of Thorner, widdour, and Ann Ward, of Barwick, widdou. Witns., Peter Slayter, John Batty.

1775, May 8. William Robshaw, batchelor, and Sarah Knapton, spinster, both of Barwick. Witns., Benjamin Jackson, Richard Waite.

1775, Sept. 25. Matthew Miller, batchelor, and Jane Pawson, spinster, both of Barwick. Witns., William Carr, Thos. Pitt.

1775, Dec. 24. Thomas Richardson, batcholer, and Mary Daniel, spinster, both of Barwick. Witns., William Richardson, John Batty.

1776, Jan. 8. John Blackburn, batcholer, and Jane Smith, spinster both of Barwick. Witns., Richard Waite, John Batty.

1776, Feb. 10. John Cullingworth, of Abberford, batcholer, and Maria Thornton, of Barwick, spinster. Witns., Thos Thornton, Richard Waite.

1776, March 17. John Thompson and Ann Mawson, both of Barwick. Witns., Jonas Vince, John Batty.

1776, Aug. 14. Thomas Jordan, of Whitkirke, and Sarah Buchanan, of Barwick. Witns., John Jordan, Richard Waite.

1776, Nov. 4. Henry Furniss, of Leeds, batcholer, and Dolly Hargrave, of Barwick, spinster. Licence. Witns., John Furniss, Richard Waite.

1776, Nov. 4. William Jowitt, of Garforth, batcholer, and Alice Dungwith, of Barwick, spinster., Witns., Thos Pitt, Richard Waite.

1776, Dec. 11. William Burland, batcholer, and Sarah Smith, spinster, both of Barwick. Witns., Thomas Perkin, Jno Smith.

1777, Jan. 19. Henry Simpson and Martha Derrick, both of Barwick Witns., John Batty, Thomas Taitt.

1777, Feb. 3. John Stead, batcholer, and Mary Akeland, spinster. both of Barwick. Witns., Samuel Webster, John Batty.

1777 Aug. 5. Thomas Outhwate, of Winmoor, of this Parish, and Eleanor Kirby, of Thorner. Licence. Witns., Richard Waite, Jno Batty.

1777, Oct. 6. Thomas Perkin, batchlor, and Mary Thorns, spinster, both of Barwick. Witns., William Rawlinson, Jno Batty.

1777, Oct. 8. John Mackontrout, batcholer, and Martha Ampshaw, spinster, both of Barwick. Witns., Jno Smith, James Robinson.

1777, Nov. 18. William Watson, batcholer, and Jane Barker, spinster, both of Barwick. Witns., David Strother, John Batty.

1777, Dec. 17. Henry Foster, batcholer, and Zilpha Cawood, spinster, both of Barwick, by J. Uttley, curate of Thorner. Licence. Witns., Saml Shippen, Jno Batty.

1777, Dec. 29. Thomas Wright, batcholer, and Hannah Brunton, spinster, both of Barwick. Witns., James Backhouse, Saml Shippen.

1778, Jan. 27. Benjamin Cromek, batcholer, and Catherine Monncy, spinster, both of Barwick. Witns., Will: Carr, Wm Munsey.

1778, April 13. John Robinson, batcholer, and Alice Tayler, spinster both of Barwick. Witns., Chas Goodall, John Batty.

1778, May 28. Thomas Thornton, batcholer, and Grace Green, widow, both of Barwick. Witns., Edward Day, John Batty.

1778, June 24th. John Hutchinson, of the parish of Calverly, and Sarah Clemishaw, of this parish, spinster. Licence. Witns., John Balme, Richard Wetherill.

1778, Oct. 28. Thomas Goodall, of Garforth, and Ann Tillotson, of Barwick. Witns., James Tillotson, Richard Waite.

1778, Nov. 17. Roger Bell and Elizabeth Forster, both of Barwick. Witns., William Shearife, Thomas Shilito.

1778, Dec. 14. John Gibson, of Witkirke, and Julia Bauckhouse, of Barwick. Witns., John Greenwood, Jno Batty.

1779, Feb. 3. John Stubs, batcholer, and Elizabeth Robinson, spinster, both of Barwick. Licence. Witns., John Robinson, John Walton.

1779, March 3. George Gummarsall, batcholer, and Mary Slayter, widow, both of Barwick. Witns., William Waite, John Batty.

1779, March 21. James Thompson and Mary Holmes, both of Barwick, by Jno Thompson, curate of Castleford. Witns., John Thompson, John Batty.

1779, March 24. John Gray, of Morwick of this parish, batcholer, and Eleanor Eamonson, of Chapel Allerton of the parish of Leeds spinster. Licence. Witns., Thos Shepley, Wm Shepley.

1779, April 11. William Dunwell, widower, and Margret Deane, spinster, both of Barwick, by Nicholas Waite Robinson. Witns., Joseph Walton, Richard Waite.

1779, May 30. William Wilson, batcholer, and Fanny Hargrave, spinster, both of Barwick. Witns., Wm. Ingham, Richard Waite.

1779, June 2. Richard How, of Sheffield, batcholer, and Elizabeth Leach, of Barwick, widow. Licence. Witns., Abraham Rawdon, Richard Waite.

1780, May 16. John Taylor, of Prestwich, and Sarah Tilney, of Barwick. Witns., John Coupland, Thos Tilney.

1780, June 12. John Shilburn and Liddy Madder, both of Barwick. Witns., Richard Waite, John Batty.

1780, July 3. Thomas Waud, of Spofforth, widower, and Hannah Stead, of Barwick, spinster. Licence. Witns., Richard Waite, John Batty.

1780, Aug. 7. Richard Braim and Ann Harper, both of Barwick. Witns., Joseph Cromek, John Batty.

1780, Nov. 6. Joseph Thompson and Rebekah Lee, both of Barwick. Witns., Richard Waite, Jno Batty.

1780, Dec. 25. Christopher Rhumbo, of Saxton, and Sarah Dodgson, of Barwick. Witns., Abraham Morritt, John Batty.

1781, Jan. 23. Joseph Wright Linley, of Witkirke, and Hannah Poppleton, of Barwick. Witns., John Porter, John Batty.

1781, Feb. 25. William Jenkinson, of Bramham, and Betty Taylor, of Barwick. Witns., Samuel Thompson, John Batty.

1781, Feb. 26. William Smith and Ann Knapton, both of Barwick. Witns., Timothy Smith, Benjamin Collite.

1781, May 28. Edward Goodall and Sarah Cook, both of Barwick, by Thomas Carr, Curate of Thorner. Witns., William Goodall, Robert Jordan.

1781, Aug. 13. Benjamin Eamonson, of Barwick, and Elianor Powell, of Bramham. Licence. Witns., Joseph Powell, Christr Powell.

1781, Nov. 5. Joseph Kitcheman and Martha Lumb, both of Barwick. Witns., Joseph Simpson, Richard Leak.

1781, Nov. 26. Thomas Baley and Ann Dickinson, both of Barwick, by Will: Hodgson, Curate of Garforth. Witns., Mary Tate, Sam Pickersgill.

1782, Feb. 18. Thomas Lumb and Ann Daniel, both of Barwick. Licence. Witns., Thos Pitt, John Batty.

1782, April 25. Samuel Pickersgill and Hannah Bullock, both of Barwick. Witns., Peter Slayter, John Batty.

1782, May 19. Robert Lee, of Kirkby Sigston, and Elizabeth Blackburn, of Barwick. Witns., Edmd Shaw, John Batty.

1782, May 20. John Nichols, of Leeds, batchelor, and Mary Taitt, of Barwick, spinster. Licence. Witns., Jos Taite, John Birkinshaw.

1782, Sept. 5. Abraham Wormild and Sarah Naylor, both of Barwick. Witns., Joseph Naylor, Thos Naylor.

1782, Oct. 13. Benjamin Rawlinson, widower, and Frances Cromeck spinster, both of Barwick. Witns., Joseph Cromek, John Batty.

1782, Nov. 18. John Naylor, of Boroughbridge, and Mary Vevers, of Barwick. Licence. Witns., John Vevers, John Batty.

1782, Nov. 24. Isaac Burckitt and Ann Hemsworth, both of Barwick. Witns., Joseph Walton, Matthew Varley.

1782, Dec. 2. John Flockton and Mary Watson, both of Barwick, by Will. Hodgson, curate of Garforth. Witns., James Robinson, John Batty.

1782, Dec. 23. Daniel Motley, of Leeds, and Mary Canwood, of Barwick, by Willm Hodgson, curate of Garforth. Witns., James Motley, Henry Cawood.

1783, Jan. 13. Peter Slayter, of Witkirke, and Ann Goodall, of Barwick, by E. Carne, Vicar of Aberford. Witns., Richard Waite, John Batty.

1783, Jan. 23. Thomas Slingsby, of Bramham, and Rebeckah Robinson, of Barwick, by Wm Hodgson, curate of Garforth. Licence. Witns., Will: Carr, John Batty.

1783, March 13. David Heaton and Maria Bullock, both of Barwick. Witns., Peter Slayter, John Batty.

1783, April 7. Robert Cocker and Sarah Thorns, both of Barwick. Witns., John Laycock, John Batty.

1783, Nov. 9. Edward Bland, of the parish of St Helens of the city of York, and Mary Gough, of this parish. Witns., Godfrey Gough, Jno Batty.

1783, Nov. 27. Joseph Cromek and Mary Wilkinson, both of Barwick. Witns., Joseph White, Ruth Butler.

1783, Dec. 3. George Darton and Ann Dungwith, both of Barwick. Witns., John Taitt; jun^r, John Batty.

1783, Dec. 8. James Goodall and Ellin Hodgson, both of Barwick. Witns., Thos Braim, John Batty.

1783, Dec. 21. Joseph Walton and Sarah Day, both of Barwick. Witns., Edward Day, John Day.

1783, Dec. 22. John Butler and Hannah North, both of Barwick. Witns., John Connell, Anthony Robinson.

1784, April 4. John Forster and Sarah Watson, both of Barwick, by Will. Hodgson, curate of Garforth. Witns., John Batty, John Varley.

1784, April 5. John Monks and Elizabeth Wadington, both of Barwick, by Will Hodgson, curate of Garforth. Witns., Abraham Wormill, John Batty.

1784, April 12. Francis Brown, of Woodhouse of the parish of Leeds, widower, and Mary Vevers, of Scholes Park of this Parish, spinster. Licence. Witns., Geo. Ogle, Bethune Green.

1784, May 16. Francis Linley, of Witkirke, and Ann Baley, of Barwick, by Will. Hodgson, curate of Garforth. Licence. Witns., Wm Linley, John Batty.

1784, Nov. 7. James Heaton and Ellen Walton, both of Barwick. Witns., Richd Lumb, Joseph Walton.

1784, Dec. 12. Joseph Simpson, of Barwick, and Sarah Clarkson, of Abberford. Witns., William Simpson, John Batty.

1785, March 28. John Loder and Sarah Deane, both of Barwick. Licence. Witns., William Carr, Jno Batty.

1785, Oct. 9. William Day and Mary Hornshaw, both of Barwick. Witns., John Day, Thomas Hornshaw.

1785, Oct. 15. Francis Syburry and Ann Taite, both of Barwick. Witns., Richd Hewitt, John Batty.

1786, Jan. 8. James Barker and Frances Morritt, both of Barwick. Witns., John Wright, John Batty.

1786, Jan. 24. John Robinson, of Bramham, and Elizabeth Barton, of Barwick. Witns., William Richardson, Theops Wilde.

1786, Feb. 5. Matthew Varley and Sarah Whitead, both of Barwick. Witns., Benjamin Jackson, John Batty.

1786, March 27. Thomas Wrigglesworth, of Rothwell, and Hannah Kirkham, of Barwick. Witns., Wm Whitehead, John Batty.

1786, April 5. Joseph Battersby, of Leeds, and Hannah Whitehead, of Barwick. Witns., Thos Charlesworth, Wm Whitehead.

1786, Nov. 6. George Hill, of Whitkirke, and Elizabeth Dean, of Barwick, by J. Jefferson, officiating Min^r. Witns., Leonard Cawwood, William Pickrsgill.

1786, Nov. 26. John Burrow, of Barwick, and Sarah Monks, of Sherburn, by Will: Hodgson, curate of Garforth. Witns., Abrahm Wormild, William Batty.

1786, Nov. 27. John Cawwood, of Barwick, and Jane Surr, of Osburn Parva, by Will: Hodgson, curate of Garforth. Witns., Henry Foster, Richard Green.

1787, Jan. 22. William Marr and Margret Slayter, both of Barwick, by W: Hodgson, curate of Garforth. Witns., Richard Parkin, William Waite.

1787, Jan. 25. John Hepworth, batcholer, and Cecilia Wharton, spinster, both of Barwick. Licence. Witns., St^{n} Moorehouse, Job Catton.

1787, Jan. 29. John Liley and Elizabeth Norton, both of Barwick, by W: Hodgson, curate of Garforth. Witns., Margaret Bean, Thomas Settle.

1787, Feb. 18. Jonathan Pearsey and Elizabeth Cawood, both of Barwick. Witns., John Cawwood, Leonard Cawwood.

1787, Apl. 29. Robert Brown and Mary Dean, both of Barwick. Witns., Jonathan Dinison, John Batty.

1787, May 6. John Hewitt and Elizabeth Barton, both of Barwick. Witns., Richd Lumb, R^{d} Hewitt.

1787, July 2. William Knapton and Sarah Lumb, both of Barwick, by Will. Hodgson, curate of Garforth. Licence. Witns., John Batty, Thos Pitt.

1787, Nov. 5. John Tillotson and Margret Hewitt, both of Barwick, by Will. Hodgson, curate of Garforth. Witns., Mark Benton, Mary Abbot.

1787, Nov. 6. William Thompson, of Barwick, batcholer, and Hannah Ward, of Saxton, widow, by Will : Hodgson, curate of Garforth. Licence. Witns., Willm Collett, Thos Calvert.

1787, Dec. 2. William Clarkson, of Aberford, and Hannah Walker, of Barwick. Witns., T. Bainbridge, Thos Pitt.

1787, Dec. 26. William Morritt, of Witkirke, and Elizabeth Moss, of Barwick. Witns., James Robinson, John Batty.

1788, Feb. 3. William Vincent and Mary Scholes, both of Barwick. Witns., John Vincent, Thomas Vincent.

1788, Feb. 19. *The Reverend Newcome Cappe, of York, Widower, and Miss Catherine Harrison, of Barwick, spinster. Licence. Witns., Wm Eamonson, Hester Deane.

1788, Feb. 28. Witham Bywater, of Tadcaster, and Ann Smith, of Barwick. Witns., Thos Shepley, Thos Bywater.

1788, April 24. Mark Carew, of Barwick, and Mary Hewitt, of Sherburn. Witns., Thos Shepley, Richd Lumb.

1788, June 9. Timothy Smith, of Bramham, and Agnes Seed, of Barwick. Licence. Witns., B. Eamonson, William Seed.

1788, July 22. William Bullock and Rebecca Daniel, both of Barwick, by William Hodgson, curate of Garforth. Witns., John Daniel, John Batty.

1788, Sept. 1. Matthew Upton, of Barwick, and Elizabeth March, of Thorner, by Wm Swaine, Vicar of Bramham. Witns., Joseph Upton, John Batty.

1788, Oct. 6. William Atkinson, of Thorp-arch, and Mary Harrison, of Barwick. Witns., Jonas Clarkson, Richard Wood.

---

*Newcome Cappe (1733—1800) unitarian; educated by dissenting ministers; pastor of St Saviourgate Chapel, York, 1756—1800; published sermons and theological tracts.—*Dictionary of National Biography*.

1788, Nov. 23. John Robinson and Susannah Stringer, both of Barwick. Witns., John Benton, John Batty.
1788, Nov. 24. William Marrison and Hannah Denison, both of Barwick. Witns., James Battey, Jonathan Denison.
1788, Nov. 27. Thomas Tillotson and Mary Hill, both of Barwick. Witns., Thomas Baley, John Batty.
1789, Jan. 31. John Reed and Martha Haist, both of Barwick. Witns. Edward Langthorn, Wm Gough.
1789, Feb. 23. John Easby, of Kirk Deighton, and Mary Challinger, of Barwick. Licence. Witns., John Chalinger, Edmund Somerton.
1789, Mar. 2. John Hewitt, of Rothwell, and Hannah Daniel, of Barwick, by William Hodgson, curate of Garforth. Witns., Elizabeth Carr, George Burwell.
1789, June 1. William Walker, of York, and Sarah Varley, of Barwick, by Thos Dikes, curate. Licence. Witns., John Varley, Mary Lumb.
1789, Nov. 1. William Peers and Elizabeth Carr, both of Barwick. by Thos Dikes, curate. Licence. Witns., Wm Carr, Sarah Carr.
1789, Dec. 7. Mark Benton and Hannah Vincent, both of Barwick, by Thos Dikes. Witns., William Hewitt, Jane Vince.
1790, Aug. 15. William Strafford and Mary Norton, both of Barwick by Thos Dikes, curate. Witns., George Scholes, John Batty.
1790, Sept. 23. William Gough and Margret Walker, both of Barwick, by Wm Sanderson, curate of Thorp Arch. Witns., Richard Lumb, James Lumb.
1790, Oct. 11. John Barker and Mary Tillotson, both of Barwick, by Wm Sanderson, curate of Thorp Arch. Witns., James Osborne, Rd Hewitt.
1790, Nov. 4. John Baley and Ann Hawley, both of Barwick, by Thos Dikes, curate. Witns., John Batty, John Wainwright.
1790, Nov. 8. John Thompson and Ann Pickard, both of Barwick, by Thos Dikes. Witns., Mary Dawson, Sarah Boffey, Isabella Atkinson, Rebecca Hey, Henry Greene.
1790, Nov. 25. Charles Fletcher, of Garforth, and Ann Abbot, of Barwick. Witns., James Whitehead, Charles Goodall.
1790, Dec. 7. Richard Hewitt and Mary Logg, both of Barwick, by Thos Dikes, curate. Witns., Wm Charter, Mary Green.
1791, Feb. 14. William Batty, of Bramham, and Mary Bean, of Barwick. Witns., Peter Newby, William Rawlinson.
1791, March 31. Joseph Cullingworth, of Fenton, and Isabella Rhodes, of Barwick. Licence. Witns., Thomas Lumb, John Scawbord.

[*All marriages were by John Graham, curate, and by banns, from here to the* 29th *Augt*, 1796, *unless otherwise stated.*]

1791, July 31. William Backhouse, of Barwick, and Ellin Nettleton, of Whitkirke. Witns., Thomas Jakues, John Batty.
1791, Aug. 22. William Little and Mary Lidster, both of Barwick. Witns., John Groves, James Jackson.
1791, Sept. 26. John Clapham and Sarah Taite, both of Barwick. Witns., John Batty, Joseph Settle.

1791, Oct. 25. James Allthouse, of Aberford, and Ann Lowreman, of Barwick. Witns., Hannah Smith, George Priestman.

1791, Oct. 31. Samuel Robinson, of Garforth, and Catherine Barker, of Barwick. Witns., Ann Hepworth, John Batty.

1791, Dec. 8. Samuel Thompson and Catherine Pickard, both of Barwick. Witns., John Thompson, Ann Picke.

1791, Dec. 13. John Scholes and Elizabeth Hemsworth, both of Barwick. Witns., Elizabeth Dawson, Ann Sch[o]les.

1791, Dec. 27. Thomas Lowreman, of Barwick, and Hannah Clarkson, of Aberford. Witns., George Priestman, John Clarkson.

1791, Dec. 27. William Smith, of the parish of All Saints, Pavement, united to Peter the Little, City of York, Taylor, and Elizabeth Ingle, of this parish. Licence. Witns., Wm Ardington, Wm Wilks.

1792, March 6. Thomas Bennet, of Garforth, and Ann Ingle, of Barwick. Witns., Laurence Barnard, John Batty.

1792, April 3. William Beanley and Hannah Waite, both of Barwick. Witns., William Robinson, John Batty.

1792, Oct. 29. Richard Dungwith and Betty Settle, both of Barwick. Witns., Sarah Calvert, John Whitehead.

1792, Nov. 26. William Pickersgill and Mary Thompson, both of Barwick. Witns., John Thompson, John Batty.

1792, Nov. 28. Joseph Upton and Mary Goodall, both of Barwick. Witns., Mary Brown, John Batty.

1793, Jan. 27. William Dawson and Mary Greenwood, both of Barwick. Witns., William Greenwood, John Batty.

1793, March 7. John Sykes, of Kirkheaton, and Elizabeth Newsome, of Barwick. Licence. Witns., William Brown, John Stubs.

1793, April 15. John Smith, of Garforth, and Mary Logg, of Barwick. Witns., George Scholes, John Batty.

1793, July 4. Thomas Stoner and Ann Bell, both of Barwick. Witns., John Batty, Benjamin Batty.

1793, July 14. John Groves and Mary Lumb, both of Barwick. Witns., Richd Lumb, James Lumb.

1793, July 29. John Goodall and Jane Dixon, both of Barwick. Witns., Thos Braim, Ann Braim.

1793, July 31. Thomas Waite and Hannah Smith, both of Barwick. Witns., Mary Smith, Richard Smith.

1793, Aug. 12. Richard Shillito and Elizabeth Wood, both of Barwick. Witns., John Harreson, Elizabeth Day.

1793, Nov. 3. William Watson and Hannah Mountaine, both of Barwick, by Robt Deane. Witns., John Robinson, Matthew Varley

1793, Nov. 4. Thomas Parker and Mary Appleyard, both of Barwick. Witns., Margaret Robshaw, John Batty.

1793, Dec. 3. Thomas Collitt and Martha Vary, both of Barwick, by R. Deane. Witns., Wm Knapton, John Batty.

1794, March 2. Alvara Thompson and Hannah Morrit, both of Barwick. Witns., James Air, John Batty.

1794, March 31. Bennitt Johnson and Mary Tillotson, both of Barwick. Witns., Hannah Atkinson, John Batty.

1794, May 6. William Rawlinson and Sarah Forster, widow, both of Barwick. Witns., Abraham Wormild, John Batty.
1794, June 17. Richard Waite, butcher, and Mary Stubbs, spinster, both of Barwick. Witns., Hannah Waite, Ann Stansfield.
1794, July 6. Joseph Turton and Hannah Murfin, both of Barwick. Witns., John Mirfin, John Batty.
1794, Sept. 29. Peter Hanson and Mary Thompson, both of Barwick. Witns., James Pawson, John Batty.
1794, Oct. 26. John Hunter and Jane Stainburn, both of Barwick. Witns., Margaret Atkinson, William Simpson.
1794, Nov. 24. William Clough, of Aberford, and Mary Slater, of Barwick. Witns., Thomas Hudson, Robt. Clough.
1794, Nov. 27. Benjamin Rawden and Ann Bell, both of Barwick. Witns., James Batty, Thos Pitt.
1794, Nov. 30. John Daniel and Betty Shillito, both of Barwick. Witns., Thos. Shillito, Abram Wormild.
1795, Jan. 12. Job Hodgson and Sarah Logg, both of Barwick, by Will. Hodgson, curate of Garforth. Witns., Jno Whitehead, John Batty.
1795, Feb. 24. Benjamin Thompson and Jane Fryer, both of Barwick. Witns., James Batty, William Abbot.
1795, July 14. John Sawyer, of Leeds, merchant, & Lucy Baines, of Barwick. Licence. Witns., Hester Deane, David Russell.
1795, July 29. Thomas Morrit and Mary Norton, both of Barwick. Witns., Hannah Slayter, John Batty.
1795, Aug. 2. William Heaton and Mary Parker, both of Barwick. Witns., Thomas Bean, John Batty.
1795, Sept. 7. John Wood, farmer, and Sarah Strother, spinster, both of Barwick. Witns., John Gough, John Batty.
1795, Sept. 30. William Tipling and Elizabeth Marshall, both of Barwick. Witns., Anthony Dunwell, John Batty.
1795, Dec. 21. Thomas Metcalfe, servant, and Ellin Mills, servant, both of Barwick. Witns., John Batty, Abraham Wormild.
1795, Dec. 25. Jeremiah Binns, of Leeds, and Mary Higgins, of Barwick. Witns., Wm Grant, John Batty.
1795, Dec. 27. Benjamin Stringer and Martha Greenwood, both of Barwick. Witns., Elisabeth Booth, John Lumb.
1796, March 21. Wm Collett, blacksmith, and Frances Pool, both of Barwick. Witns., David Heaton, William Hollings.
1796, March 21. William Hollings, of Brotherton, and Grace Pollard, of Barwick. Witns., Ralph Pool, John Acomb.
1796, May 29. John Bean and Elizabeth Collett, both of Barwick. Witns., John Collett, Benjan Jackson.
1796, May 31. Michael Prince, of Castleford, and Mary Haist, of Barwick, by R. Deane, rector. Licence. Witns., Matthew Bloome, John Prince.
1796, July 26. John Whitehead and Sarah Cowper, both of Barwick. Licence. Witns., C. Carr, Thos Pitt.
1796, Aug. 29. George Pickersgill and Elizabeth Pickard, both of Barwick. Witns., Sarah Ashbuerry, William Pickersgill.

1796, Nov. 28. George Wright and Jane Hargrave, both of Barwick, by Will. Hodgson, curate of Garforth. Witns., Randal Holmes, John Batty.

1797, March 13. George Simpson, of Sherburn, & Sarah Wright, of Barwick in Elmet, by Christ[r] Atkinson, curate. Witns., John Stubs, William Abbot.

[*All marriages were by Christ[r] Atkinson, curate, and by banns, from here to the* 28 *day of Jan[y]*, 1802, *unless otherwise stated.*]

1797, April 2. Benjamin Fowler, of Dewsbury, & Mary Benson, of Barwick. Witns., George Benson, Thomas Bean.

1797, July 4. The Rev[d] Edward Hardy, clerk, of Ripley, & Elizabeth Frances Carter, of Roundhay in this parish. Licence. Witns., Eliza Sheawood, W[m] Shearwood.

1797, July 4. Peter Higgins & Catharine Lazenby, both of Barwick. Witns., William Batty, Thomas Bean.

1797, July 15. W[m] Addeman and Jane Holmes, both of Barwick, by Rob[t] Deane, rector. Licence. Witns., T. Hutchinson, James Batty.

1797, Sept. 4. Christopher Simpson & Faith Skelton, both of Barwick. Witns., Joseph Simpson, Samuel Settle.

1797, Oct. 2. John Carrack and Mary Ross, both of Barwick. Witns., Thomas Bean, Mary Thornton.

1797, Nov. 5. Thomas Robshaw and Elizabeth Jowett, both of Barwick. Witns., W[m] Robshaw, Elizabeth Appleyard.

1797, Nov. 27. Joseph Sparling, of Aberford, & Mary Gill, of Barwick. Witns., William Batty, James Gill.

1797, Dec. 8. Robert Barker, of Harewood, & Clementina Phillips, of Barwick. Licence. Witns., J. Phillips, Mary Phillips.

1798, Jan. 10. Robert Waddingham, of Wintringham in the county of Lincoln, and Mary Green, of Barwick, by Will[m] Hodgson, officiat[g] Minis[r]. Witns., Mary Hewet, Thomas Bean.

1798, Jan. 12. George Langton and Ann Nelson, both of Barwick. Witns., John Gough, William Batty.

1798, Jan. 29. Thomas Baley, of Kirkby-overblow, & Frances Deane, of Barwick. Witns., Thomas Ingle, Benjn. Wilkinson.

1798, March 5. Joseph Bell and Mary Nettleton, both of Barwick. Witns., George Bell, William Batty.

1798, June 7. James Batty & Jane Walker, both of Barwick. Witns., Thomas Bean, Margrat Gough.

1798, June 18. William Buchanan, of Bolton Percy, & Ellen Cullingworth, of Barwick. Witns., Richard Cullingworth, Susanna Bailey.

1798, Sept. 17. Samuel Thompson and Sarah Barker, both of Barwick. Witns., Thomas Bean, William Batty.

1798, Sept. 18. John Taylor and Mary Rawden, both of Barwick, by Robert Deane, Minister. Witns., James Batty, William Batty.

1798, Nov. 15. James Dodd, a Private in the Warwickshire Cavalry, now quartered at Beverly in the county of York, & Mary Macintosh, of Barwick in Elmet. Licence. Witns., John Stubs, William Batty.

1799, Jan. 1. Edward Dixon and Ann Kirby, both of Barwick, by Will. Hodgson, officiating minister. Witns., Mary Kirby, William Batty.

1799, Jan. 28. Robert Benson, of Barwick, and Mary Waite, of Kirkby Overblow. Licence. Witns., Wm Myeirs, George Benson.

1799, March 18. Thomas Todd and Mary Rawlinson, both of Barwick, by Randh Marriott, officiating minister. Licence. Witns., Wm. Rawlinson, Joseph Rawlinson.

1799, July 8. James Tennant, of Bardsey, & Ann Newby, of Barwick, by James Drake, A.M. Licence. Witns., George Wood, Richard Burland.

1799, July 29. James Gascoigne, of Whitchurch, & Sarah Rawlinson, of Barwick. Witns., Wm. Smith, James Pawsoan.

1799, Aug. 18. Joseph Archer, of Sherburn, & Sarah Hollings, of Barwick. Witns., John Strickland, William Batty.

1799, Sept. 2. William Jenkinson, of Whitkirk, & Martha Pickersgill, of Barwick. Witns., Saml Pickersgill, Elizabeth Pickersgill.

1799, Nov. 3. John Holliday & Elizabeth Pickersgill, both of Barwick. Witns., William Batty, Abraham Wormeild.

1800, Feb. 10. George Pickersgill & Elizabeth Bell, both of Barwick. Witns., James Pawsoan, Sarah Limberts.

1800, April 28. John Robshaw, of Barwick, & Mary Wrigglesworth, of Fenton. Witns., Robert Bunting, Richard Smith.

1800, Sept. 28. Thomas Hudson & Mary Bell, both of Barwick. Witns., John Hutchinson, William Batty.

1800, Nov. 3. Bennet Johnson & Mary Hewitt, both of Barwick. Witns., E. Reynolds, Marey Dinnison.

1800, Nov. 9. Edward Briggs & Ann Maud, both of Barwick. Witns., William Batty, Thos Pitt.

1800, Nov. 17. Richard Rooke, of Leeds, & Mary Dawson, of Barwick. Licence. Witns., Elizabeth Dawson, Richard Dawson.

1801, Feb. 1. Matthew Johnson & Mary Denison [*signed* Dinnison], both of Barwick. Witns., William Mirfin, William Batty.

1801, May 4. James Whitehead and Alice Carr, both of Barwick. Licence. Witns., Thos Carr, Charles Clay.

1801, Aug. 1. Randal Holmes & Mary Barker, both of Barwick. Licence. Witns., John Butler, Sarah Butler.

1801, Aug. 30. William Dunwell & Ann Blackburn, both of Barwick. Witns., Gorge Blackbrn, William Batty.

1801, Nov. 3. Henry Raper, of the parish of St Mary in Manchester, in the Diocese of Chester, & Ann Parker, of this parish, by James Hodgson, Rector. Licence. Witns., Richard Graham, of Leeds, Elizabeth Gratton, William Batty.

1801, Nov. 8. James Rhodes, of Medley, & Ann Tilney, of Barwick. Witns., Hannah [illegible], Sarah Tilney.

1801, Nov. 22. William Watson & Christiana Lidster, both of Barwick. Witns., Edmund Rawlinson, William Batty.

1802, Jan. 7. Richard Dawson, of Kippax, and Elizabeth Todd, of Barwick. Witns., William Batty, Joseph Todd.

1802, Jan. 28. Jeremiah Maud & Ann Rumbolt, both of Barwick. Witns., George Child, William Batty.

[*All marriages were by James Hodgson, rector, from here to the end of this book, and by banns unless otherwise stated.*]

1802, Feb. 17. John Wood & Hannah Hodgson, both of Barwick. Witns., William Batty, Richd. Lumb.

1802, April 19. James Gill and Ann Jackson, both of Barwick. Witns., Benjamin Jackson, William Batty.

1802, July 25. Joseph Turpin and Ann Lambert, both of Barwick. Witns., William Batty, James Batty.

1802, Aug. 1. William Catley, of Garforth, and Mary Cawwood, of Barwick. Witns., Joshua Cood, David Cawood.

1802, Aug. 15. William Simpson, of Whitkirk, and Ann Slayter, of Barwick. Witns., William Batty, Hannah Braim.

1802, Sept. 6. William Davidson and Sarah Wright, both of Barwick. Witns., F. Green, Jas Bagnet.

1802, Nov. 28. John Beck and Rachel Rollinson, both of Barwick. Witns., Jas Rollison, William Batty.

1802, Dec. 20. James Furniss, of Thorner, & Elizabeth Wright, of Barwick. Witns., John Furniss, William Batty.

1803, Jan. 3. Isaac Ward and Rebecca Jenkinson, both of Barwick. Witns., John Wade, William Batty.

1803, Feb. 6. Thos. Eastwood and Frances Simpson, both of Barwick. Witns., Joseph Simpson, William Batty.

1803, Feb. 21. John Simpson and Eleanor Dunwell, both of Barwick. Witns., James Pawson, William Batty.

1803, Feb. 22. Matthew Hewit and Rachel Newsam, both of Barwick. Witns., Sarah Tilney, William Batty.

1803, March 3. Matthew Varley and Ann Ward, both of Barwick. Witns., John Whitehead, William Batty.

1803, May 23. George Dawson, of Sherburn, & Mary Thompson, of Barwick. Witns., Frs. Hawley, of Sherburn, Thos Dawson, Sherburn.

1803, May 30. Benjamin Blackburn & Margaret Bell, both of Barwick. Witns., Edmund Rawlinson, William Batty.

1803, Aug. 18. John Upton, junr, of Thorner, and Rebecca Clemishaw, of Barwick, by Willm Hodgson, officiating minister. Licence from Joseph Whiteley, surrogate. Witns., John Clemishaw, Rachel Clemishaw.

1803, Dec. 8. Samuel Hardisty & Sarah Chadwick, both of Barwick. Witns., James Derrick, William Batty.

1804, Jan. 23. Robert Dean, of Brayton, & Mary [*signed* Ann] Rollison, of Barwick. Witns., James Dawson, William Batty.

1804, Feb. 6. Thomas Pickersgill & Mary Waite, both of Barwick. Witns., Henry Thompson, William Batty.

1804, July 10. Charles Wood & Susanna Lumb, both of Barwick. Witns., Thos Carr, Richard Newby, James Lumb, Richard Lumb.

1804, Sept. 17. Joseph Wright and Sarah Perkin, both of Barwick. Witns., Elizabeth Wilson, Sarah Rallings, Thomas Porter, William Batty.

1804, Sept. 24. James Thompson & Hannah Lister, both of Barwick. Witns., Richard Pease, William Batty.
1804, Oct. 1. Richard Pease & Elizabeth Parker, both of Barwick. Witns., William Batty, John Jackson.
1804, Oct. 22. John Cullingworth and Hannah Daughill, both of Barwick. Witns., Barnaby Hewitt, William Batty.
1805, Jan. 9. Samuel Chadwick & Mary Flockton, both of Barwick. by Thomas Carr, curate of Thorner. Witns., Wm Batty, James Batty.
1805, Feb. 25. John Simpson, of Garforth, & Hannah Wright, of Barwick. Witns., Thos Braim, William Batty.
1805, May 27. Thomas Watterton, of Ledsham, & Margaret Hudson, of Barwick. Witns., George Hudson, Richard Pease.
1805, Aug. 19. John Sherburn & Sarah Glave, both of Barwick. Witns., John Clark, William Batty.
1805, Nov. 11. Benjamin Lunn, of Whitkirk, & Mary Brown, of Barwick. Witns., James Lumb, William Batty.
1805, Nov. 26. William Robinson, of Sherburn, & Hannah Braim, of Barwick. Witns., Wm Thompson, Ann Braim.
1805, Nov. 30. John Hutchinson, of Barwick in Elmet, and Mary Woliscraft, of the same Parish. Licence. Witn., William Batty.
1805, Dec. 23. Joseph Lodge & Mary Wright, both of Barwick. Witns., George Wright, William Batty.
1806, April 6. John Richardson & Ann Smith, both of Barwick. Witns., John Denison, Thos Smith.
1806, June 29. George Brown, of Thorner, & Mary Waddington, of Barwick. Witns., Hannah Warrington, William Batty.
1806, Aug. 11. Job Hodgson and Hannah Cowell, both of Barwick. Witns., William Batty, Joseph Turton.
1806, Oct. 30. Thomas Porter and Elizabeth Wilson, both of Barwick. Witns., Thomas Pullan, John Stubs.
1806, Oct. 30. Henry Thompson and Sarah Rollings, both of Barwick. Witns., Thomas Pullan, John Stubs.
1806, Oct. 30. Edmund Rawlinson and Ann Rollings, both of Barwick. Witns., Thomas Pullan, John Stubs.
1806, Nov. 3. John Wilkinson, of the parish of Guiseley, and Hannah Armitage, of Barwick, by Thomas Pullan, curate. Witns., William Armitage, William Batty.
1806, Dec. 10. Richard Dawson, of Sherborn, and Elizabeth Thompson, of Barwick. License. Witns., George Dawson, William Batty.
1807, Jan. 21. Michael Lumley and Ann Braithwaite, both of Barwick, by Thomas Pullan, curate. Licence. Witns., John Braithwaite, William Batty.
1807, Feb. 8. Wm Helliwell and Leah Sunderland, both of Barwick, by Thomas Pullan, curate. Witns., Ralph Hargreave, Timothy Topham.
1807, May 11. Samuel Lumb or Tomson and Sarah Shillitoe, both of Barwick, by Thomas Pullan, curate. Witns., Wm Booth, William Batty.

1807, May 18. John Steel, of Harewood, and Ann Holmes, of Barwick. Witns., Martha Steel, William Batty.

1807, Oct. 6. James Walker, of Leeds, and Ellen Hargrave, of Barwick. Witns., Thomas Collet, William Batty.

1807, Oct. 11. William Goldthorp & Mary Barker, both of Barwick. Witns., Thomas Smith, William Batty.

1807, Nov. 1. John Jakeman, of Bramham, and Mary Thornton, of Barwick. Witns., William Cullingworth, William Batty.

1807, Dec. 28. William Rhodes, of Bramham, and Ann Smith, of Barwick. Witn., William Batty.

1808, Feb. 22. James Hodgson and Ann Hawkin, both of Barwick. Witns., Nathan Ward, John Jackson, William Batty.

1808, Feb. 29. William Taylor & Sarah Plows, both of Barwick. Witns., John Lumb, William Batty.

1808, March 21. George Gummersall and Mary Atkinson, both of Barwick. Witns., Thos Pitt, John Thompson.

1808, May 9. Roger Foster and Mary Robshaw, both of Barwick, by William Crowther, officg Minr. Witns., John Walton, William Batty.

1808, May 15. William Wilson and Ann Knapton, both of Barwick, by Thos Pullan, curate. Witns., Edmd Rawlinson, Maria Smith.

1808, May 23. John Marshall, of Whitkirk, and Sarah Morritt, of Barwick, by Thomas Pullan, curate. Witns., John Barker, William Batty.

1808, Aug. 29. William Sir, of Leeds, & Jane Scott, of Barwick, by Thos Pullan, curate. Witns., Ann Naylor, Benjamin Scott.

1808, Nov. 2. Thomas Varley and Elizabeth Stead, both of Barwick, by Thomas Pullan, curate. Licence. Witns., Richard Lumb, John Bleasby.

1808, Nov. 14. *The Revd Thomas Pullan and Sarah Ward, both of Barwick. Licence. Witns., Wm Thompson, Eliz. Pullan, William Thompson, William Batty.

1809, Jan. 3. Nathaniel Bailes and Sarah Prince, both of Barwick, by Thomas Pullan, curate. Witns., George Bailes, William Batty.

1809, March 6. John Connell and Jane Addeman, both of Barwick, by Thomas Pullan, curate. Licence. Witns., Thos Pitt, William Batty.

1809, March 29. Joseph Scholes and Martha Morritt, both of Barwick, by Thomas Pullan, curate. Witns., Thos Braim, Ann Scholes.

1809, April 17. William Cheesebrough and Mary Goodall, both of Barwick, by Thomas Pullan, curate. Witns., John Goodall, William Batty.

1809, Aug. 29. Thomas Colbert, of East Cottingwith, and Mary Cawthorne, of Barwick. Witns., John Jackson, William Batty.

1809, Oct. 11. Joseph Lumb, of Barwick, and Rachel Stainburn, of Whitkirk. Licence. Witns., William Johnson, John Lum, William Lumb.

---

*Curate of Barwick Sidney Coll. Cambridge, B.A , 1806.

1809, Nov. 27. John Scruton and Alice Brown, both of Barwick, by Thomas Pullan, curate. Witns., John Jackson, William Peirse.

1809, Dec. 4. Benjamin Stringer and Elizabeth Lister, both of Barwick, by Thomas Pullan, curate. Witns., John Robinson, William Batty.

1809, Dec. 28. Matthew Thomlinson, of Wighill in the Diocese of York, yeoman, and Ann Cullingworth, of Barwick. License. Witns., William Cullingworth, James Cullingworth, John [? Ann] Cullingworth, George Cullingworth.

1810, Feb. 12. Benjamin Pickersgill and Susanna Linley, both of Barwick, by Thos Pullan, curate. Witns., John Pickersgill, William Batty.

1810, May 6. Joseph Richardson, of Aberford, and Mary Daughill, of Barwick. Witns., John Hollings, William Jowett.

1810, June 18. James Murray, of Spofforth, and Rosehannah Brownrigg, of Barwick. Witns., William Copley, William Batty.

1810, June 20. Roger Wilson and Jane Chadwick, both of Barwick. Witns., Samuel Hardisty, William Batty, James Batty.

1810, July 2. William Goodall and Rachel Clayton, both of Barwick. Witns., John Goodall, William Batty.

1810, Oct. 22. Joseph Midgley and Sarah Bell, both of Barwick, by Thomas Pullan, curate. Witns., James Midgley, William Batty.

1810, Dec. 24. Joseph Thompson and Elizabeth Hemsworth, both of Barwick, by Thomas Pullan, curate. Witns., James Hemsworth, William Batty.

1810, Dec. 25. Robert Richardson and Judith Pickersgill, both of Barwick, by Thomas Pullan, curate. Witns., Wm Pickersgill, William Batty.

1810, Dec. 26. James Sparling, of Bardsey, and Elizabeth Abbot, of Barwick, by Thomas Pullan, curate. Witns., John Gough, Thos Kemp, Ellis Wilberfoss, Sarah Connell, Elizabeth Sparling.

1811, July 3. William Johnson, of Leeds, and Elizabeth Rowlandson, of Barwick, by Richd Foster, officig Minr. Licence. Witns. James Brook, junr, Mary Johnson, Susan Rowlandson, Jos. Barritt.

1811, Aug. 19. David Strother and Mary Watson, both of Barwick, by William Bolland, officiating minister. Witns., James Lumb, William Batty.

1811, Nov. 3. William Vinces and Elizabeth Atkinson, both of Barwick, by Richd Foster, offg minr. Witns., William Batty, Edmd Rawlinson.

1811, Nov. 26. Laurence Dickenson & Catherine Wilson, both of Barwick, by Charles Wayland, off. minister. Witns., William Batty, James Batty.

1811, Dec. 23. William Smithson and Mary Goodall, both of Barwick, by Thos Pullan, curate. Witns., Joseph Jordan, William Batty.

1811, Dec. 30. John Roberts and Sarah Goodall, both of Barwick, by Thos Pullan, curate. Witns., Joseph Jordan, Henry Shippen.

1812, Jan. 21. John Williamson, of Fenton, and Mary Upton, of Barwick, by Charles Wayland, offg minr. Witns., Ann Westwood, Edmund Rawlinson.

1812, Feb. 10. James Goodall and Sarah Simpson, both of Barwick, by Thos Pullan, curate. Witns., Thos Eastwood, William Batty.

1812, May 24. Charles Turner, of Barwick, and Elizabeth Mackintosh, by Thos Pullan, curate. Witns., William Knapton, William Batty.

1812, Aug. 16. Thomas Pitt & Martha Kitchingman, both of Barwick, by Thos Pullan, curate. Licence. Witns., Edward Wales, William Batty.

1812, Aug. 31. William Oddy and Elizabeth Tetlaw, both of Barwick, by Thos Pullan, curate. Witns., Luke Bradbury, William Batty.

1812, Oct. 28. *George Mossman, M.D., of Bradford, & Ann Elizabeth Ramsbotham, of Barwick, by Lamplugh Hird, curate. Licence. Witns., Thomas Pullan, Sophia Phillips.

1812, Nov. 2. Richard Wormald & Elizabeth Keighley, both of Barwick, by Thos Pullan, curate. Witns., William Batty, Mary Wormald.

1812, Dec. 25. William Keighley, of Bradford, and Elizabeth Holmes, of Barwick, by Thos Pullan, curate. Witns., Richard Wormald, William Batty.

THE REGISTER BOOK for the Publication of BANNS OF MARRIAGE.

[*Banns of which the Marriage is not entered in the Register. The date of the 1st publication is only given.*]

1765, 24 March. Benjamin Harrison, of Barwick, & Elizabeth Hompelby, of Collingham.

31 March. Benjamin Waite, of Barwick, & Mary Barker, of Garforth.

28 April. Thomas Todd, of Barwick, & Jane Smith, of Spofforth.

26 May. Thomas Morrit, of Barwick, & Ann Robshaw, of Spofforth.

June 2. George Reedall, of Barwick, & Hannah Fowler, of Healaugh.

June 23. Jonathan Dinnison, of Barwick, & Sarah Lucy, of Whitkirk.

June 30. Lancelot Thornton, of Barwick, & Brasha Lawson, of Kippax.

Sept. 8. Joseph Thackray, of Barwick, and Mary Chambers, of Harwood.

Dec. 15. Jonathan Pennington & Izabella Wood, both of Barwick.

1766, Apl. 6. Thomas Howdle, of Aberford, & Margaret Hewit, of Barwick.

Apl. 27. Robert Dawson, of Barwick, & Ann Hodges, of Brotherton.

Sept, 14. Christopher Tezinton, of Whitkirke, & Mary Backhouse, of Barwick.

Nov. 2. Thomas Atkinson & Tabatha Crampton, both of Barwick.

*See Hunter's *Familiæ Minorum Gentium*, (Harleian Society), p. 298, and the *Northern Genealogist* 1896, p. 199.

1767, Jan. 11. William Teal, of Barwick, & Elizabeth Goodal, of Whitkirke.

Oct. 25. Frederick Whitehouse & Izabella Waud, of Kirkdeeton.

Dec. 6. James Jackson, of Barwick, and Mary Atkinson, of Kellington.

1768, Nov. 13. William Richardson, of Barwick, and Sarah Barton, of Leeds.

Dec. 11. John Peart, of Barwick, & Mary Jackson, of Tadcaster.

1769, Jan. 8. Thomas Crummock, of Barwick, and Martha Hartley, of Wakefield.

June 4. George Hewit, of Barwick, & Frances Summersgill, of Garforth.

June 4. William Thompson, of Barwick, & Jane Pickering, of Garforth.

June 18. William Hemsworth, of Barwick, & Ann Brewster, of Stillingfleet.

July 23. Thomas Burton, of Barwick, & Jane Smith, of Stillingfleet.

Aug. 20. William Booth, of Whitkirk, & Faith Madder, of Barwick

Oct. 29. James Vince, of Barwick, & Hannah Simpson, of Whitkirk.

Nov. 12. George Wright, of Barwick, & Mary Mather, of Whitkirk

Nov. 26. Thomas Bean, of Barwick, & Abigail Harrison, of Whitkirk.

1770, Sept. 30. Richard Kingsley and Mary Dawson, both of Barwick.

Oct. 14. Thomas Waite, of Barwick, and Julia Sinyard, of Ledsom

Nov. 25. James Peart, of Barwick, & Mary Geldard, of Gisburn.

1771, April 7. James Fletcher, of Garforth, & Sarah Taylor, of Barwick.

1772, March 8. William Dodgson, of Chapel-Allerton in Leeds, & Mary Dodgson, of Barwick.

April 12. John Atkinson, of Barwick, & Ann Sayner, of Belfreys in the city of York.

Nov. 8. Thomas Smith, of Barwick, & Elizabeth Scalbert, of Rothwell.

1773, Mar. 28. Jesse Borrow, in Barwick, batchelor, and Ann Bolton, spinster, in Leeds.

Oct. 31. James Bullock, of Barwick, & Sarah Abbot, spinster, in Swillington.

Nov. 21. William Barker, in Barwick, batchelor, & Hannah Graves, in Spofforth, spinster.

Dec. 5. John Lucas, in Leeds, batchelor, and Martha Abbot, in Barwick, spinster.

1774, Nov. 13. John Hewit, in Barwick, singleman, & Sarah Upton, spinster, in Thorner.

Nov. 13. William Bell, singleman, in Whitkirk, and Sarah Shilbourne, spinster, in Barwick.

1776, Jan. 28. Thomas Burton, of Bärwick, batcholer, & Hannah Gibson, of Leeds, spinster.

Nov. 3. William Dunwell, of Barwick, and Ann Marshall, of Whitkirk.

Dec. 22. William Renton, of Barwick, and Sarah Rodes, of Abberford.

Dec. 29. George Baker & Sarah Clemishaw, both of Barwick.

1777, April 13. Joseph Wigelsworth, of Barwick, and Hollaf Dixon, of Pontefract.

Aug. 17. Matthew Barber, of Tadcaster, and Margret Slayter, of Barwick.

Nov. 9. John Goodall & Betty Thompson, both of Barwick.

Dec. 14. William Slayter, of Barwick, and Martha Dawson, of Tadcaster.

1778, Apl. 19. Thomas Braim, of Barwick, and Ann Atkinson, of S. Michel le Belfrey, York.

1779, Jan. 31. Thomas Princ, of Barwick, and Mary Nicolson, of Saxton.

Mar. 14. John Goodall, of Barwick, & Ellin Goodall, of Witkirke.

Jan. 10. James Lee, of Barwick, and Sarah Smith, of Bishop-wilton.

Apl. 18. Thomas Upton, of Thorner, and Elizabeth Blanchit, of Barwick.

May 2. William Robinson, of Barwick, and Betty Thompson, of Witkirke.

May 30. William Goodall, of Barwick, and Mary Forster, of Witkirke.

Sept. 5. John Grocock, of Kippax, and Margret Lee, of Barwick.

Nov. 21. John Vary, of Barwick, and Grace Reed, of Bardsey.

1780, Mar. 26. Benjamin Otheck, of Leeds, and Mary Moncks, of Barwick.

May 21. Benjamin Cook, of Barwick, and Mary Marshall, of Witkirke.

June 4. John Walton, of Barwick, and Mary Nettleton, of Sherburn.

Aug. 6. John Husber, of Barwick, and Mary Wright, of Witkirke.

1782, Nov. 10. Benjamin Naylor and Sarah Tipling, both of Barwick

1783, Sept. 14. Edward Barrowclif, of Barwick, and Sarah Smith, of Garforth.

Sept. 28. Jonathan Richardson, of Barwick, and Mary Prince, of Witkirke.

Dec. 14. William Walton, of Barwick, and Elizabeth Pearson, of Hunsinger.

1784, Aug. 1. William Backhouse and Ann Hawkings, both of Barwick.

Dec. 26. William Beanley and Jane Stubs, both of Barwick.

1785, May 22. John Day, of Barwick, and Mary Walker, of Hunsinger.

1787, May 13. John Broughton, of Guiseley, and Sarah Marshall. of Barwick.

Oct. 14. James Hare, of Barwick, and Sarah Spencer, of Witkirke.

1788, Dec. 7. Matthew Varley, of Barwick, and Ann Taite, of Abberford.

Dec. 14. John Norton, of Barwick, and Jane Compesorton, of Riccle.

1789, Mar. 8. Thomas Taite, of Barwick, & Charlotta Thompson, of Leeds.

1790, Feb. 7. William Dickinson, of Barwick, and Elizabeth Jackson, of Aberford.

April 18. David Strother, of Barwick, & Barbary Sweeton, of Tadcaster.

Dec. 5. James Eyres, of Barwick, and Mary Bell, of Whitkirke.

1791, Jan. 23. Robert Stead, of Wolton, and Mary Lidster, of Barwick.

Jan. 23. Richard Perkin, of Barwick, and Ann Braithwaite, of St Hellins of the city of York.

May 29. James Toft, of Barwick, and Rebecca Wood, of Bardsey.

Sept. 4. John Thrach, of Barwick, and Ann Clarkson, of Whitkirk

Nov. 6. Leonard Canwood, of Barwick, and Mary Corney, of Whitkirk.

1792, Jan. 29, William Rawlinson, of Barwick, and Ellin Hey, ot Spofforth.

Mar. 11. John Hillingworth, of Thorner, and Mary Wood, of Barwick.

April 22. William Manners, of Spofforth, and Ann Haws, of Barwick.

July 27. John Deane, of Barwick, and Elizabeth Fitton of Whitkirke.

Dec. 23. John Harrison, of Thorner, and Mary Chadwick, of Barwick.

1793, June 9. Samuel Braim, of Barwick, Ann Shepperd,of Garforth

[No entries from 1793 to 1797.]

1797, Dec. 3. John Todd, of Barwick, & Ann Prince, of Ledsham.

1798, Apl. 29. Henry Taylor, of Barwick, & Mary Teal, of Leeds.

June 10. John Cawthorne, of Barwick, & Mary Stead, of Whitkirk

Aug. 19. John Spencer, of Sherburn, & Hannah Tillotson, of Barwick.

Oct. 21. James Thackray, of Barwick, & Dinah Dixon, of Copmanthorpe.

Dec. 23. Matthew Watson & Elizabeth Todd, both of Barwick.

1799, June 16. Thomas Taite, of Barwick, & Margaret Braithwaite, of Aberford.

Oct. 13. William Batty, of Barwick, & Elizabeth Carr, of Leeds.

Nov. 3. John Thompson, of Barwick, & Elizabeth Ambler, of Leeds.

1800, Feb. 2. Richard Stead, of Harewood, & Sarah Wetherhill, of Barwick.

Feb. 16. Samuel Pickersgill, of Barwick, & Hannah Fitton, of Whitkirk.

Apl. 6. Richard Baker, of Whitchurch, & Frances Denison, of Barwick.

July 27. John Rawlinson, of Barwick, & Elizabeth Clark, of Whitchurch.

Oct. 12. William Watson, of Barwick, & Hannah Harrison, of Thorner.

Dec. 14. Joseph Jackson & Mary Clarkson, both of Barwick.

1801, Feb. 8. John Connell, of Barwick, and Ann Stansfield, of Whitchurch.

June 21. John Liddle, of Saxton, & Eleanor Nettleton, of Barwick

Sep. 27. Henry Clayton, of Barwick, & Hannah Hemsworth, of Garforth.

Nov. 8. John Barker, of Barwick, & Ann Burton, of Acomb.

1802, Feb. 21. James Vince and Mary Haley, both of Barwick.

Sep. 19. George Blackburn, of Barwick, and Hannah Wood, of Whitkirk.

Nov. 21. John Butler, of Barwick, & Mary March, of Leeds.

Dec. 5. James Tomling, of Barwick, & Elizabeth Thompson, of Tadcaster.

1803, Mar. 13. John Cawood, of Leeds, & Sarah Haist, of Barwick.

Mar. 20. Joseph Newis, of Barwick, & Mary Brownrigg, of Kirkby Overblow.

Oct. 23. Thomas Wright, of Barwick, & Mary Hambler, of Whitkirk.

Oct. 30. George Johnson, of Barwick, & Sarah Hanley, of Rippon.

1804, Nov. 11. James Jackson, of Barwick, & Phebe Ellart, of Aberford.

1805, Jan. 13. Matthew Kirby and Sarah Thompson, both of Barwick.

Apl. 7. Michael Wolton, of Barwick, & Ann Eyre, of Bramham.

June 9. Richard Hemsworth, of Garforth, and Amelia Benton, of Barwick.

July 7. Thomas Cawood, of Barwick, and Elizabeth Taylor, of Whitkirk.

Sept. 15. Thomas Watson, of Knaresbro', and Elizabeth Skelton, of Barwick.

Oct. 20. James Hodgson and Mary Haley, both of Barwick.

1806, July 27. Christopher Simpson, of Barwick, and Ann Roadhouse, of Monk Frystone.

June 29. John Barret & Mary Benton, both of Barwick.

Aug. 31. John Powell & Sarah Morritt, both of Barwick.

1807, Jan. 18. John Pemberton & Sarah Ward, both of Barwick.

July 26. Joseph Scholes, of Barwick, and Sarah Speight, of Whitkirk.

July 26. Joseph Simpson, of Barwick, and Hannah Turner, of Whitkirk.

1808, July 10. Joseph Reeder, of Barwick, & Ann Connell, of Leeds,

June 19. John Prince, of Whitkirk, and Susana Jolley, of Barwick

Nov. 20. William Scott, of Brotherton, & Ellen Taylor, of Barwick

1809, July 30. Alexander Metcalf, of Barwick, and Mary Prince, of Whitkirk.

1810, May 6. Joseph Simpson, of Barwick, & Ann Vince, of Whitkirk.

July 1. Benjamin Hewitt, of Leeds, and Frances Bell, of Barwick.

July 29. George Watson, of Barwick, and Mary Smeaton, of Garforth.

Nov. 11. Thomas Perkin, of Barwick, and Margaret Booth, of Whitkirk.

1811, Dec. 1. James Bacchus, of Barwick, and Mary Marshall, of Whitkirk.

Dec. 8. William Ashton, of Barwick, and Mary Powell, of Wakefield.

Dec. 8. Robert Wright, of Barwick, and Jane Bamlet, of North allerton.

1812, Feb. 16. Matthew Heptonstall, of Heaton, and Elizabeth Sykes, of Barwick.

Mar. 22. William Copley, of Barwick, and Mary Briggs, of Aberford.

April 5. Thomas Robshaw, of Barwick, and Ann Westerman, of Whitkirk.

May 3. William Blakey, of Leeds, and Sarah Dickinson, of Barwick.

July 19. William Simpson & Elizabeth Knapton, both of Barwick

Aug. 9. Benjamin Stringer, of Barwick, and Mary Jolly, of Whitkirk.

June 28. Joseph Walton, of Barwick, and Mary Moon, of Aberford.

Sept. 20. John Jenkinson, of Leeds, & Sarah Dickinson, of Barwick.

Oct. 25. William Slater, of Barwick, & Catherine Crossland, of Aberford.

Dec. 13. Edward Brogden, of Barwick, & Elizabeth Hick, of Tadcaster.

MONUMENTAL INSCRIPTIONS.

IN THE CHURCH.

TABLET IN CHANCEL.

Sacred to the memory of the Revd Robt Deane, B.D., 25 years Rector of this parish. This venerable man, learned, pious, humble & beneficent, lived the delight of his friends, the ornament of christianity, and the father of his flock. He died in peace Feby 6th, 1799, ae^{t} 65. Erected by his affectionate relict H. Deane.

TABLET IN CHANCEL.

Sacred to the memory of Edward Wilkinson, Esqre, of Potterton, who died July 16th, 1836, aged 74 years; also of Ann, his wife, who died October 26th, 1846, aged 78 years.*

TABLET IN CHANCEL.

Sacred to the memory of John Edward Wilkinson, of Potterton, born on the 28th of October, 1789, died at Scarborough on the 14th of August, 1850; also of Catherine Wilkinson, wife of the above, who died on the 28th Dec^{r}, 1856, aged 59 years.

TABLET IN CHANCEL.

To the memory of William Eamonson, of Lazingcroft, who after having reach'd his 63^{d} year in such Vigor as seemed to promise a long continuance of his Valuable Life, was snatched from his sorrowing Family and Friends on the 6th day of March, 1781, by an inflammatory Fever in the short space of 3 days. This plain monument is erected by Elizabeth Eamonson, his widow....Also to the memory of Elizabeth and Alice, the daughters of William and Elizabeth Eamonson, who died in the bloom of (*rest decayed*)

TABLET ON SOUTH WALL.

Near this place are deposited the remains of William Ellis, Esq., of Kiddall Hall in this parish, who departed this life April the 10th, 1771, aged 64 years. He married Mary, only child of James and Elisabeth Bourne, of Mallingley, near Heckfield, Hants., and all three lie interred in Heckfield Church, by whom he had one child Elisabeth Maria who has erected this as a tribute of gratitude to the memory of a kind and affectionate father.

WINDOW IN SOUTH WALL.

To the Memory of Maria Ann Langley by her brother Bathurst Edward Wilkinson.

TABLET ON SOUTH WALL.

Sacred to the memory of James Croft Brooke, esq^{re} (of Littlethorpe, near Ripon), late Major in the 3rd or Prince of Wales reg^{t} of Dragoon Guards, 2nd son of Col: Brooke, formerly of the same reg^{t}; and of Frances, his wife, late of Scholes in this parish. He died May 14th, 1837, in the 60th year of his age, sincerely regretted by all his relations and friends, leaving three surviving sons and one daughter by Frances, his wife, 2nd daughter of the late John Brooke, esq., of Austhorpe Lodge, near Leeds, who, feeling deeply her bereavement, erected this monument to her husband's many amiable virtues.

STONE ON FLOOR SOUTH AISLE.

Here Lieth interred the Body of John Wray, who Departed this life at Lazincroft, the 17 of Feb., Anno 1759, in the .. year of his age.

STONE IN SOUTH AISLE.

Here lyeth ye body of Alvarey Vevers, of Scoles, who dyed November ye 8, [1666, aged 79].

STONE IN WEST AISLE.

Here Lyeth interred the body of Christopher Kelshaw of Roundhay, who departed this life the 12 day of December in the yeare of our Lord 1673, being 88 years old.

---

*Yesterday se'nnight was married at Woodford in Essex, Edward Wilkinson, Esq., of this town, to Miss Ann Pearce, second dau. of Nicholas Pearce, Esq., of Woodford. *Leeds Intelligencer*, 18 July, 1786.

STONE IN WEST AISLE.

Underneath this stone are deposited the remains of John Phillips, Esq., formerly of Waltham[stow], in the county of Essex, second son of Charles ..... late of the above place [*rest cut off*].

STONE IN SOUTH AISLE.

Underneath this stone lies the Body of William Vevers, of Scholes, Gent., who departed this life ... [1] Day of Feb., 1744, aged 48 years. Richard Vevers, Esq., buried here.

TABLET ON SOUTH-WEST WALL.

Sacred to the memory of Elizabeth, wife of Edward Wales, of Berwick-in-Elmet (late of Leeds), who died February 22nd, 1835, aged 62 years; also Jane, wife of the above Edward Wales, who died June 18th, 1854, in the 89th year of her age; also of the above Edward Wales, who died November 20th, 1855, in the 84th year of his age.*

TABLET ON SOUTH-WEST WALL.

Sacred to the memory of Thomas Collett, of Leeds, Batchelor, who died August 30th, 1849, aged 55 years; also of William and Mary Collett, father and mother of the above.

ON TOMBSTONE WEST END OF MIDDLE AISLE.

[Here Lies Interr]ed [the Body of] Elizabeth Haist, daughter of William Ellis, Esq. She was first married to William Dawson, of Kiddall Hall, and afterwards to Mr Benj. Haist, of Barwick.†

ON STONE SOUTH END OF MIDDLE AISLE.

Here lieth ye Body of daughter of Mr Jo... late of Leeds. She Departed September ye 12th yeare of Her Age.

ON STONE IN MIDDLE AISLE.

Underneath lie the remains of William Ellis, Esq., of Kiddall Hall in this parish, who died April the 10th, 1771, aged 64 years.

ON STONE IN MIDDLE AISLE.

Here Lyeth the Body of Wm Vevers, the son of Wm Vevers, of Morwick, who departed this life the 28 of July, 1717, aged 22; and allso of Francis, his son, who departed this life ye 13th of December in ye 20th year of his age, Anno Domini 1719; Also ye Body of Sarah, ye wife of ye sd Wm Vevers, who departed this life ye 23d day of Sep., 1729, aged 56; And also Wm, her husband, who departed this life ye 18th day of October, 1738, aged 67.

ON STONE IN MIDDLE AISLE.

In memory of the two daughters of William and Elizabeth Eamonson, of Lazincroft. Elizabeth, who departed this life December the 17th, 1772, aged 17 years and was interred here. Alice, who departed this life the 23rd of Aug., 1775, aged 18 years, and was interred in the Church at Scarborough.

ON STONE IN MIDDLE AISLE.

Here Lyeth the Body of Alice, daughter of Mr William Eamonson, of Lazincroft, who departed this life April ye 6th, 1744, In ye 30th year of her age.

ON STONE IN MIDDLE AISLE.

Here Lyeth interred Alice Eamonson, the wife of Willm Eamonson, of Austhorp, who departed this life on the [1] day of September, 1751, in the 69th year of her age

ON STONE IN MIDDLE AISLE.

Orate pro anima Johannis Grenefeld servientis ad legem qui obiit [23 Oct., 1464].—*Dr. Johnston's MS.*

ON STONE IN WEST AISLE.

Hic Jacet Milo Lodge qui obiit 7° die Sept., 1695.

TABLET ON NORTH WEST WALL.

In the Vault below lie the remains of John Phillips Esq., formerly of Walthamstow, Essex, son of Charles Phillips, died 5 January, 1814, aged 82 years, he was the younger brother of the late Rev. Charles Phillips, A.M., Vicar

---

*Edward Wales married first, 1802, to Elizabeth, only daughter of Thomas Brook of Wakefield, Surgeon, and grand daughter of the Rev Samuel Brook, M.A., Head Master of Almondbury Grammar School; secondly, 1836, to Jane, widow of John Parkinson of Hull, and daughter of the Rev. John Greenwood, M.A., Rector of Thornhill. See *Miscellanea Genealogica*, 3rd series, I. 132.

†See *Hunter's Familiæ Minorum Gentium* (Harleian Society), p. 774.

of Terling, Essex; also in the same vault are deposited the remains of Hannah, wife of the above named John Phillips, died at Whitburn, Durham, 21st December, 1815, aged 77 years.

WINDOW IN NORTH WALL.

To the honour and glory of God and to the memory of Charles Porter who died January 28th, 1880, this window was inscribed.

TABLET ON NORTH WALL.

Near this place lie Interred the Remains of William Vevers, of Scholes, Esq., who died the [1st] day of February, 1744, aged 48 years. Also his son Richard Vevers, Esqre, who died Jan. 11th, 1767, aged 35 years. Also Priscilla Atkinson [mother] to the above Richard Vevers, Esq., died ..May, 1769.

ON A TOMBSTONE IN NORTH AISLE.

R. D. ob. 1799.

ON AN UPRIGHT STONE ON THE NORTH WALL.

Hic jacet Johēs Gascoigne quōdam dñs de Laysincroft qui obiit....

EAST WINDOW IN NORTH AISLE.

Armorial window commemorating members of the Gascoigne family. [For full description see *The History of Barwick-in-Elmet*, by the Rev. F. S. Colman.]

IN THE CHURCHYARD.

[w.d.t.l.=who departed this life.]

Sacred to the memory of John, son of John and Margaret Marsland, of Roundhay, w.d.t.l. April 7th, 1828, aged 7 weeks.

In memory of Joseph Porter, of Barwick in Elmet, who died August 12th, 1835, aged 79 years. In memory of Henry, son of Joseph Porter, who died May 24th, 1842, aged 50 years. Also of Mary Ann, relict of Henry Porter, who died October 25th, 1884, aged 79 years.

Sacred to the memory of James Benson w.d.t.l. April 23rd, 1828, in the 90th year of his age. An[n], daughter of the above, who died February 2[7], 1812, aged 37 years.

In memory of Thomas Crosland, of South Milford, Gentan, who died September 11th, 1833, aged 64 years.

In memory of Mary, fourth daughter of John and Jane Crosland, of Scholes, who died December 1st, 1806, in the 2nd year of her age. Also of the above named John Crosland, w.d.t.l. June 1st, 1815, aged 51 years. Also Elizabeth Crosland, the fifth daughter of the above named John Crosland, w.d.t l. 3rd day of September, 1833, aged 24 years. Also Jane, wife of the above John Crosland, who died January 9th, 1857, aged 83 years.

In memory of Elizabeth, the wife of John Crosland, of Scholes, w.d.t.l. March 16th, 1834, in the 31st year of her age. Also of Arthur, second son of the aforesaid John & Elizabeth Crosland, w.d.t.l. April 24th, 1834, aged 6 weeks. Also the above named John Crosland who died April 23rd, 1851 aged 74 years. Also Jane, daughter of John & Jane Musgrave Crosland, of Scholes, who died April 24th, 1873, aged 4 years & 2 months.

In memory of Joseph Sparling, of Potterton, w.d.t.l. Jan. 5th, 1824, aged 82 years. Also of Mary [?] wife of the above [*rest defaced*].

Sacred to the memory of Sarah Goodall w.d.t.l. July 19 [*rest defaced*].

In memory of [*7 lines defaced*]. Also Sarah, wife of John Walton, and daughter of the above w.d.t.l. July 13th, 1814. Aged 29 years.

In memory of Jane, the wife of John Brogden, of Scholes, w.d.t.l. May 7th, 1829, aged 27 years. Also the above named John Brogden w.d.t.l. Decr 5th, 1854, aged 62 years.

In memory of the late Henry Shippen, Butcher, of Scholes, w.d.t.l. March 25th, 1849, aged 59 years. Also of Henry, son of William and Mary Shippen, and grandson of the above, w.d.t.l. Sepr 28th, 1849, aged 18 months.

R. H. B.

Obit July the 29th, 1797. John Clarkson Brooke lies buried, by his brother, Richard Herbert Brooke, under this Stone, May 8th, 1798.

Sacred to the memory of Frances, the wife of Richard Brooke, Esq., Major of the third Regt of Dragoon Guards, who died April the 23, 1789, aged 34 years. [*Verse*]. Here lie also the Remains of Mary Ann, their eldest daughter, who died August the 3rd, 1783, aged 9 months. And also of Robert Bentley, their fifth son, who died October the 3rd, 1789, aged 2 years. And likewise of Frances Catherine, their second daughter, who died July the 2, 1790, aged 9 years. Also Richard Herbert Brooke, eldest son of Richard and Frances Brooke, w.d.t.l. July 29, 1797, aged 18 years. Also John Clarkson Brooke, fourth son of the above Richard & Frances Brooke, w.d.t.l. May the 6th, 1798, aged 12 years. Also to the memory of George Charles Brooke, third son of Richard and Frances Brooke, Lieutenant in the 20th Regt of Foot, who was killed in the Battle of Vemiera in Portugal, on the 21st of August, 1808, aged 24 years.

Sacred to the memory of Richard Brooke, Esqre, of Scholes, Colonel in the Army and late Lieutenant Colonel in the third or Prince of Wales Regiment of Dragoon Guards. He married, first, Frances, the Daughter of the Revd Richard Brooke, and, secondly, Jane Marcella, late daughter of the late Revd Dr Drake, of Treaton. He was born February the 20th, 1744, and died the 16th of July, 1799. Grace Carol..., daughter of Richard and Frances Brooke.

In memory of William Dawson, who, as a Christian was sincere, candid, and consistent; as a preacher of the Gospel, original, powerful, laborious and faithful, unusually popular, and extensively useful. He was born at Garforth, March 30th, 1773, and died at Colne in Lancashire in the prosecution of his ministry, after having preached the Gospel in most parts of the United Kingdom, July 4th, 1841. This Monument was erected as a memento of private friendship and public worth by his executors Charles Smith and Edward Phillips. Also Thomas Dawson, late of Barnbow, who died September 25th, 1854, aged 67 years. Also Mary Brewer, niece of William Dawson, who died May 15th, 1884, aged 77 years.

William Slater, of this village, farmer, died 30th March, 1852, aged 68 years. Hannah Musgrave, sister of the above and Relict of Matthew Musgrave, of Leeds, wool merchant, died 19th, April 1854, aged 74 years. Also of John Charles Rawdon, late of York, Born December 24th, 1804, Died June 2nd, 1873. Also Sarah Hannah, relict of the above John Charles Rawdon, died January 14th, 1876, aged 57 years.

In memory of William Waite, of this town, who died Jan. the 8th, 1768, aged 31 years A true son of Divine Harmony

Sacred to the memory of Elizabeth Whitehead, wife of William Whitehead, of Leeds, w.d.t.l. the 24th of April, 1803, aged 42 years. Also William Whitehead, Husband of the above, w.d.t.l. the 5th day of April, 1810, aged 47 years. Also William, son of the above William & Elizabeth Whitehead, w.d.t.l. the 2nd day of December, 1810, in the 12th year of his age.

Sacred to the memory of Sarah, wife of John Whitehead, w.d.t.l. Octr 25th, 1836, aged 65 years. Also of Abraham, son of the above, w.d.t.l. Febry 25th, 1836, aged 36 years. Also of John Whitehead, Husband of the above Sarah Whitehead, w.d.t.l. April 23rd, 1838, aged 66 years. Also of Ann, daughter of the above John and Sarah Whitehead, w.d.t.l. Jany 3rd, 1840, aged 44 years.

Sacred to the memory of William Batty, of Barwick, son of John and Alice Batty, who died Febry 22nd, 1837, aged 70 years, Clerk of this parish 40 years, and Magistrate's Clerk 32 years. Near this lie the remains of Mary, wife of William Batty and daughter of James & Ann Bean, of Barwick, who died Novr 27, 1797, aged 26 years.

Sacred to the memory of John Hutchinson, of this town, w.d.t.l. the 30th day of March, 1806, in the 74th year of his age. Also Mary, second wife of the above John Hutchinson, w.d.t.l. the 15th day of May, 1828, aged 77 years. Also Elizabeth Wormald, sister to the above Mary, who died the 18th day of August, 1825, [?] in the [?] 56th year of her age.

Sacred to the memory of James Batty, late of this parish, son of William and Mary Batty. He was Born 15th February, 1793, and died 14th September, 1852, aged 59 years. Having been Apparitor of this Archdeaconry 30 years.

In affectionate remembrance of John Thompson, of Hayton House, late of Barnbow, w.d.t.l. December 9th, 1866, in the 84th year of his age. Also of Ellis, wife of the above, w.d.t.l. December 18th, 1832, in the 44th year of her age. Also of William, son of John and Ellis Thompson, who died September 24th, 1833, aged 18 years. Also their infant son, 1814.

In memory of Samuel Thompson, of Barnbow, who died June 4th, 1806, aged 61 years. Also Susannah, wife of the above, who died September 18th, 1827, aged 81 years.

In memory of Tabitha, wife of James Lumb, of this town, w.d.t.l. Augt 18th, 1818, aged 48 years. [*Verse*]. Also Mary and Saml who died infants. Also Elizabeth, daughter of the above, w.d.t.l. Novr 14th, 1821, aged 24 years. Also Thomas, eldest son of the above James & Tabitha Lumb, who died at Micklefield and is interred at the foot of this tomb, December 15th, 1840, aged 40 years. Also the above nam'd James Lumb w.d.t.l. July 21st, 1842, aged 71 years.

In memory of John Lumb, joiner, late of Chapel-Allerton, who died March 17th, 1839, aged 29 years.

In memory of William, the son of John and Sarah Kirby, of Leeds, w.d.t.l. July 22nd, 1811, aged 9 weeks. Also Sarah, the daughter of the above John & Sarah Kirby, w.d.t.l. January 21st, 1818, aged 5 years and 4 months.

Sacred to the memory of Elizabeth Whitehead, formerly of Barwick, but late of Leeds, w.d.t.l. on the 11th Day of March, 1829, aged 86 years. Also five children of William Whitehead & grandchildren of the above who all died young.

In memory of Elizabeth Lumb, only daughter of Thomas and Charlotte Lumb, of Leeds, died 8th day of Jan^{y}, 1833, aged 18 years. Also of the late Thomas Lumb, of Leeds, auctioneer, and Father of the above named Elizabeth Lumb, w.d.t.l. November 22nd, 1843, aged 63 years.

Sacred to the memory of Sarah Grundy who died January 2nd, 1834, aged 84 years.

Sacred to the memory of Robert Stead w.d.t.l. March 31st, 1839 [?] [3 *lines defaced*].

Sacred to the memory of Ann, wife of Thomas Stoner of this Town, w.d.t.l. August 10th, 1823, aged 61 years. Also Alice Stoner, daughter of the above, who died March 13th, 1798, aged 2 years. Also Hannah Stoner, daughter-in-law to the above Thos Stoner & daughter of Joseph and Elizth Roberts, of Holmfirth, who left this vale of tears at York November 8th, 1824, aged 27 years. Also Louisa Stoner, daughter of the above Hannah Stoner, who died October 24th, 1824, aged 2 years.

Here lieth interred the Body of William Taite, of this Town, w.d.t.l. the 4th day of December, 1787, aged 70 years. Also the Body of Sarah Taite, wife of the above William Taite, w.d.t.l. the 26th day of May, 1801, aged 80 years.

To the memory of Jonas Haley, of Scholes, who died Feb. 24th, 1764, aged 94 years.

Here lie interred the remains of Francis Moss, late of York, who died October 29th, 1837, aged 67 years. Also Elizabeth, his wife, who died December 29th, 1839, aged 69 years. Also Francis, only son of the above who died April 29th, 1875, aged 64 years. Also Sarah, daughter of the above Francis and Elizabeth Moss, who died July 6th, 1879, aged 72 years.

Sacred to the memory of Charles, son of William & Mary Tillotson, ... August [*rest defaced*].

Sacred to the memory of Richard Wilkinson, of Barwick in Elmet, w.d.t.l. October 15th, 1850, aged 49 years. Also Martha Ann Stubbins who died March ......, aged 29 years [*rest defaced*].

In memory of Richard Perkin, Farmer, who died Nov. 11th, 1842, aged 44 years. Also Margaret, relict of the above Richard Perkin, who died Jan. 2nd, 1874, aged 79 years.

To the memory of Elizabeth Abbot, wife of Thomas Abbot, of Barwick in Elmet, w.d.t.l. 4th July, 1816, aged 72.

Here lieth the Body of Wm Knapton, he died the 7th of Dec^{r}, 1782, aged 63 years. Also S.... Knapton................ 5th [*rest defaced*].

Here lieth the body of Robert Knapton, of Barwick, w.d.t.l. Dec^br^ ye 27, 1741, aged 55 years. Also Ann, his wife, w.d.t.l. June y^e^ ...... aged 46 years.

H.... day of Nov^r^......6 ...... 1 years, ...ah, his wife, ...of March, 1776.

Here lieth the Body of Mark Robinson .... who [5 *lines defaced*]. Also Mary, the wife of Edwd Day, of Potterton, and daughter of the above Mark Robinson, who died 1 of March, 1791, aged 61 years. Also Edwd Day, of Potterton, w.d.t.l. March 30th, 1807, aged 78 years.

Orate pro ãibus Johis Grenefeld & Johãne uxoris sue qui obiit [*rest defaced*].

Sacred to the memory of Mary, the wife of Edward Stead, w.d.t.l. the 10th of September, 1826, aged 47 years [*verse*]. Also Edward Stead, Husband of the above, w.d.t.l. February 21st, 1843, aged 71 years. [*On the back*] In memory of Mary Stead, of Brex House, Swillington, who died June 2nd, 1855, in the 47th year of her age.

Here lyeth the Body of Ann ...... w.d.t.l. Aug. the 26th, 17.., aged 32 years.

Here lyeth Francis & Eliz,: Son and daughter of Francis Holmes, of Barwick. Also Rachel, wife of Francis Holmes, mother to the above children, who died April 18, 1768, aged 60 years.

Sacred to the memory of George Holmes, of this town, w.d.t.l. the 2 day of October, 1805 [?], in the 63rd year of his age. Also of Elizabeth Holmes, wife of the above George Holmes,,w.d.t.l. the 7th day of September, 1817 [?], aged .. years.

In memory of Mary Allatt [*rest defaced*].

Here lieth the Body of [5 *lines defaced*]. Thomas, son of the above Thomas Addeman, w.d.t.l. May the 23rd, 1780, aged 45 years. Here also lieth the Body of James Plowright, of this town, son in [*rest buried*].

Sacred to the memory of William Addeman, of this Town, w.d.t.l. the .. day of November .... Also ..... wife of John Connell, and .... of the above named William Addeman, w.d.t.l. Decr 19th, 1820, aged 70 years.

Here lieth the Body of George Haist, of Barwick, w.d.t.l. April ye 22^d^, 1743, in ye 76th year of his age. Also the Body of Samuell son of the above George Haist, of Barwick, w.d.t.l. April y^e^ .., 1743, in the 49 year of his age.

Here lyeth inter'd the Body of Robert Ellot w.d.t.l. December the 27th, 1755.

[Here lie]th in[terred th]e body [of Mary] Win[ter, wife] of M^r^ [William W]inter, [daugh]ter of[...] Dineley ....ick, w.d.t.l. ... of Sep[tember,] 1702.

Ellen Hey died April 8th, 1814, aged 79 years.

In memory of Samuel Braham, Engineer at Garforth Colliery, who died June 1st, 1829, aged 57 years.

Here Lyeth the Body of Thomas, the son of William Lumb, of barwick, w.d.t.l. October the 4, 1750, aged 8 years [*verse*].

To the memory of William Greenwood, of Shippon, who died October 4th, 1848, aged 72 years. Also Ann, wife to the above, who died January 14th, 1848, aged 71 years.

Here lieth the Body of Elizabeth, the wife of Jacob Pease, of Morwick, w.d.t.l. March the 27, 1775, aged 68 years. The above named Jacob Pease died August the 7, 1779, aged 69.

In memory of Abraham Wormald who died Septr the 23^d^, 1826, aged 66 years [*verse*]. Also of Ruth, Daughter of the aforesaid, who died Novr the 12th, 1809, in the 8th year of her age. Also of Sarah, wife of the above Abraham Wormald, who died June 3rd, 1833, aged 74 years.

Sundial.—W. Lumb, 1765.

In memory of Elizabeth, wife of Benjamin Collett, of this Town, w.d.t.l. May 9th, 1811, aged 63 years. Also the above Benjamin Collett w.d.t.l. May 3rd, 1832, aged 83 years.

In memory of Ann, the wife of Benjamin Hill, of this Town, who died Novr 4th, 1832, aged 73 years.

In memory of W[illiam Scott, of] Barwick House, [who di]ed May ye 27, 1758 [*verse*]. Also Thomas, his son, [died Novem]ber ye 5th, 1763, in y^e^ ...... [*verse*]. Also Mary Scott, [widow of] William, died Nov........ [1776,] in the 66th year ..... Also William Scott ...... above died Janua.. ...... aged 6 years and .... red in the Holy ...... Church Yard, Y....

To the memory of Thomas Tilney, Mason, of Scholes, who died Novr the 2nd, 1821, aged 75 years [*verse*]. Also Ruth Hargreaves, Daughter of above, who died Octr 15th, 1826, aged 44 years. Also Sarah Tilney, wife of the above, who died April 26th, 1827, aged 79 years. [*Inscription on side defaced*].

Sacred to the memory of Louisa, Daughter of Nicholas and Grace Tilney, who died July 8th, 1822 [?], aged 1 year. Also William, son of the above, who died Decr 7th, 1824, aged 1 year and 3 months. Also Louisa Ann, daughter of the above who died Augt 3rd, 1826, aged 8 months. Also Eliza, daughter of the above, who died Novr 25th, 1830, aged 1 year and 8 months.

Sacred to the memory of William Tilney, of Chapel-Allerton, Mason, Second son of Thomas Tilney, of Scholes, w.d.t.l. Novr 29th, 1831, aged 56 years.

Sacred to the memory of Sarah, wife of William Tilney, of Chapel-Allerton, who is interred beneath the adjacent stone, who died February 28th, 1841, aged 78 years. Also Sarah Webster Lund, Daughter of the above, who died July 17th, 1854, aged 49 years.

In memory of John Atkinson, of Winmoor, w.d.t.l. December 30th, 1811, aged 67 years. Also Sarah, Daughter of the above, w.d.t.l. February 8th, 1827, aged 41 years. Also Ann, wife of the above John Atkinson, w.d.t.l. February 17th, 1830 [?], aged 79 years.

Sacred to the memory of David Parker, of this Town, w.d.t.l. Octr 9th, 1847, aged 57 years. Also Mary, Daughter of the above, who died Feby 1st, 1848, in the 26th year of her age.

In memory of Edmund Rawlinson of this Town, w.d.t.l. May 22nd, 1821, aged 38 years [*verse*].

Here lieth the Body of Joseph Cromek, who died Feby 6th, 1785, aged 33 [*verse*].

Sacred to the memory of Thomas Collett, of this Town, who died the 27 day of January, 1792, aged 85 years. Also of his son, Thomas Collett, of Garforth, who died the 13th day of January, 1794, aged 57 years. This Stone was erected by Wm Collett, of Garforth, the son of the last named T. Collett, the 4th day of March, 1817.

In memory of the late Thomas Pitt, Farmer, of Barwick, w.d.t.l. on the 12th of February, 1848, aged 72 years.

Here lieth the Body of Benjamin, the son of John Bramley, of Potterton, w.d.t.l. the 20 [?] day of Aug^st, in the .. year of his age, 1752 [?].

Sacred to the memory of Thomas Kemp, of this town, w.d.t.l. Feb^ry 18, 1838, aged 63 years, Husband to Mary Ann Kemp w.d.t.l. Aug^st th28, 1832, aged 51 years, who lies in this churchyard.

In memory of Henry Wright, of Morwick, w.d.t.l. July the 28, 1772, aged 72 [?] years. Also [Mary] Daughter .... w.d.t.l. September the 3, 1771, aged 24 years. Also of ..... wife of the [*rest defaced*].

Sacred to the memory of William Carr, of Kidhall Lane. He d.t.l. [October] the 23rd, 1801, aged 69. ...... his Relict and child [4 *lines defaced*].

John Batty died April 11, 1797, aged 53.

In memory of Mary, wife of John Batty, of Throstle-nest, who died June 24, 1811, in the 42nd year of her age. Also John, son of the above, died an infant in 1806.*

Sacred to the memory of Susanna, wife of John Batty, of Throstle-nest, w.d.t.l. October 24th, 1844, aged 61 years. Also of Richard, son of the above John & Susanna Batty, w.d.t.l. August 14th, 1844, aged 31 years. Also of the above John Batty, who died on the 5th of April, 1851, aged 82 years. Also Sarah, relict of the above Richard Batty, who died September 19th, 1865, aged 51 years.

In memory of James Batty, of this town, who [died] July 10th, 1813, aged 36 years. Also of two daughters, Mary, who died Sep. 5th, 1803, aged 3 years, Ann, who died April 3rd, 1805, aged 2 years.

Sacred to the memory of John Loder, of Kidhall Lane, w.d.t.l. 1st day of April, 1806, in the 61st year of his age. Also Sarah, wife of the above

---

*"Died on Thursday Aug. 14, 1806, at Throstle Nest, Garforth, near Leeds, Mrs. Batty, grandmother to Mr Nelson, whitesmith, in this town, at the advanced age of 100 years."—Taylor's *Leeds Worthies, Supplement*, p. 675. John Nelson of Leeds married Sarah Batty of Barwick, 5 July, 1762. See note *ante* p. 274.

John Loder, w.d.t.l. the 18th day of March, 1803, in the 51st year of his age. John, son of John & Sarah Loder; he died in his infancy, the 28th day of December, 1785. Robert, son of John & Sarah Loder, w.d.t.l. the 13th day of May, 1790, in the 2nd year of his age.

In memory of John Swaile, for Twenty years servant to E. Wilkinson, Esq., of Potterton Lodge, w.d.t.l. the 14th day of April, 1831, aged 39 years.

In memory of Mary Fatkin, wife of William Fatkin, of Potterton, w.d.t.l. March 9th, 1827, aged 48 years. Also John Fatkin, son of the above, w.d.t.l. March 8th, 1826, aged 26 years. Also the above William Fatkin who died March 30th, 1848, aged 79 years.

In memory of Mary, the wife of John Darby, of Potterton, w.d.t.l. November 19th, 1839, in the 77th year of her age.

In memory of the late James Armitage, of Scholes, who died May 13th, 1849, aged 50 years. Also Amy, wife of the above, who died March 16th, 1870, aged 72 years.

Sacred to the memory of John Cawood, of Barnbow, who died 17th of August, 1811, aged 63 years.

Sacred to the memory of Jane, the wife of William Gibson, of this Town, w.d.t.l. the 10th December, 1829, aged 63 years. Also Mary, daughter of the above who died the 20th December, 1829, aged 28 years.

In memory of Ellen, the wife of Peter Hustwit, of Leeds, and daughter of John & Ellen Clayton, of Moor Garforth, w.d.t.l. on the 12th of November, 1838 [?], aged 25 years. Also Thomas, son of the above Peter & Ellen Hustwit, who died January ...., aged 6 months [*verse*].

In memory of John Smith, late of Laverack, who died the 2^{d} of March, 1826, aged 76 years. Also Mary, wife of the above John Smith, who died July 7th, 1831, aged 87 years.

In memory of Mary, the wife of William Collett, of Garforth, who died Novr 9th, 1827, aged 61 years. Also the above William Collett, who died Novr 26th, 1832, aged 76 years. Also of Thomas Collett, of Leeds, son of the above, who died Augt 30th, 1849, aged 55 years.

In memory of James Holliday, Esqre, w.d.t.l. the 16th day of July, 1826 [?], aged 80 years.

In memory of Hannah Chadwick, of White Laith, Winmoor, who died the 28th day of April, 1828, aged 53 years.

In memory of Jeremiah Brewerton, of Wike, w.d.t.l. July 28th, 1846, aged 81 years.

Sacred to the memory of Mary Ann, the wife of Thomas Kemp, of this Town, w.d.t.l. August 28th, 1832, aged 51 years.

INDEX OF PLACE NAMES.

IN THE PARISH.

[Names of frequent occurrence are only indexed in respect of the earlier references.]

OUT OF THE PARISH.

INDEX OF SURNAMES.

Lightning Source UK Ltd.
Milton Keynes UK
UKOW06f2001210817
307653UK00011B/768/P

9 781332 212637